In Memory of
June & Edward P
Mone

fP

FORGE OF EMPIRES

EMPIRES

— *1861–1871* —

*Three Revolutionary Statesmen
and the World They Made*

MICHAEL KNOX BERAN

FREE PRESS

New York London Toronto Sydney

FREE PRESS
A Division of Simon & Schuster, Inc.
1230 Avenue of the Americas
New York, NY 10020

First Free Press hardcover edition October 2007

FREE PRESS and colophon are
trademarks of Simon & Schuster, Inc.

For information about special discounts for bulk purchases,
please contact Simon & Schuster Special Sales:
1-800-456-6798 or business@simonandschuster.com

Book design by Ellen R. Sasahara

Manufactured in the United States of America

10   9   8   7   6   5   4   3   2   1

Library of Congress Cataloging-in-Publication Data
Beran, Michael Knox.
Forge of empires, 1861–1871: three revolutionary statesmen and
the world they made / Michael Knox Beran.
p. cm.
Includes bibliographical references and index.
1. Lincoln, Abraham, 1809–1865—Influence. 2. Bismarck, Otto, Fürst
von, 1815–1898—Influence. 3. Alexander II, Emperor of Russia,
1818–1881—Influence. 4. Statesmen—History—19th century. 5. United
States—History—1849–1877. 6. Germany—History—1848–1870.
7. Russia—History—Alexander II, 1855–1881. I. Title.
E457.B44 2007
909.81—dc22   2007007021

ISBN-13:   978-0-7432-7069-4
ISBN-10:   0-7432-7069-X

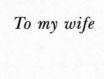

To my wife

You surely remember that we found pertaining to such
a nature courage, grandeur of soul, aptness to learn,
remembrance. . . . And it is from men of this type that
those spring who do the greatest harm to communities and
individuals, and the greatest good . . . but a small nature
never does anything great to a man or a city.

— PLATO

Contents

Note to the Reader

In *Patriotic Gore*, Edmund Wilson's book on the literature of the American Civil War, there is a passage in which Wilson compares Abraham Lincoln to Otto von Bismarck and Vladimir Lenin.

> The impulse to unification was strong in the nineteenth century; it has continued to be strong in this; and if we would grasp the significance of the Civil War in relation to the history of our time, we should consider Abraham Lincoln in connection with other leaders who have been engaged in similar tasks. . . . Lincoln and Bismarck and Lenin were all men of unusual intellect and formidable tenacity of character, of historical imagination combined with powerful will. They were all, in their several ways, idealists, who put their ideals before everything else. All three were solitary men, who lived with their concentration of purpose. None liked to deal in demagogy and none cared for official pomp: even Bismarck complained that he could not be a courtier and assured Grant and others—as he must have believed quite sincerely—that he was not really a monarchist but a republican. Each established a strong central government over hitherto loosely coordinated peoples.

In my attempt to compare three revolutionary statesmen, I have dwelt somewhat more than Wilson on differences in revolutionary characters and revolutionary methods. No doubt I have been influenced by my own (indirect) experience of the revolutions which Lincoln, Bismarck, and Alexander II made. My paternal grandfather was born a subject of the Habsburg Emperor Franz Josef. Carl Beran came from a German-Czech-Croat family which, at the beginning of the last century, was living in Croatia in Austria-Hungary. He and his family emigrated to the United States four decades after Austria's defeat by Bismarck's Prussians at Sadowa prepared the way for the German statesman's revolution.

The fate of my grandfather's cousin, who remained in Europe, testifies to the consequences of that revolution. Father Joseph Beran was a Roman Catholic priest in Prague, seventy miles west of Sadowa. He taught pastoral theology there and in the 1930s became Rector of the Seminary. Beran's biographer recounts how, one day in 1939, the rumble of German tanks and sound of German jackboots "penetrated the leaden casement windows of the cathedral school." "Symbol of the Anti-Christ," Father Beran said quietly, before he resumed his lecture. In June 1940 he was arrested by the Gestapo, and in the autumn of 1942 he was deported to Dachau as Prisoner No. 35844. In his book *Memories of Dachau,* the Communist leader Vojteck Bincak said that "Dr. Beran was one of the best and noblest characters I knew in the camp." The emaciated priest, clad in rags, was liberated by American troops—citizens of the Republic Lincoln's revolution saved—in May 1945. After celebrating a Mass of Thanksgiving, Father Beran returned to Prague, where in December 1946 he was consecrated Archbishop of Prague and Metropolitan Bishop of Bohemia in Saint Vitus Cathedral. He was later persecuted by the Russian Communists—servants of a régime which might never have come into existence had Alexander II's revolution succeeded. On a family trip to the Soviet Union in the winter of 1978 I saw with my own eyes the bleakness of the dispensation under which Cardinal Beran lived during the latter part of his life. My family was living in London at the time and I had just read Robert Massie's *Nicholas and Alexandra.* My parents, struck, I suppose, by my curiosity about Russia, took me to see the country for myself.

Very different was the experience of my mother's family. My mother's mother's family comes from Springfield, Illinois. The family's house at 413 South Seventh Street, though it is no longer in the possession of the Grahams, is around the corner from the Lincoln house at 430 South Eighth Street. My grandmother's house in Erie, Pennsylvania, was filled with souvenirs of Lincoln, among them the portrait of the President which now hangs in my living room.

Here in a small way is evidence of the different effects produced by different types of statesmanship. My father's relations were forced to flee their homeland, and my grandfather's cousin came close to perishing in a concentration camp. My mother's family prospered in Springfield and Erie, unmolested by authority.

Hundreds of books have analyzed the rise and fall of free states during the modern period, and have described the emergence of the authoritarian régimes: but none, I think, has placed a sufficient emphasis on the revolutions of 1861–1871, a decade which forms one of the most interesting chapters in the annals of human freedom, and which at the same time witnessed the emergence of novel philosophies of terror and coercion.

THREE DEATHS

TWO OF THE THREE revolutionary leaders died violently.

The first expired after a .41-caliber bullet pierced the back of his skull. The bullet passed through the soft tissue of the brain before coming to rest near one of the eye sockets, which its force fractured. The American President was carried to a nearby house, where, shortly after seven o'clock on the following morning, he ceased to breathe. A few seconds later his heart stopped beating.

The other leader saw his belly ripped open and his bowels strewed across a city street. Chunks of flesh glistened in the snow as the Russian Tsar was placed on a sleigh and taken, by his Cossacks, to his palace to die.

Of the three revolutionary leaders, only the German Chancellor died peacefully in his bed, at the age of eighty-three.

THE CORPSE OF the Russian Tsar was conveyed, in accordance with the forms of the imperial court and the Orthodox Church, to the sepulcher where his ancestors slept. But there were few signs of grief in Saint Petersburg. Alexander II died unloved. The reward for his revolutionary statesmanship was ingratitude, and his funeral was awkward. The embalmer contemplated the Tsar's body, or what remained of it, and the decision was at last taken to amputate the shattered lower extremities. While the morticians despaired over the corpse, the courtiers were vexed by a different problem, the difficulty of finding accommodation for the horde of foreign dignitaries who descended upon Saint Petersburg in a mass of special trains from Warsaw and Berlin. The German Crown Prince found himself quartered in an art gallery.

A more delicate question was presented by the imperial concubine. Ordinarily the widow of the sovereign would have been recognized as one of the principal mourners; but in this case the arrangements were complicated by the fact that Alexander had, shortly after the death of his first wife, the Empress Mary, married his mistress. The second marriage was performed in secret and was morganatic; the bride could not be countenanced openly by her husband. Doubtless it was hard on Ekaterina Mikhailovna, the young lady in question, to be the disreputable party in a mésalliance, for she was not a courtesan. She was not even an actress. Katya, as she was called, was descended from the ancient nobility of Russia. But she was of noble rather than royal or imperial blood, and what the Tsar's nephew, Grand Duke Alexander, called "a heartless law" obliged members of the imperial family to marry royalty. It was rumored that Alexander had resolved to break with this tradition; he would reveal his marriage to his people, raise Katya to the throne, and place the crown of an empress on her chestnut locks. But none of this had come to pass when he met his untimely end in a Saint Petersburg street.

Katya was shunted aside as the corpse of her lover was conveyed, past crowds of undemonstrative Russians, to the Fortress of Peter and Paul, the dungeon and crypt of the Russian tsars. The midday sun gleamed on the golden dome of Saint Isaac's Cathedral as the procession of guards and priests, mitres and chasubles, swords and scepters made its way through the city. But on history's dial darkness was falling. With the death of Alexander, the dynasty of the Romanovs began to pass into the shadows.

On the day of the interment, Katya, heavily veiled, waited with the rest of the court at the foot of the grand staircase of the Winter Palace. With her were her three children, each of whom had been sired by the late Tsar. There was George, a boy of eight, who was called "Gogo." Beside him were his little sisters, Olga and Katya. They watched as their stepbrother, the new Tsar, swept down the staircase. Alexander III resembled his father scarcely at all. The dead Tsar had been rather handsome, with intelligent, protruding eyes. Mark Twain, who saw him in the Crimea, thought him "very tall and spare . . . a determined-looking man, though a very pleasant-looking one, nevertheless." Alexander III, by contrast, was oppressively large and mentally limited. By his side was his consort, the new Tsaritsa, Dagmar of Denmark,* a diminutive brunette. Young and radiant, gliding across a marble floor she seemed scarcely to touch, she had no intimation then that her own destiny was to be darker than Katya's, and that as an old woman she would sit sobbing in a railway carriage as she watched her eldest son, Nicky, the last of the tsars, led away to captivity and death.

Katya lifted her veils at the approach of their Imperial Majesties. Dag-

---

* Upon her conversion to the Orthodox faith, Dagmar took the name Mary.

mar, the new Tsaritsa, beheld, for a moment, her tear-stained face. Young and appealing though the face was—Katya, like Dagmar, was in her thirty-fourth year—it was nonetheless the face of a stepmother. The courtiers held their breath. Before his death, Alexander had insisted that Dagmar and the other grand duchesses make Katya the obeisance traditionally accorded a Russian empress. The rôles were now reversed. Dagmar was Empress. If she held out her hand stiffly and formally, it fell to Katya to make the gesture of submissive humility. But the new Tsaritsa did not, just then, insist on her imperial dignity. She acted, not as an empress, but as a woman. She embraced Katya. Some observers leapt to the conclusion that the hearts of the new Tsar and his consort had been softened, and that Katya was henceforth to be regarded as a member of the imperial family. But the new Tsaritsa's burst of compassion sprang rather from a momentary impulse of humanity than a deliberate decision to recognize the claims of her father-in-law's seraglio. The imperial family passed out of the palace and climbed into the state coaches. Katya was not invited to ride with them.

A heavy snow fell as the carriages made their way to the Fortress of Peter and Paul. The soldiers who lined the route stood shivering in their greatcoats. The horses struggled to pull their loads of gilt and royalty through the drifting snow. At last the cavalcade reached the fortress. In the chapel, the imperial party found a solemn and gorgeous scene. Sable-mantled monks with lighted tapers in their hands stood chanting passages of Scripture. A flickering light played upon the marble tombs of the Romanovs. But there was no sense of what had been lost. As in life, so in death, Alexander contrived to smother his own poetry.

The new Tsar alone seemed to cherish a desire to linger over the dead Tsar's remains. When he went to kiss his father's lifeless hands, Alexander III was seen several times to bend over the corpse. The coffin was then sealed and lowered into the vault, into which the mourners threw sand and leaves, according to an ancient custom.

IN CONTRAST TO the cold formality of the dead Tsar's obsequies, the murdered President was borne to his tomb with such improvised ceremony as could be arranged, in the hysteria of the moment, to satisfy the somewhat morbid requirements of the citizenry. Many Americans felt the need to be close to the body, and a certain amount of democratic intimacy with the corpse was permitted, or perhaps encouraged, by members of the dead President's party, who knew that martyrdom is a potent form of publicity. In New York, where Lincoln's remains were deposited, for a time, in City Hall, the coffin was opened, and some of the mourners, when they entered the chamber, attempted to touch or kiss the face of the deceased magistrate. The corpse, which had already assumed an unnaturally dark hue, turned black with the accumulation of popular grime. An embalmer was several times summoned to wipe the greasy film which coated the President's features, and to close the sagging jaw, which had so far fallen as to reveal the teeth. It became unseemly.

But the simplicity of the country people redeemed the spectacle. The train bearing the President's body sped through the countryside, where spring was coming into flower, and at remote crossroads, in isolated villages, on the borders of desolate farms, Americans lined the tracks to salute the murdered leader. Many pressed handkerchiefs to their eyes. Women stood with babies in their arms. Schoolchildren clutched American flags wreathed in black. In gaslit railway stations, groups of maidens gathered to sing hymns; clothed in virginal white, they wore black sashes across their bosoms. Some of the mourners held aloft hand-lettered signs: "HONOR TO WHOM HONOR IS DUE." "THE ILLUSTRIOUS MARTYR." "WASHINGTON, THE FATHER, LINCOLN, THE SAVIOR OF HIS COUNTRY." "THOUGH DEAD, HE YET SPEAKETH."

The railroad car which carried Lincoln's remains had been specially acquired by the Federal government for the President's use. In life Lincoln had often traveled in it; it was comfortably furnished and contained a parlor and a bedroom. To receive him in death the car had been robed in black, and black curtains hung at the windows. Accompanying the body were members of the President's family, an assortment of friends and dignitaries, and reporters from the Associated Press, the *New-York Times*, the *Philadelphia Inquirer*, the *Boston Daily Advertiser*, and the *Chicago Tribune*. In the depths of the night, as the train raced across central New York, those aboard were astonished by the size of the crowds that waited to watch the President's coffin pass. In the little towns of Memphis and Warrens, mourners stood with flaming torches. At Rochester, at three in the morning, the train was met by the Mayor and a large congregation of citizens.

Soon the dead President was in Illinois. "COME HOME," one sign read. "GO TO THY REST," said another. After stopping in Chicago, the train cut through the prairie to Springfield, the capital of Illinois and Lincoln's hometown. His remains were brought to the statehouse, where they lay in state overnight. At noon the next day, under a bright sun, the coffin was carried down the steps to a hearse. Hundreds of mourners began to sing—

Children of the Heavenly King, as ye journey sweetly sing:
Sing your Saviour's worthy praise, glorious in His works and ways.

We are traveling home to God, in the way the fathers trod:
They are happy now, and we soon their happiness shall see.

The coffin was brought to Oak Ridge Cemetery, where it was laid in a limestone sepulcher.

OF THE THREE revolutionary leaders, the German Chancellor alone escaped a violent death. It was a dubious blessing, for Otto von Bismarck felt to the full the bitterness of his dying. Lincoln and Alexander were cut down in the vigor of power; Bismarck alone outlived his potency, and learned what it was to be cast aside by history. The accession of a new Kaiser spelled the end of his power and pre-eminence. Wilhelm II, who had recently ascended the throne of the Empire Bismarck created, was eager to be rid of his family's ancient factotum. The young Kaiser's nervous excitability, his unpredictable desires, his indiscreet lectures—half Lutheran sermon, half Neronian tirade—gave one observer "the impression of a sufferer from hysteria." Tsar Nicholas II, grandson of the murdered Alexander, was blunter in his assessment of "Cousin Willy." "He's raving mad!" exclaimed Nicholas.

Bismarck, from the Olympian heights of his power, was unable to take the imperial lunatic quite seriously. This was understandable, yet it is dangerous to condescend to a sovereign, especially one as excitable as Wilhelm. Bismarck saw too late the obstinacy of his young master, and all his maneuvers and stratagems were ineffectual. The new Kaiser was self-willed, and he was vain. He gloried in the emblems of Prussian militarism, in the Black Eagles and Death's-Heads. He possessed another, no less unnerving habit; he liked to fondle the hairs of his guard's moustache, which turned up cruelly at the ends. But the culture of the barracks formed only a part of Wilhelm's idiosyncratic mental equipment, and somewhere in that strange intelligence the swaggering soldier yielded pride of place to the quivering lover of beauty. In the rococo light of the palace at Potsdam, the sternness of the parade-ground martinet dissolved, and visitors were startled to find a sensitive young man, one who possessed artistic interests.

Bismarck had surmounted many difficulties in the course of his life, but the task of managing an aesthete in jackboots proved to be too much even for his superlative finesse. The young Kaiser appeared, one morning, on the doorstep of the chancellery complex in Berlin. He demanded to be informed of Bismarck's activities. The Chancellor, roused from his bed, came down in an ugly mood. "It was all that Bismarck could do," Wilhelm said, "to refrain from throwing the inkpot at my head." Bismarck did not throw the inkpot; he exercised his malice instead by staging one of those little comedies he delighted to contrive. He hurled a dispatch case, then pretended to be anxious lest his imperial master should read one of the papers it contained. It was now Wilhelm's turn to lose his head. His curiosity got the better of his dignity, and he snatched the paper from the Chancellor's hand. From it Wilhelm learned that the Russian Tsar had referred to him, in so many words, as a perfidious jackass.

Bismarck had made his point—but at a cost. A short time later he was ejected from his offices, and in a bitter frame of mind he boarded the train that was to take him from Berlin. "A state funeral with full honours," he said as he gazed out the window at military plumes and ostrich feathers. He was at first certain that he would be recalled by a desperate government. But time passed, and the summons did not come. The old man dreamt of returning to the Wilhelmstrasse, the center of power in Berlin. He schemed and plotted; but his ambition had lost its force. His last years were spent in fruitless resentment. He was confined to a wheelchair, yet the weakness of his body did not extend to his mind, which remained lucid, and he was able to indulge to the last the one pleasure that remained to him, that of hating. In his final delirium, he thrust out his hand. *"That,"* he declared, "is impossible, on grounds of *raison d'état."* Perhaps the statesman, who in his long career had made and broken so many laws, sought by this fiat to annul his own mortality.

If so, he failed. Six hours later he was dead.

THEIR DEATHS WERE DIFFERENT, but the lives of the three leaders were united by a common thread. In the space of a single decade, they liberated tens of millions of souls, remade their own vast countries, and altered forever the forms of national power.

Lincoln freed a subjugated race and transformed the American Republic.

Alexander broke the chains of the serfs and brought the rule of law to Russia.

Bismarck threw over the petty Teutonic princes, defeated the House of Austria and the last of the imperial Napoleons, and united the German nation.

The three men helped to forge the superpowers that during the twentieth century contended for mastery of the earth. They also made an immense contribution to human freedom. Bismarck, the least of the three liberators, swept away an archaic jumble of competing sovereignties—so many duchies and grand bailiwicks—and secured the prosperity of a region that had for a long time languished. The liberating labors of Lincoln and Alexander were as prodigious as any that history records. At the beginning of 1861 there were living, within the confines of the

Russian Empire, some twenty-two million serfs. At the same time more than four million men, women, and children in the United States were kept as slaves. By the end of the decade they were free.

How are free states made, and how are they unmade? Lincoln called his revolution a "new birth of freedom." Bismarck spoke of a revolution accomplished through an expenditure of "blood and iron." Alexander implemented what he described as a revolution "from above." Their revolutions were made in the name of freedom, and were to varying extents consecrated to the freer movement of people, goods, and ideas. They were grounded, in different degrees, in the principles that made England, in the eighteenth century, the freest and most prosperous state then existing. Even Bismarck, who deplored the English theory of freedom, understood the advantages of liberty of trade, though he was very far from being a Free Trader. Under his government industry flourished, and the mines and smokestacks of the Ruhr supplied his régime with the coal and the steel which, even more than blood and iron, underwrote the prosperity of the Reich.

The new machinery of freedom, though English in design, was universal in scope. At its core was the idea, as yet imperfectly realized, that all human beings are endowed with a fundamental dignity. This was a truth which, Abraham Lincoln believed, was "applicable to all men and all times." The machinery of freedom promised, in the early decades of the nineteenth century, to be as exportable as the steam engine, the other ingenious device of the age. The faith that all men possess a right to life, liberty, and the fruits of their industry was invoked as readily on the banks of the Rhine, the Neva, and the Potomac as on the Thames.*

Then something happened.

In the decade in which three revolutionary statesmen broadened the empire of liberty, one of the trinity revealed himself an enemy to the free state, and another lost heart. It was at this time, the poet Matthew Arnold said, that the cherishers of the free state "lost the future." What Lincoln called the "germ" of freedom, which was "to grow and expand into the universal liberty of mankind," came close to being annihilated in a world crisis that pitted the free state against new philosophies of coercion, credos that derived their moral vocabulary, Lincoln said, from "the wolf's dictionary." In the same decade which witnessed freedom's victories, a counterrevolution began, the consequences of which the world still feels.

This is the story of that decade.

---

* As well as on the banks of the Po. In 1859–60, Cavour, Garibaldi, and Victor Emmanuel unified Italy on the basis of free-state principles.

Part One

INTO THE PIT

Chapter 1

THREE PEOPLES ON
THE PRECIPICE

Saint Petersburg, January 1861

IN THE WINTER PALACE two court functionaries walked down a long gallery towards a pair of massive bronze doors. They tapped thrice with their wands, ebony batons surmounted with double-headed eagles. The doors were thrown open, and the Tsar of Russia emerged from the seclusion of his private apartments, together with his Tsaritsa.

As he passed through galleries of his palace, the Tsar acknowledged, with the merest nod of his head, the bows and curtsies of the court. Every so often he would catch the eye of some devoted servant of the state, dressed, after the fashion of the eighteenth century, in silk stockings and a coat heavy with gold embroidery. The happy courtier, his face flushed with pride, would look about to see whether those around him had observed the mark of imperial approbation.

The Tsar and Tsaritsa proceeded to the Nicholas Hall, blazing with the light of a dozen chandeliers and ten thousand candles. Diamonds and sapphires sparkled on aristocratic bosoms; the cross and star of Alexander Nevsky flashed on glittering uniforms; moiré sashes shimmered. The chevalier guards, specially selected, out of the immensity of Russia, for their good looks, stood to attention in white tunics and polished breastplates. It was a spectacle meant to impress; and it did impress. Foreign visitors struggled to do justice to the triple pomp of guards and grooms and gold-laced grandees that hedged this man whose Empire stretched from Poland to the Pacific, from the snows of Siberia to the vineyards of the Crimea, and encompassed a sixth of the land surface of the earth. Some thought the Winter Palace baroque, others likened it to a northern edition of the *Arabian Nights.* All sensed in the autocracy of which it was the symbol a refinement of coercion, the most opulent and at the same time most naked form of power. In the world struggle between freedom and oppression, Russia figured as the beau ideal of government by force.

The Tsar and Tsaritsa opened the ball with a polonaise. When the dance ended, the imperial couple mingled with their guests. Those who had never before attended an imperial ball were startled by the courtesy with which they were received by Their Majesties. A "certain democratic air prevailed," one diplomat thought. The Tsar was determined to put his guests at ease. His manner was amiable, even gentle. Nevertheless, an invisible veil hung about the person of the autocrat. An English visitor, watching the Tsar converse with an ordinary mortal, was reminded of "the Great Mogul addressing an earthworm."

Alexander II was forty-two years old at the beginning of 1861. He had for six years been the supreme ruler of Russia. His upbringing had in many ways fitted him for the exalted station he occupied. His father, Tsar Nicholas I, though of a strong and despotic nature, with acts of blood and cruelty to his name, had nevertheless been a serious and in some directions a large-minded man. The prospect of surpassing other monarchs in the education of an heir had been agreeable to his vanity, and he had taken pains to prepare little Alexander for the throne. The Tsarevitch's tutor, the poet Vasily Zhukovsky, had labored to open the boy's mind. In a letter to Alexander's mother, the Empress Alexandra, Zhukovsky described the young Prince as "the beautiful poem on which we are working." To less sympathetic eyes, Alexander appeared in a different light. There "are times," one of his teachers said, "when he can spend an hour or more during which not a single thought will enter his head."

When, at the age of thirty-six, Alexander ascended the throne of his ancestors, many predicted that he would not prosper. "He does not give the idea of having much strength either of intellect or of character," Earl Granville wrote to Queen Victoria shortly after the Tsar's coronation in Moscow. The more superstitious noted how, when Alexander was crowned in the Kremlin, the heavy chain of the Order of Saint Andrew slipped from a pillow and fell to the floor—an evil omen surely.*

No one knew better than Alexander himself the difficulty of his task. He had inherited from his father power and riches almost fabulous in extent; he was Tsar of all the Russias. But his Empire was troubled. Rus-

---

* Did Saint Andrew foretell the sovereign's violent death? During the coronation, in 1896, of Nicholas II, the last of the Tsars, the Order of Saint Andrew slipped from Nicholas's shoulder and fell to the floor. Two decades later he was murdered.

sia lay at the crossroads of Europe and Asia. Over the centuries she had been oppressed by a succession of invaders. Between the twelfth and seventeenth centuries a form of authoritarian government took hold in the land. The government of the nation that in time became Russia was modeled partly on the autocratic rule of the Byzantine despots, and partly on the tyrannical forms of the Mongolian Khans. Russia never knew the mixed constitutions which, in the Middle Ages, restrained the authority of the kings of Europe. The subjects of the tsars regarded themselves as *"kholops,* that is slaves of their Prince,"* and the tsars, in turn, looked upon the state as their personal patrimony.

Sensible that a nation of slaves will never realize the highest forms of greatness, Peter the Great, who acceded to the throne in 1682, reformed the patrimonial constitution of Russia. But he chose, as his models of civil polity, the régimes which, in France, in Spain, and in Germany, superseded the limited monarchies of the Middle Ages, and erected in their place absolute governments supported by large military establishments. In doing so Peter exchanged one form of despotism for another. Nor was his effort to break with his own patrimonial habits altogether successful. His preferred method was coercion; and in order to break the spirit of those who opposed his reforms, he made liberal use of the ancient implements of despotism, the ax, the wheel, and the stake.

Catherine the Great, who ascended the throne in 1762, relaxed somewhat the servile régime of Peter. Russia ceased, in the waning years of the eighteenth century, to be a slave state. But she did not become a free state. The country suffered from the contradiction. The decaying autocracy, strong enough to overwhelm men's energies, was too weak to suppress their hopes. The people were discontented, but they were no longer abjectly afraid. A crisis, it was evident, could not be far off.

Alexander ascended the throne determined to forestall the catastrophe. But how? Two courses of action presented themselves. One lay in a continuation of the policy of coercion, the other beckoned towards freedom. Free states like England and the United States had, in the eighteenth and nineteenth centuries, liberated their peoples' energies, and were rapidly outstripping their rivals in trade, in industry, and in the accumulation of capital. Their entrepreneurial creativity produced a series of technological revolutions that were reshaping the world. For a time the institutions of freedom seemed poised to carry all before them. But a countervailing reaction set in. Around the world, privilege rose up to defend its prerogatives. In Russia, in Germany, in America itself, grandees with their backs against the wall met the challenge of liberty with a philosophy of coercion designed to protect their power.

The new philosophy of coercion was founded on two ideas. The first was paternalism, an idea which, in different forms and under various guises, proved to be a potent weapon in the reaction against the free state. Landowners in Russia and in the American South argued that their domestic institutions embodied the paternal principle; the bondsman had, in his master, a compassionate father to look after him, and he was therefore better off than the worker in the cruel world of free labor. In Germany, the most ingenious of the Prussian aristocrats sought to implement a paternal code designed to regulate the masses and make them more subservient to the state. In the new paternal theory of government, the state was to love its subjects as a father loves a child. So Lord Macaulay, the great historian of freedom, wrote. The new paternal régime would "regulate the school, overlook the playground, fix the hours of labour and recreation, prescribe what ballads shall be sung, what tunes shall be played, what books shall be read, what physic shall be swallowed. . . ."

The second idea the grandees lighted on was militant nationalism. Shorn of the romantic rhetoric in which its apologists couched it, this form of nationalism meant the right of certain (superior) peoples to impose their will on other (inferior) peoples. Planters in the American South dreamt of enslaving Central America and the Caribbean. Germany's nationalists aspired to incorporate Danish, French, and Polish provinces in a new German Reich. In Moscow and Saint Petersburg, romantic nationalists with Pan-Slav sympathies yearned to rout the Ottoman Turks and impose Russia's will on Byzantium. By creating an enticing jingo-spectacle, the nationalists hoped to divert the imaginations of oppressed populations at home. At the same time, they sought to open new fields of exploitation—what in Germany came to be called *Lebensraum* (living space). Not least, the nationalists worked to reinforce racial chauvinism, that convenient prop of the oppressor; they argued that certain races (white, German, Slav) were superior to other races. Militant nationalism, like authoritarian paternalism, rested on the premise that all men are *not* created equal; some men are more equal than others.

The easiest course for Tsar Alexander would have been to follow the path of coercion. He had only to place himself at the head of the great Slav nation and burnish the messianic eagles Russia had inherited from Byzantium. He could then hope to rout the Turk and seat himself on a golden throne in Sancta Sophia, the jewel of Constantinople. Russia's problems would be solved in the acquisition of an even vaster empire, and she would become in fact what she had long been in mystical aspiration, the "Third Rome."

But the Tsar, breaking with the traditions of his dynasty, chose the more difficult course. At a decisive moment in the gathering world crisis,

Alexander decided that the future lay with freedom. He resolved to smash the fetters and liberate his country's forgotten potential. He did not intend to relinquish his own autocratic power; that would be going too far. But though it is tempting to scoff at the imperial hypocrite, the step the Tsar contemplated was, given the condition of his country and the doubtful stability of his throne, a daring one. He intended to free the serfs.

Icy winds swept the night as the Tsar, in the warmth of the Winter Palace, made his way from table to table. The northern landscape that lay beyond the double-glazed windows—the snow-bound plazas and stage-prop temples—strangely heightened his authority; only a superhuman authority, it seemed, could contrive to fashion a capital out of this desolate ice-world. Inside, the tables were heaped with rare and delicate dishes, all that extravagance which despotism can command and in which absolute power delights to indulge. At each table Alexander spoke a few gracious words, then raised a glass of champagne to his lips and took up an hors d'oeuvre; his guests might then say that they had dined with the autocrat. At the next table he would, machinelike, repeat the performance. Wherever he turned, he saw faces flushed with dancing, wine, and the intoxicating sense of proximity to power.

He knew how soon the happy countenances would be changed into frowns and grimaces. The revolution he contemplated would displease many of his guards and courtiers. If conducted with insufficient finesse, it might even drive them into open rebellion. The serf-owning magnificoes of the capital would doubtless embrace a policy of romantic opposition to reform. A revival of the tradition of conquest, the raising of fresh regiments, the avenging of past humiliations—the old guard never could resist the call of a bugle-horn. But would the grandees stand patiently by while the Tsar experimented with freedom, and broke the chains of the vassals who harvested their crops, cooked their meals, and polished their jewels?

Washington, January 1861

JAMES BUCHANAN had long aspired to the office of President of the United States. At length, in the twilight of life, he had attained it. He was a curious figure; and not the least curious feature of his character was his relationship with the lady who served as the mistress of his White House. Harriet Lane was the President's niece. She was also his most intimate companion. Nothing could be stranger than the intensity of the attachment that developed between the tired old bachelor and the strong and beautiful lady; but each was necessary to the other. Miss Lane organized a splendid social calendar for her uncle; she arranged exquisite dinners in the White House, and intimate champagne parties, though the President, weakly accommodating as he was in all the important questions of state, drew the line at card-playing, and he positively forbade dancing. Miss Lane, for her part, was exalted into a sphere far above that to which any young man of her acquaintance could have introduced her. In the afternoons, she would ride out, sidesaddle, on a white horse, with only a single groom in attendance. When she came in from her ride and greeted her uncle, no one who saw the pair could doubt which was the more formidable personage.

But how soon it turned to dust and ashes. In the autumn of 1860 the country was gripped by what President Buchanan could only regard as a strange hysteria. An election was on. In the North, paramilitary groups like the Wide Awakes organized torchlit processions in honor of their hero, Abraham Lincoln. Thousands of young men in flowing capes and black helmets carried their flambeaux with an almost religious fervor down the streets of Northern cities. When, in November, Lincoln was elected President, citizens in the cotton and rice counties of the South rose up to denounce his elevation. In South Carolina a flag emblazoned with the palmetto, the image of the state's patriotic defiance, was hoisted at Charleston, and in December the state declared herself independent of the Union.

President Buchanan, in the White House, lay paralyzed by nervous irresolution. He trembled on the eminence to which his grasping mediocrity had raised him, and even Miss Lane was incapable of rousing him to exertion.

What was he to do?

No state had ever before seceded from the Union. The Secretary of State, old Lewis Cass of Michigan, a hero of the War of 1812, hobbled into the White House with a red nose and a gaudy wig. He implored the President to put down the Carolina insurrection by force of arms. The Secretary of the Interior, Jacob Thompson of Mississippi, as vigorously pressed the President not to undertake measures that might kindle the spark of the Carolina revolt into a conflagration. Yet from President Buchanan himself there came neither orders nor actions, only a request for memoranda. Did a state, he asked, possess a right to secede? No, he concluded, it did not. Did the government possess a right to prevent a state from seceding? The light which the precedents threw upon the question was dubious. As the nation edged closer and closer to collapse, the President and his lawyers plunged deeper and deeper into the perplexing mysteries of sovereignty and the Constitution.

The futility of this policy was soon enough apparent. A country on the verge of civil war cannot be saved by barristers, and President Buchanan inclined to despair. The collision, in America, between the institutions of the free state and the philosophy of coercion was bound to be shattering. Here was concentrated, in a pure form, the essence of two antipathetic creeds. In the North, the principal opponents of slavery were, in temper if not dogmatic faith, Puritans, descended from men and women who, however sour might have been their characters, stoutly opposed a succession of tyrants. In the South, the leading planters were, in self-conceit if not hereditary fact, Cavaliers, who traced, or pretended to trace, their ancestry to men and women who sprang from the gentry of England, and who in the New World transmuted the principles of feudal subordination into a justification of human bondage. The characteristics of type must not be exaggerated. The planter, after the fashion of aristocracy, loved his own freedom, though he bought and sold slaves. The Puritan, having obtained liberty for himself, was often careless of that of others. But in the imagination of the Cavalier the idea of freedom slowly withered, while in the conscience of the Puritan it acquired a transforming strength.

Even in the Republic's Golden Age, when Washington and Adams, Hamilton and Jefferson, bestrode the scene, the leading statesmen saw no way to assimilate the two antagonistic cultures. Unable to reconcile the institution of slavery with the professions of the Declaration of Independence—the faith that all men are created equal—the founders of the American Republic threw onto the future a burden they could not shoulder themselves. The generation that succeeded the founders shrank from the problem their fathers had bequeathed to them. The spirit of the Republic's second epoch—its Silver Age, the age of Henry Clay and Daniel Webster—was the spirit, not of inspired creation, but of cautious compromise, the virtues of which were openly celebrated in the audacious bargaining of Clay, and darkly conceded in the polished orations of Webster.

But the Silver Age was breaking down. In the South, power passed from the tobacco counties of Virginia, where the planters had long assumed, or at least affected, a pose of anguish over their chattels, to the richer soils of Mississippi and Alabama, where a more lucrative crop—cotton—overcame any such fastidious doubts. In 1861 the leading cotton planters looked, not to Virginia, but to South Carolina for a moral and intellectual ideal. In some of South Carolina's tidewater districts slaves accounted for more than eighty percent of the population. The slave driver there could not be as careless of his bondsmen as the Virginian was or pretended to be, and the intellectuals of the Carolina master class elaborated justifications of coercion grounded in the same paternal theories advanced by grandees in Russia and Germany. Under the tuition of South Carolina, Southern political leaders ceased to be reluctant apologists for slavery; the "Fire Eaters," as they were called, pronounced their peculiar institution "a good—a positive good."

Men in the North also hastened towards the precipice. Abolitionists, touched by the light of the old Puritan conscience, demanded the immediate emancipation of the slaves, while partisans of Free Soil repudiated the conciliatory policies of the Silver Age and called for the prohibition of slavery in the virgin territories of the West.

President Buchanan, weak and dispirited though he was, attempted, after the fashion of the Silver Age, to work a compromise between the spirit of revived Puritanism and the ghost of renovated feudalism. The President was himself one of the last of the Silver Age statesmen. He had first entered Congress in 1821, when Jefferson and Adams were living. But the President had outlived his age. The accumulated burden of suspicion and mutual antipathy was by this time so great that it is doubtful whether even the arts of Clay or the oratorical skill of Webster could have effected a compromise between the contending sections and philosophies. And in vigor and ability, in imagination and courage, in all the qualities that make for greatness in politics, Buchanan was far inferior to Clay and Webster. He had, moreover, forfeited any claim to impartial arbitration. Though he came from Pennsylvania, his sympathies lay decidedly with the racial paternalism of the slaveholders and their dream of a Caribbean imperium; he was a true doughface.

Yet he had the strength of his weaknesses. He was by vocation less a leader than a diplomat; and diplomacy, he believed, might yet save the nation. He possessed the charming manners, the fawning graciousness, the half-effeminate *politesse* sometimes found in men who, through an idiosyncrasy of soul, combine a soft and yielding nature with a yearning for power and authority. Now, in the crisis of his career, James Buchanan comforted himself with the thought that his old suavity might yet save him.

Germany and France, February–March 1861

IT WAS NOT ONLY in Russia and the United States that the new decade began with a heightening of tensions between the advocates of rival conceptions of man's destiny. Germany also was torn. Some Germans spoke of the need for free constitutions and ministers responsible to elected lawmakers; others exalted an ideal of national power, to be realized in a new and potent German state. Still others wavered between the two contending points of view, and cherished the delusive hope that their country could worship at the twin altars of power and freedom.

Of the two antagonistic parties, the champions of liberty possessed, at the beginning of 1861, the superior organization. They had formed committees, drafted reports, drawn up programs of action. By contrast, those who dreamed of a new German Empire had, at this time, no strategy; they had no plan. But they had something no less vital—they had an inspiration. Revolutions begin, not in plans, but in poetry, and in music.*

"God knows," Richard Wagner wrote to a friend, "what will come out of this projected *Tannhäuser:* inwardly I have no faith in it, and that for good reasons." The composer was, he said, tired—tired "to the very depths" of his soul. He was preparing for the production of his *Tannhäuser* at the Opéra in Paris, and nothing was going right.

The tenor in particular was a fiasco. Albert Niemann was a young man with a beautiful voice. He was eager to have a success in Paris. This, he feared, would be denied him. He had heard the chatter of the boulevards; *Tannhäuser,* it was predicted, would be a failure, and he would be dragged down in its ruin. He avenged himself against the composer, whom he regarded as the author of his misfortunes, by sullenly refusing to cooperate with him during rehearsals.

Wagner's troubles were not limited to a desponding tenor. The composer was in debt, and he was reduced to humiliating shifts to raise money. "I have enormous losses," he said, and "no one who helps me!" To one of his loves, Mathilde Wesendonk, Wagner spoke of the tragic fate of the artist—his numerous ordeals, his struggles with the uncomprehending world, the unbridgeable chasm between his inner spiritual purity and the vileness of the philistines who so often thwarted his aesthetic will. "I feel myself pure," he told Frau Wesendonk. "I know in the innermost depth of me that I have never wrought for myself, but only for others; and my perpetual sufferings are my witnesses." No one, he said, understood him, though he ventured to express the hope that "some day something at least of my works will meet with understanding."

As the night of the first performance approached, Wagner was sombre. He was, he said, a German—a German to the core of his being. How could he be expected to make music for Frenchmen?

The fatal night arrived. To the Opéra carriages bearing opulent figures of the Second Empire of the Bonapartes drew up. Ancient generals and grave counselors of state handed down their ladies. Young swells from the Jockey Club, having finished their games of baccarat, came swaggering in, intent on making mischief. At last the Emperor himself

---

* Music, the ancient Greeks believed, goes deeper into the soul than utterances that lack melody: it molds the spirit more completely.

came. The audience rose, in a mass of silk and a blaze of tiaras, and Napoleon III, nephew of the great Bonaparte, took his seat in the imperial box.

The fuss over the Emperor's arrival subsided, and the first strains of the opera sounded, with their note of obscure yearning. Then came a rising, and soon the listener was borne aloft, as to some Alpine height, "into the pure air." Yet it was not the melody alone that was meant to soar; Wagner intended that his listeners, too, should ascend. He wanted them to leave behind the existing world, so sordid and prosaic, and to help him build a better, loftier one. His weapons, in this battle for men's souls, were myths, forged in music. Like other romantic poets, he found an inspiration in his people's oldest songs; he constructed *Tannhäuser*, he said, out of material with "typically German associations." "My very blood and nerves were stirred with the greatest excitement as I began to sketch and develop the music of *Tannhäuser*. My true nature, which out of disgust with the modern world was oriented toward one that was older and nobler, enveloped with ardent embrace the eternal form of my being, and mingled the two in one stream: the highest longing for love."

The Parisians in the Opéra yawned. Swathed in silks and furs, lapped in the accumulated luxuries of progress and empire, they were unable to see how soon their own repose was to be disturbed by the *Sturm und Drang* Wagner's opera betokened. Before the decade was finished, their city would be besieged by German armies, and their temples and houses and hospitals would be smashed by German shells. The waking of Tannhäuser's soul was a parable of the reawakening of Germany itself, freshly conscious of its strength. But the Parisians did not see it.

Their obtuseness was in some ways understandable, for the revolution in Germany was not, at the beginning of 1861, easy to perceive. The true extent of German power was obscured by the innumerable divisions of the German polity. Observers had, since the time of Tacitus, been astonished by the special qualities of Germany's genius, its spirit of violent activity. But in March 1861 that genius was wasted in the squabbles of two hostile parties and three dozen petty sovereignties. Those who gave their adhesion to the party of liberty were absorbed in a contentious struggle with those who upheld the dogma of force. The two leading German powers, Prussia and Austria, were locked in a sterile rivalry with one another, and the spirit of a people which, a thousand years before, had subdued much of Europe under the standard of Charlemagne languished under the sway of so many inferior diadems.

During the second act the catcalls began to sound. Not even the presence of the Emperor prevented the young blades of the Jockey Club from caterwauling for their favorite ballerinas, who Wagner in his zeal for artistic purity had banished from the stage. At a signal they raised their white-gloved hands and blew their dog-whistles. "The row was beyond belief," Niemann, the disaffected tenor, wrote to a friend in Berlin. "Princess Metternich, to whose patronage the production of the opera is mainly due, was compelled to leave the theatre after the second act, the audience continually turning round towards her box and jeering at her at the top of its voice." On the second night *Tannhäuser* was again disrupted by the genteel hooligans of the Jockey Club. On the third night Wagner withdrew the opera. *Tannhäuser* was, Niemann said, "literally hissed off, hooted off, and finally laughed off" the stage.

Wagner himself was graceful in defeat; and after the third and final performance he retired to his rooms in the Rue d'Aumale. There, at two o'clock in the morning, the prophet of the German revolution was to be found quietly drinking tea and smoking his pipe with a small party of friends. He drolly accused one of the party, little Olga Herzen, the daughter of the Russian expatriate writer, of having hissed his opera. Yet at the same time it was noticed that his hand trembled uncontrollably.

France had triumphed over Germany in the Opéra. But Wagner was not wrong in his perception of the future. The slumberers had awakened.

Chapter 2

REBELS BORN

Washington, December 1860–February 1861

WITHIN WEEKS OF the election of Lincoln, committees were appointed by the House and the Senate to determine whether the questions that divided the United States could be settled without violence. To the Senate's Committee of Thirteen came the foremost parliamentarians which America in that age could show. Chief among the proponents, on the Committee, of a peaceable adjustment of the claims of rival philosophies was old John Crittenden of Kentucky. He was a border state man, and inhabited a middle zone between the mentality of the Puritan and that of the Cavalier. He was as devoted to the cause of sectional conciliation as President Buchanan; but unlike the President, whose feeble policy was now universally despised, he retained the goodwill of men on both sides of the Mason-Dixon line.

To the Committee of Thirteen came, too, Lazarus Powell, another Kentuckian who, like Crittenden, had been bred up in the Silver Age school of compromise. Powell was an affable lawyer who had risen into power and property. A former governor of Kentucky, he was celebrated by his friends for the passion with which he both chewed tobacco and propounded the doctrines of moderation. He scorned "ambitious fanatical zealots" in the North as well as in the South.

There was another, still more potent voice in favor of compromise on the Committee. Beside the border state squires sat a short, haggard-looking man from the West. Beneath an exterior of coarse joviality, Stephen A. Douglas of Illinois concealed one of the cleverest and most resourceful minds of the Silver Age school. An unsuccessful candidate for President in the recent election and the leader of the Northern Democrats, Douglas was a man broken by drink, by debt, by the collapse of his political fortunes, and by the accumulated burdens of a long carouse. But he possessed still a quantity of that force which had made him, for a time, the most formidable man in the Senate.

Senator Crittenden, whose age and experience entitled him to precedence, was placed in the chair. With the assistance of Senator Powell, he proceeded to frame a plan of compromise. The two senators called for the restoration of the old Missouri Compromise line, and proposed that the line be extended across the nation's Western territories to California. The effect of the proposal would be to make slavery unlawful in all the Western territory north of latitude 36°30'.* To conciliate the cotton men, Crittenden proposed to guarantee slavery perpetually in all territory "now held, or hereafter acquired" by the United States south of the Compromise line, a concession that would permit the Fire Eaters to realize their dream of a tropical slave empire.

The plan was promising: but such was the procedural rule adopted by the Committee that no bargain was possible unless representatives of the two antipathetic philosophies consented to it. The cause of the opponents of territorial slavery was confided to the five Republican senators who took their seats on the Committee. In contrast to the compromisers of the Silver Age, the Republicans were, as a rule, averse to negotiation: they believed that slavery should be made unlawful in *all* the nation's territory. "Let there be no compromise on the question of *extending* slavery," Abraham Lincoln, the leader of the Republicans, wrote in December 1860. "The tug has to come, & better now, than any time hereafter."

Here was a position that the Southern men, represented on the Committee by Jefferson Davis of Mississippi, Robert Toombs of Georgia, and Robert Mercer Taliaferro Hunter of Virginia, could never accept. The question of slavery in the territories was for the slaveholders intimately bound up with the survival of their way of life. They knew that, in the early days of the Republic, the North and the South had been very nearly equal in population. By 1850, however, the population of the North had grown to more than thirteen million. The South's population had not yet reached ten million. The rapid growth of Northern power terrified men whose prosperity depended on forced labor. If the free labor system of the North prevailed in the immense spaces of the West, the balance of power in the country would shift still more dramatically in favor of the

* The Missouri Compromise of 1820 was the most durable of the Silver Age compromises. Under this law Maine was admitted to the Union as a free state; Missouri was admitted as a slave state; and slavery was declared unlawful in the remaining Louisiana Purchase territory north of latitude 36°30'.

free states. The slaves states would find themselves cornered in the South-east—a small slice of a vast continent. A loss of political power would nec-essarily follow. The incorporation, in the Union, of new free states, carved out of the territories of the West, would end Southern parity in the Senate. The paternalist institutions of the South would be doomed.

The territories of the West were the first battlefields of the Civil War. The halls of Congress were the second. In Kansas pro-slavery men mur-dered free-state men and raised the red flag of Southern Rights at Lawrence. Free-state men led by John Brown murdered pro-slavery men near Pottawatomie Creek. In the Senate, Charles Sumner of Massachu-setts denounced the pro-slavery faction's "Crime Against Kansas." Pres-ton Brooks of South Carolina, aided by fellow Southerners Laurence Keitt and Henry Edmondson, fell upon Sumner on the Senate floor, and Brooks beat him senseless with a cane. The free-state men eventually tri-umphed in Kansas; but the victory was rendered pyrrhic by the United States Supreme Court, which in the case of *Dred Scott v. Sandford* held that under the Constitution slaveholders were entitled to bring their slaves into *all* of the nation's territories.

Three of the five Republicans on the Committee of Thirteen, Col-lamer of Vermont, Doolittle of Wisconsin, and Grimes of Iowa, could all be expected to remain faithful to the uncompromising territorial policy laid down by Lincoln. The only question pertaining to the fourth, Ben-jamin "Bluff Ben" Wade of Ohio, was whether, in his intercourse with Fire Eaters and border state squires, he could be persuaded to conduct him-self with a civility becoming his office, or whether he would insist, like Preston Brooks and Laurence Keitt, on leaving blood on the Senate floor. "Bluff Ben" was a well-built Ohioan with long white hair and black staring eyes. Like many Westerners notable for their zeal in the anti-slavery cause, he was descended from old New England stock, and he regarded compromisers with the same antipathy with which he regarded slave-driving oligarchs. The man who inflicted the lash, and the man who consented that the lash should be inflicted, were in his eyes equally bloody men. When, a few years before, a Southern Senator challenged him to a duel, Wade accepted the challenge and, as was his right under the *Code Duello,* named his weapons and conditions: "squirrel rifles at twenty paces," with "a white paper the size of a dollar pinned over the heart of each combatant." The Southern Senator retracted his demand for satisfaction.

The fifth Republican on the Crittenden Committee was a more com-plicated case. William H. Seward of New York was the most illustrious member of his party after Lincoln himself. His loss to Lincoln at the party's nominating convention in Chicago in the spring of 1860 was mortifying to a man who believed his own claims to pre-eminence to be unri-valled. Seward continued, many months after the defeat, to be sullen. "Disappointment!" he told a disgruntled officeseeker. "You speak to me of disappointment. To me, who was justly entitled to the Republican nomination for the presidency, and who had to stand aside and see it given to a little Illinois lawyer. You speak to me of disappointment!"

Would Seward agree to a compromise on the question of territorial slavery? He bore the reputation of an uncompromising man. He was in many ways the antithesis of a Silver Age statesman, and he had condemned Daniel Webster when that Senator lent the force of his oratory to Henry Clay's Compromise of 1850. But ten years in the Senate had softened Seward's zeal. A small, sallow-faced man, the Senator from New York was quick, perceptive, and ambitious. His disordered clothes and slouching manners bespoke the provincial lawyer; but a careful observer might have discerned, in the pursed lips, the steady gaze, the aquiline nose, intima-tions of a strength that survives the wreck of youthful idealism.

Success came easily to Seward; perhaps too easily. At the age of thirty-seven he was Governor of New York. A decade later he was Senator. The achievement of so much splendor of fortune so early in life had its usual effect, and Seward, who began his career as an angry young man, was by degrees transformed into a cynical elder statesman. In his heart he was still a hater of slavery. In 1858 he declared the conflict between servitude and freedom to be an "irrepressible" one. But ambition is a plant that adapts itself to a variety of soils. After his bid to lead the Republican rev-olution failed, Seward cast about for other paths to glory. Little as he resembled the statesmen of the Silver Age school of Webster and Clay, he demonstrated, in the last weeks of 1860, a newfound admiration for their conciliatory policies. Whether from motives of patriotism or frus-trated desire, he proclaimed the virtues of moderation and negotiation. Shortly after the election of Lincoln, there appeared, in the *Albany Evening Journal,* a paper known to enjoy the confidence of Seward, a pro-posal for reviving the old Missouri line of 36°30'—the principle of con-ciliation at the heart of Senator Crittenden's plan. A short time later the newspaper reiterated the proposal, and in private conversation Seward promised to support a bargain arranged on this principle.

But there was a difficulty with Seward's policy. Abraham Lincoln had not endorsed it. The President-Elect opposed any accommodation between the North and the South on the territorial question. Lincoln was the most uncompromising politician of the age where territorial slav-ery was concerned, and he had labored assiduously to prevent the emer-gence of a Free Soil movement based on any principle other than the absolute exclusion of slavery from the territories.

Such an obstacle might have deterred an ordinary politician. But Seward had a supreme faith in his powers. Lincoln, he reasoned, was new to the national stage. His experience was limited. At a time when Seward himself had been Governor of a large and populous state, Lincoln had been a lawyer struggling into practice on the Illinois frontier. Seward had spent the 1850s in the Senate. Lincoln had spent the same decade trying, without success, to gain admission to that body. Surely the novice would submit to the tuition of the master statesman. Seward, flicking away the ashes of his cigar, saw that he had lost the prize. He was not to be the President. But might he not save the country from the President?

Seward opened a negotiation with Lincoln, who had asked him to be his Secretary of State. In December 1860, the New Yorker dispatched an emissary to the President-Elect, who was then residing in his hometown of Springfield, Illinois. Seward chose for the mission his closest adviser, the political boss Thurlow Weed. Weed arrived in Springfield on December 20, the same day South Carolina seceded from the Union. Lincoln received him in his house on Eighth Street. The two men spoke for six hours. The President-Elect's tone was cordial. He seemed genuinely to hope that Seward would accept the office of Secretary of State. But on one subject he was not to be moved.

He would not compromise on the question of slavery in the territories.

In order to remove any doubt as to his position, Lincoln gave Weed a paper to deliver to Seward, with instructions to govern the Senator's conduct on Crittenden's Committee of Thirteen.

Weed left Springfield and, meeting the Senator at Syracuse, delivered Lincoln's ultimatum as the two men rode the train together to Albany. In an instant all the structures of power and predominance Seward had raised in his imagination came crashing down. The choice before him was clear. He must either stoop to do Lincoln's bidding or surrender his ambition of swaying the destinies of a nation. The latter course was impossible; Seward could not bear the idea of being outside the golden circle of power. Laying aside his previous talk of compromise, he went to Senator Crittenden's Committee and declined to support the proposal to revive the Missouri line.

On December 28, the same day Senator Crittenden's Committee, having failed to reach an agreement to preserve the Union, adjourned in failure, Seward wrote to President-Elect Lincoln to accept the State Department.

Saint Petersburg, December 1857–March 1861

IN HIS BEDROOM-STUDY in the Winter Palace, Tsar Alexander rose at eight. Situated in the western wing of the palace, the room formed part of a suite of chambers that served as the Tsar's private quarters. (The Tsaritsa's apartments were adjacent to those of her husband, in the southwest corner of the building.) One reached the Tsar's study through an anteroom, which, in turn, opened on a library; this last room housed Alexander's collection of books, maps, and pornography.*

Visitors to the study were startled by a simplicity of décor which, amid the interminable splendors of a palace, was in some ways more ostentatious than luxury. The room was, like many in the Winter Palace, adorned with marble columns, yet it was plainly furnished, in the Empire style. The architect Alexander Briullov, charged with repairing the room after a fire ravaged the palace in 1837, was faithful to the eighteenth-century inspirations of an earlier designer, Giacomo Quarenghi. There was a desk, which was covered with photographs of the Tsar's family, and a circular table, piled high with state papers. Nearby was a leather easy chair. In the corner stood that fixture of Russian rooms, the glazed stove.

The Tsar affected the character of a simple soldier. He slept on a folding camp bed. Rising from it, he donned a cherry-colored robe, brought to him by his valet. Another servant brought him coffee. It was Alexander's habit to go to the window as he drank it. Looking through the double-glass, he took in the Petersburg morning. Directly below him lay the parade ground, where soldiers of the Preobrazhensky Regiment were preparing to change the guard. Beyond the parade ground lay the yellow-and-white Admiralty Building, the headquarters of the Russian navy. To the southwest lay Saint Isaac's Cathedral; to the northwest flowed the Neva.

It was said of the tsars that what they dreamt of in the night they could carry out upon waking in the morning. The reality Alexander confronted when he woke in his bedroom-study was different. Autocracy does not eliminate opposition, it drives it underground, where, like other matter that has been forced into a subterranean channel, it assumes a molten form, and becomes explosive. In England, the rowdy grandees bayed for broken glass. In Russia, they bayed for the broken heads of their sovereigns. The Empire of the Tsars was a despotism tempered by assassination.

Alexander, plotting his revolution "from above," anticipated the machinations of the opposition with a shrewdness of forecast that Lin-

---

* Alexander's collection of erotic drawings was discovered by the Bolsheviks when they invaded the Winter Palace in 1917.

coln and Bismarck—who were both to stumble in the early phases of their own revolutions—might well have envied. The Tsar knew that the fathers and grandfathers of the men who regulated his palace and drilled his regiments had not scrupled to plunge a dagger into the back of the autocrat who threatened their luxurious repose. Alexander's great-grandmother, Catherine the Great, had obtained the crown by persuading the grandees to connive at the arrest and murder of her husband, Tsar Peter III, Alexander's (putative) great-grandfather. (The integrity of the Romanov line was rendered doubtful by the infidelities of Catherine.) Alexander's grandfather, Tsar Paul, fell a victim to another palace revolution. The unhappy child of Catherine, Paul was a man of morose temper and uncertain paternity, and he struck fear in the hearts of the potentates of the army and the court. While the courtiers sighed for the looser tyranny of the mother, their murmurs inflamed the dark and suspicious nature of the son. Paul's capricious punishments exasperated the magnificoes of the capital, and on a winter night in 1801 a motley collection of generals and statesmen, heated with brandy, invaded the palace and burst into the imperial bedchamber. The seditious retainers discovered the Tsar cowering, in his nightclothes, behind a screen or drapery. It was subsequently related that Paul expired of an apoplectic seizure; but the only real question is whether he was strangled or bludgeoned to death.

Alexander's father, Nicholas I, came close to sharing the fate of Peter III and Paul I. On the day Nicholas was proclaimed Tsar, rebellious troops marched into the center of Saint Petersburg. At their head was a body of disaffected officers, some of whom were intimates of the court, and stood close to the throne. Alexander, a boy of seven at the time, was too young to understand the events that shattered the tranquility of Saint Petersburg in December 1825. But he was old enough to feel their terror. Little "Sasha," as he was called by his family, had been at his lessons in the Anichkov Palace. Attendants rushed into the schoolroom and hurried the child downstairs, where a carriage was in readiness. The Tsarevitch was taken to the Winter Palace, where his father was endeavoring to crush the revolt. When darkness fell, Nicholas ordered the artillery to be wheeled out. Flashing guns illuminated the night. Afterwards the Tsar commanded his son to be dressed in the miniature parade uniform of a Hussar of the Life Guards. In this costume the terrified child was taken out into the night. Alexander watched as his father went about in the light of enormous bonfires. Suddenly the Tsar took his son in his arms and raised him aloft. "Here, boys," Nicholas cried. "This is my heir, serve him faithfully!" A cheer went up, and the soldiers came to kiss the cheek of the trembling Tsarevitch. Little Alexander burst into tears—and learned a lesson in autocracy. He never afterwards forgot how much falseness could lie concealed in the rancid soul of a courtier.

Four decades after the revolt, Alexander found himself as little able as any other tsar to trust in the fidelity of his retainers. The courtier whose disaffection he had most to dread was Prince Alexis Fyodorovich Orlov, the leader of the party of coercion in Russia. The Prince would sooner cut off his hand, he said, than submit to a revolutionary policy of emancipating serfs and giving them land. His words could not be dismissed lightly; the Prince was one of the most powerful figures in the Empire. His family had first obtained power in the days of Catherine the Great. Gregory Orlov, the Prince's uncle, had been the lover of that ambitious Princess, and he had helped her to obtain the Crown through the deposition of her husband, the feeble Peter III. The versatile courtier had been amply rewarded both for his political and his personal services to the Empress. Honors and emoluments were showered upon Orlov and his connections; and the memory of the Tsaritsa's illicit love invested his family with an aura of romance.

The high birth and large possessions of Prince Alexis Orlov were only the beginning of his authority. In his youth the Prince had been a splendid warrior, and his uniform sagged with the medals which his valor during the Napoleonic Wars had gained him. In the years since 1812 he had evolved into a resourceful courtier, a master of the arts of intrigue that had been brought to perfection on the banks of the Neva. Elegant, courteous, and unscrupulous, with a captivating manner that recalled his eighteenth-century ancestors, the Prince had been raised by Alexander's father, Tsar Nicholas, to the highest civil honors. To his stewardship had been confided the Third Section of His Majesty's Private Imperial Chancery, which housed the Tsarist secret police; and as a reward for his fidelity he had been made President of the Imperial Council of State.

Prince Orlov was prepared to humor the Tsar, and to promise him results; but in his heart he despised Alexander's liberal impulses. To resist the revolutionary innovations was the beginning and the end of his policy; and he had reason to suppose that such resistance would not be in vain. Orlov had studied his master with care. The Tsar, he concluded, was a lazy man. He was also, he saw, a licentious one. The two qualities, artfully manipulated, might yet deliver Alexander into the hands of his courtier.

Prince Orlov knew that the domestic life of his master was troubled. Alexander had, before he ascended the throne, made a tour of Europe, and during a visit to Darmstadt, in the Grand Duchy of Hesse, he had fallen in love with a German Princess, Maximiliana-Wilhelmina. The Princess was delicately beautiful, with a slim waist and golden hair. But a cloud hung over her birth. Her mother, it was said, had passionately loved some base fellow about the court of Darmstadt, and it was this man, not Grand Duke Louis, who had in fact sired the girl. None of this, however, made any difference to the infatuated Alexander. "She is the woman of my dreams," he said. "I will never marry anyone but her." Displaying an energy of will that contrasted strangely with his habitual indolence, he broke down his parents' opposition to the marriage. The Princess was received into the Orthodox Church in December 1840; at her baptism she took the name Mary Alexandrovna. She and Alexander were married, in the spring of 1841, in the Winter Palace. They had at first been happy together. In 1842 Mary bore her husband the first of eight children. The girl, Alexandra, died at the age of six; her father preserved for the rest of his life her little blue dress. In 1843 a boy, Nicholas, was born; the child, delicate and intelligent, became the object of his parents' fondest hopes. More children followed, but the romance of Alexander and Mary faded. The Tsar's desire for fresher flesh grew more intense, and he was believed to have taken a mistress.

The violence of his desires did not yet carry Alexander to the extravagances which, at a later period, scandalized the capital; but his behavior may nevertheless have rendered him vulnerable to the stratagems of Prince Orlov and his party. If a story that went round the court can be credited, the reactionary courtiers imposed upon the Empress's confessor to do their dirty work. The priest was compliant. He insinuated, to the Tsaritsa, the necessity of reclaiming the Tsar from the epicurism and lust in which his spirit was sunk, and under the pretense of care for Alexander's soul he urged the Empress to take her husband to task for his infidelity. The result, it was said, was just what the courtiers hoped. The Tsar declined to sacrifice the concubine and instead shrank from the reproaches of the wife. Turning away from the domestic apartments of the palace, Alexander sought out the earliest companions of his pleasures. In the company of dissipated fops like the young Count Adlerberg, he forgot the cares of state and escaped the strictures of the Empress. The worthless favorites, in turn, preyed upon the sovereign and amused his looser hours. By pandering to Alexander's vices, they hoped to distract him from the laborious business of reforming Russia.

But the Tsar was not to be thus easily diverted. He did not, indeed, break openly with his adversaries. That was the mistake his grandfather, Tsar Paul, had made. Alexander reasoned instead that success lay in the appearance of vacillation. The course he chose ran contrary to all the manuals of leadership, which extol boldness and evident decision; but in the circumstances in which he found himself, the inheritor of a throne that depended for its strength on the goodwill of a powerful oli-

garchy, the strategy he embraced was an intelligent one. By adopting
what appeared to be an equivocal and vacillating course, he could hope
to conceal his true designs, while he might at the same time lull his opponents into complacency. Such a course, prompted, perhaps, less by conscious deliberation than by an instinct of survival, enabled Alexander to
disguise the strength of his reforming aspirations with shows of voluptuous idleness. Not for nothing was he compared to a chameleon, constantly changing his colors in order to elude his barons, the natural
predators of insufficiently wary autocrats.

Nor did the cause of reform suffer during these intervals of imperial
lethargy, for the Tsar was assisted, in his labors, by a party of reformers
whose energy in some measure made up for his laxity, and whose brains
and ingenuity counterbalanced the vigor and obstinacy of Prince Orlov
and the counter-revolutionary faction. The Tsar leaned particularly hard
on Adjutant General Jacob Rostovtsev, whom he placed in the chair of
the Editorial Commission, the body charged with laying the foundation
of emancipation. Rostovtsev had secured the goodwill of the Romanovs
when, in 1825, he informed Tsar Nicholas of the plot against him. A
plain, blunt man who inclined to corpulence, Rostovtsev was not as subtle or adroit a maneuverer as Prince Orlov. But the simple soldier possessed qualities of resolution and practical sagacity that enabled him to
joust confidently with the refined and devious courtier. These qualities
had enabled Rostovtsev to rise, from obscure beginnings, to great office.
He had no deep knowledge of the emancipation controversy; the question of whether a policy of freedom or a policy of coercion was most
likely to exalt the greatness of Russia interested him hardly at all. But
that which he lacked in speculative intelligence was supplied by his lieutenant, Nicholas Milyutin, an economist who had risen to be Acting
Deputy Minister in the Ministry of the Interior. As a boy, Milyutin had
been passionately interested in Russian history; later, after an interval of
romantic distress and obsession with French theater, he had entered the
civil service and become a zealous reformer. His genius and industry
soon discovered themselves, and he was generally acknowledged to possess one of the finest minds in the Empire.

The relations between Rostovtsev and Milyutin were, at first, far from
easy. The younger man, high-minded and idealistic, had nothing but
contempt for his superior, whom he regarded as an informer and tool of
the party of coercion. He doubted whether the old General, fat, merry,
perpetually cracking ribald jokes, was equal to the task of liberating the
serfs. That this "thickheaded scoundrel," this "shady political cardsharp,"
should now lead the party of reform seemed "the most howling absurdity." But no sooner had Rostovtsev taken up the business of emancipation

than his character seemed to undergo a change. The magnitude of his assignment made a deep impression on him, and the old soldier, with his wisecracks and sarcastic asides, threw himself into the work of reform with a ferocity that startled those who knew him. "I thought about history," Rostovtsev said, "and dreamed of an honorable page in its scrolls." He became a dedicated emancipator. A man like Milyutin, with his intellectual airs and earnest attachment to the cause of freedom, might once have moved the mirth of the old General; but not now. Rostovtsev was carried away by the young bureaucrat's boldness of thought and perception. He nicknamed Milyutin "Egeria," the nymph-goddess who, it was believed by the ancient Romans, had loved King Numa, and inspired his wise regulations.

Could Egeria overcome the resistance of Prince Orlov? Perhaps— but only if assistance were forthcoming from powerful personages at the court. The advocates of emancipation discovered that they had a powerful ally in the person of the Empress. Mary's life had for some time ceased to be a happy one. Her sudden removal, at the age of seventeen, from an obscure German principality to the court of the Romanovs had been almost too much for her. After the first glow of marriage faded, she wilted. Turning away from scenes of luxury and display, "Masha," as her husband called her, withdrew into an elegant but impenetrable reserve. Foreign visitors thought her charming; but Petersburg society was unimpressed. The Empress's French was poor, a disadvantage in a court where all the notables prided themselves on their proficiency in that tongue, and her old-fashioned formality rendered her unpopular with the men and women of fashion who haunted the galleries of the Winter Palace. They called her *"la petite bourgeoise Allemande,"* and they laughed at her deteriorating beauty. By nature tall and lean, the Tsaritsa became excessively gaunt. The climate of the capital was unfavorable to her constitution, and her cadaverous cheeks seemed to presage the ravages of consumption. What was more, her skin became inflamed with a hideous rash, which she imperfectly concealed with makeup.

In her aloofness and yearning for spiritual solace, Mary resembled the last Tsaritsa, Alexandra, who would one day wed her grandson, Nicholas, the last of the tsars. Both empresses preferred the boudoir to the salon. Alexandra's boudoir was mauve; Mary's was red. A rich brocatelle covered the walls of her retreat in the Winter Palace; the furnishings came from Cartier in Paris. In one respect, however, Mary was less fortunate than Alexandra. Her husband ceased to care for her. She passed her days in study and prayer; she mastered the classic literature of Russia; she devoted many hours to trying to raise the spirits of the dead. Yet she found herself, at night, constantly in tears. At the beginning of 1861 her hopes were concentrated not on this life but the next. Abandoned to the cold emptiness of a palace, she turned, for consolation, to the spiritual warmth of the Orthodox Church. In the elaborations of its liturgy and the fragrancy of its ritual she found an imperfect substitute for all that she had been denied by a wandering husband. She was a genuinely kind woman, and with a charity not, perhaps, unmixed with the desire to be revenged upon her enemies, she devoted herself to the destruction of serfdom.

The Empress was not the only figure at court to declare against the party of coercion. Her pious designs were embraced by Alexander's aunt, the Grand Duchess Hélène Pavolvna. Hélène was the widow of Nicholas I's younger brother, Grand Duke Michael. Like the Empress, she had begun life as a German Princess, but she was a more worldly figure than her niece. She had been educated in Paris, where she had acquired a taste for literature and liberal politics. Her opposition to serfdom was ethical rather than religious. Yet though she took her stand against the party of coercion, she remained a princess in the grand style, and she reveled in the intrigue of Saint Petersburg. She was at home, in the Michael Palace, on Thursday evenings, and her soirées were among the most splendid in the capital, for she was an astute collector of personalities. Her galleries resounded with the music of her protégé, Anton Rubinstein, who was soon to found the Saint Petersburg Conservatory. Statesmen mingled with artists and intellectuals in her salon; the Tsar himself liked to be present. Petersburg society was the stuff of her existence; but Hélène possessed convictions that rose above fashion. She devoted herself body and soul to the cause of freeing up Russia's obstructed potential. In her drawing room the disheartened reformer, bruised in the latest sally against the opponents of emancipation, was certain to find succor and a sympathetic ear—and perhaps something more. According to the rumor that went round Saint Petersburg, Hélène had taken the brilliant Milyutin for a lover.

Such were the men and women who sought to make a revolution.

Charleston, South Carolina, and Montgomery, Alabama,
January–April 1861

NO MAN DRIVES another man with a whip without exposing his soul to moral whiplash. Mary Chesnut knew it. She had been born to high place in the oligarchy of the South, and delighted in that brilliant world; yet she was to become, in time, a penetrating critic of the coercive psychology of her class. When, on the eve of Abraham Lincoln's revolution, she came up to Charleston, she found the metropolis of the Fire Eaters giddy in the anticipation of secession. She was inclined to cheer, and also to shudder.

While Prince Orlov, in Saint Petersburg, was busy obstructing Tsar Alexander's revolution, the Fire Eaters in the American South were readying themselves to resist Lincoln's. In her Charleston hotel, Mary Chesnut listened to their patriotic orations. She thought them exceedingly pungent, in the "hot, fervid, after-supper Southern style." Her own feelings, however, were more complicated. She was, she said, a "rebel born." She had early imbibed the skeptical attitude towards the Federal government characteristic of the states' rights school of Thomas Jefferson. Her father, who had been Governor of South Carolina, had lived and died a states' rights man. Among her friends were states' rights men like Laurence Keitt, the bullyboy who helped Preston Brooks beat Charles Sumner to a pulp on the floor of the Senate. South Carolina, she said, "had been so rampant for years." The state "was the torment of herself and everybody else." No one, she said, could live in the "state unless he were a fire-eater." She herself lived in the state. That made her a Fire Eater, too. At least in part.

The Fire Eater was a creature of fantasy, or so Mary Chesnut believed. He regarded slavery, not merely as an instrument of economy, but as a foundation of culture. He believed that the compulsory labor of blacks would free whites to realize the highest forms of liberty and virtue. On the mud-sill of slavery the South would erect a new Sparta, a second Athens. This desire to re-create, in an age of crinolines and gaslight, the slave republics of antiquity was a variant of the romantic yearning for an ideal existence. One of the principal begettors of modern romanticism had himself blessed the project. "Can liberty be maintained only on the basis of slavery?" the philosopher Jean-Jacques Rousseau asked. "Perhaps. The two extremes meet."

At the beginning of 1861, a part of Mary Chesnut sympathized with the aspirations of the Fire Eaters. She wanted them to get on with it. "Come what would, I wanted them to fight and stop talking." But her sympathy was mingled with skepticism. Her sensitivity to the element of romantic delusion in the Fire Eaters' mentality was heightened by the traditions of her husband's family. The Chesnuts were as fervent in their attachment to the United States as her father had been in professing the states' rights creed of President Jefferson. The Union was, for the Chesnuts, a family affair, almost a domestic concern. A portrait of General Washington by Gilbert Stuart hung in the hall of Mulberry, the Chesnut plantation near Camden, South Carolina. A Chesnut had served under Washington in the days when Washington bore a commission in the British service. Another Chesnut had feasted President Washington during his tour of the Southern states. Mary Chesnut's father-in-law, Colonel James Chesnut, Sr., remained true to his hereditary traditions. He was a staunch Union man without, however, being a staunch free-state man. The old Colonel was one of the most opulent gentlemen in South Carolina. He owned more than five hundred slaves, and his house at Mulberry concentrated, within its walls, the accumulated charms of a hundred years of aristocratic taste and extravagance.

Colonel Chesnut's son, Mary's Chesnut's husband, was cast in a different mold. Unlike the imperious Colonel, James Chesnut, Jr., was of a reserved and sober nature, a "modest gentleman of decent parts." He was a graduate of Princeton, a lawyer, a man at home in a library. He gave an impression of aloofness; and whether from pride or shyness or an admixture of the two he withdrew into his privacies to a degree unusual in a public man. He was a man of much coolness and moderation; but the times were not propitious to such qualities, and he was drawn by degrees into a boldness unsuited to his nature. He succumbed to the vision of the Fire Eaters. On learning of Lincoln's election, he resigned his seat in the United States Senate in order to join the resistance to the new régime. "No hope now," Mary Chesnut wrote. Her husband "was in bitter earnest." He "burned the ships behind him."

Mary Chesnut was thirty-seven years old on the eve of Lincoln's revolution. Her life had not been free from grief; and although she was now in middle age she was childless. Sadness is intelligent. In the first months of 1861, she believed that the South was at once making a nation and digging a pit. Devoted as she was to South Carolina, she feared the future, and she admitted to "a nervous dread and horror of this break with so great a power as the U.S.A."

As the crisis mounted, Mary Chesnut traveled with her husband to Montgomery, Alabama, the temporary capital of the new secessionist Republic of the South. There she encountered Varina Davis, the wife of the President of the Southern Republic, Jefferson Davis, who had taken office determined, he said, to save his people from Lincoln's revolution. The seaboard planters turned up their noses at Mrs. Davis; in their eyes the Mississippi lady was a vulgar "Western belle," bred up among six-shooters and Bowie knives in the less aristocratic world beyond the tidewater. Mary Chesnut, however, found Varina Davis's luncheons good and her gossip delicious. The two women were soon on terms of perfect unreserve. Mary Chesnut was intrigued by Mrs. Davis's intimate and probing talk; like many respectable ladies in that age, she delighted in the hushed conversations in the parlor that stripped away the velvet and muslin and laid bare the fallen flesh of her acquaintances.

But not even the most agreeably sordid revelations could dispel Mary Chesnut's unease. Tiring of tarnished petticoats, she opened her history books to study the roots of the world crisis in which she found herself caught up. She read the Earl of Clarendon's account of the English civil war, in which the historian painted the men of the seventeenth century, the Puritans and Cavaliers who fought to decide whether England was to be a free state or a servile state. As she turned the pages she began to despair. Men of the toughness and sinew of Clarendon's Englishmen were, she knew, to be found in the South. But were they valued? Were they entrusted with authority? Only by choosing "the born leaders of men," Mary Chesnut believed, could the South hope to prevail. Yet everywhere, she said, "political intrigue is as rife as in Washington." The endless jobbery too often resulted in the promotion of mediocrity. "One of the first things which depressed me," she wrote, "was the kind of men put in office at the crisis, invariably some sleeping deadhead long forgotten or passed over. Young and active spirits ignored, places for worn-out politicians seemed the rule—when our only hope is to use *all* the talents God has given us. This thing continues. In every state, as each election comes on, they resolutely put aside everything but the inefficient."

In her despair Mary Chesnut prayed that "a Caesar or a Napoleon may be sent to us." This was another romantic dream of the age; Americans were scarcely less susceptible to its appeal than Germans and Russians. A great-souled man would master the revolution and lead his people to victory. But at other times Mary Chesnut allowed herself to hope that the revolution could be averted. She seized on the report of a former Treasury official who, having resigned his post to return to the South, described the optimistic mood of the politicians in Washington. "There was to be peace," he declared.

A part of Mary Chesnut hoped that he was right.

Chapter 3

THRUST AND COUNTER-THRUST

Saint Petersburg, January 1858–March 1861

THE MAN WHO IS WARM, a Russian has said, cannot understand the man who is cold. Russians are familiar with the cold. The cradle of Russia lies in the northern forest zone, a land of short, bright summers and long, snow-saturated winters. Moscow, though it is situated on roughly the same latitude as Edinburgh, possesses a far crueler climate. Unprotected by the currents of the Gulf Stream, Russia feels the wrath of the arctic winter.

Over the centuries Russians have relied on three salves to protect them from the rigors of their climate. Fire, religion, and strong drink are the Russian's remedies against the cold. In his log *izba* the Russian peasant had his stove corner and, diagonally across from it, his icon corner—his "red" or "beautiful" corner. The icon warmed the peasant's soul. The stove warmed his body. When fire and mysticism failed to dispel the evil spirits of the winter, the Russian turned to another stimulant. According to legend, Prince Vladimir of Kiev embraced Christianity rather than Islam because "Russians are merrier drinking—without it, they cannot live." Originally a beer- and mead-loving people, the Russians eventually learnt the art of distilling grain. Vodka became the foremost national drink. To enjoy its full soul and body-warming effect, the Russian drank it on an empty stomach. At *zakouska* (hors d'oeuvres) he ate his cheese or caviar only after he drained his glass of vodka.

The longer the winter, the shorter the growing season. The question of emancipating Russia's peasants was bound up with the difficulties of farming in a cold climate. The country's agricultural yields were among the lowest in Europe. The Prussian agricultural expert August Haxt-hausen, after making a study of the subject in the 1840s, concluded that without serf labor estate farming in northern Russia would cease to be an even marginally profitable enterprise. Already the great majority of those who drove serfs were impoverished squires, unable to maintain their genteel status. Many even of the more prosperous nobles, with a hundred or more male serfs at their command, would be ruined if deprived of the unremunerated labor of the peasants.

As for the peasants themselves, they would suffer no less than their masters in the aftermath of emancipation—or so Prince Orlov and the opponents of liberation argued. Liberty, the partisans of force contended, was but another name for anarchy. The *muzhiks,* emancipated from the paternal care of their masters, would wreak havoc on the countryside. The landowners, burdened by debt and despair, would be powerless to restrain them.

But Prince Orlov had a plan to forestall the liberal revolution. If he could not resist emancipation itself, he hoped to prevent the peasants from acquiring land at the same time they obtained liberty. Without land, the peasant might be nominally free; but he would in fact be dependent on his old master. With pretended goodwill and secret malice the Prince set about raising innumerable procedural questions concerning the proposed legislation. He hoped, through this strategy of passive resistance, to break down the spirit of his adversaries. He would try their tempers. The Tsar's younger brother, the volatile Grand Duke Constantine, the most energetic of the reformers, was an especially tempting target. The reactionaries despised him. They also thought he might crack; Constantine's mind, Prince Menshikov said, had been "unhinged by masturbation." If *he* could be broken . . .

It happened largely as Prince Orlov foresaw. The question of emancipation became enmeshed in a tangle of committees. Behind the stucco façades of Saint Petersburg tempers rose, and nerves rubbed raw by the tiresome work of drafting complicated documents gave way. The Tsar became impatient. When Prince Orlov reminded his sovereign that the questions in dispute were difficult and complex, Alexander replied, "I am more than ever convinced how *difficult* and *complex* this question is, but all the same I *desire* and *demand* that your committee produce a *general conclusion as to how it is to be undertaken, instead of burying it in the files under various pretexts.*"

At last the hatreds could no longer be suppressed. The party of force charged the reformers with being "reds." The reformers accused the reactionaries of duplicity. An explosion was inevitable.

At length it came. Grand Duke Constantine accosted Prince Orlov. Imperial functionaries looked on in astonishment as the Tsar's younger brother told the Prince that he "greatly doubted" the sincerity of men who "instead of removing difficulties, did all they could to increase them." It was the moment Prince Orlov had patiently awaited. He played his part to the hilt. With a show of outraged gallantry he resorted to the language of the *Code Duello.* He told the Grand Duke that his words were an insult to the honor of the Russian nobility. The Grand Duke was not one to bear such a reproach tamely. Whether he went so far as to tell Prince Orlov that the nobility of Russia was not worthy to be spit upon, or whether he contented himself with the observation that true nobility did not exist in Russia, is a matter of dispute; but it was shortly afterwards arranged by the Tsar that the Grand Duke should undertake an extended naval cruise in the Mediterranean.

The difficulties in which the reformers found themselves did not end with the abrupt departure of Grand Duke Constantine for the fleet. General Rostovtsev began to despair of carrying out the work with which the Tsar had entrusted him. He fell sick with exhaustion. Alexander became alarmed. He did what he could to raise the old man's spirits. "Do not lose heart," he told Rostovtsev, "just as I do not despond, although I, too, have much grief to bear. Let us pray God together that He may give us strength. I embrace you with all my heart." But the Tsar's encouragement was in vain; the old soldier sank rapidly. Soon he was confined to his bed. Alexander gave orders that the sick man was on no account to be disturbed; but Rostovtsev continued to labor over his papers. With the little strength that remained to him he prepared a memorandum in which he set forth all that remained to be done. He intended his testament, as the document became known, for the Tsar's use after his death, which he foresaw must follow all too soon.

The Tsar visited the dying man in his house. Rostovtsev looked into his sovereign's eyes. "Sire," he said, "do not fear them."

While Alexander knelt in prayer at the bedside in February 1860, Rostovtsev died. The weeping monarch helped to carry the coffin. Yet no sooner had he laid his faithful servant in the grave than he determined to put in his place Count Panin, a courtier who opposed reform. The Tsar, it seemed, *did* fear them.

"Things assumed a very gloomy aspect," one observer wrote. "The question whether the liberation would take place at all was now asked." "The liberation will be postponed," it was said. The Tsar and his ministers "fear a revolution."

Washington, January–February 1861

IN AGREEING TO be Lincoln's Secretary of State, William Henry Seward appeared to abandon his pursuit of a conciliatory policy towards the South. But the love of supremacy is not easily surrendered, and Seward's aspiring nature soon found a new channel in which to work. On January 12, 1861, fifteen days after he had gone to Senator Crittenden's Committee and voted down the proposal to revive the Missouri line, Seward rose in the Senate. He spoke with an air of sadness. His tone was soft. Gone was the fervor with which he had, a decade before, denounced the peacemaking efforts of Daniel Webster. Forgotten, for the moment, was the belief he had expressed two years earlier, his conviction that the conflict between slavery and freedom was irrepressible. The question before the nation was, Seward confessed, perplexing. He himself opposed any extension of slavery into the territories; but he knew that many of his fellow citizens felt differently. He feared that these disagreements would lead to a civil war, which must in the end be fatal to the nation. He said that he did not know what the Union would be worth if it were preserved by the sword—and he opened the door to compromise on the territorial question in order to forestall what he called a "disastrous revolution."

Seward professed, in his Senate oration, to be in difficulties and doubts. But his conscience or vanity had already decided the question by which he pretended to be perplexed. He knew that if his policy of compromise were to bear fruit, he must conceal it, or show it, at most, in half-lights. He could not risk a breach with Lincoln; but in a private setting he threw away the mask. To Baron de Stoeckle, Tsar Alexander's envoy at Washington, Seward declared that, in spite of the vote he cast in Senator Crittenden's Committee, he remained sympathetic to a revival of the Missouri line, the idea which lay at the heart of Crittenden's proposed compromise. "It seems to me," Seward said, "that if I am absent only three days, this Administration, the Congress, and the District, would fall into consternation and despair. I am the only *hopeful, calm, conciliatory* person here." At a dinner party given by Stephen A. Douglas, Seward proposed a significant toast. "Away," he declared, "with all parties, all platforms, *all previous committals,* and *whatever else* will stand in the way of restoration of the American Union!" The assembled party drank off the bumper; and so forcefully did old Senator Crittenden afterwards set down his glass that it shattered on the table.

The French Minister at Washington thought Seward's pronouncements clouded with ambiguity; but Frances Seward had a surer perception of her husband's object. She shuddered to think that he was following in the steps of the man whose apostasy he had once condemned. Her husband, she saw, was taking the path "that led Daniel Webster to an unhonored grave." One of Seward's colleagues in the Senate agreed. "God damn you, Seward," the Senator said, "you've betrayed your principles and your party; we've followed your lead long enough." But Seward's pride rose high; all that was weakest, and all that was strongest, in him urged him forward, and determined him to be the preserver of the Republic in its last extremity.

Seward's transactions in January and February 1861 are obscured by sophistry and dissimulation, the usual devices with which a politician seeks to conceal his most daring maneuvers. The intrigue was a deep one; we will never know all the winks and nods. But it is certain that Lincoln himself was alarmed. The President-Elect had repeatedly disavowed any intention of compromise on the question of slavery in the territories; yet troubling rumors reached him, in Springfield, of a secret challenge to his authority. So concerned was he by the enemy within that on February 1 he wrote a letter to Seward. The letter was, in several respects, extraordinary. Lincoln reiterated his instructions to his future Secretary of State, even though those instructions had all along been perfectly clear. He did not raise the question of infidelity directly, but it is evident that he scented betrayal. He was, he said, "baffled" by the confusion which had arisen concerning what he called the "vexed question" of slavery in the territories. The President-Elect described how William Kellogg, an Illinois Congressman, had recently come to see him in Springfield. Kellogg was, Lincoln wrote, "in a good deal of anxiety, seeking to ascertain to what extent I would be consenting for our friends to go in the way of compromise" on the territorial question.

"I say now, however, as I have all the while said," the President-Elect told Seward, "that on the territorial question—that is, the question of extending slavery under the national auspices,—I am inflexible. I am for no compromise which *assists* or *permits* the extension of the institution on soil owned by the nation. And any trick by which the nation is to acquire territory, and then allow some local authority to spread slavery over it, is as obnoxious as any other. I take it that to effect some such result as this, and to put us again on the high-road to a slave empire, is the object of all these proposed compromises. I am against it."

Lincoln had reason to be alarmed. No one did faster, darker political work than the New Yorker. Seward was a master of the political trap, and although the President-Elect had so far eluded him, he knew that he might yet find himself caught up in his old adversary's nets. "Serpentine Seward," they called him. "The majority of those around me," Seward said, "are determined to pull the house down." But "I am determined not to let them."

Berlin and Saint Petersburg, February–March 1861

AT THE HEART of the German revolution lay the army.

In the middle of the seventeenth century, when princes across Europe were breaking down the limited monarchies of the Middle Ages in order to replace them with new régimes organized on principles of absolutism, those who succeeded owed their success to large bodies of professional troops. Friedrich Wilhelm, the "Great Elector" of Prussia, took note; he gathered together a few thousand men and formed them into a standing army. It was the nucleus of what would become, in time, one of the mightiest war machines the world has ever seen. In Prussia, liberty was at the mercy of those who wielded the sword.

The free-state liberals in the Prussian Chamber of Deputies, the lower house of the Kingdom's Parliament, were determined to change this. They wanted to convert the Great Elector's "soldier state"—his military régime—into a *Rechtsstaat,* a state grounded in the rule of law. To this end they sought control over the army the Great Elector had created. In 1861, they saw their chance. The Prussian arms were not quite what they had been. Albrecht von Roon, a Pomeranian nobleman and Prussian officer, drew up a plan to revive the military grandeur of the Kingdom. He proposed to enlarge the regular (or line) army—the school of Prussian valor—at the expense of the territorial militia (or *Landwehr*), which he regarded as an unreliable "citizen army" enfeebled by a middle-class officer corps.

The free-state men balked at the proposed reforms. Roon's reformation, they said, would militarize the nation. Prussia would be covered with barracks. The country would be in the grip of a military caste—the monocled, beplumed, sword-bearing Junkers. The renovated war machine would be staffed with precisely those "men known to oppose the liberal spirit of the time and resolved upon fighting that spirit with every possible means, including nationwide military indoctrination." In contrast to the French nobles, who two centuries before had been seduced by Louis XIV into a luxurious slavery, and whose remaining power had been broken by the French Revolution, the Junkers were, in the middle of the nineteenth century, a potent force in the state. Unlike the aristocrats of England, the Junkers had not been shorn of their claws by a strong and self-confident commons, a middle class jealous of its liberties. Nor had they, like the Russian nobles, been stripped of their pride by despots like Ivan the Terrible and Peter the Great.

It was precisely because the Prussian warrior class retained its fighting spirit that the Kingdom's free-state men were determined to prevent Roon's reformation of the army. They insisted that King Wilhelm did not have the power to effect a military reorganization of the state. Under the Prussian constitution, they argued, the sovereign could reorganize the army only with the consent of the legislature, which in theory controlled the purse strings of the Kingdom.

This was too much for Wilhelm, the old soldier who, in 1861, acceded to the throne following the death of his brother, Friedrich Wilhelm IV. In Prussia the King was by a long tradition the Supreme Warlord; it was only from courtesy that Wilhelm laid before the legislators his plans to remodel the army. The King flew into a rage. The reformation of the army was a cause dear to his heart; it lay close to the meaning of his life. But the liberals refused to back down. It was a question of power. A crisis loomed.

While Berlin was agitated by these events, Otto von Bismarck, forty-five years old at the beginning of 1861, was far away in Saint Petersburg, where he served as Prussian Ambassador to the court of the Tsar. The character of the envoy was not simple: Bismarck was a sphinx with too many riddles. "Faust complains of having two souls in his breast," he said. "I have a whole squabbling crowd. It goes on as in a republic." Yet the squabbling was not in vain, for it resulted in a pronounced originality of thought and utterance. Bismarck was a man who carried his own *Walpurgisnacht**** around with him. He once fantasized that he was a bomb, and he confessed himself capable of lying awake through a whole night "hating." Undoubtedly, his dreams were violent, his imagination washed in the darker oils; at the heart of Bismarckian self-culture was the question, "What have you really hated till now?"

Hatred, whatever else it may be, is a powerful mental stimulus. Bismarck had, with all his angry passions, a highly developed interior life, and a rich imagination. He was a voluptuary of power, alive to those great, sometimes wicked energies that move nations and shape the course of history. His realism was subsequently to become notorious; but what is sometimes called realism is often a cleverly disguised capacity for fantasy, the instinct of a powerful imagination to overlay the objects with which it deals with a film of fancy. Bismarck said that his imaginative faculties were the most notable element of his character; his nature, he maintained, was essentially dreamy. The great leader, like the great artist, is the most inspired fantasist: he sees the object not only as it is, but as it can be, and persuades others to submit to his hallucination.

This element of romance in Bismarck's realism gave him the keenest insight into the mysterious fatality of events; he once said that a states-

---

* Walpurgis Night, the eve of May Day, was a witches' Sabbath, an interlude of daimonic excess.

man "cannot create anything himself. He must wait and listen until he hears the steps of God sounding through events; then leap up and grasp the hem of His garment." The man who claimed to hear the historic footfall of the Deity possessed an iron will and an inordinate love of power, yet he was also nervous and oddly tender. A revolution, he knew, is the offspring of poetry and hatred; yet many years after an inspired loathing enabled him to achieve his revolutionary ends, Bismarck dismissed all the fame and authority he had acquired as insignificant compared to his greatest blessing. He was grateful, he said, that "God did not take any of my children from me."

The discrepancies of soul which, in a short time, would enable Bismarck to undertake a revolution as momentous as Lincoln's and Alexander's flowed from the deeper contradictions of his blood. Bismarck was a Junker. (The term derives from the Middle High German word for "young nobleman.") He prided himself on his descent from a race of German knights. The Junkers were, of all the hereditary aristocracies of Europe, one of the poorest. With the possible exception of the Castilians, they were the most haughty. The Junkers had not the large incomes, the splendid country seats, the palatial town houses which the greatest peers of England and France possessed. In many cases the Junker's manor was little more than a farmhouse, adorned, if it were adorned at all, with a rusting cannon or two. (The Junker's notions, even in matters of art, were all military.) The lord of the manor, as often as not, bridled his own mount, and his lady milked her own cows. Lacking the exterior attributes of an aristocratic class, the Junkers insisted all the more vehemently on the distinction of blood. Their order took on the qualities of a caste; and in Prussia the line that demarcated the patrician from the plebeian was sharper than in England or even in Russia. If the English nobility was the most democratic of the European aristocracies, the Prussian was the most peremptory and exclusive.

A Junker was thought to degrade himself if he espoused the daughter of a middle-class burgher. Although his peasants were no longer his vassals—serfdom had been abolished in Prussia in 1807—the Junker nevertheless exercised over his tenants a paternal supervision, and extracted from them many proofs of obsequious submission. A Junker might, in conversing with a man of inferior condition, employ the familiar form of the personal pronoun, *du* (thou); but his interloctutor had always to respond with the deferential *Sie* (you). To engage in trade or finance was, for a Junker, tantamount to disgrace; if he desired occupation or needed income, the Junker entered the service of the King. Commissions in the line army went, with rare exceptions, to Junkers; and in the recruitment of its officer corps Prussia continued to be guided by the maxim laid down, in the eighteenth century, by Frederick the Great, who said that the "promotion of a burgher to the status of an army officer is the first step in the decline of a state."

Bismarck sprang from the primitive nobility of Germany, but his house had fallen on hard times and could lay claim only to a slender fortune. The family estate at Schönhausen stood in a park of limes sixty miles west of Berlin. Its formal gardens had been laid out in the French style; as a boy Bismarck liked to take potshots at a moss-covered statue of Hercules which stood in one of the groves. But the parterres were overgrown with weeds, and the faded manor house, with the coat-of-arms carved into the gray stone over the door, bore witness to the degeneration of a line. The young Bismarck grew up surrounded by presentiments of decay—a familiar formula for revolutionary statesmanship, which often thrives in the soil of decadent gentility. The life of the North German gentry was a perpetual struggle to make the land pay, but the result was rarely adequate to the maintenance of seigneurial self-respect, and in their contests with a dry and sandy soil many old families sunk by degrees into debt, lost their estates, and fell into obscurity.

Such might have been the fate of the Bismarcks. Ferdinand, Otto's father, was by all accounts a man without distinction of culture or activity of mind. No one would have supposed him capable of retrieving his family's fallen fortunes. Yet retrieve them he did. Rebelling against the pride of caste, he married a daughter of the Menckens, a family which, though it was destitute of noble blood, had risen high in the service of the kings of Prussia. It was from his mother, Wilhelmine, that Bismarck inherited those vigorous qualities that enabled him to restore the honor of his scutcheons. He adored his father as the incarnation of the chivalric virtues of old Germany; but it was his middle-class mother who, having herself been educated by a scrupulous father, superintended his schooling. She enrolled little Otto in a good Berlin *Gymnasium* and laid the foundation for his subsequent intellectual development. He repaid her with enmity, and once professed "hatred" for her.

In 1861, this strange figure, a revolutionary statesman encased in the armor of a Teutonic knight, seemed to have reached the end of his road. He had made his name as a partisan of the party of coercion, a "Hotspur of reaction," an upholder of the highest pretensions of the Prussian Crown in its struggles with the free-state liberals. But ever since the death of Frederick the Great in 1786, Prussia's rulers had inclined to caution rather than boldness in the struggle against free-state principles. In the royal palace—the *Stadtschloss*—in Berlin the courtiers said that Bismarck "smelt of blood." In 1848, when much of Europe rose up in revolt against the ancient dynasties, the young reactionary went about Potsdam and

Berlin with four rounds of ammunition in his pocket and a multitude of plots swimming in his head. With an inflated sense of his own importance, he urged the army to put down the revolt with grapeshot. But the old King, Friedrich Wilhelm IV, wanted no blood on his hands. He capitulated to the free-state men and granted them their dream of a written constitution and an elected legislature.

Not long after his antics in 1848, the "mad Junker," as Bismarck was called, was sent to Frankfurt as Prussian delegate to the Bundestag, the assembly of the German Confederation (or Bund). The Bund was the handiwork of the Austrian statesman Klemens von Metternich; to it representatives of the various German states came together to endorse the policy of Austria's ruling house, the Habsburgs, who by a long tradition were the foremost of the German dynasts. (The Austrian representative was *ex officio* President of the Bund, which met in the Austrian Legation in Frankfurt.) For the greater part of four centuries the Habsburgs had worn the imperial purple; as Holy Roman Emperors, elected by the suffrage of the German princes, they claimed to be the successors of Trajan and Augustus. The Holy Roman Empire was dissolved in 1806, but the Habsburgs continued to regard themselves as the pre-eminent dynasty in Europe, and they continued to look upon their Prussian cousins in the north as vastly inferior to themselves. The royal house of Prussia, the Hohenzollerns, had obtained the marquisate of Brandenburg only in the fifteenth century; and Brandenburg, with its sterile soil and dreary bogs, was an ambiguous prize—the "sandbox of the Holy Roman Empire." Later the Electors of Brandenburg received the Duchy of Prussia from the King of Poland, but not until the eighteenth century did a Hohenzollern potentate dare to assume the title of King, and then only with the consent of the Kaiser in Vienna.

"I had been brought up," Bismarck said, "to admire, I might almost say worship, Austrian policy," but in Frankfurt he found himself repelled by the "crafty and perfidious" diplomacy of the Habsburgs. It was at this time, he said, that "I conceived the idea . . . of withdrawing Germany from Austrian pressure." He proceeded at once to dispute the pre-eminence of Austria. Bismarck was a great actor, as well as a close student of Shakespeare's plays, and he loved to disconcert his adversaries by playing the buffoon. In the Bundestag he took out a cigar and asked the Austrian delegate for a match. No Prussian delegate had ever before done such a thing; by a long tradition only the Austrians smoked in the Bundestag. It was as if Bismarck had blown smoke in the Kaiser's face.

"Germany is too small for both of us," he said in 1856. The shadow on the wall, however, was visible to him alone. At Berlin he was still regarded as an erratic figure, unreliable, perhaps unstable, certainly lacking in the self-restraint which a Prussian dignitary must possess. He was dispatched to Saint Petersburg, where, at the distance of a thousand miles, he was unable to influence the formulation of policy in the Wilhelmstrasse. He had, he said, been "put on ice."

In this frigid exile his health suffered. The rigors of the climate wrought upon his nerves, which, for all the ferocity of his passions, were never strong. But even more his unused energies left him weak and dispirited. Nothing is so frustrating to power as the inability to make its force felt.

Chapter 4

TO PROCLAIM LIBERTY
TO THE CAPTIVES

Washington, February 1861

WHILE BISMARCK, in Saint Petersburg, dreamt of power, Abraham Lincoln, at the other end of the Western world, left Springfield to take up its burdens. He arrived in Washington on February 23, about six o'clock in the morning. Only two men attended him on the train from Baltimore, Allan Pinkerton, the private detective, and Ward Hill Lamon, a lawyer from Danville, Illinois, of gigantic physical stature, who acted as the President-Elect's bodyguard.

The station was all but deserted. A crowd of hackney coachmen, most of them black, stood near the entrance to the station, looking for fares. Elihu Washburne, the Illinois Congressman, was one of the few officials present to greet the incoming President. "Abe," he called out after Lincoln stepped from the railway carriage, "you can't play that on me." It was an inglorious entrance, dictated by fear of assassination. A rumor had spread that Lincoln was to be set upon and murdered in Baltimore as he passed through that city. As a result of this intelligence the President-Elect had been advised to abandon his entourage and travel incognito to the capital.

His person and demeanor confirmed the least charitable apprehensions of those who awaited him in Washington. The capital had for weeks been giddy with stories of his boorish manners. Lincoln's appearance excited, in the polished circles of the East, something of the same uneasy malevolence which greeted the savage Goth or the exotic Syrian, recently raised to empire and invested with the purple, when he showed himself to the proud and cultivated epicures of the Roman Senate. The face of the President-Elect was stamped with the bleakness of the prairie; Henry Adams thought it a "plain, ploughed face." Yet it was not only Lincoln's looks, but his manner, too, that revealed, to those accustomed to Eastern standards of refinement, a want of taste and breeding—a vulgarity "beyond credence," one observer said, "a thing you must see before you can believe it."

The President-Elect did not always remove his hat when politeness dictated that a man must, and when, on his way to Washington, he stopped in New York, he wore black kid gloves to the Opera, when all the fine gentlemen listening to Verdi that night wore white. The merchant patriciate of New York, with its *faux* English standards, gave no quarter; and although the New York ladies condescended to give a reception for Mrs. Lincoln, even this exercise in social charity was not quite free from malice, for Mrs. August Belmont, the *grande doyenne* of New York society, did not appear. When the newspapers erroneously reported that Mrs. August Belmont had been present at the levée, the "Queen of Fifth Avenue" promptly issued a denial, and so reiterated the snub. Her husband, the New York agent of the House of Rothschild, was a Douglas Democrat.

One man claimed to see beneath the appearance of insipidity which Lincoln presented to the world. Walt Whitman, a poet who had, the previous year, brought out a new edition of his poems, *Leaves of Grass,* caught a glimpse of Lincoln as he passed through New York. A long train of equipages made their way from the Thirtieth Street Station to the Astor House. A great multitude thronged the street. The poet watched as a tall figure stepped out of a barouche. The President-Elect "paus'd leisurely on the sidewalk, look'd up at the granite walls and looming architecture of the grand old hotel—then, after a relieving stretch of arms and legs, turn'd round for over a minute to slowly and good-humoredly scan the appearance of the vast and silent crowds." Many "an assassin's knife and pistol lurk'd in hip or breast-pocket there," Whitman said, "ready, soon as break and riot came."

The poet exaggerated the hostility of the crowd; the newspapers told of a kinder reception. But whatever his deficiencies as a reporter, Whitman was a superior student of character. No less than "four sorts of genius, four mighty and primal hands," he said, could have limned Lincoln truly; he named Plutarch, Aeschylus, Michelangelo, and Rabelais. Plutarch and Michelangelo one understands—Lincoln was a hero. Rabelais, too: such was the quality of his humor. But Aeschylus? Perhaps Whitman believed that only the artist who painted the doomed Cassandra could accurately depict the superstitious dread in the President-Elect's mind. This burden of presentiment, which Lincoln was always to carry with him, was undoubtedly innate, but it had been signally confirmed by the circumstances of his boyhood. He had been born, in 1809, in Kentucky, and he had passed his early years, his law partner, William Herndon, said, among "illiterate and superstitious" people belonging "to that nomadic class still to be met with throughout the South, and known as 'poor whites.'" The rapid growth of his intellectual powers never wholly drove out Lincoln's conviction that he was privy to presages and signs that revealed the occult workings of destiny. Shortly after his election as President, he experienced a vision while reclining on a sofa in his house in Springfield. He "saw in a mirror on the wall a double reflection of his face, with one image paler than the other." He blanched: surely the paleness of the second reflection bore witness to the near approach of death. At all events he acquiesced in his wife's interpretation of the oracle, which Mrs. Lincoln said signified that her husband "would be elected to a second term but that he would not live to complete it."

He might trifle with the arts of prophecy and divination; but on the whole Lincoln's understanding was cool, lucid, and impatient of nonsense. In native power of mind he had, perhaps, few superiors. With little formal schooling he had made himself into a successful lawyer and politician, and the pattern of intellectual growth which early established itself continued to be the rule of his nature during his riper years. In every decade his mind underwent a revolution in ideas; but in no period were its workings more fierce than in the middle years of the 1850s, when he discovered his political raison d'être and revolutionary vocation. Herndon remembered how, before this revival, Lincoln would sometimes sit, in the dingy law office in Springfield, for hours at a time "staring vacantly at the windows." His opposition to the policy of militant nationalism which inspired the Mexican War had, he believed, ruined his political hopes; and living constantly with the great unhewn stones of his ambition, he was often betrayed, in the early fifties, into a moroseness or dejection of temper, for he saw no way either to rid himself of his ambitious desires or to put them to a constructive use.

Then, in 1853, Stephen A. Douglas brought a bill in Congress to organize the Nebraska Territory. In its final form the bill provided for the repeal of the portion of the Missouri Compromise legislation that prohibited slavery in the Louisiana Territory north of latitude 36°30'. The bill became law, and it instantly aroused Lincoln's wrath. Territory which had once been consecrated to freedom might now know the scourge of slavery. The more Lincoln thought about it, the more furious he became. "In the office discussions," Herndon said, "he grew bolder in his utterances." To compromise with the forces of coercion was to appease them—to palliate evil. "The day of compromise," Lincoln insisted, "has passed." The "two great ideas" of slavery and freedom, he contended,

> have been kept apart only by the most artful means. They are like two wild beasts in sight of each other, but chained and held apart. Some day these deadly antagonists will one or the other break their bonds, and then the question will be settled.

In October 1854, Senator Douglas returned to Illinois. The state fair was on; Springfield was crowded with visitors. Douglas undertook to defend his Kansas-Nebraska policy. Lincoln denounced it in what one newspaper called the "profoundest" speech he had yet given. He "quivered with emotion," and when he finished his listeners erupted in huzzas, and women waved white handkerchiefs.

In 1858 he was nominated by the Republican Party as its candidate for the United States Senate seat which Douglas held. In accepting the nomination he consigned to the ash-heap of history not only the Kansas-Nebraska policy of Douglas but the entire framework of conciliation devised by the Silver Age senators:

> We are now in the *fifth* year, since a policy was initiated [that of Senator Douglas], with the *avowed* object, and *confident* promise, of putting an end to slavery agitation.
>
> Under the operation of that policy, that agitation has not only, *not ceased,* but has *constantly augmented.*
>
> In *my* opinion, it *will* not cease, until a *crisis* shall have been reached, and passed.
>
> "A house divided against itself cannot stand."
>
> I believe this government cannot endure, permanently half *slave* and half *free.*
>
> I do not expect the Union to be *dissolved*—I do not expect the house to *fall*—but I *do* expect it will cease to be divided.
>
> It will become *all* one thing, or *all* the other.

The race was close: but in the end Lincoln lost. The defeat, however, was not complete, for the House Divided speech revealed its deliverer to be a new kind of American statesman, vigorous and uncompromising in his adherence to a revolutionary principle, yet tenacious of power and unwilling to let it slip from his grasp without a struggle.

The institutions of liberty were, Lincoln believed, in danger. A new philosophy of coercion was on the march. It was not improbable, he said, that as the new philosophy advanced, human bondage would become lawful in all the American "States, *old* as well as *new—North* as well as *South.*" If the authoritarian banners continued their progress, America would witness the "total overthrow" of free-state principles: it would become a country in which "all men are created equal, except negroes, and foreigners, and Catholics." At such a conjuncture, he would, he said, "prefer emigrating to some country where they make no pretence of loving liberty—to Russia, for instance, where despotism can be taken pure, and without the base alloy of hypocrisy."

But it was not only in America that the institutions of the free state were threatened. The new philosophy of power was, Lincoln argued, making rapid strides in other parts of the globe. He repeatedly characterized the struggle between freedom and servitude as a world struggle. The outcome of the American contest between the two philosophies would, he predicted, have a great, possibly a decisive, impact on the world crisis. Were the American Republic to be broken on the anvil of slavery, men and women around the world would suffer. If, on the contrary, the United States was saved on principles of freedom, "millions of free happy people, the world over," Lincoln said, would "rise up, and call us blessed, to the latest generations."

Scholars have criticized Lincoln for exaggerating the threat to liberty; but it is important to understand how formidable, in his day, the odds against the free state seemed. The new philosophy of coercion was dangerous precisely because it went to the heart of the free-state ideal. It attacked the principle that all men are created equal. The "definitions and axioms of free society" were, Lincoln said,

> denied, and evaded, with no small show of success. One dashingly calls them "glittering generalities"; another bluntly calls them "self evident lies"; and still others insidiously argue that they apply only to "superior races." These expressions, differing in form, are identical in object and effect—the supplanting of the principles of free government, and restoring those of classification, caste, and legitimacy. They would delight a convocation of crowned heads, plotting against the people. They are the van-guard—the miners, and sappers—of returning despotism. We must repulse them, or they will subjugate us.

Had the "van-guard" of "returning despotism" prevailed in the United States, or had two hostile republics, one slave and one free, emerged on the North American continent, it is doubtful whether America would have been strong enough, and free enough, in the decades that followed to resist effectively the slave empires that emerged in Germany and Russia, and that in the twentieth century aspired to dominion of the planet.

"I have never had a feeling politically that did not spring from the sentiments embodied in the Declaration of Independence," Lincoln said in Philadelphia as he made his way to Washington to be inaugurated as President. Yet this champion of liberty and self-government harbored within him another, secret self, a restless, darkly ambitious being, fascinated by human greatness, and passionately craving the splendor of a personal ascendancy. His ambition, Herndon said, was "a little engine that knew no rest." Many years earlier Lincoln had spoken of those men who belong to "the family of the lion, or the tribe of the eagle." It was the tribe to which he himself belonged. "Towering genius," the young Lincoln said, "disdains a beaten path. . . . It thirsts and burns for distinction; and, if possible, it will have it, whether at the expense of emancipating slaves, or enslaving freemen."

The internal antagonism between the liberal figure, content with the life and culture of the free state, and the romantic figure, yearning for something more, will always be a puzzling one. Probably the works of the romantic artists of America in that period best illuminate the desires and dissatisfactions of such a soul. Melville's *Moby-Dick* and Emerson's *Representative Men* may reveal more about the President-Elect's motives than all the newspapers of the age. Yet it is certain that the contradictions which festered in Lincoln's soul would enable him, in time, to unlock the secret of the revolution he made.

Saint Petersburg, February–March 1861

As LINCOLN WAS making his way to Washington to implement his revolution, Tsar Alexander, in Saint Petersburg, initiated a new phase in his. Prince Peter Kropotkin witnessed the dramatic events. It was a Sunday morning, the last Sunday of the Carnival that preceded Lent, and the Prince lay lounging in his bed in the Corps of Pages, the seminary of the Russian officer corps. In a short time, however, he must rise and dress, for on Sundays he was required to attend the changing of the guard at the Riding School.

Saint Petersburg, at that time, was transfixed by a single question. In between the quadrilles of the *Bal blanc* (the White Ball) and the waltzes of the *Bal rosé* (the Pink Ball), at intimate little supper parties given by the aristocracy, in the gaslit restaurants of the capital, lurid in gilt and velvet, the talk everywhere was of emancipation. Prince Kropotkin took it all in, for he was a young man, not yet twenty, with a gift of observation. As a witness to history, he was well placed; the Prince had entrée to all the fashionable personages of the capital, even to the Tsar himself, whose *page de chambre* he was soon to become.

Yet for all his intimacy with Saint Petersburg, Prince Kropotkin was not a native of the capital. He was a scion of the old *boyar* nobility of Moscow, descended from one of those princely houses that had for generations lived in proud isolation in the Old Equerries Quarter of the city, in the shadow of the Kremlin. This remnant of the ancient aristocracy of Russia, jealous of its heritage, had for many years stood aloof, unsympathetic to the changes the country had undergone since the seventeenth century. Some of the old families were rich; Prince Kropotkin's father possessed twelve hundred men-serfs. But the hereditary wealth of the primitive nobility of Russia concealed the extent of its relative decline, for many of the old families had been surpassed, in the race for honors and places, by a new class of men, the quick, vigorous souls who had risen to power in the bureaus of Peter the Great. In Saint Petersburg, the city of Peter, Prince Kropotkin was a figure almost provincial in his naïveté, the relic of an archaic race. He was an appealing young man; George Bernard Shaw, who knew him at a later period, thought him "amiable to the point of saintliness." Yet in Kropotkin's high-minded purity there was something unsettling—a suggestion of that lofty pride which would, in time, lead him to turn against the Tsar's revolution, and to offer to it a resistance more hurtful to Russia than all the clever stratagems of Prince Orlov and his party.

Kropotkin was still lounging in his bed when his servant, Ivanov, brought in the tea tray.

"Prince, freedom!" the servant exclaimed.

"Did you see it yourself?" Kropotkin asked.

"Yes. People stand around; one reads, the others listen. It *is* freedom."

The Tsar's diversionary tactics—the dispatching of Grand Duke Constantine to the Mediterranean, the installation of Count Panin in General Rostovtsev's place—had served their purpose. Alexander was ready now to act, but the deed itself he masked in another layer of secrecy. The signing of the emancipation manifesto took place two weeks before it was made public. The Tsar, after praying in his chapel and breakfasting with his family, retired to his study. With him were Grand Duke Constantine, who had returned from the Mediterranean, Tsarevitch Nicholas, and a few other trusted souls. Prince Orlov was not among those who witnessed the revolutionary act. He had fallen sick, and no other figure had emerged capable of contesting the Tsar's will.

Constantine looked on as his brother took up the manifesto. The Tsar's hands trembled as he touched it. He read it aloud. Afterwards he made the sign of the Cross. He signed the paper, and his brother sprinkled sand on the ink. The first phase of his revolution was complete. The fetters that bound more than twenty million human beings were no more.

The Tsar, however, did not, just then, announce the revolution he had initiated. Lent was approaching, and he withheld the manifesto lest the fury of the Carnival—the interval of excess that preceded the Lenten fast—furnish a pretext for violence. Behind this caution was the revolutionary statesman's apprehension that he will lose control of his revolution. Memories of the peasant revolts inspired by Stenka Razin and Emelian Pugachev lingered in the imagination of Russia. By waiting until Lent to announce the emancipation, Alexander hoped that his subjects would receive the news of his revolution in a sober and contrite frame of mind.

Two Sundays after the manifesto was signed, copies were distributed throughout the Empire, together with the text of the law itself, the Statute on the Peasants. Russians gathered in little groups to study the Tsar's message. It was by no means easy to decipher, for it had been composed, by the prelate Philaret, the Metropolitan of Moscow, in the archaic style of the Church, with many phrases drawn from the old Slavonic. "Make the sign of the Cross, thou Russian people," the manifesto began. This was the first, but not the last, error Alexander would make in his effort to remodel the state. How could he expect his people to embrace a revolution he was unable to explain to them?

While his subjects struggled to make sense of the manifesto, the Tsar went as usual to the Riding School to preside at the changing of the guard. Passing under the double-headed eagles emblazoned on the gate of his palace, he drove into Palace Square. Bells pealed, and the Tsar-Liberator was hailed by an immense throng. Some cheered. Others wept. Still others, conscious of the miraculous promise of the moment, exchanged the traditional Easter greeting, though it was the beginning of Lent.

"Christ is risen!"

"In truth He is risen!"

After the ceremony at the Riding School, Alexander remained on horseback. "The officers to me," he called out in a loud voice. The Tsar proceeded to justify his act to his horse guards. Prince Kropotkin overheard parts of the Tsar's address: "The officers . . . the representatives of the nobility in the army . . . an end has been put to centuries of injustice . . . I expect sacrifices from the nobility . . . the loyal nobility will gather round the throne."

More eloquent, to Kropotkin, was the modest exultation of a simple peasant. Seeing a fine gentleman after Mass that morning, the peasant greeted him with mirth in his eyes. "Well, sir?" the peasant said, "now—all gone?"

The task of remaking Russia had begun.

Berlin, May 1861–January 1862

IN A BRICK BUILDING on the Bendlerstrasse, a somber, neat-looking man pored over his maps. He wore the uniform of a Prussian general; but the man's delicate features, and in particular his eyes, strikingly blue, suggested nothing of the latent savagery of the warrior. At once gentle and a trifle sad, the eyes might have been those of a Lutheran pastor, or perhaps of a retiring scholar, a *Privatgelehrter,* in a quiet market town. In the spring of 1861 few even well-informed students of power were aware of the existence either of the man or the institution he directed; but he rather relished than resented this obscurity. Helmuth von Moltke, on the eve of his sixty-second birthday, had for four years been the Chief of the Prussian General Staff, and the code of this interesting body required the complete subordination of ego and ambition to the needs of the army and the state.

Germany was, at this time, teeming with would-be revolutionaries; but none was more daring or original than the self-effacing man in the Bendlerstrasse. If Wagner supplied the music of the German revolution, Moltke supplied its machinery. The forms of power he organized would reshape his age; and the shadow of his military cloak would extend far into the twentieth century. He commanded the shock troops that would soon shake the world.

In his room in the Bendlerstrasse, Moltke gloomily studied his maps. Everywhere he looked, he saw danger. Prussia was surrounded by great powers. To the west lay France, whose ruler, Napoleon III, was the nephew of the man who half a century before overran Germany and rode in triumph through Berlin. To the south was Austria, the prima donna of the German states, determined to keep the aspirant power, Prussia, in its place. To the east was the Russian colossus, while to the north lay the sea, dominated by the naval power of England. Moltke went over the possibilities. What if the Romance peoples in the west— the French, the Spanish, the Italians—formed a coalition with the Slavs in the east with the object of crushing the German center?* What if Napoleon III, lusting, as his uncle had lusted, for power and possessions, made war on Prussia in order to gain territories on the Rhine?

This perpetual imagination of disaster was morose; but it was the business of an officer of the Prussian General Staff to be morose. The work of a Staff officer consisted in nervously pondering the future and drawing up plans to meet every conceivable military contingency. War games were

---

* Moltke's fears were realized when, in the 1890s, the Franco-Russian Alliance was concluded.

the Staff officer's life. An utterly normal personality was unlikely to flourish in such an occupation; an element of neurotic morbidity was almost a prerequisite for success on the Prussian General Staff. This qualification Moltke possessed. Like the illustrious Staff officers of the past, like Scharnhorst and Clausewitz, he was touched by melancholy. The Empress Eugénie, the consort of Napoleon III, saw him once in Paris; she thought him oddly quiet, and wondered whether he were not wrung by a "continuous inner tension."

It was an indication of the genius of the Prussian army that it could make use of such a man. The prevailing idea of the Prussian officer—stolid and unimaginative, with an air of military stiffness—was true enough. But there was also, in the Prussian service, room for men of a humanistic cast of mind—men like Moltke, who at the time he became Chief of the General Staff had never commanded a regiment. The warriors, or "Plumes," led the troops, while the worriers, or "Scribes," directed the operations of the Staff. The contributions of both kinds of men, the flamboyant athletes in the field and the monocled chess players in the war room, would soon make Prussia's the most lethal military machine on the planet.

In contrast to the field commanders, with their colorful personalities, the officers of the General Staff were advisers and strategists, technical experts who were content to remain in the shadows. "My life is an existence that leaves no traces," Carl von Clausewitz, the most penetrating intellect to serve on the General Staff, once said. Clausewitz did not venture to publish, in his lifetime, *On War,* the work in which he distilled his knowledge of military art; the book appeared only after his death. *On War* is rooted in a romantic vision of the prostration of the individual before the majesty of the state. The state, according to Clausewitz, embodies the soul of the people; true freedom lies, not in the pursuit of individual happiness, but in the effort "to put king and country above all else"; war is the great creative activity of patriotism.

Moltke carried the tradition of Clausewitz into a new age. He sprang, like much of the Prussian officer corps, from the nobility of northern Germany, and he early embraced the austere creed of devotion and obedience by which his ancestors had lived. Unlike most of his brother officers, however, Moltke was intellectually curious and aware of a larger world beyond the Baltic. He owed his brains, not to his father, a Prussian officer and unsuccessful gentleman-farmer, but to his mother. Moltke's mother, like Bismarck's, had grown up in a city; she came from Lübeck, and she had absorbed something of its Hanseatic culture. Moltke himself possessed literary and artistic propensities; he seems to have aspired, in his youth, to be a universal

man on the Renaissance model. His love of art and music did not, however, deter him from becoming a soldier. After an unhappy interval in
the Danish service, he took up a commission in the Prussian army in
1821; to supplement his income, he published a prose romance and
several historical sketches, and he embarked on a German translation
of Gibbon's *Decline and Fall of the Roman Empire*. Later Moltke traveled
to Constantinople, where he became military adviser to the Ottoman
Sultan, Mahmoud II; he there undertook a survey of the Ottoman
domains as far east as the Euphrates, and penetrated regions into
which no European had strayed, he said, since Xenophon. He loved
the southern sun and the choice air of the Mediterranean, and he was
never happier than when studying the antiquities of Provence or
Rome. The "gray fogs, dripping gutters, and long evenings" of the
Berlin winter depressed him.

Moltke's ambition, upon becoming, in 1857, Chief of the General
Staff, was to adapt Prussian strategy to the technological revolutions of
the age. He was convinced that in the next war railroads and telegraph
lines would be more important than conventional fortifications. "Build
no more fortresses," he said; "build railways." He published, in 1843,
an essay on railway strategy, and one of his goals, upon becoming Chief
of the General Staff, was to supplement traditional military exercises
with railway transport drills. The first such drills took place in 1862.

Yet the principal contribution of Moltke was not technical. It was
spiritual. His delicate pallor seemed to betoken an inner purity, a quiet
grandeur of soul. Under his direction the General Staff developed an
intensity of purpose reminiscent of a monastic brotherhood. Its theology of violence would, in time, infect the entire army. War is, with slavery, the ultimate form of coercion, the art by which one man forces
another man to submit to his will. At the same time, war is the most
complete expression of the romantic desire to turn away from life; the
warrior does not merely reject the flesh, he destroys it. Not for nothing did the Prussian army, with its Death's-Heads and Black Eagles,
exalt the totems of death; the true Prussian warrior longed to seal his
faith in a sacrament of blood. Moltke, in forging a new order of Teutonic Knights, refined this spirit of fanaticism, and bred a race of men
whose souls seemed molded of the same iron as their crosses.*

---

* The Teutonic Order of Knights was a chivalrous body whose adepts, distinguished by
their characteristic habit, a white cloak adorned with a black cross, embraced the twin voca-
tions of arms and piety. In the era of the Crusades the Order formed, with the Knights of
the Temple of Solomon (or Templars) and the Knights of the Hospital of Saint John (Hos-
pitallers), the bulwark of the Christian Kingdom of Jerusalem.

Washington, February–March 1861

LINCOLN'S FIRST OBJECT, on reaching the capital, was to suppress counter-revolutionary heresy. Governor Seward must be put in his place. Gently, if possible, firmly if necessary.

Seward was mortified. Not only was his advice rejected, but the hand of his enemy was strengthened. Lincoln asked Salmon P. Chase of Ohio to be his Secretary of the Treasury. Chase was a child of the Puritans; he opposed concessions to the party of coercion and thought the politics of compromise profane. It was more than Seward could bear. He went to Lincoln and told him that he must choose. His sense both of the public interest and what was more particularly due to himself compelled him, he said, to insist on the exclusion of Chase as the condition of his own service in the Cabinet.

The President-Elect was unmoved by this appeal. Seward determined to force the issue. Two days before the inauguration, he wrote to Lincoln. "Circumstances which have occurred since I expressed to you in December last my willingness to accept the office of Secretary of State," he said, "seem to me to render it my duty to ask leave to withdraw that consent."

Lincoln saw at once the danger Seward's withdrawal posed. The expression of what amounted to a lack of confidence in his revolutionary policy, coming from one so highly placed in his own party, could only weaken his position and injure his chances as he entered into power. Yet what could he do? He could not afford to lose Seward. Neither could he afford to yield to him.

The course he chose revealed the extent of his shrewdness. He pretended that, in the perplexed hours that preceded the inauguration, he had not received Seward's letter. "I can't afford to let Seward take the first trick," Lincoln told his private secretary, John Nicolay, as he put the letter away. Seward anxiously waited for a reply from the President-Elect; but for two days no reply came.

On the eve of the transfer of power the rumble of artillery caissons was heard in the streets of Washington. Muffled batteries made their way to Twelfth Street and to Capitol Hill itself. Winfield Scott, the ranking general of the army, was taking no chances.

March 4 dawned bright. President Buchanan, too weak, the British envoy Lord Lyons observed, to wring his own hands, drove to Willard's Hotel early in the afternoon. There President-Elect Lincoln joined him in the barouche. The two presidents were driven up Pennsylvania Avenue to the Capitol, accompanied by mounted marshals adorned with blue scarves and white rosettes. Sharpshooters in green coats stood on the rooftops, and squadrons of cavalry patrolled the streets. A sullen crowd watched the presidential carriage pass. "There goes that Illinois ape, the cursed Abolitionist," a Washington lady said as the procession went by. "But he will never come back alive."

At half past one, Lincoln descended from the carriage and mounted the steps of the Capitol.

Chapter 5

MOBILIZATION

Yasnaya Polyana, Russia, April–May 1861

A YOUNG MAN, not tall, but powerfully built and muscular, sat in the train as it crossed the Russian frontier. He wore a beard, partly, perhaps, to cover up a face he thought unattractive; but undoubtedly the most remarkable aspect of his appearance was his gaze, gray-eyed and intense. "Frontier," the young man wrote in his journal as the train sped across the snowbound countryside. "Health good. Am happy." After a long tour of Europe, Count Leo Nicholaievich Tolstoy, thirty-two years old in the spring of 1861, had come home.

Early in May he reached Yasnaya Polyana, his hereditary estate south of Moscow. He followed the cart-road through fields of maize, drove past the village and the onion-domed church, and went down a narrow avenue of birches and limes. At last the whitewashed pavilion itself was before him, with its neo-classical façade—his home, or rather all that remained of it. Gone was the colonnaded mansion that had once stood on the property, the house to which his maternal grandfather, Prince Nicholas Sergeyevich Volkonsky, had retired, many years before, after long and faithful service in the court of Catherine the Great. That eighteenth-century gentleman, with his powdered wig and passion for order and activity, had determined to live aloof from the world, in the seclusion of his porticos. It was in old Prince Volkonsky's house that Tolstoy himself had been born, in 1828; but he sold the house in 1854 to pay gambling debts he contracted while serving as an officer during the Crimean War. His boyhood home was dismantled and carried off.

The loss was regrettable; but what was the disappearance of a house to the glory of the Russian spring? The season had always an enchantment for Tolstoy. "It's spring!" he would shout when the snows melted and the first blossoms appeared. "It is so good to be alive on this earth, for all good people and even for such as I." Where his grandfather's mansion once stood larch saplings now grew, along with the weeds. Tolstoy rode over the countryside, swam in the Voronka, heard the music of the nightingales, and at night gazed up at the immensity of the Russian sky. In the spring, he said, "nature, the air, everything is drenched in hope, future, a wonderful future."

Tolstoy returned to Russia filled with the spirit of reform. He wanted to contribute to the Tsar's revolution. He had agreed to serve as a local Justice of the Peace (or "Peace Mediator"), an office created to implement the Tsar's new emancipation law; and he wanted to build up the school he had started for serf children. Everyone, he said, "feels the need for action."

Every day the *muzhiks*—the peasants—came to Tolstoy with another impossible demand. "Well, lads, what do you want?" Tolstoy would ask them. After hearing them out, he would shake his head. "I am very sorry I can't do what you wish. Were I to do so I should cause your landlord a great loss."

"But you'll manage it for us some how, *batushka* [little father]," the peasants would say.

"No, I can't do anything of the kind," Tolstoy would reply.

"But somehow, *batushka*. . . . If only you want to, *batushka,* you'll know to find a way to do it."

Tolstoy would then make the sign of the Cross. "As God is holy," he would say, "I swear that I can be of no use at all to you."

"You'll take pity on us, and do it somehow, *batushka!*"

The landlords, with their own unreasonable demands, could not be disposed of quite so easily as the *muzhiks*. Tolstoy was soon quarrelling, he said, with *"all* the landowners." He received letters filled with threats. In the streets of Tula, the provincial capital, he was not safe, and a petition for his removal was laid before the responsible Minister in Saint Petersburg. Nevertheless, Tolstoy remained in office.

Like others charged with implementing the emancipation law, he soon discovered that, whatever decision he made, he must cause someone pain. The serfs had worked the land for generations. They had, they believed, paid for each field, each furrow, many times over with their sweat and blood. Anything less than an outright gift of the soil on which their families had toiled for decades was to them an injustice. "Our life belongs to you," the serfs told the landowners, "you can take it. But you have no right to move us from the land which belongs to us." Yet under the emancipation law the serfs were to receive only a portion of the land to which they believed themselves entitled. Their landlords, far from being made to feel the consequences of their greed and their brutality, were to be compensated for the loss of their property by the government. The government, in turn, looked to the peasants to be made whole. Under the emancipation legislation, liberated serfs were required to reimburse the imperial treasury, over a period of years, for the land they acquired.

The landowners, naturally enough, saw the matter in a different light. In an instant they were to be deprived, for inadequate compensation, of as much as a third of their real property. Their serfs were to be taken from them for no compensation at all. Even before the enactment of the emancipation law, a large number of noble families struggled under a heavy burden of debt. Many landowners had not yet recovered from the destruction caused by Napoleon's invasion half a century before. Other nobles, if they had been spared the desolation of war, found it difficult to afford the luxuries of peace—clothing from Paris, rest cures at Baden, winters in Nice, gaming at Monte Carlo. Many patrician families would now be ruined; most would lose much of their old dignity and influence.

Tolstoy labored at his task, he said, "in the coolest and most conscientious manner." But the endless disputes wore down his spirit. It was, he believed, life-sapping work; and he resented every type of activity that took him away from the mysterious essence of life. To gallop over the countryside on a fast horse, to plough a field of maize with his *muzhiks,* to commune with nature, to make love to a pretty peasant girl—what was politics to that? This distrust of the state was not unique to Tolstoy. A century earlier the class to which he belonged had been released, by Catherine the Great, from its obligation to serve the imperial government. After the abolition of compulsory service the nobles gained title to their lands; these they were permitted to keep regardless of whether they labored for the Tsar. The landowners cherished their freedom. Wary of being lured back into a life of official servitude, they looked with suspicion on the most innocent forms of civic responsibility. This apolitical mentality, so different from the ideal of *noblesse oblige* (nobility obligates) that inspired the aristocrats of Western Europe to toil in the public service, would have important consequences for Alexander's program of reform.

Tolstoy questioned the value of his political work; but his descents into the sweaty depths of life were as unsatisfying. At times the ache of the flesh was overwhelming. "I absolutely must have a woman," he would write. He would throw himself upon some village girl. He would go off to the Gypsies. He would debauch himself in a tavern on the outskirts of Tula or Moscow. "Girls, silly music," he wrote after one of these episodes, "girls, mechanical nightingale, girls, heat, cigarette smoke, girls, vodka, cheese, screams and shouts, *girls, girls, girls!*"

But the Bacchanalia brought him no nearer a solution to the problem of life. His excursions into ecstasy were followed by flaccid intervals of remorse and despair. He would castigate himself for "living like a beast." His "awful lust," he said, amounted "to physical illness." It was "disgusting." He yearned "for something higher, something perfect." There were moments when, looking up at the heavens, he found that "everything fainted away and became transformed into joy and love." "What is it I so ardently desire?" he asked as he gazed at the stars. "I do not know." "It is dark," he wrote, "holes in the sky, light. I could die! My God! My God! What am I? Where am I going? Where am I?"

The spring at Yasnaya Polyana brought the promise of new life, a fresh start; but it yielded no answer, and over the beauty of nature there brooded the spectre of death. "Again the same question: *why?* I am no longer very far myself from the crossing-over. Over where? Nowhere. . . ." "What's the point of everything, when tomorrow the torments of death will begin, with all the abomination of meanness, lies, and self-deceit, and end in nothingness, the annihilation of the self? An amusing trick!"

A man in such a frame of mind might possibly withdraw to a monastery. Could he be relied upon to implement an emancipation law? Tolstoy's turn towards mysticism was characteristically Russian; but from the point of view of the Tsar, such spiritual drifting was disconcerting. If his revolution were to succeed, he must find a way to mobilize the faith of men like Tolstoy.

Washington, April–May 1861

THE CAPITAL, at least, was safe.

It had, for a time, seemed not unlikely that Lincoln's revolution would end before it began. It had seemed not improbable that Washington would fall, and that the new administration would collapse, before a sufficiently strong defensive force could be transported from the North to protect the Federal city. Across the Potomac, a hostile army was being raised. A new power had come into being in the South. The Confederate States of America, once the dream of a small knot of romantics, had become a reality. Fort Sumter had fallen to the new Republic. Virginia had joined it in spirit, and would in a short time unite herself to it in fact. The government at Washington had little with which to oppose it.

There was a sigh of relief when, in response to Lincoln's call for troops, the Massachusetts 6th Regiment of Volunteers arrived after fighting its way through Baltimore. But for some time no more soldiers came. The President looked into the abyss every revolutionary leader sooner or later confronts. It is one thing to cross the Rubicon. It is another thing to know what to do when one reaches the other side.

Lincoln understood the moral necessity of a revolutionary policy; but in contrast to Tsar Alexander, he had given little thought to its practical consequences. Where, he asked, was the Massachusetts 7th Regiment? "I don't believe there is any North," he remarked in frustration. "The 7th Regiment is a myth." Lincoln was not easily frightened, but those close to him perceived, in his dark and lowering looks, an uncharacteristic agitation. He paced the floor of his office. "Why don't they come!" he was heard to say as he gazed out the window of the White House. "Why don't they come!"

The crisis passed, and Washington was soon swarming with soldiers. The Massachusetts 7th Regiment arrived. Troops from Ohio and Vermont, Maine and Minnesota, Wisconsin and Michigan poured in. Colonel Cameron's Scotch Regiment—the 79th New York—marched up Pennsylvania Avenue in tartan and plaid. Colonel Corcoran's Irish Regiment—the 69th New York—followed. By the beginning of the summer more than 30,000 soldiers were encamped in or around the Roman temples of the capital—the germ of the Army of the Potomac. The city resembled a vast bivouac. Franklin Square was covered with barracks. The East Room of the White House was converted into a guardroom. Two Rhode Island regiments were quartered in the Patent Office. Across the river, at Arlington, more troops were encamped, and a vast array of tents and standards stretched from Alexandria to Georgetown, protected by an intricate system of forts and redoubts.

With the influx of men and arms the tone of the city changed. The rudiments of a wartime society emerged. Before the outbreak of the war, Washington had been, in its social complexion, a Southern city, with French overtones. At Washington, as at Charleston, cultivated men and women piqued themselves on their intimate knowledge of the culture of France. They alluded to the novels of Balzac and Mlle Scudéry. President Buchanan conversed in French with strollers on the lawn of the White House. But the leisured, Francophile culture of old Washington was swept away in the revolution; in the spring of '61 the life of the city was regulated by the bugle, the fife, and the drum. The routines of the army formed the pattern of social existence. The city's matrons woke to reveille; their daughters made elaborate toilettes in anticipation of officers' call and dress parade; the men of the city, drowsing, after supper, over their newspapers and cigars, heard the bugle notes of tattoo ("tap-to," the call to quarters), and made their way to bed to the music of taps.

Sometimes, in the night, the ominous "long roll" sounded—a long, low, monotonous drumming, the signal that something was amiss.

By common consent the darling of the new society at Washington was Miss Kate Chase, the daughter of the new Secretary of the Treasury, Salmon P. Chase. She was a young lady of twenty, and she quickly replaced Miss Lane as the reigning *belle*. Her face was handsome, spoiled only, in the opinion of some, by a retroussé nose; her figure was "exceedingly well formed." She was always beautifully dressed, with the haughty carriage of an empress; yet with all her grandeur, Miss Chase contrived to produce an effect of simplicity, as befitted the daughter of a man who drew his inspiration from the Puritans, and who like them had emerged from the pew to grapple with the ungodly. Flowers supplied, in Miss Chase's wardrobe, the place of jewels; and she rarely went forth, from her house at the corner of Sixth and E Streets, without a rich and fragrant blossom in her hair.

Washington, anxious to escape the tension of revolution, was soon absorbed in the melodrama of Miss Chase's coming out. She was used to getting what she wanted; and what Kate Chase wanted most was not long a secret in the capital. William Sprague rode into Washington that spring on a white horse to take command of the 1st Rhode Island; and Miss Chase's destiny was sealed. How could she resist? Few gifts of nature or fortune, it seemed, had been denied this young man. Sprague was handsome, he was rich, he was powerful. He was the Governor of Rhode Island. He was thirty years old—a man of apparent splendor, and possibly of inward danger. In his dark gray eyes Miss Chase beheld the revelation of her future.

With her brusque, almost military manners, Miss Chase shone brilliantly in the firmament of wartime Washington; but the life of the city nevertheless revolved around the President. Lincoln was less awkward, in his social character, than many had expected him to be. Judge Horatio N. Taft of the Patent Office was inclined to be critical in matters of etiquette. But he never saw Lincoln embarrassed. "The President seems to be anxious," he said, "to make everyone comfortable and at their ease." This was "the essence of good breeding." When the diplomatic corps came to dine in state at the White House, the President surprised many by acquitting himself well, though his son Thomas ("Tad") observed that beside the beribboned diplomats and braided attachés, "Pa looked pretty plain with his black suit." Mrs. Lincoln was another matter: "Ma was dressed up," Tad said, "you bet." In her desire to outshine the Miss Chases of the world, Mary Todd Lincoln made, in May, an expedition to the shops of Philadelphia and New York; the result was grim.

In contrast to the egotism and display of Mrs. Lincoln, the President preserved a decent simplicity of demeanor. Judge Taft's daughter, Julia, saw him often in 1861. Miss Taft's brothers, Bud and Holly, were the play-mates of Lincoln's two youngest boys, Tad, eight years old, and William Wallace ("Willie"), ten. (Lincoln's oldest son, Robert Todd, was an undergraduate at Harvard; his second son, Edward Baker, lay buried in an Illinois graveyard.) Miss Taft was a pretty, well-bred young lady of six-teen; to her fell the lot of chaperone. She often found the President, when business was not pressing, in the family's oval sitting room on the second floor of the mansion, in the big chair by the window. He usually had a book in his lap—a "big, worn, leather-covered book." It was his Bible; and when not in use, it "stood on a small table ready to his hand." After lunch he would sit beside the window reading, "sometimes in his stocking feet," Miss Taft remembered, "with one leg crossed over the other, the unshod foot slowly waving back and forth, as if in time to some inaudible music."

Miss Taft was at first a little afraid of the President. But she soon dis-covered him to be good-humored and easy of approach. He called her "flibbertigibbet." When, in the sitting room one day, Miss Taft, in a white frock with a blue sash, professed ignorance of the term, the President looked at her in mock astonishment.

"You don't know what a flibbertigibbet is?" Lincoln asked.

Miss Taft did not.

"Well, I am surprised, child; I thought everybody knew what a flibber-tigibbet was."

"Well I don't," Miss Taft replied. "Is it a French word?" (Miss Taft took pride in her excellent French.)

"No, Julie," the President said, "it's not a French word. It's a good American word and I'm surprised you don't know what it means."

"I don't think you do either," she told the President.

"Don't know what flibbertigibbet means? Of course I know what it means and I'll tell you. It's a small, slim thing with curls and a white dress and a blue sash who flies instead of walking."

Yet suddenly the merry joking would cease; the laughter would stop; and though no sharp words escaped him, the President would sit "sad and silent under the strain." Miss Taft would find him "sprawled out in that big chair in the sitting room" with the book in his hands. It was Lincoln's habit to search the book for clues. The free state, he knew, had been forged in the heat of the English Bible; it was practically Protestant. No modern reformer, whatever might be his personal theology, could afford to overlook the reform spirit which produced the Reformation. The imagination of the American people had, moreover, been touched by the Second Great Awakening, an evangelical revival that began in the late eighteenth century. The poetry of King James's Authorized Version of the Bible lingered in the nation's consciousness.

"My friend has said to me that I am a poor hand to quote Scripture," Lincoln once remarked. Yet he had turned to the Bible in 1858 when, as Republican candidate for the Senate in Illinois, he sought what he called "some universally known figure" that would "strike home to the minds of men in order to raise them up to the peril of the times." He found what he was looking for in Mark 3:25: "And a house be divided against itself, that house cannot stand." Would the book yield another such clue?

One morning Miss Taft found the President sitting in his chair looking out the window. The Bible lay in his lap. "He spoke to me in an absent-minded way and, clasping my hand, rested it on his knee, as I stood by him. He seemed to see something interesting out the window. I stood there for what seemed to me a long time, with my hand clasped in his. I followed his gaze out of the window but could see nothing but the tops of some trees. I thought it wouldn't be polite for me to pull my hand out of his grasp, even if I could, so I stood there until my arm fairly ached." Why, she later wondered, did she not ask the President what he saw out the window? "I think," she said, "he would have told me."

At last the President turned to her. With a startled look Lincoln said, "Why, Julie, have I been holding you here all this time?"

Nothing in his life had prepared him for the violent turn events had taken. He had hoped to accomplish his revolution pacifically, and he had not permitted himself to imagine what would happen should his people throw open the gates of war. He was not a practiced man of action. He had not, like Tsar Alexander, been bred to power. He was not, like Bismarck, versed in matters of state. He had never before exercised executive authority. It is unlikely that he knew, in the spring of 1861, how to frame a military order. The highest office he had held, before his elevation to the presidency, was that of Congressman; more than a decade before he had served a single term in the House of Representatives. Still less was he a soldier. His experience of combat was, he said, limited to a struggle with the mosquitoes during the Black Hawk War. His party had, in the recent election, deployed paramilitary units like the Wide Awakes to influence the result at the polls; these companies, with their torch-light parades and "monster meetings," had been organized, Henry Adams said, "in a form military in all things except weapons." But it is one thing to connive at the acts of street thugs in an election canvass, quite another to form armies and lead a nation in an atmosphere more or less revolutionary.

A friend of Julius Caesar remarked, "For all his genius, Caesar could not see a way out." Caesar aimed to dismantle a republic, Lincoln to transform one; but both men were equally revolutionaries; and they both found themselves, once the initial revolutionary thrust was made, unsure of what to do next. In the spring of 1861 Lincoln was no more able to "see a way out" than Caesar had been.

The Secretary of State did not fail to detect the President's tremulous uncertainty. In spite of the mortification it gave Seward to serve with his enemy, Salmon P. Chase, the imperious New Yorker had agreed to sit in Lincoln's Cabinet. The State Department was too valuable a prize to sacrifice to the gratification of a personal enmity. Scarcely had he taken his seat when his sharp and jealous eye perceived an opportunity of arrogating a greater share of power to himself. Seward's judgment was, by this time, debilitated by ambition as by a form of palsy. In the spring of 1861, the Secretary of State was furtively carrying on a negotiation with the South, one which he deliberately concealed from the President. To protect his policy of conciliation, he urged Lincoln to embrace a policy of militant nationalism. By provoking a war with a European power, Seward argued, the President could distract Americans from the difficulties of their domestic politics.

Shortly before Fort Sumter fell, Seward made a play for power. In an effort to save his program of accommodation with the South, he told Lincoln that the administration was "without a policy, either foreign or domestic." If, he said, the President was unable to "pursue and direct" a coherent line of policy, he must devolve the task "on some member of his Cabinet." "It is not in my especial Province," Seward modestly added. "But I seek neither to evade nor assume responsibility."

The Secretary of State was the first man of power in the President's party to challenge his competence directly; but Lincoln knew that his own ascendancy was formal and precarious. If he did not act, other mutinies would follow.

To save his revolution, he must fight.

Berlin and Saint Petersburg, June–July 1861

IN JUNE 1861 the Prussian general, Albrecht von Roon, wrote a letter to his old friend Otto von Bismarck in Saint Petersburg. Events at Berlin, Roon informed Bismarck, had gotten out of hand; things were "ripe for a blow-up."

The letter revived Bismarck's drooping spirits. His vigorous qualities were going dormant. Unable to lay his hands on authority, he had tried to amuse himself with social life. His standard, however, was high;

he once claimed that, outside the Faubourg Saint-Germain in Paris, polite society no longer existed in the world. In this respect the Russian capital fell short of his ideal. Bismarck conceded that there were still to be found, in Saint Petersburg, men of the old school, men who had been alive in the sunset of the eighteenth century, and whose conversation preserved the light and splendor of a vanished age. Such men had come of age during the reign of the first Tsar Alexander; they had received a classical education; they spoke fluently not only French but also German. Bismarck classed them with the "cream of European civilization." But they were a dying breed, and the men of the next generation failed to come up to the lofty standard of the Alexandrine period. It was true, Bismarck said, that old Prince Orlov was remarkable both in character and courtesy. Peter Shuvalov had perhaps the "best brain" in the imperial government. But their minds were limited, their conversation confined to the commonplaces of "the court, the theater, and the army."

Yet Saint Petersburg had its consolations. Chief among them were the pleasures of the imperial court. In his various diplomatic wanderings Bismarck never encountered anything that approached the wealth and luxury of the Romanovs. Upon his arrival at one of the Tsar's palaces—if only for a meeting with Prince Gorchakov, the Foreign Minister—Bismarck would as a matter of course be assigned, for his personal use, a suite of opulent rooms. Here there was no end of delightful surprises. Lavish lunches and dinners of several courses, accompanied by "three or four superb wines," were punctually brought in—even on those occasions when he was to dine elsewhere in the palace. The food was "absolutely faultless." The wine was memorable. Cupboards in the wall were found, on inspection, to be stocked with "wines of high quality and other needful goods." The vintages were exquisite, "nothing but the very best."* The cost of the bottles, he said, "must have been terribly high." But only an absurd Stoic would deny himself a glass of Latour or Lafitte while he dressed for dinner. When Bismarck traveled with the Tsar on the imperial train, the same standard of luxury prevailed. He would be shown to a comfortable seat in one of the blue saloon cars blazoned with the double-headed eagles of the dynasty. A tray of tea and coffee would at once be brought to him, together with biscuits, meat, cigars, and an excellent bottle of Bordeaux.

---

* The "jewels" of the Romanov wine collection were stored in the cellars of the Winter Palace. These were plundered by the Bolsheviks after they stormed the palace in 1917. The exquisite vintages were promiscuously consumed by the thirsty rebels, and afterwards Palace Square was filled with besotted Communists.

There were other compensations. Bismarck rented a house on the English Quay, with a fine view of the Neva and the Nicholas Bridge. In contrast to his previous diplomatic post, in Frankfurt, he was able to spend a considerable amount of time with his three children, Mary Elizabeth Johanna, twelve years old at the beginning of 1861, Nicholas Ferdinand Herbert (Herbert), eleven, and William Otto Albert (Bill), eight. Every Saturday the children would come before their father with their exercise books to give him an account of their studies. Bismarck found time, too, to learn the Russian language, which he studied, mastered, and cherished. For exercise, there was the chase. On hunting expeditions with the great nobles, he would don a Russian hunting coat and follow the elk, the wolf, and the bear to his heart's content. His reputation as a crack shot won him the admiration of the aristocracy, and Bismarck was amused to discover that the aura of a sportsman was not useless to the success of a diplomat.

Yet he seldom appeared in society. Bismarck did not like to stay up late, and during the high season in Saint Petersburg the soirées which formed the heart of the city's social existence did not begin until eleven o'clock or midnight. In the middle of a freezing winter night, men and women of fashion, who had earlier in the evening been to the theater or the ballet, or to a ball which had grown dull, climbed into their sleighs and were driven, through snowy streets, to one or another of the city's illuminated palaces to drink champagne. Under baroque ceilings, fashionable ladies gossiped, and men of pleasure pursued pretty ballerinas. A second round of soirées, at which supper was served, began at two in the morning and did not break up until four or five. Bismarck found this social regimen injurious to heath and not necessary to diplomacy. He refused numerous invitations, though he made an exception for those of Grand Duchess Hélène, whom he pretended to like.

He derived a much greater pleasure from the society of the Empress-Dowager Alexandra, the mother of Tsar Alexander. A curious intimacy grew up between the ancient widow, dressed always in black, and the middle-aged ambassador. Bismarck came to regard her as a foster mother. She was, by birth, a princess of the blood royal of Prussia: she was the sister of King Wilhelm. She doted on Bismarck. On his visits he would dine with her at her bedside, where she took most of her meals, or he would sit beside her on one of the terraces. The aged Empress would lie on a chaise-longue, knitting and playfully scolding her protégé. Alexandra, Bismarck said, was "goodness itself to me." Her "charming naturalness has really something maternal in it, and I can confide in her as if I had known her from a child." The Romanovs were fond of Bismarck; Alexander went so far as to offer him a place in the Russian diplomatic service.

But neither the kindness nor the cellars of the imperial family could altogether assuage his bitter apprehension that history was passing him by. "Three years ago," he wrote to his sister, "I should have made a useful Minister; but now the very thought nauseates me." He had lost the season for action. Perhaps it was for the best; all that remained for him was to retire to some picturesque but insignificant diplomatic post. He rather fancied Switzerland. "Dull places with handsome surroundings," he said, "are perfect for old people."

Then Roon's letter arrived. Switzerland was forgotten. Bismarck replied immediately in a letter which was at once an analysis of the political situation in Berlin and a bid for power. He had, he told Roon, a plan to overcome the opposition of the free-state liberals—a plan to make a "break with the Chamber."

Chapter 6

VIOLENCE

Virginia, July 1861

THE SUN ROSE as the main body of the Union Army marched out of the camp at Arlington. Thirty thousand soldiers moved in four columns along the Virginia roads. At their head was Irvin McDowell. He was forty-two years old, a brigadier general, a graduate of West Point; he had devoted his life to the army. Yet he had not, as he rode out of camp, the look of a conquering hero.

He had been given the order to march by Lincoln, who was ready at last to draw blood. The President ordered a strike. General McDowell, however, felt no elation as he went down to battle. Three weeks before, at a council of war convened by the President, he had presented his plan to strike the Confederate Army near Manassas Junction, twenty-five miles southwest of Washington. The target was of strategic importance: at Manassas Junction two railway lines converged, the Manassas Gap, which connected eastern Virginia to the west, and the Orange and Alexandria, which linked southwestern Virginia to the Potomac. A victory at Manassas would not only sever the rail lines that connected the tidewater counties to the interior, it would also open the door to Richmond, which had superseded Montgomery as the capital of the Southern Republic.

Lincoln approved the plan; but McDowell's heart was not in his work. His army was by no means ready to fight. Most of the men who comprised it had, a few weeks before, been busy at the plough, in the shop, behind a desk. They did not march like soldiers. They did not act like soldiers. They left their columns at will to fill their canteens, or to pick the blackberries that grew in profusion along the Virginia roads. On the march to Manassas offenses of a more serious nature occurred. Some women were roughly handled by the troops, and several houses were plundered.

Before McDowell set out with this raw untrained soldiery, Lincoln had attempted to reassure him. "You are green, it is true," he said, "but they are green, also; you are all green alike." The President's words, however, did nothing to assuage the commander's nervous misgivings. The Southerners might be green; but they were fighting on their own ground, and they were led by men who esteemed themselves Cavaliers—country gentlemen accustomed to ride and shoot, to threaten and command.

If McDowell doubted the ability of his troops, he did not wholly trust the fidelity of his officers. Many of them, he knew, resented his promotion to command. He owed his appointment, they said, to his social connections in Ohio and New York. McDowell was descended, through his mother, from the Starlings, one of the founding families of Columbus, and he had married the daughter of Henry Burden, the master of the gigantic ironworks at Troy, New York. His fellow Ohioan, Salmon P. Chase, had vigorously advocated his elevation. McDowell knew that his officers questioned his capacity. But could he blame them? He seemed, at times, to question it himself.

On July 18, the Union Army entered the valley where Manassas Junction lay. The troops, covered with the grime and sweat of the march, pitched their tents near the little town of Centreville. McDowell dismounted and proceeded to survey the terrain. Before him lay a shallow river called Bull's Run. On the opposite bank, on a steep and rocky bluff, the Confederate battalions were arrayed in force. A bridge, known to the farmers and planters of the place as the Stone Bridge, crossed the river, and beyond it, at the edge of a sloping field, stood a farmhouse, the home of an aged widow, Mrs. Henry. In the distance McDowell could make out the faint outlines of a manor house. It was the field headquarters of his adversary, General Pierre Gustave Toutant Beauregard, the Louisiana Creole who commanded the Southern army at Manassas.

On the twentieth, a light drizzling rain fell. The air was heavy and uncomfortable. General McDowell decided against giving battle; but he ordered that an attack be made early on the following morning. Towards nightfall the sky cleared. The air, it was observed, was cooler and more delicate than it had been for many days. Taps sounded; but although many in the camp were weary, few found the oblivion of sleep. Twenty-five miles away, in Washington, President Lincoln was also restless. He woke, in the White House, from a strange dream. He dreamt, he said, of a ship—a ship sailing over unknown waters to a dark shore. The significance of the vision puzzled him.

At two o'clock in the morning drums sounded in the Union camp. The moon was full. General McDowell was himself far from well; but he gave no thought to postponing the meeting of the armies. The whole of his force was soon in motion. From the first, however, there were difficulties. Few of the men had any experience of night marches. Their efforts to muster in the moonlight were unskillful. General Tyler was slow to move his troops along the Warrenton Pike; it was half past six before he ordered his artillery to open fire on Confederate positions near the Stone Bridge. McDowell had intended the cannonade to coincide with the approach of Colonel Hunter's and Colonel Heintzelman's columns from the north, where they were to cross the river at Sudley Ford; but in the dawn light those commanders were nowhere to be seen.

The sun was high when McDowell, his patience wearing thin, mounted a horse and rode up to Sudley Ford to find out what had become of his right wing. He crossed Bull Run and soon found the dilatory columns. The march to Sudley Ford, he learned, had been far from easy; the terrain was rougher than anticipated, and much time had been lost in negotiating the obscure and treacherous ground. McDowell took personal charge of the columns.

It was now past ten o'clock. The advantage of darkness and surprise was lost. The sun was hot. The men dripped with perspiration. A cannonball struck a soldier dead. The other soldiers marched on, trampling the corpse in the dust. Ambrose Burnside's Rhode Island Brigade was the first to form and fire. A short time later William Tecumseh Sherman waded across the river with the 3rd Brigade and formed on Burnside's left.

A fierce fight commenced. The Union men, raw though most of them were, fought like veteran troopers. The Confederate forces fell back in a flash of musket fire. Even so stalwart a Southern warrior as General Barnard Bee was in despair. "They are beating us back!" he exclaimed to his brother officer, Thomas Jonathan Jackson of Virginia. "Well, sir," Jackson replied, "we will give them the bayonet." Bee could not restrain his admiration for the tenacity of a natural soldier. "There stands Jackson," he said, "like a stone wall." A short time later Bee was dead.

The roar of the battle could by this time be heard in Washington, where, at eleven o'clock, President and Mrs. Lincoln went to church. Little Tad Lincoln listened to the guns. He turned to Miss Taft. "Pa says there's a battle in Virginia," he said, and "that's big cannons going off like slamming doors."

While the President worshipped, the forces under his command advanced. They stormed the Henry house. In the intense fire that ensued, trees were shorn of their branches. The Henry house itself was rapidly reduced to a ruin. Mrs. Henry did not survive its destruction. General Beauregard's horse was hit by a shell; the head of the animal came clean off the body. Dead men lay everywhere, their faces grown black as charcoal in the sunshine.

McDowell, scenting victory, readied his troops for a last push. He ordered Captain Ricketts, the commander of Battery I, 1st U.S. Artillery, to take his guns to the high ground just above the ruins of the Henry house.

Potsdam, Magdeburg, and Berlin, January–July 1861

THE GARRISON CHURCH at Potsdam was, until it was wrecked in the last days of the Second World War, one of the holiest places in the topography of Prussian chivalry. To the crypt of the church had been brought, in August 1786, the corpse of Frederick the Great, laid out in the uniform of the 1st Battalion of Guards. In 1861 preparations were under way for another solemn ceremony in the church, the consecration, before the tomb of Frederick, of the battle-standards of new regiments of the line.

But there was a difficulty. The free-state men in the Prussian Chamber of Deputies objected to the formation of the new regiments. The regiments were intended to replace existing militia (*Landwehr*) units, and the Chamber had not consented to this change in the organization of the army. A minister with liberal sympathies, Rudolf von Auerswald, went to see the Chief of the King's Military Cabinet, General Oscar von Manteuffel, to beg him to cancel the ceremony.

The civilian was coldly received by the soldier. "I do not understand what your Excellency desires," Manteuffel told Auerswald. "His Majesty has ordered me to arrange a military ceremony. Am I to renounce this because there are a number of people sitting in a house in the Dönhoff-platz, who call themselves a *Landtag* [Parliament] and who may be displeased with this ceremony? I fail to see how these people concern me. As a general, I have never yet been ordered to take my instructions from these people."

Auerswald went away. The battle-standards were unfurled.

Otto von Bismarck was not the only Prussian who in 1861 was meditating a plan to break the Parliament and remodel the state. General Manteuffel also contemplated a renovation. The old soldier was archaic even by the primeval standards of the Prussian officer corps;

Bismarck thought him a "fantastic corporal." Manteuffel was a martinet with a turn for fantasy. His feeling for the past was intense; like
General Patton, he lived in a romance of dead commanders—
Epaminondas, Hannibal, Wallenstein. His imagination was formed on
seventeenth-century models; he found his political ideal in Thomas
Wentworth, Earl of Strafford, the statesman who labored unsuccess-
fully to make Charles I absolute ruler of England. The question, Manteuffel told King Wilhelm, was whether he would allow "power to be
wrested from his hands even before open battle had been joined." He
begged the King to remember that he still possessed "power and the
army"; that he was Supreme Warlord; that he might easily make his
authority in the Kingdom complete. He could abolish the constitution
and afterwards rule by decree.

Manteuffel's dreams were interrupted when, shortly after the dedication of the battle-standards in the Garrison Church, Karl Twesten, a
Berlin magistrate, published a pamphlet in which he criticized the generals' plans to remodel the army. Such a reorganization, Twesten said,
would "produce an atmosphere of distrust and hostility between the
military and civil society." Manteuffel took personal offense, and challenged Twesten to a duel. He shot the magistrate in the arm. Prussian
Junkers were accustomed to cudgel refractory burghers; but a duel violated army regulations. Manteuffel insisted on punishing himself. He
retired to the detention fortress at Magdeburg, where he sat for some
time in a posture of stoicism, in parodic emulation of Strafford in the
Tower of London.

Manteuffel continued, in his cell at Magdeburg, to contrive plots and
plans; he drew his inspiration from the methods which Caesar and Bonaparte had employed to subvert civil liberty. After his release, he drew up
orders to strengthen the Berlin garrisons. He hoped to form the garrisons into a Praetorian Guard capable of overawing the opponents of
royal and military authority in Berlin. A march on the capital was to follow—a "cleansing mud bath," one of the generals called it. Thirty-four
thousand men and a whiff of grapeshot. What would the free-state orators say to that?

Camden, South Carolina, and Richmond, Virginia, May–July 1861

OF ALL THE FORMS of government, an oligarchy is the most easily
roused to fight, and the most difficult to mobilize once roused. Try
though she might, Mary Chesnut could not suppress the Cassandra in
her. She knew too intimately the blood-pride of the Southern planter to
be confident in the course he had chosen. The Cavalier was bred to arro-

gance by the plantation; he must have his way, or he would, like Achilles, retire to his tent to sulk.

Not only did the plantation breed a spirit of uncooperative independence in the planter, it also sapped his will. Mary Chesnut witnessed the processes of deterioration at Mulberry. The very luxuries of the place were deadly. Sixty persons were attached to the household service alone—butlers, footmen, housemaids, picturesque in white turbans and blue dresses. Hundreds more labored outside the big house, in the kitchen and the smokehouse, the dairy and the stables, the grist mill and the lumber mill, at the cotton gin or in the fields. The result of this superfluity of labor, Mary Chesnut said, was that there was nothing to do at Mulberry. One sank into apathy, fell into a moral coma.

Mulberry was morbid. It played tricks on the psyche. Old Colonel Chesnut, Mary Chesnut's father-in-law, was the master of the house and its 12,000 acres. He was genial, courtly, and as "absolute a tyrant as the Czar of Russia." His "métier is to be an autocrat, the prince of slaveholders." The wonder was that he "was not a greater tyrant." In 1861, the old Colonel was ninety years old. He had been born a subject of George III, in the days when South Carolina was a colony of Great Britain. The patent of Mulberry bore a royal seal. During many decades of feudal pre-eminence his egotism had assumed a variety of curious forms. No lady of his family was permitted to appear before him in a red dress. Conversation at his table was strictly limited to a stream of banal pleasantries. His own opinions were never to be contradicted. He "roars and shouts," his daughter-in-law said, "if a pebble of an obstacle is put in his way." Yet he usually had his way. Mary Chesnut suspected that he had fathered children by one of his slaves. "Merciful God!" she said, "forgive me if I fail. Can I *honor* what is dishonorable? *Rachel* and her brood make this place a horrid nightmare to me."

Her father-in-law was a tyrant out of Tacitus; her mother-in-law was sprung from the pages of Gothic romance. Mary Cox Chesnut had been a Philadelphia belle in the last years of the eighteenth century; she had known George Washington and had been often in Martha Washington's drawing room. But during six decades on a cotton plantation her eccentricities had grown upon her. No less than four slaves were required to attend her each night. Two women slept in her bedroom. Two more slept in the next room, in the event the first two should need assistance. Before any garment was suffered to touch the old lady's skin, it had first to be ironed; the mistress of Mulberry could not bear the touch of anything cold or clammy. Smoothing irons had always to be kept before the fire in her dressing room, and the flame was never permitted to go out while she was at Mulberry. Her nose was as morbidly sensitive as her skin.

Candles were taken out of her rooms before they were snuffed. Lamps could be extinguished only out of doors. Violets were under no circumstances to be brought into the house, and only a certain breed of rose was tolerated.

The old lady's tenderest sensitivity was reserved for her servants. She had been used to slaves from girlhood; her father had owned them in Quaker Philadelphia. But she had never accustomed herself to the scale of Southern bondage. She could not forget the stories she had been told, when little more than a girl, of the slave insurrection at Santo Domingo. Fearful lest the people who served her should one day turn upon her, she sought to purchase their goodwill with an exaggerated courtesy. She treated each of her slaves "as if they were a black Prince Albert or Queen Victoria," and she bored her daughter-in-law by talking constantly, in a loud voice, of "the transcendent virtues of her colored household—in full hearing of the innumerable negro women who swarm over this house." She spent hours "cutting out baby clothes for the negro babies," and she was always ready with an ample wardrobe for the most recent arrival in the slave quarters. Only when she dined did the mask of benignity slip; she scented death in the pot. "I warn you," she would say as the black footmen looked on. "Don't touch that soup. It is bitter. There is something wrong about it."

In the theory of the Fire Eaters the plantation was an oasis of culture. The labor of Africans was supposed to free the paternal class to perfect its soul. The reality, Mary Chesnut knew, was different. The plantation was stupid. The inmates of Mulberry, she said, "have grown accustomed to dullness. They were born and bred in it. They like it as well as anything else." The bleating of the sheep, the dripping branches that hung low in the swamp water, the "weird sounds" of the whippoorwills on moonlit nights—they all contributed "to the general despairing effect." A "dismal-swamp feeling hangs round us" here. She had a name for it: "Southern swamp depression."

She felt relief when, at last, she fled to Richmond, to be nearer her husband, who was with Beauregard at Manassas. Amid the "stir and excitement of a live world" she was able to breathe. Her hotel, the Spotswood, was filled with Southern public men and their wives. It was a "miniature world," with as much intrigue and drama—as many quarrels and love affairs—as a student of the human heart could wish for. For that is what Mary Chesnut was, an historian of the vagaries of human character, a delver into the secret depths of personality. Perhaps she was something more . . . Might she not be an artist? She decided to keep a journal. She intended her "notes," as she called them, to be "memoirs of the times." She seems to have hoped, when she began the journal, that she might one day draw on it for material for a novel. Only in time would it become evident that the journal itself, revised and rewritten by the author in her old age, was the true masterpiece of Mary Chesnut's life.

At Richmond she threw herself into the life of Mrs. Jefferson Davis's court. But what she saw there was no more reassuring than the depressing visions of the plantation. The lords and ladies of the South carried the insolence of the big house into the forum and the senate. None would brook a superior, and few could tolerate an equal. Their meetings resembled Convocations of Nobility. One false word, and hands gripped pommels.

Mary Chesnut was instantly absorbed in the strife of antagonistic personality. There was pretty Louisa Bartow, so girlish, in her white muslin dresses, yet so cruel. Her wit was as sharp as any gentleman's saber. Mrs. Bartow was, like Mary Chesnut herself, childless, an emptiness she made up by a passionate attachment to her husband, Francis Stebbins Bartow, a lawyer who had recently been commissioned a colonel in the 8th Georgia.

Mrs. Bartow thought her husband the very first man in the South; but it was a point Mrs. Joe Johnston could never concede. Her own husband was quite obviously the most splendid specimen of masculinity in the new Republic. Was he not the highest ranking officer in the United States Army to have gone over to the Confederacy?

"If my Joseph is defeated," Lydia Johnston announced one day at tea, "I will die."

"Lydia," Mrs. Jefferson Davis said, "beware of ambition. By that sin fell the angels." The Confederacy might be big enough to contain the pride of one of the two husbands; it could not encompass both. Varina Davis had no doubt which of the two ought to have the precedence at Richmond. The First Lady of the South went about the town in a landau drawn by spanking bays, and gave brilliant levées. Mary Chesnut, with her own sensitivities of pride and rank, complained that Mrs. Davis "was not civil enough" to her at tea and kept her "bandied about for a seat."

One day, while she was sitting in Mrs. Davis's drawing room, she was startled, on looking up, to see her husband. She had thought him still at Manassas. James Chesnut had come down in haste from Beauregard's headquarters, and must go at once to see President Davis. When, at dusk, he emerged from the President's room, he told his wife almost nothing of what had taken place within; but from the few words he let fall she guessed what happened. Joe Johnston had been ordered to move his army from Winchester to Manassas to reinforce Beauregard.

"I did not know there was such a 'bitter cry' left in me," Mary Chesnut wrote after James Chesnut returned to Manassas. "But I wept my heart away today when my husband went off. Things do look so black." Mrs. Davis came into her room to try to raise her spirits; she sat by the bed telling stories. But Mary Chesnut was convinced, from the First Lady's preoccupied air, that something was wrong.

Chapter 7

A WHIFF OF POWDER

Bezdna, Russia, March–May 1861

IT IS SAID that certain followers of the *Khlysty,* the Russian cult of fla-
gellants, believed that the path to paradise lies through the "sinful
encounter." The seeker of salvation was obliged to mortify, not only his
flesh, but also his pride; for only by plumbing the depths of humiliation
could he hope to experience forgiveness, redemption, and paradisiacal
bliss. Men and women who followed the path of the *Khlysty* would gather
together and "cast all their garments from them during their wild
dance." "I flagellate, flagellate, seeking Christ," they would chant in
rhythmic ecstasy. The abyss into which the dancers descended resembled a scene from Euripides. "Here and there, one of them is seized with
convulsions and sinks to the ground senseless; the lights are extinguished, the women with unbound hair fall on the men and embrace
and kiss them passionately. In 'sinful encounter' the people of God roll
on the ground and copulate. . . ."

The most notorious exponent of the doctrines of the *Khlysty* was
Grigorii Efimovich Rasputin, the spiritual adviser to whom Tsar Alexander's grandson, Nicholas II, and his Empress, Alexandra, turned in the
desperate effort to save their son from hemophilia. Rasputin was
reproached by the Orthodox clergy for counseling penitent women to
seek salvation through sinfulness and sensual self-abasement. He humiliated "the devil of pride" in the women who came to him by forcing them
to undress in front of him, and by compelling them to stand or dance
naked in his presence. An officer's wife, who had called on Rasputin in
the hope of preventing her husband's transfer, claimed that the holy
man "told me at once to take off my clothes. I complied with his wish,
and went with him into an adjoining room. He hardly listened to my

request; but kept on touching my face and breast and asking me to kiss him." Rasputin contended that such lewdness led to grace; confronted by one of his detractors in the Orthodox priesthood, he replied, "Certainly, little father, our Saviour and the holy fathers have denounced sin, since it is a work of the Evil One. But how can you drive out evil, little father, except by sincere repentance? And how can you sincerely repent, if you have not sinned?"

The doctrines of the *Khlysty*, exaggerated perhaps by the prurience of the sect's critics, were nevertheless true to the traditions of Holy Russia. At its core Holy Russia was apocalyptic and antinomian. Paradise beckons us, here and now; we have only to learn to heed its miraculous summons. Dostoevsky distilled the essence of the millennial idea in his novel *The Brothers Karamazov.* "Mama," says a dying boy in the novel, "do not weep, life is paradise, and we are all in paradise, but we don't want to realize it, and if we did care to realize it, paradise would be established in all the world tomorrow. . . . Why count the days, when one is enough for a man to know all of happiness? My dear ones, why do we quarrel, boast in front of one another, remember wrongs against one another? We should go straight into the garden and make merry and romp, love and praise and kiss one another, and bless our lives." "Paradise," says another character in the novel, "is concealed in each one of us . . . when people understand this idea, the Kingdom of Heaven will begin for them, not in a dream, but in actual fact."

Russians differed as to how the New Jerusalem was to be attained. Some, like the *Khlysty*, emphasized the importance of intensified states of being, the ecstasies of intoxication, privation, or pain. Others regarded an abnormal physical organization as closely connected to the sources of holiness and prophetic power; epileptics, the mentally infirm, deaf mutes, and those who suffered from deformity were classed as "holy fools," and thought to live on an intimate footing with the hidden agents of grace. Old Believers (*raskolniki*), a group that broke with the established Church when the liturgy was reformed in the seventeenth century, attached importance to purity of ritual, while those who venerated pious hermits looked, in their quest for inspiration, to holy men who, through contemplation and ascetic discipline, had found "a way to God in their own hearts."

In 1861 the secular ideals of Alexander's liberal revolution collided with the millennial aspirations of Holy Rus'. To a peasant who believed that he was living on the verge of paradise, the Tsar's liberal revolution was incomprehensible. The peasant was at heart a spiritual anarch; he regarded emancipation, not as the mundane act of a secular government, but as an apocalyptic liberation from earthly bonds. The provisions of the emancipation statute required the liberated serfs to pay for the land they acquired; but the idea of payment was to the peasant an abomination. The Tsar, the peasants said, would never have imposed such onerous terms on his people. He was God's vicar on earth. Remote though he might be from those who labored in the land, he yet knew each peasant personally. His statute was written, not in ink, but in liquid gold, and in it he had granted his people "true liberty." *Tsar' dast,* the peasant said. *The Tsar will give.*

The landlords, when confronted with such arguments, insisted that the edict of ink was genuine. The peasants, in response, raised their scythes. "We no longer want the landlord," they shouted. "Down with the landlord! We have already worked enough! Now is the time for freedom!"

The refrain spread. *"Volia, volia,"* the peasants cried. "Freedom, freedom."

Anton Petrov was a thirty-five-year-old peasant from Bezdna, a village in the department of Kazan. He was a holy fool as well as a *raskolnik,* an Old Believer who repudiated the established Church; he had acquired a rudimentary knowledge of letters. He did not pronounce the Tsar's emancipation law a forgery; but after diligent study of the document he asserted that it had been misunderstood. He was convinced that he had discovered the true meaning of its strange symbols. The figure "10%" represented, he said, the Cross of Saint Anne, "by which true *volia* has been secretly sealed." After further elucidation, he concluded that the edict not only guaranteed the peasants complete and unconditional liberty, it also freed them from any obligation to pay dues and taxes.

The agreeable revelation was embraced by the local peasantry, and Petrov's progress to power was swelled by a train of deluded rustics. His claims grew more extravagant; he was a prophet; he had entered into personal relations with the Godhead, and was privy to the secret will of the Tsar. The sovereign and the Deity had confided into his hands a plenary authority; those nobles who declined to recognize either his spiritual or his temporal magistracy were to be slain with axes. The police were driven away, and thousands of peasants rallied around the vindicator of "true liberty."

At length a detachment of troops marched on Bezdna, where they found five thousand people resolved to die in defense of their saviour. The troops opened fire; fifty-one people fell dead. After the fourth volley, Holy Russia submitted to the will of the secular state. Petrov bid farewell to his mother and father, who blessed him. A witness watched as the holy fool, thin, small, and white as a sheet, emerged from his *izba.* Petrov held aloft his copy of the emancipation statute: he was convinced that the troops would not fire on a man who had invoked its iconic protection.

He was wrong.

Richmond, Virginia, July 1861

MRS. DAVIS came into the room so softly that Mary Chesnut did not know, at first, that she was there.

"A great battle has been fought," the First Lady of the Confederacy said as she leant over and kissed Mary Chesnut. "Your husband is all right." Varina Davis proceeded to relate what she knew or fondly imagined of the battle of Manassas, talking in "that calm desperate way" people have "when under greatest excitement." "Jeff Davis led the center," she said—a delusion or an unskillful fabrication; her husband reached the field only after the rout of the Union Army had begun. She went next to Louisa Bartow's room. Mrs. Bartow sat up in her bed, ready to leap to her feet at the entrance of the President's wife. But there was something in Mrs. Davis's face that took the life out of her.

"Is it bad news for me?" Louisa Bartow asked. "Is he killed?" But she knew the answer as soon as she saw Mrs. Davis's face—"knew it all in an instant."

She covered her face with her shawl.

Washington and Virginia, July 1861

"WHERE IS THE PRESIDENT?" the Secretary of State demanded when he came to the White House.

"Gone to drive," he was told by one of the ushers.

"The battle," Seward said, "is lost."

Lincoln returned from his drive and was given the news of the disaster that had befallen his army. He betrayed no emotion, and went at once to army headquarters. There he followed accounts of the débâcle.

On the battlefield, the 11th New York Infantry—a Zouave regiment, dressed in the exotic colors of Algeria—attempted to give cover to Captain Ricketts's advancing artillery. But the Zouaves were unprepared for the charge of the Confederate horse. In a moment the 1st Virginia Cavalry—Jeb Stuart's Black Horse riders, with black ostrich plumes in their hats and black Hussar's bars sewn into the facings of the coats—were upon them. Stuart himself rode into the fight, in tall boots and a yellow sash, the very image, one observer thought, of a dashing Cavaliero. Stuart's eyes, light blue in repose, seemed to acquire a darker tinge under excitement, as he went for the kill.

The battle had turned. The Cavalier spirit played a part in shifting the tide, but railroads and telegraphs were as decisive. Unbeknownst to the Union generals, General Joe Johnston had, by a series of swift and devious marches, succeeded in moving the greatest part of his army from Winchester to the rail line that connected the Valley of Virginia with the east. Johnston himself appeared on the field. He was fifty-four years old, with a high forehead and a Van Dyke beard. He was muscular and well-built, amiable in manner, molded in the traditions of Virginia chivalry. Under his direction the reinforcements bore down on the Union positions. McDowell's men, tired, hot, and thirsty, were unequal to the fresher spirit of the Army of the Shenandoah. Panic set in. "Halt and form," the Union officers cried. McDowell rode among his men and exhorted them to hold fast. But his efforts were in vain; the Union line gave way.

Entire regiments broke and ran. A crowd of Union dignitaries who had come from Washington to enjoy a picnic on the turf overlooking the fight found themselves caught up in the path of blood and history. Opera glasses and parasols lay scattered in the grass as elegant ladies raised their petticoats and raced to their carriages. The retreat became a rout. Supply wagons and artillery caissons crowded the road to Washington. Ambulances dripping with blood advanced by inches along the turnpike. Soldiers, their throats parched beyond endurance, fell on their hands and knees to lap the bloody water that filled the roadside ditches. One soldier lay dead with his canteen still at his lips. Another pleaded for a place in a wagon that was full to overflowing. Those soldiers who were too tired to walk unassisted clutched the tails of horses, knowing that sleep, for them, very probably meant death.

The hour was late when President Lincoln left army headquarters and returned to the White House. He went, not to his bed, but to his office, where he lay on a couch.* A bloody war had begun in earnest. Lincoln was still in the room when the sun, obscured by clouds, rose over the capital. A tropical rain fell. In something like desperation he telegraphed to George Brinton McClellan and ordered him to report to Washington.

Lübeck, Baden-Baden, and Hinter Pomerania, July 1861

BISMARCK HURRIED WESTWARD, riding the train from Russia. He was flushed with excitement. Roon had stated, in his letter, that the conflict between Prussia's two antagonistic parties was reaching a crisis, and

---

* The room in the White House which Lincoln used as an office is now known as the Lincoln Bedroom.

the assertion had had its effect. The lion was roused. Here, Bismarck thought, was his chance. He would personally explain to King Wilhelm his plan to break the free-state opposition in Parliament.

On the ninth, he reached Lübeck; it was five in the morning when the train pulled into the station. The only newspaper he could lay his hands on was *Ystädter,* the Swedish daily. From it Bismarck learned that the King had left Berlin to take the waters at Baden-Baden. He laid his plans accordingly, and on July 10, weary from travel, he was admitted to the presence chamber. The King was "unpleasantly surprised" to see his Ambassador. Bismarck nevertheless rallied his energies and proceeded to unfold his plan to smash the free-state men.

The plan was not original; it was a variant of the program of militant nationalism which the grandees at Saint Petersburg wanted the Tsar to embrace, and which Seward, in Washington, hoped to persuade Lincoln to take up. The King, Bismarck said, must put Prussia at the forefront of efforts to unite the German people in one nation. If he did so, Germans everywhere—even free-state Germans—would hail him for his boldness. The King could then do as he pleased; no assembly would dare to stand in the way of a man who promised to be the deliverer of his people.

The King, however, was slow to grasp the plan. Bismarck once compared his master to a horse that shinnies at every new object. How could German nationalism—the creed of dreaming revolutionists—enable him to crush the free-state opposition? The King asked Bismarck to draw up a memorandum explaining the paradoxical idea. Bismarck did so. It was really very simple. The pressure of Prussia's internal steam, Bismarck observed, was high. Open, a little, the valve of nationalism, and it could be dissipated harmlessly.

The King, once he began dimly to comprehend Bismarck's plan, seems to have felt only disgust for its Machiavellian ingenuity. Wilhelm was a simple soldier, formed in the old Prussian school. The last thing he wanted was to have at the head of affairs a man "who is going to turn everything upside down." Altogether the King thought Manteuffel's plan for a march on Berlin the more palatable alternative. The troglodytes he understood.

What was no less fatal to Bismarck's chances, the Queen detested him. Where Wilhelm was simple-minded, Augusta, his consort, was clever. She had passed her girlhood in Weimar, where she had seen the aged Goethe. She worshipped at the altar of *Kultur,* and although Bismarck was himself one of the most cultivated statesmen of his generation—a man who was at home in four or five languages, and who lived on intimate terms with Shakespeare and the Bible—Augusta nevertheless developed a passionate aversion to his character. Her feelings of dislike were fully reciprocated by

Bismarck. Augusta's admiration for the civilization of France and England exasperated a man who cherished an ideal of German greatness. The Queen, he said, "preserved from her youthful days in Weimar to the very end of her life the idea that French—and even more English—authorities and personages were superior to those of her own land." He was almost beside himself when Augusta secured for her son, Crown Prince Friedrich, an English bride—and no less a bride than the eldest daughter of Queen Victoria, "Vicky," the Princess Royal. When, in 1857, the marriage was celebrated, Bismarck was gloomy, and was heard to mutter about the "stupid admiration" for English "lords and gentlemen."

The Queen had obtained, Bismarck believed, an almost complete ascendancy over the mind of her husband. Every morning at breakfast she worked the poor man over. Letters and newspaper articles lay upon the table, apparently at random, but in fact carefully placed by the Queen for their usefulness in promoting whatever cause was just then dear to her heart. These items she obtruded upon her husband's notice while he drank his coffee. Yet when Bismarck once hinted to the King that his breakfast table was manipulated, Wilhelm waxed indignant. The King, with "his knightly spirit," defended his consort, even though appearances were against her.

At Baden-Baden Wilhelm was, after his initial fit of bad humor, perfectly cordial. He invited Bismarck to dine with him, a signal mark of favor. But nothing was said about the ministry. The next day the disappointed Junker boarded a train and went north, where he was to spend August and September at Reinfeld, the ancestral seat of his wife's family near Stolp (Slupsk) in Hinter Pomerania, at the northeastern edge of the German world. Bismarck's cleverness had once again failed in its effect; the King, he said, "thought me crazier than I was."

Scarcely had he arrived in Pomerania, however, when an event occurred which put the advice he had given the King in a new light. One morning in July, King Wilhelm went for his daily walk in the streets of Baden-Baden. Count Flemming, the scion of an old East Prussian family, alone accompanied him; neither bodyguards nor detectives were in attendance on the sovereign. As the two men strolled in the Lichtenthal Alley, they heard the report of a pistol. There was a smell of powder, and the King felt a burning sensation about his neck.

Peterhof and Yasnaya Polyana, Russia, June 1861–December 1861

IN JUNE Tsar Alexander removed to Peterhof, the summer palace which Peter the Great had reared on a bluff overlooking the Gulf of Finland, a fantastic collection of cascades, fountains, and richly adorned façades constructed in the emulation of Versailles. It was the close of the triumphant emancipation spring. The dark and despotic past, many Russians dared to hope, had been buried forever.

But the débris of ten centuries cannot be suppressed by an edict. The disturbances which followed the appearance of the emancipation manifesto were, it is true, mild in character; Prince Orlov was in this respect disappointed. There were a few hundred revolts, and a deluded peasant named Petrov was taken out and shot. But the country had not embraced the Tsar's revolution. Holy Russia operated on the tactics to which the Tsar's uncle, the first Tsar Alexander, had resorted after the invasion of Napoleon: it rarely gave battle, but instead withdrew, unbowed, into its infinite space. The Russian state had expelled the Mongols, the Poles, the Swedes, and the French, but it had never mastered the primitive power of its own people. The Romanovs co-opted the established Church, but they never converted the millennial yearnings of the country into a bulwark of the régime.

Alexander, though he was a shrewd tactician, did not know how to stir men's blood. The lawgivers of antiquity, who built for permanence, sought the sanction of the oracle for their revolutions. Russia was as rich as Delphi in spiritual metaphors, but the Tsar never pressed them into the service of reform. It would have cost him little to paint the struggle for freedom in the colors of millennial liberation. But Alexander was without pictorial capacity; his language revealed no gift of figure. He was unable to captivate Holy Russia, or make the people his partners in revolution.

In other ways the Tsar was more astute. Scarcely had the ink on the emancipation manifesto dried when he sacrificed the leading reformers to the vengeance of the party of coercion. Grand Duchess Hélène was frozen out. Her once brilliant drawing room went dark, and she herself went abroad. Nicholas Milyutin, the principal architect of the emancipation legislation, was dismissed by Alexander from his post in the Interior Ministry. Milyutin left Russia to travel in France and Italy.

To all appearances the Tsar was at the height of his prestige. A young American diplomat who saw him at Peterhof that summer was filled with admiration for the "Tsar-Liberator." William Goodloe of Kentucky was led by an equerry with enough "feathers in his hat to make an ostrich" through a series of halls and chambers. At last he reached a portal guarded by four gigantic Moors, arrayed in the livery of the Orient. The Moors threw open the doors, and the Tsar himself appeared, dressed in a sky-blue uniform and calf-skin boots, the very image, Goodloe thought, of a king, handsome of face, commanding of figure, his eyes "a beautiful light blue." Alexander spoke a few gracious words, and in a moment he was gone.

Yet his brightest days were behind him. When the euphoria that followed the appearance of the emancipation manifesto subsided, everyone was as discontented as ever. Many peasants continued to ask when true *volia* was coming. "Rumors have reached me," Alexander told a gathering of village elders, "that you are waiting for some other *volia*. There will not be any other *volia* than what I gave you."

Part of the problem was money. The Tsar was a tightfisted emancipator. Concerned for the fiscal integrity of the state and anxious over a recent banking crisis that had wrecked his Empire's primitive credit mechanisms, he threw the onus of paying for liberation on the people, particularly the peasants. As Russians awoke to a new burden of debt, high interest rates, and insufficient liquidity, the mood of the country darkened.

Alexander himself was irritable. His greatest displeasure was reserved for his oldest son. The Tsarevitch Nicholas was a charming young man, and yet . . . there was something not quite right about him. "Niks," as he was called, was handsome—perhaps, Prince Kropotkin thought, "even too femininely handsome." But his good looks and agreeable temper were deceptive; at heart the heir to the throne was "profoundly egoistic."

More troubling to the Tsar, Niks was insufficiently manly. He evinced no enthusiasm even for those activities which, to more normal specimens of Romanov manhood, were the greatest part of life. To take the salute of Cossack horsemen in Palace Square, or to go on maneuvers with the Chevaliers Gardes on the plains at Krasnoye Selo—such occupations, so delightful to Alexander, unaccountably failed to rouse up the blood of his son. The Tsarevitch, it appeared, would rather linger in the corridors of the palace, gossiping with the pages, than ride with the Horse Guards or drill with the Foot Guards. Alexander himself attended Nicholas's military examinations that summer. The Tsarevitch showed himself incapable of managing the parade ground—a signal failing in a prince descended from both the Romanov and the Hohenzollern stocks. Alexander did not conceal his anger. When Niks made yet another blunder, his father reproved him in a loud voice. "Even that," he shouted, "you could not learn!"

From the days of Marcus Aurelius and Commodus to those of the English Georges, with their recalcitrant princes of Wales, the history of relations between sovereigns and their eldest sons has been little more than a repetition of scenes of jealousy, distrust, and estrangement. The more vigorously the monarch attempts to mold the character of his heir, the more intractable does the material become; and in his attempts to strengthen the flimsy will of Nicholas, Alexander succeeded only in exacerbating his son's natural softness and timidity.

Thus did the daily round of dynasty and empire distract the Tsar from the largest questions of his revolution. The peasants, a Russian reformer wrote, "suffer much, their life is burdensome, they harbour deep hatreds, and feel passionately that there will soon be a change." They were waiting "for the revelation of what is secretly stirring in their spirits. They are not waiting for books but for apostles—men who combine faith, will, conviction, and energy. . . . The man who feels himself to be so near the people that he has been virtually freed by them from the atmosphere of artificial civilization; the man who has achieved the unity and intensity of which we are speaking—he will be able to speak to the people and must do so."

The Tsar could not do this. Might Count Tolstoy? It seemed not impossible. No high-caste in Russia had done more than Tolstoy to fathom the aspiration and potential of the common people. One night, when the clouds hung low in the sky over Yasnaya Polyana, the squire and three of his serf pupils went out into the white darkness. They crunched along in the snow. One of the students, who was called Semka, began *ah-ou-ing* as though he were a wolf. He was a big, strong boy, full of good sense. Fedka came too; Tolstoy was much taken with his "tender, receptive, poetic, yet daring nature." Fedka touched Tolstoy's sleeve with his own, then clasped two of his teacher's fingers in his hand. Pronka, the smallest of the three boys, walked behind them, careful to keep out of the bigger boys' way. He was a "sickly, mild, and very gifted lad," Tolstoy said. He lived in one of the poorest *izby* in the village—a black, dirty hut. He had not enough to eat, but he was sensitive and intelligent.

They went on in the darkness. "How was it . . . your aunt had her throat cut?" Fedka asked Tolstoy.

"Tell us! Tell us!"

Tolstoy told them the story. One of his aunt's peasants, a cook, had gone into his mistress's bedroom one night with a knife, intent on killing her. (Some half a dozen landowners were murdered by their serfs in Russia each year.) The peasant, gazing on his mistress's sleeping face, was seized by feelings of pity and shame. He went back to the kitchen and drank two glasses of vodka. He returned and slit his mistress's throat. But she continued to breathe; he had failed to sever the artery. The peasant went into the drawing room and smoked a cigarette; when he returned to the bedroom, he finished the old lady off.

Such was the peasant in the eyes of many well-to-do Russians—a semi-savage being whose brutish qualities gave the lie to the free-state idea that all men are created equal. "Human feelings," a Russian nobleman said, "were not recognized, not even suspected, in the serfs." But Tolstoy had looked more closely at the peasant than most of his peers. He had seen promise in his serf pupils—had seen in them what he called "the mysterious flower of poetry," the hope of a new and better Russia.

Could the Tsar's revolution build on that hope?

Tolstoy and his boys reached a thicket and stopped. Semka took up a stick and struck the trunk of a lime tree. The hoar frost fell from the tree on their coats and hats.

"Why are there lime trees?" Semka asked.

"Yes," Tolstoy said, "why are there lime trees?"

"To make rafters," Semka replied.

"And what about in the summer when the tree isn't cut?" Tolstoy asked.

"It's not worth anything then," Semka replied.

"No really," Fedka said, "why *does* a lime tree grow?"

They talked of the beauty of the lime tree. Then Pronka said, "Why, when we take the sap of a lime, it's like taking blood."

Chapter 8

USED-UP MEN

Washington, January 1862

GEORGE BRINTON MCCLELLAN was thirty-four years old when Lincoln summoned him to Washington and gave him the task of defending a revolution. He was a graduate of West Point and had served as an engineer under General Winfield Scott in the Mexican War; in civil life he had risen to high place in the Ohio & Mississippi Railroad. When war broke out, McClellan accepted a commission as a major general in the Department of the Ohio, though not without a pang. "The salary I gave up to re-enter the military service," he said, "was ten thousand dollars per annum." Once he received his stars, McClellan boldly crossed the Ohio. At a time when most Union generals were content to keep their camps, he won a victory before Rich Mountain in western Virginia which dazzled the North.

The adulation of the crowd went to his head, and McClellan began to fancy himself a man of destiny. The "crowds of the country-people who have heard of me and read my proclamations," he wrote to his wife, "come in from all directions to thank me, shake me by the hand, and look at their 'Liberator,' 'the General'! Of course I have to see them and talk to them. Well, it is a proud and glorious thing to see a whole people here, simple and unsophisticated, looking up to me as their deliverer from tyranny."

In Washington, where pompousness was the rule of political life, McClellan's vainglory could only become morbid. "By some strange operation of magic," he said, "I seem to have become the power of the land. . . . I went to the Senate and was quite overwhelmed by the congratulations I received and the respect with which I was treated. I suppose half a dozen of the oldest made the remark I am becoming so much used to: 'Why, how young you look, and yet an old soldier!' It seems to strike everybody that I am very young. They give me my way in everything, full swing and unbounded confidence."

It was, McClellan conceded, "an immense task that I have on my hands," but he did not think it beyond him. "I believe I can accomplish it." Indeed, he told his wife, "I see already the recent causes of our failure, and am confident that I can lead these armies to victory once more." He added, "I will endeavor to enclose with this [letter] the 'thanks of Congress,' which please preserve. I feel very proud of it. Gen. Scott objected to it on the ground that it ought to be accompanied by a gold medal. I cheerfully acquiesce in the thanks themselves, hoping to win the medal by some other action, and the sword by some other *fait d'éclat.*"

Lincoln was not a man easily imposed on, yet he fell, for a time, under the spell of the young General. He treated him with an elaborate deference, and he seems to have regarded his very fatuities as forming part of the mysterious equipment of military greatness. Here was *élan,* glamour, confidence. The "Young Napoleon," as McClellan was called, seemed true to the type of the romantic hero, a type the age was predisposed, by its poets and its philosophy, to accept. He was a young man with an odor of mastery about him. A scion of the tribe of the eagle, perhaps. True, he was not, as eagles go, very intelligent; but possibly, Lincoln seems to have thought, the military hero must be somewhat limited mentally, to preserve vigor of decision. McClellan was vain; but had not Caesar himself, fussing with his receding hair, been equally so?

Lincoln was, in his spare time, devouring books of strategy and tactics; but he was a novice in the art of war, and he knew it. He needed a general. From Caesar to Washington, in every upheaval touching the free state, the civil authorities have scurried to find a commander. Was McClellan the man? Certainly the young General believed that he was. When he strained his ears, the sound he heard was unmistakable. It was the "call of destiny." "When I was in the Senate chamber to-day," he confided to his wife, "and found those old men flocking around me; when I afterwards stood in the library, looking over the capitol of our great nation, and saw the crowd gathering around to stare at me, I began to feel how great the task committed to me. Oh! how sincerely I pray to God that I may be endowed with the wisdom and courage necessary to accomplish this work. Who would have thought, when we were married, that I should so soon be called upon to save my country?"

Perhaps if, among the many gifts that had been showered on McClellan, a sense of humor had also been granted him, he would have known a happier fate. As it was, he rode about Washington with a flashing eye, drilling his regiments and listening to the sound of popular applause. His days were crowded. "Had to work until nearly three this morning," he wrote to his wife. "I am getting my ideas pretty well arranged in regard to the strength of my army; it will be a very large one. I have been employed in trying to get the right kind of general officers. . . . Rode over the river, looked at some of the works, and inspected three or four regiments; worked at organizing brigades—just got through with that. I handed to the President to-night a carefully considered plan for conducting the war on a large scale. . . . I shall carry this thing *en grand* and crush the rebels in one campaign. I flatter myself that Beauregard has gained his last victory."

Yet already there was, in McClellan's letters, a disconcerting note; he could not conceal the contempt he felt for those with whom he was obliged to work. Generals, senators, diplomats—even presidents—were so many figures to despise. "I dined at the President's today," McClellan wrote. "I suppose some forty were present—Prince Napoleon and his staff, French Minister, English ditto, cabinet, some senators, Gen. Scott, and myself. The dinner was not especially interesting; rather long, and rather tedious, as such things generally are. . . . It made me feel a little strangely when I went in to the President's last evening with the old General [Scott] leaning on me; I could see that many marked the contrast. . . . Rose early to-day (having retired at three A.M.), and was pestered to death with senators, etc., and a row with General Scott until about four o'clock."

It soon appeared, however, that the young General was busy without being active. He was not quite so heroically fashioned as he appeared, and he was desperately afraid of subjecting his fame to the hazard of a battle. The weeks, and at length the months slipped by, while he suffered his troops to remain in idleness in their camps around Washington.

McClellan at first pretended that General Scott was responsible for this pusillanimity. He would, he said, gladly fight, but old "Fuss 'n Feathers" envied his fame and was determined to hold him back. Scott had formerly been his patron and his mentor; but McClellan now described him as "the great obstacle" to victory. The older man had won more battles than the younger one was even to fight; but McClellan regarded the aging hero as deficient in his knowledge of the military art. The "old General always comes in the way," McClellan told his wife. "He understands nothing, appreciates nothing." He would "not comprehend the danger. I have to fight my way against him." The man was "a perfect incubus. . . . I don't know whether he is a *dotard* or a *traitor*." But McClellan was confident that he would be given "absolute control independently" of Scott. "I suppose it will result in enmity on his part against me; but I have no choice. The people call upon me to save the country. I must save it, and cannot respect anything that is in the way."

General Scott withdrew from the contest with his former protégé; he retired from the army and took a house at West Point. McClellan, however, found new excuses for lethargy. He resented, with a bad grace, every effort to spur him into fighting. Did the civilian chiefs not understand that it took time to mold an army? Were they intent on squandering, in a hasty battle, the instrument which he was slowly and methodically bringing to perfection? The President was especially bothersome. His manners were primitive; McClellan thought him a "well meaning baboon." He told of going to the White House one day after tea and finding " *the original gorilla,* ' about as intelligent as ever." (Charles Darwin's *The Origin of Species* had been published in 1859.) "What a specimen to be at the head of our affairs now!" McClellan exclaimed. And the dreadful man insisted on calling on him at his house! He would put a stop to *that.* One night McClellan came home and was informed by the servant that the President was waiting for him. He turned on his heel and, ascending the stairs, went to his bedroom. He sent word to the President that he had gone to bed.

Such was Lincoln's temperament that he could accommodate himself, in his work, to men of the most disparate habits and dispositions. But he was baffled by the problem of co-operation with a timid egotist. At the end of January 1862, the President issued General War Order No. 1. He wrote it out, his private secretaries, John Hay and John Nicolay, said, "without consultation with any one, and read it to the Cabinet, not for their sanction, but for their information." The order directed that a "general movement of the land and naval forces of the United States against the insurgent forces" be made in the last week of February 1862.

Saint Petersburg, February–May 1862

NICHOLAS MILYUTIN, fresh from Rome and Paris, thought the menace palpable. "Everyone," he said, "appears to be waiting for something, fearing something. . . ."

Saint Petersburg hung in anxious suspense, but even in a revolutionary age young officer-candidates must select their regiments. A number of Prince Kropotkin's brother cadets chose the Preobrazhensky Guard, the élite regiment attached to the Tsar's household. Others looked for commissions in the Horse Guards or Her Majesty's Cuirassiers. "But you, Kropotkin?" his friends asked him. "The artillery? The Cossacks?"

No—the Prince was determined, he said, not to "enter a regiment of the Guard, and give my life to parades and court balls." While his brother cadets chose prestigious regiments near the capital, Kropotkin dreamed of assignment to a remote post, one where the heavy hand of the Tsar's government was less keenly felt.

He wanted to go to Siberia.

The Amur region had recently been annexed by Russia, and Kropotkin, who had obtained special reading privileges in the Imperial Library, got hold of every book he could "about that Mississippi of the East." He reasoned that "there is in Siberia an immense field for the application of the great reforms which have been made or are coming," and he accordingly put his name down for the Mounted Cossacks of the Amur.

His comrades in the Corps of Pages were appalled. "Kropotkin must always have his joke!" one cried. "It is so far," said another. A third, who looked up the uniform of the Mounted Cossacks of the Amur in the Officers' Handbook, found that it was atrocious. He read the description aloud, "to the horror," Kropotkin said, "of all present": "Uniform, black, with a plain red collar without braids; fur bonnet made of dog's fur or any other fur; trousers, gray." "Only look at the uniform!" Kropotkin's friend said. "Bother the cap!—you can wear one of wolf or bear fur; but think only of the trousers! Gray, like a soldier of the Train!"

Kropotkin's interests differed from those of his fellow cadets. He had grown into a high-minded, serious young man, intensely intellectual; he was becoming near-sighted and would soon require spectacles. He had been carried away by the liberal ideals that were fashionable in the early years of Tsar Alexander's reign. He had read Alexander Herzen, the expatriate writer, whose journals, *The Pole Star* and *The Bell*, though written in London, made a stir in Russia, where they were widely circulated in secret. "The beauty of the style of Herzen," Kropotkin said, seduced him, and in 1859 he had begun to edit a paper of his own. He wrote out the copies himself and slipped them into the desks of fellow cadets. He professed himself a free-state man, and he advocated the adoption, in Russia, of the rule of law and a written constitution.

Kropotkin's liberalism was the liberalism of the Decembrists, the noblemen who on a December day three and a half decades before had risen up in arms against Tsar Nicholas. The serfs, the Decembrists believed, could be citizens; Russia could be a republic. Some of the conspirators possessed wilder sympathies: they exalted the French revolutionary tradition and talked of a dictatorship of virtue. (Tolstoy, who several times tried to write a novel about the Decembrists, gave up because he found them too French.) For the most part, however, the movement was a liberal one, grounded in the ideals of the free state. Adam Smith's writings on economic freedom enjoyed a special vogue among educated young Russians of this generation; the poet Pushkin, who was closely connected to the Decembrists, celebrated Smith's work in *Eugène Onegin.* The lofty moral and intellectual qualities of the Decembrists, however, concealed their practical weakness. Their revolt in the capital was unskillfully executed, and in Senate Square their clamors for a constitution were promptly silenced by the guns of Nicholas. The liberal idealists perished on the gallows or were exiled to Siberia.

Kropotkin at first aspired to revive the Decembrist tradition of liberal heroism; but he soon began to doubt whether the flame which had once gone out could ever be rekindled. The free-state ideas propounded, at the beginning of the 1860s, by scholars like Boris Chicherin had a musty air: they stank of the study and the lecture hall. Kropotkin and those who thought like him yearned for "the grand, the elevating inspirations." They did not find such inspirations in the free state. The liberal imagination lost ground to a new sensibility, one which, though it sprung from a philosophy of coercion, possessed an appeal that the creed of freedom lacked. In March 1862, while Kropotkin was finishing up his course in the Corps of Pages, a book appeared which dramatized the new sensibility. The author was Ivan Turgenev; the novel was *Fathers and Children.* In it Turgenev described what happens when Bazarov, a young man imbued with the new spirit, encounters an older generation of liberals. "Well, and this Moniseur Bazarov, what is he exactly?" one of the characters in the novel asks his nephew.

"He is a nihilist!" the nephew replies.

Turgenev's nihilist dismisses the free-state solutions—"parliamentarianism, the bar, and the devil knows what." Our "clever men, our so-called progressives and reformers," Bazarov says, have "never accomplished anything." The nihilist disparages even the emancipation reforms which "the government is making such a fuss about." Insofar as Turgenev gives Bazarov a creed, it is a creed of violence and terror. The time has come, Bazarov argues, for Russians to stop talking and start acting. "We must," he declares, "smash people!"

The confessors of the new faith went under a variety of *nommes de guerre,* and they drew on a variety of intellectual traditions. At its core, the new sensibility was a form of romanticism, grafted on more or less bogus forms of mid-nineteenth-century science. The creed of the red romantics was utopian and coercive; it appealed to wellborn young Russians who, though they would have rejected with indignation the accusation that they were collaborating with a new species of despotism, had not broken with the spirit of *noblesse* in which they had been brought up.

In the spring of 1862, the red brigades went on the offensive. First came the leaflets. Scattered broadcast in the streets of Saint Petersburg, they bore the title "Young Russia." "Russia is entering the revolutionary stage of its existence," the leaflets proclaimed. A "revolution, a bloody and pitiless revolution," would follow, a "revolution which must change everything down to the very roots, utterly overthrowing all the foundations of present society and bringing about the ruin of all who support the present order." In language that blended the millennial impulses of Holy Russia with the romantic aspirations of scientific socialism, the leaflets declared that the

> day will soon come when we will unfurl the great banner of the future, the red banner. And with a mighty cry of *"Long live the Russian Social and Democratic Republic,"* we will move against the Winter Palace to wipe out all who dwell there. It may be that we will only have to destroy the imperial family, i.e., about a hundred people. But it may also happen . . . that the imperial party will rise like a man to follow the Tsar, because for them it will be a question of life and death. If this happens . . . we will cry, *"To your axes,"* and then we will strike the imperial party without sparing our blows. . . . We will destroy them in the squares . . . in their houses, in the narrow streets of the towns, in the broad avenues of the capital. . . .

Next came the fire.

The Feast of Pentecost, which commemorated the descent, upon the Apostles, of the Holy Ghost, was one of the most sublime in the calendar of the Orthodox Church. In the churches clouds of incense poured forth from the censers of the priests; the Pentecostal Icon, which showed tongues of flame illuminating the souls of the Virgin and the Apostles, was carried in solemn procession; and at Great Vespers the faithful knelt for the first time since Easter.

The Monday following Pentecost was specially consecrated to the Holy Ghost; shops and businesses in Saint Petersburg were closed. Prince Kropotkin, in the Corps of Pages, was dining in the apartment of one of the officers. At about four o'clock he looked out the window and saw plumes of smoke rising from the Apraxin Dvor. The market quarter, filled with wooden shops and shanties, lay in the heart of the capital. The Prince went out to the narrow lane that bounded the Dvor. "The sight," he said, "was terrific." "Like an immense snake, rattling and whistling, the fire threw itself in all directions, right and left, enveloped the shanties, and suddenly rose in a huge column, darting out its whistling tongues to lick up more shanties with their contents." The fire rapidly consumed the market, and a struggle commenced to prevent it from destroying the city.

It was not only the flames themselves, but their symbolic import that made the fire in the Apraxin Dvor so terrible an event in the psychology of Russia. In a country that had emerged from a forest, one in which most people dwelt in houses made of wood, fire, the "red rooster," was a dreaded agent of destruction. Yet in a cold climate fire was also the principal source of warmth, and it had early become connected, in the superstition of the people, with spiritual heat, prophetic illumination, and apocalyptic transformation. The revolutionist Michael Bakunin described the "childish, almost demoniac delight of the Russian people in fire." In the onion domes of their churches the Russians reproduced a stylized image of the visionary flame: the apex of a Russian church was "a tongue of fire crowned by a Cross. . . ."

Many of those who beheld the plumes of smoke rising from Apraxin Dvor wondered what cataclysm they foretold. But Prince Kropotkin did not wonder. He knew what they foretold. The end of liberalism in Russia.

Washington, February 1862

"PA DON'T HAVE TIME to play with us now," Willie Lincoln lamented. He was a quiet and intelligent child; Julia Taft thought him "the most lovable boy" she ever knew. Willie's younger brother, Tad, was a duller and more amusing boy. One day, while playing with a new ball in the White House, Tad shattered a mirror.

"Well, it's broken," Tad said. The instinct of a boy at such a moment will be to dread his father's wrath; but Tad quickly brightened. "I don't b'lieve Pa'll care," he predicted, though as a precautionary measure he threw a pinch of salt over his shoulder and attempted to say the Lord's Prayer backwards.

"It's not Pa's looking glass," Willie said gravely. "It belongs to the United States Government."

A broken mirror could add little to the troubles of a man who had on his hands a shattered country. Lincoln had by this time learned just how little real authority his office as chief executive of the United States Government conferred upon him. Leaders of free states have, notoriously, a greater difficulty in mobilizing their countries to meet an emergency than do heads of régimes despotically organized. The leader of a free state cannot simply order, or even artfully manipulate, he must persuade. His very generals feel themselves competent to criticize him. The republics of antiquity solved the problem through the institution of temporary dictatorship; but the founders of the American Republic, wary of Caesarism, did not revive it. Under the Constitution, the American President who confronts a crisis must fashion his own expedients. Every great presidency is an original invention.

But the clue eluded Lincoln. He had not yet mastered the revolutionary art. The gigantic military machine he had assembled had ground to a halt. Lincoln had entrusted to General McClellan the command of the greatest army ever deployed on the North American continent; but six months had passed, and in McClellan's hands the army remained, the President said, a "stationary engine."

In his anxiety, Lincoln pressed McClellan to attack the Confederate forces in their entrenchments southwest of Manassas. McClellan, however, refused, and when confronted with Lincoln's order calling for a general advance in the last week of February, he composed a long letter citing the insuperable obstacles to such a campaign. The Southern army encamped on the Manassas plain was not a third of the size of McClellan's army, but McClellan insisted that it was even larger than the Union force. He proposed an alternative. He wanted, he said, to bring his army by sea to one of the forks of land formed by the three great rivers—the James, the York, and the Rappahannock—that emptied into Chesapeake Bay south of the Potomac. From there the Army of the Potomac would proceed rapidly over land to Richmond, and sack the city.

While the President pondered his choices, Mrs. Lincoln threw herself into preparations for a party. Maillard's would prepare the dinner; wine and champagne would come from the Lincolns' wine merchants in New York. Five hundred invitations were sent out. In the midst of these exertions, Willie Lincoln came down with a chill. A fever, possibly typhoid, took hold of the boy. (The water used in the White House was drawn from the Potomac, which at that time served Washington as both a fountain and a drain.) The day of the party found Willie in the grip of a virulent intestinal malady. It was too late to cancel the fête; the Lincolns must go through with it. The President donned a black swallowtail coat. Mrs. Lincoln emerged from her dressing room in a gown of white silk, set off with a long train and a quantity of flounces.

Husband and wife descended the staircase to receive their guests. The affair was a splendid one, and amid the general gaiety the absence of a knot of sour-faced Republican radicals went almost unnoticed. "Are the President and Mrs. Lincoln aware that there is a civil war?" "Bluff Ben" Wade of Ohio wrote on the invitation he returned to the White House. "If they are not, Mr. and Mrs. Wade are, and for that reason

decline to participate in feasting and dancing." The President's revolution was Puritan in inspiration if not in form; Wade, a stepchild of New
England, warned the President to take care how he danced.

Official Washington was surprised by the sureness of the hostess's
taste. But Mrs. Lincoln could not enjoy her triumph. For her as well as
for her husband, the party was a hideous ordeal. Whenever they could,
they left their guests to go to the sickbed. In the weeks that followed, Lincoln spent many nights with the boy; but Willie grew weaker and weaker.
On the morning of the twentieth he appeared to be somewhat better,
and hopes were entertained for a recovery. But the revival proved fleeting. The end came, and the forms of Victorian grief were decently
observed: the open casket; the sprig of laurel, placed, on the child's lifeless breast, by his weeping mother; the reading, in the howling wind of
a winter storm, of the service for the Burial of the Dead.

Mrs. Lincoln went to pieces after Willie's death, but the President
had the duties of his office to perform. Should he authorize General
McClellan to proceed with his expedition to the lower reaches of the
Chesapeake? He was inclined to be skeptical of a plan which bore too
visibly the marks of its maker, a heavy freight of timidity and conceit. He
doubted the wisdom of a strategy which, though prodigal of time and
money, was unlikely to sever a single vital thread in the enemy's web of
communications. In a letter to McClellan, Lincoln observed that capture
of Richmond by itself would not break the rail line that connected northern Virginia with Lynchburg and the southwest, while a march on the
enemy's entrenchments southwest of Manassas (his own preferred plan)
might. McClellan replied that the entrenchments near Manassas were
too formidable to be overcome, a contention that did not redound to
his credit when, a short time later, the Confederates retired voluntarily
from those trenches, and their overpowering arsenal was discovered to
contain a number of "Quaker guns"—logs painted black.

Yet Lincoln did not lose faith in McClellan. He would, he said, "hold
General McClellan's stirrup for him if he will only win us victories." But
the painted logs detracted somewhat even from a child of destiny; and
Lincoln deprived McClellan of his position as General-in-Chief of the
armies. He did not, however, go so far as to remove him from command
of the Army of the Potomac.

Saint Petersburg, May–June 1862

A SINGLE WORD was now on every tongue.

The novelist Turgenev, who chanced to return to Saint Petersburg on
the day of the fire in the Apraxin Dvor, was startled to discover that the

word "nihilist" had been caught up by thousands of people. A short time before, the word had been virtually unknown; when Grand Duchess Hélène encountered it in *Fathers and Children,* she asked one of her protégés what it meant. Now the word was firmly ensconced in the city's vernacular; and scarcely had Turgenev stepped into the Nevsky Prospekt when an acquaintance took him to task.

"Look at what your nihilists are doing! They are setting Petersburg on fire!'"

The cause of the fire in the Apraxin Dvor was never discovered. Some believed that *agents provocateurs* in the pay of the reactionaries set fire to the market in order to give their enemies a bad name; but the suspicions of most inclined towards the red brigades themselves.

The Tsar responded with a heavy hand. He feared a revolution gone out of control, shops looted, women ravished, palaces reduced to rubble. Prince Dolgorukov, director of the Third Section, which controlled the secret police, submitted to his master a memorandum in which he urged that stern measures be taken against suspected subversives. Alexander read the report and wrote in the margin, "All this is entirely in accord with what I want." Soldiers marched down the boulevards of the capital, and mounted Cossacks patrolled the side streets. The Tsar, in a critical hour, hearkened to the same counsels which, in Berlin, inspired the Prussian generals. Like General Manteuffel, he thought only of reinforcing the garrisons. In doing so, he repelled the very people whose goodwill he needed if his revolution "from above" were to succeed.

Prince Kropotkin was one of these alienated souls. The Prince was not yet ready to join the red brigades, but he ceased to be a liberal. He had recently been named Sergeant of the Corps of Pages—an enviable appointment. The Sergeant not only occupied a privileged position in the Corps, he was also the *page de chambre* of the Tsar. To be "personally known to the Emperor was of course considered as a stepping-stone to further distinctions." As the Tsar's personal page, Kropotkin was in a position to observe Alexander closely in the spring of 1862.

He at first looked upon the Tsar-Liberator as a hero. But by degrees Kropotkin's opinion changed. The tall and dashing monarch was, he discovered, a tired man. He went through the glittering rooms of his palace with rapid strides, as though he were afraid of something. He lost his temper easily. Kropotkin sometimes found him staring vacantly into space with a worried, absent-minded gaze. His doubts multiplied. Alexander had turned away from the reforming liberals who had labored over the emancipation law; he was now constantly in the company of reactionary barons like Count Shuvalov. The Tsar, Kropotkin concluded, "retained too much of the despotic character of his father," Nicholas I, and this "pierced now and then through his easily good-natured manners." Alexander was not "a truly reliable man, either in his policies or in his personal sympathies."

In June, Kropotkin went with his fellow cadets to the annual commencement parade. The candidates were personally examined by the Tsar in the manage of their horses and the evolutions of their drill. Alexander then raised them to the dignity of officers. The young men dismounted; the Tsar himself remained on horseback. "The promoted officers to me!" he shouted. Kropotkin and his brother officers gathered round the sovereign. He spoke, at first, gently. "I congratulate you," he said. "You are officers." Then he became angry. "But if any one of you—which God preserve you from—should under any circumstances prove disloyal to the Tsar, the throne, and the fatherland, take heed of what I say,—he will be treated with all the se-veri-ty of the laws, without the slightest com-mi-se-ra-tion!" The Tsar's voice failed, his face grew peevish, "full of that expression of blind rage," Kropotkin said, "which I saw in my childhood on the faces of landlords when they threatened their serfs 'to skin them under the rods.'" Alexander spurred his horse and rode off.

"Reaction, full speed backwards," Kropotkin said to himself as he came away from the parade. He saw Alexander once more before he left Saint Petersburg. The occasion was a reception in the Winter Palace for the newly commissioned officers. The Tsar found his old *page de chambre* in the press of uniforms. "So you go to Siberia?" he asked. "Did your father consent to it, after all?"

Kropotkin replied that he was indeed going east.

"Are you not afraid to go so far?" Alexander asked.

"No," Kroptkin replied, "I want to work. There must be so much to do in Siberia to apply the great reforms which are going to be made."

The Tsar looked straight into the Prince's eyes. At last he said, "Well, go; one can be useful everywhere." Alexander's face, Kropotkin remembered, "took on such an expression of fatigue, such a character of complete surrender, that I thought at once, 'He is a used-up man; he is going to give it all up.'"

Chapter 9

PREPARATIONS FOR THE DEATH STRUGGLE

Paris, Fontainebleau, and London, May–July 1862

So ALLURING IS the sentimental image of a Paris spring, of chestnuts flowering in gardens of the Luxembourg, of acacias ripening in the Bois de Boulogne, that a spell of cold, damp, rainy weather is apt to be felt by the visitor almost as a personal affront. So at all events a thwarted revolutionist felt it as he climbed into a gilt carriage dispatched from the imperial mews.

Bismarck felt "like a rat in a barn."

He had not been made a minister. King Wilhelm had emerged unscathed from the assassination attempt in the Lichtenthal Alley at Baden-Baden. Though the bullet shredded his collar and necktie, it did no more than graze the royal neck. Oscar Becker, the would-be assassin, told the police that he had fired the shot because Wilhelm "had not done enough towards the union of Germany." Nationalism, it appeared, was too important a sentiment to be overlooked; but the King could not bring himself to embrace Bismarck's plan to adopt a nationalist program in order to crush the liberals. Instead, he formally approved Manteuffel's plan for a march on Berlin. As a consolation prize, he gave Bismarck the Paris Embassy.

The new Ambassador to France was driven through rainy streets to the Tuileries, the ill-starred palace which, before the violent events in which the decade culminated, stood on the bank of the Seine between the Louvre and the Place de la Concorde. There, in an elaborate ceremony, Bismarck presented his letters of credence to the French Emperor, Napoleon III. The new envoy professed to find such rituals boring, but he conceded that in this case the ordeal was lightened by the presence of Louis-Napoleon's consort, the Empress Eugénie. The Spanish beauty was, he said, "one of the handsomest women I know," and in the interval since he had last seen her she had "even grown more beautiful."

Bismarck was unhappy in Paris. Louis-Napoleon's court failed to dazzle him, in spite of the beauty of the Empress; the Tuileries was inferior, in splendor and elegance, to the palaces of the Romanovs. Paris, moreover, was just then destitute of agreeable society, and Bismarck was obliged to take his dinners alone in a café. Nor were his accommodations adequate; the official residence of the Prussian Ambassador, on the Quai d'Orsay, was, he said, "dark, damp and cold," and the rooms gave off an unpleasant odor, "musty and cloacic."

Such complaints imperfectly concealed the principal cause of his dissatisfaction, his incessant ambition of power. Bismarck's desire for authority had grown more intense, if that were possible, and in Paris he feverishly refined his plan to smash the liberals. He still resented his recent treatment in Berlin, where the King had all but ignored him; but Bismarck was not one to indulge his temper at the expense of his interest, and in his letters to his friend Roon he was careful to make it clear that he remained an aspirant for the first place. "You do me an injustice if you think I am reluctant," he wrote. "On the contrary, I have lively spells of the bold spirit of that animal which dances on the ice when it is happy."

The weeks that followed passed in a whirl of garden parties. Bismarck followed Louis-Napoleon's court to Fontainebleau, the ancient château of the kings of France, where he took a long walk with the Emperor in the grounds. Louis-Napoleon, fifty-four years old in 1862, talked vaguely of the possibility of an alliance between France and Prussia. Bismarck was unimpressed. The Emperor, he said, was a sphinx without a riddle.

In his boredom he went to England. In London the Industrial Exhibition was on, and the air was thick with intrigue. The French Foreign Minister, M. de Thouvenel, came up from Paris, ostensibly to award medals at the Exhibition. But the newspapers speculated that the real purpose of his visit was to discuss, with the English ministers, the possibility that their two countries might jointly intervene in the American Civil War and put an end to Lincoln's statesmanship. Bismarck himself made the rounds, and went to see the Prime Minister, Lord Palmerston. But he could play only a limited part in the diplomatic game; he was not a minister. He was, however, drawn into an interesting conversation with another man who craved, as he did, a ministerial portfolio, but who in the summer of 1862 was out of office. Benjamin Disraeli was, at this time, a leading member of the Tory opposition to Lord Palmerston's government. At a dinner in the Russian Embassy, two consummate political actors took each other's measure. On the surface the English politician, with his olive complexion and coal-black eyes, could scarcely have been more different from the massive blue-eyed Teuton; but there were curious similarities. Disraeli and Bismarck both harbored an immense ambition together with dreamy and romantic qualities; both were devoted, though in different ways, to the counter-revolution against liberalism. "Take care of that man!" Disraeli afterwards said; "he means what he says." Many years later, Bismarck returned the compliment when he said of Disraeli, *"Der alte Jude, das ist der Mann"* (The old Jew, that is the man).

Bismarck returned to Paris in not "very good health" and still in suspense as to his political fate—circumstances, he said, that left his "nerves unsettled." On July 25, he set off on "a long journey in the south of France." He intended to abandon himself to the Midi; yet he was not quite so blasé a traveler as he pretended to be. He took care to furnish Roon with his itinerary, and he worked out with his friend the code names they would use should they need to communicate by telegraph.

Virginia, April–May 1862

AT THE BEGINNING of April, General McClellan, on board the *Commodore,* steamed towards the dock at Fortress Monroe. The fortress lay at the tip of the Peninsula, the southernmost fork of the Chesapeake, a narrow tract of land bounded, on the north, by the York River, and on the south by the James River. "Mac," as he was called by his brother officers, had got his way; Lincoln had reluctantly approved his plan for a Peninsular campaign. The General came ashore at the head of the Army of the Potomac, and within days of his landing he had with him 100,000 men. When he addressed his soldiers, he told them that he had held them back thus far in order that they might now "give the death-blow to the rebellion that has distracted our once happy country." He modeled his peroration on Napoleon's Address to the Army of Italy.

It was obvious to most observers that if the campaign were to be successful, McClellan must rapidly traverse the land that lay between his army and Richmond, for each moment of delay wasted his own advantages, while it multiplied the defensive resources of his adversary. But the commander of the Army of the Potomac determined to proceed cautiously. McClellan found the enemy "altogether stronger" than expected. Days were consumed in the siege of a garrison at Yorktown, and in the elaboration of an intricate system of siege etiquette. "Yesterday made Fitz Porter 'Director of the Siege,'" McClellan wrote to his wife, "a novel title, but made necessary by the circumstances of the case.

I give all my orders relating to the siege through him, making him at the same time commandant of the siege operations and a chief of staff for that portion of the work."

The Confederate Army had, indeed, only 11,000 men in the vicinity of Yorktown when McClellan arrived on the Peninsula, while he himself had almost ten times that number under arms; but he was haunted by the idea of Confederate strength. "I am probably weaker than they are now," he reported gloomily, "or soon will be." The situation "grows worse the more you look at it." On the whole, he thought it best to proceed slowly. On the whole, it would not do "to hurry it."

After he had been before the ramparts of Yorktown for nearly a month, McClellan began to feel better about the campaign. He was always happiest contriving solutions to complicated problems of engineering. "I am getting on splendidly with my 'slow preparations,'" he reported. Visitors, he said, were impressed by the "gigantic" system of earthworks he had constructed at Yorktown. "Would be glad to have the 30-pounder Parrotts in the works around Washington," he wired Lincoln as he brought his masterwork to perfection. "Am very short of that excellent gun." Yet while McClellan labored over the placement of each mortar, each howitzer, each Parrott gun at Yorktown, the real object of his campaign, the fortifications of Richmond, were being daily strengthened through the skill and diligence of Robert E. Lee.

Lincoln was disturbed by the lassitude of his commander. "Your call for Parrott guns from Washington alarms me," the President wrote to McClellan, "chiefly because it argues indefinite procrastination. Is anything to be done?" No, McClellan replied, nothing could at present be done. The roads were "horrid," his maps were "perfectly unreliable," and the enemy was "collecting troops from all quarters, especially well-disciplined troops from the South." He would be fortunate, he said, if he could simply maintain his position. "I shall run the risk," he wrote, "of at least holding them in check here. . . . My entire force is undoubtedly inferior to that of the rebels, who will fight well."

Eventually, the Confederate Army relinquished its line at Yorktown, and McClellan advanced slowly up the Peninsula. From the first, however, the atmosphere of the place, soft, sinking, deceptive, seemed to unnerve the young General. The land appeared solid enough, but it was not; the ground was swampy, crisscrossed by sluggish rivers that flooded suddenly and without warning. The fetid air was not conducive to health. And there was the rain. Always the rain. The country was "covered with water," McClellan said, and everyone was "knee-deep in mud." He pressed on, with mounting unease, into the damp wilderness. He disliked the corps commanders Lincoln had imposed upon him and was soon barely on speaking terms with them. He retreated often to the privacy of his tent, which was after all "quite comfortable." The tent possessed its own stove, as well as a "splendid two-legged washstand" and a "floor of pine boughs—a carpet of boughs, I suppose I ought to say. . . . So you see I am living quite *en prince.*" In this sanctuary McClellan could write his long, chatty letters and talk things over with his friend Fitz-John Porter, a handsome officer who had been a year ahead of him at West Point, and who was the only one among his senior commanders whom he met on a footing of easy familiarity.

Still the rain continued to fall. "I rather like to hear it patter on the tent," McClellan wrote. But in time the drizzling weather came to seem ominous. "It is certain," he wrote to his wife, "that there has not been for years and years such a season; it does not come by chance." "Another wet, horrid day! . . . Still raining hard and dismally."

In this enervating mud-world, melting and unreal, McClellan's martial spirit once again sank. "If I am not reinforced," he wrote, "it is probable that I will be obliged to fight nearly double my numbers, strongly intrenched." He blamed his enemies in the capital for the lackluster progress of his campaign. It was their malice and perfidy, not his own want of vigor and resolution, that clouded his prospects of success. Washington, he said, was filled with "traitors" who were "willing to sacrifice the country and its army for personal spite and personal aims." Those treacherous "hounds" were determined to ruin him. Judas, he said, was an angel compared to Lincoln's Secretary of War, Edwin M. Stanton. Sinister forces were everywhere at work. Why was General McDowell's corps suffered to remain in the vicinity of Washington? It was "the most infamous thing that history has recorded." "The fate of a nation depends upon me," McClellan said, and yet "I have not one single friend at the seat of Government."

It is true that McClellan had enemies in Washington. "Bluff Ben" Wade of Ohio despised him and did what he could to undermine him. But McClellan possessed all that he needed to overcome the opposition of Wade. He commanded a vast army, and he retained the confidence of Lincoln. A victory in the field would quickly silence the radicals. Lincoln urged his commander to fight, but McClellan continued to insist that he was short of men. The President was puzzled, and not a little hurt. "Your dispatches complaining that you are not properly sustained," Lincoln wrote, "while they do not offend me, do pain me very much." He would not, however, jeopardize the safety of the capital by shifting the whole of McDowell's corps to the Peninsula. "Do you really think," he asked, "I should permit the line from Richmond, *via* Manassas Junction, to this city to be entirely open, except what resistance could be presented by less than twenty thousand unorganized troops? This is a question which the country will not allow me to evade." Lincoln nevertheless agreed to send McClellan a part of McDowell's corps—some 11,000 additional men under the command of General W. B. Franklin. He concluded his letter by reminding McClellan of the painted logs at Manassas. "The country will not fail to note—is now noting—that the present hesitation to move upon an intrenched enemy, is but the story of Manassas repeated." It was, the President said, "indispensable to *you* that you strike a blow. *I* am powerless to help this. . . . I beg to assure you that I have never written you, or spoken to you, in greater kindness of feeling than now, nor with a fuller purpose to sustain you, so far as in my most anxious judgment, I consistently can. *But you must act.*"

On the twentieth, the advance party of the Army of the Potomac crossed the Chickahominy River near New Bridge, and McClellan's vanguard approached to within a few miles of Richmond. The closer he drew to the Confederate capital the more agitated he became; the city loomed before him, and in his imagination it acquired a hideous strength. His personal radiance had by this time faded; he looked, one observer said, "prematurely old," and he appeared to be on the verge of nervous collapse. "They are concentrating everything for the last death-struggle," he exclaimed. "My government, alas! is not giving me any aid." He felt sick—indeed, he soon was sick. It was, he said, his "old Mexican enemy," dysentery. By the twenty-ninth he was somewhat better, but the long, scarcely coherent letters he wrote to Washington suggest that he did not altogether recover his mental balance. The "intentions of the enemy are still doubtful. . . . Unless he has some deep-laid scheme that I do not fathom, he is giving up great advantages. . . ."

Yasnaya Polyana, July 1862

THAT SUMMER, Tolstoy felt the wrath of the Tsar.

The Tsar's henchmen, under orders to contain the revolutionary passions which had ignited the Apraxin Dvor, were arresting reformers. In the poisonous atmosphere a wretch called Shipov, a police informer, came forward and accused Tolstoy of being a red. The school at Yasnaya Polyana was, he asserted, a front for revolutionary activity; and concealed behind secret doors in the manor house lay a printing press and stacks of revolutionary manifestos. Prince Dolgorukov, the director of the Third Section, authorized a raid.

Tolstoy was traveling when, on a July night, three troikas drove up the alley to his house. Gendarmes in sky-blue uniforms were soon swarming over the property. Yasnaya Polyana was in the grip of the Third Section. The shadowy institution was, at this time, the most powerful in Russia.

Its activities were shrouded by an impenetrable veil. Its director was a man far more dreaded in the Empire than the Tsar himself. The windows of its headquarters in Saint Petersburg were covered with iron bars, and in the dead of night carriages with drawn blinds drove mysteriously through its gates.

Yet for all the Man-in-the-Iron-Mask variety of legends to which it gave rise, the Third Section was a rational, and even a philosophical, institution. It was the child of Alexander's father, Nicholas, and it embodied that Tsar's cunning, cruel, and perceptive theory of despotism. When Count Benckendorff, the first director of the Third Section, asked Nicholas to clarify his responsibilities, the Tsar handed him a white handkerchief. "Here are your orders," Nicholas said. "Take this, and wipe away the tears of my people." The objects of the Third Section were to keep under surveillance any person who displayed unusual energy of mind, and to discover those secret or potential treacheries which, if unchecked, might in time become a danger to the régime. The ultimate purpose of the organization was to break, through intimidation or violence, the spirit of any man who might possibly become a danger to the state. To accomplish these ends, the Third Section employed an army of *agents provocateurs*. The disguised policemen did more than watch and inform; they worked subtly and ingeniously to draw forth, from the careless victim, a treacherous breath. They spread their nets, not only in Russia, but throughout Europe, in the effort to ensnare their unsuspecting prey; and however far from his homeland the Russian might fly, he could never be certain that he had escaped the hand of the despot.

In addition to secret agents, the Third Section employed a bureau of clerks who patiently scrutinized essays, novels, poems, even paintings, in the effort to uncover the latent seeds of disaffection. These critics in the pay of the government were especially attentive to thinkers and artists who displayed "audacity" in their work. Those who displayed too much audacity risked administrative arrest, torture, mock execution, consignment to an insane asylum, or deportation to Siberia, all without being brought before a regular court of law.

Under the eye of Colonel Durnovo, a functionary of the Third Section, the gendarmes searched Yasnaya Polyana thoroughly. Floorboards were pried apart, the pond was dredged, rooms were ransacked. Tolstoy's sister, Countess Mary, cowered in fear as policemen read aloud from her brother's diaries and letters. For two days it went on. The gendarmes handled the books in the library, examined the bed linen, peered behind the toilet, and cracked coarse jokes.

When Tolstoy learned of the raid, he was furious. His property had been invaded. The "slovenly Colonel" from the gendarmerie "read all my letters and diaries." "I feel malice and disgust," he said, "almost hatred, for that dear government which searches my house for lithographic and typographical machines. . . ." "We can't live like this. . . . Damocles' sword of tyranny, violence and injustice is always hanging over everyone." If he did not obtain reparation for his injuries, he would sell his estates and leave Russia; he would not remain in a country where the spirit of Ivan the Terrible still prevailed, a country "where it's impossible to know a minute in advance that they won't chain you up or flog you together with your sister and your wife and your mother. . . ."

"There are loaded pistols in my room," Tolstoy told his great-aunt. "I am waiting until the matter is decided one way or another." In the last week of August, he wrote a letter to the Tsar and went off to Moscow in a huff. Alexander had just come down for the army maneuvers in Khodynka Meadow. Tolstoy went to the Peter Palace, where the Tsar was staying, determined to lodge his complaint in person.

Near Richmond, Virginia, May–June 1862

AT THE END of May, the attack General McClellan had long feared took place. Confederate forces launched an offensive against his positions on the Chickahominy River near Fair Oaks, five miles east of Richmond.

The Confederate assault was bloody, but it failed to break the Union lines.

President Davis rode out from Richmond to watch the progress of the battle. Night came over the field, and Davis fell in with General Robert E. Lee, who had been similarly restless in the capital. In the darkness and confusion the two men encountered litter bearers carrying the broken body of the field commander, Joe Johnston. Johnston was conscious indeed, but gravely wounded. Davis and Lee turned their horses and went back to Richmond. As they rode through the night towards the lights of the city, Davis made one of the most momentous decisions of the war. He ordered Lee to take up the fallen Johnston's command.

Lee began at once to make his preparations. In three weeks he judged his defensive works sufficiently strong to permit an offensive. On June 26, he sent his men into battle. The Seven Days before Richmond began.

The Southern troops fought bravely, but in assault after bloody assault they were driven back by the tremendous firepower of the Union Army. Lee concluded that if he were to rout the Federals, he must first dislodge them from the commanding position they occupied near Gaines's Mill, a steep acclivity, bristling with guns—a place calculated to inspire dread in the hearts of attacking infantrymen. The cream of the

Southern army was sent forward, but to no avail. J. R. Anderson made three charges; and three times he fell back. W. D. Pender went off, and was similarly repulsed. Maxcy Gregg succeeded, indeed, in crossing Boatswain's Swamp, the dismal bog that lay before the Union stronghold, but he soon found himself pinned down by a heavy fire.

Lee mounted his horse and went off in search of John Bell Hood, the commander of the 4th Texas Infantry, a regiment which, on this day, was fighting as part of the Texas Brigade. Hood saluted his chief, and Lee explained his objective. "This must be done," Lee told him. "Can you break this line?"

"I will try," Hood replied.

Chapter 10

"PERICULUM IN MORA"

Bordeaux and Biarritz, July–August 1862

MAKING HIS WAY south from Bordeaux, Bismarck went at the vintage. "I drank Lafitte, Mouton, Pichon, Laroze, Latour, Margaux, St. Julien, Branne, Armeillac, and the other wines." The vineyards were hot, "but with good wine in the body this is not at all bothersome." He had not seen the German newspapers in days, nor, he said, did he miss them. At the end of July he reached Biarritz. He took rooms in the Hôtel de l'Europe, in the Place de la Mairie, and went out daily to bathe in the Bay of Biscay.

Biarritz in the 1860s was a playground of Eros, consecrated to the vitality of that nineteenth-century Venus, the Empress Eugénie, whose favorite watering hole it was. The disparity between the purity of the Empress's religion and the eroticism of her person only heightened her appeal. Eugénie was a chaste Catholic in the Mediterranean mold; the Pope had given her a Golden Rose, anointed with balsam by the papal hand, in recognition of her piety and virtue. Yet she remained the most sultry of saints, and her darkly Spanish sensuality fascinated a generation. Bismarck came alone to Eugénie's resort; but he did not come, as some husbands did, to escape domestic tribulations. His marriage was happy. The man who stood on the threshold of power and opportunity rarely granted to statesmen wrote to his wife almost daily—sometimes twice daily—whenever he was away from her. He called her "My Dearest Heart," "My Beloved Nan," "Dearest only Beloved Juanita," "Très Chère Jeanneten." He was not, he assured her, "unthankful, either for God's mercy, or for your love and truth. It is with us today as it was at the time of our wedding, and I have never thought that that was very long ago—five or six thousand happy days."

She had saved him, or so he always believed. When Johanna von Putt-kamer first met Bismarck, two decades before, he had seemed destined for a life of failure, bitterness, and fruitless eccentricity. In his chosen career, the judicial department of the Prussian civil service, he had been unsuccessful. The tasks, he said, were "petty and boring." The Prussian official was "like a member of an orchestra, but *I* want to play only the music which I myself like, or no music at all." Bismarck resigned his position and went off to Pomerania to manage his family's estates. Cows and husbandry, however, suited him no better than briefs and pleadings. He would mount his horse, Caleb, and ride off to engage in solitary reveries, passing "over many a mile, happy and sad, angry and calm, past moors and fields, past lakes and houses and people."

It was during this period of Pomeranian retirement that a change came over Bismarck. Like the young Lincoln, he had flirted with freethinking; but as he rode about rural Pomerania he wondered whether he was not like the fool in the Psalms, who "hath said in his heart, there is no God." He came to know a family called the von Thaddens, whose serenity piqued his interest. How was it that they were so contented, while he himself was so restless and dissatisfied? They adhered, he learned, to a form of evangelical Lutheranism known as Pietism. The character of young Maria von Thadden, so suggestive of peace and inner repose, held a special appeal for Bismarck. To her he opened his heart; and no sooner had he done so than he became aware of the unworthiness of his way of life. Wenching, drinking, dice—his existence was so much "champagne" fizzing to no purpose. He wanted a better, clearer wine. Maria rewarded Bismarck's confidences by talking of the secret springs of her own spiritual existence. She however took sick, and Bismarck, setting aside his scruples about the efficacy of prayer and the existence of the Deity, cried out to God. The "first fervent prayer, without my ruminating on its reasonableness, tore itself from my heart."

Maria von Thadden sank; yet it seems that, before she died, she intimated her wish that Bismarck should unite himself with her friend, Fräulein Johanna von Puttkamer, a fellow Pietist. He sought the young lady's hand, and she accepted him. The two were married in the summer of 1847. Bismarck afterwards wondered how a man who reflected on his own nature, yet knew nothing of God or family, could go on living. Life without God, without a wife, without children was, he said, a *"schmutziges Hemde"*—a dirty shirt—best cast away.

In the year of his marriage Bismarck was chosen—quite "by chance," he later said—to represent the local squirearchy in the United Diet, an assembly which King Friedrich Wilhelm IV of Prussia had reluctantly summoned in order to finance the construction of railroads. Liberalism was in the air. Bismarck rose in the Diet and condemned the liberals' favorite doctrines. With a malicious glee he played the part of the reactionary Junker. The result, he said, was "a storm." So great was the consternation that he was forced to break off his oration. He calmly turned the pages of a newspaper while he waited for the fury to subside. He then finished his speech.

Fifteen summers later, Bismarck, floating off Biarritz in the waters of the Atlantic, was on the verge of realizing the dream of his early manhood. He was on the brink of playing a decisive part in the world crisis and leading a counter-revolution against the free state. Yet he seemed to draw back. His imagination was essentially dramatic, and before any assumption of revolutionary responsibility there must be an interlude of poetry, of pastoral or erotic truancy. In the first week of August 1862 there appeared, on the promenade at Biarritz, the Prince and Princess Orlov. She was blond, beautiful, and twenty-two; her husband was old and tired. Nicholas Orlov was the son of the Prince who had vainly opposed Tsar Alexander's revolution; Bismarck had known him slightly in Saint Petersburg, but not, it seems, his pretty wife. The Orlovs were living now in Brussels, where the Prince served as the Tsar's emissary to the King of the Belgians.

On August 9, Bismarck opened his first bottle of champagne since leaving Paris. He drank it with the Prince and Princess. "Ever since the Orlovs came," Bismarck wrote to his sister, "I live with them as though we were alone in the place." A daily regimen was soon established. The morning was given over to a brisk walk and a sea-bath. The hour of siesta followed; Bismarck would lie lazily on the sofa, reading and dreaming, or watching the sea drive foam against a distant lighthouse. In the afternoons, he and the Orlovs took long walks together. They wandered about the cliffs, and picnicked in little orchards overgrown with aloe and figs. After bathing again in the sea they would return to their rooms to dress. Dinner followed, by an open window that overhung the sea; while they dined, the sun sank in the Atlantic. Princess Ekaterina would go to the piano and play something from Beethoven, Chopin, or Mendelssohn. Afterwards they would walk out to the lighthouse, where they would sit above the crash of the surf and watch the moon rise over the Pyrenees. He took to calling her *"ma chère niece"* or *"chère Kathi"*; she called him *"oncle."* "I find," he wrote, that "I am falling a little in love with *la gentille princesse.*"

Virginia, June–August 1862

JOHN BELL HOOD once boasted that he could "double-quick the Fourth Texas to the gates of hell and never break the line." Before him loomed the heights near Gaines's Mill—hell on a hill. Seventeen Federal batteries guarded the plateau. Ninety-six big guns stood ready to pour forth a lethal fire.

"Steady, steady," Hood urged as his men crawled up the hill.

The enemy's first fire came. Soldiers fell, but the line did not break. "Forward! Forward!" Hood cried. "Charge right down on them. . . ." There was a strange shriek, a sound soon to be as celebrated as the *alalag-mos*, the war cry of the Roman legions. It was the rebel yell; and under its weird inspiration the 4th Texas stormed the heights. The Union men, confounded by the appearance, on their ramparts, of warriors who seemed not to know fear, threw away their weapons. They ran for their lives or perished where they stood.

Hours later, in the stupor of despair, McClellan wrote to his superiors in Washington. "I have lost this battle," he said, "because my force was too small." The days that followed the taking of Gaines's Mill were the unmaking of George McClellan. Other successes he might have, and other victories he might yet win, but nothing he did could efface the stain of the Peninsula, and everything he said served only to make it blacker. "I again repeat that I am not responsible for this," he wired Edwin M. Stanton, the Secretary of War. The distraught commander insinuated that he had been undone by treachery at the highest levels of the Republic. "If I save this army now, I tell you plainly that I owe no thanks to you or any other persons in Washington. You have done your best to sacrifice this army."

This was always to be McClellan's claim—that Lincoln and Stanton forced him to fight, during the Seven Days before Richmond, "a terrible fight against vastly superior numbers." Yet by the *lowest* estimate McClellan had 91,000 effective troops on the eve of the first engagement. Lee had perhaps 85,000 men under arms at the same moment—a concentration of force that might never have come into being had McClellan conducted a swifter and more resolute campaign in the Peninsula. On the day the armies first clashed, each of the rival commanders believed himself to be outnumbered; but the belief that crippled McClellan raised Lee to lofty acts of military will.

"Mac" nevertheless clung obstinately to the illusion that he had been defeated, not by Lee, but by Lincoln. "If, at this instant," he wrote after the sack of the Mill, "I could dispose of ten thousand (10,000) fresh men, I could gain the victory tomorrow. I know that a few thousand more men would have changed this battle from a defeat to a victory. As it is, the government must not and cannot hold me responsible for the result."

There were fearful clashes at Savage's Station and Glendale, and a last, ghastly battle at Malvern's Hill. When the fog lifted, the survivors found an appalling scene. Some of the corpses were "swollen to twice their original size." A few had "actually burst asunder with the pressure of foul gases." McClellan retired to Harrison's Landing, where Federal gunboats in the river could protect him from the fierce sallies of Lee. He covered his retreat with petulant letters. Having lost all claim to strategic supremacy, he made his stand on moral authority. "I may be on the brink of eternity," he informed the President, but he could not allow his views with respect to slavery and the Constitution to perish with himself, even if they did not "strictly relate to the situation of this army or strictly come within the scope of my official duties."

McClellan warned Lincoln not to embrace the anti-slavery policies of his enemies, the radical Republicans; and in words that might bear an ominous construction, he suggested that the President could not survive without the support and confidence of his military commanders. "A declaration of radical views, especially upon slavery," McClellan wrote, "will rapidly disintegrate our present armies. The policy of the government must be supported by concentrations of military power."

Having failed to vindicate Lincoln's revolution, McClellan threatened to turn against it.

The South of France, Berlin, and Babelsberg, August–September 1862

SHORTLY AFTER MCCLELLAN descended to the James, Bismarck prepared to go up into the mountains. By his own report, he was "ridiculously well." He drank Madeira at breakfast, and champagne with the Orlovs. Over bottles of Möet, the conversation went on in German, Russian, and French. He wanted, he said, "only wings to fly." It was, Kathi said, a time of "foolishness, gaiety, and poetry . . . so full of dreams." The enchanted days stretched themselves into weeks; singing French *chansonettes* and snatches of Mendelssohn, the sightseers went up into the Pyrenees. They ascended the Col de Venasque, and at 7,000 feet beheld the narrow portal to Spain. To the right, Bismarck wrote, "rushed the waters of the Ebro, to the left those of the Garonne, and towards the horizon one snow cap after another looked us in the eye, far into Catalonia and Aragon." They dined on partridges, and spent the night in a hut, from which they emerged in the morning to watch the sun rise over the mountaintops.

How far did they go? Bismarck, for all the exaggeration of his rhetoric, was in many ways a prudent man. His love affair with "Catty, Katsch, *mon admirable Kathi*" had about it an artificial, almost a literary, quality; even his Bacchanalia was a masquerade. He carefully preserved, in his cigar case, the little presents Kathi made him, a yellow flower she plucked at Superbagnères, a sprig of olive from Avignon. He called them souvenirs of a "joyous time," the "sole moment" when his spirit "was free" to take the direction which was natural to it—a Garden of Eden, a "paradise lost."

If there was a strain of knight errantry in the affair, there was in it, too, an element of willful parody. To fall in love with a Russian princess was almost a necessary epoch in the life of a Continental diplomatist. Old Prince Metternich had also loved a Russian princess—Princess Lieven, whose husband, like Kathi's, had represented a Russian tsar in the courts of Europe. It was only fitting that Bismarck, who had met Metternich in 1851 and made a careful study of his life, should follow his teacher in great things as well as small. The Austrian statesman was at once the inspiration of the younger man's revolution, and the precedent he was determined to go beyond.

Bismarck had long been intrigued by the way the intellectual godfather of reaction resisted the intrusion of free-state principles into Central Europe. After the fall of the first Napoleonic Empire in 1815, Metternich led the counter-revolution against liberty. He was the prime mover in the promulgation of the Carlsbad Decrees, by which freedom of speech and of the press was abrogated in Germany. He was also the high priest of the "Holy Alliance," the league which brought Austria, Russia, and Prussia together in an effort to arrest the progress of free-state principles in Europe.

Metternich and Bismarck had more in common than a contempt for the free state and a weakness for princesses from the East. Both were masters of language; the diplomatic dispatches they composed are models of their kind. Both were notable talkers, captivating, insinuating, in certain circumstances irresistible. Both possessed a strain of gallantry and were susceptible to the charms of women; but here their characters diverged. Metternich preferred witty and clever mistresses, women who, in the tradition of the Parisian *salonnières,* were devoted to politics and intrigue. Bismarck was drawn to a less assertive type of femininity; he dreaded, perhaps he feared, a virago. He once said that he had "a horror of feminine cleverness," and he detested women who, like Queen Augusta and her daughter-in-law, Crown Princess Vicky, meddled in politics.* Kathi Orlov appealed to him precisely because she was so obviously without intellectual intensity; hers was the simplicity, he said, of a Pomeranian girl, with just enough of the great world in her to keep her from being a bore. In the interval between the state dinner and the masked ball, Metternich carried on the most complicated diplomatic and amorous intrigues; reac-

* Bismarck would later fiercely resent Tsar Alexander's mistress, Katya Dolgorukaya.

tionary though he was, he embraced the emancipated women and libertine culture of the *beau monde*. Bismarck, by contrast, conformed to the Victorian proprieties, and spurned the *liaisons dangereuses* of the old régime. His extramarital love affairs seem to have been Platonic; and although he once spoke of the "brutal sensuality" which "leads me so close to the greatest sins," he placed what he called his faculty for "depraved fantasy" in the service not of love but of power.

There were other, more profound, differences. Metternich was a creature of the eighteenth century; Bismarck was a child of the romantic revival. Metternich was, by his own confession, "a man of prose and not of poetry." He feared "disorganised excitement." Men, he said, "must not dream of reformation while agitated by passion." The fruit of his diplomacy, the Concert of Europe, was as nicely proportioned as a symphony of Haydn's. The Concert was a diplomatic minuet, intended to preserve order and prevent revolution through the maintenance of a balance of power, a state of affairs in which no single nation possesses a decisive superiority of power.

Bismarck wanted to smash the Concert. He hated it, not because it thwarted the progress of liberty, but because it protected the declining power of Austria, and was an obstacle to the rise of Prussia. He was cut out for this work of destruction; his style was less mannered and more natural, in some ways more brutal than Metternich's. Where the neoclassical Metternich had used the intellectual techniques of the eighteenth century to bring order to the European scene, Bismarck was to develop a new approach to power, rooted in the blood and passion of the romantic sensibility.

On September 16, Bernstorff, the Foreign Minister, telegraphed to him. "The King wants you to come here, and I advise you to come at once." Bismarck, however, did not bother to reply. Two days later Roon sent him, in code, a more pointed telegram. *"Periculum in mora. Dépêchez-vous"* (Danger in delay. Get going). To preserve secrecy, Roon signed the telegram "L'oncle de Maurice Henning."

Bismarck hastened to Berlin, where he learned that Wilhelm's ministers had implored the King to compromise with the free-state men. Wilhelm, however, was obstinate; he would not allow his army to rot, in Roon's phrase, in the "cesspool of doctrinaire liberalism." Yet in the fatal moment, he could not bring himself to order General Manteuffel to march on Berlin, close the Parliament, and shed his subjects' blood. The King saw no course open to him other than abdication. He summoned his son, Crown Prince Friedrich, and spoke of relinquishing the scepter to him.

Bismarck's hour had come. He had been playing a version of *A Midsummer Night's Dream* in France; in Berlin he prepared to re-enact one of

Shakespeare's history plays. The day after his arrival, he went to Wilhelm's summer palace at Babelsberg. The Gothic château stood in a quiet woods near Potsdam. The question Wilhelm confronted, Bismarck knew, lay at the heart of the meaning of the state. Did the King alone command the armed might of the nation? Or was the power of the army subject to constitutional oversight? It was the very question that had given birth to the modern free state. In England, two centuries before, a long and bloody struggle between Parliament and the Stuart kings ended with the establishment of a principle that will endure as long as freedom itself. The executive may possess the power of the sword, but ultimate control of the army rests with the legislature, which alone determines how the treasure of a nation shall be expended.

Bismarck deplored the English example. Without hesitation, he took his stand for the royal prerogative.

At Babelsberg, the King made him a little speech. "I will not reign if I cannot be true to God, my conscience, and my people," Wilhelm declared. "Yet I cannot do that if I must submit to the will of the present majority in Parliament. . . . I have therefore decided to lay down my crown." Wilhelm pointed to a document, written in his own hand, that lay on his writing table, and he lamented his inability to find suitable ministers.

Bismarck said that he was himself ready to enter the ministry. The King asked him whether he was willing to stand up to parliamentary majorities. Bismarck nodded. "Then it is my duty," Wilhelm said, "to continue the struggle with you. I shall not abdicate." The two men went out into the park. "I would rather perish with the King," Bismarck declared during the course of their walk, "than desert Your Majesty in the struggle with parliamentary power." Wilhelm was moved by these professions of fidelity; and in a short time Bismarck's appointment as both Minister-President (the principal officer of the Russian Crown) and Foreign Minister was confirmed.

Virginia, August–September 1862

THE MAN WHO SAVED Richmond from McClellan's army was fifty-five years old in the summer of 1862. Robert Edward Lee bore one of the historic names of Virginia. His father, the daring and unfortunate "Light Horse Harry" Lee, possessed in full measure the extravagant genius characteristic of the family. A hero of the Revolution, a man whom Washington loved, Light Horse Harry was undone by speculation and died a ruined man. But Light Horse Harry's fourth child, Robert Edward, was not only a Lee; he was also, through his mother, a Carter, and he inherited, in addition to the brilliant qualities of the Lees, the sober judgment and steady character that belonged to the maternal line. Where the Lees were hotheaded and unpredictable, the Carters were gracious, amiable, and sane. In Robert Edward the solid virtues of the Carters more than counterbalanced the erratic and mercurial qualities of the Lees.

Blood may not determine a man's character or destiny, but family sometimes does. The stamp of the seventeenth-century Cavaliers—the English country gentlemen who stood for King Charles I in his contests with Parliament and the Puritans—was everywhere evident in the character of Lee. His manners were those of an earlier age. His courtesy was exquisite, though some observers noted a sort of diffidence or formality in his comportment to those whom he did not know well. The great ladies of Richmond, with whose families he was intimately familiar, thought his company delightful. When he encountered them while out riding, he would make a graceful bow. One summer's day, while he rode beside the open carriage of a Richmond widow, Mrs. Stanard, that *grande dame* playfully accused him of being ambitious. Lee protested with a smile. He was not ambitious; he wanted only, he said, "a Virginia farm,—no end of cream and fresh butter—and fried chicken. Not one fried chicken or two—but unlimited fried chicken." An English officer, Viscount Wolseley, spoke of the "sweetness of his smile and the impressive dignity of the old-fashioned style of his address." His pleasures were simple and innocent, and in particular he liked to plant trees.

Lee was descended from the gentry of western England. In the 1650s his family had feuded with Oliver Cromwell's partisans, and as a result Lee was born into the oldest quarrel in America, that between the Virginia Cavalier and the New England Puritan. He was alive to the primitive antagonisms; he thought the liberal professions of New England cant. "Is it not strange," he wrote, "that the descendants of those pilgrim fathers who crossed the Atlantic to preserve their own freedom of opinion, have always proved themselves intolerant of the Spiritual liberty of others?" He was always to fear that the free-state rhetoric of New England was a mask for tyranny, a new form of Cromwellian dictatorship.

Slavery Lee knew to be evil, but he believed that the institution was slowly disintegrating and would gradually disappear. The Puritan, he maintained, sought to accomplish through violent revolution that which the "slow influences" of providence would achieve in a milder and more merciful way. When, in 1859, a knot of conspirators led by John Brown seized the engine house at Harpers Ferry and attempted to incite a slave revolt, Lee was dispatched by the War Department to suppress the insurrection. Lapsed Puritans like Emerson believed

Brown to be a noble and heroic man. Lee concluded that he was either "fanatic or madman."

Closely connected though he was to the soil of Virginia, Lee differed from many of those who held high place in the Confederacy. He had not passed his life on a plantation, nor had he passed it among politicians whose principal object was to defend the plantation. He had gone to West Point and graduated second in his class. His work as an army engineer had taken him around the country, to Savannah and New Orleans, Brooklyn and Saint Louis. He had served as Superintendent of West Point. But he was always to return to Virginia. His wife, Mary Custis, was the great-granddaughter of Martha Washington. She was as much a child of Virginia as Lee himself. The two were married, in 1831, in the shadow of the doric portico of Arlington, the Custis estate near Alexandria. Arlington became Lee's home—a place he cherished, and eventually lost. Although his military career often took him away from Virginia, he remained, even in his absences, devoted to his house, his hearth, and his roots. He was a loyal family man and an affectionate father, and in the mornings he let his young children climb into bed and "lie close to him."

Lee was never, like McClellan, self-consciously literary, yet his intellectual culture was less narrow than is sometimes supposed. As a young man he read, in French, Rousseau's *Confessions*; and in maturity he made a careful study of Bonaparte's campaigns. Though he made no special pretense to piety, he had, in middle age, experienced a kind of widening, or deepening, of spiritual perception, and at the age of forty-six he was confirmed, by the Bishop of Virginia, in the Protestant Episcopal Church. The most intense phase of his military education came during the Mexican War under General Scott, for whom he undertook a series of intrepid reconnaissances. Scott called him "the very best soldier that I ever saw in the field."

Strong as Lee's attachment to the Union was, his attachment to Virginia was stronger. He was, he said, "one of those dull creatures that cannot see the good of secession." He could not anticipate a "greater calamity for the country than a dissolution of the Union." When, however, the Union was dissolved, he returned to his native state to share, he said, "the miseries of my people." On the day he laid down his commission in the United States Army, he was calm. "Well, Mary," he said to Mrs. Lee, "the question is settled. Here is my letter of resignation and a letter I have written General Scott." "Lee," Scott told him during their last interview in Washington, "you have made the greatest mistake of your life, but I feared it would be so."

A year after he had thrown up his commission, Lee could take satisfaction in all that he had accomplished. He had done as much as any man to form the Army of Northern Virginia, and he had used the army, boldly and skillfully, to relieve the distress of the Southern capital. "The siege of Richmond was raised," Lee wrote, "and the object of [McClellan's] campaign, which had been prosecuted after months of preparation at an enormous expenditure of men and money, completely frustrated." But he could not rest; and the blood on his sword was scarcely dry when, in August, he went forth to meet a Union army under the command of General John Pope.

Chapter 11

TRUMP CARDS

London, July–August 1862

LEE MUST GRAPPLE with Pope; but Lincoln was forced to contend with England. In the summer of 1862 it seemed not unlikely that the fate of the President's revolution would be settled, not on the plains of Virginia, but in the Palace of Westminster. On the evening of July 18, a small man, slight of stature, went down to the Houses of Parliament. Such was his frigid hauteur that Lord John Russell commanded a deference scarcely less profound than royalty. In those days the ducal houses of England still possessed wealth and influence almost princely in extent. Yet even among dukes Lord John Russell's family stood high. The Russells were descended, in the paternal line, from Weymouth merchants who in the later Middle Ages had risen into wealth and gentility. The revolution of the Tudors, which completed the ruin of so much of the old medieval aristocracy of England, spelled opportunity for the Russells, and put them on the path to the ducal coronet. Together with such families as the Cecils and the Cavendishes, they formed the foundation of a new ruling class—the mighty aristocracy known to history as the Whigs.

The Whigs had, for more than two centuries, been the party of liberty in England. In the civil struggles of the seventeenth century, the Whigs had maintained, with courage and perseverance, a long contest with the Crown, one that prevented the emergence, in the British islands, of an absolute monarchy. The Whigs were zealous for liberty, yet they were no less jealous of their own prerogatives, and after the deposition of James II, the last of the Stuart kings, they formed themselves into an oligarchy hardly less powerful than that which ruled at Rome in the age of the Scipios or at Venice in the era of the Querini and the Contarini.

The anomalous qualities of the Whigs were evident in the career of "Johnny" Russell. As a young man he favored the reform of the House of Commons, which he hoped to see become a body more truly representative of the English nation; yet he owed his first seat in the House, which he entered in 1813 at the age of twenty, to the Russell interest. His father, the Duke of Bedford, told the electors of Tavistock, in Devonshire, one of the Russells' "pocket" boroughs, to return his son as their MP; and the electors of Tavistock, whose livelihoods depended on the Duke's munificence, did as they were told.

In the summer of 1862, Lord John was Foreign Secretary in the ministry of Lord Palmerston, who had been Queen Victoria's Prime Minister almost continuously since 1855. When, on the evening of the eighteenth, Lord John came down to Parliament, the lobbies were astir with anticipation. The members were agitated by a rumor that General McClellan, on the Peninsula, was on the verge of capitulating to Robert E. Lee. Lord John went, not to the House of Commons, where he had for many years played a conspicuous part, but to the House of Lords, for since 1861 he had been a peer in his own right.* Yet in spite of the rumor of a great turn of fortune in America, he found the upper House quiet. The Lord Chancellor took his seat on the woolsack at five o'clock, and their Lordships proceeded calmly to discuss a question relating to colonial fortifications.

Very different was the temper of the lower House. In the House of Commons, William Schaw Lindsay, Member for Sunderland, rose to move a resolution urging Her Majesty's government to intervene in the American Civil War. Lindsay, a shipping magnate deeply concerned in the Southern trade, foresaw in the disruption of commerce brought about by Lincoln's policies the ruin of European markets, and in both Paris and London he pressed for intervention. His talents as a speaker were such as might be expected from one who had been long engaged in commercial pursuits. He had neither the polished tone nor the forensic skill of those orators who, like Palmerston and Russell, had been bred as politicians. But Lindsay was rich, and his influence considerable. He was heard with respect by the House. It was clear, he said, that the South could never be conquered. It was still more clear that the Southerners could never be brought again into the fold of the Union. The time had come for the English government to abandon its policy of neutrality.

---

* Lord John's older brother inherited the dukedom of Bedford. Although Lord John was properly called Earl Russell after his elevation to the peerage by a fresh creation in July 1861, he continued to be known popularly as Lord John Russell, the name by which he had been called, in courtesy, as the younger son of a duke during his many years in the House of Commons.

The Confederate States had, he said, shown both the determination and the ability to support their independence. They ought therefore to be received into the family of nations; and England herself ought to offer mediation to the rival belligerents, for both humanity and England's own interests demanded that a stop be put to the war.

A long and spirited debate followed. Perhaps a trifle *too* spirited; one of the speakers, Lord Vane-Tempest, the son of the Duke of Newcastle, was said to have come down to the House drunk. At length the Prime Minister, Lord Palmerston, rose, and defended the policy of the government. He confessed that he regretted that a debate had been brought on; and he earnestly hoped that the House would leave so delicate a matter in the hands of the ministers. The contest between the North and the South had not yet, the Prime Minister said, assumed that character which would justify England in supposing that the independence of the South had been established; and no man could say what posture the conflict would next assume. Lord Palmerston sat down to cries of "Hear, hear," whereupon Lindsay rose and, on the strength of the Prime Minister's representations, withdrew his motion in favor of intervention in the American conflict.

The Houses adjourned, and Lord Palmerston and Lord John Russell went out into the London night. Although the two men continued publicly to defend the policy of neutrality, Palmerston was privately meditating a change. With sky-blue eyes and muttonchop whiskers—carefully dyed—Palmerston was an aristocrat of a type altogether different from that of Russell. Baronial juices, fermenting for centuries in the blood of the de Temples, had produced, in Henry John Temple, third Viscount Palmerston, a most potent liqueur. He had, during many decades, been at the summit of English political life. He entered Parliament in 1807 at the age of twenty-two and was made a junior Minister in the same year. He was now seventy-seven, and so little abated was his vigor that he was soon to be cited in a criminal case for improper relations with a lady who was not his wife. "Old Pam" was supposed to favor the South; and he had long desired the severance of the United States "as a diminution of a dangerous Power," one which he, like many Englishmen, regarded as their country's "great competitor for the commercial and industrial supremacy of the world." "It is in the highest degree likely," Palmerston said, "that the North will not be able to subdue the South, and it is no doubt certain that if the Southern Union is established as an independent state, it would afford a valuable and extensive market for British manufactures."

Intervention in the American war would, Palmerston knew, be popular in England, for it would strengthen the position of the South, and public opinion in the country ran, at this time, strongly against the

North. Englishmen had not forgotten how, a few months before, United States Marines had boarded RMS *Trent,* a royal mail steamer flying the Red Ensign, and carried away two Confederate diplomats, James M. Mason and John Slidell—an incident that brought England and the United States to the brink of war. (Lincoln, who needed saltpeter from British India for his guns, later released the envoys.) What was more, the cotton famine was on. The Union blockade of Southern ports had deprived England's manufacturing cities of the staple on which their prosperity depended. Factories were idle, and laborers were out of work. Some of them were beginning to go hungry.

Even in places untouched by the cotton famine, anti-Union sentiment was strong. The young Henry Adams, who had come to England with his father, Charles Francis Adams, President Lincoln's emissary to London, was astonished at its ferocity. Everyone of consequence, Adams said, "regarded the Washington Government as dead" and expected "to see Lincoln and his hirelings disappear in one vast *débâcle.*" When, on Commemoration Day in the University of Oxford, candidates for honorary degrees were solemnly proposed under the painted ceiling of the Sheldonian, the name of Lincoln was received with groans and hisses, while that of Jefferson Davis was saluted with tumultuous applause.

It was assumed by most observers that "Johnny" Russell would oppose Palmerston in the attempt at intervention. He had, not long before, helped Camillo Benso di Cavour to make a free and united nation of Italy, and he was understood, *The New-York Times* said, "to wish success to the United States." He came from a family in which the love of freedom amounted almost to an hereditary trait; the Russell pedigree, Henry Adams thought, practically guaranteed his fidelity to the Good Old Cause of a free republic.

But could Lord John resist the Prime Minister? Early in August, Palmerston wrote to Queen Victoria and informed her that England would very likely intervene in the American conflict. So strong was Palmerston's hostility to the United States believed to be that Henry Adams's father took the extraordinary step of refusing to receive further communications from the Prime Minister except through Lord Russell. At Cambridge House in Piccadilly, Palmerston's London residence, the antipathy to the Union cause was palpable. Adams remembered seeing the Prime Minister in the foyer in close conference with John Delane, the anti-Union editor of *The Times,* which had likened Americans in the North to "monkeys, grinning and chattering" at the distress they had caused in the manufacturing towns of Lancashire. Palmerston's loud, mechanical laugh haunted the young Adams as he climbed the staircase.

"Ha! . . . Ha! . . . Ha!"

Virginia and Washington, July–August 1862

FIRST ONE, then another telegraph line went dead. In the field head-quarters of the Union Army, agitation was rapidly succeeded by panic. The army was cut off from Washington. The commander, John Pope, the son of an Illinois judge in whose court Lincoln had once practiced, had a short time before boasted of his prowess as a warrior. The boasts were now forgotten. Pope was scared. Where was Lee? In front of him? Behind him? Pope could not say. He seemed to confront, in the rival commander, not a soldier but a sorcerer, one whose sinister maneuvers baffled all rational calculation.

Within a short time Pope's army was shattered. So violent were the enemy's blows that a number of Union battalions collapsed, disinte-grated by the power of opposing force. In one of his dispatches Pope said that he feared that his army would "melt away." He sat slumped in a chair, a picture of ruin. A cold rain fell as those who survived the ordeal trudged back, tired and beaten, to their camps around Washington. Others, unable to walk, were conveyed by horse-drawn ambulances to Fairfax, where they were laid upon the open ground. As darkness fell the heath resounded with the groans and shrieks of dying men, some hideously wounded, others in the last transports of feverish delirium. Clara Barton, the nurse, went among them in the night, a lantern in her hand; but not even her energetic ministrations could relieve such a mass of suffering.

All felt the sting of Lee's lash, and the heat of Stonewall Jackson's fire. In an order that revealed the full measure of his daring, Lee had, in the days before the fatal encounter with Pope, divided his army. He had given Jackson 23,000 men and ordered him to get behind Pope's lines, a strategy which, if it had been discovered by the enemy, might have resulted in the destruction of the Southern army. After many exer-tions, Jackson and his 23,000 succeeded in getting behind Pope's bat-talions. They seized Bristoe Station and severed the rail and telegraph lines that connected Pope to the world. Meanwhile Lee, astride his warhorse, Traveller, led his own detachment through Thoroughfare Gap to the plains of Manassas where, uniting his force with Jackson's brigades, he proceeded to surprise and, after fierce fighting, break the larger army of Pope.

The magnitude of the Union's defeat was indisputable; and Pope was shortly afterwards exiled to a remote command in the Department of the Northwest. But a question haunted the commanders of the van-quished army. Was it only the martial genius of the Southern soldiers that brought the Federal forces to ruin at Second Manassas?

General McClellan had by this time returned from his disastrous campaign in the Peninsula. He still commanded the Army of the Potomac. In the most charitable construction that can be placed upon his actions in August 1862, McClellan preferred to sulk in his tent rather than co-operate in the destruction of the common foe. The young General was never one to throw himself enthusiastically into work which tended, not to his own, but to another man's glory, and his pride was exasperated by the elevation of a rival commander. Pope, he said, was "a villain" who "ought to bring defeat upon any cause that employs him." Ordered to assist Pope by dispatching a corps of men under General Franklin, McClellan dithered. The order was repeated, with more vehemence; McClellan responded with excuses. Franklin's men, McClellan said, had no horses. It soon appeared that General Sumner's corps was in a similar state of unreadiness, and could not, or so McClellan claimed, "move out and fight." When, in the heat of battle, Pope begged the commander of the Army of the Potomac not for men but for supplies, McClellan surveyed with indifference the misfortunes of his competitor and coldly refused the desired succor.

A newspaper correspondent who covered the White House had never seen the President so angry. Lincoln told his private secretary, John Nicolay, that he suspected that McClellan deliberately withheld troops from Pope during the battles of Second Manassas. "He has acted badly towards Pope," the President said; "he really wanted him to fail." Such conduct was, Lincoln maintained, "atrocious," "shocking," "unpardonable." He saw at once that the egotism of McClellan had assumed a more sinister complexion; but he knew that the young man still possessed the confidence of the Army of the Potomac, for whatever his other failings, McClellan was skillful in managing the affections of his men. The humiliations of the Peninsula he had artfully laid at the feet of the government, and his officers, many of whom were secretly grateful for a commander who preferred to dream of glory rather than wrest it from the enemy, joined him in vilifying the political leadership of the Republic.

The position in which Lincoln found himself was one of extraordinary danger. England was on the verge of recognizing the Confederacy. The American Consul at Liverpool warned Lincoln that, if his armies were not soon victorious in battle, Lord Palmerston's government would be forced to recognize the South or else be driven from power. France would instantly follow England in embracing the Confederacy. The two powers would together impose armed mediation on the American belligerents. English warships would appear at the mouth of the Mississippi. The *pantalons rouges* of the French would wade ashore at New Orleans. The combined might of the two empires would pierce the North's blockade, and cotton would again reach Liverpool and Le Havre. The Southern Republic would survive, and Lincoln's revolution would end in failure.

But the President was not yet finished.

He held what he called a "last card." "I will play it," he said, "and may win the trick."

Berlin, September 1862

WHILE LINCOLN DESCENDED into the hottest places in the revolutionary furnace, Bismarck for the first time felt the heat. Even before he went down to the Prussian Chamber of Deputies to confront his adversaries on the Budget Committee, the new Minister-President was apprehensive. Bismarck was never at ease as a public speaker. "You like speaking," he once said to a lawmaker. "For you speaking is a profession, for me it is a torment." Bismarck was a big man; but his voice was high and shrill, and although in an intimate setting it could be caressing, its timbre failed him in larger assemblies.

Yet if he was nervous, the new Minister-President was also resolute. He had his plan.

He had, the week before, taken possession of the chancellery and the Foreign Ministry, Numbers 74 and 76 in the Wilhelmstrasse, and he was burning with the desire to assert himself in affairs of state. The history of his country in the last century was, he believed, one long neglected opportunity. As a result, Prussia, with its industrious population, its ancient military traditions, its fierce and warlike officer corps, could claim the title of great power only *"cum grano salis"* (with a grain of salt). But his countrymen, Bismarck believed, were ready to correct the mistakes which had in the past hindered the progress of Prussian greatness.

His face still sunburnt from travel, he informed the Budget Committee that the Crown had withdrawn, for the moment, the obnoxious army bill. He then attempted to reach an understanding with his adversaries. Prussia, he said, must take the lead in making Germany a nation. He explained how unhelpful it was for his countrymen to squabble with one another while Germany itself remained disunited. "It is not to Prussia's liberalism that Germany looks," he declared, "but to its power. . . . It is not by means of speeches and majority resolutions that the great issues of the day will be decided—that was the great mistake of 1848 and 1849—but by *Eisen und Blut* [iron and blood]."

The most famous words Bismarck would ever utter came close to ending his ministerial career before it began. The liberal lawmakers were hostile. Did the new Minister-President really expect them to surrender their principles and prostrate themselves before his authority simply because he talked of uniting Germany? It was to no avail that Bismarck assured them that "the Government was actuated by a spirit of peace and conciliation." His theatrical tricks—as a gesture of amity he took from his pocketbook the spray of olive Kathi Orlov had given him at Avignon—fell flat. Much of Berlin was soon jeering at the new Minister-President. The foreign press was hostile. *The Times* accused Bismarck of using "words of a very ominous description" and deplored his "well-known absolutist tendencies."

More troubling to the new Minister-President, the ineptitude of his performance raised questions about his competence among those who gave their adhesion to the party of coercion. Even the loyal Roon doubted the wisdom of his friend's "witty ruminations." It was rumored that King Wilhelm himself, who had gone to Baden to celebrate Queen Augusta's birthday, had begun to waver in his confidence. In his attempt to seduce the liberals from their liberalism with the bait of German nationalism, Bismarck had betrayed something worse than misjudgment—he had betrayed naïveté.

His plan to solve the constitutional problem appeared to have failed; and he had now to fight for his political life.

Washington, July–September 1862

LINCOLN'S CARD was one before which even Lord Palmerston might blanch. Emancipation. The freeing of the Confederate slaves. The end of the planters' system of coercion. "I cannot imagine that any European power would dare to recognize and aid the Southern Confederacy," Lincoln said, "if it became clear that the Confederacy stands for slavery and the Union for freedom."

Such was the card. But could he play it in the face of the hand McClellan held? The commander of the Army of the Potomac had warned the President that his men would not tolerate a war against slavery. It was not a threat Lincoln could ignore. Whatever might have been McClellan's personal intention, his officers breathed hostility to the government. His senior commanders were ready "to march upon the capital and disperse Congress as Cromwell did the Long Parliament." So Congressman George Julian asserted. Julian was a radical and perhaps exaggerated; but McClellan himself spoke of "taking my rather large military family to Washn. to seek an explanation. . . . I fancy that under such circumstances I should be treated with rather more politeness than I have been of late."

In July, when McClellan was still on the Peninsula smarting from the blows of Lee, Lincoln first raised with his advisers the possibility of emancipating the Confederate slaves. His Secretary of War, Edwin M. Stanton, had lost an infant child; the heart of the warlord was melted, and in his summer residence he lay insensible with grief. Lincoln drove to the funeral. With him, in the presidential carriage, were Secretary of State Seward and his daughter-in-law, as well as Gideon Welles, "Old Neptune," the Secretary of the Navy. The President startled his companions by raising a subject about which he had never before spoken. Ought he now to free the slaves in those lands in rebellion against the United States? He had reached the conclusion, he said, that such an act was both a "military necessity" and "absolutely essential for the salvation of the nation." A short time later, at a meeting of the Cabinet, Lincoln read out a draft of an emancipation order.

Lincoln had so far refused to characterize his revolution as a crusade to destroy slavery. He had come to power promising to overthrow the Silver Age policy of compromise where slavery in the territories was concerned; but he had always stopped short of making any attempt to extend his revolution to those states where slavery had long been lawful. It is true that, as President, he had tried, without success, to persuade the slave states of the border—Delaware, Maryland, Kentucky, and Missouri—to end slavery of their own volition, in exchange for Federal compensation. But he had done nothing more. Under the Constitution, he said, he could do nothing more. The outbreak of civil war changed the constitutional equation. In time of war the President possesses, as commander-in-chief of the armed forces, an extraordinary military authority. What these war powers are has never been ascertained with precision; but in a pinch they might enable the President to emancipate slaves under color of military necessity.

He had not yet been willing to do so. The policy of liberating blacks would, he knew, kindle the wrath of the slave states of the border; and the slave states of the border, with their rich stores of cattle and corn, were a valuable prize. Emancipation, too, would infuriate important constituencies in the North, and Lincoln had his eye on the midterm elections. The Butternut populations of the Ohio Valley, with a "corn-hog-whiskey" culture similar to that of the Upper South, were as a rule hostile to blacks. Many workers in the Northern cities were as antipathetic. On a hot day in Brooklyn four hundred Irish immigrants, armed with brickbats and stones, surrounded a tobacco factory where twenty blacks were employed. *"Kill the damn naygurs,"* they cried. *"Burn the naygurs."* A black worker was dragged from the factory, and the mob descended upon him with fury. The unfortunate man would have been beaten to death had the police not saved him. Would an emancipation edict lead to more violence? Lincoln listened, in the White House, to prophecies that differed scarcely at all from those which Tsar Alexander heard in the Winter Palace. Not Emelian Pugachev and Stenka Razin, but Nat Turner and Santo Domingo were the names on the lips of American opponents of freedom.

Such were the risks; but Lincoln nevertheless resolved to play his trump. "I felt," he said, "that we had reached the end of our rope on the plan of operations we had been pursuing; that we had about played our last card, and must change our tactics, or lose the game." Seward, however, urged him to proceed cautiously. The Secretary of State, studying the diplomatic dispatches, worried that the proclamation would be viewed by the European powers "as the last measure of an exhausted government, a cry for help." He advised the President not to promulgate the decree until he could give it to the country "supported by military success."

Lincoln was impressed by the wisdom of the advice. Were emancipation perceived to be the desperate act of a crumbling régime, Palmerston and Napoleon III could easily make out a *stronger* case for intervention—and move to partition the United States on the humanitarian plea of averting a race war. Lincoln accepted Seward's counsel. Emancipation, he said, should not "be considered our last *shriek, on the retreat*," a measure as useless as "the Pope's bull against the comet." It must be backed by power and will. He would wait for victory.

But victory eluded him.

The disaster of the Peninsula was swiftly followed by the disaster of Second Manassas. Lee was victorious in Virginia, McClellan was insubordinate at Washington. The President groped his way in an atmosphere thick with intrigue and menace. "Things," he said, went "from bad to worse." In private conversation he alluded darkly to the weakness of his position. McClellan was stronger with the Army of the Potomac than he was; the civil magistrates had ceased to be masters of the situation. Across the ocean, General Manteuffel stood ready to march on Berlin, should Bismarck's revolutionary policy fail. Why should not General McClellan march on Washington, to prevent Lincoln from implementing his? The President was sufficiently acquainted with both history and human nature to know that few things are more dangerous to constitutional government than an army which despises, but no longer fears, its civilian masters. Yet he was equally aware that the authority of his own administration was doubtful, and that continual reverses in the field had undermined its early popularity. As he pondered the transgressions of McClellan, Lincoln was by no means certain that the tottering edifice of his own power could withstand a renegade general's blows.

The draft of the Emancipation Proclamation was relegated to one of the pigeonholes of the President's desk, and Lincoln turned somberly to the disorders of the army and the government. General Pope had, he knew, forfeited the confidence of the soldiers on the plains of Manassas, while General McClellan, however despicable his character might be, retained the devotion of the troops. Early in September, Lincoln invested him with authority to superintend the defense of Washington. At the same time he entrusted him with command of the broken remnant of Pope's army. It was, Lincoln said, the "greatest trial and most painful duty" he had encountered in public life.

A short time later the Cabinet assembled in the White House. Secretary Stanton came into the room ahead of the President and announced, in a wavering voice that did not conceal his dismay, the restitution of McClellan. A ripple of consternation went round the board. The murmurs of astonishment were not yet subsided when Lincoln himself entered the chamber. Was it true, his counselors asked, that McClellan had been restored to high command? The President replied that it was. A heated discussion followed. Sharp words were uttered, though Lincoln himself preserved that mildness of temper which characterized him even when most provoked. Stanton said that no order respecting the status of the General had been issued by the War Department. "No, Mr. Secretary," Lincoln said, "the order was mine, and I will be responsible for it to the country."

But the President's troubles did not end with the restitution of General McClellan. Before the week was out he learned that General Lee, at the head of 60,000 men, had crossed the Potomac and invaded Maryland. Lincoln, who in his youth had been a freethinker, raised his eyes to the heavens. "I made a solemn vow before God," he said, "that if General Lee was driven back . . . I would crown the result by the declaration of freedom to the slaves."

Berlin, September–October 1862

WITH POWER SLIPPING from his grasp, Bismarck determined to meet the King before he returned from Baden and succumbed to the poisonous atmosphere of Berlin. The Minister-President went to Jüterbogk, thirty miles south of the capital, and waited for the King's train in the unfinished railway station. The train arrived; Bismarck made his way through the cars. He found Wilhelm sitting in an ordinary first-class carriage. The King was in a somber mood; and when, as the train got underway, Bismarck dissembled his fears and attempted to vindicate his program, Wilhelm cut him short with an allusion to the fate of Charles I of England and his Minister, Thomas Wentworth, Earl of Strafford. "I see where this will end," the King said. "In the Opernplatz, under my windows, they will cut off your head, and a little later mine."

The sun sank; the light grew dim. Bismarck summoned his histrionic powers: of all his performances, this might be the most important. In the darkened railway compartment he said, *"Et après, Sire?"*

"Après, yes, then we'll be dead," Wilhelm replied.

"Yes," Bismarck continued, "then we'll be dead. Yet we must all die sooner or later, and how can we die better? I, fighting for the right of my King, and Your Majesty sealing with your blood your rights as King by the grace of God."

Iago had not a keener insight into the springs of his master's nature. Bismarck pleaded with his sovereign to dwell, not on the sorriest, but rather on the most glorious of royal liquidations. "Your Majesty," he said, "must not think of Louis XVI. He lived and died in a state of mental feebleness, and does not make an impressive figure in history. Charles I, on the contrary, will always appear a distinguished character."

The King's honor was touched; he grew more animated; he began to see himself in the rôle Bismarck assigned him, that of an officer fighting for Prussia, under orders to hold a position to the death.

As the train sped towards Berlin, Bismarck could not resist mining so rich a vein of Hohenzollern conceit. He said nothing of his now discredited plan, which the King had never really understood; instead he urged Wilhelm to be a soldier. "Your Majesty is obligated to fight," Bismarck said, "you cannot capitulate." The words had the desired effect. The King cherished a romantic veneration for the "ideal type of Prussian officer" who goes forth to meet inevitable death with the words, *"At your command. "* In standing by Bismarck, he was doing his simple duty as a soldier.

The train arrived in Berlin; a knot of ministers and plumed equerries stood on the platform to receive the sovereign. Wilhelm, whom Bismarck had found at Jüterbogk weary and dejected, was cheerful, even "merry" as he stepped from the carriage. The conversation in the train was the real end of liberalism in Prussia: afterwards the dialogue between the Crown and the Parliament was broken off. Bismarck had attempted to persuade the free-state men to embrace his plan; the attempt had failed. He had now to find another means of emancipating the King from the restraints of the constitution.

The new Minister-President carried the army budget in the upper house of Parliament. When a majority of the lower house, the Chamber of Deputies, refused to give its assent to the bill, Bismarck persuaded the King to dismiss the recalcitrant lawmakers. Wilhelm would send them home. Bismarck then announced that, since the lower house had declined to pass a budget, the government would simply carry on without one. The Crown would continue, not only to collect taxes under existing revenue laws, but also to spend money until the matter was resolved. It was the end of constitutional government in Prussia; the principles of a free state are lost when the executive usurps the legislature's dominion over the purse. Nevertheless Bismarck affected solicitude for the constitution his policy destroyed; he pretended to believe that Prussia's laws did not contemplate a budgetary impasse, and that as a result he was not violating the spirit of the Prussian charter, but rather filling a "gap" in the legal architecture of the state.

This artifice did not for a moment deceive Prussia's free-state men. It was, for them, a terrible moment. They could either acquiesce in Bismarck's decision to consign them to irrelevance or, like the Long Parliament in England two centuries before, resort to violence, take to the streets, draw up the barricades. Bismarck was heard, during the tense autumn days, to mutter about the virtues of dying on the scaffold. There were worse modes of extinction than the ax. But this was bravado; he knew that the Prussian Crown had at its disposal an instrument no Stuart king had possessed—a standing army. The King of Prussia could dispatch, in an instant, tens of thousands of disciplined and obedient troops to the heart of his capital.

The humiliation of the legislature was accomplished without bloodshed. When, on October 13, the King dismissed Parliament, the lawmakers acted as Bismarck had prophesied: they acquiesced. Indeed there were cheers, in the Chamber of Deputies, for the King—as well as for a constitution that had practically ceased to exist.

Chapter 12

"GOD HAS DECIDED THE QUESTION"

Biebrich-on-the-Rhine, July–November 1862

THE REVOLUTION IN Germany which Bismarck initiated when he broke the Parliament in Berlin was accompanied by another, less visible, but scarcely less momentous alteration in the ideals and manners of the German people. The change could be detected in the music of Wagner, who had by this time recovered from the failure of *Tannhäuser* in Paris and was ready again to soar towards the heights. The composer had taken refuge on German soil, in Biebrich, a town on the Rhine not far from Wiesbaden. He took the lease of an apartment of three rooms overlooking the river, had his furniture brought from Paris, and meditated a production of *Tristan und Isolde,* his masterpiece of the previous decade, a work which had never yet been performed in an opera house.

Like Bismarck, Wagner was a married man who in the summer of 1862 found himself falling in love with another man's wife. Unlike Bismarck, however, Wagner was ready to go whole-hog. Cosima von Bülow was the wife of his most faithful disciple, the musician Hans von Bülow. She was the natural daughter of his closest friend, the Hungarian pianist and composer Franz Liszt. Cosima's mother, the Countess d'Agoult, had been one of the great beauties of her day; she had fallen madly in love with Liszt, and there had been a violent love affair. Cosima, the fruit of this illicit passion, was not unworthy of her romantic inheritance. She was, her mother said, "a girl of genius, very like her father. . . . She feels the *démon intérieur,* and will always resolutely sacrifice to it everything it may demand of her."

Cosima von Bülow was twenty-four when she and her husband visited Wagner at Biebrich. In the evenings the composer would take out the score of *Tristan und Isolde;* Hans would go to the piano. The work was a monument to love. Wagner had composed much of it under the inspiration of an earlier lover, Mathilde Wesendonk, the wife of one of his patrons, the Zurich merchant Otto Wesendonk. Yet *Tristan und Isolde* was also a drama of disillusion, the work of an artist who claimed to have sounded the lowest depths of despair. Cosima perceived the composer's sadness, and one day, overcome, as Wagner said, with "passionate tenderness for me," she fell at his feet, and covered his hands with tears and kisses.

Tears, rather more than kisses, were the stuff of *Tristan und Isolde*; its music was pregnant with the philosophy of Schopenhauer, who in the pages of *The World as Will and Idea* had inculcated the necessity of overcoming the "will to live." The romantic idea had taken possession of Wagner, and in *Tristan und Isolde* he had attempted to give it musical form. "The last song of the 'world' has died on my ear," he told Liszt. The world was "bad, *bad, bad to the core:* only the heart of a friend, the tears of a woman, can redeem it for us from its curse." He longed to shuffle off this mortal coil and embrace, like the Buddha, oblivion, Nirvana, the land of "Being-no-more." His profoundest desire, he said, was to die, to know, at last, "complete unconciousness, total nihility, a final end to dreaming, the last and only salvation."

Wagner had given life, in *Tristan und Isolde,* to a perennial element in the German character, the morbid idealism which found abundant expression in the old Teutonic myths and romances, but which had been obscured by the decorous, neo-classical culture of the eighteenth century. The timing of the composer's revival of the Teutonic ideal of mortal devotion was propitious. "We may go even further," one of the greatest of the Wagnerian scholars later declared, "and say that *Tristan* itself was something inherent in the German soul of that epoch that *had* to find expression some time or other, somehow or other, needing for its final perfect realisation only the coincidence of the right artist and the right moment. . . ."

By such means was hell uncorked. The infinities of human longing, which are brought to life in that music as in no other, corresponded to the mood which made the German revolution. The composer had resurrected the primitive Teutonic dance with death, and under its romantic inspiration he had created a music-drama in which death figured, not merely as a solution to the problems of life, but also as the ultimate expression of love.* A revival dangerous indeed, for as the poet Hein-

---

* Adolf Hitler expressed the wish that, at the moment of his own annihilation, he should hear what is called the *Liebestod,* the love-death song of Isolde, from the third act of *Tristan und Isolde.*

rich Heine foresaw, the excesses of German romanticism, if they led anywhere, were likely to lead to barbarism and cruelty.

London, Gotha, and Broadlands,
September 1862

IN THE MIDDLE of September word reached England of Lee's victory over Pope and his march into Maryland. Every day London expected to hear that the generalissimo of the South had erected his standard on the ruins of the Capitol. On September 13, *The Times* reported that Washington was in a perilous state, and "that within a very few hours, the good easy President may be seized, and led captive to Richmond with Mr. Seward and Mr. Stanton to bear him company."

The day after this report appeared in *The Times*, Lord Palmerston wrote to Earl Russell from Cambridge House. The Federals, the Prime Minister said, had "got a very complete smashing; and it seems not altogether unlikely that still greater disasters await them." If, Palmerston wrote, Baltimore or Washington should fall, "would it not be time for us to consider whether in such a state of things England and France might not address the contending parties and recommend an arrangement on the basis of separation [of the North and the South]?"

Lord Russell was at this time attending Queen Victoria on a sentimental journey to Saxe-Coburg and Gotha in central Germany, the homeland of Her Majesty's recently deceased consort, Prince Albert. In his reply to Palmerston, Russell did not merely endorse the Prime Minister's proposal to intervene in America, he took a more aggressive line than his chief. The question of intervention, he said, should not be made contingent on the fall of Washington or Baltimore. It was "clear," Russell wrote, that the Federal army "has made no progress in subduing the insurgent States." He argued that, whatever might be the outcome of Lee's invasion of Maryland, England and France should offer mediation "to the United States Government with a view to the recognition of the independence of the Confederates." Should the North refuse mediation, England should instantly recognize the South. At all events, he said, the Cabinet should meet as soon as practicable to decide the question.

That Johnny Russell, the "incarnate creation," Disraeli said, of "High Whiggism," should now try to put a stop to Lincoln's revolution bore witness to an astonishing change in the climate of opinion. But the tide of freedom was going out, and in the changed atmosphere even free-state men like Russell lost sight of their principles. Liberalism, the poet Matthew Arnold said, was fast descending from a power of the first to a power of the second rank.

Writing on September 23 from Broadlands, his Palladian mansion on the banks of the Test, Palmerston enthusiastically embraced Russell's suggestion that England intervene whether or not Washington fell to Lee. "My dear Russell," the Prime Minister wrote, "your plan of proceedings about mediation between the Federals and Confederates seems to be excellent." Thus encouraged by his chief, Russell set about preparing a memorandum for the Cabinet laying out the arguments for intervention.

Frederick, Sharpsburg, and Washington, September–October 1862

ON A SEPTEMBER MORNING not long after Lee invaded Maryland, a regiment of Union infantry, the 27th Indiana, marched north towards the town of Frederick. The day was warm. The regiment halted. Some of the soldiers lay down in the grass to rest. One of them saw an envelope lying nearby. The package was taken up; some cigars fell out, together with two pieces of paper—wrapping, evidently, for the cigars.

The cigar wrapper made history.

The papers in which the cigars were wrapped were found, when examined, to be covered with writing. Bearing the legend "Special Orders, No. 191," they had been issued by General Lee three days before. The papers disclosed the operations of Lee's army in the west of Maryland, and they revealed that the Southern commander had once again made a daring decision to divide his forces.

In a short time the papers were in the hands of General McClellan. Someone in the rival army had been careless, and as a result of this negligence the Union commander was privy to his adversary's plan of invasion. Before the discovery of Special Orders, No. 191, McClellan had pursued Lee with his customary caution and despair. The rebel army, he informed Washington, amounted to "not less than 120,000 men"—double its actual size—and was "numerically superior to ours by at least 25 per cent." But once reconnaissances confirmed the genuineness of Special Orders, No. 191, McClellan marched with uncharacteristic boldness on the Southern lines. Within hours of discovery of the papers, Confederate troops defending the passes of South Mountain in the west of Maryland beheld a sea of Union blue.

Lee, mystified by the unwonted resolution of his rival, ordered his men to fall back, in the night, to Sharpsburg, a village which lay between two rivers, the Potomac, to the west, and a lesser stream, Antietam Creek, which pursued its meandering course a mile or so to the east. The Federal army swiftly invested the place, and at dawn on September 17 a great battle commenced.

It would be the single bloodiest day in American history.

"Every body tears cartridges, loads, passes guns, or shoots," Major Rufus Dawes of the 6th Wisconsin wrote. "Men are falling in their places or running back into the corn." A kind of madness gripped them. "The men are loading and firing with demoniacal fury and shouting and laughing hysterically." "The mental strain was so great," another Union soldier said, "that I saw . . . the singular effect mentioned, I think, in the life of Goethe on a similar occasion—the whole landscape for an instant turned slightly red."

McClellan's massive columns seemed to foretell the doom of the Southern army and perhaps the extinction of its Cause; but just as Lee's exhausted men seemed ready to give way, four brigades, the banners of Virginia and the Confederacy waving aloft, appeared on the horizon. The arrival, in the nick of time, of General Ambrose Powell Hill's men from Harpers Ferry prevented the annihilation of the Confederate Army at Sharpsburg.

The next day the sun rose over a field strewed with corpses. Dead men lay everywhere, their bellies swelling in the sunlight. The remnant of the Southern army stood ready to fight, should battle be offered; but the spell which Special Orders, No. 191, cast over the mind of McClellan had been broken. The spasm of virtue passed, and the commander, reverting to his accustomed state of pusillanimity, did not stir. Late in the day Lee ordered his army to retire to the other side of the Potomac. "Please do not let him get off without being hurt," Lincoln wired McClellan when he learned of Lee's retreat from Antietam. The President's order, however, was disregarded. McClellan declined to pursue the flying enemy.

His indolence contrasted markedly with the vigor and ability of Lee, whose conduct as his army retired across the Potomac prevented a defeat from becoming a rout. Many years later white-haired veterans who in their prime had worn the gray could recall their commander's singular calmness during those dark hours. In the crisis of fortune, pressed by a force much greater than his own, Lee never lost his presence of mind, and only once lost his temper. During the heat of the battle, he encountered a Confederate straggler; the unhappy man was carrying away a dead pig. Lee, incensed at this dereliction of duty at a time when straggling was ruining his army, ordered the soldier to be shot. The order, however, was not carried out, and Lee recovered his equanimity.

The victory of the Union Army at Antietam was less decisive than Lincoln could have wished. It was nevertheless a victory—an almost miraculous one. But for the cigar wrapper, Lee would likely have reached the Susquehanna, destroyed the bridge that connected the Eastern seaboard to the West, and found himself in a position to threaten Baltimore, Philadelphia, or Washington as he saw fit. Instead, the bloodbath of Antietam enabled Lincoln to fulfill the vow he had made when Lee first crossed the Potomac.

Five days after the battle, the President convened a meeting of his Cabinet and initiated a new phase in a revolution which, a fortnight before, had seemed destined for failure. "Gentlemen," he began, "I have, as you are aware, thought a great deal about the relation of this war to slavery; and you all remember that, several weeks ago, I read to you an order I had prepared on this subject." All along, he said, he thought the time for acting on that order "might very probably come." "I think the time has come now. I wish it were a better time. I wish we were in a better condition. The action of the army against the rebels has not been quite what I should have liked best. But they have been driven out of Maryland, and Pennsylvania is no longer in danger of invasion."

The President disclaimed a revolutionary purpose. He was, he said, but "an instrument in God's hands." He told the Cabinet how, when Lee crossed the Potomac, he had vowed that, as soon as the Confederate Army should be driven out of Maryland, he would issue "a Proclamation as I thought most likely to be useful. I said nothing to any one; but I made the promise to myself and"—here he hesitated—"to my Maker."

Lee was driven back; the will of the Deity was manifest. "God," the President said, "had decided this question in favor of the slaves."

"I know very well," he continued, "that many others might, in this matter, as in others, do better than I can; and if I were satisfied that the public confidence was more fully possessed by any one of them than by me, and knew any Constitutional way in which he could be put in my place, he should have it. I would gladly yield to him. But though I believe that I have not so much of the confidence of the people as I had some time since, I do not know that, all things considered, any person has more; and, however this may be, there is no way in which I can have any other man put where I am. I am here. I must do the best I can, and bear the responsibility of taking the course which I feel I ought to take."

Lincoln then read his ordinance. In it he proclaimed that on January 1, 1863, all persons held as slaves in any place where the people were then in rebellion against the United States "shall be then, thenceforward, and forever free. . . ." Two minor changes were made at the suggestion of Seward, and the document, known as the Preliminary Emancipation Proclamation (it would not take effect if the insurgents returned to their allegiance within a hundred days), was issued that afternoon.

In scope and power, the act rivaled the enactments of the greatest lawgivers. But the character of its revolutionary author puzzled those who knew him best. William Herndon, Lincoln's law partner for many years, concluded that the architect of the Emancipation Proclamation was, not merely a private, but a cold man, a man capable of touching, to the depths of their beings, strangers whom he did not know, but one who was separated from those most intimately associated with him by an impenetrable barrier. Lincoln "never poured out his soul to any mortal creature at any time," Herndon said. "He was the most secretive—reticent—shut-mouthed man that ever existed."

Certainly the mastermind of one of history's most liberating revolutions was an odd man. "Mr. Lincoln," one of his closest friends, Joshua F. Speed, said, "was so unlike all the men I had ever known before or seen or known since that there is no one to whom I can compare him. In all his habits of eating, sleeping, reading, conversation, and study he was, if I may so express it, regularly irregular." Lincoln stood, like Bismarck, well over six feet, yet he ate surprisingly little, and weighed only about one hundred and eighty pounds. Unlike Bismarck, for whom the pleasures of the table were an essential part of life, Lincoln was indifferent to food; he frequently dined on nothing more than crackers and cheese and a glass of milk. During the war, his appetite failed almost entirely. "Well, I cannot take my vittles regular," he said. "I kind o' just browse round." Nor was he fond of wine. Liquor left him, he said, feeling "flabby and undone," and in maturity he never touched it.

Nature meant as little to him as haute cuisine. "I never cared for flowers," he once confessed. In Springfield he had tried, for a time, to cultivate some rose bushes; but he soon neglected them. Money bored him: he lacked what Herndon called "money sense" and had no "avarice of the *get.*" He had been, in Illinois, a leader of the bar; but his practice was not a labor of love. He could work himself up into an enthusiasm over particular cases, but the law itself, considered either as a practical pursuit or as an object of scholarly study, interested him scarcely at all. Neither was he a great reader. He delighted (as Bismarck did also) in Shakespeare and the Bible; but his contemplation was more than his reading. No man in America, Herndon said, read less and thought more.

Lincoln possessed, his law partner believed, "a strong latent capacity to love"; but he had for a long time directed his passions almost exclusively towards high and public objects. When perplexed by a problem he seemed oblivious of his surroundings. He would move about, one witness said, in a "vague, abstracted way," as though "unconscious of his own or anyone else's existence."* The continual application of prodigious mental power to the public questions of the day, if it marked Lin-

---

* Julia Taft corroborated this account of the trancelike state Lincoln entered when preoccupied by a problem.

coln out of the ordinary run of men, enabled him, too, to rise to the statesmanship of the Emancipation Proclamation, an act in which he consummated the more noble of the two ambitions which he had sketched in his youth. The genius who aspires to make a revolution, he said a quarter of a century before, "thirsts and burns for distinction; and, if possible, will have it, whether at the expense of emancipating slaves, or enslaving freemen."

Distinction he now had. There was no mock modesty. "I know very well," he said, "that the name which is connected with this act will never be forgotten."

Yet those who saw only his exterior qualities for a long time found it difficult to credit Lincoln's revolutionary genius. Oliver Wendell Holmes, Jr., a captain of infantry who had just been shot through the neck at Antietam, said that "few men in baggy pants and bad hats are recognized as great by those who see them." The proportions of genius are more accurately measured in the perspective of time and history than from the vantage of proximity, and even as Lincoln put his name to the Emancipation Proclamation, many of those who labored beside him regarded him as deficient in the attributes of leadership.

Why, they asked, did the President strike against the philosophy of coercion only in territory controlled by the Confederacy? Why did he not unbind the chains in areas actually controlled by the Union? The Emancipation Proclamation, Secretary of State Seward said, "emancipated slaves where it could not reach them, and left them in bondage where it could have set them free." But military necessity, Lincoln believed, could only be made to cover so many constitutional sins; and he was unwilling to give further offense either to the spirit of the national charter or to the sensibilities of the border states. Nor did he need to do so: slavery, he was convinced, had "been cracked."

A more searching criticism of Lincoln's statesmanship was made by those who questioned the propriety, not of the act of liberation itself, but of the manner in which it was accomplished. The freedom of millions was obtained not through the ordinary processes of liberty, but by an executive decree scarcely less arbitrary than the instrument with which Tsar Alexander effected the liberation of the serfs. The Emancipation Proclamation was the work, not of a magistrate acting within the ordinary bounds of the Constitution, executing laws enacted by the legislature, but of a revolutionary war chief who acknowledged only the authority of military necessity. Not since Oliver Cromwell, it was said, had a man of English blood exercised such an unlimited power over his fellow men.

Lincoln's detractors exaggerated the threat which his methods posed to American liberties. Free elections continued to be held in the North during his presidency, and an opposition press flourished. But the President's critics saw more clearly than many of his defenders the paradox of his revolution. Liberty he brought, but at the tip of a sword. He suspended the writ of habeas corpus, perhaps the most effective restraint ever devised to restrain tyranny, throughout the country. He disobeyed the order of a Federal court to bring a suspected rebel before a judge of the United States. He authorized the disbursement of government funds without sanction of Congress, which alone possesses the power to unloose the purse strings; and although the Constitution gives to the legislature the exclusive power to raise and support armies, he created new regiments of infantry, cavalry, and artillery on no authority other than his own prerogative, much as King Wilhelm was doing in Prussia. He then compelled Congress to act as a rubber stamp and ratify his extraconstitutional acts—a technique Bismarck would soon master in Germany.

With Lincoln's approval, Secretary of State Seward organized a secret police, not unlike Tsar Alexander's Third Section; the clandestine bureau oversaw the arrest of persons deemed obnoxious to the régime.* "I can touch a bell on my right hand," Seward told Lord Lyons, the British Minister at Washington, "and order the imprisonment of a citizen of Ohio; I can touch the bell again and order the imprisonment of a citizen of New York; and no power on earth, except that of the President, can release them. Can the Queen of England do so much?"

Seward, to do him justice, would have preferred to exercise a less execrable type of power; but his passions were versatile, his ambition was flexible, and he did not hesitate to take up a commission which Lincoln, though he condoned it, did not like to touch. One of the Secretary's communications concerning a suspected enemy of the state shows that he had at last found his place in Lincoln's revolution, in its sewers:

DEPARTMENT OF STATE,
WASHINGTON.

John A. Kennedy, Superintendent of
Police, New York:

Arrest Charles Kopperl, of Carroll County, Mississippi, now in your city, and send him to Fort Lafayette.

William H. Seward.

---

* Responsibility for domestic security arrangements was later placed in the hands of Secretary of War Edwin M. Stanton.

The jails were soon filled with those whom the rulers of the state, in their apprehension, had represented as dangerous to the government, and during the course of the war thousands of men and women were subjected to "extraordinary" or "discretionary" arrests. Some of those arrested were said to have given aid and comfort to the Confederacy; yet they were never brought before judges, nor were they permitted to confront their accusers in courts of law. Others among the detainees had done nothing more than criticize the government.

To Lord Robert Cecil, studying the Emancipation Proclamation in London, the lesson of Lincoln's revolution was simple: "if you will have democracy, you must have something like Caesarism to control it."

Chapter 13

THE SCENT OF FREEDOM

South Carolina, April 1862–January 1863

DICK WAS DIFFERENT after Lincoln proclaimed the freedom of the slaves.

"He is the first negro that I have felt a change in," Mary Chesnut said. Dick was a proud man; he had been the butler in the house of Mary Chesnut's father, the old Governor. His life was a long submission. "Yes, Marster . . . just as Marster pleases" were the words continually on his lips. Yet Dick had found dignity in his rôle, and he loved his black frock coat. When his wife, Hetty, said that he would look fine in the colorful liveries the footmen wore, Dick was scornful. "Nonsense, old woman," he said, "a butler never demeans himself to wear livery. He is always in plain clothes."

Mary Chesnut had known Dick since she was a child. She and her sisters used to be given tea by their nurses out of doors, on pine tables scrubbed white as milk.

"Do, Dick—come and wait on us," they would say.

"No, little misses, I never wait on pine tables. Wait till you get big enough to put your legs under your pa's mahogany."

The young Mary Chesnut taught Dick to read as soon as she herself learned her letters. But the world had changed since the days when she perched on his carving board and initiated him in the mysteries of the alphabet. "He won't even look at me now," Mary Chesnut said, "he scents freedom in the air."

Even before Lincoln proclaimed the freedom of her slaves, Mary Chesnut was apprehensive. She saw a new gleam in their eyes. Molly, her maid, was "full of airs." This was a blow, for Molly was one of the "upper ten" of Mulberry, a slave-aristocrat with a greater investment in the coercive system than most. James Chesnut was stung by Molly's defection.

"Tell her to go to the devil," he said, "she or anybody else on the plantation who is dissatisfied. Let them go. It is bother enough to feed and clothe them now."

Molly's impudence might give her away; but as a rule the slaves betrayed nothing. Experience had taught them to conceal their feelings. Mary Chesnut had lived among slaves her entire life, yet they were not less an enigma to her. "They go about in their black masks, not a ripple or an emotion showing. . . ."

What were they thinking? Would they rebel as Nat Turner had done? Would they kill her? Her cousin, Betsey Witherspoon, had been murdered the previous summer—killed "by her own people. Her negroes. . . . Horrible beyond words." They crept into her room in the night and smothered her with the bedding. In the midst of the murder the old lady's nightgown was soiled, and Rhody, her maid, unlocked the traveling trunk to find fresh nightclothes. Suddenly the old lady came to. She "begged them hard for life." What had she done, she asked, that they should want to kill her? The maid stopped the old woman's mouth with the blanket.

Before the murder, Mary Chesnut "never thought of being afraid of negroes. I had never injured any of them. Why should they want to hurt me?" But now she was afraid. "Why," she wondered, should they "treat me any better than they have done Cousin Betsey Witherspoon?"

Officially Mary Chesnut subscribed to the paternal theory of the Fire Eaters, who held the slaves to be overindulged children, "the idlest, laziest, fattest, most comfortably contented peasantry that ever cumbered the earth." Privately she knew this to be cant. She was remote from the ugliest facts, the branding irons, the whippings, the bloodhounds, the mutilations. But she knew enough.

The ancient Spartans struck fear in the hearts of their helots with their dagger-bearing youths, the *Krypteria*; the Southern slaveholders had the Patrol. Mary Chesnut heard dark rumors, stories of mass lynchings in the western districts, where they were "hanging negroes . . . like birds in the trees" for an attempted insurrection. She saw, too, the advertisements in the newspapers; she knew that slave families were routinely ripped apart for the profit of the master class. "NEGROES FOR SALE," one such notice read. "A negro woman 24 years of age, and two children, one eight and the other three years. Said negroes will be sold separately or together as desired." What to her was more distressing, slave women were routinely forced by their masters to have sex with them. In one respect, Mary Chesnut believed, the great indictments of slavery—*The Life of John Brown* by James Redpath and *Uncle Tom's Cabin* by Harriet Beecher Stowe—did not go far enough. A veil of Victorian prudery overhung the darkest sin. "You see, Mrs. Stowe did not hit the sorest spot. She makes Legree a bachelor." "God forgive us," Mary Chesnut wrote, "but ours is a monstrous system [of] wrong and iniquity. . . . Like the patriarchs of old our men live all in one house with their wives and their concubines, and the mulattoes one sees in every family exactly resemble the white children—and every lady tells you who is the father of all the mulatto children in everbody's household, but those in her own she seems to think drop from the clouds, or pretends so to think."

The Fire Eaters saw blacks as children; Mary Chesnut, by contrast, thought them infinitely mysterious. Hers was the racism, not of the Fire Eaters, but of the ancient Greeks, who regarded Africans as sorcerers and magicians. In her descriptions of slaves Mary Chesnut's metaphors are feline, or Egyptian. The slaves are "noiseless as panthers." Her husband's Mammy is as quiet in her "ministrations as the white cat." Old Dick is an "Egyptian Sphinx." The spiritual power of the slaves was, she believed, uncanny. Sometimes she went to the black church at Mulberry. One of the slaves, Big Jim Nelson, led the prayer. He was, she said, a great handsome man, a "full-blooded African. . . . His forefathers must have been of royal blood over there." Big Jim fell on his knees and shut his eyes. He "trembled and shook as one in a palsy." His voice "rose to the pitch of a shrill shriek." Still it "was strangely clear and musical, occasionally in a plaintive minor key that went to your heart. Sometimes it rung out like a trumpet." The enthusiasm of the congregation rose with Big Jim's ecstasy. *"Yes, my God! Jesus!"* voices shouted. *"Aeih! Savior! Bless the lord. . . ."* She wanted to shout herself.

Mary Chesnut had, by this time, lost whatever sympathy she had once felt for the philosophy of the Fire Eaters. Slavery, she believed, was finished in the South. It "has to go of course." She thought it odd that "there are people who still believe negroes to be property." If anything could reconcile her to the South's defeat, "it is Lincoln's proclamation freeing the slaves." The plantation, she maintained, was "Hell," a hell "where a big black devil dominates and a crowd of little black devils swarm around you" in the malarial heat. The white devil of the plantation she omitted to mention.

The coercive oligarchy was crumbling; but the planters would not admit it. Mary Chesnut's husband would not admit it—publicly. In South Carolina the cotton barons preferred to blame their tribulations on the Governor. In the opinion of the tidewater magnates, Francis Wilkinson Pickens was a fool. In order to prevent him from doing harm, the legislature proclaimed a regency, invested with power to restrain the incompetent executive. James Chesnut was appointed to the Governor's Council, as it was called, and Mary Chesnut followed him to Columbia, the capital of South Carolina.

She found the atmosphere of the town partly romantic, in the Southern roses-and-magnolia tradition, and partly *opéra bouffe*, in an equally venerable Southern style. She came to know one family well. She gasped; they were beautiful. Yet beauty was only the beginning of the Prestons' charm. "As Swift defines aristocracy," the Prestons had "the three essentials—brains, blood, wealth." Colonel Preston was a "splendid specimen of humanity." They called him "the Magnificent John." It was a little too much, in Mary Chesnut's opinion, "that so handsome a man—six feet four—should be clever and charming in like degree." He had been educated at the University of Virginia and at Harvard, and he had later made a fortune in Louisiana sugar. Mary Chesnut thought him "so very agreeable, so kind, so sensible." Yet in spite of these outward gifts John Preston was "a bitter, a disappointed man," for he had failed to win high office. If he could not lead, he would not hunt. (The old Cavalier story.) He had taken his family to live abroad, and had only recently returned from a long residence in Paris.

Colonel Preston's bitterness was the fruit of the accomplishment that had been the making of him—his marriage. Caroline Preston was by birth a Hampton, the daughter of old General Wade Hampton. The family was among the most formidable in South Carolina. But there was a difficulty. When they married, he was poor—the sugar empire came later—and she was rich; and in the South, at that time, rich girls did not marry poor boys. It was said that "Magnificent John" married Caroline Hampton for money, for position, for the mysterious glamour of her name; and that in exchange for these, he resigned his manhood into the hands of his new relations. "I have always treated him," an uncharitable soul confided to Mary Chesnut, "as a poodle of the Hamptons—of the family. Whenever I saw him, he was walking on his hind legs for their amusement—or rolling off the rug to get out of the way of their feet."

If John Preston's pretensions to greatness were questioned in South Carolina, his wife's were not. The grand manner Caroline Preston assumed easily and unselfconsciously, in keeping with her birth and traditions. Her beauty was undeniable. "She has a majestic figure," Mary Chesnut said, "perfectly molded. And chiseled regularity of feature." When she went to a ball, resplendent in diamonds, point lace, and velvet train, she might have vied in dignity with a reigning queen. She was, however, free from the more intimidating forms of condescension. She was "exceedingly quiet, retiring, and reserved. Indeed her gentleness almost amounts to timidity."

Such grandeur of character might have been an impediment to friendship; but an intimacy soon developed between Caroline Preston and Mary Chesnut. They went out driving together every day in Mrs. Preston's landau. Footmen, dressed in the livery of the Prestons, stood on the footboard as the carriage drove through the streets of Columbia. Mary Chesnut might have forsaken the philosophy of coercion, but she had not given up the aristocratic ideal. In the Prestons she found a fresh manifestation of all that she cherished in the seignorial manner. "I wonder if a handsomer group was ever collected in one room," she exclaimed. "I have fallen in love with a whole family. No exception whatsoever."

The Prestons had created a miniature world of rare splendor, one that in a dark hour renewed Mary Chesnut's faith in the Southern *noblesse*; yet of all the enchanting objects in the household, one creature stood apart by reason of her peculiar loveliness. This was the Prestons' daughter, Sally Buchanan Preston, who was called "Buck." Buck Preston, twenty years old in 1862, was, in spite of her beauty, singularly good-natured, with an excellent disposition. She was, her Mammy said, "the sweetest, the best, the prettiest child." She was highly accomplished, spoke excellent French, and sang beautifully; yet in spite of this she was simple and natural, without any affectation of superiority.

Mary Chesnut was from the first intrigued by the special impression of grace which the girl made upon her. "Buck," she said, was "the very sweetest woman I ever knew." Knowing, as she did, things which the cygnet could not even dimly perceive, she took it upon herself to act as her guide. For Buck was as yet unconscious of what a trial her progress towards womanhood was to be. Nor could Mary Chesnut assume, as she might have done if a duller nature were at stake, that Buck would be insulated by stupidity from the horror of the ordeal. Such was the girl's sensitivity that she was bound to feel every jolt in the road.

At no time would Buck's début have been easy, for society has always taken an unhealthy interest in the deflowering of virgin beauty. But the prurient curiosity is all the more intense when the plant happens to ripen in the last phases of an aristocracy's decay, in the shadow of an oligarchy's fallen marble. The rites then are downright barbaric; it is as though the waning hopes of the doomed order hinged entirely upon the sacrifice of the corn maiden.

Saint Petersburg and the Crimea, August 1862–November 1863

IN THE SUMMER GARDEN in Saint Petersburg, an Englishman was strolling with his lady. Coming towards them, on the path, was a Russian officer. The Russian was tall, and apparently accustomed to command; his expression, though not without gentleness, betrayed a certain heaviness and fatigue. A test of wills ensued. The Russian showed no disposition to make way for the Englishman. The Englishman was as unwilling to concede the path to the Russian. This bulldog determination seemed, at first, to surprise his antagonist. But an indulgent smile soon lighted up the Russian's face, and with a shrug of his shoulders he "deviated from his straight course, and ceded the centre of the path to the Englishman."

When the Englishman and his wife finished their walk, they found a crowd gathered at the gate of the Summer Garden. Eager to discover what the fuss was about, the Englishman worked his way to the front of the throng, where he beheld a landau emblazoned with the double-headed eagles of the Romanovs. A ripple of excitement passed through the crowd as scarlet flunkies and police detectives cleared a path for the Emperor. Hats came off, bows and curtsies were made, and in a moment the astonished Englishman found himself face to face with the officer he had encountered in the garden path. Alexander flashed a pleasant smile of recognition before driving off.

The Tsar was not quite so "used up" as Prince Kropotkin believed him to be. Even as his minions were, with his approval, flinging suspected agitators into the Fortress of Peter and Paul, raiding the houses of liberal noblemen, and condemning writers and intellectuals to Siberian exile, a part of Alexander was still the sensitive Sasha, the boy with the mild, lamb-like eyes. Nevertheless, the burdens of despotism had begun to tell. To his brother, Grand Duke Constantine, Alexander spoke of the nervous tremors that now afflicted him. "I am often seized," he said, "by an internal trembling when particularly stirred by anything. But one must control oneself, and I find prayer the best means to this end." The rumor went round that the Tsar had contracted tuberculosis. In fact he suffered from asthma, a condition that was exacerbated by his addiction to tobacco.

When a stroll in the Summer Garden proved insufficiently rejuvenating, Alexander could always escape to one of his suburban palaces. Most often he went to Tsarskoe Selo, fifteen miles from Saint Petersburg. The imperial train sped through a flat and dreary country of stunted firs and dark-leaved birch. As soon as Alexander passed through the gates of "the Tsar's village," however, the prospect changed. The rulers of Russia, reluctant to acknowledge any limitation of their power, bid defiance to nature herself. Where she was stinting and ungenerous, they waved their wands, and the wasteland was transformed into a garden. Two palaces, wrought by the art of Rastrelli, stood in a park of 800 acres. There were obelisks, canals, artificial hills, Chinese pavilions, and secluded grottoes. A lake, dug by Turkish prisoners, could be emptied and refilled like a bathtub. Six hundred men labored each day to perfect the ornamental gardens. Tsarskoe Selo seemed, to one courtier, a "terrestrial paradise," a "sort of enchanted fairy land." A French diplomat told Catherine the Great that her pleasure dome wanted only one thing.

"Indeed?" returned the Empress.

"A glass case, Madame, to protect this unique masterpiece."

At Tsarskoe Selo the Tsar could relax with friends and go for walks with his favorite setter, Milord. He was sometimes seen sitting on the grass with his guests, talking and laughing. But beguiling though Tsarskoe Selo was, its charms were too intimately connected to Alexander's official existence to afford him the solitude he craved. Accordingly it was the Tsar's custom, each autumn, to travel much farther, to the southern extremity of his Empire. The imperial train enabled Alexander to indulge a luxury unknown to his predecessors, and in a few hours he was able to exchange the frosts of the Baltic for the perpetual garden of the Crimea.

He detrained at Simferopol on the Crimean peninsula, where a carriage was in readiness. From Simferopol he was driven along a winding road, through whitewashed Tartar villages, to Livadia, one of the imperial villas overlooking the harbor of Yalta. The residence was then a comparatively simple wooden structure; the palace of white limestone which now stands on the site would not be built until the reign of Alexander's grandson, Nicholas II, the last Tsar. In the soft climate of the peninsula, washed by the waters of the Black Sea, the vine flourished, and the air was perfumed with the scent of lilacs and roses. Livadia was the Capri of the Romanovs; here they could shed the heaviness of the Russian winter and feel, for a moment, the lightness of a classical spring. Here, a thousand miles from Saint Petersburg, Alexander, dressed entirely in white, could forget the cares of the throne and come to life again amid saltwater and sunshine.

Mark Twain, who visited the Tsar in the Crimea in 1867, thought it "a vision of the Sierras." The slopes were "covered with the great parks and gardens of noblemen, and through the mass of green foliage the bright colors of their palaces bud out here and there like flowers. It is a beautiful spot." The Tsar emerged from his villa to greet Twain and the other Americans who had gathered in his garden. The "imperial family came out bowing and smiling, and stood in our midst," Twain wrote. "A great number of dignitaries of the Empire, in undress uniforms, came with them. With every bow, His Majesty said a word of welcome." "Good morning," Alexander said in English, "I am glad to see you—I am gratified—I am delighted—I am happy to receive you!" There was, Twain said, "character" in Alexander's courtesy, "Russian character—which is politeness itself, and the genuine article." The American writer was struck by the "kind expression" on the Russian monarch's face, and he judged him to be a sincere man. The Empress Mary also appeared. She wore a silk dress trimmed with blue, with a blue sash at her waist; her straw hat was edged with blue velvet, and she carried a parasol. Americans, she told her visitors, were favorites in Russia, and she hoped that Russians were similarly regarded in America. She and the Tsar then personally conducted their guests through the villa, showing them "the cozy apartments and the rich but eminently home-like appointments of the place."

While Alexander reclined in his Crimean vineyard, the grand design of his reforms continued to unfold in the capital. The acts of the red brigades had slowed but not stopped the liberal revolution. By the fall of 1862 liberal bureaucrats known as "Constantine's Eagles," protégés of Grand Duke Constantine, were directing the departments of education, justice, finance, and war. At the same time, Alexander undertook a more momentous reform, the reorganization of the Russian legal system. For almost a year a commission had been at work with a mandate to reform the laws. The commissioners proposed, among other things, that judges be made independent of the executive; that judicial proceedings be opened to the public; and that trial by jury be instituted in criminal cases. They recommended, too, that cumbersome legal procedures be simplified; under the existing system, it was difficult for a creditor to enforce payment of a debt, a circumstance which impeded the progress of commerce.

Alexander approved the proposals, and the country rejoiced. Russia's new legal system was to be "public, adversarial, and open to all estates of the realm." The country moved a step closer to embracing the free-state ideal, the faith that men and women at liberty to choose their destinies for themselves, subject only to laws that apply equally to all, will do more to make a state great than the most thoughtful commands of the most benevolent despot.

To many it seemed as though Russia stood "on the threshold of a new life." The country, the Rector of the Seminary in Kazan said, "is striving to be born again." The "Great Reforms," as they were called, were "designed to renovate" the *ancien régime* and "create the framework for a *grazhdanskoe obshchestvo* (citizen society) in place of the rigidly defined *sosloviia* (society of classes) in which autocratic politics and aristocratic class interests ruled the lives of Russians." The reforms had an anti-paternalist thrust: they were intended to transform "a body of passive subjects into one of active citizens." As such they were "decisive" in the "sphere of civil and personal rights," and "opened the way for peasant participation in other institutions that emerged from the reform process," among them juries.

Nor were the Tsar's domestic reforms his only contribution to the cause of liberty at this time. Alone among the rulers of the great powers, Alexander unequivocally took the side of Lincoln in the American Civil War. In the fall of 1862 Lincoln wrote a personal letter to Alexander. Where, the President asked, did the Tsar stand on the question of foreign intervention in America's Civil War? Alexander replied to Lincoln's inquiry through his Foreign Minister, Prince Gorchakov, who told Bayard Taylor, the American chargé at Saint Petersburg, that "Russia, alone, has stood by you from the first, and will continue to stand by you. . . . We desire above all things the maintenance of the American Union as one 'indivisible nation.'" The Prince assumed a confidential tone. *"Proposals will be made to Russia to join some plan of interference.* She will refuse any invitation of the kind. Russia will occupy the same ground as at the beginning of the struggle. *You may rely upon it, she will not change."* Gorchakov closed the interview by taking Taylor's hand. Giving it strong pressure, he said, "God bless you!"

The American was greatly moved.

Such communications, Lincoln said, were the most loyal he received from any European government. While England and France found ways to encourage the South, Alexander was true to his word: he steadfastly supported the Union. His policy was by no means purely humanitarian; Alexander was motivated in part by his desire to gain an advantage over Britain, which was determined both to counter the Asiatic ambitions of Russia and to thwart the rise, in America, of a potential threat to her commercial and naval supremacy. The enemy of my enemy, the Tsar reasoned, is my friend. But Alexander's demonstrations of support for Lincoln went beyond traditional great-power maneuvering, and at an imperial ball he went out of his way to praise the President's Emancipation Proclamation.

Yet . . . something was missing. On paper, all of Alexander's reforms were correct; they conformed to the most up-to-date methods; every decision was right. But the whole impression is of a waxwork rose, flawless in its technical craftsmanship, but without instinct of life. Alexander's tutor, the romantic poet Zhukovsky, had taught his pupil to be a liberal, but he had not been able to make him a poet. Lacking an inspiration, the Tsar's revolution was stillborn. Alexander had not, as yet, been corrupted by authority, but he had been rendered complacent by it. He did not exert himself to wring from the pulp of power the last quintessence of nectar.

A revolution, if it is successful, invents a new language. The task of the revolutionary statesman is to find the fresh accent. The Greek statesman Solon reduced his statecraft to poetry, and through his verses reconciled Athens to the revolution he made there. Lincoln and Bismarck were learning, through trial and error, to do something similar in their own countries; they succeeded in turning the romantic influences of their youth to account in their mature statesmanship. Alexander never did.

Of course only an unusually creative, one might almost say artistic, nature could have succeeded in finding a way to talk to a nation in which the different classes were, as in Russia, separated by such wide and almost unbridgeable chasms. How to explain the importance of an independent judiciary to peasants who believed, whenever they heard a peal of thunder, that the Prophet Elijah was crossing the sky in his chariot? Alexander might be forgiven his inability to touch the Russian soul; the task was difficult. What is less excusable is that he seems not to have tried.

London and Newcastle, October 1862

WITH THE VICTORY at Antietam and the issuance of the Emancipation Proclamation, Lincoln appeared to have saved his revolution. For a moment, it seemed, freedom had gotten the upper hand. After an interval of suspense, Henry Adams breathed easier. Surely the Americans were out of danger now; not even Lord Palmerston would dare to oppose a government that had defeated Lee and promised to emancipate the slaves.

Adams, for all his perspicacity, did not reckon on the influence, in Lord Palmerston's government, of William Ewart Gladstone, the Chancellor of the Exchequer. During the summer months, when the debate over whether to intervene in the American Civil War raged most fiercely, Mr. Gladstone had been preoccupied with the budget. Parliament, however, had adjourned in August, and while flocks of legislators went forth to slaughter grouse and other forms of indigenous fauna, the Chancellor, freshly liberated from the labors of the Exchequer, set himself to examine the burning public questions he had neglected during his efforts to produce a budget.

After an interval of studious retirement, Mr. Gladstone went off, at the beginning of October, on a tour of the north of England, intent on sharing with the world the fruits of his solitary meditations. He was fifty-two years old. His gifts were altogether out of the range of ordinary human nature. At Christ Church, Oxford, he had outshone myriads though bright. His activities during the very vacations of the university, duly recorded in his diary, must be the despair of lesser scholars:

> *July 6* [1830] . . . —Up after 6. Began my Harmony of Greek Testament. Differential calculus, etc. Mathematics good while, but in a rambling way. Began *Odyssey*. Papers. Walk with Anstice and Hamilton. Turned a little bit of Livy into Greek. Conversation on ethics and metaphysics at night.

July 8.—Greek Testament. Bible with Anstice. Mathematics, long but did little. Translated some *Phædo.* Butler. Construed some Thucydides at night. Making hay, etc., with S., H., and A. Great fun. Shelley.

Such a young man was unlikely to be long overlooked by the world; and before he was twenty Mr. Gladstone had a name and a reputation. At Eton he proved himself a skillful antagonist in the debates of the Literati, or "Pop" as it was sometimes called, and in the Oxford Union his performances so astonished his auditors that the Duke of Newcastle gave him a pocket borough on the strength of one of his speeches.

In the House of Commons Mr. Gladstone rose fast, and he was early marked out as a likely Prime Minister. He was undoubtedly a prodigy; but his intellect, prodigious though it was, was perpetually at the mercy of his enthusiasms. As a young man just entering the House of Commons, he was offended by the impiety of his fellow legislators, who in the profane transactions of temporal politics neglected the spiritual duties of their office. Did not their acts betray "a certain element of the Antichrist"? That the House of Commons bore little resemblance to a Bible society was a revelation unlikely to disturb the repose even of scrupulous churchmen; but the young Member for Newark could not accept this state of affairs, and in hours stolen from his parliamentary avocations he composed a large book, *The State in its Relations with the Church,* in which he elaborated the duty of the secular government to transform itself into a holy synod, to sift the claims of religious and spiritual truth, and to eject heretics from public office.

Two decades after *The State in its Relations with the Church* appeared, the House of Commons was still unregenerate; but in the mind of Mr. Gladstone a new enthusiasm had supplanted the preoccupations of the pious novice. He had forsaken the doctrines of the Tories and the High Church mandarins of Oxford; he was now entering on his liberal phase. But his liberalism was marked by the same disordered zeal that had previously characterized his Toryism. Mr. Gladstone learned, in 1858, that the peoples of the Ionian Islands, then administered by a British protectorate, were agitating for liberty and reunion with the Greek nation. His imagination was transfixed by the vision of Homer's children struggling for freedom, and he startled the cognoscenti of Westminster, who had supposed him thoroughly broken to the House of Commons, by seeking appointment as Extraordinary High Commissioner for the islands. Disraeli, who was only too delighted to consign so formidable an adversary to a Mediterranean oblivion, volunteered to facilitate the commission.

Mr. Gladstone sailed for the south, but no sooner had he made a tour of Corfu and Ithaca than the dream of Homeric warriors hurling their lances in the sun began to fade. The first transports of enthusiasm were tempered by the discovery that the degenerate inhabitants were incapable of admiring or even comprehending the virtues of their ancestors; and Mr. Gladstone learned with dismay that in the birthplace of Ulysses it was by no means easy to obtain a copy of the *Odyssey*. "The whole impression is saddening," he wrote in his diary, "it is all indolence, decay, stagnation; the image of God seems as if it were nowhere." On Cephalonia he was received as a hero and a champion of liberty; but the approbation of the Ionians quickly changed to disgust when they learned that the man they called "Greek-loving Gladstone" had no authority either to join their islands to greater Greece or grant them a genuine independence. The islanders were indifferent to the constitution Mr. Gladstone dictated to them, offended by his tone of superiority, and perhaps repelled by his pedantry. When, during one of the assemblies, a question arose as to the meaning of the word *thelesis* (will or wish), Mr. Gladstone insisted, with learned references to the literature of ancient Greece, that the Ionians did not understand their own language.

Unchastened by his Mediterranean adventure, Mr. Gladstone returned to England and cast about for new objects on which to exercise his rich and fantastic dogmatism. In Lincoln's revolution he found a topic irresistible to the lover of high-minded declamation, and his journey to the north soon became another of what Disraeli called his "pilgrimages of passion." He arrived at Newcastle flushed with the success of his tour; *The Times* compared his progress down the Tyne to a Roman Triumph. He visited the Church of Saint Nicholas; a photographer took his picture. He then repaired to the Town Hall, where a banquet was held in his honor. After dinner the cloth was removed, and a toast to Mr. Gladstone's health was proposed and drunk to applause. The Chancellor himself then rose to speak.

What Mr. Gladstone said shocked men and women on both sides of the Atlantic.

Chapter 14

"BAD TIMES, WORSE COMING"

Moscow and Yasnaya Polyana, Russia,
August–December 1862

HOWEVER MANY DECREES Tsar Alexander might issue in Saint Petersburg, a new idea of liberty could flourish in Russia, if it could flourish at all, only if men like Tolstoy were prepared to help it grow. Men who lived close to the people, and who could talk to them in a language they understood.

Tolstoy had thrown himself into the work of liberation; he had administered the emancipation law; he had tried to waken Fedka, Semka, and little Pronka to the possibilities of their existence. Yet what had he gotten for his pains, other than a visit from the secret police? He had once, perhaps, overestimated the usefulness of reform; he now succumbed too casually to the reverse delusion, and dismissed the value of all such labor.

He went to Moscow and personally presented his indictment of the Third Section to the Tsar, whom he encountered in the Alexandrovsky Gardens. But he soon forgot all about it. He fell in love with his doctor's daughter, and a short time later he married her.

When Tolstoy drove down the alley of Yasnaya Polyana with his bride that autumn, the period of reforming liberalism in his life was over. He ceased to be a teacher and a Justice of the Peace. "Have said good-bye to the students and the common people," he wrote a few days after his return to the manor. A short time later he dismissed Fedka, Semka, and little Pronka for the last time. They "are going away," he wrote. "And I feel sorry for them."

The sorrow, however, was short-lived, for in the earliest hours of his marriage to Sofya Andreyevna, née Behrs, Tolstoy was intensely happy. "I have lived to the age of thirty-four," he said, "and I didn't know it was possible to be so much in love and so happy. . . . I'm calm now and serene, as never before in my life." Yet connubial bliss was not quite as he had painted it to himself during his bachelorhood. "Living two together is such a frightening responsibility. . . . I find it terribly frightening to live now: one feels so intensely, one feels that every second of life is in earnest, and not as it was before."

The fact is that he was vexed by the small cares and petty rows of domestic life, those scrapes and annoyances from which he seems to have imagined that he, alone among the generality of husbands, would be exempted. He could only dimly comprehend the significance his bride attached to the management of the household. A month before, Sofya Andreyevna had inhabited a little room in the Kremlin, where her father practiced as a physician. Now she was a Countess, and the mistress of a vast domain. But her domestic empire, she soon discovered, though extensive, was phlegmatic. Yasnaya Polyana was mired in sloth and vodka. There was a small army of servants, a chambermaid, a laundress, a coachman, a seamstress, a charwoman; yet they were all extraordinarily lazy. The house was perpetually in disorder; the cook was drunk; the housekeeping régime was in disarray. Tolstoy himself had no regular bed linen, but rather slept, like a peasant, rolled up in a blanket. Agatha Mikhailovna, the housekeeper, appeared to be more concerned with canines than clean beds. A tall, spare woman, unbent by age, she was revered by Tolstoy, and had the care of his dogs. These she ministered to in a dirty room strewn with her own clothes, which constituted the dogs' bedding. When a puppy took sick, she would commend it to the care of Saint Nicholas, before whose icon she would light a candle.

Tolstoy, for his part, was startled, not only by the way in which his bride exalted the trivialities of housekeeping into problems of the first rank, but also by the strength of purpose she displayed in resolving them. Sofya Andreyevna threw herself unstintingly into the work of a chatelaine. She pulled the bell rope furiously, gave peremptory orders, rearranged the rooms, reorganized the linens. Her willpower was masculine in its intensity. "I can only say," Tolstoy wrote to a friend, "that her most striking feature is that of a 'man of integrity'—I mean what I say: both 'integrity' and 'man.'" But if the masculine element in Sofya Andreyevna's makeup was strong, her feminine instincts were stronger. Tolstoy was baffled by them. His wife longed to be fussed over, worshipped, caressed; and she sulked when the man to whom she had united her soul failed to offer up a sufficiently tender devotion. "My husband is ill and out of sorts and doesn't love me," she complained a fortnight after their wedding. "It is terrible to live with him." "He grows colder and colder to me every day, while I go on loving him more and more. His coldness will soon become unbearable." There was "something wrong" in their relations, and "sooner or later we will drift apart in a spiritual sense." She went about Yasnaya Polyana in a fog, a daze, a melancholy dream. If only she could rouse herself. "If I woke up, I should be a different person. . . . He would then see how much I love him, I should know how to *tell* him of my love; I should be able, as in the past, to look clearly into his soul and to realize how I could make him happy. I simply must wake up."

But she could not; and her exertions in the laundry and the linen closet contrasted markedly with the drowsy apathy of her more intimate performances. For it was not only the difficulty of joining of their souls that perplexed the newlyweds in those early days. Sofya Andreyevna's awakening on the wedding night, in the garish room in the inn, had been a rude one. A "bad dream," Tolstoy wrote afterwards in his diary. "She knows all." Her terror was "morbid." She eventually got used to the transactions of the marriage bed, but she liked them no better. "All this commerce of the flesh" was, she said, "repellent." She found no pleasure in having her naked body "crushed" to her husband's. "The physical side of love plays a very big rôle for him, and none at all for me." Her disdain for her spouse's passionate nature was heightened by the knowledge that he had adored other flesh besides her own. "When he kisses me, I think to myself, 'Well, I'm not the first woman.'"

She could not forget the diaries. Whether from a desire to put her affections to the test, or from the hope of more perfectly uniting their souls, Tolstoy had, shortly before their wedding, given Sofya Andreyevna his diaries to read. A prudent lover might seek to cast over his youthful follies a decent veil; but Tolstoy could not be content with so deceitful an expedient. Sofya Andreyevna must see his soul entire. She had taken the books from him; opened them; read. The black confessions, the brutish lusts, the numerous debaucheries, shocked her.

Her shock was closely proportioned to her naïveté. In Russia, at that time, young ladies lived a sheltered existence. Peter the Great had abolished the Eastern practice of relegating the women of the household to an apartment known as the *terem*, in order that their modesty might never be violated by the profane eye of a stranger; the habits of Oriental sequestration had died away. But the well-bred Russian girl still grew up behind a variety of screens and veils, and as a result she entered womanhood almost entirely ignorant of the less delicate aspects of relations between the sexes. Sofya Andreyevna was unprepared, at eighteen, for the revelation of her lover's erotic nature. During a sleepless night she was constantly in tears. Tolstoy's past, she wrote, "is so dreadful that I don't think I will ever be able to accept it." When, blear-eyed and pale, she greeted him the next morning, she made a show of cheerfulness; she forgave, or pretended to forgive, his transient amours. But in her soul a seed of doubt had been planted.

It now brought forth a bitter fruit. Love may be patient, but jealousy is turbulent. It "hurts me," she said, "that this love of mine, my first and last, should not be enough for him." "I, too, have been interested in men," she admitted, "but only in my imagination." At Yasnaya Polyana she was surrounded by mementoes of Tolstoy's lust. There was Askinia, the peasant girl with whom he had once lived intimately. Many years later, when he was an old man, Tolstoy spoke of the joy it gave him "to think that Askinia is still alive." And there was Askinia's son, Timofei, the spitting image of the lord of the manor himself. One night Sofya Andreyevna dreamt of an immense garden in which all the women of Yasnaya Polyana were gathered. Among them was Askinia, dressed in black silk; she had with her the little boy. Sofya dreamt that she seized her husband's natural child and tore it limb from limb. Yet before the snows of the winter came, something happened which threw a new light on the marriage. She discovered that she was herself with child.

Tolstoy's family was growing, and the sometime public man prepared to become a thorough family man. He was scarcely the only wellborn Russian to exchange public duties for domestic cares. The Tsar's reforms had briefly roused many educated Russians to a new sense of civic virtue. But their enthusiasm faded, and they sank back into apathy and indifference. Alexander had failed to persuade the best and brightest of his subjects that his revolution mattered.

Columbia and Camden, South Carolina,
March 1862–September 1862

BISMARCK'S COUNTER-REVOLUTION against the free state might succeed, though it threw the dirt of the Dark Ages in the face of parliaments and progress; but in America the romantic vision of the Fire Eaters was breaking down. In the New World feudalism was a failure. Yet the realization that their order was doomed came slowly to the grandees of the South. The war had at first been for them a parlor game, an excuse for patriotic invective. But as 1862 wore on it came closer, and ceased to be a subject of rhetorical extravagance.

"It has come home to us," Mary Chesnut said. "Half the people that we know in the world are under the enemy's guns." One by one the men donned their military cloaks and departed for the front. Her friend Laurence Keitt went off with his regiment, the 20th South Carolina, closely followed by another friend, John Hugh Means. Mary Chesnut was walking to the Prestons' house when she caught sight of Governor Means driving to the depot. She loved the Governor; he differed from the "cold, formal, solemn, overly polite creatures" who figured so largely in her Columbia existence. He loved life and did not scruple to conceal it. From his passing carriage he kissed both hands to her—a "whole-souled greeting, as the saying is." "And I returned it with my whole heart, too. 'Goodbye,' he cried—and I answered, 'Goodbye.'" She cried as she watched him drive out of sight. Two months later he was dead.

Old men died—and so, too, did younger ones, in far greater numbers. Mary Chesnut lost count of the men of eighteen or twenty who were "washed away, literally, in a tide of blood." There was "nothing to show they ever were on the earth." But the Southern mind was strong in adversity. It approached its perfection in adopting an heroic attitude towards the evils of life. Mary Chesnut was astonished by the self-control exhibited by mothers caught up in the catastrophe of blood. It was positively Spartan. When young Edward Cheves, an only son, was killed, his sister was naturally hysterical. "Oh, mother," she cried, "what shall we do—Edward is killed." But Mrs. Cheves "sat dead still, white as a sheet, never uttering a word or shedding a tear."

With the riptide of death a new strain of pessimism entered into the life of the planter aristocracy. The Union armies, Mary Chesnut said, were "three to one against us," and the Northern states had "hardly begun to put out their strength." Conversations were laconic now, shorn of the bravado of an earlier day. "Men," one officer told her, "can find honorable graves—we do not see what is to become of the women and children." Another said, "I want my wife and children out of this slaughter pen." Mary Chesnut's own husband on one occasion almost displayed emotion. He "had to own a breakdown (or nearly)," Mary Chesnut wrote. He received a letter from a mother begging him for a travel permit, one that would allow her to go to Virginia to tend her wounded son. James Chesnut began to read the letter aloud to the Governor's Council, but he broke down in the attempt. "He was awfully ashamed of his weakness," Mary Chesnut said.

James Chesnut was, if anything, too finely bred. He had as a young man read deeply in the works of Sir Walter Scott, and in middle age his soul was hardened in the stiff mold of the *Waverley* novels. He went about visibly impaired by the weight of his hereditary traditions, the burden of the ancestors whose faces stared down on him in oil from the walls of Mulberry. When, in one of his seigneurial moods, James Chesnut fell to contemplating his ideal—"behavior worthy of the Chivalry, as they call us"—his wife could not easily reach him. At such moments he was remote from her, cherishing, in some dim mental sanctuary, the *lares et penates* of the Chesnuts.

The marriage had its limitations, but it was not the principal cause of Mary Chesnut's dissatisfactions. She was still without children. Colonel Preston had once been brazen enough to touch on her sterile curse. He was anxious over a sick child. "And now, Madame," he admonished Mary Chesnut, "go home and thank God on your knees that you have no children to break your heart. Mrs. Preston and I spent the first ten years of our married life in mortal agony over ill and dying children."

"I won't do anything of the kind," Mary Chesnut replied. "Those lovely girls I see around you now—they make your happiness. They are something to thank God for—far more than anything *I have not.*"

Whatever the interior sources of her sadness, its outward form was an invalidism which, though it might at first have been an affectation, was steadily becoming habitual. It was a remarkable event if Mary Chesnut were called upon to undertake any purely mechanical labor. The work of cleaning, washing, sewing, and cooking was performed by others. She did not dress herself; her slave Molly undertook that task. Such was the "automatic noiseless perfection" of the house servants that she rarely had occasion even to ask for anything; the carefully trained domestics anticipated her desires. The servants "think for you," she wrote, "they know your ways and your wants. . . . Eben the butler at Mulberry would be miserable and feel himself a ridiculous failure, were I ever forced to ask him for anything."

Invalidism offered an escape from every form of laborious activity, but its chief attraction lay, not in its invitation to truancy, but in the social and theatrical possibilities it created. Her ongoing sickness gave Mary Chesnut an excuse to stay in the Prestons' house, where in addition to being treated with much tenderness and solicitude she was the central figure in the melodrama of the sickroom. The nineteenth-century sickroom was a shrine. Its rituals were shot through with hysterical romance. Buck's sister, Mary Preston, was appointed to hold vigil over the sickbed. Once, when Mary Chesnut experienced one of her "nervous fainting fits," the poor girl went flying downstairs to find her mother.

"Come, come," she exclaimed on finding her mother in the garden. "Mrs. Chesnut is dying, if not dead."

"Who is with her?" Caroline Preston asked.

"Nobody."

"Did you leave her alone?" Mrs. Preston cried as she raced to the sickroom.

"Surely, mama," replied the girl, "you would not have me stay there to see her die. I could not—she looked too awful."

If Mary Chesnut's invalidism was in part spectacular and histrionic, it was also faintly religious: a form of Victorian devotion, the Protestant equivalent of secluding one's self in a convent. Her body atrophied, together with the active elements of her mind, yet in taking the veil of the sickroom her contemplative and reflective faculties grew stronger. In her sequestered hours books—she read Dickens, Trollope, Disraeli, and Balzac—ministered to her as effectually as more conventional medicines. But invalidism rapidly breaks down the moral fiber, and in her despondency Mary Chesnut turned to stimulants stronger than literature. She acquired the habit of soothing her "wildly excited nerves" with opium, and during one low period she credited "D.T.'s opium" with keeping her alive.

Yet she understood her predicament perfectly. The Fire Eaters' belief that slavery left the highest spirits free to perfect their souls was a fairy tale. On the contrary, Mary Chesnut retorted, slave-bought freedom destroyed the will. The seventeenth-century men who settled the tidewater were, in the earliest phases of their history, figures of *virtù* and immense constructive power—else, she said, "they would not have been here." But "two or three generations of gentlemen planters— how changed the blood became! Of late all the active-minded men who spring to the front in our government were the immediate descendants of Scotch, or Scotch-Irish." The tidewater magnates no longer ruled the South as absolutely as they once had, nor had they, in surrendering the higher realms of public life to leaders with a more democratic style, succeeded in creating a flourishing literary or artistic culture. Her own experience was, she knew, a feminine variation on the historic pattern. The most promising males of her caste became, with few exceptions, triflers or dilettantes. The most intelligent females became invalids.

War accelerated the processes of collapse. Mulberry, the bedrock of the Chesnut fortune, was coming apart. The family fortune was daily dwindling. The old Colonel had lost half a million in railroad bonds, bank stock, and notes of hand. His "old man's croak" resounded through the rooms. "We can't fight all the world—two and two only make four—it can't make a thousand—numbers will tell. . . ." "Bad times, worse coming."

Washington, Saint Petersburg, and Berlin,
October–November 1862

LINCOLN READ WITH DISMAY the accounts of Mr. Gladstone's speech at Newcastle. The Emancipation Proclamation had been issued; Lee had been beaten at Antietam. Yet Queen Victoria's Chancellor of the Exchequer insisted that the President's revolution was a failure. The people of the Northern states, Mr. Gladstone asserted in the Town Hall at Newcastle, had "not yet drunk of the cup—they are still trying to hold it far from their lips—which all the rest of the world see they nevertheless must drink of." For there was no doubt in Mr. Gladstone's mind "that Jefferson Davis and other leaders of the South have made an army; they are making, it appears, a navy; and they have made what is more than either, *they have made a nation. . . .*"

The Chancellor's words provoked gasps in the Town Hall, followed by loud applause.

The President's trump card, it appeared, had failed to force the English Cabinet to fold its hand. Certainly the Emancipation Proclamation had not deterred Mr. Gladstone; and it was everywhere assumed that the Chancellor's panegyric upon the statesmanship of Jefferson Davis was a prelude to British recognition of the South. Nor had the Emancipation Proclamation solved the problem of General McClellan. The commander of the Army of the Potomac remained at Antietam, unwilling, or so it appeared, to fight for a government intent on freeing the slaves.

Lincoln urged McClellan to pursue more vigorously the weary army of Lee; but the General contrived new excuses for delay. His horses, he said, were "broken down from fatigue and want of flesh." "Will you pardon me for asking," Lincoln replied, "what the horses of your army have done since the battle of Antietam that fatigue anything?"

The Army of the Potomac continued to be implicated in a rumor of treachery and disaffection. It was whispered that the seditious soldiers had not given up the idea of marching on Washington. McClellan himself bitterly resented Lincoln's criticism of his generalship. It is true that he spoke, at times, of the need to acquiesce in the supremacy of the civil authorities, however stupid and perverse they might be. "The good of the country requires me to submit to all this from men whom I know to be my inferior!" he told his wife. "There never was a truer epithet applied to a certain individual than that of the 'Gorilla.'" But at other times McClellan was impatient of the yoke of the civilians. "The only safety for the country & for me," he said, "is to get rid of the lot of them."

Lincoln went to ascertain for himself the fidelity of the army. He boarded an armed train in Washington, and on a hot day in October he reached McClellan's camp at Antietam Creek. He inspected the battle-field, and afterwards he mounted a coal-black horse, specially selected, it was said, on account of its fiery nature by McClellan's staff, who sought to test the skill of the commander-in-chief in the manage of a spirited steed. Lincoln seized the bridle and, to the chagrin of the General's suite, rode off without difficulty. Drums sounded; guns thundered; battle-standards dipped. To the strains of "Hail to the Chief," the President rode through the lines to take the salute of the troops. Lincoln slept under canvas; and the next morning, waking before dawn, he sought his friend Ozias Hatch, an Illinois politician who had traveled with him to Antietam. "Come, Hatch," the President said, "I want you to walk with me." They left the sleeping camp and, after climbing one of the nearby hills, watched the sun rise over a panoply of tents and standards. The President waved his hat towards the scene and turned to his friend. "Hatch—Hatch," he asked, "what is all this?"

"Why, Mr. Lincoln," Hatch replied, "this is the Army of the Potomac."

"No, Hatch, no," Lincoln said. "This is General McClellan's body-guard."

The President returned to Washington satisfied that the army, though it might be indolent, was sufficiently submissive to his authority. The revolution had entered a new phase, and Lincoln, in spite of disap-pointments, displayed a new mastery of men and events. He saw, more clearly than ever, the global character of the struggle in which he was engaged, and using his gift of expression he tried to make his country-men understand the historical significance of the revolution they were making. Lord Palmerston, Earl Russell, and Mr. Gladstone sought through their foreign policy to defend England's interests in the world; but their conception of those interests was, Lincoln believed, too nar-row. The decisive question of the decade, the President said, was whether free constitutions could survive and prosper in the world, or whether they possessed an "inherent, and fatal weakness" that doomed them to a premature degeneration. It was a question in which England had as deep an interest as America. In his annual message to Congress Lincoln alluded to the world crisis:

We shall nobly save, or meanly lose, the last best, hope of earth.

If freedom failed in America, where else was it likely to prosper? True, it might still flourish in England; but even in England it would be vul-nerable should the island Kingdom find itself alone in a world of aggressive despotisms, armed with all the new powers of steam and coal and steel.

Lincoln read the newspapers. In the autumn of 1862 the fate of liberty hung in the balance in three great nations. It hung in the balance in Russia, where an absolute ruler sought to promote liberal reform but was unable to overcome the inertia of despotism. It hung in the balance in Germany, where a minister of the Prussian Crown applied his dark genius to the destruction of the last feeble props of the *Rechtsstaat* (a state under the rule of law). And it hung in the balance in America, where Lincoln himself struggled to preserve the free institutions of his country from the evils of domestic rebellion and the machinations of Old World powers, as well as from the temptation to meet these difficulties in a manner fatal to the very conception of liberty he sought to vindicate.

Lincoln, Bismarck, and Alexander each grasped the significance of the moment. Bismarck, the scion of knights, sought to prevent the progress of liberty by breaking the Prussian Parliament. So little did one know of the world, the new Minister-President wrote to his wife, that one was forever "going out into the dark like a child." Not even Bismarck, however, could foresee the extent of the darkness into which his country was eventually to be plunged by the decisions he made in the autumn of 1862. Alexander, the descendant of kings, sensed that freedom is the only sure foundation of greatness; but he found the principle easier to acknowledge than to implement, and he had no notion of how to communicate the insight to his subjects. Alone of the three statesmen, Lincoln, the child of common people, perceived the promise of the free state, and embodied the perception in his statecraft. But the cost of his revolution was fearful.

There was, however, one bright moment as the leaves fell from the trees that autumn. Lincoln concluded that he was finally strong enough to dispense with the services of General McClellan. A sealed envelope was brought by special train to the General's headquarters. McClellan opened the envelope and found an order relieving him of command and directing him to return to his house in Trenton, New Jersey.

Part Two

THE REVOLUTIONS
AT THEIR HEIGHT

Chapter 15

"WHOEVER HAS THE POWER"

Berlin, Gastein, and Baden, December 1862–November 1863

A PLAN LIKE BISMARCK'S, with inspirations so primitive—blood and iron and the divine right of kings—ought on every conventional estimate to have failed outright, and perished a mere archaism in an age of progress, science, and democracy. But in contrast to an older type of reactionary, in contrast to Manteuffel and Metternich, Bismarck was prepared to defend his philosophy with the most up-to-date methods. Romantic nationalism, manhood suffrage, jingo journalism—all that progress, science, and democracy could supply—he stood ready to place in the service of his revolution.

His plan was still, he believed, a perfectly good one. Only there was no use, he now saw, in *talking* about it; he must act. In December 1862, two months after assuming office, he summoned the Austrian Ambassador, Count Károlyi, to the Wilhelmstrasse. Bismarck was blunt. He told Károlyi that Austria must relinquish her claims to primacy in Germany or face war. The Habsburgs must shift their center of gravity eastward, to Hungary. If they failed to do this there would be a catastrophe.

Unfortunately for Bismarck, the chosen scapegoat was not at all co-operative. For all their ineptitude, the Habsburgs could be cunning when they felt themselves threatened. Vienna replied to Bismarck's ultimatum not by preparing for war, but by proposing to convene, at Frankfurt, a Congress of Princes to explore changes to the Bundestag, the assembly of the German Confederation (Prince Metternich's Bund).

It was a clever bluff. Bismarck did not doubt that the changes Austria sought in the Bundestag would be disadvantageous to Prussia, yet he saw at once that, by styling the affair a Congress of Princes, Vienna had fingered his own weak spot. His royal master, King Wilhelm, was a profound legitimist; the old King was bound by intimate ties to each of the princely houses of Germany, and he felt the deepest reverence for the traditions and prerogatives, for the very pedigrees and quarterings, of the venerable dynasties. The Congress of Princes would appeal to all his notions of "princely solidarity."

Wilhelm was at Gastein, in the Austrian Alps, when he learned of the Austrian proposals. Bismarck, who was with him, was wrought to a pitch of nervous apprehension over the trick the Viennese had played him. "I should like to have nothing to do," he wrote to his wife, "other than to walk on the heights, and to recline on the sunny banks, to smoke and see the snow-peaks." But such an idyll was out of the question. Flags were put out; Franz Josef, the Austrian Kaiser, was coming to make his case in person.

For once, Bismarck's jealous vigilance failed. He was bird-watching when the decisive interview took place. Franz Josef won the King over. Wilhelm wanted to go to Frankfurt. He hoped, he told Bismarck, "to turn the antagonism of Austria and Prussia into a mutual struggle against the Revolution and constitutionalism."

Bismarck at once set about trying to change the King's mind. Wilhelm, he said, must at all costs be kept "out of Frankfurt." He followed his royal master from Gastein to Wildbad, and from Wildbad to Baden. "As a result of the Frankfurt foolishness," he told his wife, "I cannot leave the King." Together the two men rode through the Black Forest in an open carriage. They avoided the German language, speaking in French so as not to be understood by the coachmen on the box. By the time they reached Baden, Bismarck believed that he had prevailed. But he found, upon arriving at the ducal palace, a new danger. Lurking in the galleries was the King of Saxony, who carried with him a message from the princes gathered at Frankfurt. They implored their brother Wilhelm to join them.

In an instant all the work of the carriage ride was undone. "Thirty reigning princes and a King as a courier!" Wilhelm exclaimed. How could he refuse such an invitation?

The two men argued until midnight when the King, "worn out," Bismarck said, "by the nervous tension of the situation," gave way. The old soldier, tears streaming down his face, agreed to be guided by his Minister's advice. Bismarck, as full of emotion, retired to his room, and smashed a vase.

In the absence of the King of Prussia, the Congress of Princes came to nothing. Yet Bismarck was far from satisfied. The free-state men continued to oppose his rule, and the weakness of his grasp on power embittered even the beauty of Baden. "I went for a walk, at midnight, in the moonlight," he wrote to his wife, "but could not get business out of my head." He returned to Berlin, where the constitutional crisis was discussed in two separate Cabinet meetings on the same day. "I had no heart" for it, he said; for he had no solution to the puzzle.

What was he to do? The free-state men were every day becoming more impatient with his rule. He imposed a censorship on the press; but this, he knew, was a shopworn tactic, and only strengthened the opposition. He must try something else. He had been intrigued by the way in which Europe's craftiest politicians used (or proposed to use) the power of the lower orders against the liberal middle—against the bourgeois and professional classes. In France, Napoleon III organized mass plebiscites to ratify his power. In England, Benjamin Disraeli envisioned a union between the common people and the aristocracy, an alliance which Winston Churchill's father, Lord Randolph Churchill, was later to christen "Tory Democracy." Others called it "neofeudal paternalism" or "English Tory Socialism."

It was an ingenious strategy. Use democratic paternalism to subvert the institutions of freedom. Today, when democracy and liberty are practically synonymous, such a policy seems paradoxical. But it did not seem so in the nineteenth century. In England and the United States, the rule of law, bills of rights, independent judiciaries, and legislative control of the purse and the army developed *before* the advent of universal suffrage. When, during the nineteenth century, democracy grew up in England and America, the institutions of the free state were relatively stable; the broader franchise did not destroy free constitutions, it made them stronger. But in countries without such stable constitutions, unscrupulous leaders used democratic instruments—plebiscites and manhood suffrage—to subvert the fledgling institutions of freedom.

Bismarck followed this lead. He employed a brutal rhetoric in the hope of winning over ordinary Germans. The *"untern Klassen"* (lower orders) were, he believed, attracted to strength; they cared little for the constitutional niceties which appealed to the educated classes. A free constitution was an idea "the practical benefits of which," Bismarck said, were "but little understood by the masses." "In the moment of decision," he believed, "the masses will stand by the monarchy," however despotic the monarch himself might be. With great psychological acuteness, Bismarck perceived how slender is the grip of free institutions on most people's minds. Across the ocean, Lincoln reached a similar conclusion; but he put the insight to a different use.

"If a compromise cannot be arrived at and a conflict arises," Bismarck said of the constitutional crisis in Prussia, "then the conflict becomes a question of power. Whoever has the power, then acts according to his opinion." Might makes right. Iron, not law, is the ultimate motive force.

Yet words, however potent, are not enough. The man of iron must act. Should he follow the example of Napoleon III and use manhood suffrage to break the free-state opposition? Bismarck discussed the possibility with Ferdinand Lasalle, who in the spring of 1863 founded the General Union of German Workers. Lasalle, the son of a silk merchant in Breslau, was a singular character, a labor leader who was at ease in the *beau monde,* a socialist orator who made love to aristocratic women, a charlatan whose egotism, inflamed by syphilis, bore at times a faint resemblance to genius. Not yet forty, with aquiline features and a fine high brow, Lasalle regarded himself as a revolutionary Cardinal Richelieu. In a nervous falsetto he unburdened himself of a load of manic cleverness.

Puffing on an expensive cigar, Lasalle explained his terms to Bismarck. "Give me universal suffrage," he told the Minister-President, "and I will give you a million votes."

Bismarck was intrigued. He had no sympathy for Lasalle's socialism, which he regarded as a delusion; but he saw in the labor leader's ideas about enfranchising the masses and regulating their lives on the paternal principle a way to squeeze the liberal middle—as well as to render the coercive authority of his government more secure.

There was, however, a problem. He knew King Wilhelm would never consent to so daring a means of outflanking the free-state men. Paternalism must wait. Yet by what other method could he maintain his grip on power? Such was Bismarck's quandary when, in November 1863, the fates came to his aid. In that month, in the castle at Glüksburg in Schleswig-Holstein, the old King of Denmark, Frederick VII, died. A new King, Christian IX, was proclaimed, and Germany prepared for war.

Virginia and Pennsylvania, April–June 1863

ROBERT E. LEE, asleep in his field headquarters, was awakened by the sound of gunfire. He did not, however, get up to investigate. He needed rest; he had only recently recovered from a severe throat infection. But on this night rest eluded him. A short time later he was again roused. Someone was calling his name. He opened his eyes and saw the face of Captain James Smith, a young officer on Stonewall Jackson's staff.

"Well," Lee said, "I thought I heard firing and was beginning to think it was time some of you young fellows were coming to tell me what it was all about."

Federal troops, Smith informed Lee, were crossing the Rappahannock in force. It appeared that the new commander of the Army of the Potomac, General Joseph "Fighting Joe" Hooker, intended to make good the boast he had uttered on taking up his command. It was not, Hooker said, a question of whether he would take Richmond, but when.*

Lee rose from his bed, and prepared to meet an army that was in all likelihood twice the size of his own. Two days later, as the sun sank behind the Blue Ridge, he was still pondering the problem. In a bivouac in a pinewoods south of Chancellorsville, he and Stonewall Jackson sat together on a log. "How," Lee asked, "can we get at these people?" Suddenly, out of the darkness, Jeb Stuart appeared. Hooker's right flank, the cavalry master reported, was exposed—it was "in the air."

In a short time Lee had his plan. Once again he decided to divide his forces in the face of superior numbers. He ordered Jackson and his II Corps to surprise the Union right.

Jackson rose and saluted. "My troops," he said, "will move at four o'clock." As he said these words, he smiled.

The men of II Corps executed Lee's orders with their customary zeal and ability. They routed Hooker's flank, and afterwards Jackson himself galloped forward into the darkness, determined to press his advantage. His pickets, however, mistook him for a Yankee horseman. Shots were fired, and three bullets shattered his left arm and hand. He was taken to a tent near Wilderness Tavern.

When the smoke cleared, it was evident that the South had won a great victory at Chancellorsville. General Hooker, stunned by the suddenness of the enemy's blows, fell into a bewildered stupor. Opportunities to take the offensive he failed to seize, and like a turtle retreating to its shell, he drew back. In the White House, Lincoln was appalled. Coming into the room with the telegram in his hand, the President was a "picture," the journalist Noah Brooks said, "of despair." His face was "ashen," and his voice trembled with emotion. "My God! My God!" he said. "What will the country say?"

Lee had triumphed; but in a glorious hour he was far from feeling elation. When he learned, from Captain R. E. Wilbourne, Jackson's signal officer, of the misfortune which had befallen his lieutenant, his brow darkened.

"Ah, Captain," Lee said, "any victory is dearly bought which deprives us of the services of General Jackson, even for a short time!"

Jackson was taken, by Lee's order, to a cottage at Guiney Station, where he was less vulnerable to the sallies of the enemy's cavalry. His shattered arm was amputated, and hopes were at first entertained for a

---

* Confronted with Hooker's vaunts, Lincoln told the story of the hen, which, he said, "is the wisest of all the animal creation, because she never cackles until the egg is laid."

recovery. But Jackson's condition deteriorated, and he soon became delirious. "Let us pass over the river," he said, "and rest under the shade of the trees." A short time later he was dead. He was thirty-nine years old.

"Such an executive officer," Lee said, "the sun never shone on. I have but to show him my design, and I know that if it can be done, it will be done. No need for me to send or watch him. Straight as the needle to the pole he advanced to the execution of my purpose." Other commanders might possess Jackson's constancy and diligence, but they lacked the enterprising spirit which attempts more than it can do, and aspires to do more than it can attempt. None of Lee's remaining corps commanders possessed the warlike genius of Jackson. Ambrose Powell Hill wanted experience. James "Pete" Longstreet wanted confidence in Lee's judgment. Robert Stoddert Ewell wanted confidence in himself.

The Army of Northern Virginia "would be invincible if it could be properly organized and officered," Lee told John Bell Hood, the young officer who had led the assault of the 4th Texas at Gaines's Mill. "There never were such men in an army before. They will go anywhere and do anything if properly led. But there is the difficulty—proper commanders—where can they be obtained?" Time and circumstance prevented the recruitment of a new officer corps. With each passing day the North, with its immense population and enormous industrial capacity, grew stronger. With each day the South, with its rudimentary manufactures and blockaded harbors, grew weaker. Lee must work with such materials as were to hand, and he must work fast.

At the end of June he marched north towards Pennsylvania in the hope of retrieving, through an act of desperate gallantry, the fortunes of the South. By taking the war to the North, Lee hoped to break the Union's will to fight. Not less important, he wanted to feed his hungry soldiers, who were growing gaunt in war-ravaged Virginia. After they crossed the border, Confederate troops seized hogs and horses, cattle and clothes. As well as shoes. General James Johnson Pettigrew's brigade set out in search of a rich supply of footgear which, it was rumored, could be found in a quiet crossroads town not far from the Mason-Dixon line. The name of the town was Gettysburg.

Paris and Mexico, March–June 1863

THE WOMAN WHO took off her clothes was handsome rather than beautiful. Although the painting for which she was to pose depicted a picnic in a park, the woman undressed indoors, in the studio; the artist to whom she was to sit would not undertake his first experiments in *pleinairisme* until the end of the decade. When Victorine Meurent stood completely naked, it was evident that her body was well formed; her legs in particular were finely shaped. She sat down and, resting her right arm on her knee, clutched her chin thoughtfully.

According to one tradition, preserved by the novelist Émile Zola, Mademoiselle Meurent had at first been unwilling to pose for Edouard Manet. The artist was at work on *Le Déjeuner sur l'herbe,** a painting which depicts, in a manner reminiscent of Goya and Velásquez, two men and two women enjoying a picnic lunch. The men are clothed, after the fashion of Parisian Bohemians. In the background, one of the women, a brunette, stoops to pick flowers; she is loosely draped in a chemise. The other woman, who sits beside the two men amid various articles of discarded clothing, is nude.

In Zola's fictional retelling, the artist was in despair as the picture progressed. Only a certain model would do for the nude study, and she hesitated to strip in a studio and expose herself to the scrutiny of a painter. One day, however, she acceded to the prayer in the artist's eyes. "Without any hurry," Zola wrote in his fictional re-creation of the episode, "she took off her hat and coat, as usual. Then she simply went on with the same tranquil movements: unfastened her bodice, dropped her petticoats, stepped out of her corset, unbuttoned the chemise that now slipped down over her hips. She had not spoken a word; she seemed to be somewhere else, as on those evenings when, lost in a dream, she would undress automatically, without paying any attention to what she was doing. . . . Still without speaking, now entirely naked, she lay down on the divan and took the pose, one arm beneath her head, her eyes closed."

Zola's account is fanciful. Victorine Meurent, nineteen years old in 1863, was a professional artist's model, accustomed to the immodesty of the studio. For all the primness of the Victorian age, the nude flourished as a form of art. Nevertheless, Manet's depiction of his naked model in *Le Déjeuner sur l'herbe* caused a sensation in the spring of 1863. The painting was immediately adjudged scandalous. The jurors of the Salon, the annual exhibition of contemporary art in Paris, refused to allow the work to be exhibited.

It was not the nudity alone of *Le Déjeuner sur l'herbe* that shocked. The Salon jurors had that very year accepted a far more provocatively posed nude by the painter Alexandre Cabanel. Cabanel's painting depicted a full-figured blonde in a posture of voluptuous abandon. Cabanel, however, prudently gave his painting the title *The Birth of Venus*. He threw over its eroticism the veil of the antique. Manet's nude, by contrast, was

---

* The painting was at that time called *Le Bain*.

not a mythical goddess but a contemporary Frenchwoman. "She is the sort of girl you might have met any day of the week hurrying up la rue Blanche," the critic Clive Bell said, "and she has unmistakably been taken out for a picnic by two young gentlemen whom you might have met any day in the quartier des Batignolles."

In the Second Empire such controversies eventually reached the throne. On a spring morning in 1863 the French Emperor, Napoleon III, went to the Palais de l'Industrie to see the painting with his own eyes. The Emperor possessed an aesthetic sense, or at any rate an appreciation of feminine form. His exertions as a lover no less than as a politician had been strenuous. But Louis-Napoleon, who now suffered acutely from a urinary complaint, was unequal to the rigors of the seraglio. The flesh was a burden to him, and in something like terror he complained to his cousin, Princess Mathilde, that he found himself pursued by lascivious maenads in the galleries of the Tuileries.

He walked the graveled paths and cast-iron mezzanines of the Palais de l'Industrie inspecting works of art. He came to Manet's painting. He studied it. The picture, he said, offended his "*pudeur,*" his modesty. The judgment might have been nothing more than the expression of a conventional taste. It might, again, have been ironical—the phlegmatic wit of an old roué. Most likely it betrayed fatigue; the Emperor was too weary to attempt a more penetrating bon mot. However, he wished to be just. He commanded that those artists who, like Manet, had been refused permission to exhibit their works in the Salon should be permitted to display their rejected art elsewhere in the building.

The Salon des Refusés was born. Yet the Emperor could not resist a gesture that revealed where his personal sympathies lay. He purchased Monsieur Cabanel's *Birth of Venus* for 15,000 francs.

Louis-Napoleon's acts were characteristic of the equivocal policy of his régime. The Second Empire of the Bonapartes was founded on a contradiction. It was an assertion of Napoleonic will, the majesty of a dynasty. Yet it was also grounded in the suffrages of the people, and consecrated to the liberation of nations. The Emperor himself was simultaneously a dictator and an emancipator. The confusion was evident in his title. He styled himself Emperor "*par la grâce de Dieu et la volonté nationale*"—by the grace of God and the national will. Despotic though his government was in form, its beau ideal was freedom. He had, ever since his accession, championed the right of nations to determine their destinies for themselves. In 1859 he passed the Alps, defeated the Austrians at Magenta and Solferino, and banished the black-and-yellow banners of the Habsburgs from Lombardy. A short time later Italy was free. A Parliament met at Turin, and a constitutional monarch, Victor

Emmanuel, took his seat on the throne of a new nation. When, in 1863, Polish patriots rose up against their Russian masters, Louis-Napoleon championed their cause. But his own subjects grumbled. The Italians were free, and if the Emperor had his way the Poles would be too. Yet the French were not.

Louis-Napoleon attempted to appease the popular clamors by granting his people rudimentary rights. But the taste of freedom only whetted the appetites of his subjects, and by degrees the spirit of opposition revived. The imperial régime became unpopular and, what was more distressing, it became unfashionable. Englishmen and Americans expect their governments to be unfashionable. It is otherwise in France, where by a long tradition the government that governs best governs glamorously. The French state exists to make manifest the formal and exquisite qualities of the French civilization. The court of Louis XIV embodied the inspirations of the *Grand Siècle;* the Versailles of the Sun King was cast in the same classic mold as the art of Poussin and Racine. A dozen decades later the court of Napoleon the Great exhibited all the splendors of a civilization passing from its classic to its romantic phase. But what *éclat* the great Napoleon's nephew still possessed was remote from the temper of his time. Mademoiselle Meurent, sitting naked on the canvas of Manet's *Déjeuner sur l'herbe,* made a mockery of the Emperor's recycled Golden Eagles, the superstitious talismans of the Bonapartes.

Constrained in his quest for mastery in Europe, Louis-Napoleon turned his eyes toward the Americas. When the Mexican President, Benito Juárez, suspended payment on foreign debts, the French Emperor affected outrage, and under the pretense of protecting creditors he sent a French army to Vera Cruz. The French force, penetrating into the interior of the country, sought to subdue Mexico City, but on May 5, 1862, it was repulsed by Mexican troops before the walls of Puebla. Louis-Napoleon dispatched fresh troops and a new commander to the scene. In July 1862, General François-Achille Bazaine was made commander of the 1st Division of Infantry, *Corps expéditionnaire du Mexique,* and the following month he sailed from the French naval base at Toulon. Bazaine resembled a prosperous shopkeeper more than he did a future marshal of France; only his eyes, which were cunning and narrow, hinted at the intelligence which lay concealed behind the façade of complacency, and offered a clue to the enigmatic character of one who would play a memorable, though not an enviable, part in the crisis in which the decade culminated.

Louis-Napoleon's mood brightened when he learned that Bazaine had avenged the French arms and taken Puebla. A short time later the Emperor rejoiced in the tidings that the commander had entered

Mexico City unopposed. Six decades after his uncle sold Louisiana to President Jefferson, Louis-Napoleon had established a new French imperium in the Americas. But it was a precarious one. Much hinged on the fate of Lincoln's revolution. Four decades before Lincoln came to power, President Monroe, on the advice of his Secretary of State, John Quincy Adams, had acted on one of Alexander Hamilton's old counsels: he had warned the European powers against interfering in the affairs of "any portion" of the New World. Should the Confederacy fall, Washington would lose little time in working to expel the French from Mexico. Louis-Napoleon affected amity towards the government of Lincoln, but he quietly did what he could to further the cause of the Confederacy.

On June 18, the Emperor received the Confederate emissary John Slidell in the Tuileries. Louis-Napoleon was gracious to the Louisianan. He expatiated on the bravery of the Southern troops, the skill of the Southern generals, and the devotion of the Southern people. He expressed his "great regret at the death of Stonewall Jackson," whom he "considered as one of the most remarkable men of the age." He was, he said, "more fully convinced than ever of the propriety of the general recognition by European powers of the Confederate States." But he regretted to say that the success of his Mexican expedition would be jeopardized by a rupture with President Lincoln. Of course, Louis-Napoleon said, it would be something else altogether were the British to join him in recognizing the South, for in the event such a step led to war with the United States, he would have the Royal Navy on his side. Might the British be persuaded to intervene? He was, he said, prepared to go to Lord Palmerston with "a direct proposition to England for joint recognition" of the Confederacy. The Emperor was as good as his word; and at his direction instructions were telegraphed to Baron Gros, the French Ambassador in London, desiring him to "inform Lord Palmerston that should Great Britain be willing to recognize the South the Emperor would be ready to follow her in that way."

Slidell emerged from the Tuileries in a state of elation. The Cause of the South had, an hour before, seemed desperate. But if Louis-Napoleon could persuade Palmerston to recognize the South, a delicious prospect would burst upon the view. Recognition would lead to intervention, and intervention would put a stop to Lincoln's revolution. The Confederacy would be saved.

Chapter 16

"THIS HORRIBLE MASSACRE
OF MEN"

Siberia, January 1863–August 1864

PRINCE KROPOTKIN went to Siberia full of hope. He was posted to Irkutsk, where he was made aide-de-camp to General Kukel, a young officer zealous for reform. Kropotkin threw himself into the work of remaking Siberia. One day Kukel said to him, "It is a great epoch we live in; work, my dear friend." Kropotkin redoubled his efforts.

But the Prince soon discovered how formidable were the obstacles to reform. Even a strong mind might lose its tone in the depths of a Siberian winter. Gaming, lewdness, and vodka broke down the forms of civility. Kropotkin learned of one police official who during the course of a Siberian magistracy progressed from the arts of peculation to those of cruelty: he had women flogged in contravention to the law. Kropotkin's indignation was roused, but he found it by no means easy to prove the man's crimes. The poorer people upon whom he preyed hesitated to give evidence against a man who might exact from them a fearful retribution. Nevertheless Kropotkin persevered, and he succeeded in gaining, first the trust, and afterwards the testimony of the victims. The official was duly cashiered—only to be rewarded, a short time later, with a more lucrative post in Kamchatka. He had, it transpired, influential connections in Saint Petersburg. "And thus it went on in all directions," Kropotkin wrote, "beginning with the Winter Palace at Saint Petersburg, and ending with Usuri and Kamchatka."

The Prince, intent on doing good, sailed down the Amur, a river in whose waters two civilizations touched. To the north lay the frigid tundra of Siberia. To the south lay the dusty plateaus of China. Count Muraviev had, not long before, claimed the Amur for Russia, and along its banks he had planted a string of settlements, populated with men and women released from the Tsarist labor camps. Kropotkin kept his wits about him as he navigated the river and succeeded in averting a famine in the region. He afterwards made a thorough study of the problem and wrote a lengthy report. His recommendations were adopted without hesitation by the authorities, and he rejoiced in having contributed to the melioration of conditions in Siberia. But his elation soon faded. The task of implementing the proposed reforms was confided to a notorious drunkard, and nothing was done.

After a few months in Siberia, Kropotkin was more than ever convinced of the futility of the Tsar's program of reform. Alexander described his work as a revolution "from above." But a liberal revolution, Kropotkin concluded, cannot be directed autocratically. "I soon realized," he wrote, "the absolute impossibility of doing anything really useful for the mass of the people by means of administrative machinery." Elaborate reforms set forth in the decrees of a remote government were, he believed, doomed to failure. Administrators in the bureaus of Saint Petersburg could not possibly know as much about the conditions that prevailed in the distant provinces of the Empire as the inhabitants of those provinces themselves, who had a most intimate knowledge of their own problems. At the same time, Kropotkin came to see how much people could do for themselves, if only they possessed sufficient liberty of action; and he marveled at "the complex forms of social organization" which ordinary men and women had evolved on their own, "far away from the influence of any civilization."

Such discoveries might have led the Prince to advocate a more thoroughly liberating revolution than the one Tsar Alexander was prepared to make; but they did not. On the contrary, he drew farther away from the ideal of the free state. The snares of power are subtle; and Kropotkin, like the rest of his class, had been bred to authority. His love of dominion assumed that ostensibly altruistic form which has not seldom proved to be the most cruel and tyrannical. He wanted passionately to raise up the masses; he longed for a new form of *noblesse oblige*. It seems never to have occurred to him that his soul might be laying a trap for itself. The man who desires most fervently to emancipate the people—is it not he who often enslaves them most completely?

Pennsylvania, June–July 1863

IF LEE AND JACKSON had not existed, the South should have had to invent them. No figure in the decade embodied more fully the romance of aristocratic paternalism than Lee, the graceful Cavalier; and none incarnated the fierce spirit of militant nationalism more completely than Jackson, the brilliant and fanatical soldier.

But Jackson was in his grave when, on June 29, Lee woke, in Pennsylvania, to a rain-soaked morning. His mood was as gloomy as the weather. He was uncharacteristically agitated and restless. A spy had, a short time before, brought news that the Army of the Potomac, now commanded by General George Gordon Meade (Hooker's replacement), had crossed the Potomac and was marching towards Pennsylvania. A great battle, Lee knew, would soon be fought. If "God grants us the victory," he said, "the war will be over and we shall achieve the recognition of our independence."

The next day Lee learned that General Pettigrew had encountered, at Gettysburg, a strong body of Union cavalry. By the time Lee himself reached the outskirts of the town, on the afternoon of July 1, thousands of troops were hotly engaged. Lee took up his field glasses, and saw before him a long ridge, one that terminated, in its northern extremity, in a commanding eminence. The names of the heights were not auspicious. The ridge was Cemetery Ridge; the hill was Cemetery Hill.

A short time before, Lee would have turned, at such a moment, to Stonewall Jackson. But R. S. Ewell now commanded Jackson's II Corps. Lee gave Ewell discretionary orders to "push those people" off Cemetery Hill. Ewell, however, failed to do so. Night fell on an already bloody field. The next day opened with a fierce Confederate cannonade. Amid the hiss and roar of shells the 26th North Carolina Regimental Band played polkas and waltzes. The veterans of "Pete" Longstreet's I Corps were to deliver the principal blow; but Longstreet, who had no faith in Lee's plan, was dilatory.

Savage fighting now took place in the shadow of Cemetery Ridge, in Devil's Den and the Peach Orchard; and Longstreet's men moved to take the position of mastery in that part of the battlefield, Little Round Top, which lay at the southern end of Cemetery Ridge. A quick-witted Union officer perceived the importance of the hill and interposed. Colonel Strong Vincent, a twenty-six-year-old lawyer from Erie, Pennsylvania, who commanded a brigade in the Army of the Potomac's V Corps, raised his colors on Little Round Top. "Don't give an inch!" he cried as Confederate troops commanded by John Bell Hood went forward. A short time later Vincent was struck by a bullet and mortally wounded. Nevertheless, his 3rd Brigade saved Little Round Top for the United States.

On the third day, more than 12,000 Confederate troops made a final attempt to break the Union line and with it the Union itself. Thirty-eight-year-old General George Pickett sallied forth on a black charger. He was descended from an old Virginia family, and had been graduated from

West Point, where he was the "goat"—the lowest-ranked cadet—of his class. (His classmate George McClellan ranked second.) Pickett's long hair flowed in ringlets almost to his shoulders, like that of the seventeenth-century Cavaliers whom Van Dyke painted. "Up, men," he cried, "and to your posts! Don't forget today that you are from old Virginia!"

But Pickett's charge failed. Lee, astride Traveller, found Pickett in the midst of the carnage.

"General Pickett," he said, "place your division in the rear of this hill, and be ready to repel the advance of the enemy should they follow up their advantage."

"General Lee," Pickett replied, "I have no division now."

Lee seldom spoke of his invasion of the North in the months and years that followed. But he once speculated on the effect which Jackson's death had on the outcome. "If I had had Stonewall Jackson with me," he said, "so far as man can see, I should have won the battle of Gettysburg."

Washington, July 1863

WALT WHITMAN was walking up Pennsylvania Avenue with bottles of blackberry and cherry syrup in his satchel. He was on his way to the Armory Hospital to bring refreshment to convalescent soldiers. He saw the tidings posted outside a newspaper office:

Glorious Victory for the Union Army!

Whitman was at first jubilant, but afterwards, when he learned the quantity of blood that had been spilled at Gettysburg, he was somber. Seven thousand men perished in the decisive battle of the Civil War. Tens of thousands more were wounded.

"I say stop this war, this horrible massacre of men!" he cried out.

Whitman had come to Washington the previous December in search of his brother, George, of the 51st New York Volunteers, who had been wounded in the bloodbath at Fredericksburg, where the Union commander, Ambrose Burnside, sent thousands of Union troops forward in a futile attempt to take the well-entrenched Confederate positions on Mayre's Heights, to the west of the town. ("If there is a worse place than Hell," Lincoln said after he learned of the débâcle, "I am in it.") Whitman found his brother at Falmouth, alive and only slightly hurt. Afterwards he returned to Washington, where he took a room in a lodging house. He hoped to find work in one of the government departments. But although he had obtained, from Ralph Waldo Emerson, letters of recommendation, no job was forthcoming.

Whitman remained in the capital, earning a living as a copyist, and in his spare time nursing wounded soldiers. By far the worst cases he encountered were those in the Armory Hospital. "I am very familiar with this hospital," Whitman said, "have spent many days & nights in it—have slept in it often—have seen many die here." In the hospital he tended his "boys," as he called them. He was pierced to the marrow by their courage, as well as by the "shining beauty" of their hair, "dampened with clots of blood." "Poor fellows . . . too young they are, lying there with their pale faces and that mute look in their eyes. O how one gets to love them. . . ."

As much as the soldiers, President Lincoln cast a spell over Whitman. The poet liked to study the President's face on summer afternoons, when Lincoln went out on horseback or for a drive in his barouche. "I see the President nearly every day," he said. "We have got so that we exchange bows, and very cordial ones." The President's face, he said, was that of "a hoosier Michael Angelo, so awful ugly it becomes beautiful, with its strange mouth, its deep cut, criss-cross lines, and its doughnut complexion." Whitman told his mother, Louisa Van Velsor Whitman, that he thought Lincoln "a pretty big President—I realize here in Washington that it has been a big thing to have just kept the United States from being thrown down and having its throat cut."

The President himself, riding out in the capital, could not have named the man with the florid face and baggy trousers who gazed at him in the street. Yet he knew him. His law partner, William Herndon, had a few years before purchased *Leaves of Grass*. One day, in the law office in Springfield, Lincoln took up the book. He read the poetry silently at first, afterwards aloud. "Time and again," one of the clerks in the office recalled, "when Lincoln came in, or was leaving, he would pick [the book] up, as if to glance at it for only a moment, but instead he would often settle down in a chair and never stop reading aloud such verses or pages as he fancied."

Whitman was the strangest of the prophets who arose at this time to interpret the meaning of the American free state. He professed himself a seer, a saviour, a demiurge: a revealer of mysteries, a sexual healer, a not minor divinity. He was the oracle who, through his "prophetic screams," would give the United States a "translucent mould" in which it could realize its poetry.

I speak the password primeval . . . I give the sign of democracy. . . .

Whitman's inspiration was not classic; there was in him nothing of the Greek instinct of compression, or tendency to purity of form. But he had done what no one else had yet been able to do.

He had found poetry in the American free state.

Everyone knew that the American free state was destitute of poetry. A "great void exists in the civilization over there," Matthew Arnold said. There was in America, Nathaniel Hawthorne wrote, "no shadow, no antiquity, no mystery, no picturesque and gloomy wrong," only a "commonplace prosperity, in broad and simple daylight." America, Ralph Waldo Emerson said, was "formless," and had "no terrible & no beautiful condensation." A democratic state, Alexis de Tocqueville maintained, was bound to be "less brilliant, less glorious" than an aristocratic one: aristocracy, he concluded, was "much more favorable to poetry."

To the contrary, Whitman argued, America, too, possessed poetry; it lay in its citizens. There was no need to go to the troubadours of feudalism for an inspiration, or to Wagner or Walter Scott. Coercion had no monopoly of beauty. "Nature's cunningest work," Whitman said, was "the human frame, form and face." He was drawn to a variety of performance art, then popular in America, in which women known as "model artists" enacted *tableaux vivants*. Lady Godiva on her horse and Venus in her shell were among the *"poses plastiques"* they adopted. Whitman applied the lesson in his poetry. The experiment which Manet had commenced in oils he undertook in verse. In *Leaves of Grass* he portrayed "superb persons"—omnibus drivers, Brooklyn boys, clam-diggers, Indian girls, mothers of children, emptiers of privies, kept women, slaves, trappers, flatboatmen. *Leaves of Grass* uncovers a democratic dance . . . the butcher-boy sharpening his knife . . . the carpenter dressing his plank . . . the Yankee girl working her sewing machine.

I hear America singing . . .

The bodies and souls of Americans, Whitman said, were "unrhymed poetry," the constituent parts of what was "essentially the greatest poem," the United States themselves. For he had penetrated "the broadcloth and gingham"; had beheld the primal American, "hankering, gross, mystical, nude."

If Whitman was right, Arnold and Tocqueville were wrong. America, the prototype of the free state, *did* possess poetry, culture, a distinction of spirit. Well might Lincoln have found *Leaves of Grass* suggestive; for he too was in quest of an American poetry. More than ever the President sought, in the aftermath of Gettysburg, the clue that might enable him to thread the labyrinth of his revolution.

Chapter 17

DUST UNTO DUST

Schleswig, London, Berlin, and Copenhagen, February–April 1864

A COATING OF SNOW lay on the ground as Prussian troops crossed the border of Schleswig. Not since the conquest of Silesia by Frederick the Great more than a century before had a Prussian army traversed a peaceful frontier intent on spoliation and conquest. In the dim light of a Baltic dawn the Danish dragoons who guarded the bridges of the Eider beheld with dread the approaching eagle standards. They fired a few ineffectual shots at Bismarck's brigades and retired.

The invasion of Schleswig had begun. As the sun rose over the frigid landscape of Jutland, massive columns of Prussian infantry could be seen advancing north from Kiel. The roads were crowded with artillery caissons, baggage wagons, and commissariat carts. In spite of the bitter cold, the Prussian soldiers were in high spirits. "Hurrah for Schleswig-Holstein!" they shouted, and they sang the anthem of Prussia, *"Ich bin eine Preusse"* ("I am a Prussian! See my colors gleaming . . .").

The Prussians advanced on a pretext: to rescue their fellow Germans in Schleswig and Holstein from the yoke of the Danes, who had imposed a new constitution on the duchies. Bismarck had, at last, found a field on which to shed blood and brandish iron. He cared nothing for the justice of the cause; he had himself ridiculed those Germans who cried tyranny whenever a drunken Teuton in Holstein was handled roughly by a Danish magistrate. No matter; the Schleswig-Holstein question had inflamed the patriotism of millions of Germans, and Bismarck had for some time believed that romantic nationalism was the instrument on which the free state would be broken in Germany.

Marching beside the Prussians were Austrian troops whom Franz Josef had summoned from the far-flung provinces of his Empire in the hope of retrieving his dynasty's prestige north of the Danube. Bismarck, having failed to humble Austria, was willing to use her. Recruits from Hungary, Croatia, and the Tyrol chattered and sang in such a diversity of accents and dialects as might have perplexed the most learned philologist. But the warriors of the Habsburgs lacked the fiery enthusiasm of the soldiers who marched beneath the black-and-white standards of the Hohenzollerns. To the higher inspirations of German nationalism the Austrians were insensible. Few of them spoke the language of Goethe. Fewer still professed the faith of Luther. Scarcely any cared whether the German-speaking peoples of Schleswig and Holstein were governed by Teutons or by Scandinavians.

A fortnight before the invasion of Schleswig, Austrian and Prussian diplomats at Copenhagen had delivered to Chamberlain Van Quaade, the Danish Foreign Minister, an ultimatum demanding the repeal of the new constitution which Denmark had imposed on the duchies in an attempt to bind them more closely to Copenhagen. Van Quaade referred the ultimatum to King Christian IX. The King, who had ascended the throne upon the death of Frederick VII in November, was not eager to open his reign with a display of weakness. The reply he instructed his diplomats to make, though it was couched in conciliatory language, stated that it was impossible for him to comply with the German demands. The new constitution would remain in force.

King Christian was a spare man with a sharp face and a slender hope that England would help him to resist the Germans. Princess Alexandra, his second child, had, the previous winter, wed Edward Albert, Prince of Wales, presumptive heir to the throne of England. (Christian's younger daughter, the sixteen-year-old Princess Dagmar, was as yet unmarried; she would however soon be betrothed to the Tsarevitch Nicholas, "Niks," the eldest son of Tsar Alexander.) Christian did not rely solely on the compassion of his daughter's relations: he had another, weightier reason for supposing that England might assist him in opposing the Germans. A dozen years before, a treaty had been solemnly subscribed by the great powers, and by this instrument the Concert of Europe pledged itself to respect the unity and integrity of Denmark.

At Pembroke Lodge, his suburban haven overlooking the Thames, Lord John Russell fretted. He dispatched Lord Wodehouse to Copenhagen in an effort to persuade the Danes to reduce the size of their army and withdraw their controversial constitution.* He also issued a diplomatic note menacing the Germans with the risks they ran in undertaking a campaign of conquest against the Danes.

When, in spite of these efforts, the Germans resorted to arms, Russell pressed his colleagues in the Cabinet to offer naval and military assistance to Denmark. But Lord Palmerston, he found, was cool to the idea of intervention. As he neared the end of his eightieth year, the Prime Minister was at last beginning to show his age. He suffered from gout and sleeplessness. His eyesight was failing. His mind, however, was singularly lucid. As he revolved in his mind the difficulties of intervention in the Danish conflict, Palmerston conceived that they were not such as a prudent minister could disregard. "I doubt," he wrote to Russell from Cambridge House, "whether the Cabinet or the country are yet prepared for active interference." He had recently rejected Gladstone's and Louis-Napoleon's appeals to intervene in Lincoln's revolution, in large part because Tsar Alexander was hostile to the idea. A new crisis had now arisen; but to the Prime Minister, a cautious man masquerading as a buccaneer, the fjords of the Baltic appeared no more inviting than the tidal waters of the Chesapeake. "I believe Palmerston has no wish to go to war at all," Queen Victoria told Russell.

Soon, however, the old man's pugnacious spirit began to revive. Accounts of German armies on the march in Jutland infuriated him; his Anglo-Irish blood was up. But Palmerston could not carry the Cabinet. When his colleagues declined to send in the Channel Fleet, he lamented their "timidity and weakness." On his own initiative he summoned the Austrian Ambassador, Count Apponyi, to Downing Street and warned him that the Germans were playing a dangerous game.

Bismarck was unimpressed by Palmerston's whirling words. He had made his own calculations and concluded that England would not go to war for the sake of the Treaty of 1852. "England is excessively noisy," he believed, "but will not fight." This confidence was not misplaced. Not only was a majority of the English Cabinet averse to war over Denmark, so, too, was the English Queen. "With regard to this sad S. Holstein question," Victoria wrote to her daughter Vicky, the Crown Princess of Prus-

---

* The plea for a smaller nation to be reasonable in order to appease German aggression was to have its twentieth-century echo. In the summer of 1938, Neville Chamberlain dispatched Lord Runciman to Prague with instructions to arrange an accommodation, one that would be acceptable to Berlin, between the Czechoslovak government and the German-speaking population of the Sudetenland. Lord Robert Cecil observed in 1864 that English ministries preferred to urge, not Germany, but the weaker powers upon which Germany preyed, "to swallow the cup of humiliation to the dregs."

sia, "my heart and sympathies are all German." Her daughter-in-law, Princess Alexandra, was Danish; but her departed husband, Prince Albert, was German.

While the Queen and her ministers dithered, Bismarck's brigades advanced. They carried the day at Missunde and Sankelmarkt, and the corpses of Danish officers were laid on the dusty pavement of Ulkeböl. The hope of many a Danish family perished on the ramparts of Dybböl, and in Copenhagen many a noble house went dark. Callers were politely informed (under the most trying circumstances the courtesy of the Danes never failed) that the inmates were in mourning; and an observer might detect, in so many pairs of steel-gray eyes, traces of stifled tears. The dirges of military bands sounded in the streets, and the red-and-white banners of Denmark, which had been set out in the first ebullition of patriotic enthusiasm, were covered with crêpe. Children with flaxen hair followed their fathers' coffins to forlorn little churchyards, where clergymen in limp gowns and starched ruffs pronounced the words, "dust unto dust," as caskets were lowered into the earth.

Pennsylvania and Virginia, July 1863–January 1864

Amid the ridges and round tops of Gettysburg, between Seminary Ridge and Cemetery Hill, the Cause of the South, too, was laid in its death shroud. Yet the Cause, having died, was reborn. Mary Chesnut witnessed its death and experienced its mysterious regeneration. She learned of the failure of Lee's invasion of the North at Richmond, where her husband had been made an aide-de-camp to President Davis. In that unhappy capital, where factious cabinet secretaries and contumacious senators harangued and intrigued over a disintegrating empire, she became convinced of the futility of Southern exertion. The Cause had ceased to be real, but it did not cease to be holy. Turning away from the coercive philosophy of the Fire Eaters, Mary Chesnut continued to cherish the dream of aristocracy which it inspired. In the darkest days of 1863 she continued to revere the confessors, the martyrs, the apostolic succession of heroes who labored to defend the ethereal vision.

Her young friend, Dr. John Darby, an army surgeon, introduced her to John Bell Hood himself, the commander of the 4th Texas. Hood was at this time in the meridian splendor of his fame. Thirty-two years old, "Sam" Hood—his West Point comrades still called him by his Academy nickname—was among the South's anointed ones. He had been consecrated by Stonewall Jackson himself, and he was now a general of the army. He "won his three stars &c under Stonewall's eyes," Mary Chesnut wrote, and was promoted "by Stonewall's request." He was tall, thin, and shy, with blue eyes, light hair, and an appearance of awkward strength. Mary Chesnut looked at his "sad Quixote face" and thought him a sword-bearing mystic, reviving, by an improbable atavism, the prophetic militancy of a Templar knight. Hood's face was "the face of an old crusader who believed in his cause, his cross, his crown." Mary Chesnut's friend, Colonel Venable, had seen Hood in battle, in "the hottest of the fight." "The man was transfigured. . . . The fierce light of his eyes—I can never forget."

In the light of such eyes the mythology of the Lost Cause began to take shape.

Mary Chesnut came to know Hood well. She had taken into her rooms in Richmond the Preston sisters, Buck and her sister Mary. General Hood, enchanted by the beauty of the young ladies, invited them to join him in a picnic at Drewry's Bluff, six miles below Richmond. (In 1862 Confederate batteries on the Bluff had prevented Union gunboats from sailing up the James to batter the Southern capital.) Here the Texas Brigade had fixed its camp. There was to be turkey, chicken, and buffalos' tongues; dancing was also mentioned. But the next morning, just as the ladies were about to step into the carriage, Dr. Darby came striding up, his clanking cavalry spurs sounding a note of despair. "Stop!" he cried. "It's all up. We are ordered back to the Rappahannock. The Brigade is marching through Richmond now." He suggested, however, that they might watch the brigade as it passed along the turnpike. They at once set off. They reached the turnpike and, standing on the sidewalk, watched a great army march by.

They were accustomed to seeing soldiers beautifully turned out in fresh uniforms. Now they saw only shabbiness. "Such rags and tags— nothing alike—most garments and arms taken from the enemy—such shoes!" Girt round with pots and pans, the motley troops marched with bread and bacon stuck on the ends of their bayonets.

"Oh, our brave boys!" Buck Preston groaned.

Just then General Hood came galloping up. The men of the Texas Brigade might have marched to the tune of their favorite song, "The Yellow Rose of Texas," but Hood himself had his eye on a Carolina blossom. Standing on the curb, Buck's sister, Mary, presented him with a garland of flowers. Hood, taking a Bible from his pocket, pressed one of the petals into its pages. With mirth in her eyes the young lady suggested that the book appeared not previously to have been opened.

Hood's El Greco countenance grew less gloomy. "Not hurt by daily use—eh?" He doffed his hat and took leave of the ladies. Before riding off, however, he turned to look at Buck, who stood somewhat aloof. He bent down and whispered something to John Darby.

"What was that he said to you?" Buck asked Darby after Hood had gone. "About me?"

"Only a horse compliment," Darby replied. "He is a Kentuckian, you know. He says, 'You stand on your feet like a thoroughbred.'"

Buck had a knack, Mary Chesnut said, of "being fallen in love with at sight and of never being fallen out of love with." Sam Hood rapidly succumbed to her charms. When he returned from the war in autumn of 1863, he was a greater hero than ever. At Chickamauga, where Confederate troops under Braxton Bragg routed a Union force led by William S. Rosecrans and prepared the way for the siege of Chattanooga, he led the decisive charge. But his state was in other ways as sere as the season. His body was smashed. At Gettysburg shrapnel from an artillery shell (it exploded as he led the doomed assault on Little Round Top) deprived him of the use of one of his arms. At Chickamauga he lost one of his legs. There would be no more dancing for Sam Hood.

Mary Chesnut was in her dining room giving orders to Laurence, her husband's manservant, when Mary Preston called out to her. "Come here, Mrs. C. They are lifting Hood out of his carriage, here, at your door." The maimed man was borne into the drawing room and laid upon a sofa. There was a flush of fever in his face. "This is the first house I have had myself dragged to," Hood said. Luncheon was brought to him, as well as oranges. "How kind people are. Not once since I was wounded have I ever been left without fruit, hard as it is to get now." Mary Chesnut saw that he looked wistfully towards the door of the apartment. She surmised the reason for his glances; but Buck Preston did not appear.

Sam Hood was determined, he said, "to be as happy as a fool, well, as a one-legged man, can be." He found his principal happiness in the company of Buck, and he was soon driving out with her nearly every day. One day they went to the Richmond fairgrounds. Mary Chesnut was with them, and so was Henry Percy Brewster, a lawyer who had served as Secretary of War in Texas during the interval when the state had been an independent republic. Brewster was now on Hood's staff. The day was cold, and they were swathed in rugs and furs. Buck was regal and remote in black velvet.

Hood asked Brewster to enumerate the symptoms of a man's being in love. He was, he said, ignorant of the characteristics of that particular malady. He admitted that he had once, at the age of seventeen, fancied himself in love. But that was a "long time ago."

Brewster described the condition of a lover in the first uneasiness of desire. When the swain beheld the object of his passion, his breath was apt to come short. "If it amounts to mild strangulation, you have got it bad. You are stupidly jealous, glowering with jealousy, and [have] a gloomy, fixed conviction that she likes every fool you meet better than she does you, especially people that she has a thorough contempt for. . . ."

"Well," Hood said, drawing a breath of relief. "I have felt none of these things so far, and yet they say I am engaged to four young ladies— liberal allowance, you will admit, for a man who cannot walk without help."

"To whom do they say you are engaged?" Buck asked. Her eyes were fixed on the bobbing heads of the horses.

"Miss Wigfall is one."

"Who else?"

"Miss Sally Preston"—that is, Buck herself.

Mary Chesnut watched Buck's reaction. The girl was as icy as ever. She did not move an eyelid. "Are you not annoyed at such a preposterous report?"

"No," Hood replied.

"God help us," Brewster said under his breath to Mary Chesnut. "He is going to say everything right out here before our faces."

Buck, however, wanted no proposals. She spoke with great coolness. "Richmond people are liberal, as you say. I never heed their reports. They say *I* am engaged to [Charles] Shirley Carter and to Phil Robb."

Hood looked at Buck. "I think," he said, "I will set a mantrap near your door and break some of those young fellows' legs too." He dismissed her other suitors as "light-winged birds."

Buck Preston and Sam Hood made a striking couple. Each was an embodiment of the Southern ideal—an incarnation of the spirit of the Confederacy. But after Gettysburg the Confederacy wore a ghoulish aspect. Their *pas de deux* was in danger of becoming a *danse macabre*.

Washington, July–September 1863

IN THE DAYS after Gettysburg, the question gnawed.

Why had Bobby Lee escaped?

"Our army held the war in the hollow of their hand," Lincoln said, "and they would not close it."

The President wrote in anger to General Meade. "I do not believe you appreciate the magnitude of the misfortune involved in Lee's escape. He was within your easy grasp, and to have closed upon him would . . . have ended the war. As it is, the war will be prolonged indefinitely. . . . Your golden opportunity is gone, and I am distressed immeasurably because of it."

He did not send the letter. Meade, he saw, had done his best. But he continued to lament the narrowness of his generals' vision. A succession of commanders—McClellan, Burnside, Hooker—regarded the capture of Richmond as the key to the war. Meade and his staff seemed to share this view. Lincoln thought differently. "To avoid misunderstanding," he wrote in September 1863, "let me say that to attempt to fight the enemy slowly back into his intrenchments at Richmond, and there to capture him, is an idea I have been trying to repudiate for quite a year." "Lee's army, and not Richmond," he said, was the "objective point."

Yet the problem, he knew, was not a purely military one. War is not only a contest of opposing armies: it is also a conflict of rival wills. In 1863, Lincoln had not only to instruct his commanders in the precepts of strategy, he had, too, to stimulate the North's will to fight. Enthusiasm for the war had fallen off sharply, and it had been necessary to resort to conscription. But the Enrollment Act of 1863 brought difficulties of its own. There were disturbances in a number of Northern counties, and riots in New York City claimed more than a hundred lives.

The President's task was to raise the nation's morale at a time when his own was suffering. The slaughterhouse atmosphere had begun to tell. The President looked like an old man, and had bloody dreams. Frustrated though he was by the course of events, there was no one to whom he could unburden himself. Mary Lincoln inhabited a world of her own. She had made her life into a mausoleum for her dead son Willie, and like Tsar Alexander's Mary, she spent many hours attempting to communicate with the departed. In July she was thrown from a carriage, and was never afterwards quite right in the head. Lincoln's relations with his oldest boy, Robert, were strained. He had given Bob the "best of educations," and had provided him with a better start in life than he himself had known; but the two were not close. With ungenerous disdain Lincoln "guessed Bob would not do better than he had." He cherished his youngest son, Tad; the boy frequently slept in his father's bed. But the President had not enough time for the child, who was curiously stunted; at the age of nine he could neither dress himself nor read a book.

Lincoln was a lonely man in the White House; but his solitude cannot by itself explain his darkening mood in 1863. He was, after all, used to being alone. He had gone so far as to elaborate a pet theory to explain the qualities that separated him from the lesser lights that surrounded him. His mother, he surmised, was the natural child of a high-souled Virginia planter, and from this source came his uncommon powers of mind and tenacity of purpose. "God bless my mother," he once said, "all that I am or ever hope to be I owe to her." That Lincoln should have attributed his genius to the very patrician culture he set himself, in his public career, to destroy, might seem odd; but he was a creature of paradox.

Power, however, was relentlessly exposing his paradoxes. The tension between the democratic vindicator of equality and the great-souled man born to "ride in triumph through Persepolis" had once existed only in the shadows of his imagination. The necessities of his revolution now made the contradiction nakedly visible; they forced Lincoln to play the part that had long beguiled him, that of the romantic strongman, the scion of eagles—a type that at once fascinated and repelled him.

The President's detractors were quick to seize on the discrepancy between his professed principles and his actual deeds. His solicitude for the rights of slaves was, they said, a pretense, and they pointed to his ambiguous statements about blacks, who he once said could never live with whites "on terms of social and political equality." As late as August 1862, Lincoln spoke of the need for blacks to go away—to leave the United States and form colonies elsewhere. He invoked the equality of opportunity that lay at the heart of the American idea; yet he supported protective tariffs and other giveaways to well-connected businessmen. To overcome, in the South, the last resistance to prohibitory tariffs was, the President's opponents said, the real object of his revolution. And now men were dying, by tens of thousands, for his bloody ambition.

The accusations were painful to Lincoln in part because there was an element of truth in them. He *was* an ambitious politician; and like all ambitious politicians, he had at times to trim his sails to the prevailing wind, though to do so were to deviate from the course of absolute right. Yet the charges were not the whole truth, and Lincoln exerted himself to set the record straight. He consented to the enlistment of blacks in the army, and by this act invested precious political capital in the cause of black equality. He defended his "strong measures" in the field of civil liberties as essential to the safety of the state, and argued that their emergency character was too patently transitory to form the foundation of a permanent despotism. America would no more come to rely on such measures in time of peace, he said, than a man would "contract so strong an appetite for emetics during temporary illness as to persist in feeding upon them during the remainder of his healthful life."

The President had considerable success, in the North, in overcoming opposition to his leadership, and in convincing his fellow citizens that he was not a wolf in sheep's clothing. His letter defending his "strong measures" was issued as a pamphlet; more than half a million copies were printed. Overcoming an earlier ambivalence, he pressed for black citizenship in those portions of the South occupied by Union armies. Writing to political ally Michael Hahn to congratulate him on having fixed his "name in history as the first-free-state Governor of

Louisiana," Lincoln asked "whether some of the colored people may not be let in" and enrolled in the state's reconstructed franchise, "as, for instance, the very intelligent, and especially those who have fought gallantly in our ranks."

Yet a wartime leader who can do no more than refute his critics is bound to fail. He must energize his supporters. In 1863, Lincoln was still struggling to find the moral clue, a means of mobilizing the spirit of those who remained faithful to his revolution.

His efforts in this direction met with a degree of success, but something was missing. In July he described the principle for which Americans in the North were contending, the spirit of 1776. "How long ago is it?" he asked in a speech at the White House,

> —eighty odd years—since on the Fourth of July for the first time in the history of the world a nation by its representatives, assembled and declared as a self-evident truth that "all men are created equal."

Alexander H. Stephens, the Vice President of the Confederacy, said that in Lincoln's imagination the Union rose "to the sublimity of religious mysticism." But the President had yet to find a way to convey the impassioned quality of this inner vision to his people.

Chapter 18

FIGHTERS FOR THE FUTURE

Munich, August 1863–October 1864

DINING IN STATE in the Nymphenburg Palace near Munich, Crown Prince Ludwig, the eighteen-year-old heir to the throne of Bavaria, was dreamy and remote. Ignoring both his mother, Queen Mary, and the dignitaries beside whom he was seated, he rapidly drained his champagne glass. The footman who carried the bottle did not, however, refill the Prince's glass. Annoyed, Ludwig held his glass over his shoulder. The footman looked in perplexity to the Queen, and only at her direction was the Prince's glass replenished.

Taciturn and gloomy in the company of state dignitaries, Ludwig in his solitary reveries burned with obscure enthusiasms. Later the nature of these yearnings would become clearer to him, but at eighteen he felt only bafflement and frustration, and a desire, vague yet intense, for some momentous form of greatness. At Hohenschwangau in the Bavarian Alps, where he passed much of his boyhood, Ludwig had evolved into a parody of German romanticism. The castle itself, which his father, King Maximilian II, had built on the ruins of an older edifice, might have been the Alpine retreat of Byron's Manfred. Here, in the shadow of lofty pinnacles and castellated towers, Ludwig developed that taste for *Schwärmerei* (romantic rapture) which was to have such fatal consequences in his life. The Prince's eyes were sensitive to light, and as a boy he had liked nothing better than to hide himself in the dark recesses of the castle, where he could more easily elaborate his visions. One day his tutor, the learned von Döllinger, found him nearly lost to sight in the depths of an enormous sofa.

"Your Highness should have something read to you," the tutor ventured to suggest, "that would serve to pass the tedious hours."

"Oh, they are not tedious to me," little Ludwig replied. "I think of lots of things, and I am quite happy."

The boy's love of swans and beautiful knights might not by itself have been unhealthy; but there were other signs that the mind and imagination of Ludwig were not happily constituted. He could not bear the sight of common humanity. He would turn his face to the wall rather than look at an ungainly footman. He felt for members of the lower and middling orders an aversion which he had not always the good sense to conceal. Yet his nature was not essentially frigid. His eye and mouth were those of a lover and a voluptuary. He longed for intimacy with a few chosen spirits. But here there was an obstacle. He was morbidly sensitive of his own dignity, and he could not forgive, even in a favorite, a breach of the rigid etiquette that hedged his person. The pride of the House of Wittelsbach, so evident in the way he threw back his head and thrust out his chin when he walked, made him imperious, and this superbity of manner thwarted his desires for stimulating relations with artistic persons.

A little experience of the world, if it could not have altered the nature of Ludwig, might have softened his youthful egotism and hauteur. But such an education in reality was denied him when, in March 1864, his father, the King, died in the royal residence in Munich. Ludwig passed, in an instant, from the nursery to the throne. The young man who had needed his mother's consent to drink a glass of champagne was now the ruler of nearly five million people.

Ludwig ascended the throne determined to foster an artistic revolution. He aspired to be such a promoter of art and encourager of genius as his hero, Louis XIV of France, had been. Ludwig carried the emulation far. He posed for a painter in a costume and posture that recalled one of the portraits of the Grand Louis by Hyacinthe Rigaud, and he constructed, at Herrenchiemsee, a palace modeled on Versailles. Yet self-absorbed though he was, Ludwig had sense enough to perceive that the Sun King's style, however entrancing it might have been, was remote from the spirit of his own age. Only a new and powerful art, he believed, could effect the spiritual regeneration of his people. He cast his eyes far and wide, but he saw only one man who, by virtue of his peculiar genius, could be of use to him.

"Find Richard Wagner for me!" the King is said to have exclaimed in the earliest days of his reign.

Wagner had for some time fascinated Ludwig. A performance of *Tannhäuser* sent him into convulsions of ecstasy. Wagner's essay, *The Work of Art in the Future*, made no less deep an impression. He longed to hear the composer's revolutionary but as yet unperformed music-drama, *Tris-*

tan und Isolde. Here, Ludwig believed, was an artist who might redeem Germany by purging the land of the "soulless utilitarianism" which disfigured it. Art could transform the "utilitarian man" of the present into a spiritual being, the "artistic man" of the future. "It was this one word 'Future,'" the historian Leopold von Ranke said, "which gained Ludwig for Wagner's music."

The man on whom the King's hopes for the future hung was, at this time, a fugitive, flying from creditors and bailiffs. Wagner had left Biebrich and gone to Vienna. He had fled Vienna and gone to Mariafeld. Ludwig dispatched his secretary, Franz von Pfistermeister, to find him. The emissary found Wagner in Stuttgart. He left his card, but the composer, who suspected the ruse of a disgruntled lender, hesitated to see him. When, at last, the interview took place, Pfistermeister told him that his royal master admired him deeply and desired him to repair at once to Munich. The composer shed tears. It was the sign he had long awaited.

Early in May the two men met. They were both deeply moved. Wagner, bending low over the royal hand, was entranced by the beauty of Ludwig. "Alas," the composer wrote, "he is so handsome and intelligent, so splendid, and so full of soul, that I tremble lest his life should dissolve like a fleeting dream of the Gods in this vulgar world." Ludwig, for his part, promised to free Wagner from the constraints that had for so long hampered his art. "Rest assured," the King said, "that I will do everything in my power to make up for what you have suffered in the past. The mean cares of everyday life I will banish from you for ever; I will procure for you the peace you have longed for in order that you may be free to spread the mighty wings of your genius in the pure aether of rapturous art."

The King paid Wagner's debts and established him in a villa near the royal residence of Berg. Every day the royal carriage was sent to the Villa Pellet to fetch the composer. The King loved him, Wagner said, "with infatuation." He flattered himself that he figured, in Ludwig's imagination, as an incarnation of the "first beloved," that "ultimate object of desire" which, according to Plato, is "the source and origin of all friendship between human beings." Yet on his own side Wagner was not less enamored. He flew to the King "as to a mistress." Were Ludwig to die, he would die "the moment after." Under the inspiration of the King he might even liberate himself from the bondage of feminine beauty. "Shall I be able to renounce women completely?" he asked. "With a deep sigh I confess I could almost wish it! One look at his dear picture helps me again! Oh, the lovely youth! Now he is everything to me, world, wife and child."

Wagner found it always easier to talk of renunciation than actually to renounce, and when Ludwig went off to take the waters of Kissingen in the company of other royalties, the composer in his loneliness ceased to proclaim the virtues of a chaste aloofness from women. "My solitude," he said, "is terrible." Fortunately Cosima von Bülow arrived in Bavaria at the end of June. Wagner had not seen her since the day, six months before, when with tears and sobs they had made to each other a mutual confession of love, or what Cosima styled "death-in-love." Cosima's husband, the faithful Hans, did not accompany his wife on her journey to Bavaria; he was in Berlin suffering another nervous breakdown, and would not be able to travel for a week. The interval seemed to the lovers of the Villa Pellet a happy eternity. "I have been here three days," Cosima wrote to a friend from the villa, "and it seems as though it were already a century. . . ." When poor Hans finally arrived from Berlin, he discovered that his wife belonged to his friend. Tristan now monopolized the cave of Isolde's love.

In the meantime Wagner's power in Bavaria grew and grew. The soft mind of the King was unequal to the arts of so accomplished a seducer, and Wagner's ascendancy over Ludwig became, for a time, almost complete. The composer had been brought, by suffering and study, to renounce the world, but neither adversity nor philosophy had purified his mind of its innate love of power. Wagner soon ceased to be a protégé of the King of Bavaria. The King of Bavaria appeared rather as a proselyte of Wagner. The visions of the composer became the policy of the state. The treasure of the Kingdom was diverted to the purposes of music and art. Preparations were made, not only for a production of *Tristan und Isolde,* but for the establishment of a new school of music and a new festival theater in Munich.

Wagner himself, forsaking the isolation of the Villa Pellet, came to Munich, where he was enabled, by the King's munificence, to make an appearance not unworthy of his exalted status. He took a house on Briennerstrasse. A handsome income was settled upon him, and he furnished his rooms in rich velvets, silks, and satins. After many struggles, the prophet of the German revolution had found a home.

Washington and Pennsylvania, November 1863

AT HALF PAST EIGHT on a November night, in her father's house on the corner of Sixth and E Streets, Kate Chase married William Sprague. Rhode Island's "Boy Governor" had been chosen to represent Rhode Island in the United States Senate, and not long after he took his seat the couple became engaged. The match was steeped in the spirit of the revolution in which the two were caught up: the daughter of Puritan idealism was to be joined in flesh to the son of Puritan industry.

In the parlor of the Chase house, the great figures of Washington assembled. Some anxiety was manifested on account of the President. At twenty-five after eight, Lincoln had not yet appeared. The diplomats and statesmen gathered in the parlor knew that the President's relations with Kate's father, Salmon P. Chase, the Secretary of the Treasury, were far from good. So cunningly have desire and jealousy been woven into our nature that even the purest spirits can surmount them only with difficulty; and the spirit of Salmon P. Chase was not pure.

He was tortured by the desire for power. He felt for those who possessed a greater share of it than he feelings not far removed from hatred. He reviewed, in an agony of envy and rapacity, the disappointments of his life. He had, when Abraham Lincoln was still an obscure lawyer in Illinois, been elected Senator from Ohio. Later he had governed the state. He had done as much as any man to transform the anti-slavery movement in the North from a quixotic moral crusade into a revolutionary force in national politics. These early successes, he believed, marked him out as a man of destiny, the anointed figure who would lead the Republicans to victory and greatness. But in 1860 the obscure lawyer from Illinois had wrested from him the mantle of glory. Three years after the Republican Convention in Chicago, Chase continued to be unreconciled to the pre-eminence of Lincoln. Even now, as he waited for the President to cross his threshold, he was preparing to challenge him for the party's nomination in 1864.

The sound of cheering in the street heralded the near approach of the President. A crowd of gawkers watched as the presidential carriage drove up to Chase's door. The President came alone. Mrs. Lincoln, who still grieved for Willie and nursed an antipathy towards the bride, pleaded a cold. As the President ascended the steps, he was met by his Treasury Secretary. The two potentates greeted each other cordially, but between them there was no bond of trust or friendship. The previous autumn, Chase had, in an attempt to cultivate those senators who might in the future prove useful to his ambitious designs, poured into the ear of William Pitt Fessenden of Maine a stream of malignant gossip concerning the administration. The aspirations of a lifetime were mingled in his poisonous talk. Chase told Fessenden that Secretary of State Seward had obtained an evil ascendancy over the mind of the President, and that his "back-stairs influence" effectively controlled the executive. The rumor of Seward's power was the signal for a revolt on Capitol Hill. Radical Republicans like "Bluff Ben" Wade had long distrusted the Secretary of State as an enemy to their cause. They clamored for the dismissal, from the President's councils, of the Judas of the revolution. A delegation of Republican senators went to the White House and remonstrated with Lincoln. The war, they told him, "was left in the hands of men who had no sympathy with it or the cause," and they urged him to make such changes in the Cabinet as would give "unity and vigor" to the government.

Lincoln met the challenge to his leadership with energy, and with cunning. He brought the senators face to face with the Cabinet for what he called a "free and friendly conversation." In fact, he set a trap. Lincoln asked each Cabinet member (other than Seward, who was not present) to state before the senators whether there had been any want of unity in the Cabinet. Chase saw at once that he was in an untenable position. He must either defy President Lincoln to his face or disavow his words to Senator Fessenden. In vain did he attempt to extricate himself from the consequences of his tale-bearing. He said that "he should not have come here had he known he was to be arraigned by a committee of the Senate." But he knew that he had been outwitted, and he at last conceded that "there had been no want of unity in the Cabinet."

A year after the revolt was quelled, Lincoln watched Chase give his daughter away in marriage. The costume the bride had chosen for the occasion was simplicity itself. The dress, of white velvet, was from a good Paris maker; it was the last word in fashion, yet it was plain and unadorned. Washington was of two minds concerning her character. Some pronounced her an amiable woman, "modest and retiring in her manners." Others thought her grasping and aspiring. Certainly she was adept in the arts of social flattery. Her conversation, which was singularly winning, was the net with which she snared the unwary—and even the wary. Charles Sumner of Massachusetts, the chairman of the Senate Foreign Relations Committee, succumbed to her charms. Lord Lyons, the British envoy in Washington, fell in love with her. Before her marriage she was often seen riding with James A. Garfield of Ohio.

Those who held Kate Chase to be a young woman without shame or scruple fully believed her capable of contracting a mercenary alliance with the Spragues in order to improve her father's political chances. The mill which William Sprague's forebears had established on the Pocasset River had grown into an industrial empire. Each week the Sprague looms wove and printed immense quantities of cotton and calico. The family commanded an array of houses, yachts, racehorses, and banks. The government of Rhode Island itself might almost be considered a domestic possession. Kate Chase was already the leading political hostess in the capital. The Sprague fortune would allow her to do things on a scale which Washington, with its tradition of republican simplicity, had not yet seen. She would be, in America, all that a Duchess of Devonshire or a Duchess of Bedford was in England. No, she would be more. She would make her father President, and reign triumphantly over the White House.

In the Chases' parlor the Bishop of Rhode Island read the marriage office. The dignitaries watched as Sprague slipped the ring onto Kate's finger. He was a small man, slight of build. Some thought him handsome, but his eyes gave his face a drooping aspect. It was the outward sign of a life that was less golden than it seemed. His father had been murdered when Sprague was little more than a boy. At fifteen he had been taken from school and set to learn the cotton and calico trade. His education had been sacrificed to the exigencies of business, and he possessed, one observer thought, only a "limited mental capacity." Yet he had sense enough to be conscious of his deficiencies, and in the Senate he rarely opened his mouth. His heart, moreover, was better than could be reasonably expected in one who had from infancy been brought up in the knowledge that a great fortune was one day to be his. In one of his letters he expressed the hope that his and Kate's love for one another would make good the losses each had suffered. "I have not had a father's care for twenty years," Sprague wrote, and "Katie has missed a mother." (Kate was five years old when her mother died.) As a pledge of his devotion, Sprague vowed, three weeks before the wedding, to give up smoking and drinking. Tobacco, he said, led to "brandies and whiskies." Brandy and whiskey led to "dyspepsia and an unhappy life." He was sorry for his dark carouses, but he warned his fiancée that he would "be very cross for a few days" after forswearing his habitual stimulants.

The marriage rite was followed by champagne and dancing, and afterwards Senator and Mrs. Sprague retired to their nuptial bed. President Lincoln, in the meantime, returned through the dark streets of the capital to the White House. In a week's time he was to speak at Gettysburg, where a national cemetery was to be dedicated on the battlefield. He had received the invitation only the week before; in preparing his remarks he would not have the luxury of time. The President intended to use the opportunity the ceremony afforded to say something about why his revolution to save and transform the United States was worth making, in spite of the cost in blood.

It was a subject close to his heart. The fragility of his country's liberties had long been a source of concern to Lincoln. Twenty-five years before, in his address to the Young Men's Lyceum in Springfield, he had argued that, although America had nothing to fear from a foreign foe, her institutions might nevertheless perish from the indifference or apathy of her citizens, should they cease to find in those institutions any-thing to inspire fidelity or attachment. The possibility that "the feelings of the best citizens will become more or less alienated" from the Repub-lic was, the young Lincoln said, real. Across the ocean, in Germany, Bis-marck said that the Prussians, forced to choose between the institutions of freedom and those of despotism, would stand by the despot. Lincoln, in America, wondered whether his countrymen might not permit their free constitution to degenerate into a form of despotism. To "fortify" the country against this civic dissipation, he proposed the development of public myths and rituals, a "*political religion* of the nation. . . ."

This was a romantic solution. It was not enough to appeal to people's minds. One must touch their hearts. So romantic statesmen such as Giuseppe Mazzini (during his Young Italy phase) and Benjamin Disraeli (during his Young England period) contended. So Abraham Lincoln, in his youthful romantic phase, believed. Though one's "cause be naked truth itself," he declared in one of his early essays, one could never per-suade others with reason alone. One must employ the "drop of honey which catches the heart."

A quarter of a century later, the nightmare Lincoln had envisioned in his youth had come to pass. Americans *were* alienated from their gov-ernment. In the South, the Fire Eaters had walked away from it. In the North, the peace-at-any-price men, or Copperheads, did not want to fight for it. Lincoln had, by this time, outgrown the cruder romantic impulses of his youth, when, like Bismarck, he read Byron and suffered from "hypochondriasm," a form of ostentatious melancholy. As a mature statesman, Lincoln did not seek a "political religion of the nation"; that strain of romanticism led inexorably to coercion, a cult of the state. He could never believe, as Disraeli did, that the "divine right of govern-ment" was "the keystone of human progress." But he believed as firmly as ever that free states, if they were to survive, must have a higher inspi-ration, a poetry that fortifies.

Romanticism supplied the revolutionary statesmen of the nine-teenth century with a new set of tools, implements with which they might mold opinion in an age of telegraphs and daily newspapers. In the period 1861–1871, men who had in their youth had been influenced by the romantic school attained power and influence in the world. Disraeli (born 1804) and Marx (born 1818), Bismarck (born 1815) and Lincoln (born 1809)—they had all been inspired, in their different ways, by the romantic revolution, which was, when they were young men, just begin-ning to reach a wide audience. They were all touched by the romantic enthusiasm for lofty, high-souled ideals; they all felt that reverence for the past, for the "mystic chords of memory," which Burke and Coleridge,

Fichte and Father Jahn, had inculcated in their disciples. (Marx, the least sentimental man in the romantic school, venerated ancient Greece.) They all felt the truth of what the English priest John Henry Newman said when he spoke of the need for something "deeper and more attractive" than the "dry and superficial philosophy" of the eighteenth century. But where Bismarck and Marx placed their romantic myths in the service of coercion, Lincoln placed his in the service of freedom. The genie unleashed by the romantic conjurors, which had promised to destroy the free state, might yet be made to work its salvation.

At noon on November 18 the President boarded a special train bound for Gettysburg. He arrived at nightfall. The next morning, after breakfast, he retired to his room to work on the address which he had begun to compose in Washington. At ten o'clock he emerged with the manuscript in his hand. Surrounded by an eager crowd, he mounted the horse he would ride to the cemetery. After various delays, the procession went forward, led by a squadron of cavalry, a regiment of infantry, and two batteries of artillery—the funeral escort accorded the bier of the highest ranking officer in the service.

The cemetery, when he saw it, was unfinished. Graves had still to be dug, and the skeletons of Confederate soldiers lay unburied in Devil's Den. He was greeted by a military salute, and as he ascended the platform, all the men present uncovered. A heavy fog obscured the field, yet some men told how, during the prayer offered by the Reverend Mr. Stockton, the sun broke through the mists. The scholar-statesman Edward Everett delivered the principal oration of the day, and afterwards a hymn was sung. Lincoln then rose to make what were styled, in the ceremony's program, "dedicatory remarks."

Yasnaya Polyana, June 1863–January 1867

"DARLING," Tolstoy urged his wife, "try to wait until midnight."

Sofya Andreyevna was in labor. In a few hours it would be the twenty-eighth, and Tolstoy had a superstitious regard for the number signified by this date. It happened as he wished, and early the next morning the baby, a boy, was born. The child came into the world on the same leather sofa on which Tolstoy himself had been born, thirty-five years before. The proud father wanted to name his son Nicholas, after his own father and his older brother. But Sofya Andreyevna objected that the name was unlucky; both men had died young. They named the baby Sergei instead.

Tolstoy was no longer, he said, a "free man." He was instead "lucky enough to be fettered by chains of rich liquid green-and-yellow children's s**t." But happy families are not all alike: some of them harbor, beneath a placid surface, depths of discontent. Sofya Andreyevna was downcast. Her husband, she said, "constantly frustrates my spontaneous outbursts of love." She accused his coldness and neglect: now that his passion had spent its novel force, he thought her not much better than his borzois, Lubka and Krylat, a little dearer than Mashka, his English thoroughbred. "I am to gratify his pleasure and nurse his child," she said. "I am a piece of household furniture, I am a *woman.*"

When his wife threw a tantrum, "everything collapses," Tolstoy said, and "I stand there as though I had been scalded. I am afraid of everything and I see that there can be no happiness or poetry for me except when I am alone." The problem, he concluded, lay, not in Sofya Andreyevna, but in himself. "I am happy with her," he said, "but I am dreadfully unhappy with myself." "Where is it—my old self, the self I loved and knew, who still springs to the surface sometimes and pleases and frightens me? I have become petty and insignificant."

He needed to do something. But what? He spoke of going off to the army to serve "the fatherland," a ridiculous enthusiasm, his wife thought, "in a man of thirty-five." The fit of romantic nationalism passed, but Tolstoy was no happier. He could not go on running the estate. "I'm not cut out for it." He once thought his vocation lay in teaching. But the "teacher that used to be in me," he said, was "there no longer." Teaching was too arduous a calling, involving as it did a constant struggle to conceal the fact that he did not know what to teach. Still less did he envision himself as a reformer, an actor, however minor, in Tsar Alexander's liberal revolution.

As he pondered history and watched his family grow, Tolstoy was seized by an idea. The belief that the world was shaped by the acts of revolutionary statesmen was a gross error. Almost as though he were trying to justify the choices he had made, he argued passionately that families did more to shape history than political and military leaders. In 1812, Napoleon the Great invaded Russia, entered Moscow, and was compelled to make his disastrous retreat. Historians told the story as though the leaders of the age—Napoleon himself and his marshals, Tsar Alexander I and his generals—shaped its historic contours. Tolstoy maintained that this conception of historical causation was flawed. He was determined to tell the story of those years in a different way. He would show how insignificant and blind were the great figures of the epoch. He would reveal the true character of the age in stories the historians overlooked. Napoleon and Alexander would figure in the work he projected; but they would not be its heroes.

By the fall of 1863 Tolstoy was hard at work. "I've never felt my intellectual powers, and even all my moral powers," he wrote in October, "so free and so capable of work. And I *have* work to do. This work is a novel of the 1810s and 1820s, which has been occupying me fully since the autumn." He soon ceased to call the book a novel. It "is not a novel and is not a story," he insisted. But neither was it a history. He was, he believed, working out a new kind of art, one that combined elements of history and fiction, but was free from the vices of these genres. "There are marvelous people in it," he said. "I love them very much." He thought of calling the book *All's Well That Ends Well.* He held out no great hopes for its reception. "Probably," he said, "it will pass unnoticed."

One day he went out riding and fell from his horse. When he came to, a thought flashed in his mind. "I said to myself, *'I'm a writer.'*" He kept repeating aloud, "I am being reborn." ("What *does* he mean?" Sofya Andreyevna wondered.) In the mornings, after taking coffee with his family, he would retire to his study with a quantity of tea. When the writing went well he would come away from his desk in a state of exultation, saying that he had left "a bit of his life" in the inkstand.

Art and family, which he now took to be his portions in life, were higher callings than politics; and he took another step away from the Tsar's liberal revolution. Although Tolstoy did not hesitate, in his work-in-progress, to obtrude numerous asides about politics and history, he insisted that the "aims of art are incommensurate (as the mathematicians say) with social problems." He wanted to write, not a solution to social and political controversies, but a book "to make people love life in all its countless inexhaustible manifestations." Questions about the reform of Russia were trivial. All "these problems splash about in a little puddle of dirty water which only seems like an ocean to those whom fate has set down in the middle of the puddle." It was "a matter of complete indifference" to him "who suppresses the Poles, or captures Schleswig-Holstein. . . . Butchers kill the oxen we eat, but I'm not obliged to accuse them or sympathize with them."

Sofya Andreyevna was at first skeptical of her husband's literary passion. She raised her eyebrows as he slipped away with his pitcher of tea to work "on *The History of 1812*." "He is writing about Countess So-and-So, who has been talking to Princess Whosit. Insignificant." She was relieved, however, "that his mental state has improved, for I was afraid."

As *War and Peace* began to take form, she changed her mind about its value. It was "so *clever.*" She saw to it that her husband was not disturbed when he was working. She relieved him of the task of looking after the estate, and while he was writing, she went round Yasnaya Polyana herself, an assortment of barn-door keys hanging at her waist. She cared for little Sergei and the other children who came, Tatyana in 1864 and Ilya in 1866, and devoted many hours to the nursery. She took her husband's rough drafts and, using a magnifying glass to decipher his scarcely legible revisions, wrote out the fair copy.

"As I copy I experience a whole new world of emotions, thoughts, impressions," Sofya Andreyevna said. "Nothing touches me so deeply as his ideas, his genius." Her husband was now writing furiously; he was "irritable and excited," and tears often stood in his eyes. "All the parts he has read to me," she said, "have moved me almost to tears too; whether this is because, as his wife, I feel so much for him, or because it really is very good I cannot say for certain—although I rather think the second."

Chapter 19

THAT A NATION MIGHT LIVE

Pennsylvania, November 1863

Four score and seven years ago . . .

The truth enshrined in the Declaration of Independence was in danger. History, the President told the citizens gathered on the battlefield, was testing it. At home, a great civil war threatened to destroy the nation conceived in liberty. Abroad, the world crisis was working against the faith of the Declaration, the belief that all men are created equal. Freedom was losing the future to new forms of coercion.

At Gettysburg, Lincoln attempted to get the future back.

Every revolution mortifies the flesh. The successful ones exalt the spirit. On the battlefield that saved his revolution, Lincoln raised up his altars. He had found his clue. In his address he allied America's free institutions to what he found to be still living in the country's original spiritual inspirations.

He had not searched his Bible in vain. The men who gave "the last full measure of devotion" at Gettysburg had, he said, "consecrated," not only the soil of the battlefield, but also the truths of the Republic. They had washed the principles of the Declaration of Independence in their blood. In doing so they had "hallowed" those principles—purified them, after the fashion of Hebrews 9:22.*

The implication was strange, yet obvious. The Republic was twice-born. It would have a second birth—what Lincoln called a "new birth"—of freedom.

Lincoln at Gettysburg identified the "new birth of freedom" which his revolution made possible with the multiple-birth theory of John 3:3

---

* "And almost all things are by the law purged with blood: and without shedding of blood is no remission."

("except a man be *born again,* he cannot see the *kingdom of God*"). The improbable conceit *ought* to have failed, perished a mere piece of rhetorical sentimentality. But it worked. Amid the pressures of the world crisis, the child of the romantic revival used an older poetry—a drop of honey—to consolidate his revolution and fortify the free state.

After the President spoke a dirge was sung, and a short time later he boarded a train and returned to Washington. He was by this time sick with a fever, and upon returning to the White House he went to bed.

Denmark, Berlin, and Biarritz, June 1864–October 1864

IN THE DEAD of a June night the Prussian transports slipped quietly from their moorings. Under cover of darkness they made their way to Alsen Island, the last of the enemy's strongholds in southern Denmark. At dawn on the twenty-sixth, the transports debouched their loads. Prussian troops fell upon the unsuspecting Danes in their batteries and redoubts. The Prussians were in a short time masters of the island.

The war in Denmark had reached its crisis. The Germans moved with lightning speed. A new spirit of method and celerity characterized their operations. The old commander in the field, Field Marshal Wrangel, was withdrawn. He was a veteran of the Napoleonic Wars, and with a misplaced confidence in his abilities he dispensed with the advice of the General Staff. Helmuth von Moltke's war plans he contemptuously flung aside. So ponderous were the tactics of the old Field Marshal that the Danes were able to retire behind their fortifications without serious loss. Many in Germany became indignant, one diplomat observed, when it appeared that the Prussians were "not crushing [Denmark] fast enough." Wrangel was recalled to Berlin, and Moltke became the principal director of the war; he was made Chief of Staff to the new commander in the field, King Wilhelm's nephew, Friedrich Karl, the "Red Prince," so called because he was partial to the scarlet coat of the Ziethen Hussars.

The distress of the Danes was by this time great. Their capital was menaced. Their military power was broken. Their fortifications, some of which, like Dannewerke, had stood for centuries, had been leveled to the ground by the Prussian field guns. The Prussian infantry corps, with their breech-loading needle guns, poured a lethal fire on the remaining Danish positions.* The whizzing bullets made a pinging sound which,

---

* Across the ocean, the breech-loading revolution had not yet taken place; in America, Union and Confederate infantrymen continued to rely on muzzle-loading rifles like the Springfield and the Enfield.

during a hot engagement, sounded like a swarm of insects. Many bullets found their mark, and the black coffins of the Danes piled up.

King Christian was in a short time forced to sue for peace. The *Dannebrog* would fly over Schleswig and Holstein no more. The duchies were extorted from the Danes as a condition of peace, giving the Germans a prize of immense strategic value. The duchies touched two seas—the Baltic and the North—and might, in the hands of a large and populous nation, form the base of a formidable naval force. The harbor of Kiel alone, Lord Robert Cecil wrote, was a "splendid prize for which the mightiest nations would be glad to compete."

In Prussia, the architects of the victory over Denmark were liberally rewarded. Moltke was showered with medals and honors. As he made his way from the seat of battle, he was chagrined to discover that he had become famous. Wherever he went he was pointed out and saluted with cheers. The Danish war was, he believed, the crowning glory of his career, and he went at once to King Wilhelm to broach the subject of his retirement from the army. But the old King was not about to part with so valuable a lieutenant; Moltke was informed that his services were too important to be relinquished.

Bismarck, too, tasted the fruits of victory. The Exalted Order of the Black Eagle was now his. He found a more substantial benefit in the new stability of his power. He was, one contemporary said, "completely master of the situation in Prussia." Europe marveled at the way in which Fortune, that fickle strumpet, had smiled upon his audacity. In October 1864 he felt himself entitled to a vacation, his first since becoming premier. For a fortnight he sauntered about Biarritz. He saw Kathi Orlov, swam in the ocean, toured the Basque villages. During his sojourn he had a dream. He was climbing a mountain. The defile grew steeper. He found himself confronted by a mass of rock, and a profound abyss. He hesitated, and wondered whether he ought not to turn back. But he resolved to press on, and taking up his stick, he struck the rock. The rock vanished; and Bismarck resumed his ascent.

The obstacles to his revolution were falling fast. The plight of the Prussian liberals was by this time scarcely less acute than that of the Danes. The free-state men in the Prussian Chamber of Deputies were inundated with letters from across Germany beseeching them to support Bismarck. "We know," one of these correspondents wrote, "that you have important domestic dissensions, a great home question to settle, but we wonder at your regarding it otherwise than as dust in the balance compared to the immeasurably greater interests at stake in the duchies." The liberal deputies found themselves in an unfortunate position. If they stood firmly on their constitutional principles, they confessed themselves traitors to the German nation. If they urged the Crown to proceed vigorously in the matter of the duchies, they could not consistently refuse it supplies for the army. They chose a middle course. They continued to withhold monies from the Crown. The budget which Bismarck submitted they again refused. A request for an emergency supply of twelve million thaler was rejected. Permission to raise a loan was denied. Yet on the whole the opposition of the free-state men to Bismarck's régime was less fierce than it had been. The lawmakers sympathized with the Minister-President's efforts to liberate their brethren in the duchies, and they allowed themselves to believe that his policy would in time strengthen the cause of the free state. War, they reasoned, was productive of civil turmoil, and might "bring a relief from some of the dynastic influences that press down the liberal element" in Germany.

The Concert of Europe, another obstacle to the rising power of Bismarck, proved to be as unavailing as the Danish arms. The European powers, in declining to enforce the Treaty of 1852, were careless of the principle of collective security. Bismarck, it is true, pretended that there was no violation of the Treaty, and that Prussia had acted in accordance with its provisions. His sophistry could persuade only those who desired to be deceived. Certainly Denmark, too, had breached the Treaty: she had, in contravention of the document's terms, imposed a constitution that bound Schleswig more closely to Copenhagen. But the breach by the Danes of their obligations did not justify the Prussians in forsaking theirs. It took no great sagacity, one diplomat observed, to see that "under her zeal for the enforcement of treaties" Prussia concealed a multitude of "ambitious projects." Those with eyes to see knew that "territorial aggrandizement" was "among the dreams of Herr von Bismarck."

England, too, proved to be a less formidable stumbling block to Prussian ambition than Bismarck could reasonably have expected. For three hundred years England had been the umpire of the balance of power in Europe, and had opposed the emergence, on the Continent, of a military power capable of threatening her own liberties. Even now England aspired to the role of arbiter. "A great many paper missiles," Lord Robert Cecil wrote in the *Quarterly Review,* "were projected from the Foreign Office." Bismarck ignored them.

The result, for the English, was humiliation. "The friendship of England," one diplomat observed, "has been the bane of Denmark." English diplomacy "is a jest and causes sneers throughout all Europe." The cartoonists of the Continent depicted John Bull in a variety of humiliating postures, and German writers sneered at decadent Carthage, sunk in "cowardice and sensuality." The pledges and the threats of Her Majesty's Government, Lord Robert Cecil wrote, were equally ineffectual, and the Danes in consequence of their reliance on England's good faith suffered one "of the most wanton and unblushing spoliations which history records." Bismarck drew his own conclusions. "I wasted several years of my life," he said, "by the supposition that England was a great nation."

One by one the lights went out, and step by step Bismarck's revolution proceeded. He had opposed power to domestic law, and he had survived. He had opposed power to international law, and he had triumphed. The first victories of the new régime marked the re-emergence of a wildness in the diplomatic atmosphere of Europe. Though as a rule Bismarck devoted more time to revising his lies than publishing his truths, he was candid about the moral character of the revolution he had initiated. A French diplomat who came to the Wilhelmstrasse struggled to express his disapproval of the Minister-President's conduct towards Denmark without, however, transgressing the bounds of conventional politeness. Bismarck cut him short. "Don't put yourself out," he said, "nobody but my King thinks that I acted honorably."

Yet he was pleased with himself. The German foray into Jutland had reawakened his royal master's "taste for conquest." Like an animal who, after a long interval of domestication, sinks its teeth into a carcass, the old King had regained a lust for blood. Bismarck, too, possessed such a sanguinary instinct. "When I have an enemy in my power," he said, "I must destroy him." "I am going my own way; whoever goes with me is my friend, who goes against me is my enemy—to the point of annihilation."

Virginia and Alabama, June–May 1864

"God help my country," Mary Chesnut exclaimed.

In the elegiac phase of the Confederacy, gloom hung "like a pall everywhere." Frank Hampton was dead. His heroic end—he fell at the Battle of Brandy Station—eclipsed his ridiculous self-conceit. Mary Chesnut followed the bier to the Capitol in Richmond. Inside Mr. Jefferson's neo-classical temple, she and her friend, Mrs. John Coles Singleton, opened the coffin.

"How I wish I had not looked! I remember him so well in all the pride of his magnificent manhood. He died of a saber cut across the face and head and was utterly disfigured." Mrs. Singleton broke down at the sight. "We sat for a long time on the front steps of the State House. Everybody had gone. We were utterly alone." They remembered the happy week they had all passed together at Mrs. Singleton's house. A beaming Frank Hampton had brought his bride. "And now . . . only a few years . . . nearly all that pleasant company are dead—and our world, the only world we cared for, literally kicked to pieces."

The great personages of the South, Mary Chesnut found, were all more or less dejected. Mrs. Jefferson Davis could give her no ground for optimism. She was "utterly depressed." The two ladies went for drives together around Richmond with the Davis children. Mary Chesnut was struck by their "unbroken wills." The exception was five-year-old Joseph Evans, who was called Joe. He was the "good child" of the family.

President Davis was as gloomy as his wife. As a political mechanism the Republic over which he presided did not work. The purest oligarchies have typically been characterized by a jealousy of executive power. In ancient Sparta, where a warrior caste lived parasitically on the labor of enslaved helots, the Heraclid kings were practically impotent. In the Venetian Republic, the Doge was at times little more than a shadow. At Richmond, President Davis contended with a legislature dominated by proud and luxurious planters who were unwilling to shoulder the burdens of war. When, in 1862, the Confederate Congress raised the upper age limit of the draft to forty-five, it provided that "one white man on every plantation with twenty or more slaves" should be exempted from conscription. As a result, many fine gentlemen stayed home.

Yet even if a greater spirit of sacrifice had prevailed among the planters, Davis would still have found it difficult to vindicate the South's independence. There was not enough money. As in Tsar Alexander's Russia, liquid assets were scarce in the Confederacy; the greatest part of the planters' wealth was invested in land and slaves. Capital and credit mechanisms were primitive. To meet his obligations, Davis turned to the printing presses. The Confederacy's paper money, however, commanded little confidence, and prices soared.

Nor could Davis reasonably expect to alleviate his domestic troubles through a *coup de main* in foreign affairs. In the fall of 1863 Lincoln's ally, Tsar Alexander, sent his fleets to the coastal waters of the United States. The Russian navy anchored, during the winter, in American harbors— the Atlantic fleet at New York, the Pacific fleet in San Francisco Bay. The flagship *Alexander Nevsky* called at Alexandria on the Potomac. Davis knew that Russia's demonstration of support for Lincoln's revolution all but ended his hope that England and France would intervene in the American conflict.

Mary Chesnut saw Davis at a Richmond soirée. He was given to pacing. He "walked with me slowly, up and down that long room." Our "conversation was of the saddest." "Nobody knows so well as he does the difficulties which beset this hard-driven Confederacy. He has a voice which is perfectly modulated. I think there is a melancholy cadence in it which he is unconscious of as he talks of things as they are now."

Mrs. Robert E. Lee was no less downcast. Her home, Arlington, was gone; it had been confiscated by the United States Government, and would soon be converted into a Federal cemetery. Her daughter, Annie—"my sweet Annie," General Lee called her—was dead. Her son, William Henry Fitzhugh Lee, who was known as "Rooney," had been taken prisoner. While he was in captivity his young wife, Charlotte, had sickened and died. Mrs. Lee was a charming woman, cultivated and pious. She had borne her husband seven children, and she had managed the household while he followed the peripatetic life of a soldier. Yet like many women of her class, Mary Lee had receded into invalidism. Rheumatism confined her to a wheelchair, and she was constantly in pain. "Poor lame mother," she said of herself. "I am useless to my children." Over tea she and Mary Chesnut found solace in the past. They talked of how, in the "old Revolutionary times," Mary Chesnut's mother-in-law had greeted Mrs. Lee's relation, General Washington, as he made his way to New York to become the first President of the United States.

The despair of General Lee, though it was also great, was in a manly and heroic mold. Mary Chesnut thought him "the very first man in the world." When, after the fashion of an earlier age, he made her one of his low bows and flashed her one of his charming smiles, she blushed like a schoolgirl. She was a little afraid of the General, but his manner to her was full of gentle consideration. He spoke to her of his son, Rooney. "Poor boy," Lee said, "he is sadly cut up by the death of that sweet little wife of his." Mary Chesnut thought she saw tears stand in the General's eyes. When ladies were present Lee invariably concealed the iron that lay just beneath the surface of his exquisite courtesy. With meddlesome officers he was apt to be more direct. When Wade Hampton III, who had questioned Lee's judgment concerning the deployment of some brigades, threatened to quit the service and return to his plantation, Lee dismissed the planter with a wave of casual disdain. "I would not care if you went back to South Carolina with your whole division," Lee told him. Hampton pronounced the rebuke "*immensely* mortifying."

At times it appeared as though Lee's graceful and ingenious chivalry was all that held the Confederacy together. The country was sinking fast. President Davis was, by this time, one of the most unpopular men in the South. He had, it was said, less to fear from the vengeance of the Yankees than from the passions of his own enraged constituents. He could still rely on the soldiers to cheer him whenever he passed them by; but much of the civilian population regarded him with contempt. In Richmond itself the anxiety was great. The shrieks of wounded soldiers wrought upon the nerves of the townspeople as they went about their business. When, in the churches of Richmond, the congregations sat down to worship of a Sunday, there was an ominous thudding as amputees laid aside their crutches. Most disturbing of all, there was a scarcity of bread. The prospect of famine loomed.

So, too, did the possibility of revolt. The slaves were restive. President Davis's manservant, Jim, absconded with Mrs. Davis's maid, Betsy. One morning Mary Chesnut, coming down to breakfast, was startled to find her husband's man, the fastidious Laurence, drunk. Ordered to move a chair, the slave raised it above his head and smashed a chandelier. James Chesnut watched the exhibition with mounting indignation. "Mary," he said, "do tell Laurence to go home. I am too angry to speak with him." Laurence was sent home to Mulberry, where he was followed, in a short time, by Molly, Mary Chesnut's maid. "I am to be left," Mary Chesnut said, "for the first time in my life, wholly at the mercy of hired servants."

The agitation of Richmond found its analogue in the depths of the country. The report of her mother's illness brought Mary Chesnut deep into the interior of the Confederacy. She took the train to Montgomery, and from there traveled by steamer to Portland. During her journey she encountered much bitterness towards the régime. "This horrid, horrid, Confederacy!" a woman at Montgomery shrieked. "It is unendurable. My God! This den of thieves. I have lost everything but my virtue. My clothes all gone. This dress—it is an old toilette table cover."

"Do you not wish Lincoln was dead and the war over?"

"No," the woman replied. "There are worse men—worse presidents on this continent than Lincoln."

On the steamer to Portland, Mary Chesnut's cousin, James William Boykin, told her of the bales of cotton he had lost in Mississippi. He "charged it all to Jeff Davis in his wrath." When they disembarked, her cousin rode off, and Mary Chesnut waited for the coach in an unlit shanty. The proprietor was a white-trash grotesque; he was drunk and stared at her with a queer look on his face. "Well, Madam," he slobbered, "what can I do for you?" She had reached the heart of the Confederacy, the "jungle South," they called it, where the air was miasmic and men and morals equally dilapidated. In the shanty there were no lamps or candles, and although it was a hot night Mary Chesnut kept close to the fire. Her temples throbbed.

At last the carriage came and took her to her sister's house. She went at once to her mother. "I knew you would come," the old woman said as she took her daughter's hands.

Her sister Sally's appearance shocked her. "As she lifted the candle over her head to show me something on the wall, I saw that her pretty brown hair was white." Her sister's eyes were without life, and "in a stony way, pale and cold as ice," she told Mary Chesnut of the deaths of her children. Kate, the baby of the family, was a beautiful gray-eyed girl. "Strange," Sally said, that "one of my children . . . has lived and has gone, and you have never seen her at all. She died first, and I would not go to the funeral. I thought it would kill me to see her put in the ground." Then thirteen-year-old Mary fell sick. "I did not leave her side again in that long struggle between life and death." "Mama," the girl said, "put your hands on my knees. They are so cold." "I put my hand on her knee. The cold struck to my heart. I knew it was the coldness of death." "I did everything for her," Sally told her sister. "I even prepared my darling for the grave."

As soon as her mother recovered, Mary Chesnut left the Black Belt and returned to Richmond. On the way to the capital she passed troop trains that extended for miles along the tracks. Soldiers on platform cars lay covered in gray blankets. A feeling of "awful depression" laid hold of her as she passed them by. "All these fine fellows going to kill or be killed," she reflected. "Why?"

When she reached Richmond, she found her friends gripped by a giddy hysteria. They resembled "sailors who break into the spirits closet when they find the ship must sink." For the first time she encountered a "resolute feeling to enjoy the brief hour and never look beyond the day." Her husband's resistance to wine and to "hospitality run mad" disappeared. "Your plan for a solitary life in Richmond seems to have failed," she teased him as she prepared one of her elaborate menus. A typical dinner began with soup *à la reine*, followed by mutton, ham, wild duck, and partridges. The wines were as copious as the dishes—a Sauternes with the first course, a Burgundy with the second, then sherry and Madeira.

The senators and patricians of Richmond crowded Mary Chesnut's soirées, eager to drown consideration. Foreign officers came too, among them a Prussian cavalry officer on Jeb Stuart's staff, Heros von Borcke, a young man destined to play a part in two of the three great revolutions of the decade. Yet in whatever exuberance of spirit Mary Chesnut's parties began, they ended now on a note of lamentation and regret.

"After the battles around Richmond [when McClellan was before the city]," one of her guests said, "my hope was strong. All that has insensibly drifted away."

"I am like David," said another, "after the child was dead. Get up, wash my face, have my hair cut . . ."

"I now long, pine, pray, and grieve—and—well, I have no hope," said a third. "Have you any of old Mr. Chesnut's brandy here still?"

James Chesnut took the key to the cellar from his pocket. In a moment the decanter was set down. As the men sat over their brandy, the conversation was grim.

"One more year of Stonewall would have saved us," said one.

"General Lee can do no more than keep back Meade," said another.

Oppressed by such a feeling of doom, Mary Chesnut might, at Mulberry, have sought relief in morphine. In Richmond, she was comforted by the nearness of Buck. She still watched the lovely girl from across the room. "The darling!" she exclaimed. "She has her peculiarities. Who can describe her? This I know. I would not have, if I could, anything altered about her mentally, morally, physically. Of how many people can one say that?" In Mrs. Ives's house she saw her favorite with General Hood. Buck was protecting the crippled warrior from the crush of admirers. John Cabell Breckinridge, Vice President of the United States under Buchanan (he now wore the uniform of a Confederate general), bustled up to Mary Chesnut and interrupted her reverie. "That is a beautiful picture," he said, catching the direction of her gaze. "Will she marry him?"

Mary Chesnut shook her head.

Breckinridge growled. "He cares awfully for her. No wonder. She is so sweet. Poor old battered hero. . . ."

Hood was by this time able, with the help of crutches, to walk, and he could again mount his horse. He and Buck often went out together to ride. Yet she continued to elude him.

Did the stump repel her? She said that it did not. The "Cause glorifies such wounds," she said. Perhaps the lugubrious face disturbed her, those features, so reminiscent of a Mannerist painting, strangely grafted onto a mass of Kentucky flesh. Certainly the violence of Hood's passions gave her pause. When, at a later time, he caught the briefest glimpse of her naked flesh, she was frightened by the desire she aroused in him. Yet she insisted that she was not one of those beauties who was afraid to be pawed by the beast, and she told Hood that if only her parents had not forbidden the match, she could "care for him."

This, however, was a lie. No explicit prohibition touching Sam Hood had been laid down by Colonel and Mrs. Preston. Buck confessed her untruthfulness to Mary Chesnut. "You foolish child!" the older woman scolded. In a softer tone she warned Buck that it was dangerous to encourage, in a man like Hood, a passion she could not return. "Why," Mary Chesnut asked, "are you playing with him in that way?"

Chapter 20

THE VALIANT MEN

Washington and Virginia, March–June 1864

IN THE SAME MOMENT the German revolution found, in Helmuth von Moltke, a victorious captain, Lincoln's revolution, too, found its commander.

Not that the man who entered the lobby of Willard's Hotel on a March afternoon in 1864 looked like a conquering hero. He stood just five feet eight, and he slouched in a way that made him seem shorter. He was slightly built, weighing about a hundred and thirty-five pounds. His major general's uniform was shabby. A cigar hung at his mouth. Five days earlier, he had been summoned to Washington from the West, where he commanded the Army of the Tennessee. The lofty rank of lieutenant general of the Army, once held by George Washington, had been restored by act of Congress. It was now to be bestowed upon him.

The man who signed the register of Willard's— *"U. S. Grant and son, Galena, Ill."*—knew himself to be one of destiny's more puzzling children. Ulysses S. Grant sometimes reflected on the inscrutable motions of providence. "It seems that man's destiny in this world," he said, "is quite as much a mystery as it is likely to be in the next." Three years before his arrival in Washington, in the spring of 1861, Grant had been, at the age of thirty-nine, a failure in the race of life. Although he had graduated from West Point and served with distinction in the Mexican War, he felt no vocation for the profession of arms, and he had been unhappy in the peacetime army. Sent to a remote outpost on the Pacific coast, he had been unable, on his officer's pay, to bring his family with him. The unhappy man sat down beside a barrel of whiskey and "drank himself out of the army." Grant resigned his commission and returned home without prospects. His father-in-law gave him eighty acres near Saint Louis. Grant turned farmer. He chopped down trees and rode into town in his old blue army coat to sell firewood. The farm did not prosper, and he tried to sell real estate. He failed as a real estate agent and attempted to secure the position of county engineer. The place was given to another man, and Grant, in his old army coat, went about the town looking for work. "He was actually the most obscure man in Saint Louis," the wife of his onetime real estate partner said. "Nobody took any notice of him." In May 1860 he took his family to Galena, Illinois, where his father gave him a job as a sales clerk in the family's leather goods business. He met with no more success in this line of work than he had in the others he had tried, and in the spring of 1861 he saw only the prospect of more failure before him. "I was no clerk," he said, "nor had I any capacity to become one."

In the interval since he had relinquished his clerkship to rejoin the colors, Grant had risen fast. He was now the ascendant hero of the North. He had, during more than two years, been the brightest star in the Union officer corps. Early in 1862, when the other Union commanders were paralyzed by fear and vanity, Grant, in Tennessee, took Fort Henry and Fort Donelson, feats which had gladdened the heart of Abraham Lincoln. When, at Shiloh, he was taken by surprise and regained the field only after a copious expenditure of blood, Lincoln refused to censure him. "I can't spare this man," the President told one of Grant's detractors, "he fights." In July 1863 Grant took Vicksburg, the most important Confederate citadel then remaining on the Mississippi. (New Orleans, the gateway to the river, had fallen to Admiral David Glasgow Farragut in April 1862.) Lincoln rejoiced. "The Father of Waters," he said, "again goes unvexed to the sea." Grant's victory at Chattanooga in the autumn of 1863—his men succeeded in taking Missionary Ridge and breaking Bragg's siege of the city—confirmed the superiority of his abilities and sealed his reputation as the most formidable of the Union commanders. "Grant," Lincoln said, "is my man."

After dining at Willard's with his thirteen-year-old son, Fred, who had accompanied him to Washington, Grant went to the White House. He had never before seen the President. He had only once before been in Washington. Lincoln, receiving guests in the Blue Room, recognized him at once from likenesses that had appeared in the press. "Why, here is General Grant!" the President said as he grasped his hand. "Well, this is a great pleasure, I assure you!" Lincoln thought his guest the "quietest little fellow you ever saw," a contrast to the more familiar type of military swagger and verbosity. The next day, when he awarded Grant his commission, the President expressed the "nation's appreciation of what you have done, and its reliance upon you for what remains to be done. . . ." Grant, who did not like to speak in public, thanked the President for the honor he had conferred upon him. His voice was tremulous, and he was at first unable to make himself heard. If, he said, he succeeded in meeting the responsibilities which now devolved upon him, his success would be due to the armies he commanded and "above all, to the favor of that Providence which leads both nations and men."

Grant went at once to the headquarters of the Army of the Potomac. He saw, with the glance of genius, what so many commanders had overlooked. The materials for victory were there. But they were disorganized. There was a need for system and discipline in the deployment of men and matériel. The auxiliary departments that supplied the army with food and munitions were independent of the field commanders; the commissary and ordnance personnel acknowledged no masters other than those in the bureaus of Washington. Grant fixed the problems. Lincoln was amazed. He "makes thing *git,*" the President said. "Wherever he is, things move."

His most important changes were in the realm of strategy and command. The methods he adopted bore a remarkable resemblance to those which his counterpart in the Prussian army, Helmuth von Moltke, had lighted on across the ocean. But where Moltke's ideas were the product of years of studious brooding, Grant's were formed rapidly in the bloody cauldrons of Shiloh and Vicksburg. Both Grant and Moltke turned their minds to an eternal problem of war. A battlefield, the Prussian strategist Clausewitz said, is inevitably a scene of confusion. Innumerable reports, some true, more false, most distorted, reach the ears of the commander. He begins to doubt the strategy he set out to execute, and issues orders not from conviction but from despair. This age-old problem had been rendered more acute by the conditions of modern warfare. The advent of the railroad and the telegraph greatly enlarged the field of operations which the commander must consider in making his dispositions; and it was all but impossible for him to attend to the many technical tasks involved in the deployment of his army and at the same time retain a sense of the overall strategic picture.

Moltke and Grant, independently of one another, solved the problem by means of a division of labor. Under the new system, the offices of strategist and field commander were separate and distinct. Yet the specialists who performed these discrete rôles were obliged to work in close concert with one another. The commander in the field was accompanied by, or was in constant communication with, the principal strategist of the war. Grant, accordingly, did not take for himself the position of commander of the Army of the Potomac: he left General Meade in that place. But he established his own headquarters near Meade's, and he assumed in his camp a rôle similar to that which Moltke, in the Danish War, had undertaken in the camp of the Red Prince. In the past the field commander relied on an intuitive *coup d'œil* to penetrate the fog of war. The new system endowed him with a "better angel" (or evil genius), an officer who had strategy constantly in his mind.

Grant understood the importance of two other qualities which under Moltke were to become articles of faith in the Prussian high command. The first was speed. Grant did not, like McClellan, spend months laboring over the war machine. He used it. Within six weeks of assuming command of the armies, he went down to battle. On May 4, he led 116,000 Union soldiers across the Rapidan towards the Army of Northern Virginia, which under the command of Robert E. Lee continued to hold the line of the Rapidan and the Rappahannock.

Grant's second article of faith was co-operation. The Army of the Potomac did not take the offensive alone: it marched as part of a concerted attack on the vitals of the South. On May 5, General Sherman, for whom Grant felt an affection and respect akin to that which Lee had conceived for Stonewall Jackson, rode out of Chattanooga in the direction of Atlanta. Simultaneously, General Benjamin F. Butler and the Army of the James embarked on steamers at Fort Monroe and proceeded up the James River towards Petersburg and Richmond; and General Franz Sigel went forth to seize cattle and corn in the Shenandoah Valley. This movement "all along the line" opened the series of campaigns known as Operation Crusher. Lincoln, who had for some time pressed for concerted action, helped in an unobtrusive way to shape Grant's strategy. "Those not skinning," he said, "can hold a leg."

The sun was bright as the Army of the Potomac crossed the Rapidan. Battle-stained standards fluttered in the breeze. General Grant, who had taken a degree of care in his dress not usual to him, wore a sword and a sash as he rode his bay horse, Cincinnati, to Germanna Ford. Upon his hands were a pair of yellow thread-gloves, a gift, it was thought, from Mrs. Grant. Having crossed the river, Grant and his troops entered the desolate country known as the Wilderness. The region, with its tangled underbrush, was in many places almost impenetrable, and the few roads which cut through it were far from good. Union skirmishers soon encountered the enemy.

Lee's army could muster only between 60,000 and 80,000 men in the spring of 1864, but although they were outnumbered, the Southern soldiers retained an ardent spirit, and they were intimately familiar with the terrain on which they fought. Jeb Stuart rode out with his cavalry, followed by Lee himself and A. P. Hill at the head of III Corps. The hostile armies were in a short time hotly engaged. The struggle on both sides was obstinate and bloody. The Confederate line buckled, and seemed ready to break, but was saved by the onset of darkness. The next day the Union ranks twice began to give way, but afterwards recovered. Bursting shells ignited the thickets, and the odor of charred flesh hung in the air.

While the battle raged, Grant chain-smoked cigars. He had never witnessed more desperate fighting. Yet he retained his mental poise. Other Union commanders emerged from their first encounter with Lee stunned and dazed, and never afterwards regained their composure. If Grant felt a similar distress, he did not show it. Others, he observed, clothed Lee "with almost superhuman abilities." But he himself had served with the great commander in the Mexican War. "I had known him personally," he said, "and knew that he was mortal."

In refusing to acquiesce in the mystique of Lee, Grant acquired in the eyes of his men an aura of his own. The Army of the Potomac had been ready, one soldier said, "for an explosion at the first mistake Grant made." But the animosity towards the new commander passed away, and Grant soon had the eastern army as firmly in hand as ever he had that of the west. Men noticed the look in his face. It was the look of a man who had "determined to butt his head through a brick wall and was about to do it." He has "the *grit* of a bull-dog," Lincoln said. "Once let him get his 'teeth' *in,* and nothing can shake him off."

Neither side gained a clear victory in the Wilderness, and the spring passed in a succession of battles as Grant marched south towards the James. Lee's forces reached Spotsylvania Court House first and had the advantage. Repeated Union assaults failed to dislodge the enemy. So great was the rate of mortality in one place, where the trench turned sharply, that it lives in history as the Bloody Angle. The fighting was savage. Muskets crossed, and skulls were crushed with the club ends.

The thread-gloves with which Grant opened the campaign had by this time disappeared. They were never afterwards seen. In a dispatch to Washington he announced his "purpose to fight it out on this line if it takes all summer." The war of attrition had begun.

The cost was enormous; but the balance turned. The initiative passed, in Virginia, from one side to the other, for although Lee's lines held, the situation of his army became every day more desperate. Union cavalry under the command of Philip Sheridan rode towards Richmond and severed the lines of supply which enabled the Confederate Army to live. Jeb Stuart sallied forth gallantly to engage Sheridan's cavalry. But at Old Yellow Tavern he received a mortal wound. Heros von Borcke was with him when he died. "My dear Von," Stuart said, "I am sinking fast, but before I die I want you to know that I never loved a man as much as yourself. I pray your life may be long and happy; look after my family when I'm gone, and be the same friend to my wife and children that you've been to me."

"We must," Lee said, "destroy this army of Grant's before he gets to the James River. If he gets there it will be a siege, and then it will be a mere question of time." What might have been Lee's greatest opportunity to break the Union forces came at the beginning of June. As the Army of the Potomac advanced on Cold Harbor, eight miles from Richmond, Lee saw a chance to catch the Federals on the march. He ordered an attack. Mary Chesnut's friend Laurence Keitt was in the vanguard: he led the 20th South Carolina to the fight. He was instantly cut down. The regiment broke, and the whole Confederate line fell back, retiring behind their works. A series of costly assaults ordered by Grant failed to pierce them. Lee's own losses were comparatively light, but the moment of opportunity had passed. He had failed to break the Army of the Potomac, and he now saw no way to do so.

By the middle of June, Grant's army was south of the James.

Berlin and Washington, September 1864

ACROSS THE OCEAN, Bismarck watched the progress of Lincoln's statesmanship with dismay. He detested the American President; his personal sympathies lay wholly with the aristocratic landowners of the South. Yet he made no effort to hinder the President's revolution as it unfolded. He steadily rejected proposals for European intervention in the Civil War—not from love of Lincoln, but from a desire to undermine an enemy closer to home, Louis-Napoleon of France, whose Mexican Empire could not long survive the victory of the United States.

Bismarck lives in history as a practitioner of *Realpolitik;* but the hatred of the free state which drove his statesmanship had its origin, not in what he called the "clockwork" side of his nature—the cunning realism that enabled him to baffle all the diplomatic chess players of the age—but in a less accessible part of his mind that was curiously tender and poetical. He spoke once of being touched with the melancholy of one who, on an autumn morning, beholds the sere foliage and feels within himself immortal longings—a yearning for forests and oceans, for sunsets and the music of Beethoven. His statesmanship, for all its fierce realism, was elegiac. He was alive to the fragility of the civilization into which he had been born, and he saw how easily its treasures, wrought of intricacy of soul and a nobly erotic instinct for good form, might be swept away in the deluge, that flood of disintegrating vulgarity which Lincoln seemed to him to embody. "If there is to be a revolution," Bismarck said, "we would rather make it than suffer it."

But could he act purposefully in history to save the things he loved? In his private speculations Bismarck doubted man's ability to unlock the secrets of providence and master events:

> It was borne in upon me that God had denied man the possibility of knowledge, that it was presumption to claim to know the will and the plans of the Lord of the World, that man must wait in humility to see how his Creator will dispose of him at his death, and that we on earth have no other means of knowing God's will than through conscience, which has given us a feeler with which to find our way through the darkness of the world.

"As God will," he concluded. He however distinguished sharply between the destinies open to a man in his private condition and those which beckoned when he assumed a public character. The moral limits which applied in public life were, Bismarck believed, less narrow than those which governed the private realm: they permitted a wider scope for intelligent action. Providence, too, wore such a Janus-face. The private man must feel his "way through the darkness of the world" with no other guide than conscience; but the public man could avail himself of the special providence which discloses itself to gifted leaders. The statesman might not be able to steal a look at "God's cards," Bismarck said, but he could "see where the Lord wishes to go" and "stumble after Him."

Four thousand miles away, Lincoln, in Washington, was as conscious of the mysteries of time and history. He, too, had meditated on the divinity that shapes man's ends:

> The will of God prevails. In great contests each party claims to act in accordance with the will of God. Both *may* be, and one *must* be, wrong. God cannot be *for*, and *against* the same thing at the same time. In the present civil war it is quite possible that God's purpose is something different from the purpose of either party—and yet the human instrumentalities, working just as they do, are of the

best adaptation to effect His purpose. I am almost ready to say this is probably true—that God wills this contest, and wills that it shall not end yet. By his mere quiet power, on the minds of the now contestants, He could have either *saved* or *destroyed* the Union without a human contest. Yet the contest began. And having begun He could give the final victory to either side any day. Yet the contest proceeds.

Lincoln said that "probably it is to be my lot to go on in a twilight, feeling and reasoning my way through life, as questioning, doubting Thomas did." He and Bismarck held similar ideas of providence: both viewed the mysteries of time and destiny through the dark glass of old-fashioned Protestantism. But where the German kept his theology to himself, the American began to work his into his public utterances. God's will might be inscrutable; but Lincoln nevertheless began to speak, with cautious optimism, of a providential design in which man's better impulses would prevail. "God disposes," he said in 1864. But looking over the past three years, Americans could, he believed, fathom something of His purposes, and could therefore "feel more hopeful and confident for the future."

Events seemed, for a time, to justify the President's optimism. At home, General Grant, though he had not succeeded in outmaneuvering Lee, was wearing him down. Abroad, Europeans in ever greater numbers viewed the contest in America (so Minister Adams in London reported) as "plain between vested rights and popular liberty." Lincoln was pleased, too, that Russia seemed to be moving towards freedom. Bayard Taylor, the chargé in the American Legation in Saint Petersburg, had returned to the United States and given a lecture on Russia. Lincoln attended the lecture in person and afterwards wrote to Taylor. "I think a good lecture or two on 'Serfs, Serfdom, and Emancipation in Russia' would be both interesting and valuable," the President said. "Could not you get up such a thing?"

But much remained doubtful. The coming elections filled Lincoln with foreboding. Not since 1832, when Andrew Jackson was re-elected, had an American President been granted a second term of office. In June 1864 delegates to the Republican* Convention at Baltimore nominated Lincoln for President. But his difficulties were not ended with his victory over those in his party who, like Salmon P. Chase, questioned his leadership. His popularity in the North as a whole was uncertain. Grant's campaign, though it promised eventually to be successful, was costly;

---

* The party styled itself the National Union Party in 1864.

more than 60,000 Union soldiers had fallen dead or wounded since the opening of the Army of the Potomac's campaign of 1864. Many in the North yearned for a settlement that would restore peace at once, even if the terms of the armistice stipulated the maintenance of slavery in the South. Lincoln, however, rejected this moral equivalent of a separate peace—such a truce would force him to repudiate the Emancipation Proclamation and return to bondage blacks who had fought bravely for the faith that all men are created equal. "I should be damned in time and in eternity for so doing," the President said.

Yet he knew that his opposition to slavery was likely to prove costly in the canvass. The Copperheads stigmatized the Emancipation Proclamation as the Miscegenation Proclamation. In the summer of 1864 these peace-at-any-price men appeared to be winning the war of public opinion. George McClellan, the most prominent Democrat in the nation, seemed poised to ride a wave of Copperhead sentiment into the White House. It "seems exceedingly probable," Lincoln wrote in August, "that this Administration will not be re-elected." Unless "some great change takes place," he would, he said, be "badly beaten" by McClellan in the autumn.

Berlin, Paris, and Nice, April 1865

THE IMPERIAL TRAIN sped across the frontier of Russia at an unprecedented speed, hurtling the Tsar towards France. Alexander's son, Tsarevitch Nicholas, lay languishing in a villa on the Riviera. The spinal malady from which he suffered had worsened. The health of members of the imperial family was a closely guarded secret in Russia; but word spread that Niks was gravely ill.

Alexander went first to Berlin, where his uncle, King Wilhelm, embraced him. He went next to Paris, where the eastern railway joined the line which led to Lyons and the south. Napoleon III was waiting on the platform. As the Tsar emerged from the railway carriage the rivalry of empires was, for a moment, forgotten. A newspaper correspondent who glimpsed Alexander's face thought that it betrayed a profound depression. Louis-Napoleon stepped forward and, with the peculiar grace which not even his detractors denied him, offered his sympathy to the Tsar. After exchanging a few words of courtesy with his host, Alexander went back into the railway carriage.

His paternal intuition ought to have told him long before that his oldest son was ill. Niks had grown frightfully thin. Ordinary tasks were painful to him. Once, during a foxhunt at Peterhof, he grimaced in pain after leaping into the saddle. When Alexander asked him what was wrong, Niks was too proud to reply. He put spurs to his horse and rode on. Later, when Alexander saw the emaciated youth dragging himself about the palace, he chided him for walking like an old man. A future Tsar must carry himself like a soldier.

Alexander's conscience must now have smote him. The behavior he had attributed to his son's effeminacy was in reality the result of illness, possibly tuberculosis of the spine. Caused by the same bacterium that causes pulmonary tuberculosis, Pott's disease attacks the vertebrae and slowly destroys them.

The imperial train pulled into the old station at Nice, and the Tsar went at once to his son's bedside. Niks, it is said, was able to recognize his father; but Alexander could not mistake the gravity of his son's condition. The Tsarevitch was dying.

Chapter 21

POWER AND ENCHANTMENT

Richmond and South Carolina, May–August 1864

IN THE DEAD OF NIGHT the windows of President Davis's house were open, and the curtains blew wildly. Little Joe Davis, the "good child," had fallen from a railing. Mary Chesnut, hearing the news, went at once to the mansion. She found the boy white and beautiful in death. Mrs. Davis did not appear; but Mary Chesnut, seated in the drawing room, heard the heavy footfall of the President. In the room above Jefferson Davis paced and repaced the floor.

The death was ruled an accident, but it dripped doom. The bloody child, spattered on the pavement, seemed to Mary Chesnut an evil omen. She left Richmond shortly after the boy's funeral and readied herself to witness the annihilation of her class. Her husband had a short time before been made a brigadier general, and he had been ordered to return to South Carolina. The train took her as far as Kingsville, where she sought accommodation in a dingy hotel.

"No room," she was informed by the *hôtelier* at the desk. "Who are you?"

Mary Chesnut gave her name.

"Try something else," the woman said as she eyed the traveler's torn dress and dusty petticoat. "Mrs. Chesnut don't travel round by herself, no servants, no nothing." When, at last, Mary Chesnut convinced the clerk of her identity, she professed astonishment. "The Lord sakes alive," she exclaimed, "and to think *you* are *her.* Now I see—dear! dear me! Heaven sakes, woman, but you are *broke!*"

At last she reached Mulberry. She found the place greatly changed. Old Mrs. Chesnut, her mother-in-law, was dead. Her father-in-law, the aged Colonel, was left alone in the darkness. Mary Chesnut felt pity for the parent she had long regarded as a tyrant. When his wife was living he used each morning to don a dressing gown and go to her room, where he brushed his hair before her mirror. He continued to go to her room in the mornings now that she was in her grave. One morning Mary Chesnut saw him there. He was kneeling beside the empty bed, sobbing bitterly.

Mary Chesnut fled to Columbia. She found the town wild with excitement. General Sherman was marching on Atlanta at the head of 100,000 men. The innards of the Southern Republic would soon be within his grasp. Columbia itself was not safe. In the Prestons' house Mary Chesnut came upon Buck. The girl was now Sam Hood's fiancée. She stood at the head of the stairs in a flowing dressing gown. Her blue eyes, wide open, shone black with excitement.

Had Mary Chesnut heard the news? President Davis had relieved Joe Johnston of command of the army charged with saving the South from Sherman. In his place he had appointed Sam Hood. "I have prayed God," Buck said, "as I never prayed him before." The eyes of the world now rested upon her fiancé; and Buck Preston, the *belle* of the Confederacy, sank to her knees in prayer.

Washington, March 1865

AFTER THE PRESIDENT HAD, as was his custom, received the day's petitioners in his office on the second floor of the mansion, he ordered the door to the chamber to be closed. Joshua F. Speed, the friend of his youth, was paying a visit to Washington, and Lincoln wanted to talk to him of private things. As the President beckoned Speed to a place by the fire, he saw that they were not alone. Two women, whose dress bespoke the humbleness of their station, had contrived to remain in the room after the dismissal of the other petitioners. Their presence seemed to provoke the President.

"Well, ladies, what can I do for you?" Lincoln asked.

The older of the two women begged the President to release her son from the prison in western Pennsylvania in which he had been confined for draft evasion. The younger woman begged him to release her husband from the same place.

"Where is your petition?" the President asked.

"Mr. Lincoln," the old woman said, "I've got no petition; I went to a lawyer to get one drawn, and I had not the money to pay him and come here too; so I thought I would just come and ask you to let me have my boy."

"And it's your husband you want," the President said to the young woman.

"Yes."

Lincoln rang the bell and asked for a paper. In a moment Mr. Dana entered the room with the document. On it were set forth the names of men held by the Federal government for draft evasion in western Pennsylvania.

"Well," the President said as he gazed out the window, "these poor fellows have, I think, suffered enough; they have been in prison fifteen months. I have been thinking so some time, and have so said to Stanton, and he always threatened to resign if they are released. But he has said so about other matters, and never did. So now, while I have the paper in my hand, I will turn out the whole flock." He took up a pen. "*Let the prisoners named in the within paper*," he wrote in his neat hand, "*be discharged.*" He signed the paper and turned to the two women. "Now ladies," he said, "you can go. Your son, madam, and your husband, madam, is free."

The young woman knelt to him.

"Get up," Lincoln said as he raised her to her feet, "none of this."

The old woman went to the President and, wiping the tears from her face, looked into Lincoln's eyes. "Good-bye, Mr. Lincoln," she said, "we will never meet again till we meet in Heaven."

The President took the old woman's hand. A change came over his face. "With all that I have to cross me here," he said, "I am afraid I will never get there; but your wish that you will meet me there has fully paid for all I have done for you."

After they left, the door to the chamber was again closed. Lincoln took off his boots and stretched his feet towards the fire. "That young woman," he said to Speed, "is a counterfeit, but the old woman is a true mother."

The end of the war was in sight. The noose was tightening around the neck of the South. Atlanta had fallen to General Sherman. General Grant was before Petersburg and Richmond. In Tennessee, Sam Hood and his army had been routed and crushed. Lincoln himself, in spite of his forebodings of defeat at the polls, had been re-elected to a second term. The sentiments of the peace-at-any-price men were less pervasive in the North than he had feared, and General McClellan, who was for a time the darling of the Copperheads, had received only 21 electoral votes. Lincoln himself had received 212. A free people had endorsed his revolution.

The President, in victory, was tired, and not entirely well. His feet and hands, he said, seemed always to be cold. A good night's sleep, the usual remedy for life's smaller shocks, did not allay the sensation of fatigue. Nothing, Lincoln said, seemed to touch the "tired spot." To his friend he confessed his apprehensions. "Speed," he said, "I am a little alarmed about myself; just feel my hand."

Speed touched the President's hand. It was cold.

On March 4, the day on which his first term of office was to expire, Lincoln went early to the Capitol. There had been a great storm in the night. The wind howled, and the rain beat down on the glass roof of the hall of the Capitol. The morning dawned dark, leaden, soaking. The streets were so many rivers of mud. The authorities feared mischief, and the President was accompanied, as he made his way to the Capitol, by a bodyguard of soldiers. He rode at a sharp trot. The lines cut deeper than ever into the brown face; but the old goodness, one observer thought, was still visible underneath the furrows.

Rain and fog obscured the recently finished dome that now dominated the approaches to Capitol Hill. Upon reaching the seat of the legislature, the President went to the Vice President's room. There he sat for some time transacting business and affixing his name to freshly enacted laws. The Thirty-Eighth Congress was approaching its demise, and weary lawmakers, many of whom had labored through the night in the gaslit chambers, were preoccupied with negotiating provisions for the taxation of income and the supply of the gigantic army which in the last four years had been called into being.

The President did not fret over the address he was to deliver in the afternoon. He had composed it in the days preceding the inauguration, and he had it with him now, printed on a half-sheet of foolscap. The newspapermen had been informed that the oration would be brief. The address, the Associated Press reported, would in all likelihood not exceed a column in the newspapers.

In the chamber of the Senate, the great figures of Washington assembled. Diplomats, generals, and politicians presented their tickets and were admitted to the chamber. Ladies and newspapermen crowded the galleries. The heads of the executive departments came, led by the ranking member of the Cabinet, Secretary of State Seward. He was a man greatly changed from what he had been on the same day four years before. He was now submissive in all things to a President whom he recognized as his superior in political strength, and possibly in wisdom and judgment as well. Lincoln, Seward had for some time believed, was "the best of us." The President's re-election had placed him, he said, "beyond the pale of human envy."

A hush came over the chamber as Lincoln's new Vice President made his entrance. Andrew Johnson was a staunch Union man. He had served as military governor of Tennessee, and he was credited with exertions that had done much to keep alive, in that state, the cause of the United States. But those near to him were anxious for him on this day. They watched uneasily as he approached the rostrum, arm-in-arm with the outgoing Vice President, Hannibal Hamlin of Maine. Johnson had earlier called for whiskey to soothe his nerves, and his friends wondered whether he had not consumed too much.

He now addressed the assembly. He was, he said, a man "from the ranks." Yet he had come to occupy the second highest office in the land. He was a plebeian . . . and he thanked God for it. He then turned to Salmon P. Chase, whom Lincoln had recently raised to be Chief Justice of the United States. "And your exaltation and position," he said, "depend on the people." (In fact the Chief Justice, like all judges under Article III of the Constitution, held his office during good behavior.) Johnson next turned to the Cabinet. "And I will say to you, Mr. Secretary Seward, and to you, Mr. Secretary Stanton, and to you, Mr. Secretary—" Here he hesitated; in his befuddlement he could not remember the name of the Secretary of the Navy. He turned to someone sitting near him. "Who is the Secretary of the Navy?" he asked. "Mr. Welles," he was told. "And to you, Mr. Secretary Welles, I would say, you all derive power from the people . . ."

"There is evidently something wrong," Secretary Stanton whispered.

"Johnson is either drunk or crazy," said Secretary Welles.

"The man is certainly deranged," said Attorney General Speed.

A ray of sunshine penetrated the chamber, and it was determined that the President should go out of doors to take his oath and kiss his Bible. (Had the bad weather continued, the inauguration of the President would have taken place in the Senate chamber.) Lincoln passed from shadow into light. "Don't let Johnson speak outside," he instructed the marshal of ceremonies, Ward Hill Lamon, the gigantic lawyer. A platform had been erected before the east front of the Capitol, and at the appearance of the President the Marine Band played "Hail to the Chief." Lincoln delivered his address.

> On the occasion corresponding to this four years ago, all thoughts were anxiously directed to an impending civil-war. All dreaded it— all sought to avert it. . . . Both sides deprecated war; but one of them would *make* war rather than let the nation survive; and the other would *accept* war rather than let it perish. And the war came. . . .

"Probably no other speech of a modern statesman," Lord Charnwood said of this address, "uses so unreservedly the language of intense religious feeling." In language closer to that of John Winthrop and John

Cotton than that of James Madison and Alexander Hamilton, Lincoln invoked the "living God" of the Bible.* The history of the country was, he said, providential. It was a story of sin, suffering, and redemption. The sin (or offense) was slavery; the suffering (or woe) was the Civil War; the redemption (or grace) lay in the possibility of peace, and the binding up of wounds that would follow the revolution.

With malice towards none; with charity for all . . .

Lord Charnwood said that Lincoln's oratory, which differed from that of most of the other great speakers in history, was "perhaps more like that of some of the great speeches in drama." Such dramatic exertions take their toll, and when the inaugural fêtes were concluded, Lincoln collapsed in fatigue. He had uttered his tragic valediction; but the tragedy itself was not yet complete.

Saint Petersburg, June 1865–March 1866

THE WINTER WAS a memory in Saint Petersburg. The White Nights came. Dusk merged into dawn without an interval of blackness. The days were hot, and the canals emitted a foul odor, the Petersburg stench. In the taverns people sat at sticky tables drinking beer and vodka. Out of doors drunken men staggered in the sunshine. The music of street singers filled the air.

Oh, my handsome soldier
Don't beat me for nothing

The newspapers reported an alarming increase in incidents of crime. Sleep was difficult in the White Nights; and much that in other seasons is buried in the oblivion of darkness was acted out in the light.

The frigate *Alexander Nevsky*, which had recently paid a call at Alexandria, Virginia, to demonstrate Russia's support for Abraham Lincoln, steamed towards Kronstadt. The wind blew fiercely. The imperial standard flapped on the mizzenmast. Eighteen men-of-war were drawn up in line of battle to receive the flagship, and a hundred batteries thundered. The Tsar himself, who had come up in his yacht *Strela*, sailed out to the London Buoy to meet the ship. He went aboard, received the

* "*It is* a fearful thing to fall into the hands of the living God"–Hebrews 10:31. This chapter of Scripture made a deep impression on another nineteenth-century psychologist, Dostoevsky, who cited it in Book VI of *The Brothers Karamazov.*

salutes of the officers and sailors, and proceeded to the principal cabin. From it came the sounds of plaintive chanting. The monks were there. They were praying for Niks, whose mortal remains, brought from Nice, lay on a catafalque. Father Pachcmi, a monk from the Saint Sergius Monastery of the Trinity, read the *panichide* for the repose of the Tsarevitch's soul. While the *Nevsky* was towed into Merchants' Harbor, the Tsar knelt before his son's coffin.

Two days later the body was interred. The imperial family came to the capital early that morning from Tsarskoe Selo. The Tsar and the other pallbearers—the Crown Prince of Denmark, Prince Albert of Prussia, and the dead Tsarevitch's brothers—went up to Merchants' Harbor in the *Alexandria* to collect the corpse. (The Neva was too shallow for the draft of the *Nevsky*.) In a few hours they returned with the remains of Niks. The vessel docked at the English Quay. Bells tolled, and minute guns fired. The pallbearers carried the coffin to the street, where the funeral car waited. The horse of the Tsarevitch, in the velvet housing of the Ataman Cossack regiment, snorted and pawed. The cortège went forward to the strains of a dirge. The Ataman Cossacks, in uniforms of sapphire blue, carried the dead man's flag and mace. The Tsar followed his son's bier past dense crowds to the fortress. Nik's coachman, his box draped in black velvet, drove the eight horses which pulled the car. (Tradition required that the man never drive again. In exchange for renouncing forever the exercise of his calling, he received a pension from the Romanovs.) At eight o'clock a funeral Mass was sung in the fortress. Two hours later the distraught Empress arrived. Supported by her husband, Mary came to weep and pray before the coffin of her son.

The death of the Tsarevitch plunged Russia into mourning. The peasantry was in those days still loyal to the dynasty. The workers were scarcely less devoted. "At that time," one radical said, "it was dangerous to speak badly of the Tsar in the factories." Students who went among the workers to distribute revolutionary literature were booed. "As a rule the worker does not love the students just because he looks upon them as enemies of the Tsar," one observer said. "The Tsar is for him the personification of truth and justice." When they learned that the Tsar's eldest son was dead, ordinary Russians were sad.

Still the students came. Some were nihilists, others socialists. Most were intent on practicing on the workers a romantic version of *noblesse oblige* derived from the philosophy of Bakunin, Marx, and Eugène Sue, in which the love of power was disguised into a universal pity. One who went among the people had a wild look in his eyes. His face was pale and his hair hung down to his shoulders. Dmitri Karakozov came from the decaying gentry of Saratov, where his family, before emancipation, possessed some fifty peasants. He had been expelled from the university in Moscow, and had become a teacher in one of the free schools there. Karakozov possessed the inverted holiness often found in revolutionary circles. He was connected to a socialist cell called "Hell"; its dogmas were a garbled mixture of Saint Paul, Machiavelli, and Robespierre. The sect's disciples repudiated the Tsar's liberal revolution; Karakozov's cousin, who held a high place in the priesthood of Hell, said that if the free-state men won, they would "invent some sort of constitution and push Russia into the Western way of life. This constitution will find support among the upper and middle classes, as it will guarantee individual liberty and give a stimulus to industry and business."

The young revolutionists were always to blame what they called the "abnormality of the social organization" of Russia on the selfishness of the middle and upper classes. But those among them who talked to the people knew better. The peasants and workers, it transpired, had as little love for socialist altruism as the well-to-do. The toiling masses "gave unmistakable evidence of an acquisitive spirit of the worst bourgeois type combined with moral cynicism and politically reactionary attitudes." If the revolutionists were to avert a liberal-bourgeois catastrophe and at the same time shatter the Tsarist régime, they could not rely on the goodwill of the people. They must instead be cruel. Only after the revolution, when "all men will become righteous in one instant," could they afford to be kind.

Karakozov, haunted by the suspicion that he would die before he had accomplished a noble deed for the people, longed to contribute to the revolution. But what could he do? In his despair he contemplated suicide. He went so far as to acquire poison. The winter came, and he withdrew to the Saint Sergius Monastery of the Trinity. (Although he had converted to socialism, Karakozov had never freed himself from the grip of the older faith.) In March 1866 he arrived in Saint Petersburg.

He had, by this time, acquired a revolver.

Chapter 22

MUFFLED DRUMS

Richmond and Chesapeake Bay, April 1865

THE SUN SHONE as the President went up the James River towards Richmond. The capital of the Confederacy had fallen. Jefferson Davis had fled. In the global struggle for liberty, those who were fighting on the side of the President were on the verge of a great victory.

The President wanted to be there, wanted to inspect the abandoned camp of "the other fellow," as he sometimes called Jefferson Davis. "Thank God I have lived to see this," he was heard to say. "It seems I have been dreaming a horrid nightmare for four years, and now the nightmare is gone. I want to see Richmond."

He came up from City Point, a bluff south of the fallen Capitol which overlooked the converging waters of the James and the Appomattox. There he had maintained, since March 24, a floating White House aboard the steamer *River Queen*. He had later transferred his headquarters to the *Malvern*. Its accommodations were less spacious than those of the *River Queen*; but though the quarters were cramped, the President declined Rear Admiral Porter's offer of the principal cabin, and he contented himself with a smaller berth, just six feet in length. He pretended to find it comfortable; yet he admitted that "you can't put a long blade into a small scabbard."

The *Malvern* and its escorts steamed up the winding river past the seats of a fallen aristocracy. Death and decay mingled strangely with the life and hope of a spring morning. The flotilla paddled past Shirley, the stately seat of the Carters and the Hills; it was at Shirley that Anne Hill Carter had been born, the mother of Robert E. Lee. The boats passed Turkey Island, a plantation of the Randolphs, the family which had given America one of her greatest presidents, Thomas Jefferson, and one of her greatest jurists, John Marshall. The convoy steamed past Varina; here John Rolfe had cultivated tobacco, and here he had taken his bride, Pocahontas, after their marriage in 1614. It was Rolfe who described the fateful day, five years later, when a Dutch man-of-war appeared in the bay and "sold us twenty Negars"—the beginning of the story which Lincoln came to end.

At length the spires and chimneys of Richmond came into view. As the flotilla drew near to the city, the presidential party found débris blocking the channel. Live torpedoes bobbed amid the corpses of horses and the wreckage of boats. The President descended into the captain's barge, and a detachment of Marines towed him towards the Southern capital. When the Marines could do no more, the sailors rowed Lincoln to the landing. The President stepped onto the dock and walked up the hill towards Mr. Jefferson's statehouse. "I want to see the Capitol," he said.

All around him there was devastation. In the brief span of time— less than forty-eight hours—since Jefferson Davis and the other high dignitaries of the Confederacy had abandoned the city, Richmond had plumbed the depths of the inferno. A devil was loosed in the city. Pillage and rapine were rapidly followed by conflagration. Fires, intended by the fleeing Confederates to destroy the warehouses, were whipped by the winds, and ignited the artillery shells. A hundred thousand explosions shook the city to its foundations. After a night of horror the Mayor begged the Union forces to come in to "preserve order and protect women and children and property."

Lincoln, guarded by a small contingent of sailors, walked amid shattered glass and smoking rubble. The sun was hot as he passed broken walls and houseless chimneys. He took off his overcoat, and was several times seen to remove his hat and wipe perspiration from his brow.

The words, at first, were indistinct.

"Glory to God!"

Soon there were more voices.

"Glory! Glory! Glory!"

First one, then another black man recognized the President. Lincoln was in a short time surrounded by those whom he had liberated. Some of the former slaves knelt to him. Others sang. An old man dropped his spade. "Bless the Lord," he said, "there is the great Messiah! I knew him as soon as I saw him. He's been in my heart for long years, and he's come at last to free his children from their bondage! Glory, Hallelujah."

So Simeon had sung, many centuries before.

He begged them not to kneel. "Don't kneel to me. That is not right. You must kneel to God only, and thank Him for the liberty you will hereafter enjoy. I am but God's humble instrument."

Lincoln gazed at Mr. Jefferson's statehouse, where the Stars and Stripes again flew. He went next to Jefferson Davis's house. Whatever feelings of triumph he felt he carefully suppressed. He entered the rival President's study and sat down in a chair. "This," he said, "must have been President Davis's chair." He spoke softly. He wondered whether he might have a glass of water. The Davises' butler brought him the water. The butler brought, too, a bottle of whiskey; this Lincoln left untouched. There must be no gloating, and no revenge. "I want no one punished," he said, "treat them liberally all round."

On April 8 the President returned to Washington on the *River Queen*. Before sailing he asked the band to play the *Marseillaise*. He then requested that "Dixie" be played. "That tune is now Federal property," he said. It was "good to show the rebels that, with us in power, they will be free to hear it again." On the voyage back to his own capital the President was pensive. He took up a volume of Shakespeare and began to read aloud from it. *Macbeth*—his favorite play. The tragedy of the man of ambition, the creature of destiny. He recited the lines—

> *Duncan is in his grave;*
> *After life's fitful fever he sleeps well . . .*

Lincoln lingered over the poetry. He tried to fathom Macbeth's state of mind. The "dark deed achieved," he said, "its tortured perpetrator came to envy the sleep of his victim. . . ."

The idea of destiny is the great elixir of revolution. Nothing so rouses a people as the belief that their nation has a rendezvous with it. Nothing so legitimizes a ruler or a régime as a myth that purports to offer a nation control of the future. Yet no revolutionary leader can offer such a vision of futurity convincingly unless he has a corresponding feeling within himself, a belief that he has been marked out by fate, a belief that he can, in Bismarck's words, hear the footsteps of God sounding through events.

Lincoln understood this. The man who surveyed the prostrate capital of his adversaries felt the allure of destiny. But he who steals a glance into the Sibylline books of his country pays for the privilege. Macbeth suffered for his colloquies with the Weird Sisters.

Washington, April 1865

A FEW MINUTES after ten o'clock on Good Friday, April 14, John Wilkes Booth entered the lobby of Ford's Theatre. He carried with him a Derringer pistol loaded with a .44-caliber lead ball.

Brooklyn, April 1865

WALT WHITMAN, visiting his mother, was awakened by the tolling of bells. Something had happened. He went out for the newspapers. It was a dark, dripping Saturday, redeemed only by the lilacs. They had bloomed early that spring. Their fragrance would linger in his memory to remind him of a day "black, black, black."

Darmstadt and Saint Petersburg, April–May 1865

REFLECTING ON THE life and death of his fellow liberator, Tsar Alexander spoke of Lincoln's "noble career." "Tried himself," Alexander wrote, "by a woeful loss" (the death of Niks), he sympathized with Americans in their hour of bereavement, and he asked that his condolences be conveyed to Mrs. Lincoln. He commanded that a solemn requiem be chanted in Kazan Cathedral at Saint Petersburg. When someone objected that Lincoln was not a communicant in the Orthodox Church, the Tsar became angry. "He was the noblest and greatest Christian of our generation," Alexander said. "He was a beacon to the whole world— nothing but courage, steadfastness and the desire to do good."

Berlin, April 1865

NORMAN BUEL JUDD, the American Minister at Berlin, learned the news from a telegram dispatched by Minister Adams in London. A few days before, Judd, a fifty-year-old Illinois lawyer, had hung out his banners to honor the triumph of Lincoln's statesmanship. Now he draped his Legation in black in memory of his friend's life. Berlin, he said, talked of nothing else, and there was much weeping.

But in at least one house no tears fell. In the Wilhelmstrasse, the eyes of Bismarck were dry. Lincoln's cause was not his, and the condolences he extended to the American people were perfunctory. The Minister-President did, however, attend a memorial service for Lincoln in Saint Dorothea's Church.

In the Prussian Chamber of Deputies the news was very differently received. On the floor of the Chamber, Dr. William Loewe, who had once found refuge from despotism in New York, bowed his head before "the modest greatness" of Lincoln. He asked the Chamber to unite with him in paying tribute to the dead President's memory.

The address the Prussian lawmakers framed described the joy with which they had, a short time before, hailed the triumph of "right and law" in America; and it expressed the sorrow they felt upon learning that the architect of that triumph was no more. More than two hundred deputies subscribed their names to the document, and a delegation of the most eminent members carried it to the American Legation.

Chapter 23

SHAME

Paris and Biarritz, September–October 1865

THE WEATHER IN EUROPE was unseasonably warm, and there had been no rain for weeks. Asiatic cholera, issuing from the swamps of the Ganges, was carried westward along the trade routes to Damascus and Acre. The pestilence raged at Beirut and Jaffa, and was brought by Levantine shipping to the ports of the western Mediterranean, to Tripoli, Malta, and Gibraltar. At Rome, the Holy Father, Pius IX—*Pio Nono*—proclaimed a quarantine. In Toulon, the disease appeared with startling suddenness. The blackened corpses of four Italian sailors were found in a soiled garret, and from that moment the progress of the plague was violent and rapid.

Caused by the bacterium *Vibrio cholerae,* Asiatic cholera is one of the swiftest of death's messengers. The most fortunate victims perish within two or three hours of the onset of symptoms. Others, less happy, linger in agony for a few days. Weakened by ricewater stools and incessant vomiting, they appear like hideous changelings, with sunken eyes and a ghastly coloration. Their skin, which emits a foul odor, is cold to the touch, yet the sufferers feel themselves to be inwardly burning. Early in October there were reports that the disease had reached Paris.

Bismarck, undeterred, rode the train to the French capital. He had absented himself from felicity for too long. He *must* go to Biarritz and see Kathi Orlov again. He had recently been raised by King Wilhelm to the rank of Count, and for the moment his power was secure. His health, moreover, was bad. The loyal Roon, with an eye on "Otto's Herculean industry," said that his friend had "now to reckon with the rebellion of his truest and most submissive subject, his stomach." Bismarck, alarmed by his "deranged digestion" and "tortured nerves," needed a vacation.

Sunshine, Moët and beer (he liked to mix the two in a concoction he called "Black Velvet"), and Kathi Orlov were the medicines he required.

He found Paris hot and dry. The waters of the Seine were at the lowest point in memory, and mudlarks dug in the flats which the receding river had exposed. The drains and sewers of the city were stagnant, the fountains were dry, diarrhea was rife. Visitors were advised to drink seltzer water, and the wards of the Charité and the Hôtel-Dieu swelled with the sick. Yet a kind of levity prevailed, and at nine o'clock in the evening the dining gardens of the Moulin Rouge and the cafés of the Champs-Elysées were crowded. Bismarck went to the Quai d'Orsay to pay his civilities to Drouyn de Lhuys, the French Foreign Minister. Drouyn, a sixty-year-old career diplomat in the French service, was the friend of Austria, not Prussia, and the rumor went round that Bismarck spoke to him "in a very bellicose and proud way."

Afterwards he took the train to Biarritz. He was chagrined to learn that Kathi Orlov had canceled her visit. Fearful for the health of her children, she had decided to take her holiday in England, at Sidmouth, instead. Although Bismarck did not know it, he was not to see her again.

In the absence of Kathi, he devoted his energies to revolution. He went to see Napoleon III, who was in residence at Biarritz. The weather had by this time changed. The barometer had fallen, the sea was rough, and the wind blew from the northeast. The horizon was black as Bismarck drove up to the Villa Eugénie. An autumn storm lashed the coast, and the surf foamed as the two potentates exchanged greetings.

Bismarck found the French Emperor in a poor state. Louis-Napoleon's bladder was an agony to him. His face was ashen. He walked with difficulty. Wherever he looked he saw danger. France was querulous. Mexico was a quagmire. His protégé, Archduke Maximilian of Austria, had sailed, the preceding year, to Vera Cruz to take his seat on the throne of Louis-Napoleon's Mexican Empire; but the blond Prince was innocent of those arts which are indispensable to the politician who finds himself in a difficult position. Maximilian's only resource, when confronted with an obstacle to his will, was a peevish obstinacy. Before the birth, in 1858, of a son to Franz Josef, Maximilian had been next in line to the throne of Austria. With the birth of the dark-starred Rudolph, however, he was relegated to second place in the succession. It was assumed, at Vienna, that he would relinquish his rights to the Austrian Crown upon accepting Louis-Napoleon's invitation to sit on the throne of Mexico. But as the day of his departure drew closer, it became evident that Maximilian had no intention of surrendering his chance of a second empire. There were unpleasant scenes in the baroque antechambers of Vienna; archducal potentates lost their tempers; and Maximilian, after a hot exchange with Archduke Rainer, the President of the Council of Ministers, quitted the city in disgust. Only when General Frossard brought a stern warning from Louis-Napoleon himself did Maximilian relent.

The willful Prince was by that time absorbed in another dispute, this one concerning his right to the throne not of Austria but of Mexico. Maximilian contended, a trifle fancifully, that in taking up the Mexican crown he did but avail himself of his hereditary prerogative as the right male heir of the body of Charles V, the Habsburg Emperor who had united in his person the crowns of Spain and the Holy Roman Empire. By contrast, Louis-Napoleon insisted, with perhaps even less justice, that Maximilian's authority derived from the will of the nation of Mexico. The quarrel was resolved in favor of Louis-Napoleon, whose advance of twenty-five million francs enabled Maximilian to purchase, among other necessary items, the liveries in which he and his consort, Archduchess Charlotte, intended to dress the imperial household at Mexico City.

The prospect brightened, for a moment, when Maximilian reached Vera Cruz, and all had at first gone well for the Habsburg adventurer. Indians and mestizos had pressed adoringly around the imperial carriage. Maximilian's appearance was the fulfillment of a prophecy the Indians had long cherished. A fair-haired prince, it was said, would one day liberate them from the yoke of the *hacendados*. "You are the white man with light hair and blue eyes," the Indians told him, "whom we have been so long expecting." But Maximilian's prospects were darkened by the triumph of Lincoln's revolution. The establishment of a foreign despotism on the ruins of the Mexican Republic alarmed Americans. Already a knot of millionaires in New York had formed a committee dedicated to ensuring that "this continent is for ever devoted to the cause of liberal institutions and republican government." More ominously, General Grant had dispatched, to the vicinity of the Rio Grande, Philip Sheridan, with orders to assemble an army.

Louis-Napoleon was unwilling to be drawn into a contest with the United States. In October 1865 he thought only of extricating his troops from Mexico in the least humiliating way. Maximilian he must leave to his own devices. This abandonment of a friend would doubtless cost the French Emperor a pang, and leave a stain upon the scutcheons of the Bonapartes; but he saw no other way. The situation in which his unfortunate vassal would find himself, after the last French battalion embarked at Vera Cruz, would, indeed, be one from which even the most dexterous statesman might shrink. And Maximilian, in abilities and mental power, did not exceed the limits of mediocrity. His days were passed in vain pageantry, in fruitless tourism, and in the prescription of elaborate rules of etiquette for his court. The real work of directing the administration was carried on not by the Mexican Emperor, but by the French commander, François-Achille Bazaine, the soldier upon whom Louis-Napoleon had recently conferred the highest military gift in his power. Bazaine was now a Marshal of France, one of the few men promoted from the ranks to attain that dignity. Benito Juárez, who with the rest of the Republic of Mexico had retired to the hills, respected the potent truncheon of Bazaine. But the barren scepter of Maximilian excited only his contempt.

At the Villa Eugénie, Louis-Napoleon roused himself from his Mexican despair to receive Bismarck. What passed between the two men is not exactly known, but it is certain that they discussed the deteriorating relations between Prussia and Austria. Ostensibly Berlin and Vienna were partners in the occupation of the Danish duchies they had together overrun. By the terms of a recent treaty, Prussia was to administer Schleswig, while Austria was to govern Holstein. In fact Bismarck was determined to carry out his plan of expelling Austria from northern Germany; and a factitious dispute over the duchies might well enable him to accomplish this.

The attitude of the French towards such a quarrel was likely to be dispositive. What, Bismarck asked Louis-Napoleon, would France do in the event relations between Berlin and Vienna came down to a "war to the knife"?

Europe was agitated by rumors that the two men struck a sinister bargain in the Villa Eugénie. Bismarck, the newspapers observed, emerged from the meeting pleased, a circumstance which could only excite unease in many places on the Continent. In fact, he had extracted from Louis-Napoleon a promise of French neutrality in the event of a war between the two German powers.

What could Bismarck have offered the French in exchange for so valuable a pledge? Some speculated that Louis-Napoleon promised him that, should Prussia emerge victorious in the contest with Austria, he would reward France with a slice of Rhenish territory, or assist her in the subjugation of Belgium. Louis-Napoleon himself, who kept details of the talks a secret even from his closest advisers, later said that Bismarck did indeed promise him territorial compensation. But the bargain was never reduced to writing. Prussia, Louis-Napoleon believed, was certain to be defeated. When Austria emerged the winner, he could go to Bismarck's aid—and name his price.

Chester, South Carolina, April–June 1865

SHE HAD TO KEEP MOVING. South by southwest. Out of the enemy's grasp. The train raced on, carrying Varina Davis deeper and deeper into what remained of the shrinking Confederacy. She detrained at Chester. Mary Chesnut, who had fled to the town to escape the advancing armies of Sherman, met her at the station. She found the First Lady of the South was "as calm and smiling as ever."

Chester was at this time filled with the élite of the Confederacy. One encountered them like shades in Hades, pale copies of their former selves. The town took on the desperate qualities of a diaspora camp. Living space was at a premium. Men of high rank slept on stairwells and under dining room tables. Tubs of water cluttered the rooms as the fugitives did their best to keep themselves clean. Everyone strained their ears for the sound of approaching guns. And everyone dreaded the proscription they feared would follow all too swiftly the arrival of the enemy's columns. Most civil ruptures, they knew, are sealed with the blood of the losers.

Mrs. Davis's reception at Chester threw a curious light on human nature. Some who had quarreled with her in her prosperity treated her, in her adversity, with a delicate consideration. Others who had obsequiously flattered her greatness now scorned her fallen dignity. A few still rose from their chairs when she entered a room. Others kept their seats.

She could not remain long in the town. She went off, cherishing the hope that she would soon be reunited with her husband. Jefferson Davis was, at this time, at Danville, Virginia. But his situation there was becoming every moment less tenable, and he was preparing to quit the town. He intended to abandon his railroad cars and light out for the West, accompanied by a squadron of Tennessee cavalry. Refusing to surrender to the despair he must inwardly have felt, he spoke of leading an irregular offensive against the Federals. But the vision of a guerrilla campaign, conducted by a peripatetic government in the hills, was already passing into the realm of fantasy. Shortly after Varina Davis left Chester, a friend dashed into Mary Chesnut's rooms.

"General Lee has capitulated."

Some wept when they heard the news. Others were incredulous.

"That is a lie," Kate Hampton exclaimed.

"I do not believe it," Buck Preston said.

"Now we belong to negroes and Yankees!" shrieked Buck's sister Mary.

The belief that it was a mistake, perhaps a deliberate falsehood, was, for a time, strong. Lee, it was said, would never have allowed himself to be taken alive. Soon, however, the accumulated evidence was too strong to admit of doubt. Lee had surrendered his sword to Ulysses S. Grant in a little crossroads town in Virginia called Appomattox Court House.

The revelation was a blow to what little remained of the Fire Eaters' fighting spirit. Already the strength of the most romantic partisans of the Cause was shattered. Edmund Ruffin, the prince of the Fire Eaters, prepared to commit suicide in Virginia. Other Fire Eaters set out for Mexico, where they hoped to find protection at the court of Maximilian. More gave way to despondency. Where once there had been defiance, there was now only "croaking and dismay, infirmity of purpose and irresolution."

One of the broken spirits was Sam Hood. When he appeared, shorn of honors and prestige, at Mary Chesnut's door, a friend counseled her not to receive him. "Send word you are not at home."

"Never," Mary Chesnut replied. "If he had come here, with Sherman dragging, a captive at his chariot wheels, I might say 'not at home'—but now . . ."

She ran downstairs and greeted the unhappy man. She gave him a glass of what remained of the Chesnuts' wine. But black care was upon his brow. Hood sat in silence, morosely staring into the fire, "going over some bitter hour" in his mind. Huge drops of perspiration stood on his forehead. He looked as though he were undergoing "the torture of the damned." Everywhere he was reviled as the man who failed to stop Sherman. He ought, it was said, to have engaged Sherman's army as it marched through Georgia. His decision to withdraw to Tennessee to obstruct Sherman's communications was judged foolish and naïve. His generalship, indeed, seemed to confirm the truth of Robert E. Lee's observation: the man was all lion and no fox. In December 1864 Union forces under General George Thomas had annihilated his army in desperate fighting south of Nashville. A month later he tendered his resignation. "Hood is dead," Mary Chesnut's friend Louis Wigfall said, "smashed, gone up forever." Not literally dead, of course: fourteen years of physiological life remained to him. His was rather the living death of a defeated general.

The fall of Hood placed Buck Preston in a quandary. It was one thing to receive a fallen hero in one's parlor. It was another to unite oneself for life to his miserable ruin. When Mary Chesnut informed her of Hood's removal from command, Buck "turned as white as the wall." She had now to look her "future in the face." Her gaze was not soft. The girl sat for hours alone on Mary Chesnut's piazza. "She rarely speaks now," Mary Chesnut said. Her eyes were "devoid of all expression." But her vision itself was mercilessly acute.

The throat settled the matter.

It was, Hood said, so soft, so white. It fairly demanded to be kissed. And the legs; for Buck was standing by the fire when he came in. She had lifted her petticoats to warm her limbs. On her legs were her best stockings—the "beautiful, beautiful silk stockings that fit so nicely." Hood could not help himself. The legs were so shapely. In the Victorian age young ladies who did not want to be thought "fast" wore high collars, and they concealed their legs beneath an abundance of drapery. But Hood had caught his fiancée in *déshabillé*. He was driven wild by the sight. As "I stood by the fender, warming my feet," Buck told Mary Chesnut, "he seized me round the waist and kissed my throat—to my horror—and when he saw how shocked I was, he was frightened in a minute and so humble and so full of apologies. . . . I drew back and told him to go away, that I was offended. In a moment I felt a strong arm so tight around my waist I could not move. He said I should stay [there] until I forgave his rash presumption, and he held me fast."

Buck told Hood that she could never forgive such conduct. But to Mary Chesnut she admitted that she had merely "pretended to be in a rage." The unauthorized kiss gave her the excuse she needed to break off the engagement. She later claimed that she wished Hood had persevered in spite of this to all appearances definitive rebuff. If he had been persistent, she said, she would have married him despite the kiss, despite his diminished stature. If she could not marry him in Mary Chesnut's house, "well, I would have gone down on the sidewalk. I would have married him on the pavement, if the parson could be found to do it. I was ready to leave all the world for him, to tie my clothes in a bundle and, like a soldier's wife, trudge after him to the ends of the earth."

Mary Chesnut raised her eyebrows.

"It was a shame," Buck told her mentor. "Now, would you believe it, a sickening, almost an insane, longing comes over me, just to see him once more." But "I know I never will. He is gone forever."

Saint Petersburg, April 1866

IN THE AFTERMATH of Niks's death, the Tsar's day still followed its predictable course. In his bedroom-study in the Winter Palace, Alexander rose at eight and drank his coffee. After a brisk walk round the Palace, he went to see the Empress. He kissed her when he came in. She still called him Sasha. He still called her Masha. They ate breakfast together. The forms of domesticity were decently observed, but the marriage itself, many believed, was hollow. Husband and wife were still, it is true, united by their love for their children; in the autumn Grand Duke Alexander, their clumsy second son, was to wed Niks's former fiancée, Dagmar of Denmark. But even that happy occasion would be tinged with regret; the Empress continued to mourn her firstborn son. Her principal consolation lay in the contemplation of God. Her rooms were filled with icons. She was obsessed by relics. She surrounded herself with monks and visionaries, holy men who, it was said, could fathom the whole of a man's destiny in his gaze. The Tsar could not follow his wife in these pious pursuits; mysticism was not his cup of tea. Perhaps he did not want to know his destiny. Ever since his predecessor Tsar Peter ascended the throne of the Romanovs nearly two centuries before, the destiny of every Tsar had been dark.*

After breakfast the Tsar went to his bedroom-study and sat down at the desk from which he governed an empire. It was here that he received his ministers. The Minister of War and the head of the Third Section came every day; the Foreign Minister came every second day. After lunch, the Tsar went for another walk.

On a spring afternoon in 1866, he set out as usual for the Summer Garden to take his post-prandial stroll. He was accompanied by his niece and nephew, Mary and Nicholas, the children of his sister Mary. His favorite setter, Milord, came along. The day was sunny, the snow had melted, but there was a chill in the air, and the Tsar wore an overcoat. Some time after three o'clock he went back to his carriage. The crowd watched, white gloves flew up, a policeman came to attention. The Tsar was in the midst of donning a cloak for the ride back to the palace when the shot rang out.

* Peter the Great (reigned 1682–1725) murdered his son; Peter II (reigned 1727–30) died of smallpox; Ivan VI (reigned 1740–41) was deposed, while yet an infant, and flung into Schlüsselberg, where he was murdered on the orders of Catherine the Great; Peter III (reigned 1761–62) was deposed by Catherine and executed by her partners in crime and sensuality; Paul I (reigned 1796–1801) was murdered in a *coup d'état;* Alexander I (1801–25) died in mysterious circumstances in Taganrog on the Sea of Azov; and Nicholas I (reigned 1825–55) died a broken man, cast down by the defeats suffered by Russia in the Crimea.

Chapter 24

"BETTER TO DIE"

Berlin and Vienna, January–May 1866

BISMARCK OPENED HIS BIBLE. The Ninth Psalm: *"When mine enemies are turned back, they shall fall and perish at thy presence."* "We have good confidence," he wrote, "but we must not forget that Almighty God is very capricious."

He was ready to roll the dice. He could, he believed, defray the charge of a war with Austria (or part of it) by selling Prussian railway interests. He could win the war because he had, through his diplomacy, taken care to secure his flanks. France he had disposed of in the Villa Eugénie, where he had received from Louis-Napoleon a pledge of neutrality. He now considered his southern front. In April 1866 he entered into a secret agreement with the Italians that would go far to relieving Prussia's underbelly. The Italians were hungry for Venetia, still in the hands of the Habsburgs; and they promised that, if Prussia should go to war against Austria within three months, Italy would join her in the fight. Franz Josef would be obliged to defend two fronts.

Every hour the animosity between Vienna and Berlin grew. Bismarck announced that Holstein, now a province of Austria, was "a nest of democrats, intriguers and revolutionary agents under the protection of the Austrian double eagle." The Viennese saw the writing on the wall and prepared for the worst. They feared a Prussian descent on Bohemia, in what is now the Czech Republic. Austrian troops were rushed northward towards the frontier. The technical requirements of their army placed the Austrians in an unfortunate position; they could not mobilize their forces in less than seven weeks. Prussian mobilization, by contrast, required only three weeks—Moltke's railway drills had resulted in an immense strategic advantage.

Bismarck seized on the intelligence of Austrian troop movements and at the end of March accused Vienna of "warlike activity" which compelled Prussia to take countermeasures. Austria "without any recognizable cause has been, since the thirteenth of March, moving considerable masses of troops in a threatening manner towards the Prussian frontier." Vienna, Bismarck pretended, was the aggressive party; Berlin was merely attempting to defend itself. At the end of March, an order instructing the Prussian army to prepare for partial mobilization was handed down.

Vienna promptly denied the accusation that it possessed warlike intentions. Bismarck repeated his charges in a provocative communiqué. The Austrians replied with some warmth. It was almost beneath the dignity of Austria, they said, to deny again accusations that had been repeatedly denied in the past. Prussia was the true aggressor in the matter, as that Kingdom's own extensive military preparations proved. Count Mensdorff, the Austrian Foreign Minister, pointed to Bismarck's long record of militant rhetoric. Had not the Prussian leader said many times that war between Austria and Prussia was inevitable? Had he not openly evinced his desire to annex both Schleswig and Holstein for Prussia? "All this," Count Mensdorff said, "must be mere delusion, and to the realm of reality must belong only those threatening masses of Austrian troops . . . moving to the Prussian frontier!" He categorically demanded that Berlin withdraw its mobilization order.

But the diplomats in the Ballhausplatz, the Austrian Foreign Ministry, were unequal to a mind as resourceful, penetrating, and unscrupulous as Bismarck's. Conscious of the menacing character which Prussia had assumed in the eyes of Europe, the Minister-President judged it prudent to extend to his adversaries an olive branch. If, he said, Austria stood down from her military preparations, Prussia would do the same in respect of her own. Vienna at once embraced the specious offering, not comprehending how empty it really was. As Bismarck well knew, Prussia's secret ally, Italy, was on the verge of mobilizing her forces. Intelligence of these preparations soon reached Vienna, and the Austrians naturally took steps to confront the threat to their southern frontier. On April 21 an order mobilizing the Austrian Army of Italy was handed down at Vienna.

Bismarck took care that his friends in the German press were kept abreast of the Austrian preparations. In a German paper known to enjoy the confidence of the Prussian ministry, it was claimed that Austria was mobilizing her southern army, not indeed to counter the Italians, but in order to attack Prussia. Ordinary Prussians were angered by what they took to be the duplicity of the Viennese. Bismarck withdrew his olive branch, and persuaded King Wilhelm to summon his people to arms.

Early in May Prussia mobilized six army corps and called up the reserves.

London, September 1865–June 1866

THOSE WHO FEARED the progress of Bismarck's battalions still nursed the hope that England, France, and Russia would intervene to preserve the peace of the Continent. Amid rumors of war, there was talk of invoking the Concert of Europe and convening a Congress. But nothing came of it. England and the other powers, one diplomat observed, "contented themselves with moral lectures and appeals to Prussia with, I suppose, the usual effect."

England was largely oblivious of the gathering world crisis. Bathed in the soft complacency of commercial prosperity—the British Empire was, at this time, at the zenith of its supremacy in trade—the English failed to perceive, in Prussia's advancing columns, the outriders of a philosophy that would one day threaten their own freedom and greatness. In London, Bismarck observed, they "are much better informed about China and Turkey than about Prussia. Loftus [the English Ambassador in Berlin] must write to his Minister much more nonsense than I imagined."

Insofar as the English were concerned by developments on the Continent, they continued to fear that any attempt by England to interpose herself in Germany would redound to the benefit of France, which in their minds was the most dangerous power in Europe. Certainly France was, the English believed, a more dangerous power than Prussia. Lord Loftus, writing from Berlin, "could not view with any dissatisfaction or fear of danger to England an increase of power to Prussia." Prussia was "the great Protestant State of Continental Europe." She represented "the intelligence, the progress, and the wealth of Germany. . . . We have nothing to fear from her. She will become a Power of great importance in maintaining the peace of Central Europe. She will gradually advance in a constitutional system of government, and she will play the part of a moderator in Europe." And France? She was no moderator. She was not even Protestant. And she was (the English believed) very strong. Englishmen marveled at the "enormous armies of the French," her "commanding territorial position," her "instinctive readiness for war." The French arms were "in a state of perfect preparation." So dire was the threat of French power believed to be that a volunteer movement had sprung up in England to resist it, and wellborn young men engaged in shooting practice at Wimbledon and Scrubbs.

No less a figure than Palmerston himself spoke of the alarming power of France. Like many statesmen, the Prime Minister had learned, too well, the lessons of the last war. He remembered how, when he was a young man, the Continent had languished in the grip of a Bonaparte. He had himself played a part in the earlier volunteer movement which had been formed to resist the usurper who, in preparation for a descent upon England, had massed his barges at Boulogne. Almost with his dying breath Palmerston uttered a prophecy of French aggression. Prussia, the Prime Minister wrote to Earl Russell in September 1865, "is too weak as she now is." It was, he said, "desirable that Germany, in the aggregate, should be strong, in order to control those two ambitious and aggressive powers, France and Russia, that press upon her east and west."

Shortly after composing the letter, Palmerston went out for a drive at Brocket and caught a chill. The great Prime Minister died on October 18, two days before his eighty-first birthday.

Alone among the high figures of the government, Queen Victoria believed that England must intervene to stop Prussian aggression. She had changed her mind about Bismarck since the Danish War. Having been apprised by her daughter, Crown Princess Vicky, of the Minister-President's tactics, the Queen was indignant, and she wrote to King Wilhelm beseeching him not to go to war on account of the "faults and recklessness . . . of *one* man." "The Missus," Lord Clarendon, the new Foreign Secretary, wrote, "is in an awful state about German affairs." But Earl Russell, who had kissed hands as Prime Minister after Palmerston's death, curtly rejected his sovereign's arguments. It "would be an injustice to the people of England," Russell said, "to employ their military and pecuniary resources in a quarrel in which neither English honour nor English interests are involved."

Vienna and Berlin, May–June 1866

IN THE HOFBURG, the vast palace of the Habsburgs, Franz Josef rose from his iron cot at four in the morning. His valet waited outside the imperial bedchamber, listening intently. When he heard the unmistakable sounds of awakening humanity, the servant entered the room. "I am at Your Majesty's feet!" he intoned. "Good morning!" The valet was followed by the bath attendant, who, after making a low bow, gave the All Highest a sponge bath. By five o'clock, as the June sun penetrated the baroque plazas of his capital, Franz Josef, having washed, prayed, and donned a uniform, went through the door into his study.

Seated at his desk, the impresario of empire went to work. Thirty-five years old in June 1866, Franz Josef had little insight into the technical needs of his autocracy. His infantry was armed with inferior rifles, his bureaucracy was corrupt, his treasury was exhausted, his diplomatic initiatives were for the most part inept. But he had his strengths. People who knew the Kaiser personally thought him dull; but they failed to perceive the delicacy of his imperial choreography. Franz Josef's happiest hours (other than those he spent hunting chamois or reviewing regiments) were passed in the Imperial Theater. There he developed an instinct for gesture. His soldiers might not have the best guns, but they wore the most beautiful uniforms. His capital possessed the most splendid palaces. He had married the most beautiful woman the nobility of that age could boast. The slim, neurotic Elisabeth was a work of highest Wittelsbach art. She had, by 1866, become estranged from her husband, and she was often abroad, in Madeira, in Spain, in Corfu, cultivating exquisite impressions. She was not at all the Emperor's type; Franz Josef preferred banality to originality, and he had, besides, a love of pudgy legs and plump derrières. But his personal tastes did not matter. Elisabeth, slender, spiritual, ascetic, gave him something he needed more than the fleshy Viennese *Topfenstrudels* he favored—she supplied his régime with style.

But style could not save him on this June morning. His people were on the verge of *Bruderkrieg*, civil war. He himself signed the order that precipitated the outbreak of hostilities. The All Highest commanded his ministers to transfer his Empire's rights in Schleswig and Holstein to the German Confederation (old Prince Metternich's Bund). Let the Bundestag in Frankfurt settle the vexed question. In transferring his rights to the Bund, Franz Josef formally breached his agreements with the Prussians: those agreements stipulated that Austria and Prussia would resolve, jointly and exclusively, all questions concerning the disposition of the duchies. By placing his interests in the duchies in the hands of the Bund, the Kaiser hoped to rally the German-speaking peoples to his cause. For war, he believed, was now inevitable. He was convinced that nothing he did—short of surrendering Holstein outright to Prussia and relinquishing Austria's claims to leadership in Germany—could prevent violence. "How can one avoid war," he asked, "when the other side wants it?"

The Kaiser's decision gave Bismarck the excuse he needed to implement the next phase of his revolution. His path to war was not hindered by the appearance of a gunman in Unter den Linden. One evening, as he was returning to his residence in the Wilhelmstrasse, three shots rang out. In the shadow of the blossoming lime trees, Bismarck grappled with his assailant, and seizing him by the arm and throat, held him until the 2nd Foot Guards arrived. The gunman, a student named Ferdinand Cohen, opposed Bismarck's war policy; he was carried off to the police bureau, where he died after repeatedly stabbing himself in the throat with a pocket knife. Bismarck himself was not seriously hurt. One of the bullets passed through his garments and produced a slight contusion on his shoulder; the concussion of another blast bruised one of his ribs. "I consider it good fortune to give one's life for our King and Country," Bismarck said afterwards, "and I pray to God to grant me such a death. This time God has decided otherwise." The incident only strengthened his reputation as a man of iron.

A short-lived peace movement did no more to deter Bismarck from his revolutionary path. When peace meetings were held in a number of German cities, he professed to be undismayed. "Events change public opinion," he told a group of diplomats in the Wilhelmstrasse, "and a battle won, or even a battle lost, strangely alters men's minds." Lord Loftus, the English diplomat who believed that Prussia represented the cause of European progress, attempted to impress upon him the virtues of pacific statesmanship. Bismarck brushed him aside. "Why, after all," he said, "Attila was a greater man than your Mr. John Bright. He has left a greater name in history."

On June 12, Prussian troops stormed into Holstein. The single Austrian brigade withdrew without firing a shot. In the Bundestag in Frankfurt, members rose to accuse Prussia of taking the law into her own hands. Determined to resist Prussian coercion, they resolved to mobilize the Confederation's feeble army. Prussia declared the Confederation dissolved and launched a lightning invasion of neighboring German states. Bismarck, sitting in his garden in the Wilhelmstrasse, gave General von Moltke the watchword.* The Chief of the General Staff went off to the telegraph. The sun sank, and Bismarck sat there under the old elms chatting with Lord Loftus. The clock struck midnight. Bismarck rose from his chair. "The war has begun!" he announced. "At this hour troops are marching into Hanover, Saxony, and the Electorate of Hesse—long live the King."

Europe, Lord Loftus said gravely, would never tolerate an attempt by Prussia to subdue sovereign powers simply because they disapproved of Prussia's policies.

"Who is Europe?" Bismarck asked.

Outwardly he projected an iron confidence; but inwardly all was turmoil. "When you start a war," Bismarck said, "you know when the first

---

* Seven decades later the Wilhelmstrasse gardens were excavated and a network of underground bunkers was constructed for another German leader, Adolf Hitler, who perished in one of the bunkers in 1945. His corpse was doused with petrol and burnt in the chancellery garden.

shot is fired, but you can *never* tell when the last one will be." He spoke of the consequences of a Prussian defeat. "The struggle will be severe. . . . If we are beaten, I shall not return here. I shall fall in the last charge. One can die but once; and if beaten, it is better to die."

Once again Europe heard the crunch of Prussian jackboots; but the swiftness of the advance took the Continent by surprise. Within hours of Bismarck's announcement to Lord Loftus, the Prussian Army of the Elbe crossed the frontier and entered Saxony. Three infantry divisions (drawn principally from the Prussian VIII Corps) together with twenty-six squadrons of horse and more than a hundred field guns proceeded rapidly to Dresden, the capital of the Saxons. The Prussians entered the city unopposed. At the same moment a Prussian division entered and subdued the Electorate of Hesse. The Elector himself was made a prisoner. Only in the Kingdom of Hanover did the Prussians encounter resistance. The Prussian commander was slow in moving his divisions, and the Hanoverians repulsed the invader at Langensalza. But their valor yielded, at length, to the weight of numbers, and the King, George V, a scion of the Guelphs, was forced to flee his Kingdom.

The Prussian war machine rolled on.

The armies did not stop with the subjugation of Hanover, Saxony, and Electoral Hesse. Scarcely had Prussia's enemies north of the River Main been subjugated when the invasion of Austria commenced. The first prong of the Prussian thrust, the Army of the Elbe, crossed the Austrian frontier and entered Bohemia (now the Czech Republic) on June 22. Leading the van were the 7th Regiment of King's Hussars, the 8th Battalion of Rhenish Jaegers, and four battalions of fusiliers. The next day the second prong of the offensive, the Prussian First Army, descended on Bohemia from the north. At the head of this force, drawn from Prussian II, III, and IV Corps, was King Wilhelm's nephew, Prince Friedrich Karl, the Red Prince. Among those under his command was Heros von Borcke, who had recrossed the Atlantic to draw his sword in the service of a more effectual romance. Now a second lieutenant in the 3rd Neumarkt Dragoons, he still carried within him the .58-caliber Minié ball that had lodged in his lung when he was aide-de-camp to Jeb Stuart in Virginia. In his quarters von Borcke kept two pictures, one of his old commander and the other of his present one. The Red Prince, visiting him one day, saw that his own portrait hung above that of General Stuart. "You must change the position of the pictures," the Red Prince said, "and put mine below."

The third element in the Prussian thrust, the Second Army, crossed into Bohemia from its base at Fürstenstein in Prussian Silesia. This army, which encompassed V and VI Corps, was led by Crown Prince Friedrich, the son of King Wilhelm. "Fritz" was thirty-four years old when he took command of the Second Army. He and his wife, Crown Princess Vicky, lived in the New Palace at Potsdam. Their seven-year-old son, Wilhelm, was a true Prussian. A willful boy with a withered arm, he once referred to his maternal grandmother, Queen Victoria, as an "old hag," and in a fit of temper he bit his uncle, Prince Arthur, in the leg. Friedrich and Vicky were pacific liberals; they disliked Bismarck's militarism and opposed his war with Austria.

But the Crown Prince was determined to do his duty.

Chapter 25

THE BLOODLETTING

Saint Petersburg, May–September 1866

THE GATES OF THE Fortress of Peter and Paul swung open, and a cart drove out. On it sat the culprit, Dmitri Karakozov, the revolutionist who had fired at the Tsar in the Summer Garden. He was a poor shot; Alexander had walked away unscathed.

A young officer of the Cuirassiers watched as the cart made its way down the rough escarpment of the fortress. A large crowd had gathered. Some of the onlookers groaned. Others made the sign of the Cross. *"Lord, forgive his sins and save his soul."* The wagon jolted on the stones, and its occupant quivered, as though made of jelly. The Cuirassier wondered whether they were not "bringing out an India-rubber doll to be hanged." The thought flashed in his mind that Karakozov was already dead, and that for the sake of appearances the authorities had resolved to hang a corpse.

In fact Karakozov was not dead, but he had, for many days, been in the hands of the Third Section. His head, his hands, his joints were entirely loose. "It was a terrible thing to see," the Cuirassier said, "and to think what it meant."

Two soldiers helped Karakozov to ascend the scaffold. Opinion was divided concerning the prisoner's state of mind as he approached eternity. Some say that he had gone out of his mind and was now insane. Others say that he had, like the older brother of Father Zosima in *The Brothers Karamazov*, experienced redemption, and that his last hours had been passed "on his knees in passionate prayer."

The period of reformation was coming to an end in Russia. The disenchantment that follows every revolutionary thrust was exacerbated by Karakozov's pistol shot, and by the interval of reaction that followed.

When, in the past, tsars had been assailed, the dark facts of treason and murder had been concealed from the masses. In the eyes of the people the monarchy continued to embody a remote and lofty perfection. When Karakozov fired at Alexander in broad daylight, a veil fell away.

The Tsar himself emerged from the line of fire shaken and suspicious. Perhaps some awful curse did hang over the Romanovs. In his terror he raised one of his old boon companions, Peter Shuvalov, to the most powerful place in the government. The young courtier became head of the Third Section. He was descended from a family that had risen high in the eighteenth century, and he possessed gifts of wit and repartee reminiscent of the courts of that vanished age. The Shuvalovs aspired to a French ideal of culture, and they had helped to import, into Russia, the ideals of the French Enlightenment. That a scion of the luminaries should now become a policeman and a torturer might at first seem an historical irony; but the inquisitorial vocation comes easily to those who have embraced Voltaire's faith in the virtues of enlightened despotism. Count Shuvalov organized the White Terror that followed Karakozov's attempt on the life of the Tsar. Reformers were ousted from the Ministry of Justice, the Ministry of Education, and the Ministry of the Interior, and hundreds of people were subjected to arbitrary arrest.

No man, the Greeks said, is less free than the despot. He lives constantly with his fears, and falls victim to morbid suspicions. Alexander, who during the first ten years of his rule had retained his mental equanimity, succumbed at last to the afflictions of power. He trusted no one—not even Shuvalov, whom he placed under counter-surveillance. A man notably courageous when confronted by immediate physical danger, Alexander broke down under the lurking threat of assassination. In vain did he set out on fantastic hunting expeditions, accompanied by a train of huntsmen and dancing girls. A troupe of French performers was employed to divert him with renditions of scenes from the Marquis de Sade; but like bear-slaying, erotic indulgence provided only a momentary relief from the distresses of authority.

Alexander's earlier policy might be defended as a creative vacillation between reform and reaction, an approach that allowed for change, yet at the same time maintained the social equilibrium. In ten years he had done more than free the serfs and institute the rule of law. He had relaxed restrictions on the press, liberalized the universities, emancipated dissenting religious sects, and made it easier for Russians to travel beyond the borders of their country. The state budget, which had previously been shrouded in administrative secrecy, he had ordered to be published; and he had abolished the pernicious practice of tax farming. At his behest, the Minister of War, Dmitri Milyutin (Nicholas's brother), reformed the army. The crueler forms of corporal punishment were abolished, and the term of service for conscripts was reduced. A new office, that of Chief of the General Staff, was created on the model Moltke had developed in Prussia. In what was perhaps his most daring measure, Alexander had, in 1864, signed a law creating local assemblies or *zemstvos* in parts of his Empire. These assemblies, elected by people of all classes, embodied, in a rudimentary form, the principle of a legislature.

But if the Tsar at one moment acted the liberal, he at the next played the reactionary. He freed the serfs, and suppressed the Poles. He promoted education, and closed the Sunday Schools. He relaxed the censorship, and sentenced journalists to hard labor in Siberia. He eased religious restrictions, and persecuted Jews. He promoted the rule of law, and detained obnoxious subjects in lunatic asylums. He sanctioned local *zemstvos,* and refused to grant a national legislature. When the Tsarevitch lay dying at Nice, the nobility of Moscow petitioned him for a national assembly. He rejected the petition. What "he had already done in the past," he said, "must remain a sufficient pledge for all his faithful subjects." No one had the right to "anticipate him in his incessant aims for the good of Russia." "The right of initiative . . . belongs exclusively to ME, and is indissolubly bound to the autocratic power entrusted to ME by God. . . ."

The apparent contradictions of his rule owed something to the astuteness of his policy. Those who criticized him, he said, did not understand the difficulties involved in implementing a program of reform in a country like Russia. A too rapid course of constitutional change would, he believed, fatally undermine authority and terminate in the dissolution of the Empire. He told Bismarck that in the eyes of the Russian people the monarch was an "all-powerful lord, the emissary of God. This feeling almost has the force of religious sentiment. . . . If the people should lose this feeling for the power that my crown imparts to me, the nimbus that the nation possesses would be ruptured." Russia would fall to pieces.

But during the White Terror that followed Karakozov's pistol shot, Alexander's régime acquired a different complexion. He sensed this himself. He "would fall into a gloomy melancholy, and speak in a sad tone of the brilliant beginning of his reign, and of the reactionary character it was taking." The revolution that stops in place, Mazzini said, is lost; but Alexander made no effort to re-create the earlier, revolutionary atmosphere.

General Trepov, the Governor of Saint Petersburg, preyed upon the Tsar's fears. If Trepov were a few minutes late for a briefing, Alexander would become anxious. "Is everything quiet at Saint Petersburg?" he would ask as soon as Trepov came in. (Trepov was later shot and gravely wounded by the Marxist terrorist Vera Zasulich.) The reactionary courtiers took advantage of their master's terror to plunder the state. Stalled liberal revolutions often spawn forms of crony capitalism; the tyrant acquiesces in the pillage, not because he likes to be robbed, but because he regards the thieves as "his protectors from the revolution."

In one area alone did Alexander conduct affairs with his old vigor. He continued to enlarge the Empire. China recognized Russian claims to the Amur and the Ussuri. Vladivostok, the San Francisco of the Russians, rose on the Sea of Japan. The Caucasus was finally subdued; Turkestan and Tashkent were enrolled among the metropolises of the Empire; and General Kaufman was deputed to complete the subjugation of Central Asia.

Each of the three powers that in the twentieth century would contend for leadership of the planet felt the allure of romantic nationalism; each, in the middle decades of the nineteenth century, added to its dominions. Prussia, under Bismarck, had already dismembered Denmark, and was poised to take over Germany and portions of France. The United States continued, in the midst of the Civil War, to pursue its policy of Manifest Destiny. The Homestead and Pacific Railway acts of 1862 strengthened the country's transcontinental grip. The Legal Tender Act of 1862 created a transcontinental currency. But although each of the three pivotal leaders of the decade flirted with romantic nationalism, they did so in different ways. Bismarck used the nationalist romance to crush the free state in Germany. Lincoln understood the dangers which the nationalist ideal posed to the principle that all men, wherever they come from, are created equal; but he at the same time believed that the United States, in becoming a transcontinental "empire of liberty," would be better able to defend the principles of freedom in the world struggle against despotism. Alexander, for his part, proved to be the least imaginative of the empire builders; he failed to use Russia's tradition of messianic imperialism to stir patriotic hearts and save his liberal revolution.

The Tsar's own heart was elsewhere.

Alexander had known Princess Ekaterina Mikhailovna Dolgorukaya since she was a girl. Katya, as she was called, possessed a pedigree unsurpassed, in antiquity and splendor, by any in Russia. But her fortune had been squandered through the caprice and folly of her father, Prince Michael. After the death of the Prince in 1860, the Tsar himself took charge of her upbringing. Alexander enrolled her in the Smolny Institute for Noble Maidens, a finishing school for daughters of the aristocracy which Catherine the Great had founded in emulation of Mme de

Maintenon's Saint-Cyr. During the course of a visit to the institute, the Tsar discovered that Katya had become a young woman. She had "skin of ivory," and magnificent chestnut hair. Her eyes, it was said, were like those of a startled gazelle. When he invited her to accompany him on his walks around Saint Petersburg, she dutifully complied. Alexander's passions were always impetuous; and he soon found that he was in love.

Vienna and Bohemia, June–July 1866

IN THE RINGSTRASSE the Viennese gathered in little knots to read the imperial proclamation. The year before, Franz Josef, in another attempt to smother daylight with magic, had opened the first section of the boulevard, with its parks and public buildings. He was perpetually touching up his Empire—so many daubs of Habsburg paint. But the painting stopped when the proclamation appeared.

A people lulled by aesthetic sedatives found itself roused from its slumbers and thrust into the world crisis. "Prussia," Franz Josef declared, "now publicly places might before right," and he had little choice, he said, but to order his Army of the North to march to Berlin to try to stop Bismarck's revolution.

On a hot day in June the Army of the North filed out of its base in Olmütz (Olomouc) in Bohemia in obedience to the Kaiser's command. It was, to say the least, a handsome army. There were regiments of pink trousers and sky-blue coats, and regiments of blue trousers and snow-white coats. There were Hussars in scarlet, and Tyrol riflemen in green. The Cuirassiers wore crested helmets, while the blond Jaegers of Styria were adorned with the feathers of the capercaillie.

The troops marched in three columns towards the fortress of Josephstadt (Josefov) on the upper Elbe. At their head was Ludwig August von Benedek. The dapper Feldherr was sixty-one years old in June 1866. He had, in a succession of battles, earned the reputation of a brave corps commander. But he had never before commanded a large army. He had, it is true, more experience of fighting than his Prussian counterpart, General von Moltke. Unlike Moltke, however, Benedek was unacquainted with the higher realms of military art. "I am too little the scientifically arrogant strategist," he once confessed. "I conduct the business of war according to quite simple rules and am no friend to complicated combinations."

Benedek had, too, another weakness. He had passed the greatest part of his career with the Austrian Army of Italy. He knew, he said, "every tree as far as Milan." But his knowledge of Austria's northern frontier was slight. "So now I am to study the geography of Prussia!" he exclaimed upon learning that he was to be Feldherr. "How can I take in things like that at my age?" "It would really be better," he told his wife, "if a bullet hit me."

Into such hands was the fate of Austria confided. Benedek knew that in order to defeat the Prussians he must swiftly engage and dispatch the enemy's First Army, commanded by the Red Prince, Friedrich Karl. If he failed to destroy this army quickly enough, the Prussian Second Army, commanded by Crown Prince Friedrich, would fall upon his right flank while he was contending with the Red Prince. He would find himself caught in the Prussian pincers.

Everything depended on the boldness and celerity of Benedek; but he seemed to put off the fatal reckoning. The Red Prince drew closer, and the Feldherr fell back upon the fortress of Könnigrätz on the Elbe. There he convened a council of war. The officers who gathered round the board were gloomy. The council broke up, and Benedek wired Franz Josef. "I beg Your Majesty urgently," he said, "to make peace at any price. Catastrophe for the army is unavoidable." The Kaiser rejected the advice: the dignity of the House of Austria required that the Army of the North hazard a battle. Benedek recovered his equanimity and prepared to fight. He determined to make his stand on the banks of the Bistritz, a river that flowed some eight miles northwest of Könnigrätz. Here, amid orchards and corn fields, stood a little Bohemian village of pinewood cottages and watermills.

It was called Sadowa.

The Austrians had the vantage of ground; and they improved such natural defenses as the terrain afforded by digging trenches and throwing up breastworks.

In the meantime the Prussian high command arrived by rail at Reichenberg (Liberec) in Bohemia. Bismarck, upon reaching the castle where the King and his suite were to lodge, was astonished to find it guarded by only a few hundred train-soldiers with rusty carbines. Enemy cavalry, he knew, lay but a few leagues off. He turned to General von Moltke, who by royal edict had been made strategic mastermind of the campaign, and asked him whether this was not dangerous.

"*Ja,*" Moltke replied, "in war everything is dangerous."

Bismarck found himself scorned by the military men as a trembling civilian, one who had never fleshed his sword in battle. He was, indeed, no soldier. As a young man he had attempted to evade military duty. "I feel pain when I raise my right arm," he claimed. (Bismarck never was one for saluting.) His experience of soldiering was limited to the garrison duty he had been forced to perform at Potsdam. Nevertheless, the man of iron was wounded by the aspersion of cowardice. He quitted the castle and took lodgings in the town, which lay open to the enemy. He was bored and nervous. In a letter to his wife he begged her to send him cigars, a French novel, and a big revolver.

The campaign moved rapidly towards its catastrophe. On the evening of July 2, the Prussian high command learned that the Austrians were massed in force on the opposite bank of the Bistritz. Moltke, who had retired early, was roused from his bed. *"Gott sei dank!"* he said. *God be thanked!* The moment was at hand. He had worried that Benedek would shrink from a decisive contest. But the struggle, it now appeared, would be short and tumultuous. The Prussian commanders passed a sleepless night making their final dispositions, and at four o'clock the Red Prince's First Army was in motion.

The morning of the third dawned raw and rainy. A mist overhung the valley. In the Austrian camp Benedek wrote a last letter to his wife. His nerves, he admitted, were stretched thin, but he predicted that all would be well when the cannon began to thunder. He then went out among the troops and looked his soldiers in the eye. They were ready. At seven o'clock the Prussian trumpets sounded, and the Uhlans went forward, their lances and banners waving in the rain. Next came the Prussian infantrymen in gray-green field uniforms. Few wore the spiked *Pickelhaube* helmet; most wore field caps. Bismarck himself appeared in a long gray coat and cuirassier's helmet.

Moltke, who was coming down with a cold, put aside his pocket handkerchief and ordered the Red Prince to attack the Austrian line. A fierce artillery bombardment heralded the offensive. The guns flashed, and in a short time the village of Sadowa was in flames. The Prussian assault was valiant; but it failed to dislodge the enemy. The slaughter was great, and a number of Prussian units were almost wholly annihilated.

At noon, the Austrian line appeared to be as solid as ever. In Prussian headquarters there was consternation. Moltke alone was serene. "Your Majesty," he assured the King, "will today win not only the battle but the campaign." The Chief of the General Staff enjoyed the reputation of a man who never promised unless he meant to pay; but Wilhelm was unconvinced. About this time Bismarck surveyed the field with a telescope. He was puzzled by the appearance, in the distance, of a series of plough furrows. The furrows, curiously enough, appeared to be moving. "Those are not plough furrows," he exclaimed at last, "the spaces are not equal." He handed the glass to Moltke. What Bismarck had at first taken to be plough furrows were in fact soldiers of the Prussian Second Army. Crown Prince Friedrich had arrived.

"The campaign is decided," Moltke told the King, "and in accordance with Your Majesty's desires!" Wilhelm, who saw before him only the fog of war, continued to profess doubt. "No," Moltke said firmly, "the success is complete. Vienna lies at Your Majesty's feet."

The arrival of Crown Prince Friedrich and the Second Prussian Army decided the battle. Nearly half a million men were soon in full grapple. The right wing of the Austrian army collapsed. The Prussians took the Austrian works by storm, and drove their opponents from position to position. The nerves of Habsburg military discipline broke down as soldiers deserted their standards. "Oh, you cowards!" the officers cried. "Stand there, you yellow dogs!" Benedek, informed that his army was in full retreat, was at first incredulous. "Don't be silly," he said. He galloped off with his staff to survey the field for himself. He soon found himself under a withering fire. A number of his officers fell dead from their saddles.

The Feldherr now proved his worth. Nothing so became Benedek at the battle of Sadowa as the manner in which he lost it. All the alacrity of spirit which he had wanted in the days leading up to the contest he instantly recovered. Careless of his life, he went among his men and strove by an example of fearlessness to turn the tide. His troops, inspired by his courage, made a gallant stand. Jaeger horns sounded, and military bands played "God Save the Kaiser." The Austrians moved forward with bayonets fixed. They marched on, unflinching, even as their ranks were decimated by the Prussian guns.

It was too late. Incapable of further resistance, the Austrians retired in the direction of Könnigrätz. The sluices of the fortress were opened to forestall pursuit by the enemy, and the moats filled with water. Many were drowned in the inundation. Benedek himself, guarded by a squadron of Uhlans, crossed the Elbe with what remained of his staff. His ruin was complete; there was nothing left but to despair and die. Moltke, in the pride of fortune and victory, did not neglect to pity his vanquished rival. "A defeated Feldherr!" he exclaimed. "Oh, if civilians had even the remotest idea of what that means! . . . Oh, when I try to imagine it to myself!" The Chief of the General Staff was by this time feverish with fatigue, illness, and the intoxication of success. While his soldiers sang *Nun Danket* ("Now thank we all our God . . .") Moltke retired to his bed.

Paris and Bohemia, July 1866

THE CHÂTEAU OVERLOOKING the Seine squeaked and gibbered with ghosts. In the neo-classical galleries of Saint-Cloud, Marie-Antoinette had once dallied, and Napoleon Bonaparte had once plotted. The château was said to have been Bonaparte's favorite residence. Certainly it was his most fortunate. It was here that he had, in November 1799, carried out the *coup d'état* that created a dynasty. It was here, sixty-seven years later, that his nephew learned of the battle that presaged the end of the House of Bonaparte. Many years later, the aged Eugénie recalled that fateful time. It "still quivers within me," the fallen Empress said, "like a sensitive nerve."

The period after Sadowa was "the date of doom for the Empire."

"It is France," people said, "that is beaten at Sadowa." In his heart Louis-Napoleon knew the words to be true, and in the days and weeks that followed the battle he seemed like one in a trance, powerless to avert his fate. Drouyn de Lhuys, the French Foreign Minister, urged the Emperor to act forcefully to retrieve the honor of France. If, Drouyn said, France imposed armed mediation on Austria and Prussia and brokered the peace, the Emperor could yet regain the prestige which Bismarck had wrested from him at Sadowa. The monarch nodded with a smile of apathy, and a peremptory telegram was dashed off to the Prussians.

The next day a council of state was held in the château. The Emperor presided. The Empress was present. Drouyn again pressed for a policy of forcefulness. It was not enough for France to proclaim herself an arbiter. She must make a demonstration of military might. The Empress spoke next, and in French tinged with a coloring that betrayed her Spanish birth she embraced the policy of Drouyn. France, she said, must be strong. She turned to Marshal Randon, the Minister of War, and asked whether the army was in a position to make a show of force on the Rhine.

"Yes," Randon replied. "We can concentrate 80,000 men on the Rhine immediately, and 250,000 within twenty days."

The Emperor said nothing.

The Marquis de La Valette, the Minister of the Interior, took advantage of the silence to speak. He utterly opposed the policy of Drouyn. If France fought Prussia, she must, he said, become the ally of Austria. Austria was the enemy of Italy, France's friend. The liberation of the Italians from the tyranny of Austria, on the nationalist principles so dear to the Emperor's heart, was one of the historic achievements of the Empire. How could the Emperor now turn on his heel, abandon the Italians, throw up the ideal of nationalism, and embrace the arch enemy Austria, the breaker of nations?

Louis-Napoleon, in the depths of his fatigue, seemed struck by La Valette's arguments, or so the Empress thought; but still he said nothing. La Valette went on. A war with Prussia was, he said, unnecessary. Berlin, he argued, would be generous in compensating a friend who by remaining neutral had made possible its victory. France would get all that she needed without the waste of war.

The Empress listened to the Minister with mounting impatience. At last she leapt to her feet. "When the Prussian armies are no longer tied up in Bohemia," she said, "and can turn back against ourselves, Bismarck will simply laugh at our claims!"

Despairing though he was, Louis-Napoleon tentatively inclined to the warlike counsels of Drouyn and the Empress. He ordered a French force to march to the Rhine, and he requested that the lawmakers of the Corps Législatif be summoned to approve the monies needed for mobilization.

But the Emperor's resolution was hollow. Later in the day he reversed his decision.

"I am not ready for war," he said.

Vienna, July 1866

WHILE THE BATTLE RAGED at Sadowa, the Hofburg was tranquil. The household guards paced back and forth before their yellow-and-white sentinel boxes. Footmen in silver braid and black knee breeches stood at polished doors. Soldiers of the Imperial Bodyguard watched over the private apartments of the Emperor with halberds in their hands. The meticulously regulated ballet was in keeping with the character of the imperial choreographer. "No breach of traditional court rules, however slight, ever escaped" the notice of Franz Josef, his adjutant, General Baron von Margutti, said. "What do you mean by not being dressed according to the regulations?" the Kaiser once demanded of a lieutenant reporting for orderly duty. "You've no buttons on your sleeves. Didn't you know it?"

"No, Your Majesty, indeed I did not."

"Then you don't know the regulations. It's monstrous."

The regulations. Emanating from the Hofburg, they extended to the remotest corners of Franz Josef's Empire. The intricate web of rules and commands was assiduously maintained by an army of policemen and paper-pushers, the foremost of whom was the Emperor himself. A continuous stream, in fact a flood, of missives issued daily from the desk of the All Highest. "You can take it from me," Franz Josef said, "that in important matters written communications are not only the safest but also the quickest method." Every day the Kaiser sat at his desk writing orders, instructions, minutes, memoranda. He made notes touching every military review and special audience. The habit became so ingrained that he committed even the fleeting impressions of the day to slips of paper, setting forth in a cryptic shorthand the names of people he liked and ministers he did not want to see. "Wekerle—here again already—*ach Gott!* not this time! no! no!" Papers covered in the neat hand of the Emperor piled up on the desks of his ministers, adjutants, chamberlains, equerries. From their desks more paper issued, the life blood of the immense bureaucracy of the Habsburgs.

On this summer evening, however, all the paper was black.

As with every other part of the Kaiser's day, the dinner hour was regulated by fixed customs. As soon as the settings were laid, Franz Josef came to inspect the table. He took up a knife, and looked for his reflection in the blade. A telegram was brought in. The commander of the fortress at Könnigrätz was reporting that the fugitive remnant of the Austrian army was clamoring to be admitted to the citadel. Such news was sufficiently disturbing; but Franz Josef did not yet give up hope. Then came a telegram from Feldherr Benedek himself.

"General rout."

Franz Josef turned as white as his uniform.

The news spread fast. Beyond the gates of the palace astonishment was, at first, curiously mingled with apathy, and even with levity. Men and women sat up late eating and drinking in the dining gardens of the Prater, unmoved by the disaster that had befallen the Army of the North. The music of Strauss wafted over the frivolous scene, and prostitutes with painted faces plied their trade. The nonchalance appalled those of a graver cast of mind. "Does not such scum deserve its fate?" one onlooker asked as he gazed upon the indolent sensuality of the Prater. But the spirit of blasé indifference could not long be maintained even by the most cynical, and by degrees insouciance was succeeded by terror. A "gloom almost amounting to despair," one diplomat wrote, "took possession of the city."

The terrified populace fixed angry eyes on the architects of its humiliation. When the Kaiser drove out to Schönbrunn, the summer palace of the Habsburgs, precautionary measures were taken, and he was for the first time in his reign escorted by a detachment of Household Cavalry. The silence of the crowd was broken by shouts of "Long live the Emperor Maximilian." Such tributes to the younger brother, who was now in Mexico, were thought to annoy Franz Josef intensely.

The imperial scribes made a feeble attempt to defend the régime. In the *Wiener Abendpost* apologists for the court contended that the appointment of Benedek as Feldherr had been forced upon the Kaiser by public opinion. The admission reassured no one, and only strengthened the impression that the government was incompetent. The Kaiser, sensible of the danger in which he stood, condescended to receive a delegation of his subjects. Zelinka, the Mayor of Vienna, told the Kaiser that his constituents feared that the city would soon be besieged by the Prussians. Franz Josef replied that the "trenches were very far away."

But they were coming closer.

The Prussian Second Army marched on Olmütz. The railway and telegraph lines which ran through that city were severed, and Vienna was cut off from the north. The Prussian First Army continued its advance and was soon less than sixty miles from the capital. The population of the city was swollen by an influx of refugees desperately seeking to escape the invaders. Foreign nationals, fearful for their lives, crowded the lobbies of embassies and legations. Outwardly the Kaiser displayed a serene confidence; but this appearance of strength was belied by the trembling prudence of his bureaucrats. Steamships in the Danube were loaded with the ancient treasures of the dynasty, and quantities of gold bullion were sent away from the danger.

At length the Prussians were at the gates of the city. The massive armies lay down on the Marchfeld, the great plain east of the capital. From the belfries of Vienna frightened residents saw a line of tents and standards that stretched for miles. The left flank of the invading army extended almost as far as Pressburg (Bratislava). A "sickening expectation" prevailed, one observer said, that the victorious Prussians would enter the city in a matter of days.

Bohemia, July 1866

AS HE GAZED ON the corpses of Sadowa, Bismarck thought not of his revolution but of his son. "It makes me sick," he said, "when I reflect that Herbert may be lying like that some day." The champion of blood and iron was appalled by the sight of real blood, but sentimentality vied, in that labyrinthical brain, with the demands of an iron will. When, shortly after the battle, he received the telegram informing him that Louis-Napoleon sought to impose mediation on the belligerents, he was indignant. This was a violation of the promise of neutrality the French Emperor had made at Biarritz. "I will be revenged on the Gauls," he said, "when opportunity offers."

He mastered his anger. Moltke assured him that Prussia was strong enough to resist the French should they attempt to march on the Rhine; but Bismarck would run no unnecessary risks as he prepared to harvest the bloody fruits of Sadowa. The Prussians telegraphed their acceptance of French mediation.

Bismarck was nevertheless determined to outwit the French. He ordered his deputy, Baron Robert von der Goltz, the Prussian Ambassador at Paris, to repair to Saint-Cloud and extort Louis-Napoleon's assent to

Prussia's terms. Goltz enjoyed the confidence of the French, with whom he was at home; he was the son of a Prussian diplomat and had been born in the Prussian Embassy in Paris. He conducted his mission with notable skill. He pointed out to Louis-Napoleon that the terms Prussia sought were more moderate than might have been expected given the overwhelming character of the Prussian victory. Goltz further observed that King Wilhelm favored a more far-reaching settlement, and that only with difficulty could Bismarck restrain his sovereign from making more extensive demands. If France did not approve the proposed terms quickly, there was a danger that Bismarck would lose control of the King.

Louis-Napoleon took the words to heart. He, too, needed an armistice. The longer the war continued, the more the prestige of the mediator suffered. He accepted Bismarck's terms.

An obstacle fell away; but Bismarck's work was by no means finished. He had now to stare down his own sovereign. For Baron Goltz was not altogether bluffing when he threatened Louis-Napoleon with the rage of Wilhelm. Victory had gone to the King's head. He was intoxicated by the prospect which opened up after Sadowa. Like Alexander gazing on the Punjab, he yearned to carry his conquering arms still farther. He would march into Vienna. He would strip the Habsburgs of their fairest possessions.

Bismarck mocked the King and the more adventurous generals. Why not "go on to Constantinople," he asked, "establish a new Byzantium, and leave Prussia to its fate?" To his wife he spoke of the difficulty of overcoming the romantic temptation. We are "carried away as easily as we fall into despair," he wrote, "and I have the thankless task of pouring water into the sparkling wine and trying to make it plain that we are not alone in Europe but have to live with three other powers who hate us and envy us." Bismarck was a man of proportion as well as of will; extravagant claims would, he knew, bring reaction. The other powers would not stand by indefinitely while Prussia remodeled vast swaths of Europe.

But the King was obstinate. The Austrians must, he said, be punished for their evil deeds. Bismarck replied that it was no business of theirs to sit in judgment over the moral character of the Habsburgs; their task was to unite Germany under Prussia. The wounding of Austria would only leave her thirsting for revenge, and might drive her into the arms of France: it would contribute nothing to the interest or security of their own Kingdom. Such arguments were, however, lost on the King, and Bismarck was haunted by the suspicion that all that he had gained would be snatched away as a result of his master's intransigence.

His nerves gave way. He begged to be relieved of his duties in the Cabinet and allowed to join his regiment. He quitted the council chamber and, going to his bedroom, fell into a fit of weeping. He wondered whether it would not be best for him to fall out the window. (His room, he noted, was on the fourth story.) At this dark moment, he felt a hand on his shoulder. It was Crown Prince Friedrich. He told Bismarck that, though he had opposed his policy towards Austria, he was prepared to go to the King and support his plan for peace.

Half an hour later the Crown Prince returned. It was a nasty business, he said; but *Pater* had relented.

The terms dictated by Bismarck were embodied in the armistice concluded at Nikolsburg (Mikulov). The result was a revolution. Austria, though she was not required to part with any of her territory,* was banished from Germany, and Prussia's suzerainty over the German-speaking peoples was henceforth assured. The King of Hanover and the Elector of Hesse were stripped of their ancient patrimonies, and their subjects were constrained to obey the dictates of Berlin. Nassau, Holstein, Lauenburg, a slice of Hesse-Darmstadt, a sliver of Bavaria, and the greatest part of Schleswig were annexed to the Prussian state. Hundreds of square miles were added to the territory controlled from Berlin, and more than four million Germans became subjects of the King of Prussia. Saxony was suffered to retain a precarious independence; but it was otherwise with Frankfurt, which was forced to surrender her old municipal freedom. The submission of the city was ratified by plunder, and the despondent Burgomaster hanged himself in order to escape the depredations of the Prussians. Louis-Napoleon asked Baron Goltz whether it was true that thirty million florins had been extorted from the city. "Surely that is too harsh," the French Emperor said. "Oh dear no," replied the Baron with a smile, "Your Majesty forgets that Frankfurt is the city of the Rothschilds." Frankfurt would henceforth form part of Prussia.

With the stroke of a pen the schism of northern Germany was repaired. The resulting state was called the North German Confederation. In fact, it was a Prussian superstate, with Bismarck as its Chancellor. The last remnant of old Prince Metternich's vision of Germany perished. The Bund which that statesman had prophesied would be the salvation of Europe had expired in fecklessness. The security of the German people, Metternich believed, lay in the existence of two strong German powers.† Bismarck thought differently, and Germany was recast. "In 1866," Wilhelm Roepke wrote, "Germany ceased to exist." Prussian Germany took its place.

---

* Other than Venetia, which pursuant to an agreement between Franz Josef and Louis-Napoleon was ceded by Austria to France, and was a short time later united with Italy.

† "Each weakening of one of the Central Powers," Metternich declared, "represents the most direct blow at the existence of the other."

There was shock in France when it was learned that Prussian supremacy north of the Main involved the outright annexation of immense tracts of land. Louis-Napoleon shrugged his shoulders and tried to dismiss the question as "a matter of detail"—as though the compulsory naturalization of millions was a diplomatic rounding error. But he agreed to ask Bismarck for a reward for his (not altogether benign) neutrality. Just as the armistice was about to be signed, Louis-Napoleon's emissary, Count Benedetti, a slight, bald-headed Corsican, came begging for scraps from the Prussian table. Bismarck was angered by his intrusion. "Louis shall pay for it," he is said to have exclaimed. But the crafty Junker instantly recovered his self-command. He feigned sympathy for the French claims. Of course, he was ready to do justice to France. Only he was loathe, just now, to take any steps that might jeopardize the armistice. There would time enough in the future to address such matters. Deceived by these plausible words, the French acquiesced. The armistice was signed, and the siege of Vienna was raised.

A little more than a year after the American Civil War ended, the German civil war was completed, and Bismarck concluded the first phase of his revolution. The war between the American states ended after four years of fighting; the war between the German states was finished in six weeks. In each case the result was momentous; in the crucible of war, two revolutionary statesmen gave a new inflection to the world crisis, and forged powers that were destined to play a memorable part on the stage of history. Undoubtedly, what is most interesting in the German revolution is the way in which its architect, having unleashed the philosophy of blood and iron, refused to push it to its limit. Bismarck did not repeat the mistake of the conquerors of the past. The purest type of romantic conquistador—Alexander, Caesar, Bonaparte—does not know when to stop. Bismarck was different. He never forgot the faintly perceptible line that separates victory from hubris.

Paris, Berlin, and Vichy, July–September 1866

THE SHADOWS LENGTHENED as the French Emperor, strolling with his Empress amid the shrubberies of Saint-Cloud, found himself face to face with an image of death. He saw it rise before him in the summer evening, luminous and inexorable—the epitaph of his Empire, written by Bismarck in the blood and dust of Sadowa. The fault, he knew, was his own. To Eugénie he admitted that he had made a mistake. It could not now be undone. The "hour of fate had passed by." Louis-Napoleon lapsed into silence. He "seemed so utterly crushed," the Empress said, "that I trembled for our future." Unable to "get a single word out of him," she began

Before the revolution:
Abraham Lincoln in
the spring of 1860.
Library of Congress

Before the revolution:
Otto von Bismarck in
the summer of 1862.
*Bildarchiv Preussicher
Kulturbesitz*

In the midst of a revolution:
Tsar Alexander II. *Corbis*

Prince Alexis Fyodorovich Orlov, front row, third from right,
in Paris in 1856. *Corbis*

Helmuth von Moltke,
the Chief of the Prussian
General Staff. *Corbis*

William Henry
Seward, the American
Secretary of State.
Library of Congress

Leo Tolstoy. *Collection of the author*

James and Mary Chesnut. *Granger Collection*

Richard Wagner at the piano, playing a selection from *Parsifal*. *Vincente de Paredes*

Mary Todd Lincoln. *Library of Congress*

Empress Mary of Russia,
by Winterhalter. *Collection of the author*

Johanna von Bismarck.
Bildarchiv Preussicher Kulturbesitz

George McClellan and his
wife, Ellen. *Library of Congress*

Robert E. Lee.
Library of Congress

The western wing of the Winter Palace in Saint Petersburg. Tsar Alexander's private apartments were situated in the middle of the wing, above the carriageway
known as the Saltykov Entrance. *Library of Congress*

Prince Peter Kropotkin in
1864. *Collection of the author*

President Lincoln and
General McClellan confer
at Antietam, October 1862.
Library of Congress

Edouard Manet, *Le Déjeuner sur l'herbe,* 1863.
Musée d'Orsay, Paris

Walt Whitman.
Library of Congress

Friedrich Nietzsche in 1864,
when he volunteered in a
Prussian cavalry regiment.
Corbis

Napoleon III, Emperor of the French.
Library of Congress

The Empress Eugénie.
Library of Congress

Ekaterina "Katya" Dolgorukaya.
Collection of the author

John Bell Hood.
Corbis

Kate Chase.
Library of Congress

A Union soldier disemboweled by a shell at Gettysburg, July 1863.
Library of Congress

Ulysses S. Grant in Virginia in 1864.
Library of Congress

Lincoln reads his Second Inaugural Address, March 1865.
Library of Congress

The cost of revolution: the ruins of Richmond, April 1865.
Library of Congress

The burden of revolution: Lincoln in April 1865.
Library of Congress

The cost of revolution: damaged buildings in the Rue de Lille, Paris, after the Prussian bombardment. *Corbis*

The burden of revolution: German troops parade in the Champs-Elysées in Paris, March 1871. *Corbis*

Bismarck leaves Berlin
after his fall from power.
*Bildarchiv Preussicher
Kulturbesitz*

The assassination of the Tsar. *From periodicals of the time*

to sob. "My soul was on the rack. . . . From this moment we were on the slope leading to the abyss, the slope up which there is no return."

Public opinion turned violently against her husband. The Emperor was scorned as a "painted Jove." Newspapers spoke of the shame of the Empire, and politicians lamented the plight of a nation that confronted, on its eastern frontier, an immense new supremacy, controlled by a country which the Emperor's own uncle said had been "hatched from a cannon ball," a kingdom in which war had long been the national industry. Why, they asked, had Louis-Napoleon abandoned the policy, pursued by French statesmen since the days of Richelieu, of dividing Germany against herself? Why had he helped to foster the union of the Teutons under "*ces maudits Prussiens*"?

In a morose frame of mind, the Emperor retired to Vichy. His health had taken a turn for the worse. The "moral shock he had undergone," Eugénie said, "reacted violently on his physical condition." He could neither walk nor sleep and could hardly eat.

Perhaps there was still time. It might be that he could yet redeem himself, in the eyes of his people, by obtaining a slice of Germany for France. At Vichy, he and Drouyn drafted instructions for Benedetti. The sad-eyed Corsican went once more to Bismarck. Some territory on the Rhine, perhaps the fortress at Mainz, would be most helpful to his master.

While Benedetti attempted to bargain with Bismarck, Louis-Napoleon was forced to interrupt his cure and drag himself back to Paris. Archduchess Charlotte, the consort of Maximilian—she was now known as Carlotta, Empress of Mexico—had arrived in the city and taken rooms in the Grand Hotel, a new establishment on the Rue Scribe. She begged to be received at Saint-Cloud. Louis-Napoleon sent a state carriage and a squadron of Cuirassiers to fetch her. He and Eugénie greeted her at the door of the château and conducted her, past busts of Roman emperors and paintings of the Olympian Gods, to the private apartments of the Empress. Here, amid furniture that had once belonged to Marie-Antoinette, Carlotta painted in dark colors the position of her husband, the blond Prince who reigned on the heights of Chapultepec. In the summer palace of the Spanish viceroys, Maximilian presided over a disintegrating Empire. Carlotta implored Louis-Napoleon to reconsider his decision to withdraw the French expeditionary force in Mexico. But the French Emperor, preoccupied with the demise of his own imperial adventure, could only counsel her to surrender her dreams and urge her husband to come home. A glass of orangeade was brought to the suppliant Empress; she looked at the glass queerly. She screamed; the world was against her; her enemies were trying to poison her. Carlotta fled to Rome in the hope of securing the protection of the Pope; and the word "hysteria" began to be whispered in the princely and diplomatic drawing rooms of Europe.

The news from Mexico was bad, but that from Berlin was worse. The solicitations of Count Benedetti were in vain. Now that the armistice was signed, Bismarck would not part with an inch of German soil to nourish the Empire of a competitor. It would have been different, he said, if France had actively aided Prussia in the subjugation of Austria; but the Emperor had scarcely acted as a friend when he imposed mediation on the belligerents. Bismarck then resolved on the public humiliation of Louis-Napoleon. He published both Benedetti's demand for territorial compensation and his own refusal in the French newspaper *Le Siècle*.

The decision reflected motives of policy as well as of revenge; for when the peoples of southern Germany learned of Louis-Napoleon's interest in their territory, they ceased to have any desire to revive their historic alliances with France. The German states of the south instead concluded defensive treaties with Bismarck.

This, however, was not quite the end of the matter. The revelation of Louis-Napoleon's impotence provoked the rage of France. Benedetti went again to see Bismarck. His master needed something, anything, to shore up his drooping prestige. The two men considered the possibilities. If Germany was out of the question, what about . . . Belgium? Bismarck appeared to be receptive; there was no reason, he said, why the French Empire should not extend wherever French was the language of the people. Prussia, he intimated, might be willing to co-operate with Louis-Napoleon in such a project. Would the Count be good enough to draft an agreement? Only it was a *sensitive* question; the Count really must be careful. One could never trust subordinates. He ought to write out the draft in his own hand. Blood and—irony. Benedetti obliged, and took out his pen. Bismarck soon had the paper in his hands. The Count went away, expecting to receive a telegram informing him when the document was to be signed. It never came. Bismarck, however, carefully retained the draft in the poor Count's handwriting.

It might prove useful one day.

Yasnaya Polyana, January 1867

"BISMARCK THINKS he has outwitted all Europe," Tolstoy wrote to a friend. But the Prussian statesman was only one of a thousand other causes which, he maintained, made "the blood-letting of Germany necessary in 1866." Bismarck, Tolstoy said, was another of the "old jades" walking the "tread-wheel" of politics. Statesmanship was a swindle. Tossing aside the newspapers, he returned to dirty diapers and the pages of *War and Peace*. Could he have foreseen the remoter consequences of the world crisis—could he have known that in seventy-five years a German army would carry the philosophy of blood and iron to Yasnaya Polyana itself (the manor house would serve as the headquarters of a German general), he might have spoken differently.

Berlin, September 1866

AT THE END of the summer the victorious Prussian armies returned in triumph to the capital. The helmets of the Great Elector's Life Guard Cuirassiers, the oldest of the Prussian cavalry regiments, flashed in the September sunlight, and breastplates gleamed.* The 3rd Neumarkt Dragoons trotted past. Riding with them was Jeb Stuart's former aide-de-camp, Lieutenant von Borcke, who wore the Order of the Red Eagle, a tribute to his gallantry in the (largely ineffective) cavalry charge at Sadowa. Bismarck and Moltke rode with the other commanders in the first rank of the procession, just ahead of the King. The Minister-President wore the spiked helmet and white uniform of a major general of the 7th Heavy Landwehr Regiment of Horse, of which he had recently been named chief; across his chest was draped the orange sash of the Exalted Order of the Black Eagle.

The crowd hailed the architect of the German revolution with a passionate enthusiasm as he went down the alley of the Linden, past the captured guns and standards of the Austrians. At the Brandenburg Gate, he was showered with rose petals. Astride his horse, the man of iron appeared a tower of strength, but in reality he was unwell, and only with difficulty did he maintain himself erect in the saddle.

"But I have beaten them all!" he exclaimed. "All!" In the aftermath of Sadowa the free-state opposition to his authority collapsed. A puny band of liberals continued to resist the Minister-President, but the rest acquiesced in his régime, and voted to indemnify or pardon him for whatever unconstitutional actions he might have taken in the past. The dream of ministerial responsibility and parliamentary control of the army died away. Bismarck accepted the submission of his adversaries; he did not, like the old-fashioned reactionaries, seek to destroy the Parliament altogether. A relic, he concluded, was more useful than a ruin. The legislature lapsed into impotence, and the light of liberty, which had flashed for a time in the hearts of the opponents of the government, was put out.

* The unit was subsequently reorganized as the 2nd Panzer Regiment.

The first communiqué of the victor raised a shudder in Europe. The right of conquest, Bismarck announced, was a "sacred right." Even more sacred were conquests undertaken in order that Germany might live. Prussia's actions followed, he said, from the "right of the German nation to exist, to breathe, to be united; it is the right and the duty of Prussia to give the German nation the foundation necessary for its existence." The right of the German nation to live and to breathe—*zu leben und zu athmen*—superseded both private right and international law.

This was an extension, into the jurisprudence of nations, of the poetry of militant nationalism. Like other statesmen of the romantic school, Bismarck believed that people craved myths, and required the stimulus of an ideal; he knew that poetry (in the words of the German scholar Jacob Burckhardt) is "a national force and power." Nothing in his theory of diplomatic prudence was so influential as his myth of a "living" Germany, a Germany which, in its path to vitality, might subdue and extirpate peoples and nations. For Bismarck constituted the state he founded in such a way that he alone possessed the power to restrain the military chiefs of the General Staff, who instinctively embraced his theory of German vitalism. The most durable part of his revolution proved to be, not his diplomacy of moderation, but his cult of blood and iron; a romance that inspired innumerable Germans to "dream on, dream on, of bloody deeds and death."

Washington, June 1866

IN THE MONTHS that followed the surrender of Lee and the death of Lincoln, Walt Whitman thought often of the revolution which killed more than 600,000 human beings and liberated four million more. The true story of it, he was convinced, would never be told. "Future years will never know the seething hell and the black infernal background of countless minor scenes and interiors, (not the official surface-courteousness of the generals, not the few great battles) of the secession war; and it is best they should not—the real war will never get in the books."

Only "a few stray glimpses into that life" and "into those lurid interiors" would be "convey'd to the future." Lincoln himself, "the leading actor in the stormiest drama known to real history's stage," would be known only imperfectly in aftertimes. The President's death, Whitman believed, made America a nation: his spilt blood condensed "a Nationality." But no artist could truly portray even Lincoln's physical appearance, "the peculiar color" of his face, the "lines of it, the eyes, mouth, expression." If Lincoln's face must be forgotten, what hope for his spirit and his poetry? "The current portraits are all failures," Whitman said, "most of them caricatures." Yet he could not forbear to make an attempt of his own. The previous autumn he had brought out a new edition of his war poems. The book was called *Drum-Taps*. The edition contained, as an appendix, eighteen poems which the poet published under the title *Sequel to Drum-Taps*. The first of these was called "When Lilacs Last in the Dooryard Bloom'd." It was his elegy of Lincoln.

Peterhof, July 1866

THEY MET IN a pavilion near Peterhof. On the second floor lay a suite of private rooms. Here the Tsar and Katya became lovers. Afterwards he made a vow, one which Katya later confided to a friend. "Today, alas," Alexander said, "I am not free; but at the earliest possible moment I will marry you. I consider you, now and forever, as my wife before God."

Putbus, Isle of Rügen, September–December 1866

AFTER THE TRIUMPH in Berlin, Bismarck collapsed. He went to Putbus, on the Baltic Isle of Rügen, for a rest cure. He found it difficult even to read; much of the time he sat and stared. "When he sits still," his wife said, "and looks at the blue sky and green meadows, or turns the pages of a picture book, he is tolerably well."

Part Three

_____

FREEDOM AND TERROR

Chapter 26

TOWARDS THE ABYSS

Camden, South Carolina, April–December, 1865

THEY WENT DOWN the road, past burned towns, deserted plantations, blackened chimneys. "This is Sherman's track," Mary Chesnut thought. She wept.

James Chesnut tried to console her. He pointed to the roses, which had flowered abundantly that spring. "Nature is a wonderful renovator," he said. There had been no frost since early March, and the vegetation was much advanced; but to Mary Chesnut the effect was funereal. The soft lights, the velvet shadows—nature, fecund and cruel, was mocking her.

They crossed the river at Chesnut's Ferry. When the ferryman asked his fee, they were unable to pay him. "There was poverty for you," Mary Chesnut said. They went on to Mulberry. The plantation was in ruins. The cotton was gone, the mills and the gins were wrecked, the big house had been plundered. Doors were smashed, windows had been broken, furniture destroyed. James Chesnut's father, the old Colonel, was still in nominal possession; but he was a blind, bewildered dotard. He was ninety-three, and walked with faltering steps, feeling his way through the wreckage with his cane.

They had enough to eat, and much domestic help; the poverty of a ruined planter was relative. Cuffee, the gardener, promised to stay as long as "old Marster" lived, and the kitchen garden was in a flourishing condition. Scipio, the old Colonel's man, also elected to remain, to care for his former owner; and Molly continued to look after her mistress. But there was no cash, other than the small sums Molly brought in; she went about Camden hawking eggs and butter.

James Chesnut was bitter about his losses. Other planters had gone home before the war ended and saved something of their estates. He had stayed at his post, and had returned to find a desolation. He was, at first, wild for scapegoats. It was "the habit of all men," Mary Chesnut wrote, "to fancy that in some inscrutable way their wives are the cause of all evil in their lives." But he later begged her pardon; he had only himself to blame for his misfortunes.

There remains yet something of honor and pride, of life.

It was his consolation. He could now act the final part of the tragedy. A ruined Cavalier, a knight of sorrowful countenance. Adversity was a test of virtue, the trial that separated the true gentleman from the impostor. Stripped of his plumage, a walking anachronism, James Chesnut would never be nobler. Ruin suited him—was in his case a more natural vocation than politics. At last he could live proudly aloof, in the shade of his shattered porticos.

Her husband had still his "smatch of honour," his fragment of romance. What, Mary Chesnut asked, had she? She was forty-two when the war ended, but "a hundred, in thought and feeling." She had no children. She no longer had even Buck. Her protégée had, since breaking off her engagement to Sam Hood, been seen riding out with Rawlins Lowndes, a handsome rice planter. But Buck was miserable—a sacrificial virgin, vainly seeking an altar. She was said to have lost twenty pounds and to have become a "perfect wreck." Her family took her away, to spend the winter in Paris.

The revolution had come, and it had destroyed. "A feeling of sadness hovers over me now, day and night, that no words of mine can express," Mary Chesnut wrote. There "are nights here with the moonlight, cold & ghastly & the whippoorwills, & the screech owls alone disturbing the silence when I could tear my hair & cry aloud for all that is past & gone."

Paris, Saint Petersburg, and the Crimea, May–December 1867

WHATEVER THE TRAGIC FLAW that dooms a revolution, accountability ultimately rests with the leadership. In the spring of 1867, Tsar Alexander traveled to Paris. One night, shortly before the clocks struck twelve, he left his room in the Elysée Palace and knocked on the door of Count Adlerberg's chamber. The Tsar wanted to go for a walk.

The startled Count suggested that His Majesty would perhaps like someone to accompany him.

"But I don't need anyone to accompany me," Alexander said. "I'll manage on my own. But, my dear man, give me a little money."

"How much does His Majesty require?"

"I have no idea, how about a hundred thousand francs?"

The money, though it was a great sum, was instantly procured, and the Tsar went out into the Paris night. He was not quite alone. French and Russian police detectives discreetly shadowed the master of eighty millions. Alexander hailed a cab and drove to the Rue Basse-du-Rempart. There he alighted and, taking out a piece of paper, examined it in the lamplight. Evidently it was an address. He turned and passed into a courtyard, only to discover that it was the wrong house. In the meantime, however, the gate had shut behind him. The Tsar was unable to open it. As he stood there puzzled, one of the agents who had been following him came over and pointed to a rope that hung near the gate. Alexander pulled the rope and the gate opened. He soon found the house he sought.

Katya was waiting for him. Their affair had progressed since the summer of 1866, but the secret had become known, and in order to avoid scandal it had been arranged that Katya should leave Russia and live, for a time, abroad. She dutifully boarded a train. Alexander, however, found the separation painful; he was now deeply in love with the girl. His letters to her were written in a strain of romantic adoration. She was the "dear Angel" of his soul, "my life, my all," *"ma petite femme adorée."* He resolved that she should quit her place of exile at Naples and go to Paris, where he could meet her when he visited the city during the World's Fair which Louis-Napoleon had organized to prop up his sagging régime.

The Tsar's visit had a diplomatic as well as an amorous purpose. After Sadowa, the pressures of the world crisis became more intense. As Bismarck's revolution unfolded and the power of Prussia grew, her neighbors to the east and west attempted to put their differences aside and draw closer to one another. Louis-Napoleon was waiting on the platform of the Gare du Nord when the Tsar's train pulled in, and he had thoughtfully arranged that, in driving to the Elysée Palace, their cavalcade should avoid the Boulevard Sébastopol, which commemorated the Anglo-French victory over Russia in the Crimean War.

Paris, with its degenerating *mœurs,* dripped decadence. The crinolines favored by the Empress Eugénie had gone out of style, and women no longer concealed their figures beneath accumulations of drapery. It was an age of *décolletage;* and at a ball in the Tuileries the beautiful women of the Second Empire flaunted their bosoms. The Tsar appeared to enjoy himself immensely, and for a time his diplomatic projects seemed to prosper no less signally than his romantic ones. But there was to be no *entente*. During a military review at Longchamp in the Bois de Boulogne, a Polish patriot drew a revolver and fired two bullets at the Tsar. Alexander came away unhurt, but the second attempt on his life threw an unflattering light on the contradictions of his revolution. The autocrat who freed the serfs continued to oppress the Poles. Alexander, preferring to overlook the perplexities of his policy, blamed the French. Surely Louis-Napoleon's security services—his army of gendarmes and mouchards—could have done a better job of protecting a guest. The dream of a Franco-Russian *rapprochement* faded.

Several times during the visit, Alexander was seen to stare vacantly into space, with the curious faraway look that Prince Kropotkin had once noticed in his eyes. When the great Napoleon had stared thus into the vacancy, his expression, men recalled, was that of one who "looks into another world" and beholds visions of power and possibility. By contrast, the vacant gaze of Alexander betrayed, not the ecstasies of prepotency, but its apprehensions. During what remained to him of life, Alexander was never quite free from dread of assassination. "Why," he asked, "do they hound me down like a wild beast?"

He must have guessed the answer. The reds hounded him precisely because he had allied his dynasty, however tenuously, with the forces of freedom, and in doing so had threatened their apocalypse. The dreamers hated him with a hatred they never extended to his more reactionary predecessors, Alexander I and Nicholas I, or to his more reactionary successors, Alexander III and Nicholas II. They were determined to break the liberal sovereign, in body and spirit.

The Tsar returned to Russia, and Katya became his professed mistress. Her detractors insinuated that she was privy to the machinations of the Pan-Slavs, who urged the Tsar to solve his problems by marching on Constantinople in the name of militant nationalism. But there is no evidence that she played a part in the formulation of policy. Alexander seems to have sought in Katya a respite from the burdens of politics and diplomacy. He installed her, in Saint Petersburg, in a house on the English Quay, with servants and carriages, and he arranged that she should visit him regularly in the Winter Palace. There was a low door in the façade, to which she was given the key. Having passed into the palace, she would ascend a staircase that led to a suite of rooms on the third story. The Tsar's father, Nicholas, had once occupied the apartments, and ever since his death they had been left undisturbed. In Nicholas's study, beneath paintings of battles and portraits of illustrious tsars, the two lovers dallied.

When Alexander went to Tsarskoe Selo, Katya accompanied him, and was settled in a nearby villa. Her assignations with the sovereign took place in a wing of the Catherine Palace, in a little room that overlooked the rose gardens. But the favorite rendezvous of the lovers was the Crimea. Driving through a country with charms to rival those of Greece, the Tsar sometimes ordered the carriages to stop at the Gates of Baidar, an eminence that commanded striking views of the Black Sea and the Iayla Mountains. Here the imperial party, forgetting, for a moment, the stresses of autocracy, could dine al fresco on the terrace of a taverna. When the lovers reached Livadia, they threw off all constraint. The Tsar visited Katya openly, and rode over to her house on one of his Arabian stallions.

While Alexander dwelt in his alternative world, Count Shuvalov administered the Empire. He was a capable vizier, one whose aristocratic manners belied uncommon talents and real abilities. The Count was a *grand seigneur* to his fingertips, at ease in every drawing room, at home with every pretty woman. He was an adroit dispenser of praise, that art which, when practiced unskillfully, is called flattery, but which, when undertaken by a master, is known as charm. A thorough man of the world, he had learnt the art of making profligacy appealing. "Count Shuvalov is out driving in his carriage," his majordomo would inform callers when the Count was making love. His enemies loudly condemned, and secretly envied, his numerous seductions. Yet they could not assert that the exertions of the voluptuary detracted from the labors of the statesman. Disraeli, who sat across the table from Shuvalov at the Congress of Berlin, testified to the Russian's skillfulness as a negotiator. "Schu" fought his battles "with marvelous talent and temper," Disraeli wrote to his friend Lady Bradford. "He is a first rate parliamentary debater, never takes a note, and yet in his reply never misses a point."

Alexander himself did not yet wholly lose the power of initiative; he sold Alaska to the United States in the face of considerable opposition, hoping through this gesture to strengthen Russia's relations with a rising free state. But Shuvalov was now the dominant figure in Russia. His views of the world crisis differed from those of his master. He "prepared one reactionary measure after another," Prince Kropotkin said, "and when Alexander showed reluctance to sign any one of them, Shuvalov would speak of the coming revolution and the fate of Louis XVI, and, 'for the salvation of the dynasty,' would implore him to sign the new additions to the law of repressions." But such speechmaking eventually became tiresome, and Shuvalov dispensed with it. He discovered an easier method of governing the Tsar. When Alexander went off to hunt bears in the forests of Novgorod, Shuvalov followed with a portfolio of orders and decrees. "A couple of bears would be killed by Alexander," Kropotkin wrote, "and there, in the excitement of the hunting festivities, Shuvalov would obtain his master's signature to any scheme of repression, or robbery in the interests of his clients, which he had concocted."

Lucerne, Switzerland, May 1869–March 1870

IN A SPRING NOON in 1869, a young professor of philology made his way to a villa overlooking Lake Lucerne. Passing through the gate, the professor heard the notes of a piano, and an anguished voice repeating a refrain—

Verwundet hat mich
der mich erweckt . . .

He who has awakened me
Has dealt me this wound . . .

It was a fatal moment: the young professor was enchanted. Germany could never afterwards be the same. The young professor was Friedrich Nietzsche, and he had been pierced by the genius of Wagner.

The two men who between them created the music of the German revolution soon became close friends. Nietzsche, who earlier in the year had been installed in the chair of philology at Basel, became an intimate of the circle at Triebschen, Wagner's villa overlooking Lake Lucerne. He was just twenty-four, yet it was evident that he possessed astonishing depths. These, however, he carried lightly, and even the arrogant Cosima, the mistress of the house, found him sympathetic. (Cosima had, by this time, left her husband, Hans von Bülow, and she was now pregnant with Wagner's son, Siegfried, who was born in June 1869.)

To Nietzsche, Wagner unfolded his hopes for art and revolution. More than ever, the composer identified his music with the resurrection of the German nation. "One thing is now clear to me," he said, "with Germany's well-being stands or falls my art-ideal." Without Germany's greatness, his art was only a dream; if the dream were to become reality, "then as a matter of course Germany also must achieve its predestined greatness." Wagner did not doubt that Germany would triumph; he shared the confidence of his patron, King Ludwig, who believed that "the other peoples of the earth will pay homage to ours and bow before its spirit." The difficulty lay, not in the revival of Germany, but in the realization of the art-ideal. Wagner had given the world *Tristan und Isolde,* which received its first performance in Munich in 1865. But much remained to be done. How was he to establish the little artistic city-state which alone could create the proper mold for German culture? He soon found a solution to the problem. He would erect, in northern Bavaria, a temple of the muses at Bayreuth.

His new disciple seemed to comprehend it all. Nietzsche was convinced that Wagner had discovered the "Dionysian power" of the German soul. The composer's art was "the earthquake through which some primeval force that had been dammed up for ages finally liberated itself." He called Wagner *"Pater Seraphicus"* (the epithet of Saint Francis of Assisi), a being who, like the Seraphim of Isaiah, was distinguished by the fervor of his love.

The rule of flattery proposed by Disraeli in connection with royalty pertains to artists as well: it must be laid on with a trowel. Wagner grew fond of the young man who seemed likely to burn a quantity of useful incense in his name. "At that time," Nietzsche later wrote, "we loved each other and hoped everything for each other: it was truly a profound love, without a single *arrière-pensée.*" Only when, at dinner, the meat was served did Wagner's brow darken. Nietzsche was a vegetarian. The composer reproved his acolyte for this; the "contest of all against all," he said, "ran through the whole of creation, so that it was necessary for man to get strength through his food in order to accomplish great things." Nietzsche nodded his head in agreement, but continued to abstain. This obstinacy, one witness said, "made the Meister really cross." Evidently it was necessary to retreat to the safer conversational ground of the art-ideal.

Still the friendship flourished. "I'd let go cheap the whole rest of my human relationships," Nietzsche later said: "I should not want to give away out of my life at any price the days of Triebschen—days of trust, of cheerfulness, of sublime accidents, of *profound* moments." But what he called the "secret work and artistry" of his instinct (the call of "heights that no bird ever reached in its flight," the summons of abysses "into which no foot ever strayed") would not suffer him to remain forever in a condition of discipleship. Had Wagner looked more closely into the eyes of his nearsighted proselyte, he might have detected in them a gleam of apostasy, one that flashed something more than an antipathy to carnivorousness.

Possibly the young professor was a throwback to an older European type; for in his later life, after he broke with Wagner and the world, Nietzsche conformed to the pattern of the itinerant shaman, seeking the secret of existence while passing back and forth between the mountains and the Mediterranean littoral. He possessed the reflexive asceticism of a mage. Not only was he a vegetarian, he was also, it would seem, a celibate, shunning the flesh of women as well as of beasts; there was something in the intensity of his daydreaming that was compatible only with chastity, or with some close approximation to it.* He was a myopic, migraine-burdened dreamer, "a philosopher and solitary by instinct," searching for the elixir of vitality betwixt the Alps and the Riviera.

Nietzsche's progress would possess only a personal and a psychological interest had he not, during his chase after health, conceived a poetry which was to play a part in the world crisis. Nietzsche created his myths in a mood of hostility to Wagner and to Germany's romantic aspirations—but as he himself observed, the artist knows not what he does.

---

* Aloof though he seems generally to have kept himself from women, Nietzsche is said to have made several proposals of marriage, which were refused. His subsequent breakdown may have been caused by syphilis, possibly contracted from a prostitute.

Chapter 27

UNRIPE FRUIT

Berlin and Madrid, July 1870

COUNT BENEDETTI, stepping into the train at Berlin, had at last got away, and was about to begin a holiday journey to Wildbad, in the south of Germany. The Prussian capital was a cruel post for the French diplomat, who had been bred under Mediterranean stars; his escape from the court of Wilhelm must have come as a relief. Europe, to his chagrin, still talked of the way Bismarck had tricked him four years before, in the aftermath of Sadowa. Nor had his old antagonist in the Wilhelmstrasse ever helped him to obtain, for his poor master in Paris, compensatory territory in the Low Countries. The omission seemed to Benedetti all the more unaccountable when he recollected how eager Bismarck had been, four years before, to have him write out a draft of a treaty for the subjugation of the Belgians—in his own hand, no less, the better to preserve the secret. At all events, Benedetti could breathe more easily now; the mercurial Prussian was far away, in the woods of Pomerania, undergoing another cure for his unruly digestive tract. Riding the train southward, the French Ambassador could look forward to a spell of unbroken tranquility at Wildbad, where, in the depths of the Black Forest, he intended to enjoy a much needed rest.

Across Europe, envoys and *élevé consuls* were forsaking the labor of their dispatch boxes for the pleasures of the promenade, the curehouse, and the gaming table. Rarely had the peace of Europe seemed more assured than it did in the first days of July 1870, and the spas and resorts of the Continent were crowded with diplomatists in mufti, seeking an interval of repose. Fatigued by the sun and the rigors of their cures, many of those who drowsed over their newspapers on the morn-

ing of July 5, 1870, doubtless failed to perceive the significance of a little item of news that appeared that day. It was announced from Madrid
that the Spanish Cabinet was to assemble in the palace at La Granja, at
the foot of the Sierra de Guadarrama, to consider the candidature, for
the Crown of Spain, of Prince Leopold of Hohenzollern-Sigmaringen, a
thirty-five-year-old Prussian colonel connected, by a remote affinity of
blood, to the ruling house at Berlin.

Two years before, a revolution had taken place in Spain. The stout
and easygoing Queen, Isabella, had been driven from her throne. After
toying with the idea of establishing a republic, the victorious rebels, led
by Don Juan Prim, Count of Reus and Marquess of Castillejos, had
endeavored to settle the Crown. It was suggested that Prince Leopold of
Hohenzollern-Sigmaringen would make a suitable king. The Prince, it
was admitted on all sides, was without distinction of mind or manner, but
he looked splendid in a uniform, and his very aristocratic dullness, in a
position so tediously ceremonial, might almost be a virtue. Leopold
spent his winters drilling on the parade grounds of Berlin, and his summers lounging at Benrath, his seat on the Rhine; his most notable
achievement in life, before he succeeded in disturbing the peace of
Europe, was his marriage to a Portuguese Princess who was both beautiful and (it was said) accomplished. But there were difficulties. In France
the prospect of a Prussian Prince ruling at Madrid was regarded with passionate aversion; and the Prince himself was reluctant to surrender himself to the hazards of Spanish destiny. The prospect of a Hohenzollern
candidature faded.

Here the matter might have ended, and Leopold's name might today
slumber in placid obscurity in the pages of the *Almanach de Gotha*. But
one man, vigilant, artful, and patient, was watching developments at
Madrid closely, and was determined that the candidature of Leopold
should not die.

Bismarck secretly embraced the cause of the Hohenzollern Prince.

He dispatched to Spain one of his secret agents, the military attaché
Theodor von Bernhardi, and he supplied him with £50,000 drawn on
the "reptile funds"* to smooth the way for Leopold. A final step
remained. In the last days of June 1870, Bismarck obtained, for his strat-
agem, the tepid approval of King Wilhelm, who had for some time
opposed the scheme.

The trap was laid, and it only remained for Louis-Napoleon to fall
into it.

---

* What Bismarck called his "reptile" or "Guelf" funds encompassed assets sequestered from
the demesnes of the exiled House of Hanover.

Boston, Washington, and Utah Territory, July 1868–May 1869

ON A HOT JULY NIGHT, Henry Adams returned to America after seven years in Europe. He and his parents disembarked from a Cunard steamer at the mouth of Boston Harbor. A government tugboat conveyed them to the North River Pier. From the moment they set foot on shore, it was evident that a revolution had taken place. "Had they been Tyrian traders of the year B.C. 1000, landing from a galley fresh from Gibraltar," Adams wrote, "they could hardly have been stranger on the shore of a world, so changed from what it had been ten years before."

Henry Adams returned eager to obtain power in the Republic Lincoln's revolution had remade. But he was perplexed by the absence, in America, of a path to it. There was no *cursus honorum*—course of honors—like those of the aristocratic societies of the Old World. In the United States, one must blaze one's own trail. Adams sought a path through British precedents. He intended to become a literary journalist on the model of Lord Macaulay and Lord Robert Cecil. He went to Washington as a newspaper correspondent, hoping to make a name for himself by exposing corruption. The age of Lincoln had been succeeded by the age of the robber baron; Adams intended to reveal the lucrative trade in favors that enabled men like Jay Gould and Jim Fisk to establish their ascendancies. Once he made his reputation, he would lay his hands on power.

He was soon disillusioned. Politics, if it was amusing as a spectacle, was greasy as a way of life. There was in America no place, Adams came to believe, for the kind of cultivated intelligence he admired in European political figures, men who in temperament if not in blood were more or less aristocratic. There was another, deeper problem. Could Adams have believed that, in descending to the arena, he should be battling for an idea, he might have brought himself to do it. His ancestors, in founding the Republic, had been building a city on a hill; his great-grandfather, John Adams, in serving his country, was serving his God. But for Henry Adams, God was dead. No great idea drove him to enter the lists of power—the reforms he advocated were all little ideas; and (so much of the old New England spirit did he retain) he thought power divorced from ideal purpose poison. "I suppose every man who has looked on at the game," he wrote to his friend Henry Cabot Lodge, "has been struck by the way in which politics deteriorate the moral tone of everyone who mixes in them. The deterioration is far more marked than in any other occupation I know of except the turf, stock-jobbing, and gambling. . . . Politicians as a class must be as mean as card-sharpers, turf-men, or Wall Street curb-stone operators. There is no respectable industry in existence which will not average a higher morality."

What had gone wrong? Why had the idea, part Puritan, part Plutarch, which had sustained John Adams amid all the perplexities of politics failed to inspire his great-grandson? The "inner light" of Protestantism could not yet be wholly archaic; it had precipitated the country's most recent revolution. But the flame which had burned so brightly during the Civil War proved to be the last radiance of a candle before it is put out. No sooner had the children of the Puritans defeated the sons of the Cavaliers than their own energies dissipated. The best and brightest Yankees of Henry Adams's generation found themselves, after Appomattox, sitting on the ashes of their youth, disheartened by the world Lincoln's revolution had made.

Some of Adams's friends attempted to suppress their ideal instincts and make a place for themselves in business or the professions. Adams himself was almost driven to wish that he possessed the soul of a banker. He pictured himself making an expiatory pilgrimage to State Street in Boston, to seek the fatted calf of his grandfather Brooks. (Peter Chardon Brooks, his maternal grandfather, had left at his death an estate worth two million dollars.) But the thing was impossible; he was not cut out for a clerkship in the Suffolk Bank.

After offending President Grant by writing an article on Jay Gould's conspiracy to corner gold, Adams returned to Massachusetts, accepted a professorship at Harvard, and began to teach history. When, several years later, he went again to Washington, he did so in the capacity not of a power-seeker but of an historian, one who devoted his leisure to cultivating a select circle of friends, each as exquisite, as a type, as the carefully chosen volumes of his library. He fell into the vocation of a *flâneur*, and like many of his peers he became a moral tourist. He traveled to Chartres, and found solace amid its roses and apses. He went to Rome, and sat musing on the silent oracles of paganism.

In the course of their pilgrimages the most gifted figures of Adams's generation found new inspirations; but only a few, like Wendell Holmes, who was furiously applying himself to the law, discovered anything that could be of use to them in the public service. Most shunned civic virtue, or failed in the effort to practice it. Some left the country altogether. Henry James crossed the ocean to seek the "denser, richer, warmer European spectacle." There he remained; for he was, he told his friend William Dean Howells, "less a sufferer in Europe than in America." Howells himself did not flee; he stayed home, vowing to "speak out plainly about the life men lead in America." But he too became disenchanted, and would in time confess to James that, though he lived in New York, he also was an "exile from America."

On May 10, 1869, two rail lines were joined at Promontory Summit, in the Utah Territory. The Central Pacific's locomotive, *Jupiter,* and the Union Pacific's engine, *No. 119,* kissed cowcatchers. The country had gained a continent. Leland Stanford, the President of Central Pacific, brought with him a golden spike, one of several commemorative devices furnished for the occasion. (The ornamental spikes were for show; ordinary iron spikes were used to secure the last tie.) Engraved on Stanford's spike were the words: "May God continue the unity of our Country, as the Railroad unites the two great Oceans of the world."

The United States was now what its founders had dreamt it would become, a transcontinental "empire of liberty." Cars and engines thundered down its rails, smoking, rumbling, roaring, flaming; Walt Whitman, counting freight trains on the railway that ran along the Hudson, said that "there cannot be less than a hundred a day." But Henry Adams shook his head. The country, he said, was rapidly becoming little more than a "mechanical consolidation of force," one that threatened to consign men of his type, men of culture and idealistic aspiration, to the ash-heap.

Saint-Cloud and Paris, July 1870

THE FRENCH EMPEROR stood on the balcony off his dressing room at Saint-Cloud, languidly smoking a cigarette as the sun rose over the valley of the Seine. The fates had woven for him another net of troubles. Three days before he had learned of the attempt by Bismarck to place Prince Leopold of Hohenzollern-Sigmaringen on the throne of Spain.

The Emperor likened the prospect of a Prussian dynast reigning at Madrid to a dagger pointed at the heart of France. Of course, he must bestir himself to meet the threat to his Empire, but—alas—it would be no easy thing. Bismarck's *démarche* could scarcely have come at a worse time. The torment to which Louis-Napoleon's bladder subjected him had grown more excruciating, and the opiates to which he had now a frequent recourse clouded his mind and debilitated all his powers of decision. He found it difficult to walk unassisted, and in the privacy of the palace he supported himself on the arms of his chamberlains. *"Le vin est tiré,"* he was heard to say, *"il faut le boire"* (The wine is drawn; it must be drunk).

His throne was in as sorry a state as his urinary tract. The dynastic inspirations of the Bonapartes had always been paleolithic, but never had the Golden Eagles seemed more obsolete than they did in the summer of 1870. The Second Empire had lost its will, and even its self-respect. Grave personages were appalled by the spectacle of the imperial residences, where amid the gilt and parquet men staggered about drunk, and women abandoned themselves to the voluptuous motions of the Can-Can. The Emperor himself ceased to believe in his romance. He knew that his régime was an anachronism, and in order to save his dynasty and appease the growing discontent of his people he had, the previous winter, relinquished, or affected to relinquish, the last tattered shreds of his despotism. He summoned one of his opponents and asked him to form a government. Emile Ollivier, an idealistic barrister devoted to the free state, was designated a "constitutional minister," responsible for his acts to the legislature.

But six months after Ollivier kissed hands, the state of France was not good. In parts of the country the harvest had failed, and the authorities would soon be forced to look to America for bread. The financial markets, it is true, were in a flourishing condition, but the workers were discontented. Nor was Louis-Napoleon able, at this conjuncture, to draw on reserves of success in foreign affairs to pay his domestic debts. His most recent adventure, in Mexico, had ended in ruin. Three years before, Marshal Bazaine had returned to Toulon with the last of the French forces, and the puppet-Emperor Maximilian, fallen into the hands of the rebels, had been taken out and shot in a ragged courtyard at Querétaro. Now a new shadow had fallen across Louis-Napoleon's path, and so peevish was the temper of his people that any miscalculation on his part was likely to prove fatal to his dynasty.

Shortly before noon, Ollivier arrived at Saint-Cloud. He was ushered, past the Roman motifs of the château, into the presence of the Emperor. The slim, bespectacled premier more nearly resembled a student leader in the Quartier Latin than he did a successor to Richelieu and Mazarin. Forty-five years old in the summer of 1870, Ollivier had met with success at the bar, but his inner vocation was philosophical. To those who knew him well, it was obvious that he was more suited to pursuing, inwardly and imaginatively, the life of the mind than he was to playing the mixed game of power and politics that was carried on in the palaces of Paris.

A third figure soon joined the Emperor and the premier at Saint-Cloud. Ollivier might seem to possess the principal authority of the government, but he was not, in reality, the moving power in Louis-Napoleon's Cabinet. The pre-eminent figure, both in abilities and in influence, was the Foreign Minister, Antoine-Alfred Agénor, Duc de Gramont. Gramont was descended from the ancient *noblesse* of France, and he possessed in a high degree the haughtiness of his race. He had nothing but contempt for the plebeian who in theory presided in the Cabinet, and he regarded Ollivier's pacific liberalism as dangerously naïve. With each passing day, Prussia, Gramont argued, was growing stronger. Her population, her industry, her armaments were all rapidly growing. Unchecked, the rising power of the Prussians would soon over-throw the existing balance of power: the Kingdom would extend her dominion over Europe: she might possibly, and not unreasonably, aspire to rule the world. France's wisest course, the Foreign Minister con-tended, was to fight the Prussians now, before they became so irresistibly strong that no power on earth could stop them.

Such advice was not uncongenial to Louis-Napoleon. Among the Emperor's projects, during this time, was the formation of a military alliance with Austria. He and Franz Josef would jointly make war on Prus-sia. But the proposed *entente* was still, in the summer of 1870, speculative in character, and Louis-Napoleon was far from having resolved on a resort to arms. Even in the flower of youthful vigor his character tended toward vacillation rather than decision; and he was now old and sick. Yet he could not but own that there was something in his Foreign Minister's argument. If a struggle with Prussia must come, was it not, perhaps, bet-ter that it should come now rather than later?

Ollivier, for his part, though he did not positively dissent from these counsels, was less convinced of their wisdom. He however repressed his scruples, and submitted to the policy of Gramont. The next day, the Duc went to the Palais Bourbon, the seat of the legislature. In the Corps Législatif, he read out a declaration which he had composed jointly with Ollivier and the Emperor. France, he told the lawmakers, would never suffer a foreign power to place a prince on the throne of Spain. Such an act would disturb the equilibrium of Europe: it would "imperil the interests and the honour of France." He relied, he said, on the wis-dom of the Germans and the friendship of Spain to avert the calamity; but, in the contrary event, he told the assembly, "with your support and the support of the nation, we shall know how to do our duty without hesitation or weakness."

Gramont sat down to tumultuous cheers, and Europe shuddered. The declaration in the Corps Législatif made it plain that France regarded the Hohenzollern candidature as a *casus belli*.

War, it appeared, was imminent.

Saint Petersburg and Moscow, June 1867–May 1871

REVOLUTIONS SUCCEED WHEN rhetoric is taken seriously. Yet Tsar Alexander had not even the rudiments of a verbal art. Those Russians who, like Prince Kropotkin, yearned for poetry and reform looked else-where for an inspiration. The Prince had, in his pursuit of the ideal, got as far as China, but he found the dusty plateaus of Manchuria to be as destitute of poetry as the palaces of Saint Petersburg. He must go back, and begin over again.

The Prince returned to European Russia early in 1867. Attaching himself to the Imperial Geographical Society, he devoted himself to science. But other thoughts possessed him. "It often happens," he said, "that men pull in a certain political, social, or familiar harness simply because they never have time to ask themselves whether the position they stand in and the work they accomplish are right; whether their occupations really suit their inner desires and capacities, and give them the satisfaction which everyone has the right to expect from his work." The Prince was determined to avoid the fate into which so many of his contemporaries had fallen. He wanted to take a stand in the world crisis.

A visit to Moscow strengthened him in his resolution to break out of the conventional mold. His father lay dying in his house in the Old Equerries Quarter. The Prince went to his bedside. He had not been home for many years, and he was startled by what he found. Henry Adams returning to Boston in the aftermath of Lincoln's revolution was not more bewildered. However incomplete the Tsar's statesmanship might have been in some directions, it had changed the face of the Old Equerries Quarter. The noble families that had once dominated the Quarter had almost entirely disappeared. Some had perished after the fashion of aristocratic debauchery, victims of drink, dice, or courtesans. More had been ruined by the emancipation law. The houses of the fallen nobles had been taken by a new class of men. Kropotkin's father called them "the intruders"—merchants, bankers, men who had made fortunes in the railways or in the new industrial concerns. Genteel dilapidation has never been the style of the *nouveaux riches*, and Russia's rising entrepreneurial class conformed to the familiar pattern of parvenu ostentation. The new men enlarged the old aristocratic houses, or tore them down and erected pretentious palazzos in their place. Fifth Avenue was not more gaudy.

Few were left, Kropotkin said, who remembered the Quarter as it was in the old days. The streets were alive for him with ghosts others did not see. He recalled how, when he was a boy, Nicholas I had come to celebrate the silver jubilee of his reign. The gigantic Tsar had made much of the seven-year-old Kropotkin; he had taken him by the arm and presented him to his daughter-in-law, Mary, who was then in the full bloom of her young beauty. She was expecting a child, and was unconscious of the fate that awaited her in her declining years, when as a lonely Empress she would be forsaken by her husband, Nicholas's son Alexander, for a schoolgirl. Kropotkin still remembered the blush that came into Mary's cheeks when Nicholas, pointing to him, said, "That is the sort of boy you must bring me."

It had all passed away. "A couple of retired generals, who cursed the new ways, and who relieved their griefs by predicting for Russia a certain and speedy ruin under the new order, or some relative occasionally dropping in, were all the company my father had now," Kropotkin said. The dying man lamented the passing of the old order, but Kropotkin himself shed no tears. The landed gentry into which he had been born was, he believed, a cruel and tyrannical class: it deserved its fate. Yet he did not love the new men who replaced the moribund nobility. Some of the tycoons were, to be sure, distinguished in their way; they were men of force and ability, who by raw strength had made their way to the top. But they bore the stamp of a machine age. In character they were mechanical, uniform—sterile; they lacked tone and nuance; their culture was vulgar, their taste second-rate.

Not long after Kropotkin visited his father's sickbed, the old man died. His coffin was borne aloft through the narrow streets of the Old Equerries Quarter, and he was buried in the crypt of Saint John the Precursor, the little red church in which he had, many years before, been baptized. Kropotkin could now act as he pleased, and need not worry whether his actions would distress his father. The choices he made would doubtless have appalled the old man, yet they were at the same time true to the highest ideals of his aristocratic training. In the house next door to his family's in the Old Equerries Quarter—a house he had known from childhood—a group of revolutionists now gathered to meet. The Prince crossed the threshold and entered the conclave.

Wildbad, July 1870

AMBASSAOR BENEDETTI ARRIVED at his hotel in Wildbad to find a telegram from the Quai d'Orsay. *"Very grave news from Spain."* Shortly afterward another telegram arrived, ordering him to repair in all haste to Ems, in the Rhineland, where King Wilhelm had gone to drink the waters. His holiday ruined, the hapless Benedetti boarded a train. As the German countryside passed him by, he reflected on his desperate errand, and revolved in his mind every imaginable argument he might use to persuade the King to forbid Prince Leopold to accept the Spanish Crown. At the station at Ems he was met by Prince Radziwill, one of the King's adjutants, and together the two men went off, in the summer night, to Benedetti's hotel.

Varzin and Berlin, July 1870

WHEN COUNT BENEDETTI arrived at Ems, Bismarck was at Varzin, the estate in Pomerania which the Prussian Parliament had granted him in gratitude for his services during the war against Austria. There he had secluded himself for some time, putting out that he sought, in this retirement from affairs, a restoration of his health, which the hurry of business had somewhat broken. Yet his rustication also served another purpose, to lull the French into complacency, and to induce them to relax their suspicious vigilance while his machinations ripened at Madrid.

The gathering diplomatic storm recalled him to the capital. Bismarck detrained at the station near the Brandenburg Gate and went at once to his residence in the Wilhelmstrasse. The mansion had once belonged to La Barberina, the dancing courtesan who had beguiled Berlin in the age of Frederick the Great. It was a curious house.* Bismarck never bothered to furnish it properly; eight years after he moved in, unhung paintings lay against the walls, and the rooms were cluttered with the débris of official life, papers, railway timetables, gifts from foreign governments. This domestic negligence Bismarck excused by saying that whoever "is interested in furnishing is not interested in food; the essential thing is to eat well."

He was in high spirits. Like many great men, Bismarck required the stimulus of a catastrophe. The ends which he had pursued with skill and vigor, though not, perhaps, with real wisdom, were almost in his grasp. At times he was to be seen in the garden of his residence, "repeatedly pacing up and down that evergreen avenue" in a "meditative mood, swinging a big stick." At other times he was to be found in his office, lying on a dark red sofa, surrounded by newspapers, smoking a Havana cigar. Nearby stood his writing table, covered with green baize and illuminated by two candles. In the porcelain writing stand were four or five large lead pencils, the Chancellor's usual writing implements, and half a dozen quill pens with the feathers cut short. Every so often an idea would strike him, and he would ring for one of his assistants. Were the French railways being watched? Someone must see to it that they were. Was the General Staff being kept abreast of developments? It was imperative that General von Moltke be given all the latest information. Nor could pub-

---

* Bismarck and his family occupied No. 76 in the Wilhelmstrasse from 1862 until 1878, when they moved into the adjacent residence, No. 77, the renovated Radziwill Palace, which thereafter served (together with an annex) as the Reich Chancellery. Sixty years later, the new Chancellor of the Reich was appalled by the shabbiness of the place. Pronouncing it "fit for a soap company," Adolf Hitler ordered Albert Speer to build a massive new structure nearby, at No. 6 in the Voss Strasse. All of the buildings have since been destroyed.

lic opinion be neglected. As *"l'affaire Hohenzollern"* progressed, Bismarck was studious in fomenting, through a secret patronage of the press, the patriotic fury of Germany. He drew on his "reptile funds" to stimulate the zeal of newspaper editors, and he set members of his own staff (the "Literary Office") to work preparing articles for publication.

In the final phases of the revolutionary struggle, no subject was too minute to engage the Chancellor's attention. Bismarck personally dictated to Moritz Busch, one his secretaries, an anonymous op-ed piece in which he argued that French manners were sadly fallen off. "As a matter of fact," Bismarck said, "the idea that Paris is the home and school of good manners is now only to be met with in other countries, in old novels, and amongst elderly people in the most remote parts of the provinces. . . . Travelers who have visited the country at long intervals are agreed in declaring that the forms of polite intercourse, and even the conventional expressions for which the French language so long served as a model, are steadily falling into disuse. . . . The French show themselves to be a decadent nation, and not least in their manners."

France, Bismarck believed, was a nation in decline. A people that has ceased to master history must be prepared to be used by her: the degradation of the French would seal the union of the Germans. But . . . was the whole business not possibly premature? Bismarck seemed, for a moment, to draw back. "That the unification of Germany would be enhanced by policies involving force, I think is self-evident," he wrote in 1869. "But there is quite another question, one that has to do with the precipitation of a violent catastrophe and the responsibility of choosing the time for it. An arbitrary intervention in the course of history, on the basis of purely subjective factors, has never had any other result than the shaking of unripe fruit." "That German unity is an unripe fruit today is in my opinion obvious," he asserted. Those who pressed for unification were, he said, novices in the art of statesmanship. They did not understand that a statesman can neither manipulate time nor substitute legerdemain for the slow unconscious processes of history. "We can set our watches," Bismarck said, "but the time will not go any faster."

He seemed, for a moment, to tremble before the forces he had unleashed.

Chapter 28

THE VIPER CASTS ITS SKIN

Paris, July 1870

JUST BEFORE THREE O'CLOCK, Emile Ollivier made his way to the Tuileries. The premier found his master seated in an antechamber, surrounded by his officers. Louis-Napoleon was in high spirits. He had in his hands a letter from Prince Leopold's father, Prince Charles-Antoine, the head of the House of Hohenzollern-Sigmaringen. The father, who trembled at the prospect of a war brought about by his family's weakness for a scepter, had decided that it would be unseemly for a scion of the Hohenzollern-Sigmaringens to ascend the throne of Spain in blood and obloquy. The candidature of his son was accordingly withdrawn. "This dispatch of Prince Antoine means peace," Louis-Napoleon said. "What has happened is a vast relief to me. A war is always a very great risk."

The exhausted Ollivier, relieved by the peaceful resolution of the crisis, went home to sleep; after all, it had been a close call.

Scarcely had he quitted the Tuileries when the Duc de Gramont was announced. The nobleman was greatly agitated. The withdrawal of the Hohenzollern candidature was, he said, altogether inadequate. What, he asked, was to prevent the son from repudiating the act of the father? Prince Leopold, for all they knew, was at this very moment wending his way towards Madrid to claim his crown. The Prussians said that the Prince was on a walking tour in the Alps; but who was to say the story was not a ruse, devised by Bismarck to catch the French offguard?

The weary Emperor sighed. But of course Gramont was right. The French people—the French lawmakers—would never accept so flimsy a thing as Charles-Antoine's word concerning the withdrawal of his son's candidature. France must have guarantees from Wilhelm himself. Just before he departed for Saint-Cloud, Louis-Napoleon authorized his Foreign Minister to transmit revised instructions to Benedetti, who remained at Ems.

The imperial carriage swept through the gates of the Tuileries, past the burnished eagles of the Bonapartes, into the Place de la Concorde. Forty-five minutes later, while Gramont was telegraphing the new instructions to Benedetti, the Emperor crossed the threshold of Saint-Cloud. He found his court disappointed by the turn events had taken. Encountering General Bourbaki, a fierce warrior of Cretan ancestry, the Emperor said lightly, "It will not be necessary for you to get ready your war-gear, for every cause of conflict is now removed."

Bourbaki threw down his sword.

General Lebœuf, the Minister of War, was no less unhappy. Mobilization must begin at once, he said, or France would lose her advantage in the death grapple that must come. The Empress, too, was discontented. Why was the Emperor playing the diplomat? Had he forgotten that he was a Bonaparte?

The Emperor bowed his head, and telegraphed to Gramont. In particular, Louis-Napoleon said, Wilhelm must be made to understand that, until France received the assurances she sought, she would continue her armaments. With these words the Emperor raised the stakes: in effect he declared that he was mobilizing his army. General Lebœuf assured him that the troops were ready. "Never have we been so ready," the General said, "never shall we be so ready. . . . Not even a gaiter-button is missing."

In the meantime Ollivier had waked from his sleep. By an uncanny inspiration he went to the Quai d'Orsay. The hour was late, but he found Gramont still busy in his office. The Foreign Minister was telegraphing the Emperor's latest dispatch to Benedetti at Ems.

Ollivier started. He had thought the crisis over. The main question had been settled, and no reasonable ground for disturbing the peace of Europe remained. In an instant his eyes were opened. The Emperor had acted, in the gravest of matters—a question of war and peace—without consulting him. The premier felt the sinking nausea of a man who has lost contact with power. He had been left out of the secret. His advice concerning the latest French demands had not been sought or even, as a matter of courtesy, asked.

The premier's first instinct was to drive to Saint-Cloud and beg the Emperor to retract the new instructions. But his courage failed him, and he went instead to his office in the Place Vendôme, where during a sleepless night he debated with himself the line of conduct he should pursue.

A struggle now took place in the soul of the premier. In theory he subscribed to the high Roman theory of public virtue, but in practice he was unable to resist the blandishments of the brilliant and luxurious, but deeply degenerate, court in which he had determined to push his chances. To converse *tête-à-tête* with the Emperor, and to instruct him in the finer points of liberal political theory, to be on almost familiar terms with the Empress, and to be invited to little supper parties at the Tuileries—men of sterner stuff than Ollivier might have succumbed to so seductive a flattery.

Had he been a greater man, he would at once have thrown up his portfolio and tendered his resignation to the Emperor. But he had grown used to the caresses of the court, and he knew that he would find it painful to descend to the impotence and obscurity of a private station. The fate of a fallen French politician was not, in those days, an enviable one. "My children," says a mother in one of Balzac's novels, "so long as a man is in office, adore him; but if he falls, help to drag him to the refuse dump. When he has power he is a minor god, but when he has lost it and is ruined he is viler than Marat, for he is living, and Marat is dead and put away." Ollivier's indignation was tempered, too, by the knowledge that he had no place to go. His old comrades among the republican opposition regarded him as an apostate, and in his fall from power they would show him no mercy. He was, he said, "conscious of being ill-served, humiliated, betrayed on all sides." Nevertheless, he remained in office.

Berlin, July 1870

Bismarck, too, had thoughts of resignation. Dining in his residence in the Wilhelmstrasse with Generals von Roon and von Moltke, the Chancellor was angry. When he was vexed his eyes lit up "with a threatening gleam," like "sheet lightning across a landscape of a summer's eve." The withdrawal of Prince Leopold's candidature had deranged all his plans. His master, King Wilhelm, had, in his negotiations with Benedetti at Ems, acted as his own Foreign Minister—or rather, Bismarck contended, as Queen Augusta's Foreign Minister. Their Majesties' sentimental diplomacy had not only tarnished Prussia's prestige; it would, Bismarck believed, impede the German revolution. "My first thought was to resign," he later wrote, "because after the insulting provocations [of the French], I saw in [the King's] extorted compliance a humiliation for Germany, one for which I did not want to be officially responsible. . . . Given the posture of France, it seemed to me that our national sense of honor obliged us to go to war; and that if we did not accede to the claims of this emotion, we should lose the whole impulse towards national development. . . ."

While Bismarck was dining morosely with the generals, a telegram from the King was brought in. In it Wilhelm described an encounter with Benedetti that had taken place earlier that day in the Cure-Garden at Ems. The King had taken his waters in the *Kurhaus,* and he was sitting on a bench in the park, reading a newspaper, when Benedetti sent word through one of the King's aides-de-camp, Prince Radziwill, that he desired an audience of His Majesty. The King responded by sending Radziwill back to Benedetti with a copy of the newspaper he had been reading; in it was printed the news of Charles-Antoine's letter withdrawing his son's candidature. What more, the King asked, could Benedetti need to know? A short time later Wilhelm rose from the bench and set out for his lodgings. He was just coming down the promenade when Benedetti appeared in his path. The King, catching sight of the Ambassador, greeted him amiably, and as his adjutants restrained a crowd of onlookers, he indicated that he was pleased that the affair was ended, for, he said, the candidature "might have embroiled us in complications, in view of the way in which it has been regarded in France."

Benedetti could not be content with this reply; he had his instructions from Paris. How, he asked the King, could the French government be certain that the renunciation of the candidature was definite? The King protested that there was no doubt about that. Benedetti then informed Wilhelm of France's demand that the King personally guarantee the renunciation. Wilhelm replied that this was impossible. Benedetti persisted. "Well, Sire, I can, then, write to my government that Your Majesty has consented to declare that you will never permit Prince Leopold to renew the candidature in question?"

The King stepped back. "It seems to me, Monsieur l'Ambassadeur, that I have clearly and plainly expressed myself to the effect that I could never make such a declaration, and that I have nothing more to add." He raised his hat and walked on.

Benedetti later in the day pressed for another audience; but Wilhelm declined to receive him. "Be kind enough to inform Count Benedetti," the King told one of his adjutants, "that there is no reply, and that I cannot receive him again."

In his dining room in the Wilhelmstrasse, Bismarck read the telegram with dismay. It was true that the King had refused the new French demands; but the withdrawal of the Hohenzollern candidature still stood. His own humiliation was unrelieved: and his revolution was not less threatened. The "position of a Foreign Minister," Bismarck said, "is, at the best of times, the precarious one of a tightrope dancer." He stood now on one of the highest wires, and he had somehow to recover his balance. He reread the telegram, and as he did so a light flashed in his mind.

He turned to Moltke. Was the army ready for war?

Moltke replied that it was.

Bismarck went to a side table. He might before have speculated about the unripeness of Germany for the revolution he envisioned, but now, in the heat of the moment, he was as ready as Lincoln or Alexander had been to act. "The tug has to come," Lincoln had said at the beginning of the decade, "& better now, than any time hereafter." It was precisely Bismarck's own frame of mind when, on a July night in 1870, he took a pencil and proceeded to mark up what would come to be called the "Ems Telegram."

In a short time the work was done. The scene which the old King and the French Ambassador had acted out in the Cure-Garden was artfully rewritten. The new edition betrayed the hand of an inspired dramatist. Wilhelm, in his dispatch from Ems, had conveyed something of the mild irritation he had felt in the face of Benedetti's "importunate manner" on the promenade in the *Kurgarten*. Yet the King, with the chivalrous spirit of a gentleman of the old school, was conscious that he, too, had spoken "rather sternly at last." Neither he nor Benedetti seems to have thought that the other had given personal offense; and indeed one witness said that nothing could have been more gentle and forbearing than the conduct of the King towards the Ambassador. Bismarck could not be content with this; in rewriting the Ems Telegram, he made it seem as though the King had coldly and haughtily refused to talk to Benedetti at all. The telegram in its original form implied an ongoing negotiation. In Bismarck's revised version, Wilhelm appeared to deliver to the Ambassador a definitive rebuke.

EMS, *13 July.*

Subsequent to the reception by the French Government of the official communication that Prince Leopold of Hohenzollern had withdrawn his pretensions [to the Spanish throne], the French Ambassador addressed a demand to the King of Prussia to authorise him to telegraph to Paris that he (the King) engages at all future times to refuse his consent, should the Prince of Hohenzollern be again nominated. The King refused to receive the Ambassador again, and sent word to him by His Aide-de-Camp that His Majesty had no further communication to make to him.

"If I not only publish this text at once in the newspapers," Bismarck told Moltke and Roon, "but also transmit it by telegram to all our embassies, it will be known in Paris before midnight . . . it will have the effect of a red cloth upon the Gallic bull."

Washington and Rhode Island, September 1865–December 1871

A romantic revolutionist like Bismarck has this advantage over his free-state counterparts: his object is to create illusions, while the task of the free-state leader is to superintend a process which, by stripping away the comforting distortions of romance, will always be disillusioning. In a free-state revolution, old verities crumble; men lose their way, and so, too, do women.

William Sprague's family had, in its earlier phases, been the abstemious embodiment of Puritan industry. As much as the Chases represented the idealistic aspirations of Puritanism, the Spragues incarnated its tendency to laborious thrift. But the bloodstock had deteriorated. On the eve of his marriage, Sprague promised his bride that he would forswear whiskey and brandy; but he soon reverted to his old habits. He got drunk, groped the chambermaids, pursued midnight hags in the brothels. When, in 1866, Kate took their little boy, Willie, on a tour of Europe, Sprague remained at home, where he abandoned even the pretense of virtue. "You know I am fond of the ladies," he wrote to his wife after she sailed, "and you must not blame me for indulging in that fondness. . . . I have taken to whiskey since you left also. . . . I must I think get some young woman to live with me. . . . If I may be permitted to try to love a little in your absence, it will be but to be stronger and stronger in my love to you when you return."

Kate's father counseled her to be patient. The "happiness of a wife," Chief Justice Salmon P. Chase told his daughter, "is most certainly secured by loving submission and loving tact." Kate must always remember that her husband was the head of his family, and that her marriage vow required her to "acquiesce cheerfully and affectionately" even in his errors. This advice to submit calmly to one's fate came strangely from a man who was himself tortured by his failure to win the White House, yet Kate took it to heart. Acquiesce she did, and it seemed, at first, as though she did not acquiesce in vain. Sprague knew his mind to be "sadly disconnected," and he was convinced that unless he changed his habits he would "go down hill fast, or faster than I have." Little Willie, his son, awakened in him a hope of reformation. Sprague described how Kate sometimes took the child into their bed. She would lay the boy on his arm, and he "would feel a holy feeling come over me."

But the holiness was fleeting. At a state dinner in the White House, Sprague was visibly drunk. "I would not take more if I were you," a fellow diner admonished him. "There are a pair of bright eyes looking at you."

"Damn them," Sprague said, "they can't see me!"

"Yes they can see you," Kate said, "and they are thoroughly ashamed of you."

She trembled for her family's reputation. Sprague himself became alarmed. "I will *not* let you see the newspaper slips," he wrote to Kate. "I have shown the slips to your father. . . . He does not understand such weakness as *mine*." The Senator was now an object of pity or contempt in Washington, but Mrs. Sprague's own social position remained one of unchallenged splendor. A charming woman who is both rich and hospitable will always be forgiven a boorish husband. Kate threw the most magnificent balls in the capital, and her afternoon receptions were crowded with the great. She maintained her connections with the august personages who in the summer gathered at Newport, and her husband built for her, at Narragansett, an immense mansard-roofed monstrosity in the latest style. The slouch and furtiveness of the Senator betrayed his habitual vice, but Kate herself remained beautiful; and Mr. Worth, the dressmaker in Paris, confessed that even after childbirth her figure was perfectly developed.

Yet in other ways she was much changed from what she had been before she became a wife and a mother. Kate had once preferred flowers (respectable republican flowers) to intricately cut jewels, and she had fashioned for herself a style of utmost simplicity. But her dress was now as rich and ornamental as her rococo rooms. She blazed with precious gems. Flitting into a ballroom of beaten gold, she seemed to outshine the gilt of a Gilded Age. She and her father had opposed the slave power as fervidly as their ancestors had opposed the royal and the papal power. But Kate now exhibited all the impatience of a frustrated sensuality, an avidity of money and power and pleasure. The viper had cast its skin. Her husband had strayed. Might not she?

On the eve of the fifth anniversary of her marriage, she burned with enmity. "I almost hate this man at times who calls himself my husband," she wrote in her diary, "and yet has so little title to the name. . . . A wild tumultuous storm is raging without and my heart, in attune with the elements, [is] as turbulent and stormy."

Henry Adams, preparing for his rôle as *pontifex maximus* of the Washington well-to-do, mounted his social pulpit to censure Kate's conduct. Preaching on the text of Judges 11, he pronounced his anathema on "Jephtha's daughter," as he called Kate, and on her aspiring father, Chief Justice Chase. Jephtha was a Judge of Israel who sacrificed his daughter to the Lord in order that he might get the children of Ammon into his hands. The Chases, Adams said, made a more bitter bargain. The Chief Justice laid his daughter as a burnt offering on the altar of Sprague's millions, but in contrast to the Israelite, who really had gotten the children of Ammon into his hands, the American never was able to lay his on the White House.

The decline of the Chases and the Spragues was another sign of disintegration in the aftermath of a revolution that was meant to give the nation a new birth. The combination of virtues possessed by such families as theirs had made the American free state; but revolutions are morally corrosive. They end by consuming the qualities that nourished them.

Paris, July 1870

Evening came, and the domes and palaces of the city glittered in the fading midsummer light. *Le Soir,* the latest of the evening papers at Paris, went on sale in the kiosks. The headline might have been traced in characters of blood:

Public Insult to Our Ambassador!

Beneath the legend was printed Bismarck's revised Ems Telegram. People fought over copies, and the edition was soon sold out.

All that day the atmosphere in the city had been tense. Fear and ecstasy blended together in the anticipation of momentous events. The Emperor left Saint-Cloud in the morning and arrived at the Tuileries at a quarter past noon. The sovereign's presence in the capital on a hot summer day was itself, in the eyes of many, an omen of evil augury. Yet across the Seine, in the Palais Bourbon, the Emperor's principal Minister still cherished a hope that peace could be preserved. Emile Ollivier was putting the finishing touches on an oration in which he professed himself satisfied with the letter of Charles-Antoine withdrawing his son's candidature. Then the Duc de Gramont came into the room and showed Ollivier the Ems Telegram. Was it not, Gramont said, a "slap in the face" of France?

Ollivier could but nod his assent. "It is now beyond the power of man to avert this war," he said.

Still the Emperor hesitated to take the last step. A council of state was convened that day in the Tuileries. The sovereign entered the council chamber—it was hung with red silk and dominated by a painting of Eugénie in her state robes and coronet—and took his seat at the oblong table. He appeared to be under the influence of drugs. His face was waxen, his eyes half-closed. He spoke vaguely of summoning a European Congress to broker a settlement with Prussia. The council broke up without reaching a decision, and Louis-Napoleon withdrew to Saint-Cloud. After dinner the principal dignitaries of the Empire gathered in the château, and sat till a late hour. The sentiment of the council was now manifestly in favor of a resort to arms. "Napoleon has no option," one observer said, "but between the dangers of a war and the dangers of a revolution." The "depth of French feeling on this subject," said another, was such "that it might be dangerous, if not fatal, for the Government to oppose it."

The next day the Emperor returned to Paris, and France declared war on Prussia.*

In the Place de la Concorde Louis-Napoleon was acclaimed by immense crowds. The words *"la Guerre"* were on every tongue. The city was reeking hot, too hot to sleep, and at night everyone except the very old and the very young remained out of doors. Snatches of war-filled talk floated through the streets.

"After the first battle . . ."

"It seems that the Prussians . . ."

"He left with his regiment . . ."

Soldiers went about drunk; women shrieked; and when Marie Sass, the soprano who had taken the part of Elisabeth in Wagner's *Tannhäuser* in 1861, climbed aloft with a tricolor in her hand and sang the *Marseillaise* in a voice that rang like a silver trumpet, the ecstasy of the Parisians rose to a new height.

Not every Frenchman could share in this enthusiasm. The day after the declaration of war, Marshal Bazaine, who for the past year had commanded the Garde Impériale at Paris, bid farewell to his bride, Josefa de la Peña, whom he had married during the ill-fated expedition to Mexico. He then went to the Gare de l'Est, carrying with him the emblem of his marshalcy—a baton covered in blue velvet, studded with Golden Eagles, and capped with a vermeil calotte bearing the legend *Terror belli, Decus pacis* (Terror of war, Ornament of peace). Bazaine's mandarin gaze was acute as he entered the railway station. Stepping into the train that would take him to the headquarters at Metz, the fortified city on the Moselle, he confessed to a dark premonition.

"Nous marchons à un désastre," the Marshal said—we march to a disaster.

---

* The declaration of war was formally delivered to the Wilhelmstrasse four days later by Le Sourd, the French chargé d'affaires at Berlin.

Chapter 29

DEAD OR VICTORIOUS

Germany, July 1870

A SPECIAL TRAIN conveyed King Wilhelm and the German high command to the front. Bismarck rode luxuriously in a saloon car he had confiscated from King George V, the exiled King of Hanover. The Chancellor, his clerks observed, was in his "rosiest humor." He was about to consummate one of history's most memorable revolutions, yet he was almost relaxed. His assistants marveled at their chief's "incredible napping powers," and during the journey towards the seat of war they sometimes found the gigantic figure so heavily asleep that only with difficulty could they rouse him.

It was otherwise with King Wilhelm. He kept largely to himself, riding glumly in his own railway carriage, the simplicity of which he preferred to the sumptuous adornments of the Guelphs' saloon car. In contrast to Bismarck, Wilhelm was perplexed by dark thoughts, and he slept poorly. The Machiavellian qualities of his Minister's statecraft, though he had reluctantly condoned them, weighed heavily on his conscience. "It is terrible to contemplate what we have before us," the King said. "No one better than myself, who had to pronounce the decisive word, knows what sacrifice the whole German country must expect."

The royal train was hailed by vast crowds as it passed through the old towns of western Germany. Here the streets, narrow and winding, still reeked of the Middle Ages. The landed aristocracy paid, as a rule, scant attention to the *Städtmenschen,* the townspeople; but Bismarck knew the power of the petty bourgeoisie. He was one of the few Junkers who had taken the trouble to learn the language of the plebs. His publicity machine was the most effective of the age, for just as Moltke divined the revolutionary potential of telegraph wires and railway lines in the mobilization of armies, so Bismarck perceived the revolutionary potential of telegraph wires and newspapers in the mobilization of public sentiment.

The intensity of feeling displayed in the towns through which the train passed showed that his labors had not been in vain. Already he heard his royal master saluted by the most fervid patriots in the crowd not as *König* (King) but as *Kaiser* (Emperor). Bismarck must have smiled at this manifestation of his handiwork, for he had lost no time in preparing the public for the new Empire he intended to found in the event of Prussia's victory. The propaganda carried on under his auspices was directed at an ugly constellation of passions. Benedetti was the first to be sacrificed on the imperial altars. German newspapers ludicrously distorted the French Ambassador's conduct on the promenade at Ems. The little Corsican was represented as having behaved like a malignant organ grinder, hectoring the poor old King all the way to his lodgings. Partly as a result of this astute invective, "forty millions of Germany are," one diplomat reported, "as one man." Everywhere the people had an "absolute confidence" in Bismarck and Moltke.

This confidence was not misplaced. As the high command sped towards the front, the intricate processes of mobilization unfolded with an efficiency and precision that bore all the marks of Moltke's tenacious organizational abilities. The sixty glittering officers who served on the General Staff had matters well in hand; and so sanguine was their Chief that, after the mobilization order was given, he was said to have passed the time reading French novels. Observers were astonished as regiment after regiment went forward in perfect order, in accordance with their timetables. There "was neither confusion nor hurry nor haste." Nor were the Prussians and their confederated brethren the only Germans to mobilize; Bavarians, Badeners, and Württembergers also heeded Bismarck's trumpet.

By the beginning of August, more than a million Germans were under arms.

Saint Petersburg, June 1870–May 1874

IF BISMARCK'S REVOLUTION appeared destined to succeed, the Tsar's was ending in fatigue, and in horror. Disraeli saw Alexander after his vitality was spent. "His mien and manners are gracious and graceful," the English statesman said, "but the expression of his countenance, which I now could very closely examine, is sad. Whether it is satiety, or the loneliness of despotism, or the fear of violent death, I know not, but it was a visage of, I should think, habitual mournfulness." There are some natures, Disraeli observed, which experience power as the most exalted of sacraments, "an inward and spiritual grace." But the mystic pleasures of authority were unknown to Alexander; it was not for him the exquisite narcotic that Bismarck (and Disraeli himself) found it to be.

Once, he had inclined to leniency. When an informer reported "an insolent expression used at the Saint Petersburg Chess Club when someone's king was in jeopardy," Alexander threw the report in the wastepaper basket, summoned the spy, gave him twenty-five rubles, and dismissed him from the service. But power and fear were ruining the Tsar. His hatred now encompassed those who expressed even a mild opposition to his régime. The formerly magnanimous man began cruelly to mistreat the most modest of his adversaries. A young man was arrested for possessing a copy of Emerson's essay "Self-Reliance." A teenaged girl was sentenced to nine years' hard labor in Siberia for putting a socialist pamphlet into the hands of a worker. A teenaged boy was hanged for posting a revolutionary proclamation in a railway station. If the Tsar forbore to execute the darkest of the terrorist princes who had been caught up in his nets, Sergei Nechaev, it was perhaps because he could not decide whether it would be more agreeable to kill him outright or bury him alive in a ravelin of the Fortress of Peter and Paul.*

There were moments when Alexander saw all too clearly what he had become; he would break down in tears; he would reproach himself for his acts. More often he turned away from that which he found painful. Courtiers were forbidden to mention subjects which were distressing to the Tsar. He did not like to be reminded that his wife, the Empress Mary, was still living; he had wronged her, and she now led an existence almost entirely separate from his own. "Don't speak to me of the Empress," the Tsar said, "it makes me suffer too much." The name of Katya could only be whispered in the palace; but gossip, like politics, may be carried on by indirection. Was it true, the fashionable personages who haunted the court asked one another, that Count Tolstoy was at work on a new novel, the subject of which was the bad end to which adulterers came?

Alexander had in the past been a light drinker, but he now drank to excess, or so it was said. And whenever he could, he disappeared into the parallel world he had constructed for himself and Katya. The bond

---

* Nechaev, who was at one time the protégé of Bakunin, was confined in the most dreaded of the fortress's dungeons, the Alexis Ravelin. In the 1870s Tolstoy visited the fortress, where Nechaev was then languishing; he was researching his never-finished novel about the Decembrist conspirators. The commandant, under whom Tolstoy had served in the Crimea, showed him over most of the fortress but would not permit him to see the Alexis dungeons. He told Tolstoy that anyone might enter the dungeons, but that only three persons in the Empire—the Tsar, the commandant, and the director of the Third Section—"having once entered them, could again leave them."

between the lovers was strengthened when Katya gave birth, in the study of Nicholas I, to a son, whom the parents named George. Alexander installed mother and child in a suite of rooms in the Winter Palace just above his own; an elevator made for ease of communication between the two apartments. The Tsar was fond of his natural child, who seemed to absorb him more than his legitimate offspring did. "Gogo," as the boy was called, was, Alexander said, "a true Russian," something which could not be said of the other Romanovs, with their mostly German blood. In 1868 the first of a new generation of legitimate Romanovs was born. Grand Duchess Mary, the former Dagmar of Denmark, presented her husband, Tsarevitch Alexander, with a baby boy. They named the child Nicholas, after his great-grandfather and his uncle, the dead Tsarevitch. But the boy who was destined be the last of the tsars saw little of his grandfather Alexander, and experienced nothing of his personal influence.

Count Shuvalov disapproved of his master's relations with Katya; she was, he believed, a tool of the Pan-Slavs. (Reactionary though he was, the cosmopolitan Shuvalov had no patience for utopian visions of Russia's romantic nationalists.) A vizier is always jealous of the harem, and the Count sensed in the concubine a threat to his own pre-eminence. He continued to carry himself with the voluptuous arrogance of an aristocrat who adores every type of pleasure and scorns every form of sentimentality, but for a moment his cynicism failed, and forgetting to sneer, he became almost tender, and exhibited all the pathos of a jilted courtier. He remonstrated with the Tsar, and when he was in his cups he railed against Katya. Alexander, he said, was "completely dominated by her, unable any longer to see save through her eyes, and capable now of the worst follies to prove his love for her."

Shuvalov's interference in the domestic affairs of the Romanovs was not wise. It irritated not only the Tsar, but other members of the imperial family as well. It seemed at times as though the Count cherished the hope that by aggravating the family's troubles he would make the Romanovs more dependent on his counsels. But Alexander was not to be thus managed. His counter-intelligence services kept him apprised of Shuvalov's activities, and he determined to strip him of his powers as director of the Third Section.

"I congratulate you, Peter Andreivich," the Tsar said to the courtier one morning when he came in to make his report.

"May I ask, Sire, in what way I have deserved Your Majesty's congratulations?"

"I've just appointed you my Ambassador in London."

The fall of Shuvalov did not, however, result in a return to the earlier policies of the reign. The old energy and the old idealism were gone; and the initiative, in Russia, passed into other hands.

London and Paris, July 1870

SOME STATESMEN EXCEL in the art of leveling, of knocking things down. Others expend their energy in repairing what is broken, and in making the shattered vessel whole. Mr. Gladstone, however, possessed a twin vocation: he aspired to be both a breaker and a restorer. In the earliest phases of his career he dreamed of reconstructing Holy England; in his mature statesmanship he was iconoclastic, and sought to shatter the idols of conventional England. Mr. Gladstone's very hobbies reflected the duality of his nature. He chopped down trees at Howarden Castle; and pursuing streetwalkers in London, he attempted to restore them to virtue.

In the summer of 1870, Mr. Gladstone was in a destructive frenzy, and like an Oxford-educated dervish he whirled about, a fantastic vision of motive power, working feverishly to break down the shibboleths of the civil service, the army, the schools, Ireland. Bismarck, always vigilant, watched the maniac carefully; here was a force which, should it ever comprehend the meaning of his own revolutionary purposes, might utterly disconcert them. Ridiculing him as a "big Utopian Babbler," he took to calling Mr. Gladstone "Gloucester," after the prince in Shakespeare's *Richard III.* "England, beware of Gloucester," Bismarck was fond of saying.

Plainly, Mr. Gladstone did not understand the significance of Bismarck's statesmanship. His powers of foresight were as defective in 1870 as they had been eight years before, when, in the heat of Lincoln's revolution, he declared that Jefferson Davis had made a nation. On the eve of Bismarck's triumph, Mr. Gladstone failed to comprehend how much England must lose were France to fall, and were a German Reich to be constituted under Prussia.

The data on which he might have founded a more accurate judgment of men and events were there. France was, in the 1860s, a power in decline. Gone were the days when she had offered the world a path to modernity. The neo-Roman forms of her government, the massive monuments of power raised up by her statesmen and extolled by her intellectuals, the immense regulatory structures reared by the diligent mandarins who labored in her bureaucracies—these had once inspired the world with envious awe. Here, surely, was the formula of national greatness. But the centralizing ideal of the French state—an ideal which the disciples of the French Republic cherished scarcely less than the partisans of the Bourbons and the Bonapartes—had been gradually eclipsed, during the eighteenth and early nineteenth centuries, by the English approach to political and economic order. England's freedoms, her laws, the reach of her commerce, the extent of her capital—her gold standard and naval supremacy—had given the world a new model to emulate, and afforded it a new formula of power.

Now Germany was rising, and preparing to counter the English revolution with one of its own. China and India, Greece and Rome, France and England—the German philosophers demonstrated that each of these nations had, for a time, offered the world a vision of its destiny, a distinctive conception of human possibility: each had been a "World-Historical people," an incarnation of the advancing "World-Spirit." But history had passed these nations by; and Professor Hegel conclusively proved that the "German Spirit" was now destined to fill the earth.

The speculations of the German philosophers heralded the appearance of a power that would, within the lifetime of Mr. Gladstone's own grandchildren, pose the gravest threat to English liberties since the Spanish Armada. But Mr. Gladstone did not see it. Bismarck, eager to stave off English interference in his projects, was determined that he should not see it. He told Lord Loftus, Her Majesty's Ambassador in Berlin, "that if Germany should be victorious . . . the balance of power in Europe would be preserved; but if France should unfortunately obtain the upper hand, she would be mistress of Europe and would impose her law on other States." This was precisely the opposite of the truth; but Mr. Gladstone, who believed that Germany, under Prussia, would establish a mild and liberal form of government, found the prediction persuasive.

He stipulated only that the belligerent powers respect the integrity of Belgium. The point was a sensitive one in England, where the Belgian fortresses had long been regarded as "the outworks of London." Three decades before, in 1839, Lord Palmerston put the plains of Flanders and Brabant out of reach of an aspiring Continental power: he secured an international treaty guaranteeing the inviolability of Belgium. Ever since then the principle that Belgium was an untouchable breakwater had been a cardinal article of English policy.

Bismarck was quick to assure Mr. Gladstone that Prussia had no intention of violating the Treaty of 1839. He then slyly released to the world photographic copies of the draft treaty which Count Benedetti had given him four years before in the aftermath of Sadowa. The document boldly flouted the Treaty of 1839 and lay bare France's designs on the territory of the Belgians. Bismarck summoned the diplomatic corps to the Wilhelmstrasse and showed the envoys the autograph manuscript in the poor Count's hand. Those in England who distrusted. Louis-Napoleon had for some time attributed to him an appetite for the precious bulwark, but there had never been any proof of his intentions. With the release of Benedetti's draft, however, France's desire to strip England of her prophylactic barrier was nakedly exposed; and any reservations the English might have harbored concerning Prussian aggression were swept away in a rising tide of indignation at the perfidy of the French.

In the Quai d'Orsay, the Duc de Gramont could only shake his head. Bismarck, the most warlike statesman on the Continent, had succeeded in painting France as the sole aggressor in the crisis. Gramont, who had once aspired to be the "French Bismarck,"* saw all his work undone by the fraud, the violence, and the genius of the object of his pathetic emulation. He looked on in horror as his country went to war without an ally or even a friend. The Austrians and the Italians, on whom Gramont had counted for support, declared that they would await the outcome of the first battles before deciding whether to join the fight; the Russians appeared to have entered into some mysterious understanding with Bismarck; and the English were in an uproar over Belgium. Gramont bravely, though not very convincingly, issued a communiqué in which he stated that "France seeks no alliance, but prefers single-handed conflict."

South Carolina, Louisiana, Massachusetts, and Washington, January 1867–July 1877

THE MARRIAGE OF Buck Preston and Rawlins Lowndes, which took place in the Prestons' house in Columbia, was an unsatisfactory dénouement. After the ceremony, the newlyweds withdrew to Oaklands, the Lowndes plantation on the Combahee River. Buck bore her husband three children, and went into a steep decline.

A month after the wedding, Sam Hood married a young lady in New Orleans, where he had gone into business. "Poor wounded hero and patriot," Mary Chesnut said. Buck ought to have married him; he was the "only true man" she ever saw in her protégée's train.

Mary Chesnut herself was now very poor, living between regret and fear. All that remained of her brilliant personality she invested in the journals she had kept during the war. If she could only save something out of time, that undammable river. It was a labor of tears.

She did not regret the passing of slavery; but she continued to cher-

---

* Bismarck did not return the compliment; he called Gramont "the stupidest man in Europe."

ish the aristocratic ideal. Together with Dixie School writers like Thomas Nelson Page and Mary Johnston (Joe Johnston's niece), she helped create a romance of the Old South. "Everybody knows a gentleman when he sees one," she wrote, quoting Lord Byron. "I have never met a man who could describe one." Yet she made the attempt. Though she criticized the coercive system of the antebellum "Chivalry," Mary Chesnut was as enamored as ever of the planters' vision of nobility.

She and the other Dixie School writers endowed planter paternalism with a retrospective appeal it could never have possessed in the heyday of Cavalier prosperity. At the height of their power, the great landowners of the South had inspired resentment in poorer whites whose democratic impulses they had stifled. But the planters had fallen, and white Southerners of all conditions could now dwell with nostalgic satisfaction on a class that had ceased to threaten and command. At the same time, many Southerners—and not a few Northerners—found in the planters' philosophy a justification, not indeed for slavery, but for a new caste system, one in which every (white) man was an aristocrat, separated from the untouchable class by the mystic virtues of skin color.

Lincoln had defeated the Southern partisans of coercion, but he had not changed their hearts. Radical Republicans like "Bluff Ben" Wade, viewing with dismay the servile "Black Codes" which Southern whites imposed on former slaves after the war, tried to force the South to embrace equality. Early in 1867, legislation dividing the former Confederate states into military districts under the jurisdiction of the United States Army passed both houses of Congress.* President Andrew Johnson, Lincoln's successor, vetoed the legislation; the intent of the bills, he said, was "to protect niggers." Congress overrode the vetoes, and the House of Representatives impeached the President.† Under the Reconstruction Acts, the South was governed by the sword, and blacks were given the vote.

Radical Reconstruction did not last. In 1877, Rutherford B. Hayes took office as President after a disputed election. A "let alone" policy towards the South prevailed. The last Federal troops were withdrawn from the statehouses in Louisiana and South Carolina, and Southern "Redeemers" proceeded to erect a new fabric of white supremacy.

---

* Tennessee alone was permitted to retain its government as originally reconstructed.
† After his impeachment, Johnson was tried in the Senate. The votes of two thirds of the Senators were necessary to convict him and remove him from office. When the roll was called, the advocates of conviction were 1 vote short. Had the Senate convicted Johnson, "Bluff Ben" Wade, president *pro tempore* of the Senate, would have succeeded him as president, for the office of vice president was then vacant.

Not all the gains of Lincoln's revolution were erased. Blacks moved about the reconstructed South with a degree of freedom unknown under slavery. Some enrolled in schools, others went into business. The freshly ratified Fourteenth Amendment to the Constitution—which holds that no state may deprive a person of life, liberty, or property without due process of law—provided hope for the future. But the reconstructed South fell short—far short—of the vision of a "new birth of freedom" which Lincoln, in his prophetic fury, had foreseen. For a "brief moment," the Harvard-trained black scholar W. E. B. Du Bois wrote, the former slave stood "in the sun." But he soon "moved back again toward slavery." Like the liberated serfs of Russia, the former slaves in the South found themselves, two decades after they received their freedom, in a condition not much better than servitude. "They have taken the bridle out of our mouths," one freedman said, "but the halter is round our necks still."

The myths of paternalism prevailed. In his book *In Ole Virginia* (1887), Thomas Nelson Page invoked a sentimental version of the planters' system in order to justify the new régime of Jim Crow, which like the old régime treated blacks as childlike creatures incapable of freedom. "Dem wuz good ole times, marster," Page makes a former slave say of the old plantation days, "de bes Sam ever see! Dey wuz in fac'! Niggers didn' hed nothin' 'tall to do."

In the North, too, Lincoln's revolution was in danger of betrayal. The new money power appeared to many to be as great a threat to liberty as the old slave power had once been. The United States had, at that time, no law capable of addressing the problem of economic monopoly. In the aftermath of the Civil War, a small number of industrialists and financiers acquired the lion's share of critical markets. By the end of the century J. P. Morgan's firm alone held directorships in corporations with an aggregate capitalization exceeding twenty-two billion dollars. The plutocrats intimidated competitors, overcharged consumers, exploited employees, bought and sold senators. In the summer of 1877 workers on the Baltimore & Ohio Railroad struck; their pay had been cut for the second time in less than a year. The strike spread. Chicago and Saint Louis came to a standstill. In Philadelphia militiamen opened fire on protestors. Twenty people were killed. Enraged workers torched the railroad yards; a hundred locomotives and two thousand cars were consumed. In the spring of 1886 a bomb was thrown during a labor rally in Haymarket Square in Chicago. One policeman died on the spot; seven others were mortally wounded. The police opened fire; eleven people fell dead.*

* Four agitators were hanged for the murders of the policemen. Prince Kropotkin paid tribute to the "Chicago Martyrs" at a meeting in England to honor their memories.

Four years later, in 1890, the Sherman Anti-Trust Act became law; but not until the twentieth century was an effective antitrust régime established in the United States.

Disheartened by racial chauvinism in the South and plutocratic monopoly in the North, some Americans questioned whether Lincoln's political philosophy was capable of meeting the challenges of an age he never lived to see. The America Lincoln knew was overwhelmingly rural; in 1860 just sixteen percent of Americans lived in cities of eight thousand or more. But the country was changing fast. In their quest for a solution to problems created by the growth of cities and the rise of an industrial economy, some, like W. E. B. Du Bois, looked to the new forms of paternalism which Lasalle and Marx hoped to erect in place of the antiquated structures of medieval feudalism. Du Bois at first believed that Lincoln's principles offered blacks a path to a better place; but as the liberal tide receded he, too, became disenchanted with free-state solutions.

Like Du Bois, Henry Adams wondered whether a form of paternal control was not the answer. The Constitution Lincoln preserved had, he said, "broken down." The American governing machinery was "the poorest in the world,—the clumsiest,—the most inefficient." Studying the savage markets of his age, Adams came to the conclusion that the Constitution needed to be amended and the government given greater power to manage the economy. The eighteenth-century constitutional machine "was never meant," Adams said, "to do the work of a 20-million horse-power society."

Without quite articulating his vision, Adams foresaw the triumph of the modern administrative state. A new paternal clerisy would emerge; but unlike that which held sway in the Middle Ages, the modern master class would be technocratic rather than theocratic. Like others in the North who were appalled by the world the Civil War had made, Adams developed a secret fondness for the paternal ideal. His daydreams, like those of other discontented Brahmins, are as revealing as the fantasies of the defeated Confederates. The Southerner wallowed in Walter Scott; the disoriented Yankee, abjuring his native inspirations, went directly to the Middle Ages themselves. Shuddering at the vulgarity of the figures who were rising to power around them, the Northern high-castes walled themselves off in little Romanesque citadels of privilege. (Adams's Harvard friend, Henry Hobson Richardson, delighted to design them.) To sift more effectually the coarse democratic light, they substituted for windows the stained glass which Adams's friend John LaFarge was teaching himself to make. They sent their children to be educated in schools modeled on the medieval foundations of Eton and Winchester; and however agnostic they might have been in their own hearts, they were pleased that their progeny should gather together every morning in Gothic chapels designed by Henry Vaughan.

While Mary Chesnut, in the South, composed her encomium to the seignorial vision of the dispossessed planters, Henry Adams, in the North, made his own obeisance to the feudal ideal.

Paris, July 1870

PRINCESS MATHILDE would later remember the shock she felt when she saw her cousin in his study at Saint-Cloud. Louis-Napoleon's face "was ashen, his eyelids puffy, his eyes dead, his legs wavering, his shoulders bowed." His hair, which had once been brown, was now unnaturally black. It had been dyed by his *valet-coiffeur.*

"Is it true that you are taking command of the army?" Mathilde asked her cousin.

"Yes."

"But you're not in a fit state to take it!" she protested. "You can't sit astride a horse! You can't even stand the shaking of a carriage! How will you get on when there is fighting?"

"You exaggerate, my dear," the Emperor said in a muffled voice, "you exaggerate."

"No," the Princess said, "I'm not exaggerating. Look at yourself in a glass!"

"Oh, I dare say," he replied, "I'm not very beautiful, I'm not even very dapper."

Yet when the Princess continued to insist that he was not fit to be generalissimo, Louis-Napoleon brushed her objections aside with a gesture of resigned fatalism. He had little choice, he believed, but to assume personal command of his armies. The nephew of Napoleon the Great could do no less. A Bourbon, anointed with all the precious oils of legitimacy, might remain at Versailles, or in a sumptuous tent a few leagues off from the battle, while his marshals wielded his sword in his name; a Bonaparte, if he were to prove himself something better than a usurper, must go to the front.

The day of departure arrived. The air was heavy as the imperial family went to Mass. In the chapel the Archbishop of Paris, Monsignor Darboy, a saintly prelate, raised aloft the consecrated wafer; and in the spirit of the Eucharistic sacrifice the Empress silently offered up the life of her son, the Prince Imperial, as an oblation to the Deity. "I gave it as a burnt offering to God," she said of her boy's life.

The little Prince was to accompany his father to the front. "I had no doubts of his courage, the dear boy!" Eugénie recalled long after the

Prince met his tragic end. "But after all, he was fourteen! And I could not but fear, I was bound to fear, that he might be somewhat put out when he first heard the whiz of bullets. . . ."

"Ite missa est," Archbishop Darboy intoned; and the Emperor and his family rose from their knees and went to the principal salon of the château. There Louis-Napoleon took leave of his household. Some detected a sadness in his eyes as he shook hands with his retainers. He spoke to each of them with a peculiar tenderness.

"In a fortnight Your Majesty will be in Berlin," one of his courtiers ventured to suggest.

"No, don't expect that," the Emperor said, "even if we are successful." He was smoking a cigar, which some thought odd, for he usually smoked cigarettes.

The imperial family went down to the railway siding. The Prince Imperial, who had cried earlier in the day at the prospect of a separation from his mother, was now filled with excitement, and was constantly asking questions of his aides-de-camp, Major Lamey and Captain Duperré. "Lulu," as the boy was called, had led a sheltered life. He had rarely been beyond the walls of his father's palaces, and on those infrequent occasions when he had ventured forth from the imperial enclosures, he had been protected by a retinue of vigilant guardians—a governess, a nurse, an equerry, a body of strapping soldiers. Now he was to be ripped from this dreamworld and thrust into the atmosphere of war. The Empress had with her own hands packed the trunk he would take with him to the front, and although she delighted in the curls of his unscissored locks, she had consented to their being cropped in conformity to the military regulations.

A sad parting took place. The Empress kissed her husband mournfully: she knew as well as he that he could return in one of only two ways—dead or victorious. Eugénie then took her son in her arms, and after embracing him traced an image of the Cross on his forehead.

The whistle blew, and the train got underway. Members of the court doffed their hats and cried *"Vive l'Empereur."* The Emperor and the Prince waved from the window; and the Empress struggled to repress a sob.

Alsace, August 1870

THE PLAINS OF ALSACE, sloping downward towards the Rhine, are among the most fertile in Europe. At the beginning of August 1870 the rich fields were covered with the white field tents then used by the French army. In the camps the soldiers stacked their arms and sat down to eat their dinners. Many a *"merde"* and *"foutre"* was heard, for there was a dearth of hot food. The supply wagons had lost their way, and in the ranks most of the men would have to content themselves with hardtack and brandy—unnourishing fare after a day's march in the heat. Some soldiers turned resentful eyes towards the officers' quarters, where elaborate kitchen wagons stocked with poultry, game, and vintage wines stood in readiness.

Taps sounded, and those who found it impossible to sleep in the close atmosphere of the tents lay outside in the twilight, scanning the eastern horizon as it grew steadily blacker.

Where were they?

Already rumors were abroad in the camps. A million Germans, it was said, had risen in the east and were moving, with a strange fervor, towards the Rhine. Meanwhile, in their own camps, the French soldiers found only confusion and disorder. General Lebœuf might have been right in saying that not a gaiter-button was missing. But much else was.

Leaders, for instance. The first appearance of the Emperor at Metz was not encouraging. Louis-Napoleon drove up the Rue Serpenoise in an open carriage, surrounded by his *Cent Gardes*. A young man who, half a century later, would lead French armies against another German onslaught, saw him pass by. The Emperor gave the impression, said the future Marshal Foch, "of a man utterly worn out." Louis-Napoleon's soldiers took to calling him "the old woman." He seemed to personify the rot that had crept into the army. In contrast to the Prussian army, which as a result of compulsory military service was an army of young men, the French army was filled with men like the Emperor, aging career soldiers. This in theory gave the French an advantage in experience, but in reality many of the men who were supposed to lead had soured in the barracks; they looked forward not to the next victory but to the next drink.

The graying, gouty army might have had gaiter-buttons, but it had no plan of campaign. For days the men marched and counter-marched, often on empty stomachs, under a hot sun; but at the end of these expeditions they found themselves no nearer the German frontier. The Emperor spoke, vaguely and expansively, of taking the war to Germany, but the staffwork which might have allowed the army to act on the Emperor's conception had not been undertaken. There were neither sound timetables nor accurate military maps, neither arrangements for the co-ordination of the railways nor machinery for the pooling of intelligence.

Most disastrous of all, there were not enough troops to launch an offensive. A fortnight after the mobilization order was given, only about 200,000 men were concentrated on the frontier, somewhat less than half the number General Lebœuf had promised. Nor were the regiments which had been successfully mobilized adequately supplied. Critical stores and arsenals were found, on inspection, to be dangerously depleted. Transport had in many places broken down. Long trains filled with provisions raced eastward at every hour of the day and night, yet when they reached their destinations there was no one to unload the precious matériel. The cars sat on the tracks, blocking the path of other trains.

Fear and frustration drove many soldiers to drink. Others threw down their arms and their kits in mutinous rage. A few blew their brains out. But mostly the soldiers waited. Turning their eyes constantly to the eastern horizon, they wondered what it held.

Chapter 30

"DÉCHÉANCE! DÉCHÉANCE!"

Paris, August 1870

EUGÉNIE, who had been designated Empress-Regent by her husband before he left for the front, was lunching with her ministers at Saint-Cloud when suddenly she burst into tears. The ministers looked about uneasily; the footmen who stood behind the chairs, in powdered hair and coats of Napoleonic green, stared impassively ahead. The Empress was seized by an hysterical vision. "I saw as it were a death's-head on everything around me," Eugénie remembered. "I was waiting in horrible anguish for the fatal message which I felt was on its way."

One night, as she was preparing to go to bed, her maid brought news of a telegram. The message she dreaded had arrived.

The German invasion of France had begun. Tens of thousands of troops streamed onto French soil. On August 6 the invaders struck near the forest of Forbach in Lorraine and drove the French from the heights of Spicheren. The Corps of General Frossard, the Prince Imperial's military instructor, was enveloped and crushed. At the same time, 100,000 Germans fell upon Marshal MacMahon's positions at Woerth and Froeschwiller, where the plains of Alsace rise to meet the wooded slopes of the Vosges.

Eugénie fought back tears as she read the telegram. "In a flash," she said, "I saw the abyss yawning, and thought I should swoon." But the Empress quickly recovered her presence of mind, and before climbing into her carriage she gave orders for her ministers to assemble that night in Paris. "When I reached the Tuileries at one o'clock in the morning," she said, "I was a different woman. I was no longer agonized, no longer excited, no longer weak. I felt calm and strong, I was lucid and resolved." A strange light seemed to fill her whole being. "I felt," she said, "as if I were raised above myself."

Her moment had come. "The dynasty, sir, is doomed," she told the Marquis de Piennes, "we must now think only of France." She said this purely for effect; as her own actions were to demonstrate, she did not believe that the Napoleonic Empire was lost. Her husband's star had been eclipsed; but Eugénie believed as passionately as ever in the romance of the Bonapartes. She could yet save the Empire for her son. She treasured in her soul the feeling of transfiguration she had experienced, fourteen years before, as she rode with the Emperor in a state coach to Notre Dame. There, in the baptistery, the Prince Imperial was to be christened. Eugénie wore a dress of light blue silk; the Regent diamond blazed in her crown. "The sun was just beginning to sink," she said, "and the Rue de Rivoli was glowing purple; we filed along in this dazzling light. Beside me the Emperor remained silent, doing nothing but returning salutes. I myself was equally silent, for my heart was uplifted by an inexpressible joy, and I kept inwardly repeating to myself, 'It is through this child, through *my son*, that the dynasty of the Napoleons will take final root in the soil of France, just as eight centuries ago the House of Capet was there implanted; it is *he* who will put the final seal on the work of his father.'"

All her life had been a preparation for this moment and this trial. She had long known the fascinations of power. "Even as a girl I had a taste for politics," she said. "It is one that I inherited from my mother, in whose house I used to hear statesmen, diplomats, generals, publicists, orating from morning till night." "What stirred me were the broad questions, where national interest, national prestige, were at stake. It was even through this that I first felt drawn to my future husband, before I ever knew him personally. His chivalrous follies . . . his heroic bearing . . . his proud proclamations . . . the noble accents of his patriotism—all these things exalted me." Her whole being quivered with the desire for mastery, an emotion which in some natures is as strong as that of love, and unites as mysteriously the desires of the body and the aspirations of the soul. She remembered how once she was taken out onto the lake of Annecy, in a barge festooned with purple silk, and towed by twenty rowers. "The sky was ablaze with stars. . . . Now and then the whole landscape would be lit up by Bengal lights or showers of fire, or sheaves of rockets. It was magical. . . . I was in a low-dress, with my diadem and my most splendid jewels. It was a warm evening, but I had flung a great scarlet *burnous* with gold fringes over my shoulders, and for a moment, so as to enjoy the spectacle more fully, I stood up on our deck. Immediately, from every vessel, the cry broke out 'Long live the Empress!' I was beaming with joy."

The joy had vanished. Passing into the Tuileries, the Empress-Regent went at once to the council chamber. Her bearing was queenly. She held herself so erect that, when she took her seat, her shoulderblades scarcely touched the back of the chair. Fragile though she was, she possessed, one observer thought, an "almost virile courage." Her husband's vigor had disappeared, but Eugénie, in spite of her beauty, radiated authority. She had no patience for the belief that women were unfit to rule. Nothing "used to irritate me more," she said, "than to hear myself denied a political sense because I was a woman. I longed to reply, 'Indeed. Women have no political sense? What about Elizabeth? Maria Teresa? Catherine II?'"

She strained every nerve to revive the courage of her weak and tremulous ministers. Emile Ollivier, agitated by the thought of the retribution that awaited him should the government fall, babbled incoherently about the need to arrest enemies of the state. The Empress silenced him. There must be no arbitrary measures. The first task of the government was to prepare Paris to receive the news of the defeats. The full extent of the disaster must be made public, not at once, but by degrees. The Empress gave the necessary orders. She then turned to the task of putting Paris in a posture of defense. Her aide-de-camp, Admiral de la Gravière, could not but admire the energy and resolution which the delicate woman displayed in that terrible hour. "Madame," he said, "at this moment you are like one of Corneille's heroines."

Tragedy might be her destiny; but Eugénie was determined that it should be of the heroic rather than the pathetic variety. She would go down, not meekly, like Lady Jane Grey, or in the grip of a tender insanity, like Ophelia. She would go down as a fighter. She would inspire France as Joan of Arc had done—and if courage had its reward, she might yet live to see her son crowned Emperor. Her first communiqué as Empress-Regent, drafted in the depths of that dark night of defeat, bore witness to the heroic rôle she conceived for herself:

THE TUILERIES.

Frenchmen! The opening of the war has not been in our favour. Our arms have suffered a check. Let us be firm under this reverse, and let us hasten to repair it. Let there be among us but a single party, that of France; but a single flag, that of our national honour.

I come into your midst. Faithful to my mission and to my duty, you will see me first, where danger threatens, to defend the flag of France.

Eugénie.

Moscow, Zurich, and Saint Petersburg, September 1871–March 1872

THE CIRCLE TO WHICH Prince Kropotkin had attached himself, known by the name of a prominent revolutionist who belonged to it, Nicholas Chaikovsky, was one of many which appeared in Russia at this time. It drew its inspiration, as did so many of Russia's red brigades, from the various and interconnected tissues of the red romance—nihilism, anarchism, socialism, terrorism. If the Circle of Chaikovsky differed from other revolutionary cells, it did so by being more intensely moral and intellectual than the others. Its members were dedicated to an ideal of ethical excellence; Prince Kropotkin called them "visionaries," and compared their philosophy to that of a "religion which gave a more or less simple symbolical form" to its communicants' "aspirations to purity and total sacrifice."

There were no formal requirements for admission to the Circle. The only credential the members recognized was an honest soul; the only bar to entry was falseness or conceit. The Prince likened the cell to "a closely united group of friends." An almost monastic atmosphere pervaded it, and the adepts labored zealously to purify their souls. Never, Kropotkin said, "did I meet elsewhere such a collection of morally superior men and women as the score of persons whose acquaintance I made at the first meeting of the Circle of Chaikovsky."

The Chaikovskists were enjoined not only to overcome their baser passions, but also to help the common people. He who would lead a revolution in the state, they believed, must first cleanse his own soul, and afterwards teach himself to love his neighbors as himself. The only question was how best to do this. The Circle devoted many hours to the puzzle of the masses. In what way, they asked, could they be most useful to peasants and workers? "Gradually," Kropotkin said, the group "came to the idea that the only way was to settle amongst the people, and to live the people's life." Like so many aspiring revolutionists in Russia at this time, the Chaikovskists resolved to go "to the people." Throughout the Empire, young men of fortune and education were going to the villages—and young women, too. They went "as doctors, doctors' helpers, teachers, village scribes, even as agricultural laborers, blacksmiths, woodcutters, and peasants. Girls passed teachers' examinations, learned midwifery or nursing, and went by the hundred into the villages, devoting themselves entirely to the poorest part of the population."

The extremes of purity and the diabolic meet. Dostoevsky, on his deathbed, spoke of writing a sequel to *The Brothers Karamazov.* "I am taking Alyosha out of his holy retreat in the monastery," he said, "and am making him join the nihilists. My pure Alyosha shall kill the Tsar!" Like

Dostoevsky's Alyosha, Kropotkin's Chaikovskists were gentle people, treading unwittingly on the precipice of hell. Romantic revolutions begin, not in the discontents of the masses, but in the obscure hurts of disaffected gentility. Such revolutions are made by men like Bismarck, the son of the degenerate Junkers; by men like Lenin, the child of the *petite noblesse,* the minor nobility, of Russia; by men like Marx, the scion of a lapsed rabbinical line.* The romantic revolutionist is an aristocrat of the spirit who, like Bismarck, has read too much Dumas and Walter Scott, or who, like so many of the Russian revolutionists, has taken too closely to heart the tales of Eugène Sue and Nicholas Chernyshevsky, and has aspired to become the virtuous avenger of a class or a people.

The apostles of the new religion called themselves atheists, but in chasing the Holy Grail of the peasant and the proletarian, they adhered to the older pattern of Orthodox Christianity. In their wanderings they resembled Russia's itinerant holy men, and like them they devoted their lives to acts of charity and acts of penance. They read the Gospels assiduously, not from religious conviction, but in order to persuade the peasants that their socialist teachings were true to the Word of God. No less central to the faith of the Chaikovskists was their belief in the efficacy of education, philosophy, the Western tradition of poetic culture. Kropotkin shared this enthusiasm for intellectual training; his yearning to perfect his soul was closely connected to his desire to enlarge his mind. Like others in his circle, he read the works of the romantic philosophers who descended from Hegel, among them Marx and Lasalle. (Bismarck's favorite socialist was no longer living; having fallen, a few years before, into a syphilitic mania, Lasalle had been killed in a duel over a girl.)

Yet there were, the Chaikovskists discovered, obstacles on the road to self-knowledge. The Tsar had relaxed the censorship, but many books were still proscribed. Kropotkin went abroad. He traveled to Switzerland, where he accumulated a library of revolutionary pamphlets, books, and newspapers. In a little room on the Oberstrasse in Zurich he experienced an intellectual as well as a moral revelation. His mind was inspired by the discovery of new methods of thought and action; his spirit was touched by the knowledge that men were willing to suffer and even die for them. He was not, however, content with paper advances, and wary of being betrayed into a book, he went out, in Zurich and Neuchâtel, to find the workers themselves. He joined a

* Contemporaries noted that the delegates in the Petrograd Soviet, which waxed in power after the fall of the Tsarist régime in 1917, "had lilywhite hands which had obviously never touched lathe or plow."

section of the Workers International, and after the meetings he would talk to the members over glasses of wine—sour, he noted, and very different from the delicate vintages to which his palate had become accustomed in the Winter Palace. If there was an odor of Orthodox piety in the Prince's altruism, there was an element of aristocratic *noblesse oblige* in his charity.

Kropotkin returned to Russia a professed revolutionary; the former *page de chamber* of the Tsar sought a commission in the red brigades.

Lorraine, August 1870

IN THE FIELD Bismarck wore the undress uniform of the 7th Heavy Landwehr Regiment and a pair of boots so big they reminded one observer of engravings of the Thirty Years' War. In the mornings he took breakfast—a cup of tea and one or two eggs—and afterwards went to his field headquarters to work. His capacity for exertion amid the mayhem of war was, his assistant Moritz Busch thought, "well-nigh superhuman." "Even in those places where we stayed only for one night he, incessantly active himself, kept his assistants almost continuously engaged until a late hour. Messengers were constantly going and coming with telegrams and letters. Councilors were drawing up notes, orders, and directions under instructions from their chief. . . . Reports, questions, newspaper articles, etc., streamed in from every direction, most of them requiring instant attention."

Bismarck cared little where he slept at night, though when he found a bed he was careful always to have his revolver near him before he lay down. Dinner was another matter. He abhorred the frugality of King Wilhelm's field kitchen and was determined not to imitate it. "There is seldom any champagne," Bismarck complained after dining at the royal table, "and in the matter of food also short commons is the rule. When I glance at the number of cutlets I only take one, as I am otherwise afraid that somebody else would have to go without." His own table was more lavish than the King's, to the chagrin of the Frenchmen whose houses, kitchens, cellars, and coops he commandeered. He professed himself unable to understand the surliness displayed by some of his hosts; he seemed to think they should be grateful to him. Would they rather the house be turned into a German field hospital? In that case, Bismarck said, the "wife's fine underlinen" would "be torn up for lint and bandages." He complained of being unfairly accused of purloining items of value, yet he had no compunction about taking what he wanted. He was particularly keen to get to Ferrières, the seat of the Rothschilds, in order to have a go at the cellar.

Bismarck lives in history as the "Iron Chancellor," the stout, lion-hearted statesman. "Let me play the lion too," he liked to say, quoting Bottom's lines in *A Midsummer Night's Dream.* "I will roar, that it will do any man's heart good to hear me. . . ." Yet if the Chancellor was a lion, he was a sensitive and apprehensive one. "My temperament is dreamy and sentimental," he once said. "People who paint me all make the mistake of giving me a violent expression." He had prepared the way for the French war in order to complete his revolution; but he found it difficult to stomach the violence which was the necessary consequence of his statesmanship. Naked bodies, dark gray in color and swollen from the heat, lay unburied in the road. The stench was in some places unbearable; and Bismarck, riding across fields strewed with clotted gore, took to fortifying himself with gulps of brandy. Cato said of Caesar that he was the only statesman to undertake a revolution while he was sober; Bismarck—in contrast not only to Caesar but also to Lincoln—conformed to the more common pattern of revolutionary statesmanship, and found in wine and cognac a respite from the intolerable pressures of his vocation.

The carnage that repelled the Chancellor was due in part to the French infantry rifle, the *chassepot,* which proved to be a more effective instrument of destruction than the Prussian needle-gun. The French weapon had a longer range, and its bullets, which were capable of smashing bones and shredding muscle, inflicted more horrific casualties. To overcome this disadvantage, the Germans threw immense numbers of men at the French lines. Bismarck, sickened by the bloodbaths, criticized the generals for abusing the "gallantry of our men" and being "spendthrift of blood." The commanders were "squandering" the "best soldiers in Europe." He leveled at the German high command the same accusations which Americans hurled at General Grant, who was also called a butcher. But the brother officers of the Staff contended that the sacrifice of the infantry was necessary in order to give cover to the advancing artillery. Once the new steel guns manufactured by Herr Krupp were brought up close to the enemy's positions, the French battalions lost their *élan,* and battles that might have dragged on for days ended in quick German victories.

Bismarck gave the impression of a man at war, not only with France, but also with his own sensitivity. General von Moltke, by contrast, knew only one enemy. The Chancellor was uneasy as the last and bloodiest act of his revolution unfolded: but the Chief of the General Staff was imperturbably calm. One of Bismarck's assistants lamented the fact that the statesman had not such iron nerves as the commander. The serenity of Moltke's fine-drawn, clean-shaven face seemed to express "perfect content and satisfaction" as he surveyed scenes from which other men turned away fighting the urge to vomit. The whistle of bullets, so far from disconcerting him, "quickens his clearness of vision," one diplomat said: it "multiplies his power, and makes him the most terrible antagonist an enemy could encounter." War, indeed, seemed strangely to rejuvenate the septuagenarian warrior. Moltke had such a "love of fighting and joy in the battle," Bismarck said, that his whole personality seemed to undergo a change as soon as he smelled powder. He who was usually "dry and taciturn" became "amusing, lively, I might say jolly."

Bismarck, who was never personally close to Moltke, sometimes tried to fathom the meaning of the soldier's enigmatic calm. He himself, with all his strength of will, was never able to overcome what the poet Keats called "Negative Capability, that is when man is capable of being in uncertainties, Mysteries, doubts. . . ." Moltke, by contrast, seemed to have purified himself of this negative break on the will, a circumstance which Bismarck attributed to his highly developed faculties of self-denial. The General, he observed, was "a very moderate man all his life in everything, and I have always burned the candle at both ends. . . . " The Chief of the General Staff, spare, serene, ascetic, could deny himself even doubt. He had merged the whole of his being in the battle.

Paris, August 1870

OBSERVERS FOUND IT difficult to convey the state of feeling which the news of the defeats in Alsace and Lorraine precipitated in Paris. The city had not known such a day since the great Revolution eight decades before. Some thanked God that rain was falling when the first bulletins were posted; the weather seemed to dampen the angrier passions of the crowd. Parisians stood about on the boulevards in little knots, reading the newspapers and discussing the tidings from the front.

When the weather cleared, the city exploded. All the suppressed hatreds and resentments of the populace burst forth. A strong body of troops was dispatched to the Palais Bourbon to restrain the crowd as the lawmakers of the Corps Législatif assembled to question the government. Inside the chamber, the unfortunate Ollivier mounted the tribune and attempted to vindicate his administration. Weak, nervous, and afraid, he read his words from a manuscript. Scarcely had he begun to speak when angry legislators interrupted him.

"The country has been compromised!" one lawmaker cried.

Jules Favre, the most prominent of the opponents of the government, leapt to his feet. "Yes," he exclaimed, "by the imbecility of its chief!" His fierce gesticulations betrayed the gloomy passions and malignant temper of one who had no rival, among his peers, in the arts of invective and denunciation. Turning his massive head towards Ollivier, Favre sternly reprimanded the premier. "Come down from the tribune," he said. "It is a shame!"

Before the day was out, Ollivier relinquished the tribune, the ministry fell, and the Empress-Regent summoned new counselors. The rise of the premier had been rapid. His fall was swifter still. Fearful for his life, Ollivier made arrangements to flee into Italy.

Virginia, September 1865–May 1870

THE OLD MAN pursued his road alone, riding westward through the dust and the heat. His mount was gray, and so, too, was his uniform, though it gave no clue to his rank, for it was shorn of buttons and insignia, in accordance with Federal orders. The man was, in fact, a prisoner of war; but he had given the Federal officers his parole, and he was free to go where he liked.

Ahead of him lay the line of the Blue Ridge, and a sinking sun. At last he reached the crest of the ridge. Spread out before him lay the Valley of Virginia and, farther west, the blue-gray mass of the Alleghenies. He stopped at several farmhouses, and, dismounting from his horse, inquired whether he might have shelter for the night. No, he was told. Life was hard for the raw-faced piedmont people; hospitality was a luxury they could ill afford. The old man mounted his horse and rode on. Soon, however, he had better luck, and found a kindly farmer's wife who was willing to take him in.

The next day he rode down into the Valley. In Lexington he was recognized at once, and the townspeople saluted him as he approached the inn. General Robert E. Lee doffed his hat and bowed from the saddle. A number of his old soldiers were in the street, lounging in the late summer sunshine, and they helped him to dismount from Traveller.

Lee had come up to Lexington to assume his duties as President of Washington College. This institution, which had been founded in 1749 at Greenville (it was then called Augusta Academy), had been moved to Lexington in 1802 after a fire destroyed its original home. (In 1870 the name of the college was changed, and it was thenceforth known as Washington and Lee.) The former commander of the Army of Northern Virginia might have chosen a different line of work. Romania, it was said, had invited Lee to lead its army. An insurance company offered him $10,000 a year. But he turned the offers down. He had ceased to be a warrior, and he would not become a businessman. He instead became a teacher. "I consider the proper education of youth," he wrote, "one of the most important objects now to be attained, and one from which the greatest benefits may be expected." Nothing else, he said, promised to do so much for the "standard of our moral and intellectual culture."

In his work at Washington College, Lee sought to preserve what was best in the old Virginia tradition of honor, which was the tradition of his family and his class. When a new boy asked for a copy of the rules, Lee told him, "We have no printed rules. We have but one rule here, and it is that every student must be a gentleman." Yet unlike others who labored to salvage the ideals of old Virginia, Lee, in instituting the honor system at Washington College, looked, not to the past, but to the future. He rarely spoke of the war or of the Old South, nor did he complain of his family's fortune, which was ruined, or of the manor at Arlington, which was a graveyard. He preferred to talk of the New South his people must build. "I have a self-imposed task," he wrote, "which I must accomplish. I have led the young men of the South in battle; I have seen many of them fall under my standard. I shall devote all my life now to training young men to do their duty in life." His boys, in preparing themselves for "the great work of life," must find new fields of honor, different from those which had in the past defined the Southern ideal. Lee retained the old classical and literary curriculum of the college, which he knew to be valuable; but to it he added branches of knowledge other than those intended to form the tongue of the orator and the mind of the public man. His students must learn, not only Greek and Latin, but also business, science, and engineering.

His heart grew weaker, and his hair turned white. Nevertheless, he exerted himself. He learned the names of all of the boys and watched carefully over their progress—a demanding task, for the enrollment of the college soon exceeded four hundred. His work had also a religious dimension; he believed, as Lincoln had come to believe, that durable reform will always be closely connected to the spiritual sensibilities of a people. Lee wanted his college to minister, not only to the minds, but also to the souls of the undergraduates. He was, however, shy of sermon-making, and he preferred to lead by example rather than exhortation. "I find it so hard," he wrote, "to keep one poor sinner's heart in the right way that it seems presumptuous to try to keep others."

He dined early, and afterwards rode out on Traveller, to see the last of the sun. He was not without faults. His charity was circumscribed by the prejudices of his age, and he spoke slightingly of blacks, in a manner unworthy of his greatness. Yet line by line, precept by precept, he gave the South a new ideal. To cling, as Mary Chesnut did, to the tradition of the *preux chevalier* seemed to him an extravagance. It was observed that, during exercises with the nearby military academy, Virginia Military Institute, he would not march in time. When a mother brought him her baby and asked his blessing, Lee said, "Teach him he must deny himself." It was no good living elegiacally, in the past, or in cultivating self-pity; one must deny oneself those pleasures; one must forget to hate. A clergyman spoke hotly, in his presence, of the iniquity of the Federals, but Lee said, "Doctor, there is a good old book which I read and you preach from, which says, 'Love your enemies, bless them that curse you, do good to them that hate you, and pray for them which despitefully use you and persecute you.'" The old wounds counted now only because, like all forms of suffering, they had a creative potential, and could lead to something better. "We failed," Lee said, "but in the good providence of God apparent failure often proves a blessing." He cited the words of the Stoic Emperor, Marcus Aurelius: "Misfortune nobly born is good fortune."

In whatever task he undertook, Lee had the ability, Douglas Southall Freeman has written, "to visualize his fundamental problem as though it had been worked out in a model and set before his eyes." In his imagination he pictured a reconstructed South as readily as he had once envisioned the turning of the Federal flanks at Chancellorsville and Second Manassas.

He knew that he would not live to see the new vision realized. He seemed not to regret this; such beauty and order as a man finds in this life are, he supposed, but intimations of a more ideal pattern. "My interest in Time and its concerns," he wrote as the end drew closer, "is daily fading away and I try to keep my eyes and thoughts fixed on those eternal shores to which I am fast hastening."

Lorraine, August–September 1870

LOUIS-NAPOLEON, reclining on cushions intended to soften the jolting and lurching of his carriage, left the front and hurried westward towards Verdun. The Frenchmen who watched his cavalcade pass were dismayed. The Rhine lay in the other direction. But the only concern of the ailing Emperor was to get away as rapidly as possible, while the roads were still passable, for he dreaded the prospect of falling alive into the hands of the Germans. Reports of Prussian cavalry led him to cover his escape with a heavy guard. In addition to the gendarmes of the provost-guard and his personal bodyguards, the *Cent Gardes,* distinguished by their sky-blue uniforms and glittering breastplates, the Emperor was escorted by detachments of Dragoons and Lancers, as well as by a battery of artillery. The heavy cavalry, however, proved cumbersome, and the Emperor, anxious to move quickly, ordered that they be replaced by swifter *Chasseurs d'Afrique.*

A long line of equipages followed the Emperor's carriage along the white road. They carried the personnel and baggage of Louis-Napoleon's suite and retinue. In addition to his staff officers and equerries, his physician, his police agent, and his confessor, the Emperor was accompanied by more than seventy members of the imperial household. There were footmen, chefs, chamberlains, stewards, cooks, scullions, and grooms. The pomp and luxury of the imperial train reminded some observers of the days of Louis XIV. The Emperor appeared to be modeling his conduct on that of the Sun King, re-creating in the camp the splendors of the palace, and shunning in the field the hazards of the battle. This behavior, at once weak and arrogant, was the cause of much grumbling. A Bonaparte was supposed always to seek the hottest fire; yet here was the Emperor, in the act of fleeing from the battle.

Before he departed for Verdun, Louis-Napoleon devolved upon Marshal Bazaine the command of the Army of the Rhine. Bazaine at once resolved to remove his army from the bloody amphitheater of Lorraine by means of a prudent retirement. He told the Emperor that he would as soon as practicable follow him on the western road, in order that he might unite the Army of the Rhine with the troops commanded by Marshal MacMahon at Châlons. Once joined together, the two armies could hope to resist the multitudes of Germans: and their combined force might yet succeed in preventing the enemy from reaching Paris.*

But the juncture of the two armies never took place. After bloody fighting in the vicinity of Mars-la-Tour and Gravelotte, Bazaine found himself surrounded, in Lorraine, by the enemy; and he was in a short time forced to fall back on the fortifications of Metz.

The failure of Bazaine to escape encirclement by the Germans gave rise to numerous conspiracy theories. It was said by some that he sullenly refused to co-operate with Louis-Napoleon because he had, after his return from Mexico, been coldly received at court. Others traced Bazaine's supposed petulance to the anger he felt when, at the outbreak of the war with Prussia, he received only a corps command. Still others, with an even smaller show of probability, claimed that the Marshal had struck a bargain with the Prussians: he betrayed his country, and worked to subvert the Empire to which he owed the highest honors, in exchange for Prussian lucre, or in the hope of obtaining Prussian assistance in the establishment of a new régime in France, of which he was to be the head.

The truth was different. It is possible, though far from probable, that Bazaine nourished in his heart a secret grievance against the Emperor.

---

* This strategy resembled somewhat the one which, in 1914, led to the French victory at the Marne.

He was, however, a seasoned soldier, accustomed to disappointments, and it is not likely that he would have allowed a personal antipathy to affect his military judgment after he became generalissimo. In a struggle to the death, in the battle for a nation's life, the petty vexations of the past, the trifling disappointments of private life, sink rapidly into nothingness. Selfishness itself is suspended in the emergency. Yet even if it were true that Bazaine still burned, after the first disasters befell the army, with an implacable yearning for retribution against the régime, he must soon have discovered, as the German armies pressed closer, that the path of vengeance coincided with the path of duty. To succeed where the Emperor failed—to win the victory that eluded a Bonaparte—would surely have been the most splendid revenge the Marshal could have wreaked on Louis-Napoleon.

The failure of Bazaine's generalship had its origins, not in personal malice or treacherous ambition, but in the Marshal's acuity of vision, and in his realism and his pessimism. He had not been long in the field when he saw, with the eye of one practiced in the art of appraising the strength of an adversary, that the Germans had more men than the French; that they had a more potent artillery; that they had a superior form of martial organization; that they possessed a deeper, a revolutionary, fervor. The blows they inflicted on the French forces in August 1870 were "absolutely stupefying in their suddenness and severity." Bazaine rapidly formed the judgment that the war could not possibly be won; and no sooner had he reached this conclusion than he fell into the same enervating fatalism which would grip the French high command seventy years later in the face of another German onslaught. In such circumstances, amid so many presages of defeat and ruin, the will tends naturally to break down. A great commander like Robert E. Lee might overcome the forces of disintegration, as well as the paralyzing inertia that co-operates with them in undermining the fighting spirit, but Bazaine, though he was a good soldier, was a mediocre general.

While the commander-in-chief of the Army of the Rhine, shut up in Metz, succumbed to an ever deeper pessimism, the Emperor, who had been powerless to inspire in Bazaine that confidence which despair had annihilated in his own soul, reached the camp of Châlons-sur-Marne. He was by this time little more than a mock Emperor. He had relinquished his military authority to Bazaine, and his civil powers to the Empress-Regent. People spoke of him as one already dead; and in the camp soldiers insulted his name with impunity. "I seem to have abdicated," he was heard to say. As his mind became more clouded, not only by bodily suffering but by intense mental anguish, he lost the last habits of action, and became, at length, the passive spectator of his own tragedy.

For a brief moment, the Emperor showed some faint symptoms of a reviving spirit. Forgetting his earlier resolution to conquer or die, he toyed with the idea of returning to Paris and superintending the defense of the city. This, considered from a purely military point of view, would have been his wisest course. What remained of the French army might, in the vicinity of the capital, have operated with success against German armies hampered by long and precarious supply lines. But politically such a course was impossible. The Empress telegraphed at once to disabuse her husband of the notion that he should be welcome in his capital. The sight of his receding standards would infuriate the Parisians. His head would not be safe. He would be torn to pieces by the mob. He would "never reach the Tuileries alive," Eugénie said.

The Emperor relapsed into apathy, and the Empress and her councilors unfolded their own plan of campaign. If little Lulu were to have any chance of succeeding his father and ruling France, Louis-Napoleon must redeem his failures through an act of heroic gallantry. He and Marshal MacMahon must set out at once to relieve Metz and rescue Bazaine. The plan was a desperate one, for MacMahon's force comprised only some 130,000 troops, and would be greatly outnumbered by the German armies operating in the valley of the Meuse, the backdoor through which MacMahon hoped to enter Lorraine.

The broken Emperor followed MacMahon's army as it marched north towards Rheims, then east towards Mézières. Seldom has a great prince appeared a more pitiable or a more contemptible figure. Makeup had been applied to Louis-Napoleon's face to conceal his deathly pallor, and a cruel fate dictated that this dyed and painted scion of the Bonapartes should in the last extremity of power resemble a rouged matron.* The Emperor still dragged a princely retinue, but the splendor of his entourage seemed now to mock his dwindling authority. In provincial houses, he sat down to solitary repasts, sumptuous indeed, but cheerless. Once, while at table, he began to shake violently; and an aide-de-camp saw tears streaming down his face.

On another night he was interrupted while dining and told that he must instantly board a train. He did so, and was taken northward in the direction of the Belgian frontier. Louis-Napoleon stepped off the train into the darkness, and found himself in a little fortified town on the banks of the Meuse.

It was called Sedan.

---

* In fairness to Louis-Napoleon, it should be noted that a number of other nineteenth-century statesmen used rouge to disguise the pallor of their complexions, among them Palmerston and Disraeli.

Near Metz, September 1870

NIETZSCHE LAY IN the darkness of the freight car, nursing wounded Germans.

He had, a short time before, taken a leave of absence from his professorship at Basel. He was a German, and he believed that it was his duty to fight for Germany. But he had not been permitted to shoulder arms; the previous year, in order to take possession of his professorial chair, he had become a Swiss citizen, and he was therefore prohibited from serving as a combatant. He volunteered instead as a medical orderly. After the German victory over Marshal MacMahon at Woerth, he was charged with the task of collecting dead and wounded soldiers. An interval of comparative tranquility followed, when he was attached to the German force besieging Marshal Bazaine at Metz. Then came the three days and nights in the freight car. The wailing "seemed as if it would never end." The grotesqueness of those hours was heightened, for Nietzsche, by his fever-distorted vision, for he was himself succumbing to dysentery and diphtheria.

Amid the wreckage of the car, he experienced a moment of illumination, touched with feverish delirium. While the "earth trembled under the thudding strides of Ares," he was able, he told Richard Wagner, "to remain aloof and engaged with my theme even in the midst of the terrible direct effects of the war; indeed, I recall lying together with wounded men in the freight car in the lonely night, and although I was charged with their care, my thoughts turned to the three abysses of tragedy: their names are 'delusion, will, woe.'"

The revelation Nietzsche experienced in the watches of that night he elaborated in a book he published a year after the war ended. *The Birth of Tragedy,* his first book, is a work of prose-poetry, a series of meditations on the nausea of life and the origins of Greek tragic drama. How, Nietzsche asked, can a man live, and act, when he "sees everywhere only the horror or absurdity of existence"? To experience life is to feel nausea; "and nausea inhibits action." Tragic poetry, he argued, enabled the Greeks to overcome this nausea: it allowed them to live and to act, in spite of the "wound" of existence.

The war, though it reduced him in blood and muscle, had, he believed, sweetened and spiritualized the powers of his mind. One "would never dream," he wrote, that *The Birth of Tragedy* "was begun amid the thunder of the battle of Woerth." The thunder foretold revolt. *The Birth of Tragedy* anticipates themes Nietzsche was to pursue during his wandering years, after he suffered a nervous breakdown and resigned the chair of philology at Basel. He traveled with a single trunk, two suits, three shirts, and numerous books, manuscripts, and medicines; he passed his days in boardinghouses and cafés in Genoa and Rapallo, in Rome and Nice, in Messina and Mentone, in Sorrento and Sils Maria. The simplicity of his exterior life concealed the voluptuous quality of his inward existence, a perpetual banquet of culture, the revelry and amusement of the symposium. He would solve the riddle of the Greeks, and use the secret to destroy the delusions of the romantics, whose credos, he believed, were the bane of his time. The antidote to romanticism lay, he said, in a recovery of the murderous life force of the Greeks, and in a revival of their "godlike selfhood," which, he contended, derived from "Dionysian" sources.

Nietzsche deployed his Dionysian batteries against the "cadaverous perfume" of Schopenhauer and the "decadent" fantasies of the nationalists and the socialists—against all those who did not say "yes" to life with a sufficiently affirmative zeal. He was the ablest student of the romantic phenomenon since Rousseau; yet so far from escaping from the ideas he deplored, he cast them in a new, more vehement, and perhaps more alluring form. In retrospect, Nietzsche's avowal of Dionysian willpower appears to have been a charade, the most ironic, the most decadent— the most romantic—of his deceptions. When a sickly man, dancing naked in a rented room, dreams of hurling lances with the supple-sinewed Hellenes, he has not embraced life—he has invented a new mode of myth.

"Zarathustra is a dancer."

His "will to power" was a deception within a deceit. Nietzsche glorified strength and condemned compassion, but when, in January 1889, he broke down in Turin, he wept to see a coachman flog a horse in the Piazza Charles Albert. The philosopher of power threw himself upon the mare's neck to protect it.* Nietzsche's writings were conceived in sick-

---

* The flogging of horses made a deep impression on Dostoevsky and Tolstoy as well. In *Crime and Punishment,* Dostoevsky describes how Raskolnikov, dreaming that he has become a child again, watched as drunken peasants outside a tavern beat a little mare to death. "Hit her in the face, in the eyes, in the eyes," the nag's owner cried, while the young Raskolnikov, horrified by the sight, "made his way screaming through the crowd to the sorrel nag, put his arms round her bleeding dead head and kissed it, kissed the eyes and the lips." Tolstoy relates that little Pronka, his serf pupil, told him how, as he was going to school one morning, he came upon Gavruka, one of the villagers. "He was coming from the pub," Pronka said, "as dru-u-unk as could be." Gavruka began to beat his nag. The creature was soon in a lather, but he "kept on beating [the] horse over the eyes." "Why should he beat it?" Pronka asked Tolstoy. "He got down and just flogged it."

ness and ironic ambiguity; but his fellow countrymen overlooked the nuances. They construed literally his call for the "relentless destruction" of everything that is "degenerating and parasitical," for the annihilation of morality, the segregation of the sick, and the destruction of the unbeautiful.

Some Germans saw a resemblance between Nietzsche's Dionysian dowry and Bismarck's yoking together of blood and iron. Nietzsche indignantly rejected the suggestion; he was at pains to distinguish his own romantic charlatanry from that of Bismarck, whose myths he denounced as the work of an overgrown fraternity boy.* In one of the last letters he wrote before his final breakdown, he said that the "horned-beast race" of Germans was "utterly alien" to him. "To think German, to feel German—I can do anything, but not that."

His provisos and qualifications went unheeded. Germany embraced him as a native prophet of coercion. "I know my fate," he wrote near the end of his memoir, *Ecce Homo*. "One day my name will be associated with the memory of something tremendous—a crisis without equal on earth, the most profound collision of conscience, a decision that was conjured up *against* everything that had been believed, demanded, hallowed so far. I am no man, I am dynamite."

His dæmon did not deceive him.

Paris, August–September 1870

"THE EMPRESS!" the plumed *Suisses* exclaimed as they struck the floor with their staves. Eugénie appeared. Like the other great ladies of Paris, she wore only black now, and her diadem was of jet. She was in mourning for France. She greeted the American envoy, Elihu Washburne, the man who at the beginning of the decade had welcomed Lincoln to Washington, and she inquired after the latest news from the United States.

Washburne replied that all the news was good.

"Unfortunately," Eugénie said, "it is not so here. It is all very bad. We have had very bad news now. We have had great reverses."

Washburne, who as a Congressman from Illinois nine years before helped bring Ulysses S. Grant back into the army, said that reverses were incident to all military operations. In the revolution through which his own country had passed, he observed, the Union armies had at first suffered great defeats.

---

* There was in Bismarck's rhetoric, Nietzsche said, something that "repels and disgusts. . . ." "But the Germans tolerate it" because they "are becoming militarized in the sound of their language."

"Yes," the Empress said, "it was at Bull Run, was it not?"

"It was," the American replied.

"But," the Empress continued, "unfortunately our people are not like yours. The French people give up so quickly and become so dissatisfied and so unreasonable, while your people have more patience and more fortitude. However I don't despair, but keep up my courage and try to give an example. I think we can retrieve all our disasters."

The dissatisfactions of her people were rarely absent from Eugénie's mind in the last days of August 1870. She was in constant communication with the Prefect of Police, and she made liberal use of her husband's intelligence services, among them the *Cabinet Noir* of the Post Office, where private letters were secretly opened and transcribed. Yet thickly encompassed as she was by guards and detectives, she lived in an atmosphere of terror. She drank coffee in the mornings to stimulate her spirits, and in the evenings she took chloral, a sedative, to soothe her nerves. The nights were the worst. It was during the night, Eugénie seems to have feared, that they would come for her.

Minutely informed though she was concerning the discontent of Paris, the Empress knew little of what was passing at the front. Towards the end of the month communications from the army slowed to a trickle, then stopped altogether. For three or four days no dispatches came. The prolonged silence "kept me in a frightful state of anguish," Eugénie said. "I could not eat, I could not sleep; I was endlessly choked with sobs."

Then, on September 3, Chevreau, the Minister of the Interior, brought a telegram. The Empress was standing at the top of the private staircase that communicated between her own apartments on the first story of the Tuileries and those of the Emperor on the ground floor. There she learned that her husband had been surrounded by German armies at Sedan. The last of the imperial Bonapartes had surrendered his sword and his person to the King of Prussia, and had afterwards been carried away a prisoner to Germany.

A terrifying wail resounded through the palace. "No," Eugénie shrieked, "the Emperor has not surrendered! A Napoleon never surrenders! He is dead! Do you hear me? I tell you he is dead and they're trying to hide it from me!"

A gloomy silence followed. When, at last, she acknowledged the shameful facts, she fell into a rage. "Why didn't he kill himself?" she screamed. "Why didn't he have himself buried under the walls of Sedan? Could he not feel he was disgracing himself? What a name to leave to his son!" The father of her child had aspired to be a second Caesar, but in the eyes of the world he more nearly resembled the unskillful Valerian, the only Roman Emperor to fall alive into the hands of an enemy.

The storm passed, and the Empress, repenting of her words, fell upon her knees. She invoked her husband's name, and implored him to forgive her trespasses against him.

The next day, September 4, dawned bright. The Empress rose from a sleepless bed and went to her oratory to pray. Already crowds of Parisians, inflamed by the tidings of Sedan, were pressing against the railings of her palace. *"Déchéance! Déchéance!"* they cried—"Fall! Fall!" Luncheon was served at half past eleven; but few of those in attendance had any appetite for the cuisine. With every passing minute the fury of the mob grew more intense; and cries of *"Vive la République!"* were distinctly heard by those servants of the dynasty who remained in the Tuileries.

The imperial régime was melting away. The regular operations of government were suspended as imperial functionaries, fearful for their lives, fled the city and the awful retribution which they foresaw must come all too soon. Evil tidings poured in from the faubourgs, as well as from Belleville and the other "red" arrondissements of the city. The dispatches from the Prefecture of Police were grim. Some counseled the Empress to take strong measures to suppress the rebellious Parisians; but this advice she wisely dismissed. "Anything rather than civil war," she said. Already it was doubtful whether repressive orders would be obeyed, and violent instructions, although they could not avert the calamity, would forever blacken the name of the Bonapartes.

The Empire fell with a great ruin. An angry crowd stormed the Palais Bourbon and invaded the legislature. A young lawmaker, distinguished by the proud and intellectual cast of his features and by the brilliance and vigor of his rhetoric, mounted the tribune; and Léon Gambetta, whose energy and genius were soon to be felt throughout France, pronounced the dynasty of the Napoleons extinct. The chief antagonists of the Empire, accompanied by a great mob of Parisians, went in motley procession to the Hôtel de Ville and proclaimed a Republic. A provisional authority, styling itself the Government of National Defense, was formed, and the new masters of France, or at least of Paris, harangued the crowd, and promised to vindicate the liberty and honor of the nation. Amid such doubtful omens the Third Republic was born.

The gilded eagles which adorned the gate of the Tuileries were struck off and smashed by the crowd. Inside the palace itself all hope was extinguished. Staff officers with revolvers in their hands—it was no longer prudent to trust the fidelity of the troops—stood guard while the Empress bade farewell to her ladies. "Go, go, I beg you!" she said. The sobbing women departed. Eugénie then went to other end of the salon, turned, and made a bow. The Chamberlain addressed those who still remained. "Her Majesty thanks you," he said, "and invites you to withdraw."

A few faithful companions attended the Empress to her private apartments. Among them were Prince and Princess Metternich; theirs was a family practiced in the art of fleeing revolutionary mobs. Also in attendance was Eugénie's confidante, Madame LeBreton, the sister of General Bourbaki; she held the sinecure of reader to the Empress. Eugénie went through her rooms, collecting jewels and other precious items; these she entrusted to Princess Metternich. The Empress cast a last, melancholy look on those rooms which were the scene of her long prosperity and her final distress. They were charming, though some visitors complained that they were a little too new, and a little too gilded. The *Salon Bleu* bore the impress of Eugénie's style and her peculiar femininity: white satin curtains hung at the windows, and cartouches over the doors depicted the beautiful women of the age. (Like that other handsome sovereign, Elisabeth of Austria, Eugénie was fascinated by the gorgeousness of rival beauties; they provided her with a standard against which she could measure her own.) Not less distinctive was her boudoir. Its walls were hung with green satin; the curtains and upholstery were of purple silk. To this room she and her husband would repair after luncheon each day; the Emperor would light a cigarette, she herself might dabble with her watercolors, and together they would discuss the day's events—an interlude of intimacy stolen from the relentless labor of politics and power.

The decisive moment drew near. Ominous sounds emanated from the courtyard, and the tread of boots sounded on the staircase. Eugénie and her attendants stole down a secret passageway that led to the Louvre. Hurrying through the empty galleries of the palace, they gained the street at the easternmost end, near the tower of Saint-Germain l'Auxerrois. The fugitive Empress, heavily veiled, climbed into a hackney cab. For several harrowing hours she searched for a place in which to shelter herself for the night. At last she found refuge in the house of her American dentist, Dr. Thomas Evans. The next day Eugénie concealed herself in a closed landau, and Dr. Evans mounted the box.

In terror and suspense they drove towards the northern suburbs. Would they be stopped? Would she be recognized? Would she suffer the fate of her heroine, Marie-Antoinette, who had also tried to fly from a revolution? That unfortunate Queen and her husband, Louis XVI, got as far as Varennes before they were discovered, betrayed, and delivered up to the vengeance of the Parisians. Eugénie now felt the cold fear that once gripped them.

At last, however, the carriage gained the open road. As it vanished from sight so did the vision of Empire which, seven decades before, had possessed the first Napoleon, and which his nephew and his consort had vainly attempted to perpetuate.

Chapter 31

VINUM DAEMONUM

Yasnaya Polyana, June 1869–March 1878

EVERYONE IS, at some time or another, conscious of a mysterious dread. Something is looming over one's head. But what? It might be an obligation one has promised to fulfill, but has put off. Perhaps it is a debt one must pay, that has fallen past due. Sometimes, however, it happens that a person is conscious of this feeling of dread and yet, on reflection, can find no reason for it. He searches his mind, anxiously seeking the clue to his unease. His debts are paid, his duties are performed, yet still he feels fear.

The fear, Tolstoy said, is the fear of death.

He ought to have been in the best of spirits. He was in every outward sense content. He had completed *War and Peace,* and in his life he was faithful to its thesis that truth and happiness are to be found, not in the empty caprices of politics, but in the ordinary cycle of domestic joys and tribulations. His reward for these domestic labors was a large and loving family, and a tranquil home. He had, too, engrossing work to do. He had begun to teach the peasants again, and he was full of plans for the reform of the Russian schools. His mind and his pen were also active; he learnt Greek, and he began to write *Anna Karenina.*

But he could not rid himself of the feeling of dread. "I felt lost," he said, "and became dejected." The mood passed, and he went on living as before; but soon the feeling returned. The crisis became acute. "My life came to a standstill. I could breathe, eat, drink, and sleep . . . I could not help doing these things; but there was no life. . . ." His existence, he said, was "a stupid and spiteful joke someone has played on me."

He opened his Schopenhauer, and found in those pages what seemed to be an answer. "Life," Schopenhauer said, "is that which should not be—an evil; and the passage into Nothingness is the only good in life." Evidently the problem was life itself. Existence was a mistake—a blunder of the universe, an error to be evaded. Tolstoy eyed the crossbar in his study, and thought of hanging himself from it.

But Schopenhauer's rejection of life—his dream of a romantic escape into nothingness and Nirvana—did not wholly persuade him. Tolstoy later said that, had he swallowed Schopenhauer whole, he should have committed suicide straight off. But he chose rather to live. "I feared life," he said, "desired to escape from it; yet still hoped something of it."

It chanced that Tolstoy engaged, as a mathematics instructor for his children, a young man called Vasily Alexiev. Alexiev had once belonged, with Prince Kropotkin, to the Circle of Chaikovsky; he was now living the life of a mendicant revolutionist. "I was literally starving," Alexiev remembered. "Through some acquaintances, a place as tutor at Count Tolstoy's was offered me. I was so frightened by the Count's title, that I at first declined." But eventually he went to Yasnaya Polyana, and he and Tolstoy became friends. Alexiev confessed to his employer his dream of going to the people, and of escaping the evils of life by building a new form of communal existence. Tolstoy sympathized with Alexiev's aspirations, though he opposed the violent methods espoused by some of his comrades in revolution. The rebels hated the Tsar and despised his revolution, but Tolstoy insisted that Alexander was "a kind man who has done much good," and he regretted that the red brigades, with their "godless and inhuman methods, incendiary fires, robberies, and murders," had "poisoned" the monarch's life and warped his character. Alexiev told Tolstoy of Chaikovsky's own doubts on this score; he related how the socialist leader, disenchanted with Russia, had led a group of disciples to the "steppes of Kansas" (so the Russian phrased it) to found a new faith.

A new faith. Here, Tolstoy thought, was a path that might lead him out of perplexity and despair. Alexiev "made me believe in the possibility of what had always dimly stirred in my soul." Even before he knew the young socialist, Tolstoy had begun to re-examine the question of faith. He had, at an earlier period in his life, turned away from the Orthodox Church, but he had never ceased to find in its liturgy an echo of the eternal. When he was married in the Kremlin, he felt the power of the Church's mysticism. When his brother lost a young child, he found a consolation in the Church's rituals. "The priests were there," Tolstoy wrote, "and a small pink coffin, and everything as it should be." How else, he asked, was his brother "to remove the putrefying body of the child from the house? . . . There is no better way (at least, I could devise none) than to do it with a requiem and incense. . . . For me at least those Slavonic words evoke quite the same metaphysical ecstasy one experiences when one thinks of Nirvana."

Tolstoy began to attend Mass every Sunday, and he talked late into the night with the priest who came to teach his children theology. He fasted, he prayed, he visited the monastery of Optina Pustyn and the Saint Sergius Monastery of the Trinity. "Faith still remained to me as irrational as it was before," he said, "but I could not but admit that it alone gives mankind a reply to the questions of life; and that it consequently makes life possible." Turning his gaze on himself, he realized that he only lived at those times when he believed in God. "I need only be aware of God to live. I need only to forget him, or disbelieve in him, and I die. . . . To know God and to live is one and the same thing. God is life. Live seeking God, and then you will not live without God. And more than ever before, all within me and around me lit up, and the light did not again abandon me." He was ready now to live, and ready also to die.

He did not, however, become, or at any rate he did not remain, an Orthodox Christian. A church, he said, was but "power in the hands of certain men." What was precious in Christianity, he maintained, was to be found, not in the hierarchy of the Church, but in the teachings of Jesus, and in the faith of the people. The Gospels he perused with diligence, and he devoted much labor to elucidating the meaning of Jesus' words. The peasants he studied as closely. The more he looked at them, the more he became convinced that "they have a real faith, which is a necessity to them and alone gives their life a meaning and makes it possible for them to live. . . . While we think it terrible that we have to suffer and die, these folk live and suffer, and approach death with tranquility, and in most cases gladly." In order to learn the secret of the inward peace of the *muzhik*, he began to copy his outward dress. He wore a homespun blouse and shoes of bast or hemp, and so far did he carry this rustic affectation that he was sometimes mistaken by his friends for a peasant.

At peace with himself, Tolstoy was tormented by the suffering of others. The misery of the peasants was acute. Their condition was in some respects worse than it had been before the enactment of the emancipation law. The former serfs languished under a heavy burden of debt. There was a need, one historian has written, for a "more liberal, more flexible" agrarian law, but Alexander's government, in its reactionary phase, frowned upon innovations in the state. The provincial councils which the Tsar had established attempted to play a remedial rôle; but in the repressive atmosphere that now prevailed, the *zemstvos* were not permitted to take the initiative in solving their constituents' problems.

"What then must we do?" Tolstoy asked. He might, like Alexander himself in the earliest days of his reign, have sought a remedy in the institutions of freedom—institutions which, in America at any rate, seemed to offer the masses a chance to escape from poverty and oppression. But Tolstoy rejected the free-state ideal; it led, he believed, to the decay of the soul. Russia might be poor and miserable—but how much holier, how much more spiritually graceful, were her people than those of the supposedly more advanced nations of the West, with their anemic constitutions and bills of rights.

Lincoln had attempted to endow the free state with a new grace; Tolstoy rejected the constitution of liberty altogether. He rejected it even though he believed that Lincoln was the greatest man of the age. Lincoln, Tolstoy said, "was a Christ in miniature, a saint of humanity, whose name will live thousands of years in the legends of future generations." We are, he maintained, "still too near to his greatness, and so can hardly appreciate his divine power; but after a few centuries our posterity will find him considerably bigger than we do. His genius is still too strong and too powerful for the common understanding, just as the sun is too hot when its light beams directly on us. . . . The greatness of Napoleon, Caesar, or Washington is only moonlight by the sun of Lincoln." Tolstoy's tribute to the dead President possessed every virtue except comprehension of the subject. He enumerated the noble qualities of Lincoln's character, his simplicity, his charity, the love he bore his enemies. But the essential drama of Lincoln's life, his struggle to refine the institutions of freedom, Tolstoy overlooked.

Only when the shadow of authority darkened his path did he speak of the desirability of free-state reform. Once, when one of his bulls gored its keeper to death, he was obliged by the investigating magistrate to promise that he would not leave Yasnaya Polyana while the inquiry proceeded. Tolstoy was outraged, and spoke again of settling in a country where free institutions prevailed. "It is absurd, and shows how utterly arbitrary these gentlemen are," he said. "I shall sell all I have in Russia and go to England, where every man's person is respected. Here every police-officer, if one does not grovel at his feet, can play one the dirtiest tricks."

But the mood passed.

Versailles, October 1870

THE SUN WAS SETTING when Bismarck reached Versailles. He had reached the end of his revolutionary road. "I am God's soldier," he said, "and wherever He sends me I must go. . . ." In the sanctuary of the kings of France, the soldier would conclude the last battles of the German revolution. Bismarck hoped, when he arrived, to complete these battles within a few weeks' time; but he soon confronted difficulties familiar to the student of such cataclysms. There was too little revolutionary spirit in some directions, too much in others; and five long months elapsed before he attained his ends and broke up the house he had commandeered in the Rue de Provence.

To unite Germany by bringing the German states of the south into the fold of his Confederation was the great point of his ambition. Bismarck could influence popular opinion in southern Germany through the vitriol of the newspapers, but he found the hereditary princes less tractable. Bavaria, the largest of the southern principalities, was the greatest prize. Ludwig, however, was jealous of his sovereignty; he found abhorrent the idea that he should subordinate his Wittelsbach blood to that of a mere Hohenzollern.

The task of negotiating a peace with the French was no less arduous. Jules Favre, the Foreign Minister of the French Government of National Defense, which had been formed in the aftermath of the fall of the Napoleonic Empire, came to dine with Bismarck and announced the French position: not "a clod of our earth or a stone of our fortresses." Such a position could not easily be reconciled either with the demands of German opinion or the requirements of the General Staff. A large number of Germans regarded the cession by France of Alsace and Lorraine, the vestibule that connected two empires, as the sine qua non of a peace settlement; and—what in Prussia was of greater moment—so did the sixty glittering officers of the Staff.

Such were the obstacles the revolutionist confronted. The French might, indeed, be browbeaten, and Paris, which was now surrounded by German troops, could be starved into submission. The Bavarians could be bribed. But General von Moltke was another matter. Relations between the Chancellor and the Chief of the General Staff had long been cool. They now broke down altogether.

Moltke was determined to preserve unblemished his prerogatives as the principal military counselor of King Wilhelm, the Supreme Warlord. He regarded himself not merely as the director of an army, but as the high priest of a military orthodoxy, the guardian of an ancient warrior tradition. He insisted that in time of war he possessed the *"exclusive* right to advise the King." He excluded Bismarck from the army's councils, and left the Chancellor to deduce from the newspapers the designs of the General Staff.

At the heart of the dispute was the question of the postwar settlement. Moltke maintained that the problems raised by the settlement were purely military in character and lay outside the sphere of a statesman's competence. Bismarck argued that the narrow proficiency of a soldier was unequal to the task of concluding a durable peace; the postwar order must be fashioned by a man of more comprehensive vision.

Moltke favored a Carthaginian peace. The security of Germany required not merely the defeat but the subjugation of France; only by breaking once and for all the will of the French nation could Germany "cap the volcano that has been shaking Europe for a century now with its wars and revolutions." Paris must be captured and converted into a base for further operations. A series of fresh campaigns could then be launched, and German troops would march deep into the heart of France. Bismarck smiled. As if one could "draw the fangs" from a nation of forty million. The attempt to destroy France, he observed, would not only prove impracticable, it would also draw upon Germany the wrath of the other European powers. The rowdy vigor which had served Germany's turn while her revolution was making would only complicate her existence now that her nationhood was virtually assured. Germany's post-revolutionary security, Bismarck maintained, lay in her moderation, and in the ability of her people to persuade their neighbors that their nation's immense power was not a threat to the civilization of the Continent.

Yet Bismarck was himself partly to blame for the errors of Moltke and the Staff. In order to justify the earlier phases of his revolution, he had announced the theory of German vitalism; he had asserted the right of a nation to live and to breathe—and to nourish itself on the carcasses of its neighbors. The doctrine had been embraced by the General Staff and now formed an article of its creed. Here, surely, was the paradox of Bismarck's revolution. To make it, he was compelled to unleash forces which, if not properly restrained, would eventually destroy it. Like the French Revolution, the German revolution, too, would in time devour its children.

Bismarck failed to persuade the General Staff that discretion was the better part of valor, and throwing away the mask of Falstaff, he began to storm like Lear. He made violent scenes; he raved and ranted; he opened the sluice gates of his dark wit. Moltke he depicted as a vulture feasting on the entrails of his power. The General's silhouette "gets more buzzardlike day by day," he said. He ridiculed the Staff as a group of pompous "demi-gods" who after Sedan had bungled the war.

Moltke was not to be moved by such antics. He had studied Bismarck's tactics in the aftermath of Sadowa, and he was ready for them. Confronted with the Chancellor's rage, the Chief of the General Staff fixed a cold eye on his adversary, and said nothing. Not even Bismarck's sharpest darts pierced the armor of the General's self-control. "What some day settles the value of a man's life," Moltke said, "is not the glamour of success but purity of purpose, loyal adherence to duty." He knew where his duty lay.

Metz, August–October 1870

IN REVOLUTIONS, it has been said, men live fast. In a matter of days or hours, reputations, careers, fortunes—the slow laborious work of decades—are ruined irretrievably. Marshal Bazaine was said by some to have compiled the best record of his generation of French soldiers. He had joined the colors forty years before; had risen from the ranks; had demonstrated courage and ability in Africa and in the Crimea, in Italy and in Mexico. Then, in August 1870, he encountered an enemy unlike any he had previously known. He lost his nerve, and was shut up with his army in Metz.

Conditions in the city swiftly deteriorated. Supplies were limited, and the troops were put on short rations. They were soon compelled to eat their horses; but there was no salt, and the flesh was unappetizing. The aqueducts having been broken up by the enemy, the besieged inhabitants dipped their buckets in the polluted waters of the Moselle. Disease was rife, and the air was heavy with the odor of death and the latrine. Apathy spread, and discipline deteriorated. When the rains came, the camps were transformed into pestilential swamps, and even strong men cracked. Bazaine retired to a suburban villa at Ban Saint-Martin; he was said to have sought relief from despondency in games of billiards.

There was a glimmer of hope. Bismarck, frustrated by the intransigence of the new French government, and uncertain whether a peace concluded with so precarious an authority would be worth the parchment it was printed on, opened a curious negotiation with Bazaine. The Chancellor conceived the idea of restoring, with Prussian arms, the régime of the Bonapartes. Louis-Napoleon, who had been carried off to Germany and given a palace for a prison, would be seated again on his throne, and as he valued his life could be relied upon to sign a treaty satisfactory to Prussia. As part of this plan, the Germans would lift the siege of Metz, and Marshal Bazaine, having pledged himself to defend the restored régime, would use his army to prop up the revivified dynasty. Bazaine, for his part, seems to have conceived himself bound in honor to listen to any proposal that promised to restore to the Tuileries the master to whom he had sworn undying allegiance. But he listened in vain, for the scheme was little more than a figment of Bismarck's imagination, and it came to nothing. Bazaine went back to billiards and despair.

The prospect of starvation now loomed before him; and in a dark hour the Marshal resolved to surrender both himself and his army to the

Germans. "Let us all be thankful," says an historian in his account of the fall of another French warrior, that "we have never had to face the trials under which he broke." At the end of October, 170,000 soldiers, the largest body of troops remaining to France, laid down their arms and marched into captivity.

Versailles, October–November 1870

BISMARCK WAS OFTEN SEEN, in the bright moonlit nights of the French autumn, pacing the garden of his house in the Rue de Provence. His anxiety was great. The longer the French, the Bavarians, and the General Staff resisted his will, the greater the likelihood that the rest of Europe, awakening to the meaning of his revolution, would intervene and demolish all his work.

The French especially drove him into rages. Léon Gambetta was his bête noire. The young barrister was "almost certainly" a Jew, Bismarck said, "judging from his physiognomy." Gambetta was the soul of France's Government of National Defense. Casting a glance on the map of operations, he perceived the vulnerability to which the German army, like all armies of occupation, was subject. The French leader had little in the way of a regular army with which to oppose the gigantic battalions of Moltke, but he made good this deficiency in professional troops by organizing a guerrilla force, and by converting the war into a people's struggle. Snipers known as *francs-tireurs* ambushed German patrols and instilled in the invader a fear he had not previously known.

Gambetta's efforts to field mass armies were no less disturbing to Bismarck, who sought an armistice with the defeated enemy in accordance with the precepts of conventional diplomacy. His antagonist declined to accommodate him. Gambetta threw convention to the winds; by sowing confusion and disorder, he intended to break the Germans' will to fight. He was just thirty-three. His black hair was cut long, and he wore a beard that did not, however, conceal his under-lip, which was full and sensual. In his fervid oratory the defiance of France, and more especially of Paris, received its classic expression. The besieged capital possessed only a limited supply of food, but the patriotism of the people was intense. Those members of the French government who regarded as visionary Gambetta's belief that he could expel the Germans without first submitting to their terms did not dare to defy him. For Gambetta was supported by the "red" arrondissements of the city, where the zealots of revolution yearned to punish all who sought to betray their romantic dream.

In October, Gambetta escaped from Paris in a balloon in an effort to rally the French nation. His guerrillas continued to demoralize the German armies. Young Prussians who had once marched down French roads singing Luther's Hymn or "Watch on the Rhine" now left a trail of broken wine bottles behind them. They swaggered into little towns shouting, *"Mademoiselle, voulez-vous baiser?"* ("Miss, do you want to kiss?"). Bismarck vented his anger in wine and angry talk. He took a justifiable pride in his drinking abilities; at Versailles he boasted that he had once drunk off three quarters of a bottle of champagne "at a draught." "Everybody," Bismarck said, "was immensely surprised; but I said, 'Give me another.'" Yet he was not Socrates, for wine had its effect on him. Some have supposed that his most objectionable words were spoken under its influence. "And their treacherous *franctireurs,*" he exclaimed one day, "who now stand in blouses with their hands in their pockets, and in the next moment when our soldiers have passed by take their rifles out of the ditch and fire at them. It will come to this, that we will shoot down every male inhabitant."

"Count Bismarck," Vicky wrote to her mother, Queen Victoria, "may *say* the wildest things. But he never *acts* in a foolish way." Bismarck was not a man to sacrifice his real interests to fanaticism; but in the autumn of 1870 he concluded that there are times fanaticism may further one's real interests. Passion, he believed, drives revolutions; and the fuel must be heated to a sufficiently high temperature to produce the necessary explosion. The advice of Philip Sheridan, General Grant's cavalry master, made a deep impression upon him. Sheridan had come to the Prussian camp as an observer. He urged the Germans to embrace the policy of total war to which Lincoln and Grant had been driven during the Civil War. "The proper strategy," Sheridan told Bismarck over dinner at Rheims, "consists in the first place of inflicting as telling blows as possible on the enemy's army, and then in causing the inhabitants so much suffering that they must long for peace, and force their Government to demand it. The people must be left nothing but their eyes to weep with over the war. . . ." "You know how to hit an enemy as no other army does, but you have not yet learned how to annihilate him. One must see more smoke of burning villages, otherwise you will not finish with the French."

Bismarck had at first resisted calls for the bombardment of Paris. He now changed his mind. If he were to break the will of the French, he must, he believed, employ tactics of terror against civilians. "The more Frenchmen suffered from the war," he said, "the greater would be the number who would long for peace, whatever our conditions might be." Bismarck never accepted Moltke's thesis that France must be subjugated and destroyed, but he was now convinced that the necessities of his revolution demanded that the Germans exercise cruelty. They must drink of the *vinum daemonum.* They need not drain the cup—if they did, they would invite European retribution. But if their revolution were to succeed, they could not suffer it to pass untasted.

The Chancellor followed his usual practice of mounting a press campaign to prepare public opinion for the step he intended to take. The campaign was successful, and Germans everywhere were soon clamoring for the bombardment of Paris. Let fire devour the temples and palaces of the enemy, their theaters and museums, the Immortals of their Academy, the polluted altars of their Panthéon. Working herself into a pious rage, Bismarck's wife, Johanna, urged that the entire French population be "shot and stabbed to death, down to the little babies." Wagner was roused by newspaper feuilletons that appealed to two of his strongest instincts, the love of the pyre and the desire for revenge. Paris, he said, was the *"femme entretenue"* (kept woman) of the world and should be reduced to rubble. Cosima remembered how eager he was "to write to Bismarck and beg him to bombard" the city, though there is no evidence that the composer desired the Chancellor to train his batteries specifically on the Opéra.

The guns were soon wheeled up.

Bavaria, May 1867–December 1870

THE STORY OF Bavaria's capitulation to the German revolution begins with the appearance of a handsome young man at Schloss Berg, a castle of the Wittelsbachs shrouded in the shadows of the Bavarian Alps. The young man, with his well-proportioned body and blond and wavy hair, was a groom in Ludwig's stables; his name was Richard Hornig. Dressed in a sky-blue Eton jacket, he was leading a mount when the King's eye fell upon him.

Ludwig swooned. An intimacy soon grew up between the two men, in spite of the difference of their stations, and together they set out on a sort of honeymoon journey to France, where Ludwig, traveling incognito as the Count of Berg, made a pilgrimage to Versailles, the Mecca of his cult of kingship. When he returned to Bavaria, he dismissed his fiancée, Sophie, the daughter of Duke Max of Bavaria. Ludwig had, a few months before, thrown himself enthusiastically into preparations for their wedding; he had studied the precedents of Versailles, and had ordered a special coach to be built, more splendid than that of the Sun King. But no amount of frippery could conceal the fact that he was not to be the bride, and that in embracing a woman he would be compelled to forsake his groom. "Sophie got rid of," he wrote in his diary after the engagement was broken off. "The gloomy picture fades. I longed for, am athirst for, freedom. Now I can live again after this torturing nightmare."

"Heaven be praised," he wrote on the day the wedding was supposed to have taken place, "the horror has not come to pass."

At last, Ludwig knew—love. But his was a love divided against itself. His soul aspired to a chaste and Platonic eroticism; his instincts demanded a carnal fulfillment. The royal diary bore witness to the ferocity of the inner struggle. "Only spiritual love is permissible," Ludwig wrote, "the sensual is accursed. I call down solemn anathema upon it." He sought to wash himself "of all mire," that he might be "a pure vessel for Richard's love and friendship." His vows of chastity became more fervid. He swore "by the pure and holy sign of the Royal Lilies" to "resist every temptation; and never to yield if at all possible either in acts, words, or even in thoughts." He and Hornig sealed one of their mutual pledges of continence with a kiss, "holy and pure . . . only one. *Ich der König*. I the King. . . ."

"Accursed be I and my ideals," Ludwig said, "if I fall again." Yet he did fall.

While his soldiers were dying for Germany on French battlefields, Ludwig remained in Bavaria. His spiritual opium-eating grew more exotic. He passed his days adoring the moon, invoking the magical properties of lilies, and sighing for the Wagnerian atmosphere of the mountains. "On the mountains there is freedom," he wrote on the eve of the battle of Sedan, "and there men never bring their pain."

Romanticism is disease, Goethe declared near the end of his life. Ludwig had contracted the malady in one of its most virulent forms. He was the Emma Bovary of Bavaria, and his gorgeous abandon prepared the way for the rape of his Kingdom. He dreamt of flight. He would escape to a remote mountain fastness, and revive in a fairy-tale castle the last enchantment of the Middle Ages. He would leave Bavaria altogether and live out the remnant of his life in a charmed zone, in Cyprus or in Crete. All he needed was money. He once confided to Hornig his intention to sell Bavaria in order to pay for his romantic dream. He now saw the chance to do so. Bismarck's revolution, uncongenial though it otherwise was to a scion of the Wittelsbachs, had this merit—it would allow him to replenish his coffers.

A deal was cut. The King of Bavaria submitted almost meekly to the wand of the magician. Bismarck made various concessions to the Bavarian negotiators, and obtained a treaty incorporating Ludwig's Kingdom into the new German Confederation.* Another, more secret bargain was shortly thereafter struck. It was agreed that a handsome pension should

---

* Of the other southern states, Baden and Hesse subscribed treaties of incorporation shortly before the Bavarian convention was concluded; the instrument incorporating Württemberg was concluded shortly thereafter.

be paid annually to Ludwig out of the "reptile funds." Certain other transfers of cash were made or promised. Bismarck then dictated a letter. It was no easy thing for Ludwig, with his Wittelsbach hauteur, to swallow the product of a Prussian statesman's pen; but he needed money, and he did as he was told. He tendered to King Wilhelm of Prussia an invitation to become, not President of a new German Confederation, but Kaiser of a new German Reich.

Chapter 32

"YOU HAVE A NEW WORLD"

The United States of America, April 1870

THE FIFTH ANNIVERSARY of the murder of Abraham Lincoln passed almost unnoticed in America. The country was absorbed in more vivid crimes. There was a sensational murder trial in New York. A man named Daniel McFarland was accused of killing his wife's lover, Albert Deane Richardson, a crack correspondent on *The New-York Tribune* and an heroic escapee from a Confederate prison. In Reading, Pennsylvania, a petulant husband shot his wife and her paramour. In the North End of Boston a man was stabbed and beaten to death by desperadoes. William Marcy "Boss" Tweed and the Tammany Ring controlled New York, and stockholders of the Erie Company filed suit against those "notable bad men," Jim Fisk and Jay Gould, on account of the millions of dollars they allegedly misappropriated.

Perhaps it is unfair to deplore the crime and filth of that age—the dirt of the Dismal Decades that followed the death of Lincoln. Other ages have been as lurid as the Gilded one. In point of wantonness the Borgias and Viscontis exceeded the standard of Fisk and Tweed, though they had a prettier style. Jay Gould might have been a Medici prince, had his taste not been so bad. The thespian family of Booth, which, in the spring of 1870, continued to operate a theater in New York, had the audacity to stage, on the eve of the anniversary of John Wilkes's murder of the President, a play about the killing of a virtuous political leader. On April 13, 1870, Edwin Booth acted *Macbeth,* and offered a subtle rebuke to those who were inclined to be sentimental about the death of Lincoln. Murdered Duncans come and go, but Babylon is eternal.

The Brown Decades, if they were no more morally grotesque than the mean, were more dramatically disappointing. The country, having been brought to the highest pitch of nervous tension, went suddenly slack. No remedy has yet been found for the moral hangover that follows a free-state revolution. The first such revolution, England's Glorious one of 1688, appeared to Swift and Pope as unsatisfactory as Lincoln's revolution appeared to Henry Adams and Henry James.

Lincoln attempted to solve the problem of disillusion by giving the country a new method of understanding its problems—or rather, by reviving an old method. In the theory of history then held by many free-state men (it is sometimes called the "Whig interpretation of history"), the story of man is a providential drama of the progress of liberty. Lincoln had, before his death, come to regard this theory as naïve and Panglossian. The progress of freedom, he contended, is morally complicated; it is intimately connected to the processes of redemption, and directly related to the purification of souls. Sin must be expiated in suffering, and crime must be remitted in punishment. Only then is progress possible.

Lincoln's insight into the reality of evil and the possibility of grace distinguished his statesmanship from that of the other pivotal leaders of the decade. In Germany, Bismarck sought to divorce morality from politics; he developed the morally agnostic science of *Realpolitik*. In Russia, no statesman emerged capable of bridging the chasm between the ethical yearning of the people for the New Jerusalem and their secular and pragmatic desire for the mundane forms of freedom: between Dostoevsky and Alexander lay a gulf of misapprehension. In America, by contrast, Lincoln united the two apparently antithetical conceptions of moral and material progress. He painted the free state in the light of an ongoing struggle in every soul between good and evil, and he connected that struggle to (what he argued was) a providential design in which, after a period of suffering and expiation, man's better impulses would prevail. In doing so he gave Americans a moral ideal, a shaping fantasy, one that kept alive, in a barren time, the country's faith in its future.*

Versailles and Paris, January–March 1871

In the Hall of Mirrors Bismarck read aloud the proclamation of the new German Empire. A tremendous *"Hoch"* shook the old mirrors, and the assembled princes and generals sang "Now Thank We All Our God." King Wilhelm of Prussia was proclaimed Kaiser Wilhelm of the German Reich.

---

* Lincoln's Freevangelical politics would have enduring appeal; Franklin Roosevelt, Martin Luther King, Jr., and Ronald Reagan were among those who in their different ways embraced his idea of an American rendezvous with destiny.

Some witnesses were moved by the pageant. Others were repelled. A Bavarian observer shook his head—it was all "so cold, so proud, so glossy, so strutting and boastful and heartless and empty."

Wilhelm himself was in a foul mood on the day of the investiture. It was, he said, the most unhappy day of his life. The title "King of Prussia" was dear to his heart; the imperial dignity meant little to him. It seemed to him yet another of his Chancellor's conjuring tricks. But if he must after all be Emperor, he was determined to be "Emperor of Germany." Bismarck, however, maintained that the territorial title was impermissible: Wilhelm, a national sovereign, must be the "German Emperor," the ruler not of a particular extent of land but of an entire people. The King thought that he had got his way. When, however, the decisive moment came round, he heard himself saluted, in the Sun King's hall, as the "Emperor William." Wilhelm seethed with indignation, and when he stepped down from the dais he refused to shake his Minister's outstretched hand.

Ten days after the ceremony Bismarck concluded an armistice with the French. The defeated country was exhausted by the ordeal through which it had passed. More than 100,000 Frenchmen had fallen since July. Half a million German troops were bivouacked on French soil. Gambetta had fled, and Paris had been bombed. The Panthéon had been damaged, hospitals had been shelled, and civilians had been killed—among them a number of children. Yet it was hunger, not bombs, that broke the spirit of Paris; to survive the Parisians had been forced to eat their cats and their dogs, the animals in the zoo, and the rats in the sewers.

Favre, the chief French negotiator, was standing on a balcony of the Quai d'Orsay with his fifteen-year-old daughter when, at midnight, the armistice took effect. He burst into tears. The price his country paid for peace was high. The terms of the armistice, afterwards embodied in the Treaty of Frankfurt, fastened on France a huge indemnity, and provided that German troops should remain on French soil until it was paid. The loss of Alsace and Lorraine was a heavier and more humiliating forfeiture. The French were permitted to retain Belfort in Alsace; but in exchange for this concession they were obliged to allow a German army to goose-step through the streets of Paris. The settlement, however, was not nearly as draconian as the one Moltke hoped to obtain. Bismarck prevailed over the Chief of the General Staff. At the behest of Wilhelm, two Cabinet decrees were promulgated: the limits of Moltke's jurisdiction were acknowledged and the supremacy of the Chancellor was confirmed. It was a personal rather than a constitutional victory. Bismarck fought the last battle of his revolution for the sake of his own honor and prestige, not in order to vindicate the principle that the army must answer to civilian leaders. Lincoln's revolution confirmed the subordination of the army to the constitution; Bismarck's confirmed the subordination of the army to Bismarck himself.

For a moment the Chief of the General Staff was disposed to sulk; the King, he said, had treated him "ungraciously." But no sooner had the emotion of resentment made itself felt than Moltke mastered it. During the armistice negotiations he acted, without a trace of bad temper, as the Chancellor's subordinate rather than as his co-equal; duty required no less. Bismarck, whose revenges were mild unless policy dictated otherwise, behaved handsomely towards his defeated rival, and did not abuse the victory he had gained. Although he doubted the wisdom of retaining Metz as a spoil of war—"I don't like so many Frenchmen in our house who don't want to be there"—he demanded that the French cede the city to Germany. It was a concession to Moltke.

Shortly after the conclusion of the armistice, three Prussian Hussars rode into Paris by the Porte Maillot. They cantered up the Champs-Elysées to the Arc de Triomphe. More Germans followed—Bavarian riflemen, Prussian Uhlans, "Bismarck cuirassiers" with white coats and waving plumes. Some rowdy youths known as *tapageurs* (noisies) hurled insults at the invaders. The Germans halted and methodically loaded their pieces. The *tapageurs* fled.

At last came the Prussian Royal Guard. The music of military bands filled the air, and as Parisians looked on in awe and hatred Bismarck himself entered the city. He found himself, after the victory parade, in the Place de la Concorde, where he was accosted by a crowd of hostile Frenchmen. His sang-froid did not desert him. Turning to one of the angry faces, he took out a cigar and asked for a light.

Paris was impressed.

London, December 1870–February 1871

THE FALL OF FRANCE awakened Mr. Gladstone from his dream of reform. He was dismayed by the mutilation of France. The cutting away of Alsace and Lorraine heralded a return, he said, to "the old and cruel practice of treating the population of a civilized European country as mere chattels."

The nature of the German revolution began to dawn on "Professor Gladstone," as Bismarck called him. "I have an apprehension," Mr. Gladstone said, "that this violent laceration and transfer is to lead us from bad to worse, and to the beginning of a new series of European complications." The Prime Minister had earlier supposed the emerging American empire to be the greatest threat to England's grandeur, and he had worked strenuously to wreck Lincoln's work. But he now foresaw that Germany rather than the United States would pose the real threat to his country's liberties in the coming decades.

Mr. Gladstone's great rival was similarly alive to the danger of Bismarck's statecraft. The Prussian's triumph "represents the German Revolution," Benjamin Disraeli said, "a greater political event than the French Revolution of the last century. . . . You have a new world. . . . The balance of power has been entirely destroyed."

Brooklyn, August 1870

Walt Whitman was gloomy. He was bringing out a book, *Democratic Vistas,* in which he hoped to refute European critics of the free state. Matthew Arnold, twisting his mouth contemptuously, declared that America had no poetry in it. The British prophet Thomas Carlyle went further. There was no poetry in any free state, and never could be.

Whitman in rebuttal invoked the beauty of the American man and the American woman. They were, he said, "freedom's athletes." But the more he looked about him, the more he began to doubt his own premises. "Are there, indeed, *men* here worthy of the name?" he asked in *Democratic Vistas.* "Are there athletes? Are there perfect women, to match the generous material luxuriance? Is there a pervading atmosphere of beautiful manners? Are there crops of fine youths, and majestic old people? . . . Confess that to severe eyes, using the moral microscope upon humanity, a sort of dry and flat Sahara appears, these cities, crowded with petty grotesques, malformations, phantoms . . . everywhere the youth puny, impudent, foppish, prematurely ripe—everywhere an abnormal libidinousness, unhealthy forms, male, female, painted, padded, dyed, chignon'd, muddy complexions, bad blood, the capacity for good motherhood deceasing or deceas'd, shallow notions of manners. . . ."

The poet wondered whether there was not something ruinous in the very success of Lincoln's revolution.

Paris and Lyons, September 1870–May 1871

While the Germans marched home under the banners of romantic nationalism, the Parisians raised aloft another romantic standard.

Shortly after the last Prussian dragoons left Paris, the French General Claude-Martin Lecomte, acting on the instructions of the newly installed President of the French Republic, Louis-Adolphe Thiers, rode up to Montmartre at the head of a body of troops. M. Thiers had ordered General Lecomte to retrieve assorted pieces of artillery which were then in the possession of the National Guard. A hostile crowd watched the troops march in. The poorer Parisians bore the line army little love; but they sympathized with the National Guard, a body imbued with the spirit of revolution.

An altercation ensued; a member of the National Guard was wounded. A woman with a red belt and a rifle ran through the streets crying treason. Her name was Louise Michel. The natural daughter of a French aristocrat, she was known, among the habitués of radical circles, as *"la Vierge rouge"* (the Red Virgin). The mob went wild. General Lecomte was dragged from his horse and savagely beaten. Afterwards he was taken to a nearby house, at the back of which lay a garden of gooseberries and clematis. A second General, Clément Thomas, was also captured, and he too was brought in. The young Mayor of Montmartre rushed over; his name was Georges Clemenceau. He begged his constituents to be merciful. "No blood, my friends, no blood," he implored. But he was too late. Montmartre had new martyrs. The officers were dead in the garden, and drunken harridans were squatting over their corpses.

Georges Clemenceau burst into tears.

All Paris was soon in ferment. M. Thiers fled with the rest of the magnificoes of the Third Republic to Versailles. A red flag was hoisted over the Hôtel de Ville. The Commune had begun.

The greatest terror prevailed in the city, one diplomat wrote, as the Communards moved from the theory of extermination to the practice. The new masters of Paris were unable indeed to agree on a policy concerning the spoliation of private property; but where human life was concerned they were decisive. Citizens who gathered to protest the illegality of the Commune's authority were massacred in the street. A Committee of Public Safety was established; and the cruel and lascivious Raoul Rigault became director of police. Those accused of being enemies of the Commune were hunted down like animals, among them many Catholic priests, who were paraded through the streets wearing placards which declared them to be thieves. By the middle of May 1871 more than three thousand people had been taken into custody by the new régime. Some of these victims the Communards executed, others they kept as hostages. Among the hostages was Monsignor Darboy, the Archbishop of Paris, who was seized in his episcopal palace and carried off to prison.

The Commune controlled Paris; but Adolphe Thiers controlled France. The seventy-four-year-old President of the Republic was, in intellect and judgment, one of the first statesmen of the age. His mind, like his pen, was bold, copious, and penetrating; and it was richly stocked with information gathered during a long course of study and scholarship. But the brilliant qualities of M. Thiers were overbalanced by an imagination which, though singularly rich and fertile, was at the same time violent, peremptory, and unforgiving. Light vied with darkness in that complicated intelligence; and though it is not easy to say which of the two contending forces got the upper hand, their friction endowed M. Thiers with remarkable powers of command, and enabled him to perform, not merely with resolution, but with a strange elation the work of putting to the sword those of his fellow citizens who had raised the standard of rebellion. An army was organized at Versailles. Marshal MacMahon, who had recently been released from German captivity, was placed at its head.

In the third week of May the army of Versailles entered Paris through the gate of Point-du-Jour at the western limit of the city. The Communards, in an act of romantic extravagance, determined to destroy the city rather than surrender it. The column of triumph in the Place Vendôme was toppled. Barrels of gunpowder were ignited in the Tuileries. Flames appeared in the windows of the Palais-Royal and the Palais de Justice. In a short time the Hôtel de Ville itself was on fire, as was one of the wings of the Louvre. "Paris," an English resident wrote, "is burning."

The Communards next took steps to ensure that the enemies of the régime did not survive its demise. Paris swam in blood. Mr. Washburne, the American envoy, was greatly affected by the report of illegal executions. He obtained from the Communards a permit to visit the most illustrious of the prisoners, Archbishop Darboy, who was incarcerated in the Mazas. The American Minister was one of the few diplomats then remaining in Paris; he had determined to follow the precedent of his predecessor, Gouverneur Morris, the only envoy who, eight decades before, had remained in the city during the darkest days of Robespierre's Terror. Washburne found Archishop Darboy in a small and gloomy cell. "I was deeply touched," the diplomat said, "at the appearance of this venerable man . . . his slender person, his form somewhat bent, his long beard, for he has not been shaved apparently since his confinement, his face haggard with ill health." But although the priest was broken in body, he was in spirit unbowed. Washburne was charmed by his cheerful animation. The Archbishop was prepared for the worst; but he "had no word of bitterness or reproach for his persecutors." On the contrary, the prelate said, the world judged his captors "to be worse than they really were." Before Washburne left the cell, he gave the priest a bottle of Madeira. A short time later Darboy was taken by cart from the Mazas to the bastion of La Roquette. On a May evening he was taken out into an alley and shot.

Versailles, October 1871–December 1873

Unable to avenge themselves against the Germans, Frenchmen turned against those of their own who, they believed, had brought about their defeat. Louis-Napoleon and his Empress, dethroned and disgraced, were, indeed, beyond the reach of their former subjects' vengeance. Eugénie had made her way to the coast of Normandy, where a yacht conveyed her safely to England. Louis-Napoleon joined her there after his release from his prison in Hesse-Cassel. The last of the imperial Napoleons and his consort were soon settled comfortably at Chislehurst in Kent, under the personal protection of Queen Victoria.

Disappointed of revenge against the Bonapartes, angry Frenchmen turned their eyes towards Marshal Bazaine. It must have been with a degree of trepidation that the soldier returned to France after his internment in Germany. Raoul, a Constable of France, had been put to death for having allowed himself to be taken alive by the enemy. Six centuries later the processes of retribution in France were scarcely less medieval. Bazaine, however, was determined to vindicate his honor.

The mandarins of the Third Republic plunged into *"l'affaire Bazaine."* There was to be a trial: and the proceeding must satisfy the public craving for a sanguinary revenge. There was no question of the offense which was to be brought home to Bazaine: it was in its nature capital. The questions with which the bureaucrats struggled pertained rather to the style than the substance of the court-martial. In lengthy memoranda they debated where the proceeding could best be staged. The château at Compiègne? Fontainebleau? Blois? How many stenographers would be needed? Where were the newspapermen to sit? Eventually a body called the Permanent Council of War was seated in the Grand Trianon at Versailles.

A verdict was handed down. French military tradition required that the Marshal quit the room before judgment was pronounced; Bazaine accordingly retired with his family to an upper chamber of the pavilion. He was there talking freely, as though unaware his life was at stake, when his adjutant, Colonel Villette, came in together with his advocate, M. Lachaud. Bazaine turned, and saw Villette stagger. He advanced toward Lachaud, who informed him of the verdict.

"*A mort,*" the lawyer said. "To death."

Bazaine grasped Lachaud's hand.

"By what majority?" he asked.

"Unanimously."

"Ah," the Marshal said.

Bazaine resumed the conversation he had broken off, but his family was by this time in tears. Colonel Villette went to grasp his commanding officer's hand but collapsed in the attempt; and the Marshal betook himself to another room to conceal his emotions.

Bazaine had been condemned *"à mort et à la degradation militaire"*—to death and to military degradation—for treating with, and capitulating to, the enemy before doing all that was prescribed by duty and honor. His defense—that he had surrendered Metz because his men were starving and that a further effusion of blood would not have changed the result of the war—was dismissed. Pursuant to the Code of Military Justice, he was to be stripped of his epaulettes before being shot, and compelled to relinquish his truncheon. His sword was to be broken before his eyes, and he was simultaneously to be ejected from the Legion of Honor and shorn of the Médaille Militaire which had been conferred upon him for his valor and conduct in Mexico.

Bazaine went downstairs, where he found twelve soldiers of the line armed with rifles, together with their officers. He bore himself with a Stoic self-mastery not unworthy of a Marshal of France. Where, he asked, was he to stand? He took his place, and said that he was ready.

Saint Petersburg and Moscow, December 1871–March 1874

PRINCE KROPOTKIN adopted the *nom de guerre* Borodin, and went about in peasants' boots and sheepskins. (Beneath this costume he wore a silk undergarment.) He lived ascetically, dining on rye bread, cucumbers, and weak tea. What remained of his income, after he had thus meagerly provided for himself, he devoted to the cause of the people. He printed pamphlets, helped friends to evade the police, and attempted to relieve the suffering of the masses.

His efforts were soon ended. Kropotkin was arrested by agents of the Third Section, and after a long interrogation was taken to the Fortress of Peter and Paul. He passed through a series of iron gates, and was taken down a passageway that led to a cell. A heavy oak door shut behind him, a key turned in the lock, and he was alone.

THE ORDEAL OF LIBERTY

SIX YEARS AFTER the culmination of the revolutionary events of 1861–1871, Ulysses S. Grant, having completed two lackluster terms as President of the United States, went on a tour round the world. Among the capitals in which he stopped was Berlin, where he called on Chancellor Bismarck in the Wilhelmstrasse.

"What always seemed so sad to me about your last great war," Bismarck told Grant during their interview, "was that you were fighting your own people. That is always so terrible in wars, so very hard."

"But it had to be done," Grant replied.

"Yes," said Bismarck, "you had to save the Union just as we had to save Germany."

"Not only save the Union," Grant said, "but destroy slavery."

"I suppose, however," Bismarck rejoined, "the Union was the real sentiment, the dominant sentiment."

"In the beginning, yes," said Grant, "but as soon as slavery fired upon the flag it was felt, we all felt, even those who did not object to slaves, that slavery must be destroyed. We felt that it was a stain to the Union that men should be bought and sold, like cattle."

Bismarck changed the subject. Lincoln had made one sort of revolution, he another. The awkward break in the dialogue between the Chancellor and the President was a hint of the chasms the world crisis of 1861–1871 opened up. The struggles that began during those years would continue for a dozen decades and engage the passions of the whole world. Germany's challenge to the free state would lead, in the twentieth century, to two world wars; the fires lit by Russia's red brigades would not be extinguished until the 1990s, when the Cold War ended.

AFTER THE FAILURE of Alexander's liberal revolution, Russia hurtled with ever greater rapidity towards catastrophe. The Tsar acquiesced in a policy of romantic nationalism, and in 1877 he went to war with the Ottoman Empire. Russians rallied to their sovereign's throne, eager to subdue the "turbaned Turk." The Russian army, after many disappointments, reached the suburbs of Constantinople. But Great Britain, the traditional protectress of the Ottoman régime, was determined to defend her interests in the Near East, which since the opening of the Suez Canal was the principal highway to her Indian Empire. Disraeli turned the screws, and Alexander pulled back. Although the final settlement left the Empire with gains in Asia Minor and Bessarabia, Russia was dissatisfied. The Tsar had revived the ancient dream of a redemption of Byzantium, but to the consternation of his subjects, he had failed to make the vision come true.

The red brigades contributed to the domestic unhappiness of the Empire. A series of attacks on Tsarist officials took place. The director of the Third Section was assassinated in a Saint Petersburg street. Trepov, the Governor of the city, was shot and seriously wounded by the Marxist terrorist Vera Zasulich. In April 1879 a revolutionist fired five shots at Alexander himself outside the Winter Palace. The Tsar dodged the bullets. In September the terrorist group People's Will conducted what was called a trial and condemned Alexander to death *in absentia*. Afterwards terrorists mined the tracks on which the imperial train traveled, and in December 1879 the Tsar narrowly escaped with his life when a bomb exploded and wrecked the imperial baggage train. Two months later, in February 1880, a powerful explosive was detonated in the Winter Palace itself, in a cellar beneath the Tsar's dining room. Dozens perished, but Alexander, who had not yet gone in to dine when the explosion occurred, survived.

He was now a prisoner of his office. He went about surrounded by Cossacks, and traveled in steel-plated carriages specially built by French craftsmen. Thousands of soldiers with bayonets fixed lined the railway tracks when he traveled by train. He trusted no one. The valet who brought him his robe in the morning, the butler who poured out his coffee, the maid who cleaned his room, the sentinel who guarded his door—any one of them might be in the employ of the nihilists. His heart grew harder, his attitude more cynical. The more good he tried to do, he believed, the more he would be hated. When he was told that a man had spoken uncharitably of him, he said, "Strange, I don't remember ever having done him a favour; why then should he hate me?"

In 1880, the Empress Mary died, alone and neglected. In the days that followed the Tsar was strangely giddy. One day, at Tsarskoe Selo, he donned the blue uniform of a Hussar of the Life Guards and went to fetch Katya, or the Princess Yurievskaya as she was now styled, in her room in the Catherine Palace. They were married that day in a drawing room of the palace.

The Tsar insisted that his morganatic consort be accorded by members of the imperial family the same deference which the deceased Empress had been shown. When Alexander and his young wife entered a room together, the master of ceremonies tapped thrice with his stave and cried out, "His Majesty, the Emperor, and Princess Yurievskaya." The beaming Tsar watched as the Princess seated herself in a chair formerly reserved for Mary. "At sixty-four Alexander II acted as a boy of eighteen," the Tsar's nephew, Grand Duke Alexander, said. "He whispered words of encouragement into her small ear; he wanted to know whether she liked the wine; he agreed with everything she said; he looked at his relatives with a friendly smile inviting them to enjoy his idyllic happiness." "I am so happy at present," the Tsar said one evening as he took Katya into dinner, it "frightens me."

There was a last suggestion of promise. While Alexander dawdled in his daydream, General Loris-Melikov directed the government. In contrast to Count Shuvalov, the new vizier was a reformer, and he proposed the creation of a number of advisory commissions, the gossamer threads of what might eventually become the more substantial fabric of a parliament and a constitution. Such a reform, Loris-Melikov told Alexander, would perhaps reconcile the country to a step the Tsar longed to take— the crowning of Katya as Empress. Alexander tentatively approved the idea. He then went off to preside at the changing of the guard in the Riding School, just as he had two decades before, on the day the emancipation law was promulgated. After the ceremony, he climbed into his carriage. "To the Winter Palace," he instructed the coachman, "by the same route." As the cavalcade went down Catherine Street, a student threw a bomb. The device exploded, killing a Cossack of the Escort and mortally wounding a young boy. The Tsar, who was unhurt, alighted from the carriage and, after making the sign of the Cross, went towards the victims. A crowd gathered, and someone asked the Tsar whether he was hurt.

"Thank God, no," Alexander said.

"Thank God?" cried a voice. A second terrorist tossed a bomb at the Tsar's feet.

The shattered body was taken to the Winter Palace. Drops of black blood spattered on the marble staircase as the Tsar was carried to his bedroom-study on the second story. Doctors and grand dukes crowded round the couch on which the mangled body was laid. Alexander was by this time unconscious; one of his eyes was shut, the other fixed in a glassy stare.

Katya burst in. She had not had time to dress, and wore only a pink-and-white negligée. She threw herself on her husband. "Sasha, Sasha!" she screamed as she kissed him. The court surgeon took one of the Tsar's hands and felt the pulse. At length he let the hand drop.

"The Emperor is dead."

Alexander's nephew, Grand Duke Alexander, looked at Katya. She "gave one shriek and dropped on the floor like a felled tree. Her pink-and-white negligée was soaked in blood."

In the years after Alexander's death, his successors, Alexander III and Nicholas II, pursued a reactionary course. Their efforts to quench the flame of rebellion with a policy of severity brought the country ever closer to civil upheaval, and in March 1917 the dynasty quivered, then fell. Nicholas and his family were taken prisoner, and in July 1918, in the Siberian city of Ekaterinburg, they were shot dead by order of Lenin, né Ulyanov. The red brigades had triumphed.

As for Katya, she survived the fall of the Romanovs. She died at Nice in 1922, at the age of seventy-four. The youngest of her three surviving children by the Tsar, who was also called Katya, lived into the era of Chairman Khrushchev and President Eisenhower. She for a time earned a meager living as a dance-hall performer; later she pawned her last piece of jewelry for forty pounds and a bottle of gin. Born in a Romanov palace, the youngest child of Alexander spent her last years in a bungalow in England. She died, alone and impoverished, just before Christmas 1959.

PRINCE KROPOTKIN was transferred from his cell in the Fortress of Peter and Paul to one of the Tsarist prison hospitals. He escaped from the hospital and fled to England. He was for many years active in anarchist circles, though after 1900 he grew markedly less radical. He expressed sympathy for Russia's free-state liberals: Russia, he said, must have a constitution and a legislature. When revolution broke out in 1917, the former *page de chambre* of the Tsar returned to his native land after more than forty years in exile. He supported the provisional government formed after the abdication of Nicholas; Alexander Kerensky, the leading figure in the new government, offered him a place in the Cabinet. (Kropotkin declined to accept the portfolio.) He was dismayed when, in the autumn of 1917, the Bolsheviks seized power. "This buries the revolution," he said. The Prince died in the town of Dmitrov outside Moscow in February 1921.

Count Tolstoy, who spent his final years advocating Christian anarchism, was recognized throughout the world as Russia's greatest living prophet. In August 1910 his family celebrated his birthday; he was eighty-two. In spite of the mythic proportions of his reputation, he was still very much a man, crawling between heaven and earth. At times, his wife wrote in her diary, he lived a "spiritually exalted" life, denying himself all luxuries, and striving to be "good, honest, open and spiritually pure." At other times, "he enjoys himself quite openly, loves good food, a good horse, cards, music, chess, cheerful company. . . ." On his birthday, Countess Tolstoy said that she hoped he "would soon be completely *at peace with himself*" now that he was "reaching the end of his life." "At this," she said, "he pulled an angry face." Their life together in 1910 resembled nothing so much as their life together in 1862—quarrels, tears, tantrums, and reconciliations.

One day in October 1910 the Countess rejoiced when "my dear husband, the *old* Lyovochka, noticed my existence twice. . . . Later on he ate a delicious pear and brought one for me to share with him." At the end of the month, at five in the morning, Tolstoy slipped out of the house, accusing his wife of having rummaged through his papers. In a letter he said that he wanted to give up the world and live alone, in silence. "I thank you for the forty-eight years of honorable life you spent with me," he wrote, "and I ask you to forgive all the wrongs I have done to you." He and a friend, Dr. Makovitsky, went to the railway station and boarded a train. "What you need, Father," a peasant told Tolstoy in the car, "is to get away from the affairs of this world, to go into the monastery and labor to save your soul." Tolstoy smiled. At Kozelsk he wired his daughter Alexandra, and asked her to send him copies of Montaigne's *Essays,* the second part of *The Brothers Karamazov,* and Maupassant's *Une Vie.* He and Makovitsky engaged a carriage and drove to a hostelry near the monastery of Optina Pustyn. The next day they visited Tolstoy's sister, Mary, who was a nun in the Shamardino Convent. Here Alexandra joined them. Tolstoy spoke of settling at Optina, or of remaining in the shadow of Shamardino; at other times he talked of going to the Caucasus, or to Bulgaria and Turkey. In fact his journey had a single object, that of avoiding the path that leads to the grave.

Accompanied by Alexandra and Makovitsky, the restless man went back to Kozelsk and boarded a train. The flight of the prophet was front-page news. "The old boy's played her a pretty trick!" a young dandy on the train said. "It must not have made Sofya Andreyevna very happy to see him skip out like that. . . ." But when he learned that Tolstoy himself was aboard, he closed his mouth.

The Count had, by this time, developed a fever. The party detrained at Astapovo, and Tolstoy was put to bed in the stationmaster's cottage. "God is that infinite whole of which man is conscious of being a finite part," he said. In his delirium he talked of the peasants. "What about the *muzhiks?*" he asked. "How do the *muzhiks* die?" Pneumonia set in, and after a vigil of several days he breathed his last. He was buried at Yasnaya Polyana.

Countess Tolstoy survived her husband. After the Revolution of 1917, her pension from the Tsar ceased to be paid, and Yasnaya Polyana became a state farm. The aged Countess was, however, permitted to stay on, and a few rooms were set aside for her use. Bolshevik soldiers later commandeered the house and raised the red flag over it. Countess Tolstoy died in November 1919.

ALEXANDER'S REVOLUTION never reached those places in the Russian spirit where Tolstoy delighted to linger. Bismarck, by contrast, touched Germany's spiritual nerve all too skillfully. After 1871, the Chancellor's principal task was to prevent his countrymen from destroying their Empire in a euphoria of violence.

The General Staff was not merely ready, it was eager for battle. No sooner had Moltke returned to Germany than he began to draw up mobilization plans for the next campaign. He foresaw a war on two fronts, with Russia coming in on the side of France. In 1877 he refined these plans: his new strategy called for a "great decisive battle" against the French in the earliest phases of the war, after which Germany would be free to throw her might against the Russians. It was a premonition of 1914.

Bismarck by no means ignored the external dangers to the Empire which preoccupied the Staff. The French, he saw, were full of bitterness. Louis-Napoleon escaped the vengeance of his former subjects; he perished at Chislehurst, in January 1873, after surgeons opened his bladder.* Bazaine, too, cheated the executioner; Marshal MacMahon, who succeeded M. Thiers as President of the French Republic, commuted his sentence to twenty years' penal servitude.† Germany's Staff officers sought to frustrate the French yearning for *la revanche* (revenge) with mobilization plans; Bismarck preferred to meet the challenge through an intricate diplomacy designed to prevent the emergence of a Franco-Russian military alliance. In this he was successful, and it was only after his ejection from office that the French and the Russians negotiated their *entente*.

Moltke acquiesced in the diplomatic design which Bismarck communicated to him. The Field Marshal (for such he now was) dropped his

---

* The former Empress Eugénie survived her husband; she died in Spain in July 1920, in her ninety-fifth year. Their son, Lulu, the former Prince Imperial, was slain by Zulu warriors while fighting with the British in South Africa in June 1879.
† Bazaine subsequently escaped from his prison on the Ile Sainte-Marguerite, and afterwards lived in exile in Madrid.

"decisive battle in the West" plan, and in time he ceased to advocate a pre-emptive strike against Russia, in which Austria was to be the stalking horse. Bismarck persuaded him that a break between Vienna and Saint Petersburg, with their antagonistic interests in the Balkans, would spell doom for Germany. But others on the Staff were unreconciled to the Chancellor's pacific policy. Moltke's deputy, Count Alfred von Waldersee, who succeeded him as Chief of the General Staff in 1888, was a warmonger, and so, too, was Count Alfred von Schlieffen, who succeeded Waldersee. Schlieffen favored a mobilization plan that drew on Moltke's discarded strategy of a massive initial thrust against France. While Bismarck remained in power his immense prestige enabled him to stare down the generals, but after he fell the Staff came into its own.

At home, Bismarck's policy combined elements of authoritarian nationalism and paternalistic socialism. His own authority was great, for although his constitution granted universal manhood suffrage, he himself, the principal Minister of the Empire, was not responsible to the elected lawmakers. The Reich, though it was in appearance a constitutional monarchy, was in fact a coercive superstate, tempered only by the prudence and moderation of the Chancellor. Such opposition as Bismarck encountered he crushed, or attempted to crush. He suppressed the socialist parties—and, ingeniously, appropriated their paternal theory of government. "Give the workingman the right to employment as long as he has health," he said, "assure him of care when he is sick and maintenance when he is old, and the socialists will sound their birdcall in vain."

Such reforms might have been salutary had they been implemented in a different spirit; but they were intended less to help people than to liquidate their will. Bismarck's object, the historian A. J. P. Taylor wrote, was not to improve the condition of the workers, but to make them subservient to the state. "Whoever has a pension for his old age," Bismarck said in 1881, "is far more content and far easier to handle than one who has no such prospect."

The Reich was at once the consummation and the tomb of Bismarck's genius. Through his policy, the historian Theodor Mommsen said, the Black Prince broke his nation's back. He liberated a people without freeing them, and became yet another manifestation of a problem that drove Machiavelli to despair. The leader who is strong enough to make a nation is rarely good enough to give it freedom. In certain moods Bismarck was himself inclined to lament the repercussions of his statecraft. "Had it not been for me," he said, "there would not have been three great wars; 80,000 men would not have perished; and parents, brothers, sisters would not be in mourning. But that is something I have to settle with God." Presumably, however, the Chancellor was confident that these negotiations with the Deity would have an outcome favorable to himself.

In 1888, Wilhelm I, the aged Kaiser, died. He was succeeded by Crown Prince Friedrich, the son-in-law of Queen Victoria. The new Emperor was in the grip of cancer, and he died just three months after ascending the throne. His son, Willie, became Kaiser Wilhelm II. The young ruler was impatient of restraint, and he forced Bismarck to retire. The ex-Chancellor passed his last years as a country squire, railing against the stupidity of the Reich's leadership, and against those danger-ous policies which were the fruit of his own craft and subtlety; for his Empire never did escape the crookedness and violence in which it was begot. The old man's principal consolation lay, not in the memory of his statesmanship, but in the devotion of his family. His marriage continued to be a happy one, and he remained close to his three children. At the same time he cherished the memory of Kathi Orlov, who had died young, in 1875. Bismarck himself died in 1898 at his estate at Friedrichs-ruh. He was eighty-three.

Field Marshal von Moltke died in Berlin, in his apartment in the headquarters of the General Staff, in April 1891, full of years and honor. He left no children; but his nephew and namesake, the younger Hel-muth von Moltke, carried on the family's military tradition, and in 1905 he succeeded Schlieffen as Chief of the General Staff. Moltke the Younger modified the mobilization orders for war with France that he inherited from Schlieffen. "It must come to a fight," Schlieffen is said to have exclaimed on his deathbed. "Only make the right wing strong." But the younger Moltke weakened the right wing; and it was his revised war plan that Germany followed into battle in the summer of 1914.

During the battle of the Marne in September 1914, when the German advance was halted twenty miles from Paris, the soft, nervous nephew col-lapsed. The genius of General Joseph Galliéni, the Military Governor of Paris, and the gallantry of Tsar Nicholas II saved France. Galliéni attacked the exposed flank of General von Kluck's army, as it marched within sight of the Eiffel Tower; the Tsar threw his armies at the Germans, and forced them to transfer two army corps and a division of cavalry from the West-ern to the Eastern theater. Thirty-two German troop trains raced eastward to meet the fortitude of Russia. It was the last great liberal act of the Tsarist régime, one in which Nicholas showed himself not unworthy of the mem-ory of his grandfather Alexander. "Majesty," Moltke the Younger is said to have informed the Kaiser after the Marne, "we have lost the war." Relieved by the Kaiser of his command, the nephew died in June 1916, while the battle raged at Verdun. Two years later the military power of Germany was broken, and in September 1918 the last offensive of General Ludendorff, who was by then virtually the military dictator of Germany, failed. A desperate Kaiser proclaimed Germany a free state on the English model, with ministerial responsibility. But the concession came too late, and the Kaiser fled to Holland.

The dynasty of the Hohenzollerns was at an end, but the General Staff, though restricted in its operations by the Treaty of Versailles, continued not merely to function but to dominate. The ascetic ideal of discipline and obedience which the elder Moltke had inculcated in the Staff ensured that its traditions would survive the wreck of the Reich. Behind "the veneer of republican governments and democratic institutions, imposed by the victors and tainted with defeat," Winston Churchill wrote, "the real political power in Germany and the enduring structure of the nation" lay with the officers of the General Staff. Under General Hans von Seeckt, the brethren of the Staff secretly planned the revival of the army, and they ensured that the precious institutional knowledge of their order did not perish with themselves.

As FOR RICHARD WAGNER, he at last succeeded in erecting his temple of art. The first Bayreuth Festival was held in 1876; the Kaiser himself was present, as were many notables of the Empire. Through the munificence of his patron, Ludwig of Bavaria, the composer was enabled to build, at Bayreuth, a splendid villa for himself; he called it *Wahnfried,* or Peace from Illusion. Wagner died of a heart attack at Venice, in the Palazzo Vendramin-Calergi on the Grand Canal, in February 1883. He was sixty-nine.

Ludwig survived his friend; he died in mysterious circumstances in June 1886, at the age of forty. Wagner's widow, Cosima, lived to a great age. She was still residing at Wahnfried when, in 1923, her son Siegfried Wagner welcomed to his father's house a young agitator who, in the aftermath of Germany's defeat, was rising into prominence. The guest's name was Adolf Hitler. The Nazi leader stood silently before Wagner's grave. Winifred Wagner, whom Siegfried married to beard his homosexuality, became a close friend of Hitler; she and her children were among the very few who were permitted to call the Fuehrer by his nickname, "Wolf." "Frau Wagner—and that is her historic service—linked Bayreuth to National Socialism," Hitler said. Wagner's temple of art became the Fuehrer's court theater; it was at Bayreuth, Hitler said, that "the Master . . . forged the spiritual sword with which we fight today." Hitler delighted in the atmosphere of Wahnfried, which he said "radiates life," and in the company of the Wagners. "I love these people and Wahnfried," he once exclaimed.

Nietzsche broke with Wagner a decade before Hitler was born. The estrangement deepened when the philosopher saw the Christian motifs in the composer's late work, *Parsifal.* "Incredible!" Nietzsche exclaimed after he received the text from Wagner. His friend had "turned pious." Nietzsche might have forgiven Wagner *Parsifal*—he dissolved in tears when he first listened to the prelude—but he could not forgive him for having become *reichsdeutsch,* a chauvinist of the Empire. Bayreuth, in Nietzsche's opinion, was but a prop of the Reich. After his breakdown in Turin, in January 1889, the philosopher was taken to the clinic at Basel; he insisted on calling the attendant charged with restraining him "Bismarck." He died insane at Weimar in August 1900, at the age of fifty-five.

IN MAY 1873, Chief Justice Salmon P. Chase was laid in his grave. Six months later his daughter, Kate Chase Sprague, saw her husband's business fail. William Sprague lapsed into an inebriated stupor. Kate turned for companionship to Roscoe Conkling, the handsome New York politician. Henry Adams thought Conkling the preening epitome of senatorial pompousness, with an egotism so mannered "it became Shakespearian and *bouffe.*" There were rumors of a love affair, and in the summer of 1879 the newspapers reported that Sprague threatened Conkling with a rifle. Kate sued for divorce, and the marriage was dissolved. In 1890 her son, Willie, having failed at various jobs, went west looking for work. He committed suicide at Seattle. Kate lost her beauty as well as her wealth; her hair turned gray, and her face grew puffy. She died in Washington in July 1899. She was fifty-eight. William Sprague died fifteen years later in Paris.

Henry Adams relinquished his Harvard professorship and became a writer, composing works of history and fiction. His wife, Marian "Clover" Hooper, committed suicide in December 1885. In 1904 Adams privately printed his paean to the Middle Ages, *Mont Saint Michel and Chartres*; three years later he brought out a private edition of his memoir, *The Education of Henry Adams*, which traced his growing disenchantment with American democracy. He suffered a stroke in 1912, and six years later, in March 1918, he died in Washington. In 1919 he was posthumously awarded the Pulitzer Prize for *The Education of Henry Adams*.

In spite of the doubts he expressed in *Democratic Vistas*, Walt Whitman insisted that the American free state was the world's last, best hope. He entertained various, somewhat obscure ideas about how the latent poetry of the country could be brought out; he imagined that a race of "orbic bards" would emerge and restore the country's democratic faith. After suffering a stroke in January 1873, he moved to Camden, New

Jersey. In his final years he was a celebrity, "the good gray poet." His lectures on Lincoln widened his fame; Oscar Wilde made a pilgrimage to his house; Thomas Eakins painted his picture. Walt Whitman died in March 1892, at the age of seventy-two.

James and Mary Chesnut moved into a new house in Camden, South Carolina, in 1873. Money was scarce, and the couple were obliged to sell their Gilbert Stuart portrait of President Washington. James Chesnut continued his political labors, without much success, and Mary Chesnut continued her literary work, with about the same result. She never published the diary into which she formed the journals she kept during the war, and during her lifetime her literary talents were unrecognized. Early in 1885, James Chesnut suffered a seizure and died. Mary Chesnut died the following year, in November 1886. She was sixty-three. Two decades after her death, a portion of her work was published under the title *A Diary from Dixie*. Subsequent editions appeared in 1949 and 1981. In his book *Patriotic Gore* (1962), Edmund Wilson paid tribute to the "brilliant journal of Mary Chesnut, so much more imaginative and revealing than most of the fiction inspired by the war." He called her diary "an extraordinary document—in its informal department, a masterpiece . . . a work of art."

Sam Hood's insurance business failed in 1879. He died that summer in a yellow-fever epidemic in New Orleans. His former fiancée, Buck Preston Rawlins, died the following year, at the age of thirty-eight. She was buried in Magnolia Cemetery at Charleston.

LINCOLN'S REMAINS LIE in the vault at Oak Ridge Cemetery in Springfield. Mary Todd Lincoln never recovered from the shock of his death. She died in Springfield in July 1882, at the age of sixty-three. Only one of her four children survived her. The Lincolns' youngest boy, Tad, died six years after his father, in July 1871. Their oldest child, Robert Todd Lincoln, married Mary Eunice Harlan, the daughter of Senator James Harlan of Iowa, the man H. L. Mencken called the "damndest ass" in America for his dismissal of Walt Whitman from a clerkship in the Department of the Interior (Bureau of Indian Affairs). Robert Todd Lincoln prospered as a railroad executive. He became Secretary of War under President Garfield and Minister to England under President Harrison. He died in Vermont in July 1926.

After the passing of Lincoln, America confronted new problems. The North was beset by commercial oligopoly; in the South the system of segregation known as Jim Crow flourished. The former Confederacy was as little redeemed as the land of Jay Gould and Jim Fisk—or was rather redeemed in a way Lincoln could scarcely have approved.

And yet. America did not become a slave empire. Had Lincoln not forced his revolution in 1861, slavery, in some perhaps modified form, under some perhaps prettier name, might have survived into the twentieth century. The institution would have derived fresh strength from the novel weapons in the coercive arsenal—"scientific" racism, social Darwinism, jingo imperialism, the ostensibly benevolent doctrines of paternalism. The coercive party in America, unbroken in spirit, might have realized its dream of Caribbean empire; Cuba and the Philippines, after their conquest by the United States, might have become permanent slave colonies. Strengthened by a policy of militant nationalism, the coercive party might, in the twentieth century, have worked to prevent the United States from playing a part in the struggle against such coercive régimes as the Kaiser's Second Reich and Hitler's Third one.

The historical probabilities would have been no less grim had Lincoln, after initiating his revolution, failed to preserve the United States as a unitary free state. The Southern Republic, having gained its independence, would almost certainly have formed alliances with régimes grounded in its own coercive philosophy. The successors of Jefferson Davis would not improbably have linked arms with the successors of Otto von Bismarck. Young German officers, in the tradition of Heros von Borcke, would have traveled to the Military Institute at Staunton to instruct cadets in the latest refinements of military art; and young Southern patricians would have crossed the ocean to complete their educations in the schools at Berlin.

None of this came to pass. The virtue of Lincoln preserved the liberties of America. In the decades that followed, the nation he saved played a part in vindicating the freedom of peoples around the world.

Four score and seven years ago our fathers brought forth on this continent, a new nation, conceived in Liberty, and dedicated to the proposition that all men are created equal.

Now we are engaged in a great civil war, testing whether that nation, or any nation so conceived, and so dedicated, can long endure. We are met on a great battle-field of that war. We have come to dedicate a portion of that field, as a final resting place for those who here gave their lives that that nation might live. It is altogether fitting and proper that we should do this.

But, in a larger sense, we can not dedicate—we can not consecrate—we can not hallow—this ground. The brave men, living and dead, who struggled here, have consecrated it, far above our poor power to add or detract. The world will little note, nor long remember, what we say here, but it can never forget what they did here. It is for us the living, rather, to be dedicated here to the unfinished work which they who fought here have thus far so nobly advanced. It is rather for us to be here dedicated to the great task remaining before us—that from these honored dead we take increased devotion to that cause for which they gave the last full measure of devotion—that we here highly resolve that these dead shall not have died in vain—that this nation, under God, shall have a new birth of freedom—and that government of the people, by the people, for the people, shall not perish from the earth.

—*Address at Gettysburg, Pennsylvania,*
November 19, 1863

Abbreviations in Notes and Sources

AA	Archives de l'Armée française, Château de Vincennes
AAAPSS	*Annals of the American Academy of Political and Social Science*
ALH	John G. Nicolay and John Hay, *Abraham Lincoln: A History,* 10 vols. New York: Century, 1890
AMH	*American Historical Review*
B	C. Grant Robertson, *Bismarck.* New York: Howard Fertig, 1969
BE	*The Bradenham Edition of the Novels and Tales of Benjamin Disraeli,* 12 vols. London: Peter Davies, 1927
BGE	Erich Eyck, *Bismarck and the German Empire.* New York: W. W. Norton, 1964
BMS	A. J. P. Taylor, *Bismarck: The Man and the Statesman.* New York: Vintage, 1967
C	Walt Whitman, *The Correspondence 1842–1867,* ed. Edwin Haviland Miller. New York: New York University Press, 1961
CP	Fyodor Dostoevsky, *Crime and Punishment,* trans. Constance Garnett. New York: Random House, 1956
CSP	*Canadian Slavonic Papers*
CW	*The Collected Works of Abraham Lincoln,* ed. Roy P. Basler, 9 vols. New Brunswick, NJ: Rutgers University Press, 1953–55
D	*Dædalus: Journal of the American Academy of Arts and Sciences*
DGW	Gideon Welles, *Diary of Gideon Welles,* 3 vols. Boston: Houghton Mifflin, 1911
DST	Sophia Tolstoy, *The Diaries of Sophia Tolstoy,* ed. O. A. Golinenko, S. A. Rozanova, B. M. Shumova, I. A. Pokrovskaya, and N. I. Azarova, trans. Cathy Porter. New York: Random House, 1985

DTW	Sofya Tolstoy, *The Diary of Tolstoy's Wife,* trans. Alexander Werth. London: Victor Gollancz, 1928
EHA	Henry Adams, *The Education of Henry Adams,* ed. Ernest Samuels and Jayne N. Samuels. New York: Library of America, 1983
FA	*Foreign Affairs*
FP	*Foreign Policy*
Gedanken	Otto Fürst von Bismarck, *Gedanken und Erinnerungen,* 2 vols. Stuttgart: Cotta, 1898
Gesammelten Werke	*Bismarck: Die gesammelten Werke.* Berlin: Otto Stollberg, et al., 15 vols., 1925–33
GR	*Georgia Review*
HLL	William H. Herndon, *Herndon's Life of Lincoln.* New York: Da Capo, 1983
IO	*International Organization*
JAH	*Journal of American History*
JHI	*Journal of the History of Ideas*
JMH	*Journal of Modern History*
JPE	*Journal of Political Economy*
JSH	*Journal of Southern History*
L	Douglas Southall Freeman, *Lee.* New York: Touchstone, 1997
LBD	W. F. Monypenny and George Earle Buckle, *The Life of Benjamin Disraeli, Earl of Beaconsfield,* 6 vols. New York: Macmillan, 1910–20
LDD	*Lincoln Day by Day: A Chronology 1809–1865,* ed. Earl Schenk Miers, 3 vols. Washington, DC: Sesquicentennial Commission, 1960
LG	Walt Whitman, *Leaves of Grass.* New York: Vintage and Library of America, 1992
LGT	Edvard Radzinsky, *Alexander II: The Last Great Tsar,* trans. Antonina Bouis. New York: Free Press, 2005
LHJTVP	Evelyn Ashley, *The Life of Henry John Temple, Viscount Palmerston,* 2 vols. London: Richard Bentley, 1876

LLJR	Spencer Walpole, *The Life of Lord John Russell,* 2 vols. London: Longmans, Green, 1889
LO	Noah Brooks, *Lincoln Observed: Civil War Dispatches of Noah Brooks,* ed. Michael Burlingame. Baltimore: Johns Hopkins University Press, 1998
LRW	Ernest Newman, *The Life of Richard Wagner,* 4 vols. Cambridge: Cambridge University Press, 1976
LSWPF	Francis Fessenden, *Life and Services of William Pitt Fessenden,* 2 vols. Boston: Houghton Mifflin, 1907
LWEG	John Morley, *The Life of William Ewart Gladstone,* 3 vols. London: 1903
MCCW	Mary Boykin Chesnut, *Mary Chesnut's Civil War,* ed. C. Vann Woodward. New York: Book-of-the-Month Club, 1994
MHM	*Maryland Historical Magazine*
MOS	George B. McClellan, *McClellan's Own Story: The War for the Union: The Soldiers Who Fought It: The Civilians Who Directed It: And His Relations to It and to Them.* New York: Charles L. Webster, 1887; Scituate, MA: Digital Scanning, 1998
MR	Peter Kropotkin, *Memoirs of a Revolutionist.* New York: Dover, 1971
NC	*The New Criterion*
NCMH	*The New Cambridge Modern History,* ed. J. P. T. Bury, 14 vols. Cambridge: Cambridge University Press, 1960
NYPL	New York Public Library
Origines Diplomatiques	*Les Origines Diplomatiques de la Guerre de 1870–1871, Recueil de Documents Publié,* ed. Ministère des Affaires Étrangères, 29 vols. Paris: Imprimerie Nationale, 1910–32
ORTW	*On the Road to Total War: The American Civil War and the German Wars of Unification, 1861–1871,* ed. Stig Förster and Jörg Nagler. Washington, DC, and Cambridge: German Historical Institute and Cambridge University Press, 2002
PMUSG	Ulysses S. Grant, *Personal Memoirs of U. S. Grant,* ed. E. B. Long. New York: Da Capo, 2001
RAL	John Bigelow, *Retrospections of an Active Life,* 2 vols. New York: Baker & Taylor, 1909
REL	Douglas Southall Freeman, *R. E. Lee,* 4 vols. New York: Scribner's, 1935; Safety Harbor, FL: Simon Publications, 2001

RGR   *Russia's Great Reforms, 1855–1881,* ed. Ben Eklof, John Bushnell, and Larissa Zakharova. Bloomington: Indiana University Press, 1994

Rheinpolitik   Hermann Oncken, *Die Rheinpolitik Kaiser Napoleons III von 1863 bis 1870,* 3 vols. Stuttgart: Deutsche Verlags, 1926

RP   *Review of Politics*

RR   *Russian Review*

SCHM   *South Carolina Historical Magazine*

SDC   Walt Whitman, *Specimen Days & Collect.* Mineola, NY: Dover, 1995

SD NARA   State Department Archives, National Archives and Records Administration

SR   *Slavic Review*

SS   Gerhard Ritter, *The Sword and the Scepter: The Problem of Militarism in German History.* Vol. I: *The Prussian Tradition, 1740–1890,* trans. Heinz Norden. Princeton Junction, NJ: Scholar's Bookshelf, 1988

SSH   *Social Science History*

SW, 1832–1858   *Abraham Lincoln: Speeches and Writings 1832–1858,* ed. D. E. Fehrenbacher. New York: Library of America, 1989

SW, 1859–1865   *Abraham Lincoln: Speeches and Writings 1859–1865,* ed. D. E. Fehrenbacher. New York: Library of America, 1989

T   Hernri Troyat, *Tolstoy,* trans. Nancy Amphoux. Garden City, NY: Doubleday, 1967

TE   Maurice Paléologue, *The Tragic Empress: A Record of Intimate Talks with the Empress Eugénie, 1901–1919,* trans. Hamish Miles. New York: Harper & Bros., 1928

TL   *Tolstoy's Letters 1828–1879,* trans. R. F. Christian. New York: Charles Scribner's Sons, 1978

VMHB   *Virginia Magazine of History and Biography*

WLM   *The Works of Lord Macaulay,* ed. Lady Trevelyan, 8 vols. London: Longmans, Green, 1879

WPQ   *Western Political Quarterly*

WWHS   *The Works of William H. Seward,* ed. George E. Baker, 5 vols. Boston: Houghton Mifflin, 1884

Notes and Sources

Note to the Reader

xiii   *"The impulse"*: Edmund Wilson, *Patriotic Gore: Studies in the Literature of the American Civil War* (Boston: Northeastern University Press, 1984), xx–xxi.

xiv   *"penetrated the leaden"*: John Petek, *Archbishop Joseph Beran*, ed. Michael Novak (Notre Dame, IN: University of Notre Dame Press, 1964), 8.

xiv   *"Symbol"*: Ibid.

xiv   *"Dr. Beran"*: Ibid., 12.

xiv   *persecuted:* Albert Galter, *The Red Book of the Persecuted Church* (Westminster, MD: The Newman Press, 1957), 343–93; "Freedom for a Fighter," *Time*, October 11, 1963; Maria Teresa Carloni, *Il Cardinale Scomodo: Il Card. Giuseppe Beran, Arcivescovo de Praga* (Urbania: Bramante, 1972).

xiv   *413 South Seventh:* Floyd S. Barringer, *Historic Homes of Springfield* (Springfield, IL: Privately printed, 1966), 54–55.

Prologue: Three Deaths

1   *fractured:* "Our Great Loss–Assassination of President Lincoln," *The New-York Times*, Monday, April 17, 1865, 1.

1   *shortly after seven o'clock:* "Our Great Loss–Death of President Lincoln," *The New-York Times*, Sunday, April 16, 1865, 1.

1   *his belly ripped:* Bernard Pares, *A History of Russia*, 5th ed. New York: Vintage, 1965), 403.

1   *died unloved:* W. E. Mosse, *Alexander II and the Modernization of Russia*, rev. ed. (New York: Collier, 1970), 138, 141–42, 146.

1   *amputate:* "The Assassination of the Emperor of Russia," *The Times*, Wednesday, March 16, 1881, 10.

1   *The German Crown Prince:* "Russia," *The Times*, Friday, March 25, 1881, 5.

1   *shortly after the death:* Elizabeth Narishkin-Kurkakin, *Under Three Tsars*, ed. René Fölöp Miller, trans. Julia E. Loesser (New York: E. P. Dutton, 1931), 66.

2   *"a heartless law"*: Alexander, Grand Duke of Russia, *Once a Grand Duke* (New York: Cosmopolitan Book Corp.–Farrar & Rinehart, 1932), 44.

2   *undemonstrative Russians:* "Russia," *The Times*, Tuesday, March 22, 1881, 5.

2   *the dungeon:* H. Sutherland Edwards, *The Russians at Home and Abroad: Sketches, Unpolitical and Political, of Russian Life Under Alexander II*, 2 vols. (London: W. M. H. Allen, 1879), i, 5.

2   *golden dome:* Maurice Paléologue, *The Tragic Romance of Alexander II of Russia*, trans. Arthur Chambers (London: Hutchinson, 1927), 24–25.

2   *Katya, heavily veiled*: A. A. Mosolov, *At the Court of the Last Tsar*, ed. A. A. Pilenco, trans. E. W. Dickes (London: Methuen, 1996), 71–72.

2   *rather handsome:* Frederic Hamilton, *The Vanished Pomps of Yesterday* (Garden City, NY: Doubleday, 1934), 116.

2 *"very tall"*: Mark Twain, *The Innocents Abroad* (New York: Library of America, 1984), 311.

2 *lifted her veils:* Mosolov, *At the Court of the Last Tsar,* 71–72.

3 *Alexander had insisted:* Alexander, *Once a Grand Duke,* 48, 50.

3 *embraced Katya:* Mosolov, *At the Court of the Last Tsar,* 71–72.

3 *A heavy snow:* "The Funeral of the Late Emperor of Russia," *The Times,* Monday, March 28, 1881, 6.

3 *chanting passages of Scripture:* "Russia," *The Times,* Tuesday, March 22, 1881, 5.

3 *to bend over the corpse:* "The Funeral of the Late Emperor of Russia," *The Times,* Monday, March 28, 1881, 6.

3 *threw sand and leaves:* Ibid.

3 *potent form of publicity:* David Donald, *Lincoln Reconsidered: Essays on the Civil War Era* (New York: Vintage, 1961), 4–5.

3 *attempted to touch:* "The Obsequies," *The New-York Times,* Tuesday, April 25, 1865, 1.

4 *turned black:* Ibid.; "The Obsequies," *The New-York Times,* Wednesday, April 26, 1865, 1.

4 *An embalmer:* "The Obsequies," *The New-York Times,* Tuesday, April 25, 1865, 1.

4 *pressed handkerchiefs:* "The Obsequies," *The New-York Times,* Saturday, April 22, 1865, 1.

4 *"HONOR TO WHOM":* Ibid.

4 *"THE ILLUSTRIOUS MARTYR":* "The Obsequies," *The New-York Times,* Sunday, April 23, 1865, 1.

4 *"WASHINGTON":* "The Obsequies," *The New-York Times,* Tuesday, April 25, 1865, 1.

4 *"THOUGH DEAD":* "The Obsequies," *The New-York Times,* Tuesday, May 2, 1865, 1.

4 *The railroad car:* "The Obsequies," *The New-York Times,* Saturday, April 22, 1865, 1.

4 *robed in black:* Ibid.

4 *Memphis . . . Rochester:* "The Funeral Cortege," *The New-York Times,* Friday, April 28, 1865, 8.

4 *"COME HOME" . . . "GO TO THY REST":* "The President's Obsequies," *The New-York Times,* Thursday, May 4, 1865, 1.

4 *"Children of the Heavenly King":* "The Burial," *The New-York Times,* Friday, May 5, 1865, 1.

5 *a limestone sepulcher:* Ibid.

5 *"sufferer from hysteria":* Mosolov, *At the Court of the Last Tsar,* 202.

5 *"He's raving mad!":* Ibid., 203.

5 *"It was all":* B, 473.

6 *He hurled:* BMS, 247.

6 *snatched the paper: The Kaiser vs. Bismarck: Suppressed Letters,* trans. Bernard Miall (New York: Harper, 1921), 100–201. John. C. G. Röhl, *Wilhelm II: The Kaiser's Personal Monarchy, 1888–1900,* trans. Sheila de Bellaigue (Cambridge: Cambridge University Press, 2004), 297.

6 *in so many words:* Alexander said, "C'est un garçon mal élevé et de maivaise foi" BMS, 247. The Tsar also called the Kaiser a "rascally young fop" and a "pipsqueak"–Röhl, *Wilhelm II,* 37; George F. Kennan, *The Decline of Bismarck's European Order: Franco-Russian Relations, 1875–1890* (Princeton: Princeton University Press, 1980), 398.

6 *"A state funeral":* BMS, 253.

6 "That": BMS, 265 (emphasis added).

7 *twenty-two million serfs:* Terence Emmons, *The Russian Landed Gentry and the Peasant Emancipation of 1861* (Cambridge: Cambridge University Press, 1968), vii, 3. Also affected by emancipation, though far less dramatically, were twenty-five million Crown peasants—ibid., 3. The state peasants had been given title to their land and certain other freedoms during the reign of Nicholas I, and from that time "were, for all purposes, freemen"–Richard Pipes, *Russia Under the Old Regime* (Harmondsworth, Middlesex: Penguin, 1979), 146.

7 *four million men, women:* According to the Census of 1860, there were 3,954,000 slaves in the United States, but this was almost certainly an undercount.

7 *free states:* Rather than democratic ones; for although the freest state will always be in some degree democratic, a democratic state may not be free. France, in 1861, was in some respects more democratic than England at that time; its suffrage was broader. Yet it was less free. Democracy is only one element in the mixture which secures freedom. Compare F. A. Hayek, *The Constitution of Liberty* (Chicago: University of Chicago Press, 1960), 20, 103–17.

7 *"from above":* Larissa Zakharova, "Autocracy and the Reforms of 1861–1871 in Russia: Choosing

Paths of Development," trans. Daniel Field, RGR, 20; Michael T. Florinsky, *Russia: A History and an Interpretation,* 2 vols. (New York: Macmillan, 1969), ii, 883.

7 *deplored the English theory:* Bismarck "has always hated the English," Lord Granville wrote to Mr. Gladstone in 1870–Lord Edmond Fitzmaurice, *The Life of Granville George Leveson Gower, Second Earl Granville, K.G.,* 2 vols. (London: Longmans, Green, 1905), ii, 67.

7 *liberty of trade:* Bismarck's revolutionary path was blazed by those who made the *Zollverein,* the customs union which eliminated numerous restraints on trade in Germany. The *Zollverein,* Friedrich List said, did away with more barriers to trade and national unity "than had been swept away by the political whirlwinds of the American and French Revolutions"–Edward Earl Meade, "Adam Smith, Alexander Hamilton, Friedrich List: The Economic Foundations of Military Power," in *Makers of Modern Strategy: Military Thought from Machiavelli to Hitler,* ed. Edward Meade Earle (New York: Atheneum, 1967), 141; Handels-Vertrag zwischen dem Zollverein und Großbritannien, SD NARA M44/ROLL 13.

7 *a Free Trader:* Otto Pflanze, "Bismarck's 'Realpolitik,' " RP, vol. 20, no. 4 (October 1958), 498–99; James Wycliffe Headlam, *Bismarck and the Foundation of the German Empire* (New York: G. P. Putnam's Sons, 1899), 421–22.

7 *Under his government:* Henry W. Littlefield, *History of Europe Since 1815* (New York: Harper & Row, 1963), 96–97; Fritz Stern, *Gold and Iron: Bismarck, Bleichröder, and the Building of the German Empire* (New York: Vintage, 1979), 93.

7 *"applicable to all men":* Lincoln to Henry L. Pierce, et al., April 6, 1859, SW, 1859–1865, 19.

7 *"lost the future":* Matthew Arnold, *Culture and Anarchy* (1869), in *English Literature: The Victorian Period,* ed. George Morey Miller (New York: Scribner's, 1930, 1933), 439. Compare F. A. Hayek on the receding of the liberal tide in *The Constitution of Liberty,* 202. In this book I use the terms "liberal" and "free state" interchangeably, and have generally preferred the latter to the former. I have done so in order to avoid the ambiguities inherent in the terms "liberal" and "liberalism." In the nineteenth century, and in Europe to this day, "liberalism" refers to the principles of liberty ascendant in England after the Revolution of 1688–constitutional government, the rule of law, and the liberty of the individual in political, spiritual, and economic matters. In the United States, "liberalism" acquired, during the course of the twentieth century, a somewhat different meaning.

7 *"germ":* Lincoln, "Address to the Washington Temperance Society of Springfield, Illinois," February 22, 1842, SW, 1832–1858, 89.

7 *"the wolf's dictionary":* Lincoln, "Address at Sanitary Fair, Baltimore, Maryland," April 18, 1864, SW, 1859–1865, 590.

Part One: Into the Pit

1. Three Peoples on the Precipice

11 *Saint Petersburg, January 1861:* This section heading and those that follow are intended to give the reader a rough idea of the time and place with which each segment of the narrative is concerned. Not every incident or quotation in a particular section falls within the temporal and geographic limits set forth in the heading.

11 *the Winter Palace:* Geraldine Norman, *The Hermitage: The Biography of a Great Museum* (London: Jonathan Cape, 1997), 67–71.

11 *their wands:* A. A. Mosolov, *At the Court of the Last Tsar,* ed. A. A. Pilenco, trans. E. W. Dickes (London: Methuen, 1996), 198.

11 *catch the eye:* MR, 143.

11 *silk stockings:* Mosolov, *At the Court of the Last Tsar,* 194–196.

11 *Diamonds and sapphires:* E. A. Brayley Hodgetts, *The Court of Russia in the Nineteenth Century,* 2 vols. (New York: Charles Scribner, 1908), ii, 70.

11 *good looks:* That student of beauty, Kaiser Wilhelm II, remarked, "The Chevalier Garde and *Garde à Cheval* recruits were a nice-looking lot, though the fact that hardly any of them had any hips

made their white capes look as though they had been poured over their slim bodies"–Wilhelm II, *My Early Life* (New York: George H. Doran, 1926), 256.

12 *polonaise:* MR, 143; Mosolov, *At the Court of the Last Tsar,* 198–99.

12 *courtesy:* Hodgetts, *The Court of Russia in the Nineteenth Century,* ii, 70.

12 *"democratic air":* Bayard Taylor to James T. Fields, January 24, 1863, in *Life and Letters of Bayard Taylor,* ed. Marie Hansen-Taylor and Horace E. Scudder, 2 vols. (Boston: Houghton Mifflin, 1885), i, 407.

12 *His manner was amiable:* E. M. Almedingen, *The Emperor Alexander II: A Study* (London: Bodley Head, 1962), 204.

12 *"the Great Mogul":* Frederic Hamilton, *The Vanished Pomps of Yesterday* (Garden City, NY: Doubleday, 1934), 116.

12 *Vasily Zhukovsky:* Irina M. Semenko, *Vasily Zhukovsky* (Boston: G. K. Hall, 1976).

12 *"beautiful poem":* Edward Crankshaw, *The Shadow of the Winter Palace: Russia's Drift to Revolution 1825–1917* (New York: Da Capo, 2000), 155.

12 *"are times":* W. Bruce Lincoln, *The Romanovs: Autocrats of All the Russias* (New York: anchor, 1981), 431.

12 *"He does not give":* John Van der Kiste, *The Romanovs 1818–1959* (Stroud: Sutton, 2003), 31.

13 *authoritarian government:* Richard Pipes, *Russia Under the Old Regime* (Harmondsworth, Middlesex: Penguin, 1979), 24, 73.

13 *Russia never knew:* "The locus of original political authority," Richard Pipes writes, "was the private domain of the prince or tsar, his *oikos* or *dvor*. Within this domain the prince reigned absolute, exercising authority in the double capacity as sovereign and proprietor. Here he was in full command, a counterpart of the Greek *despotes,* the Roman *dominus,* and the Russian *gosudar',* that is lord, master, outright owner of all men and things"–Ibid., 21–23, 48–51, 65–73.

13 *mixed constitutions:* Thomas Babington Macaulay, *History of England,* WLM, i, 22, 119.

13 *"kholops":* Pipes, *Russia Under the Old Regime,* 85.

13 *exchanged one form:* Macaulay, *History of England,* WLM, i, 22, 34.

13 *Catherine the Great:* During Catherine's reign, the highest servants of the Crown (*dvoriane*) obtained title to their estates, and a tradition of private property grew up. Numerous restrictions on trade were abolished, among them most of the imperial monopolies–See Pipes, *Russia Under the Old Regime,* 69, 113–14, 131–33, 211.

13 *forestall the catastrophe:* Valerie Bunce, "Domestic Reform and International Change: The Gorbachev Reforms in Historical Perspective," IO, vol. 47, no. 1 (Winter 1993), 119; Terence Emmons, *The Russian Landed Gentry and the Peasant Emancipation of 1861* (Cambridge: Cambridge University Press, 1968); W. Bruce Lincoln, *The Great Reforms: Autocracy, Bureaucracy, and the Politics of Change in Imperial Russia* (DeKalb, IL: Northern Illinois University Press, 1990), xiii. For a different perspective, see Daniel Field, *The End of Serfdom: Nobility and Bureaucracy in Russia, 1855–1861* (Cambridge, MA: Harvard University Press, 1976).

13 *rapidly outstripping:* See Elie Halévy, *The Liberal Awakening 1815–1830,* 2d ed. (London: Ernest Benn, 1949), vii; A. J. P. Taylor, *The Struggle for Mastery in Europe 1848–1914* (Oxford: Oxford University Press, 1971), xxx; Henry W. Littlefield, *History of Europe Since 1815* (New York: Harper & Row, 1963), 1–12; and James McPherson, *Battle Cry of Freedom: The Civil War Era* (Oxford: Oxford University Press, 2003), 9–21.

14 *paternalism:* Shearer Davis Bowman, "Antebellum Planters and Vormarz Junkers in Comparative Perspective," AMH, vol. 85, no. 4 (October 1980), 779–808; Eugene D. Genovese, *Roll, Jordan, Roll: The World the Slaves Made* (New York: Pantheon, 1974), 4–7, 317. Compare Louis Hartz, *The Liberal Tradition in America: An Interpretation of American Political Thought Since the Revolution* (San Diego, CA: Harcourt Brace, 1983), 146–48, 178–83; Elizabeth Fox-Genovese and Eugene D. Genovese, *The Mind of the Master Class: History and Faith in the Southern Slaveholders' Worldview* (Cambridge: Cambridge University Press, 2005), 312.

14 *Landowners in Russia:* MCCW, 245; Peter Kolchin, "In Defense of Servitude: American Proslavery and Russian Proserfdom Arguments, 1760–1860," AHR, vol. 85, no. 4 (October 1980), 811–17. For a different perspective, see Field, *The End of Serfdom: Nobility and Bureaucracy in Russia, 1855–1861,* 22.

24 *parity in the Senate:* Ibid., 109–10.

24 *"Bluff Ben" Wade:* A. G. Riddle, *The Life of Benjamin F. Wade* (Cleveland: William W. Williams, 1886), 17.

24 *"squirrel rifles":* T. Harry Williams, *Lincoln and the Radicals* (Madison, WI: University of Wisconsin Press, 1972), 65.

25 *"Disappointment!":* David Herbert Donald, *"We Are Lincoln Men": Abraham Lincoln and His Friends* (New York: Simon & Schuster, 2003), 147.

25 *He bore the reputation:* Frederic Bancroft, *The Life of William H. Seward,* 2 vols. (Gloucester, MA: Peter Smith, 1967), ii, 82–83.

25 *Seward's zeal:* "Seward's reputation for radicalism was in large measure undeserved"–Eric Foner, *Free Soil, Free Labor, Free Men: The Ideology of the Republican Party Before the Civil War* (Oxford: Oxford University Press, 1982), 222.

25 *proclaimed the virtues of moderation:* The historian Glyndon Van Deusen has argued that Seward in November 1860 "felt compromise was not the answer" and changed his mind only in December, when he proposed that the territories be divided into two parts, with "New Mexico coming in as a slave state, the rest of the territory north of the compromise parallel being free"–Glyndon G. Van Deusen, *William Henry Seward* (New York: Oxford University Press, 1967), 243. Such an interpretation, if accepted, would add another layer of perversity to Seward's actions: unconvinced of the need for territorial compromise in November, he embraced it, in December, only after he learned that Lincoln was dead against it. It is more likely, however, that Seward was sympathetic to a revival of the Missouri line in November, when Weed first floated the idea in the *Albany Evening Journal.* In early December the rumor spread that Seward "wanted to make a great compromise like Clay and Webster!" Seward to Weed, December 3, 1860, in Thurlow Weed Barnes, *Memoir of Thurlow Weed* (Boston: Houghton Mifflin, 1884), 308. When Seward was summoned to a Republican caucus and asked whether he had authorized the proposals in the *Albany Evening Journal,* he pointedly refused to answer the question. "I kept my temper," he wrote to Weed. "I told them they would know what I think and what I propose when I do myself. . . . The Republican Party to-day is as uncompromising as the Secessionists in South Carolina. A month hence each may come to think that moderation is wiser." Seward to Weed, December 3, 1860, in Ibid., 308.

25 *the most uncompromising:* Harry V. Jaffa, *Crisis of the House Divided: An Interpretation of the Issues in the Lincoln-Douglas Debates* (Garden City, NY: Doubleday, 1959), 25. Lincoln was quietly prepared to compromise on several lesser questions; but on the critical question of territorial slavery he was uncompromising. See Kenneth M. Stampp, "Lincoln and the Strategy of Defense in the Crisis of 1861," JSH, vol. 11, no. 3 (August 1945), 299, and Harold Holtzer, *Lincoln at Cooper Union: The Speech That Made Abraham Lincoln President* (New York: Simon & Schuster, 2005), xix, 30. New Mexico, the apparent exception to this uncompromising policy, in fact proves the rule. David Herbert Donald noted that Lincoln was "willing for New Mexico to be admitted without prohibition of slavery, 'if further extension were hedged against.' But on one point he was immovable: the extension of slavery into the national territories"–David Herbert Donald, *Lincoln* (New York: Simon & Schuster, 1996), 270; David M. Potter, *Lincoln and His Party in the Secession Crisis* (New Haven: Yale University Press, 1962), 223. New Mexico, Lincoln knew, was not the key to compromise: the key to compromise lay in the application of the Missouri line principle, not merely to territory now held by the United States, but hereafter acquired by it. Lincoln could therefore offer the sop of New Mexico to the compromisers in his party without jeopardizing his revolution. His determination not to compromise any *significant* point was real. He believed that "the Missouri line extended [to territory now held or hereafter acquired], or Douglas's and Ely Thayer's popular sovereignty would lose us everything we gained by the election." Lincoln to Weed, December 17, 1860, in Barnes, *Memoir of Thurlow Weed,* 310–11. Lincoln said that, were he to consent to the extension of the Missouri line, the Fire Eaters would soon demand more: "a year will not pass," he said, " 'till we shall have to take Cuba as a condition upon which they will stay in the Union." Lincoln to James T. Hale, January 11, 1861, in Potter, *Lincoln and His Party in the Secession Crisis,* 160, 233.

26 *dispatched an emissary:* Lincoln had earlier extended an invitation to Weed to come to Springfield. Barnes, *Memoir of Thurlow Weed,* 293; Van Deusen, *William Henry Seward,* 240; Potter, *Lincoln and His Party in the Secession Crisis,* 69.

26 *Weed arrived:* LDD, ii, 302; Floyd S. Barringer, *Historic Homes of Springfield* (Springfield, IL: privately printed, 1966), 68; Thurlow Weed, *Autobiography of Thurlow Weed,* ed. Harriet A. Weed (Boston: Houghton Mifflin, 1883), 604; Van Deusen, *William Henry Seward,* 240.

26 *He seemed genuinely to hope:* John M. Taylor, *William Henry Seward: Lincoln's Right Hand* (New York: HarperCollins, 1991), 128.

26 *But on one subject:* Potter, *Lincoln and His Party in the Secession Crisis,* 165–69.

26 *gave Weed a paper:* Bancroft, *The Life of William H. Seward,* ii, 10.

26 *Seward could not bear:* Taylor, *William Henry Seward,* 127.

27 *pornography:* LGT, 58–59.

27 *Empire style:* Alexander, Grand Duke of Russia, *Once a Grand Duke* (New York: Cosmopolitan Book Corp.–Farrar & Rinehart, 1932), 60.

27 *cherry-colored robe:* LGT, 128.

27 *It was Alexander's habit:* Ibid.

28 *intimates of the court:* Orlando Figes, *Natasha's Dance: A Cultural History of Russia* (New York: Metropolitan, 2002), 72–74.

28 *"Here, boys":* LGT, 34.

29 *cut off his hand:* Bernard Pares, *A History of Russia,* 5th ed. (New York: Vintage, 1965), 363.

30 *"She is the woman":* W. E. Mosse, *Alexander II and the Modernization of Russia,* rev. ed. (New York: Collier, 1970), 30.

30 *had at first been happy:* Hodgetts, *The Court of Russia in the Nineteenth Century,* ii, 40–41.

30 *little blue dress:* Van der Kiste, *The Romanovs 1818–1959,* 15.

30 *a mistress:* MR, 144; LGT, 173; Stephen Graham, *Tsar of Freedom: The Life and Reign of Alexander II* (New Haven: Yale University Press, 1935), 70.

30 *The priest was compliant:* Mosse, *Alexander II and the Modernization of Russia,* 39.

30 *shrank from the reproaches:* Ibid.

30 *Count Adlerberg:* MR, 149; Sidney Harcave, *Years of the Golden Cockerel: The Last Romanov Tsars 1814–1917* (New York: Macmillan, 1968), 175; Mosse, *Alexander II and the Modernization of Russia,* 38.

31 *By adopting:* Compare Norman Peirera, "Alexander II and the Decision to Emancipate the Russian Serfs, 1855–1861," CSP, vol. 22 (March 1980), 99–115. See also Daniel Field, *The End of Serfdom: Nobility and Bureaucracy in Russia, 1855–1861,* 95.

31 *Editorial Commission:* Zakharova, "Autocracy and the Reforms of 1861–1871 in Russia: Choosing Paths of Development," RGR, 29–30; Field, *The End of Serfdom,* 164–65.

31 *practical sagacity:* Pares, *A History of Russia,* 365.

31 *no deep knowledge:* Field, *The End of Serfdom,* 166.

31 *Nicholas Milyutin:* W. Bruce Lincoln, *Nikolai Milyutin: An Enlightened Bureaucrat of the Nineteenth Century* (Newtonville, MA: Oriental Research Partners, 1977), 3, 5, 15.

31 *zealous reformer:* Milyutin's liberal credentials are open to question; he seems to have owed much to the traditions of the French Enlightenment, in which reform was regarded as the province of enlightened mandarins in the service of the state–Rieber, "Alexander II: A Revisionist View," JMH, vol. 43, no. 1 (March 1971), 53.

31 *the finest minds:* Zakharova, "Autocracy and the Reforms of 1861–1871 in Russia: Choosing Paths of Development," RGR, 29.

31 *informer:* Ibid., 27; Field, *The End of Serfdom,* 165.

31 *tool of the party:* Lincoln, *Nikolai Milyutin,* 44–45.

31 *"thickheaded scoundrel":* Field, *The End of Serfdom,* 165.

32 *sarcastic asides:* Graham, *Tsar of Freedom,* 42; see also Harcave, *Years of the Golden Cockerel,* 174.

32 *"I thought":* LGT, 125.

32 *dedicated emancipator:* Zakharova, "Autocracy and the Reforms of 1861–1871 in Russia: Choosing Paths of Development," RGR, 27; Field, *The End of Serfdom,* 166.

32 *"Egeria":* Graham, *Tsar of Freedom,* 43.

32 *a powerful ally:* MR, 151.

32 *Foreign visitors:* Bayard Taylor to James T. Fields, February 18, 1863, in *Life and Letters of Bayard Taylor,* ed. Hansen-Taylor and Scudder, i, 408.

32 *formality:* MR, 151.

32 "la petite bourgeoise": Van der Kiste, *The Romanovs 1818–1959,* 13.

33 *genuinely kind:* MR, 151.

33 *Grand Duchess Hélène Pavolvna:* MR, 129, 151.

33 *educated in Paris:* Elizabeth Narishkin-Kurkakin, *Under Three Tsars,* ed. René Fölöp Miller, trans. Julia E. Loesser (New York: E. P. Dutton, 1931), 23–24.

33 *reveled in the intrigue:* Count Paul Vassili [Ekaterina Rzewska Radziwill], *Behind the Veil at the Russian Court* (London: Cassell, 1914), 40–41.

33 *Thursday evenings:* Narishkin-Kurkakin, *Under Three Tsars,* 33–34.

33 *the Tsar himself:* Countess Kleinmichel, *Memories of a Shipwrecked World* (London: Brentano's, 1923), 60.

33 *According to the rumor:* Vassili, *Behind the Veil at the Russian Court,* 39–40.

34 *"hot, fervid":* MCCW, 3.

34 *"rebel born":* MCCW, 4.

34 *"had been so rampant":* Ibid.

34 *"was the torment":* Ibid.

34 *"state unless he were":* Ibid.

34 *"Can liberty":* Jean-Jacques Rousseau, *The Social Contract,* in Rousseau, *Political Writings,* trans. Frederick Watkins (Madison, WI: University of Wisconsin Press, 1986), 105.

34 *"Come what would":* MCCW, 4.

35 *"modest gentleman":* James Henry Hammond, *Secret and Sacred: The Diaries of James Henry Hammond,* ed. Carol Bleser (Oxford: Oxford University Press, 1988), 214.

35 *"No hope now":* MCCW, 4.

35 *"a nervous dread":* Ibid.

35 *to save:* McPherson, *Battle Cry of Freedom,* 245.

35 *"Western belle":* MCCW, 136.

36 *read the Earl of Clarendon's account:* MCCW, 7.

36 *"the born leaders":* Ibid.

36 *"political intrigue":* Ibid.

36 *"One of the first":* MCCW, 5 (emphasis in original).

36 *"a Caesar":* MCCW, 10.

36 *"There was to be":* MCCW, 11.

3. Thrust and Counter-Thrust

37 *The man who is warm:* Solzhenitsyn says this in *A Day in the Life of Ivan Denisovich.*

37 *forest zone:* Pipes, *Russia Under the Old Regime,* 1.

37 *his icon corner:* H. Sutherland Edwards, *The Russians at Home and Abroad: Sketches, Unpolitical and Political, of Russian Life Under Alexander II,* 2 vols. (London: W. M. H. Allen, 1879), i, 188.

37 *"red" or "beautiful" corner:* Pipes, *Russia Under the Old Regime,* 144.

37 *The stove:* Mary Matossian, "The Peasant Way of Life," in *The Peasant in Nineteenth-Century Russia,* ed. Wayne S. Vucinich (Stanford, CA: Stanford University Press, 1968), 5.

37 *"Russians are merrier":* Pipes, *Russia Under the Old Regime,* 157; Pares, *A History of Russia,* 31.

37 *beer- and mead-loving:* Edwards, *The Russians at Home and Abroad,* 249–50; Pipes, *Russia Under the Old Regime,* 157; Mary Matossian, "The Peasant Way of Life," in *The Peasant in Nineteenth-Century Russia,* ed. Vucinich, 13.

37 *Vodka:* James H. Billington, *The Icon and the Axe: An Interpretive History of Russian Culture* (New York: Vintage, 1970), 86.

37 *zakouska:* Edwards, *The Russians at Home and Abroad,* i, 251.

37 *agricultural yields:* Pipes, *Russia Under the Old Regime,* 7.

38 *Haxthausen:* Ibid., 11.

38 *unable to maintain:* Ibid., 175, 178.

38 *acquiring land:* Serge A. Zenkovsky, "The Emancipation of the Serfs in Retrospect," RR, vol. 20, no. 4 (October 1961), 284.

38 *passive resistance:* Field, *The End of Serfdom,* 65.

38 *"unhinged by masturbation":* Ibid., 207.

38 *"I am more":* Ibid., 71 (emphasis in original).

38 *"reds":* MR, 132.

39 *"greatly doubted":* Mosse, *Alexander II and the Modernization of Russia,* 53.

39 *Russian nobility:* Ibid.

39 *He fell sick:* Compare Edward Crankshaw, *The Shadow of the Winter Palace,* 171.

39 *"Do not":* Mosse, *Alexander II and the Modernization of Russia,* 61.

39 *The Tsar visited:* Field, *The End of Serfdom,* 167, 346.

39 *"Sire":* LGT, 126.

39 *Count Panin:* David Saunders, *Russia in the Age of Reaction and Reform* (London: Longman, 1992), 231.

39 *"Things assumed":* MR, 132.

40 *rose in the Senate:* Seward, "Speech in the Senate of the United States," January 12, 1861, *WWHS,* 651–69.

40 *what the Union would be worth:* Ibid., 652.

40 *opened the door:* Ibid., 667–68; Bancroft, *The Life of William H. Seward,* ii, 14–15; Van Deusen, *William Henry Seward,* 245; Albert D. Kirwan, *John J. Crittenden: The Struggle for the Union* (Lexington, KY: University of Kentucky Press, 1962), 398.

40 *policy of compromise:* Seward's policy in the secession crisis is analyzed by Eric Foner in *Free Soil, Free Labor, Free Men: The Ideology of the Republican Party Before the Civil War,* 223.

40 *Baron de Stoeckle:* Van Deusen, *William Henry Seward,* 247–48.

40 *"It seems to me":* Bancroft, *The Life of William H. Seward,* ii, 37.

40 *"Away with all parties":* Ibid., ii, 22.

40 *shattered on the table:* Robert W. Johannsen, *Stephen A. Douglas* (New York: Oxford University Press, 1973), 828.

40 *The French Minister:* Van Deusen, *William Henry Seward,* 245.

41 *"unhonored grave":* Ibid.

41 *"God damn":* Ibid., 249.

41 *"baffled":* Lincoln to Seward, February 1, 1861, SW, 1859–1865, 197.

41 *"in a good deal":* Ibid.

41 *"I say now":* Ibid. (emphasis in original).

41 *"Serpentine Seward":* Williams, *Lincoln and the Radicals,* 19.

41 *"The majority":* Allan Nevins, *The Emergence of Lincoln: Prologue to Civil War 1859–1861* (New York: Charles Scribner, 1959), 439.

42 *a few thousand men:* Hans Delbrück, *History of the Art of War,* 4 vols. Vol. IV: *The Dawn of Modern Warfare,* trans. Walter J. Renfroe, Jr. (Lincoln, NE: University of Nebraska Press, 1990), 244–45; Gordon A. Craig, *The Politics of the Prussian Army 1640–1945* (Oxford: Oxford University Press, 1964), 4–5.

42 *"soldier state":* SS, 154.

42 *Pomeranian nobleman:* Roon was decended, in the paternal line, from a family originally Dutch.

42 *He proposed:* Craig, *The Politics of the Prussian Army 1640–1945,* 140–41.

42 *"citizen army":* Edward Crankshaw, *Bismarck* (Harmondsworth, Middlesex: Penguin, 1990), 109.

42 *militarize the nation:* SS, 129.

42 *"men known to oppose":* SS, 129.

43 *Supreme Warlord:* Walter Goerlitz, *History of the German General Staff, 1657–1945,* trans. Brian Battershaw (New York: Frederick Praeger, 1953, 1956), 4.

43 *The reformation:* SS, 130.

43 *It was a question:* SS, 135–36.

43 *"Faust complains":* BMS, 12.

43 *"hating":* Hajo Holborn, "Bismarck's Realpolitik," JHI, vol. 21, no. 1 (January 1960), 88.

43 *most inspired fantasist:* Compare Isaiah Berlin, "Winston Churchill in 1940," in Berlin, *Personal Impressions,* ed. Henry Hardy (Harmondsworth, Middlesex: Penguin, 1982), 3–17.

44 *"cannot create":* BMS, 115.

44 *"God did not"*: BMS, 13.
44 *Middle High German:* Shearer Davis Bowman, "Antebellum Planters and Vormarz Junkers in Comparative Perspective," AMH, vol. 85, no. 4 (October 1980), 781.
44 *the most democratic:* Macaulay, *History of England,* WLM, i, 31.
45 *"promotion of a burgher":* Emil Ludwig, *Hindenburg,* trans. Eden and Cedar Paul (Philadelphia: John G. Winston, 1935), 20; Delbrück, *The Dawn of Modern Warfare,* 256.
45 *as a boy:* Sidney Whitman, *Personal Reminiscences of Prince Bismarck* (New York: D. Appleton, 1903), 60.
45 *a familiar formula:* Witness the careers of Julius Caesar and Franklin D. Roosevelt. See Ronald Syme, *The Roman Revolution* (Oxford: Oxford University Press, 1989), 15, 25; Joseph Alsop, *FDR: 1882–1945: A Centenary Remembrance* (New York: Viking, 1982), 30.
45 *Ferdinand:* BMS, 10–11.
45 *"hatred":* Fritz Stern, *Gold and Iron: Bismarck, Bleichröder, and the Building of the German Empire* (New York: Vintage, 1979), 97.
45 *"Hotspur of reaction":* Heinrich von Treitschke, *Treitschke's History of Nineteenth-Century Germany,* trans. Eden and Cedar Paul, 7 vols. (New York: AMS Press, 1968), vii, 445.
46 *four rounds of ammunition:* Gedanken, i, 21; Crankshaw, *Bismarck,* 50–51.
46 *The Austrian representative:* Henry A. Kissinger, "The White Revolutionary: Reflections on Bismarck," D, vol. 97, no. 3 (Summer 1968), 901.
46 *"sandbox":* Friedrich Nietzsche, *Beyond Good and Evil: Prelude to a Philosophy of the Future,* trans. Walter Kauffman (New York: Vintage, 1989), 180.
46 *consent of the Kaiser:* Thomas Carlyle, *History of Friedrich II of Prussia, called Frederick the Great,* 10 vols. (London: Chapman & Hall, 1872), i, 38.
46 *"I had been brought up":* Vilbort, *Siècle* (June 1866), in Ludwig Bamberger, *Count Bismarck* (Breslau: Günther, 1869), 124.
46 *"Germany is too small":* Gesammelten Werke, ii, 139ff.
47 *"put on ice":* BMS, 43.
47 *his health:* Bismarck to his sister, June 29, 1859, *Gesammelten Werke,* xiv (1), 530.

4. To Proclaim Liberty to the Captives

48 *hackney coachmen:* William Howard Russell, *My Diary North and South,* ed. Eugene H. Berwanger (New York: Knopf, 1988), 40.
48 *"Abe":* Donald, *Lincoln,* 278.
48 *his boorish manners:* Bayne, *Tad Lincoln's Father,* 6–7.
48 *polished circles of the East:* Russell, *My Diary North and South,* 45
48 *savage Goth:* Edward Gibbon, *The History of the Decline and Fall of the Roman Empire,* ed. J. H. B. Bury, 7 vols. (London: Methuen, 1909), i, 156–58, 183–87.
49 *"plain, ploughed":* EHA, 817.
49 *"beyond credence":* MCCW, 13.
49 *Mrs. August Belmont:* See the thinly veiled portrait of this lady in the character of Mrs. Julius Beaufort in Mrs. Wharton's novel, *The Age of Innocence* (1920; New York: Library of America, 1985), 1030–31.
49 *When the newspapers:* Jay Monaghan, *A Diplomat in Carpet Slippers: Abraham Lincoln Deals with Foreign Affairs* (Lincoln, NE: University of Nebraska Press, 1997), 31.
49 *Her husband:* Niall Ferguson, *The House of Rothschild: The World's Banker, 1849–1999* (London: Penguin, 1999), 115–17. Mrs. August Belmont was the daughter of Commodore Perry and the niece of John Slidell, afterwards Jefferson Davis's emissary to the court of Napoleon III.
49 *"paus'd leisurely" . . . "an assassin's knife":* Walt Whitman, "Death of Abraham Lincoln," SDC, 308.
49 *"four sorts":* Ibid., SDC, 309.
50 *"illiterate":* HLL, 14.
50 *"saw in a mirror":* Edmund Wilson, *Patriotic Gore: Studies in the Literature of the American Civil War* (Boston: Northeastern University Press, 1984), 128.
50 *dingy law office:* HLL, 365.

50   *"staring vacantly"*: Donald, *Lincoln,* 163.
50   *His opposition:* HLL, 246.
50   *aroused Lincoln's wrath:* HLL, 290.
50   *"In the office":* HLL, 295.
50   *"The day of ":* Ibid.
51   *"two great ideas":* Ibid.
51   *"profoundest":* HLL, 296.
51   *"quivered":* HLL, 296.
51   *"We are now":* Lincoln, "House Divided Speech," June 16, 1858, SW, 1832–1858, 426 (emphasis in original).
51   *"become lawful in all":* Ibid.
52   *"total overthrow":* Lincoln to Henry L. Pierce, et al., April 6, 1859, SW, 1859–1865, 18.
52   *"all men are":* Lincoln to Joshua F. Speed, August 24, 1855, SW, 1832–1858, 363.
52   *a world struggle:* Jaffa, *Crisis of the House Divided,* 84–85, 86, 186, 344.
52   *"millions of free":* Lincoln, "Speech on the Kansas–Nebraska Act at Peoria, Illinois," October 16, 1854, SW, 1832–1858, 340.
52   *Scholars have criticized:* See Richard Hofstadter, *The American Political Tradition and the Men Who Made It,* 142–50, and J. G. Randall, *Lincoln the President,* 2 vols. (New York: Dodd, Mead, 1945), 107–08. Other scholars have taken Lincoln's arguments seriously. See Jaffa, *Crisis of the House Divided: An Interpretation of the Issues in the Lincoln-Douglas Debates;* Don E. Fehrenbacher, *Prelude to Greatness: Lincoln in the 1850s* (Stanford, CA: Stanford University Press, 1962), 81; and James McPherson, *Battle Cry of Freedom: The Civil War Era,* 181.
52   *"definitions and axioms":* Lincoln to Henry L. Pierce, et al., April 6, 1859, SW, 1859–1865, 19. The struggle in America between the philosophy of freedom and the philosophy of coercion was, Lincoln said, "essentially a People's contest. . . . a struggle for maintaining in the world, that form and substance of government, whose leading object is, to elevate the condition of men–to lift artificial weights from all shoulders–to clear the paths of laudable pursuit for all–to afford all, an unfettered start, and a fair chance, in the race of life"–Lincoln, Message to Congress in Special Session, July 4, 1861, SW, 1859–1865, 259.
53   *"I have never had":* Lincoln, "Speech at Independence Hall, Philadelphia, Pennsylvania," February 22, 1861, SW, 1859–1865, 213.
53   *"a little engine":* HLL, 304.
53   *"the family of the lion":* Lincoln, "Address to the Young Men's Lyceum of Springfield, Illinois: The Perpetuation of Our Political Institutions," January 27, 1838, SW, 1832–1858, 34 (emphasis in original omitted).
53   *yearning for something more:* HLL, 176.
54   *old boyar nobility:* MR, 2.
54   *a new class of men:* Ibid.; Pipes, *Russia Under the Old Regime,* 95.
54   *"amiable to the point":* Barbara W. Tuchman, *The Proud Tower: A Portrait of the World Before the War 1890–1914* (New York: Ballantine Books, 1996), 71.
54   *"Prince, freedom!":* MR, 133.
54   *contesting the Tsar's will:* On the question of why Russian planters were, as rule, less effective in opposing Tsar Alexander's revolution than their counterparts in the American South were in opposing Lincoln's, see Peter Kolchin, "In Defense of Servitude: American Proslavery and Russian Proserfdom Arguments, 1760–1860," AHR, vol. 85, no. 4 (October 1980), 820–26.
54   *hands trembled:* Vassili, *Behind the Veil at the Russian Court,* 52.
54   *Afterwards he made:* LGT, 131.
55   *Lent:* Daniel Field, "The Year of Jubilee," RGR, 42.
55   *Memories:* Serge A. Zenkovsky, "The Emancipation of the Serfs in Retrospect," RR, vol. 20, no. 4 (October 1961), 286; Field, *The End of Serfdom,* 45.
55   *Philaret:* MR, 134.
55   *Others wept:* Vassili, *Behind the Veil at the Russian Court,* 52.
55   *"Christ is risen!":* Irina Paperno, "The Liberation of the Serfs as a Cultural Symbol," RR, vol. 50, no. 4 (October 1991), 426.

55   *"The officers"*: MR, 134.

55   *"Well, sir?"*: MR, 133.

56   *delicate features . . . his eyes*: Otto Friedrich, *Blood and Iron: From Bismarck to Hitler, the von Moltke Family's Impact on German History* (New York: HarperPerennial, 1996), 29.

57   *"continuous inner tension"*: Goerlitz, *History of the German General Staff, 1657–1945,* 74.

57   *"Plumes"*: Ibid., 32.

57   *"My life"*: Ibid., 61.

57   *"to put king"*: SS, 49, 54.

57   *not to his father*: Friedrich, *Blood and Iron,* 22–24.

58   *art and music*: Friedrich August Dressler, *Moltke in His Home,* trans. Mrs. Charles Edward Barrett-Lennard (London: John Murray, 1907).

58   *prose romance*: Moltke, "The Two Friends," in *Moltke: His Life and Character Sketched in Journals, Letters, Memoirs, a Novel and Autobiographical Notes,* trans. Mary Herms (New York: Harper, 1892), 39–95.

58   *since Xenophon*: Ibid., 22.

58   *"gray fogs"*: Helmuth von Moltke to Adolf von Moltke, January 28, 1867, in *Letters of Field-Marshal Count Helmuth von Moltke to His Mother and Brothers,* trans. Clara Bell and Henry W. Fischer (New York: Harper, 1892), 180.

58   *"Build no more fortresses"*: Philip Neame, *German Strategy in the Great War* (London: Edward Arnold, 1923), 2.

58   *railway strategy*: Von Treitschke, *Treitschke's History of Nineteenth-Century Germany,* vii, 277.

58   *His delicate pallor*: Moltke: His Life and Character, 251.

58   *War*: "War therefore is an act of violence intended to compel our opponent to fulfill our will." Carl von Clausewitz, *On War,* ed. Anatol Rapoport (London: Penguin, 1982), 101.

59   *"Circumstances which"*: Seward to Lincoln, March 2, 1861, in CW, iv, 273; ii, 43–44.

59   *"I can't afford"*: Donald, *"We Are Lincoln Men,"* 149.

59   *Muffled batteries . . . Sharpshooters in green coats*: Bayne, *Tad Lincoln's Father,* 7.

60   *A sullen crowd*: Ibid.

60   *"There goes that Illinois ape"*: Ibid., 8.

5. Mobilization

61   *"Health good"*: T, 207.

61   *"It's spring!"*: T, 185.

62   *"nature, the air"*: Ibid.

62   *Justice of the Peace*: Tolstoy to Countess A. A. Tolstaya, May 14, 1861, TL, 142; Marc Raeff, *Plans for Political Reform in Imperial Russia, 1730–1905* (Englewood Cliffs, NJ: Prentice-Hall, 1966), 121; Field, "The Year of Jubilee," RGR, 43–44.

62   *"feels the need"*: Tolstoy to Botkin, January 4, 1858, in Boris Eikhenbaum, *Tolstoi in the Sixties* (Ann Arbor: Ardis, 1982), 3.

62   *"Well, lads"*: Aylmer Maude, *The Life of Tolstoy: The First Fifty Years* (New York: Dodd, Mead & Co., 1917), 227.

62   *"all the landowners"*: T, 215 (emphasis in original).

62   *a petition*: T, 213; Maude, *The Life of Tolstoy: The First Fifty Years,* 226–28.

62   *"Our life"*: Franco Venturi, *Roots of Revolution: A History of the Populist and Socialist Movements in Nineteenth-Century Russia* (New York: Knopf, 1960), 68–69; compare Field, "The Year of Jubilee," RGR, 48–49.

63   *imperial treasury*: The Tsar, conscious of the need for fiscal prudence, was unduly parsimonious in designing his emancipation settlement; his reforms left both the nobility and the peasantry in a desperate condition—Rieber, "Alexander II: A Revisionist View," JMH, vol. 43, no. 1 (March 1971), 50–51.

63   *struggled under a heavy burden*: Emmons, *The Russian Landed Gentry and the Peasant Emancipation of 1861,* 26.

63   *not yet recovered*: Ibid., 28–29.

63 *"in the coolest and most conscientious":* Tolstoy to V. P. Botkin, January 26, 1862, TL, 153.

63 *wore down his spirit:* Tolstoy, *A Confession and Other Religious Writings,* trans. Jane Kentish (Harmondsworth, Middlesex: Penguin, 1987), 27–28; Tatyana Andreyevna Kuzminskaya (née Behrs), *Tolstoy As I Knew Him: My Life at Home and at Yasnaya Polyana* (New York: Macmillan, 1948), 67.

63 *its obligation to serve:* Pipes, *Russia Under the Old Regime,* 113, 133, 184.

63 *compulsory service:* Ibid., 89.

63 *civic responsibility:* Ibid., 189.

63 *apolitical mentality:* Ibid., 188.

63 *"I absolutely must":* T, 82.

63 *"Girls":* T, 129 (emphasis added).

64 *"living like a beast":* T, 66.

64 *"awful lust":* T, 142.

64 *"everything fainted":* T, 168.

64 *"What is it":* T, 175.

64 *"Again the same question":* T, 200.

64 *"What's the point":* Tolstoy to A. A. Fet, October 17/29, 1860, TL, 142.

64 *Massachusetts 6th:* Charles B. Clark, "Baltimore and the Attack on the Sixth Massachusetts Regiment, April 19, 1861," MHM, 56 (March 1961), 39–71.

65 *"I don't believe":* John Hay, Diary, April 24, 1861, in *Inside Lincoln's White House: The Complete Civil War Diary of John Hay,* ed. Michael Burlingame and John R. Turner Ettlinger (Carbondale and Edwardsville, IL: Southern Illinois University Press, 1997), 11.

65 *"Why":* ALH, iv, 152.

65 *79th New York:* Bayne, *Tad Lincoln's Father,* 52.

65 *a Southern city:* Henry Adams recalled "the simple, old-fashioned, Southern tone" of Washington society in 1860–61–EHA, 816.

65 *French overtones:* Bayne, *Tad Lincoln's Father,* 3ff.

65 *conversed in French:* Ibid., 8, 26–27.

65 *regulated by the bugle:* Ibid., 36.

66 *reigning belle:* Ibid.

66 *"exceedingly":* Peg A. Lamphier, *Kate Chase and William Sprague: Politics and Gender in a Civil War Marriage* (Lincoln, NE: University of Nebraska Press, 2003), 23.

66 *Miss Chase:* Bayne, *Tad Lincoln's Father,* 36; Lamphier, *Kate Chase and William Sprague,* 24.

66 *getting what she wanted:* Bayne, *Tad Lincoln's Father,* 36.

66 *"The President seems":* Ibid., 67–68.

66 *"Pa looked":* Ruth Painter Randall, *Lincoln's Sons* (Boston: Little, Brown, 1955), 107; Bayne, *Tad Lincoln's Father,* 30–31.

66 *an expedition:* Jean H. Baker, *Mary Todd Lincoln: A Biography* (New York: W. W. Norton, 1987), 184–87; Justin G. Turner and Linda Levitt Turner, *Mary Todd Lincoln: Her Life and Letters* (New York: Knopf, 1972), 88.

67 *the lot of chaperone:* Bayne, *Tad Lincoln's Father,* 43.

67 *"big, worn":* Ibid., 13, 69.

67 *"sometimes":* Ibid., 13.

67 *"You don't know":* Ibid., 5.

67 *"sad and silent":* Ibid., 32.

67 *"sprawled out":* Ibid., 69.

68 *"My friend":* Lincoln, "Speech at Chicago Illinois," July 10, 1858, SW, 1832–1858, 458.

68 *"some universally":* HLL, 325.

68 *"He spoke to me":* Bayne, *Tad Lincoln's Father,* 69.

68 *"Why, Julie":* Ibid.

68 *a military order:* T. Harry Williams, *Lincoln and His Generals* (New York: Vintage, 1952), 7; compare David Herbert Donald, *Lincoln,* 439.

68 *paramilitary units:* Donald, *Lincoln,* 254.

68 *"monster meetings":* Ibid., 254.

68 *"in a form military":* EHA, 810.

69   *"For all his genius"*: Ronald Syme, *The Roman Revolution* (Oxford: Oxford University Press, 1960), 56.

69   *the Secretary of State was furtively carrying on:* Donald, *Lincoln,* 289–92; McPherson, *Battle Cry of Freedom,* 268.

69   *policy of conciliation:* Glyndon G. Van Deusen, *Thurlow Weed: Wizard of the Lobby* (Boston: Little, Brown, 1947), 270.

69   *"without a policy"*: Seward, "Some Thoughts for the President's Consideration," in Bancroft, *The Life of William H. Seward,* ii, 132–33; CW, iv, 317–18.

69   *"ripe"*: Roon to Bismarck, June 27, 1861, *Gedanken,* i, 240.

70   *Faubourg Saint-Germain: Gedanken,* i, 223.

70   *not only French: Gedanken,* i, 219.

70   *"cream": Gedanken,* i, 219.

70   *"best brain"*: Ibid.

70   *"the court"*: Ibid.

70   *suite of opulent rooms: Gedanken,* i, 225.

70   *"three or four"* . . . *"absolutely faultless"*: Ibid.

70   *"wines of high quality": Gedanken,* i, 226.

70   *"nothing but the very best"* . . . *"terribly high": Gedanken,* i, 225.

70   *"jewels"*: Mosolov, *At the Court of the Last Tsar,* 231.

70   *plundered by the Bolsheviks:* Ibid.

70   *the imperial train:* Bismarck to his sister, October 19, 1859, *Gesammelten Werke,* xiv (1), 541.

71   *the Russian language:* BMS, 44.

71   *the soirées:* Bismarck to his sister, March 26/14, 1861, *Gesammelten Werke,* xiv (1), 567–68.

71   *Grand Duchess Hélène:* Vassili, *Behind the Veil at the Russian Court,* 39.

71   *The aged Empress:* Bismarck to his wife, June 28, 1859, *Gesammelten Werke,* xiv (1), 529.

71   *"goodness itself"*: Bismarck to his sister, June 29, 1859, *Gesammelten Werke,* xiv (1), 530.

71   *"charming naturalness"*: Bismarck to his wife, June 28, 1859, *Gesammelten Werke,* xiv (1), 529.

71   *fond of Bismarck:* Bismarck to his sister, July 1/13, 1860, *Gesammelten Werke,* xiv (1), 556.

72   *Russian diplomatic service:* BMS, 45.

72   *"Three years ago"*: Bismarck to his sister, January 17/5, 1862, *Gesammelten Werke,* xiv (1), 581.

72   *"Dull places"*: Bismarck to his sister, March 7, 1862, *Gesammelten Werke,* xiv (1), 582.

72   *"break with the Chamber"*: Bismarck to Roon, July 2, 1861, *Gesammelten Werke,* xiv (1), 571.

6. Violence

73   *blackberries:* William T. Sherman, *Memoirs of General William T. Sherman by Himself,* 2 vols. (New York: D. Appleton, 1875), i, 181.

73   *On the march:* Robert S. Harper, *Irvin McDowell and the First Battle of Bull Run* (Columbus, OH: Ohio State Museum, 1961), 4.

74   *"You are green"*: Williams, *Lincoln and His Generals,* 21.

74   *If McDowell doubted:* James B. Fry, *McDowell and Tyler in the Campaign of Bull Run* (New York: D. Van Nostrand, 1884), 13–14; Harper, *Irvin McDowell and the First Battle of Bull Run,* 2; Williams, *Lincoln and His Generals,* 18–19.

74   *The air:* Edwin S. Barrett, *What I Saw at Bull Run* (Boston: Beacon Press, 1886), 15.

74   *a strange dream:* Bayne, *Tad Lincoln's Father,* 75.

75   *At two o'clock:* This account of the battle of Bull Run is drawn primarily from James B. Fry, *McDowell and Tyler in the Campaign of Bull Run;* Edwin S. Barrett, *What I Saw at Bull Run*; James Longstreet, *From Manassas to Appomattox: Memoirs of the Civil War in America* (Philadelphia: J. B. Lippincott, 1896); William T. Sherman, *Memoirs of General William T. Sherman by Himself,* i, 181–88; and Benton J. Lossing, *Pictorial History of the Civil War,* 2 vols. (Philadelphia: David McKay, 1866), i, 584–608.

75   *"Pa says"*: Bayne, *Tad Lincoln's Father,* 53.

76   *While the President:* Doris Kearns Goodwin, *Team of Rivals: The Political Genius of Abraham Lincoln* (New York: Simon & Schuster, 2005), 371.

76 *To the crypt:* Thomas Carlyle, *History of Friedrich II of Prussia, called Frederick the Great,* 10 vols. (London: Chapman & Hall, 1872), x, 194.

76 *The regiments were intended:* Craig, *The Politics of the Prussian Army 1640–1945,* 151.

76 *A minister with liberal sympathies:* Ibid., 152.

76 *"I do not understand":* Ibid.

77 *"fantastic corporal":* Ibid., 149.

77 *dead commanders:* Ibid.

77 *"power to be wrested":* SS, 141.

77 *"power and the army":* SS, 141, 135.

77 *abolish the constitution:* Crankshaw, *Bismarck,* 112.

77 *"produce an atmosphere":* Craig, *The Politics of the Prussian Army 1640–1945,* 153.

77 *Manteuffel took personal offense:* Ibid.

77 *Strafford in the Tower:* Ibid.

77 *"cleansing mud bath":* Goerlitz, *History of the German General Staff, 1657–1945,* 80.

77 *Thirty-four thousand:* Craig, *The Politics of the Prussian Army 1640–1945,* 155.

78 *"absolute a tyrant":* MCCW, 262.

78 *"métier is to be":* MCCW, 255.

78 *"was not a greater":* MCCW, 191.

78 *The patent:* MCCW, 249.

78 *During many decades:* Elisabeth Muhlenfeld, *Mary Boykin Chesnut: A Biography* (Baton Rouge: Louisiana State University Press, 1981), 47.

78 *"roars and shouts":* MCCW, 250.

78 *"Merciful God!":* MCCW, xix.

78 *known George Washington:* MCCW, 201.

78 *Smoothing irons:* MCCW, 202–03.

79 *Candles . . . Violets:* MCCW, 77.

79 *"as if they were":* MCCW, 211.

79 *"the transcendent virtues":* MCCW, 217.

79 *"cutting out":* MCCW, 202.

79 *"I warn you":* MCCW, 217.

79 *stupid:* See, e.g., MCCW, 242, 365–66.

79 *"have grown accustomed":* MCCW, 250.

79 *"weird sounds":* MCCW, 256.

79 *"memoirs of the times":* MCCW, xviii.

80 *Louisa Bartow:* MCCW, 84.

80 *Francis Stebbins Bartow:* MCCW, 3.

80 *"If my Joseph":* MCCW, 90.

80 *spanking bays:* MCCW, 123.

80 *"was not civil enough":* MCCW, 83.

80 *One day:* MCCW, 100.

80 *she guessed what happened:* MCCW, 101.

81 *"I did not know":* Ibid.

81 *Mrs. Davis came:* MCCW, 102.

7. A Whiff of Powder

82 *"sinful encounter":* René Fülöp-Miller, *Rasputin: The Holy Devil,* trans. F. S. Flint and D. F. Tait (Garden City, NY: Garden City Publishing, 1928), 32.

82 *"cast all their garments":* Ibid.

82 *"I flagellate":* Billington, *The Icon and the Axe,* 177.

82 *"Here and there":* Fülöp-Miller, *Rasputin: The Holy Devil,* 32.

82 *"the devil of pride":* Ibid., 223.

82 *forcing them to undress:* Ibid., 36.

82   *"told me at once"*: Ibid., 184–85; Robert K. Massie, *Nicholas and Alexandra* (New York: Ballantine, 2000), 337.

83   *"Certainly, little father"*: Fülöp-Miller, *Rasputin: The Holy Devil*, 54–55; see also 215.

83   *"Mama"*: Fyodor Dostoyevsky, *The Brothers Karamazov*, trans. David McDuff (Harmondsworth, Middlesex: Penguin, 2003), 374–75.

83   *"Paradise"*: Ibid., 392.

83   *New Jerusalem:* Compare CP, 236.

83   *Others regarded:* Fülöp-Miller, *Rasputin: The Holy Devil*, 121.

83   *"a way to God"*: Figes, *Natasha's Dance*, 293.

83   *Holy Rus':* Dostoyevsky, *The Brothers Karamazov*, 368.

83   *spiritual anarch:* Compare Richard Pipes, *Russia Under the Old Regime*, 162; Irina Paperno, "The Liberation of the Serfs as a Cultural Symbol," RR, vol. 50, no. 4 (October 1991), 429.

84   *He was God's vicar:* Pipes, *Russia Under the Old Regime*, 161.

84   *each peasant personally:* Ibid.

84   *liquid gold:* Venturi, *Roots of Revolution*, 211; compare Field, "The Year of Jubilee," RGR, 46.

84   *"true liberty"*: Venturi, *Roots of Revolution*, 212.

84   "The Tsar will give": Pipes, *Russia Under the Old Regime*, 162.

84   *"We no longer"*: Venturi, *Roots of Revolution*, 211.

84   "Volia": Daniel Field, *Rebels in the Name of the Tsar* (Boston: Unwin Hyman, 1989), 44.

84   *Old Believer:* Venturi, *Roots of Revolution*, 214.

84   *The figure "10%"*: Ibid.

84   *"true volia"*: N. A. Krylov to A. P. Ermolova, April 13, 1861, in Field, *Rebels in the Name of the Tsar*, 72.

84   *His claims:* P. F. Kozlialinov, Governor of Kazan Province, to the Minister of Internal Affairs, April 13, 1861, in ibid., 37; Paperno, "The Liberation of the Serfs as a Cultural Symbol," RR, vol. 50, no. 4 (October 1991), 428.

84   *slain with axes:* Venturi, *Roots of Revolution*, 215.

84   *"true liberty"*: Ibid.

84   *Bezdna:* Ibid., 215–16.

84   *fifty-one people:* Apraksin's Second Report to the Tsar, April 19, 1861, in Field, *Rebels in the Name of the Tsar*, 58.

84   *thin, small:* Venturi, *Roots of Revolution*, 216.

84   *Petrov held:* Field, *Rebels in the Name of the Tsar*, 47; Paperno, "The Liberation of the Serfs as a Cultural Symbol," RR, vol. 50, no. 4 (October 1991), 431;

85   *"A great battle has been fought"*: MCCW, 106–06.

85   *"Where is the President?"*: ALH, iv, 353.

85   *black ostrich plumes:* Heros von Borcke, *Memoirs of the Confederate War for Independence*, 2 vols. (New York: Peter Smith, 1938), i, 22.

85   *tall boots and a yellow sash:* Ibid.

85   *the very image:* Ibid.; Edgar Erskine Hume, "Colonel Heros von Borcke: A Famous Prussian Volunteer in the Confederate States Army," in *Southern Sketches, First Series*, no. 2, ed. J. D. Eggleston (Charlottesville, VA: Historical Publishing, 1935), 5.

85   *Stuart's eyes:* Von Borcke, *Memoirs of the Confederate War for Independence*, i, 21–22.

86   *General Joe Johnston:* Fry, *McDowell and Tyler in the Campaign of Bull Run*, 37–38; Harper, *Irvin McDowell and the First Battle of Bull Run*, 5; Gamaliel Bradford, *Confederate Portraits* (Boston: Houghton Mifflin, 1914), 3–7.

86   *Panic set in:* Longstreet, *From Manassas to Appomattox*, 50; Barrett, *What I Saw at Bull Run*, 26.

86   *a rout:* Barrett, *What I Saw at Bull Run*, 27.

86   *Lincoln was still:* ALH, iv, 355.

86   *he telegraphed:* The telegram to McClellan was sent at two in the morning–McPherson, *Battle Cry of Freedom*, 348.

87   *The only newspaper:* Gedanken, i, 245.

87   *"unpleasantly surprised"*: Gedanken, i, 248

87 *The plan:* Lothar Gall, *Bismarck: The White Revolutionary,* trans. J. A. Underwood, 2 vols. (London: Allen & Unwin, 1986), i, 167.

87 *a memorandum:* Bismarck, "Denkschrift über die deutsche Frage," July 1861, in *Gesammelten Werke,* iii, 266–70.

87 *The pressure:* Bismarck to Roon, July 2, 1861, *Gedanken,* i, 243.

87 *"who is going to":* Gall, *Bismarck,* i, 167.

87 *Altogether the King thought:* The plan for a march on Berlin was formally approved in January 1862–Craig, *The Politics of the Prussian Army 1640–1945,* 159.

88 *"preserved from her youthful days":* *Gedanken,* i, 121.

88 *"stupid admiration":* BGE, 39.

88 *at breakfast:* *Gedanken,* i, 123.

88 *"his knightly spirit":* *Gedanken,* i, 123.

88 *"thought me crazier:"* *Gedanken,* i, 249.

88 *As the two men strolled:* H. W. Dulcken, *Life of the Emperor William the First of Germany and King of Prussia* (London: Ward, Lock, 1888), 48; Paul Wiegler, *William the First: His Life and Times,* trans. Constance Vesey (London: Allen & Unwin, 1929), 200.

88 *In June:* William Cassius Goodloe to General David S. Goodloe, June 19, 1861, in James Rood Robertson, *A Kentuckian at the Court of the Tsars: The Ministry of Cassius Marcellus Clay to Russia* (Berea College, KY: Berea College Press, 1935), 46.

89 *a few hundred revolts:* Venturi, *Roots of Revolution,* 208, 216; Field, "The Year of Jubilee," RGR, 42.

89 *Grand Duchess Hélène:* Radziwill, *Behind the Veil at the Russian Court,* (London, Cassell, 1914), 44.

89 *Nicholas Milyutin:* MR, 132.

89 *"feathers in his hat":* William Cassius Goodloe to General David S. Goodloe, June 19, 1861, in Robertson, *A Kentuckian at the Court of the Tsars,* 45.

89 *"a beautiful light blue":* William Cassius Goodloe to General David S. Goodloe, June 19, 1861, in ibid., 46.

90 *"Rumors":* Field, "The Year of Jubilee," RGR, 48.

90 *banking crisis:* Steven L. Hoch, "The Banking Crisis, Peasant Reform, and Economic Development in Russia, 1857–1861," AHR, vol. 96, no. 3 (June 1991), 795–820.

90 *"even too femininely":* MR, 152.

90 *gossiping:* Ibid.

90 *"Even that":* Ibid.

91 *"suffer much":* Herzen, quoted in Venturi, *Roots of Revolution,* 35.

91 *Semka:* Viktor Shklovsky, *Lev Tolstoy,* trans. Olga Shartse (Moscow: Progress Publishers, 1978), 287.

91 *"tender, receptive":* Maude, *The Life of Tolstoy: The First Fifty Years,* 254; Shklovsky, *Lev Tolstoy,* 287.

91 *Pronka:* Maude, *The Life of Tolstoy: The First Fifty Years,* 255.

91 *"How was it":* Ibid., 256 (emphasis added).

91 *Some half a dozen:* Venturi, *Roots of Revolution,* 64–65.

91 *The peasant:* Tolstoy, "Why Do People Stupefy Themselves?" in *The Complete Works of Lyof N. Tolstoï: Essays, Letters, Miscellanies* (New York: Thomas Y. Crowell & Co., 1899), 127–31.

91 *"Human feelings":* MR, 57.

92 *"the mysterious flower":* T, 217.

92 *"Why are there lime trees":* The dialogue is recounted by Tolstoy in his essay, "The Yasnaya Polyana School in November and December [1861]."

8. Used-Up Men

93 *"The salary":* MOS, 43.

93 *"crowds of the country-people":* MOS, 59.

93 *"By some strange":* MOS, 82–83.

94 *"an immense task":* MOS, 83.

94 *"I see already":* MOS, 82.

94 *"call of destiny":* Williams, *Lincoln and His Generals,* 24; compare MOS, 85.

94   *"When I was in the Senate"*: MOS, 83.

95   *"Had to work"*: MOS, 82–83.

95   *"I dined"*: MOS, 84.

95   *"the great obstacle"*: MOS, 85.

95   *"old General always"*: MOS, 84.

95   *"not comprehend"*: MOS, 85.

95   *"a perfect incubus"*: McPherson, *Battle Cry of Freedom,* 360.

95   *"absolute control"*: MOS, 85.

96   *"well meaning baboon"*: Stephen W. Sears, *Landscape Turned Red: The Battle of Antietam* (New York: Book-of-the-Month Club, 1994), 22.

96   " 'the original gorilla' ": McClellan to Mrs. McClellan, November 17, 1861, in McClellan, *The Civil War Papers of George B. McClellan: Selected Correspondence, 1860–1865* (New York: Ticknor & Fields, 1989), 135, 152.

96   *"without consultation"*: ALH, v, 160.

96   *"Everyone"*: Lincoln, *Nikolai Milyutin,* 70.

96   *"But you"*: MR, 154.

97   *"enter a regiment"*: Ibid.

97   *"Mississippi of the East"*: MR, 113, 155.

97   *"there is in Siberia"*: MR, 155–56.

97   *"Kropotkin must always"*: MR, 155–56.

97   *"The beauty of the style"*: MR, 127.

97   *wilder sympathies*: Venturi, *Roots of Revolution,* 1–10; Adam B. Ulam, *The Bolsheviks: The Intellectual and Political History of the Triumph of Communism in Russia* (New York: Collier, 1968), 22–24; Figes, *Natasha's Dance,* 72, 76–77, 84–86; Nicolas Berdyaev, *The Russian Idea* (London: Centenary Press, 1947), 24.

98   *Eugène Onegin*: Emmons, *The Russian Landed Gentry and the Peasant Emancipation of 1861,* 37. N. A. Beshtuzhev, a Decembrist who had studied economics, was a Free Trader who in 1831 published an essay, *On Free Trade and Economic Activities.* Later, however, he advocated a form of "populist socialism" grounded in the communal practices of the *obshchina*–Venturi, *Roots of Revolution,* 7–8.

98   *The liberal idealists*: Ulam, *The Bolsheviks,* 22–24; Sidney Monas, *The Third Section: Police and Society in Russia Under Nicholas I* (Cambridge, MA: Harvard University Press, 1961), 16.

98   *free-state ideas*: See Andrzej Walicki, *A History of Russian Thought from the Enlightenment to Marxism* (Stanford, CA: Stanford University Press, 1979), 150; Andrzej Walicki, *Legal Philosophies of Russian Liberalism* (Oxford: Clarendon Press, 1987), 131; and Emmons, *The Russian Landed Gentry and the Peasant Emancipation of 1861,* 42–46.

98   *a musty air*: Venturi, *Roots of Revolution,* 24. See also Billington, *The Icon and the Axe,* 450: "Russian liberalism was–more than any other current of ideas in nineteenth-century Russia–the work of college professors."

98   *"the grand"*: MR, 277.

98   *"Well, and this Monsieur"*: Ivan Turgenev, *Fathers and Sons,* trans. Rosemary Edmonds (Harmondsworth, Middlesex: Penguin, 1975), 93–94.

98   *"parliamentarianism"*: Ibid., 126.

98   *"We must"*: Ibid., 271.

99   *"revolution, a bloody and pitiless"*: Venturi, *Roots of Revolution,* 292–96.

99   *"The sight"*: MR, 158.

100   *a dreaded agent*: Billington, *The Icon and the Axe,* 24.

100   *"childish, almost demoniac"*: E. H. Carr, *Michael Bakunin* (New York: Vintage, 1961), 187.

100   *"a tongue"*: Billington, *The Icon and the Axe,* 47.

100   *"Pa don't"*: Bayne, *Tad Lincoln's Father,* 48.

100   *"the most lovable"*: Ibid., 3.

100   *"Well, it's broken"*: Ibid., 49.

100   *"It's not Pa's"*: Ibid., 48.

101   *"stationary engine"*: Francis F. Browne, *The Every-Day Life of Abraham Lincoln* (New York: N. D. Thompson, 1887), 528.

101 *Lincoln pressed:* Lincoln to George B. McClellan, February 3, 1862, SW, 1859–1865, 304; ALH, v, 161.

101 *McClellan insisted:* ALH, v, 152–54, 162–63.

101 *party:* Baker, *Mary Todd Lincoln: A Biography,* 205–06.

101 *chill:* Turner and Turner, *Mary Todd Lincoln: Her Life and Letters,* 121.

101 *black swallowtail coat:* David Herbert Donald, "This Damned Old House: The Lincolns in the White House," in *The White House: The First Two Hundred Years,* ed. Frank Freidel and William Pencak (Boston: Northeastern University Press, 1994), 63.

101 *"Are the President":* Williams, *Lincoln and the Radicals,* 105.

102 *Willie:* Randall, *Mary Lincoln: Biography of a Marriage,* 283–84.

102 *In a letter:* Lincoln to George B. McClellan, February 3, 1862, SW, 1859–1865, 304.

102 *logs painted black:* Williams, *Lincoln and the Radicals,* 122–23.

102 *"hold General McClellan's stirrup":* Lord Charnwood, *Abraham Lincoln* (New York: Henry Holt, 1928), 290.

103 *Grand Duchess Hélène:* Narishkin-Kurkakin, *Under Three Tsars,* 34.

103 *"Look at what your nihilists":* Ivan Turgenev, *Literary Reminiscences and Autobiographical Fragments,* trans. David Magarshack (New York: Farrar, Straus & Giroux, 1958), 194.

103 *agents provocateurs:* Ulam, *The Bolsheviks,* 64.

103 *a memorandum:* Venturi, *Roots of Revolution,* 175; Ronald Hingley, *The Russian Secret Police: Muscovite, Imperial Russian and Soviet Political Security Operations 1565–1970* (London: Hutchinson, 1970), 49, 51.

103 *"All this":* Venturi, *Roots of Revolution,* 175.

103 *"personally known":* MR, 140.

103 *a hero:* MR, 141.

103 *absent-minded gaze:* MR, 147.

104 *"retained too much":* MR, 149.

104 *"The promoted officers":* MR, 165–66.

104 *"full of that expression":* MR, 166.

104 *"So you go":* MR, 166–67.

9. Preparations for the Death Struggle

105 *"like a rat":* Bismarck to Countess von Bismarck, June 1, 1862, in *Gesammelten Werke,* xiv (2), 589; Bismarck to Roon, June 2, 1862, *Gedanken,* i, 251.

105 *the bullet:* Wiegler, *William the First: His Life and Times,* 200.

105 *Oscar Becker:* Dulcken, *Life of the Emperor William the First of Germany and King of Prussia,* 48.

105 *elaborate ceremony:* Bismarck to Roon, June 2, 1862, *Gedanken,* i, 251.

106 *Empress Eugénie:* Bismarck to Countess von Bismarck, June 1, 1862, *Gesammelten Werke,* xiv (2), 589; Bismarck to Roon, June 2, 1862, *Gedanken,* i, 251

106 *a café:* Bismarck to Countess von Bismarck, June 1, 1862, *Gesammelten Werke,* xiv (2), 589.

106 *"dark, damp and cold":* Bismarck to his sister, June 16, 1862, *Gesammelten Werke,* xiv (2), 589–90.

106 *still resented:* Gedanken, i, 251.

106 *"You do me":* Bismarck to Roon, Whitsuntide 1862, *Gedanken,* i, 255.

106 *a sphinx:* Wetzel, *A Duel of Giants,* 18.

106 *ostensibly to award medals:* "France and America," *The New-York Times,* Tuesday, July 29, 1862, 2.

106 *the newspapers speculated:* Ibid.

107 *a dinner:* LBD, iv, 341, 558.

107 *"Take care of that man!":* LBD, iv, 341. According to Count Charles Frederick Vitzthum von Eckstædt, Disraeli claimed that at the Russian dinner Bismarck (1) unfolded to him his plan of German unification, and (2) intended the revelation as a communication to "the Queen's Ministers"—Count Charles Frederick Vitzthum von Eckstædt, *Saint Petersburg and London in the Years 1852–1864,* 2 vols. (London: Longmans, Green, 1887), ii, 172. The story must be regarded with skepticism. Bismarck was not a minister at the time and would not have made unauthorized communications of policy (through a member of the opposition, no less) to the English

Ministry. Moreover, had Disraeli really been in possession of Bismarck's plan as early as 1862, he himself would almost certainly have been more prescient in his approach to the German revolution, which by his own subsequent confession "destroyed" the existing balance of power.

107   "Der alte Jude": Robert Blake, *Disraeli* (New York: St. Martin's Press, 1967), 646.

107   *"nerves unsettled"*: Gedanken, i, 259.

107   *"a long journey"*: Gedanken, i, 258.

107   *100,000 men:* But he estimated his effective force at 86,000–MOS, 266.

107   *"give the death-blow"*: Stephen W. Sears, *To the Gates of Richmond* (New York: Ticknor & Fields, 1992), 21.

107   *Napoleon's Address*: Ibid.

107   *"altogether stronger"*: ALH, v, 360.

107   *"Yesterday made"*: MOS, 315.

108   *"I am probably"*: ALH, v, 364–65; MOS, 312.

108   *"I am getting"*: MOS, 313.

108   *"Would be glad"*: ALH, v, 374.

108   *"Your call"*: MOS, 295; ALH, v, 374.

108   *"horrid"*: MOS, 357, 264, 276; ALH, v, 380

108   *"covered with water"*: MOS, 276, 309.

108   *disliked the corps commanders:* Williams, *Lincoln and the Radicals*, 135.

109   *"quite comfortable"*: MOS, 312–13.

109   *Fitz-John Porter:* ALH, v, 414; Sears, *To the Gates of Richmond*, 211.

109   *"I rather like"*: MOS, 312.

109   *"It is certain"*: MOS, 402, 357.

109   *"If I am not"*: ALH, v, 380.

109   *"traitors"*: MOS, 310.

109   *"hounds"*: MOS, 359.

109   *Judas:* Sears, *Landscape Turned Red*, 36.

109   *"the most infamous thing"*: MOS, 308.

109   *"The fate"*: ALH, v, 370.

109   *"Bluff Ben"*: Williams, *Lincoln and the Radicals*, 124–40.

109   *"Your dispatches"*: Lincoln to McClellan, April 9, 1862, SW, 1859–1865, 313.

109   *McDowell's corps:* Williams, *Lincoln and His Generals*, 78–87.

109   *"Do you really think"*: Lincoln to McClellan, April 9, 1862, SW, 1859–1865, 314 (emphasis in original); ALH, v, 363.

110   *"The country will not fail"*: Lincoln to McClellan, April 9, 1862, SW, 1859–1865, 314 (emphasis in original).

110   *"prematurely old"*: "McClellan Before the Battles," *The New York-Times*, Wednesday, July 30, 1862, p. 8.

110   *"They are concentrating"*: MOS, 356.

110   *"old Mexican enemy"*: MOS, 397.

110   *letters:* Williams, *Lincoln and His Generals*, 93–95.

110   *"intentions of the enemy"*: MOS, 395.

110   *authorized a raid:* Tolstoy to Countess A. A. Tolstaya, July 1862, TL, 158–61; Kuzminskaya (née Behrs), *Tolstoy As I Knew Him*, 83.

110   *most powerful:* MR, 335–36.

111   *far more dreaded:* MR, 336.

111   *The windows:* Monas, *The Third Section*, 92.

111   *"Here are"*: Ibid., 48.

111   *potential treacheries:* Ulam, *The Bolsheviks*, 29.

111   *agents* provocateurs: Ibid.

111   *They spread their nets:* Venturi, *Roots of Revolution*, 176.

111   *"audacity"*: Monas, *The Third Section*, 152.

111   *Those who displayed:* MR, 252, 254–56, 335–42; Hugh Seton-Watson, *The Decline of Imperial Russia, 1855–1914* (New York: Frederick Praeger, 1952, 1956), 15; Monas, *The Third Section*, 91; Ulam, *The Bolsheviks*, 28–29.

111 *Floorboards:* Maude, *The Life of Tolstoy: First Fifty Years,* 286.

111 *For two days:* T, 224.

111 *"slovenly Colonel":* Tolstoy to Countess A. A. Tolstaya, July 1862, TL, 157–58.

112 *"I feel malice":* Ibid., 158.

112 *"We can't live":* Tolstoy to Countess A. A. Tolstaya, August 7, 1862, TL, 160–63.

112 *"There are loaded":* T, 226.

112 *In the last week of August:* Tolstoy to the Emperor Alexander II, August 22, 1862, TL, 163–64.

112 *Fair Oaks:* Map of the Military Department of Southeastern Virginia, in *The Official Atlas of the Civil War* (New York and London: Thomas Yoseloff, 1958), plate XVI.

113 *J. R. Anderson:* REL, ii, 148–49.

113 *"This must":* L, 205.

10. *"Periculum in Mora"*

114 *"I drank":* Bismarck to his wife, July 27, 1862, in *Gesammelten Werke,* xiv (2), 605.

114 *"but with good wine":* Bismarck to his wife, July 29, 1862, in *Gesammelten Werke,* xiv (2), 605.

114 *At the end of July:* Bismarck to his wife, August 1, 1862, in *Gesammelten Werke,* xiv (2), 607.

114 *Golden Rose:* Ernest Alfred Vizetelly, *The Court of the Tuileries, 1852–1870* (London: Chatto & Windus, 1922), 99.

114 *"My Dearest Heart":* Bismarck, *The Love Letters of Bismarck,* trans. Charlton T. Lewis (New York: Harper, 1901), 376, 185, 91, 93.

114 *"unthankful":* Bismarck to his wife, August 14, 1862, *Gesammelten Werke,* xiv (2), 612.

115 *"petty and boring":* Gedanken, i, 13.

115 *The Prussian official:* BGE, 14; Gall, *Bismarck: The White Revolutionary,* i, 140.

115 *"over many":* Erich Marcks, *Bismarck: Eine Biographie, 1815–1851,* in *Otto von Bismarck: A Historical Assessment,* ed. Theodore S. Hamerow (Boston: D. C. Heath, 1966), 3.

115 *freethinking:* Kissinger, "The White Revolutionary: Reflections on Bismarck," D, vol. 97, no. 3 (Summer 1968), 896–98.

115 *"hath said":* Psalm 14.

115 *Pietism:* Ronald Knox, *Enthusiasm: A Chapter in the History of Religion, With Special Reference to the Seventeenth and Eighteenth Centuries* (Notre Dame, IN: University of Notre Dame Press, 1994), 398–99.

115 *unworthiness:* Gall, *Bismarck,* i, 25.

115 *Wenching:* Bismarck to his wife, July 3, 1851, *Gesammelten Werke,* xiv (1), 229.

115 *"first fervent prayer":* Gall, *Bismarck,* i, 26.

115 *Johanna von Puttkamer:* Ibid., i, 25.

115 "schmutziges Hemde": Bismarck to his wife, July 3, 1851, *Gesammelten Werke,* xiv (1), 230.

116 *"a storm":* Gedanken, i, 18.

116 *pages of a newspaper:* Ibid.

116 *essentially dramatic:* William L. Langer, "Bismarck as a Dramatist," in *Studies in Diplomatic History and Historiography in Honour of G. P. Gooch, C.H.,* ed. A. O. Sarkisissian (London: Longmans, Green, 1961), 199–216.

116 *since leaving Paris:* Bismarck to his wife, August 10, 1862, *Gesammelten Werke,* xiv, 610.

116 *"Ever since":* "Lettres à la Princesse Orloff," *Revue des Deux Mondes,* March 15, 1936, vol. xxxii, 306.

116 *daily regimen:* Bismarck to his wife, August 14, 1862, *Gesammelten Werke,* xiv (2), 611–12. It has been recently reported that documents in the archives of the Biarritz Swimming Committee reveal that Bismarck was swept out to sea by the undertow, and that he was saved by a "quick-thinking French lifeguard, Pierre Lafleur," who "plucked a floundering Bismarck from the waves." French patriots were quoted as saying, "it might have been better [for France] if Lafleur had let Germany's future Chancellor sink"—Luke Harding, "How France Missed a Chance to Sink Bismarck," *The Guardian,* Tuesday, August 22, 2006.

116 *on the sofa:* Bismarck to his wife, August 11, 1862, in *Gesammelten Werke,* xiv (2), 611; Bismarck to his wife, August 4, 1862, in *Gesammelten Werke,* xiv (2), 608.

116 *figs:* Bismarck to his wife, August 10, 1862, in *Gesammelten Werke,* xiv, (2) 610.

116 *Dinner followed:* Bismarck to his wife, August 22, 1862, in *Gesammelten Werke,* xiv (2), 614.

116 *Chopin:* Nicholas Orloff, *Bismarck und die Fürstin Orloff* (Munich: Becksche, 1936), 58; Bismarck to his wife, August 15, 1862, in *Gesammelten Werke,* xiv (2), 616.

116 *the moon rise:* Bismarck to his wife, August 14, 1862, in *Gesammelten Werke,* xiv (2), 612.

116 *she called him:* Orloff, *Bismarck und die Fürstin Orloff,* 66.

116 *"I find":* "Lettres à la Princesse Orloff," *Revue des Deux Mondes,* March 15, 1936, vol. xxxii, 306.

116 *"double-quick the Fourth Texas":* Sears, *To the Gates of Richmond,* 241.

116 *Seventeen Federal batteries:* Ibid., 215.

117 *"Steady, steady"* . . . *"Forward! Forward!:* Ibid., 241.

117 *"I have lost":* McClellan to Stanton, June 28, 1862, MOS, 425.

117 *"I again repeat":* Ibid. At the time neither Lincoln nor Stanton saw the last two lines of the letter: Colonel Sanford in the telegraph office deleted them—Sears, *To the Gates of Richmond,* 251. When his wife questioned the wisdom of such communications, McClellan replied: "Which dispatch of mine to Stanton do you allude to? The telegraphic one in which I told him that if I saved the army I owed no thanks to any one in Washington, and that he had done his best to sacrifice my army? It was pretty frank and quite true. Of course they will never forgive me for that. I knew it when I wrote it; but as I thought it possible that it might be the last I ever wrote, it seemed better to have it exactly true"—MOS, 452.

117 *"a terrible fight":* MOS, 442, 346; ALH, v, 426, 431. "That I have to a certain extent failed," McClellan said of the Peninsula Campaign, "I do not believe to be my fault, though my self-conceit probably blinds me to many errors that others see"—MOS, 453. Probably.

117 *91,000 effective:* Williams, *Lincoln and His Generals,* 88.

117 *Lee had:* L, 197; Williams, *Lincoln and His Generals,* 114.

117 *"If, at this instant":* McClellan to Stanton, June 28, 1862, MOS, 425.

117 *"swollen to twice":* McPherson, *Battle Cry of Freedom,* 477.

118 *"I may be":* McClellan to Lincoln, July 7, 1862 (the "Harrison's Bar Letter"), MOS, 487–89; ALH, v, 448–52.

118 *ominous construction:* Williams, *Lincoln and the Radicals,* 146.

118 *"A declaration":* McClellan to Lincoln, July 7, 1862, MOS, 488–89.

118 *"ridiculously well":* Bismarck to his wife, August 19, 1862, *Gesammelten Werke,* xiv (2), 612.

118 *Madeira . . . Möet:* Bismarck to his wife, August 22, 1862, *Gesammelten Werke,* xiv (2), 614.

118 *"only wings to fly":* Bismarck to his wife, August 11, 1862, *Gesammelten Werke,* xiv (2), 611.

118 chansonettes: Bismarck to his wife, September 9, 1862, *Gesammelten Werke,* xiv (2), 618.

118 *narrow portal:* Ibid.

118 *"rushed":* Ibid.

118 *"Catty":* "Lettres à la Princesse Orloff," *Revue des Deux Mondes,* March 15, 1936, vol. xxxii, 306.

118 *a yellow flower:* Bismarck to Princess Orlov, September 16, 1863, in Orloff, *Bismarck und die Fürstin Orloff,* 144.

119 *"joyous time":* Bismarck to Princess Orlov, ca September 16, 1863, and Bismarck to Princess Orlov, February 11, 1863, both in Orloff, *Bismarck und die Fürstin Orloff,* 144, 143. Compare "Lettres à la Princesse Orloff," *Revue des Deux Mondes,* March 15, 1936, vol. xxxii, 310, 311–12.

119 *high priest:* Ludwig Bamberger, *Count Bismarck* (Breslau: Günther, 1869), 42.

119 *he detested:* George F. Kennan, *The Decline of Bismarck's European Order: Franco-Russian Relations, 1875–1890* (Princeton: Princeton University Press, 1980), 71.

119 *Pomeranian girl:* Bismarck to his wife, August 11, 1862, *Gesammelten Werke,* xiv (2), 611.

120 *"brutal sensuality":* Wetzel, *A Duel of Giants,* 16.

120 *"a man of prose":* Henry A. Kissinger, *A World Restored: Metternich, Castlereagh and the Problems of Peace 1812–1822* (Boston: Houghton Mifflin, 1973), 10.

120 *"disorganised excitement":* Metternich, "Confession of Faith: Metternich's Secret Memorandum to the Emperor Alexander" in *The Documentary History of Western Civilization: Metternich's Europe,* ed. Mack Walker (New York: Walker, 1968), 125, 123.

120 *Concert of Europe:* Kissinger, *A World Restored,* 10, 41–61.

120 *techniques of the eighteenth century:* Kissinger, "The White Revolutionary: Reflections on Bismarck," D, vol. 97, no. 3 (Summer 1968), 909.

120 *romantic sensibility:* Pflanze, "Bismarck's 'Realpolitik,' " RP, vol. 20, no. 4 (October 1958), 499.

120 *"The King":* BMS, 50–51.

120 "Periculum in mora": *Gedanken,* i, 266.

120 *compromise:* BGE, 54–56.

120 *"cesspool of doctrinaire liberalism":* Thomas Nipperdey, *Deutsche Geschichte 1800–1866: Bürgerwelt und starker Staat* (Munich: C. H. Beck, 1983), 755.

121 *Babelsberg:* Lord Ronald Charles Sutherland Leveson Gower, *My Reminiscences,* 2 vols. (London: Kegan Paul, 1883), i, 186.

121 *"I will not reign":* Gedanken, i, 267.

121 *"Then it is my duty":* Gedanken,, i, 268.

121 *"I would rather perish":* Gedanken, i, 269.

121 *"Light Horse Harry":* Bertram Wyatt-Brown, *Southern Honor: Ethics and Behavior in the Old South* (Oxford: Oxford University Press, 1983), 105–06.

122 *"a Virginia farm":* MCCW, 116.

122 *"sweetness of his smile":* Lord Charnwood, *Abraham Lincoln,* 230.

122 *"Is it not":* L, 93.

122 *Slavery:* Wyatt-Brown, *Southern Honor,* 107. It has been alleged that Lee ordered the whipping of two runaway slaves; and that, after witnessing the whipping himself, he ordered brine to be poured on the wounds–Ibid., 371–72.

122 *"slow influences":* L, 92–93.

123 *"fanatic":* L, 103.

123 *"lie close":* Wyatt-Brown, *Southern Honor,* 107.

123 *"the very best":* L, 76.

123 *"one of those dull":* L, 111.

123 *"greater calamity":* Robert E. Lee to William Henry Fitzhugh ("Rooney") Lee, January 29, 1861, in William M. Rachal, " 'Secession Is Nothing But Revolution': A Letter from R. E. Lee to His Son Rooney," VMHB, vol. 69, no. 1 (January 1961), 3–6.

123 *"the miseries of my people":* Ibid.

123 *"Well, Mary":* L, 111.

123 *"Lee":* L, 110.

124 *"The siege":* L, 221.

11. Trump Cards

125 *frigid hauteur:* Disraeli's characterization, LBD, iv, 390.

125 *the Whigs:* The history of the Whig aristocracy is full of anomalies. The houses of Cavendish and Russell, later so staunchly Whig, adhered during the English Civil War to King Charles. In the sixteenth century the Cecils helped to lay the foundations of the Whig order; yet in the seventeenth century James Cecil, Earl of Salisbury, was attached to James II and converted to Roman Catholicism. The family did not again attain political prominence until the rise, in the nineteenth century, of Lord Robert Cecil, afterwards third Marquess of Salisbury, a great Tory. The Bentincks, a family that played a leading part in the Revolution of 1688, later switched sides, and in the nineteenth century promoted the career of Disraeli.

126 *rumor that general McClellan:* "Three Days Later from Europe," *The New-York Times,* Thursday, July 31, 1862, 1; "Parliamentary Intelligence," *The Times,* Saturday, July 19, 1862, 8–10.

126 *colonial fortifications:* "Parliamentary Intelligence," *The Times,* Saturday, July 19, 1862, 8.

126 *Lindsay:* RAL, i, 482–86; Margaret Antoinette Clapp, *Forgotten First Citizen: John Bigelow* (Boston: Little, Brown, 1947), 175; James Morton Callahan, *Diplomatic History of the Southern Confederacy* (New York: Frederick Ungar, 1964), 150–53; *The New-York Times,* "The American Question in Parliament," Thursday, July 31, 1862, 2; *The Times,* "Civil War in America," Saturday, July 19, 9.

127 *spirited debate:* "Parliamentary Intelligence," *The Times,* Saturday, July 19, 1862, 8–10.

127 *drunk:* Howard Jones, *The Union in Peril: The Crisis over British Intervention in the Civil War* (Chapel Hill, NC: University of North Carolina Press, 1992), 135.

127 *Lord Palmerston:* "Parliamentary Intelligence," *The Times,* Saturday, July 19, 1862, 8–10. Palmerston's was an Irish peerage, and he was thus permitted to sit in the House of Commons.

127 *meditating a change:* On July 29, 1862, Gladstone wrote to his wife that Palmerston "has come exactly to my mind about some early representation of a friendly kind to America, if we can get France and Russia to join." Gladstone to Mrs. Gladstone, July 29, 1862, LWEG, ii, 75

127 *sky-blue eyes:* "Palmerston, whose eyes are sky-blue, she [Mrs. Beecher Stowe] calls dark-eyed." Thomas Babington Macaulay in Trevelyan, *The Life and Letters of Lord Macaulay,* ii, 367.

127 *carefully dyed:* Lytton Strachey, *Queen Victoria* (1921; New York: Harcourt Brace, 1978), 154.

127 *improper relations:* Blake, *Disraeli,* 434.

127 *favor the South:* "American Topics in England," *The New-York Times,* Thursday, August 7, 1862, 4; *The New-York Times,* Saturday, August 9, 1862, 2.

127 *"as a diminution":* Gladstone's characterization of Palmerston's position—EHA, 824.

127 *"great competitor":* John Bigelow to Seward, April 17, 1863, RAL, i, 641.

127 *"It is":* Philip Guedalla, *Palmerston, 1784–1865* (New York: G. P. Putnam's Sons, 1927), 464.

127 *Intervention . . . would be popular:* There were, it is true, many in England who sympathized with the North. Harriet Beecher Stowe's novel *Uncle Tom's Cabin* had been a sensation in England as well as America; Queen Victoria was said to have wept over the story of Uncle Tom. *The Times,* the organ of the upper classes, was hostile to Lincoln; but the newspapers read by the merchants and lawyers of the provinces were in many instances sympathetic to the Union. The mute approbation of the mercantile and professional classes, however, was as nothing compared to the passionate avowals of many workingmen. In Manchester and Blackburn, workers with anxious wives and hungry children passed resolutions in favor of the preservation of the United States and the policy of Lincoln. Their expressions of sympathy touched both George Eliot, who paid tribute to the workers in her novel *Daniel Deronda* (1876), and Lincoln himself, who said that the workers "know that the destruction of the American Republic—whatever else it may mean—means no good to the common people." Scholars have in recent years questioned the pervasiveness of sympathy for the Union cause among the workers; but James M. McPherson has argued persuasively that the "revisionist interpretation overcorrects the traditional view"—Sir Edward Cook, *Delane of The Times* (London: Constable, 1916), 131–32; *The New-York Times,* Wednesday, July 30, 1862, 2; Thursday, July 31, 1862, 3; George Eliot, *Daniel Deronda* (Harmondsworth, England: Penguin, 1995), 124; and McPherson, *Battle Cry of Freedom,* 550–51.

128 *Red Ensign:* MCCW, 238.

128 *saltpeter:* James McPherson, *Battle Cry of Freedom,* 390.

128 *anti-Union sentiment:* John Lothrop Motley to Seward, June 18, 1864, SD NARA T157/ROLL 6.

128 *"regarded the Washington Government":* EHA, 832, 831.

128 *Commemoration Day:* "English and American Aristocracy," *The New-York Times,* Wednesday, July 30, 1862, 3.

128 *"Johnny" Russell:* "Intervention," *The New-York Times,* Thursday, August 7, 1862, 4; EHA, 844, 868.

128 *Early in August:* Palmerston to Queen Victoria, August 6, 1862, in Jones, *The Union in Peril,* 150, 258 n. 23.

128 *took the extraordinary step:* EHA, 844.

128 *"monkeys":* New-York Times, Tuesday, July 29, 1862, 1.

128 *"Ha!":* EHA, 842.

129 *First one:* Sears, *Landscape Turned Red,* 2.

129 *John Pope:* Williams, *Lincoln and the Radicals,* 120, 122–23.

129 *scared:* So his calls "for reinforcements, for supplies, for guidance" on August 25, 1862, suggest—Sears, *Landscape Turned Red,* 2.

129 *Where was Lee?:* Ibid.

129 *"melt away":* Ibid., 15.

129 *slumped in a chair:* Ibid., 11.

129 *A cold rain:* Browne, *The Every-Day Life of Abraham Lincoln,* 521; Allan Nevins, *The War for the Union: War Becomes Revolution, 1862–1863* (New York: Charles Scribner's Sons, 1960), 181, 183.

129 *All felt:* REL, ii, 300–01, 309, 312–16.

130 *sulk in his tent:* McPherson, *Battle Cry of Freedom,* 525.

130 *"a villain":* Ibid.

130 *Ordered to assist Pope:* Halleck to McClellan, August 27, 1862, MOS, 510.

130 *The order was repeated:* Halleck to McClellan, August 28, 1862, in Nevins, *The War for the Union,* 183.

130 *"move out and fight":* "not a moment must be lost in pushing as a large a force as possible towards Manassas. . . ."–Ibid.

130 *Pope begged:* See ibid., esp. note 28. Historians disagree in their estimate of McClellan's motives during Second Manassas. T. Harry Williams argued that McClellan's decision to withhold Franklin and Sumner was reasonable–*Lincoln and His Generals,* 163. Allan Nevins painted a darker picture of McClellan at this time–*The War for the Union,* 180–84. Lincoln himself, who was in some ways in a better position to judge than historians, believed that McClellan was deliberately "trying to break down Pope"–Williams, *Lincoln and His Generals,* 163. See also Sears, *Landscape Turned Red,* 4–6.

130 *A newspaper correspondent:* Sears, *Landscape Turned Red,* 8.

130 *"He has acted badly":* ALH, vi, 23. See also W. D. Kelley, *Lincoln and Stanton: A Study of the War Administration of 1861 and 1862* (New York: G. P. Putnam, 1885), 72.

130 *"atrocious . . . unpardonable":* Nevins, *The War for the Union,* 185. Lincoln told Gideon Welles that "there has been a design, a purpose in breaking down Pope, without regard of consequences to the country. It is shocking to see this and know this; but there is no remedy at present. McClellan has the army with him"–Williams, *Lincoln and His Generals,* 163. Nevertheless, Lincoln let the matter drop. In November he told Orville Browning that he suspected no one's good faith in the débâcle of Second Manassas other than Fitz-John Porter, whose fidelity he thought open to question–Orville Hickman Browning, Diary, November 29, 1862, in Browning, *The Diary of Orville Hickman Browning,* ed. Theodore Calvin Pease and J. G. Randall, 2 vols. (Springfield, IL: Illinois State Historical Library, 1925–33), i, 589.

130 *possessed the confidence:* Kelley, *Lincoln and Stanton,* 71; Browne, *The Every-Day Life of Abraham Lincoln,* 519.

130 *skillful in managing the affections:* Kelley, *Lincoln and Stanton,* 70–71.

130 *artfully laid at the feet:* See McClellan to Stanton, June 28, 1862, MOS, 425.

130 *The American Consul:* Sears, *Landscape Turned Red,* 40.

130 *English warships:* Ibid.

131 *"last card":* Allen C. Guelzo, *Lincoln's Emancipation Proclamation: The End of Slavery in America* (New York: Simon & Schuster, 2005), 171.

131 *"I will play it":* Ibid.

131 *public speaker:* Bamberger, *Count Bismarck,* 39; Kissinger, "The White Revolutionary: Reflections on Bismarck," D, vol. 97, no. 3 (Summer 1968), 890–91.

131 *"You like speaking":* Golo Mann, *The History of Germany Since 1789,* trans. Marian Jackson (New York: Frederick Praeger, 1968), 157.

131 *"cum grano salis":* *Gedanken,* i, 276.

131 *"It is not to Prussia's":* *Gesammelten Werke,* x, 140; *Berliner Allgemeine Zeitung,* October 2, 1862. The speech was not transcribed by an official stenographer; it was, however, reproduced with what Bismarck called "tolerable accuracy" in the newspapers–*Gedanken,* i, 283. Bismarck later reversed the order of the words and in January 1886 spoke of "blood and iron," the more familiar formulation–James Wycliffe Headlam, *Bismarck and the Foundation of the German Empire* (New York: G. P. Putnam's Sons, 1899), 166.

132 *"the Government was actuated":* "Foreign Intelligence," *The Times,* Thursday, October 2, 1862, 7; Bamberger, *Count Bismarck,* 69.

132 *spray of olive:* Headlam, *Bismarck and the Foundation of the German Empire,* 167.

132 *"words of a very ominous description":* "Foreign Intelligence," *The Times,* Monday, October 6, 1862, 8; see also "Foreign Intelligence," *The Times,* Saturday, October 4, 1862, 9.

132 *"witty ruminations":* *Gedanken,* i, 284.

132 *even Lord Palmerston:* Did Lincoln expect Palmerston to blanch? On this question, see Guelzo, *Lincoln's Emancipation Proclamation: The End of Slavery in America,* 253–54.

132 *"I cannot imagine":* Sears, *Landscape Turned Red,* 334.

132 *McClellan's personal intention:* Must remain a mystery. On June 9, 1862, McClellan wrote to his wife: "The secretary [Stanton] and President are becoming quite amiable of late; I am afraid that I am

a little cross to them, and that I do not quite appreciate their sincerity and good feeling.... *How glad I will be to get rid of the whole lot*"–MOS, 402 (emphasis added). Whether the last sentence refers to his departure from the service or to some darker intention is not clear. The language McClellan held, in his letter of August 9, 1861, is scarcely less ambiguous: "As I hope one day to be united with you for ever in heaven, I have no such aspiration [to dictatorship]." Yet: "I would cheerfully take the dictatorship and agree to lay down my life when the country is saved. I feel sure that God will give me the strength and wisdom to preserve this great nation.... I feel that God has placed a great work in my hands"–MOS, 85.

132 *"to march upon"*: Guelzo, *Lincoln's Emancipation Proclamation*, 120.
132 *"taking my rather large"*: Sears, *Landscape Turned Red*, 38; Guelzo, *Lincoln's Emancipation Proclamation*, 120.
133 *With him, in the presidential carriage*: DGW, i, 70–71; Guelzo, *Lincoln's Emancipation Proclamation*, 124.
133 *The President startled*: Donald, *Lincoln*, 362.
133 *"military necessity"*: ALH, vi, 121–22.
133 *meeting of the Cabinet*: ALH, vi, 123–26.
133 *done nothing more*: The bill Lincoln signed in April 1862 freeing slaves in the District of Columbia did not interfere with slavery in particular states.
133 *slaves states of the border*: Guelzo, *Lincoln's Emancipation Proclamation*, 34; Hans L. Trefousse, "Unionism and Abolition: Political Mobilization in the North," ORTW, 105–08.
133 *"corn-hog-whiskey"*: McPherson, *Battle Cry of Freedom*, 31, 493.
133 *four hundred Irish*: *The New-York Times*, August 5, 1862, 8.
134 *prophecies*: See Guelzo, *Lincoln's Emancipation Proclamation*, 16, 53, 82, 135–36, 254.
134 *"I felt"*: ALH, vi, 128.
134 *"as the last measure"*: Guelzo, *Lincoln's Emancipation Proclamation*, 136.
134 *"supported by military"*: Ibid., 137.
134 *Lincoln was impressed*: ALH, vi, 130.
134 *Were emancipation perceived*: Guelzo, *Lincoln's Emancipation Proclamation*, 254.
134 *"be considered our last"*: Francis Bicknell Carpenter, *Six Months at the White House with Abraham Lincoln* (New York: Hurd & Houghton, 1867), 22 (emphasis in original).
134 *"the Pope's bull"*: Guelzo, *Lincoln's Emancipation Proclamation*, 169.
134 *intrigue and menace*: Sears, *Landscape Turned Red*, 1.
134 *"Things" he said, went*: ALH, vi, 128.
134 *McClellan was stronger*: Kelley, *Lincoln and Stanton*, 74–75; Ellis Paxon Oberholtzer, *Jay Cooke*, 2 vols. (Philadelphia: G. W. Jacobs, 1907), i, 203–05.
135 *The draft of the Emancipation*: Guelzo, *Lincoln's Emancipation Proclamation*, 144. Guelzo raises doubts about the claim by David Homer Bates that Lincoln composed the first draft of the Emancipation Proclamation in the cipher room of the War Department telegraph office–Ibid., 143–44.
135 *Early in September*: A. K. McClure, *Abraham Lincoln and Men of War-Times: Some Personal Recollections of War and Politics During the Lincoln Administration* (Philadelphia: Times Publishing, 1892), 167; ALH, vi, 21.
135 *"greatest trial"*: Guelzo, *Lincoln's Emancipation Proclamation*, 164.
135 *Secretary Stanton*: Kelley, *Lincoln and Stanton*, 69–70.
135 *a wavering voice*: Nevins, *The War for the Union*, 186.
135 *mildness of temper*: Kelley, *Lincoln and Stanton*, 70.
135 *"No, Mr. Secretary"*: Browne, *The Every-Day Life of Abraham Lincoln*, 519.
135 *"I made a solemn"*: Guelzo, *Lincoln's Emancipation Proclamation*, 169.
135 *Jüterbogk*: Gedanken, i, 283.
136 *"Et après"*: *Gedanken*, i, 284–85.
136 *"Your Majesty"*: *Gedanken*, i, 285.
136 *"obligated"*: Ibid.
136 *"At your command"*: Ibid.
136 *"merry"*: *Gedanken*, i, 286.
136 *send them home*: BMS, 58.
137 *existing revenue laws*: Norman B. Judd to Seward, February 2, 1864, SD NARA M44/ROLL 13.
137 *"gap"*: The technical questions raised by Articles 99 and 109 of the Prussian constitution are intricate and dull–see BGE, 54–55.

137   *no Stuart king:* In the seventeenth century each of the principal Continental powers maintained a large standing army; England, an island nation, did not. Charles II, the penultimate Stuart king, began to form a regular army; but at his death in 1685 it consisted only of about 7,000 infantry and 1,700 cavalry and dragoons—a number scarcely sufficient to protect Whitehall, and far from the number needed to awe a London mob. Charles's brother, James II, the last of the Stuart kings, enlarged this force, and on the eve of his downfall was able to bring some 40,000 men into the field, exclusive of militia. In the same era, the Elector of Brandenburg-Prussia, then a state scarcely even of the second rank, was able to support 30,000 men in arms and idleness; and the army of Louis XIV of France included more than 300,000 regular soldiers, a force larger than any seen on the Continent since the days of the Roman Empire.

137   *cheers:* "Foreign Intelligence," *The Times,* October 16, 1862, 10.

137   *ceased to exist:* Norman B. Judd to Seward, February 2, 1864, SD NARA M44/ROLL 13.

12. "God Has Decided the Question"

138   *Biebrich:* LRW, iii, 173. Extracts from *Tristan und Isolde* had, indeed, been performed before this date, but not the opera as a whole.

138   *"a girl of genius":* LRW, iii, 297.

139   *"passionate tenderness":* LRW, iii, 299.

139   *Schopenhauer:* George Santayana, *Egotism in German Philosophy* (New York: Charles Scribner's Sons, 1916), 110–13.

139   *"The last song":* LRW, ii, 434.

139   *"bad,* bad, bad": LRW, ii, 434 (emphasis in original).

139   *"Being-no-more":* LRW, ii, 476, 435.

139   *"We may go":* LRW, ii, 435 (emphasis in original). The connection between Wagner's music and German nationalism has been traced more recently by Joachim Köhler in *Richard Wagner: Last of the Titans,* trans. Stewart Spencer (New Haven: Yale University Press, 2004), 316–17, 532–33. For a different conception of the relation of Wagner's music to German nationalism, see Roger Scruton, "Wagner: Moralist or Monster?" NC, vol. 23, no. 6 (February 2005).

139   *Adolf Hitler:* Spotts, *Hitler and the Power of Aesthetics,* 115–15.

140   *Heine foresaw:* Isaiah Berlin, "Nationalism," in Berlin, *Against the Current: Essays in the History of Ideas,* ed. Henry Hardy (Oxford: Clarendon Press, 1989), 336; Berlin, "The Life and Opinions of Moses Hess, in ibid., 250; and Berlin, "Two Concepts of Liberty," in Berlin, *Four Essays on Liberty* (Oxford: Oxford University Press, 1984), 119.

140   *"that within a very few":* "The Civil War in America," *The Times,* Saturday, September 13, 1862, 9.

140   *"got a very complete smashing":* Palmerston to Russell, September 14, 1862, LLJR, ii, 349.

140   *"would it not be time":* Ibid.

140   *attending Queen Victoria:* Court Circular, *The Times,* Wednesday, September 10, 1862, 6.

140   *"clear":* Russell to Palmerston, September 17, 1862, LLJR, ii, 349; Ephraim Douglass Adams, *Great Britain and the American Civil War,* 2 vols. (New York: Russell & Russell, 1925), ii, 38.

140   *England should instantly:* Russell to Gladstone, September 26, 1862, in Adams, *Great Britain and the American Civil War,* ii, 40.

140   *"incarnate creation":* LBD, iv, 390.

140   *the second rank:* Matthew Arnold, *Culture and Anarchy* (1869), in *English Literature: The Victorian Period,* ed. George Morey Miller (New York: Scribner's, 1930, 1933), 439.

141   *"My dear Russell":* Palmerston to Russell, September 23, 1862, LLJR, ii, 350.

141   *a memorandum:* LLJR, ii, 351.

141   *The day was warm:* John M. Bloss, "Antietam and the Lost Dispatch," in *War Talks in Kansas* (Kansas City, MO: Franklin Hudson, 1906), 83–84.

141   *some cigars:* Ibid., 84.

141   *"Special Orders, No. 191":* MOS, 572–73; Williams, *Lincoln and His Generals,* 165–66.

141   *In a short time:* MOS, 572–73.

141   *careless:* Sears, *Landscape Turned Red,* 114–15.

141   *customary caution:* Ibid., 105–06.

141 *"not less than"*: Ibid., 106.

141 *mystified:* REL, ii, 410.

142 *"Every body"*: Sears, *Landscape Turned Red,* 193.

142 *"The men are loading"*: McPherson, *Battle Cry of Freedom,* 540.

142 *banners:* REL, ii, 400–01.

142 *stood ready:* REL, ii, 405–06.

142 *"Please"*: ALH, vi, 145.

142 *a Confederate straggler:* REL, ii, 390.

142 *ruining his army:* REL, ii, 411.

142 *But for the cigar:* Sears, *Landscape Turned Red,* 67–68.

143 *"Gentlemen"*: Salmon P. Chase, *Inside Lincoln's Cabinet: The Civil War Diaries of Salmon P. Chase,* ed. David Donald (London: Longmans, Green, 1954), 149–50.

143 *"I think the time has come now"*: Ibid.

143 *"an instrument"*: Guelzo, *Lincoln's Emancipation Proclamation,* 167.

143 *"God"*: Ibid., 172.

143 *"I know"*: Chase, *Inside Lincoln's Cabinet,* 149–51.

143 *Two minor changes:* Donald, *Lincoln,* 375.

143 *issued:* "A Proclamation by the President of the United States . . . A Decree of Emancipation," *The New-York Times,* Tuesday, September 23, 1862, 1.

144 *"never poured"*: Kenneth M. Stampp, "Lincoln and the Strategy of Defense in the Crisis of 1861," JSH, vol. 11, no. 3 (August 1945), 297.

144 *an odd man:* HLL, 411.

144 *"Mr. Lincoln"*: HLL, 420.

144 *one hundred and eighty pounds:* HLL, 471.

144 *"Well, I cannot"*: Donald, *Lincoln,* 358.

144 *Liquor:* HLL, 96, 421.

144 *"flabby and undone"*: Benjamin P. Thomas, *Abraham Lincoln: A Biography* (New York: Modern Library, 1968), 37.

144 *"I never cared"*: HLL, 411, 474.

144 *"money sense"*: HLL, 139, 279 (emphasis added).

144 *the law itself:* HLL, 485.

144 *Shakespeare and the Bible:* Lincoln to James H. Hackett, August 17, 1863, SW, 1859–1865, 493; HLL, 420, 777.

144 *read less:* HLL, 209, 477, 258.

144 *"a strong latent"*: HLL, 483.

144 *"vague, abstracted"*: HLL, 411.

145 *"thirsts and burns"*: Lincoln, "Address to the Young Men's Lyceum of Springfield, Illinois: The Perpetuation of Our Political Institutions," January 27, 1838, SW, 1832–1858, 34.

145 *"I know very well"*: Guelzo, *Lincoln's Emancipation Proclamation,* 210.

145 *"few men in baggy pants"*: Wilson, *Patriotic Gore,* 785.

145 *"emancipated slaves"*: Nevins, *The War for the Union,* 235.

145 *"been cracked"*: Donald, *Lincoln,* 397.

145 *scarcely less arbitrary:* Compare Carl N. Degler, "The American Civil War and the German Wars of Unification: The Problem of Comparison," ORTW, 66.

146 *the most effective restraint:* Macaulay, *History of England,* WLM, i, 524–25.

146 *throughout the country:* Donald, *Lincoln,* 380.

146 *compelled Congress:* Degler, "The American Civil War and the German Wars of Unification: The Problem of Comparison," ORTW, 66.

146 *"I can touch"*: Taylor, *William Henry Seward: Lincoln's Right Hand,* 169.

146 *"DEPARTMENT OF STATE"*: Bancroft, *Life of Seward,* ii, 261.

147 *"if you will have democracy"*: Lady Gwendolen Cecil, *Life of Robert, Marquis of Salisbury,* 4 vols. (London: Hodder & Stoughton, 1921), i, 139. Compare Degler, "The American Civil War and the German Wars of Unification: The Problem of Comparison," ORTW, 63, 66; Gabor S. Boritt, *Abraham Lincoln, War Opponent and War President* (Gettysburg, PA: Gettysburg College, 1987), 21.

13. The Scent of Freedom

148 *"He is the first"*: MCCW, 464.

148 *"Yes, Marster"*: MCCW, 465.

148 *"Nonsense"*: MCCW, 464.

148 *scrubbed white:* Ibid.

148 *"Do, Dick"*: Ibid.

148 *"He won't even"*: Ibid.

148 *"full of airs"*: MCCW, 375.

148 *"upper ten"*: MCCW, 282.

149 *"Tell her to go"*: MCCW, 375.

149 *"They go about"*: MCCW, 464; see also MCCW, 234.

149 *"by her own people"*: MCCW, 198.

149 *"begged them hard"*: MCCW, 211.

149 *"never thought"*: MCCW, 199.

149 *"Why"*: MCCW, 199.

149 *"the idlest"*: MCCW, 428. Russian paternalists similarly insisted on the "lazy, childlike" characteristics of their serfs—Kolchin, "In Defense of Servitude: American Proslavery and Russian Proserfdom Arguments, 1760–1860," AHR, vol. 85, no. 4 (October 1980), 811.

149 *But she knew:* See, e.g., MCCW, 249.

149 *"hanging negroes"*: MCCW, 234.

149 *"NEGROES FOR SALE"*: McPherson, *Battle Cry of Freedom,* 38.

149 *In one respect:* MCCW, 307, 428.

149 *"You see, Mrs. Stowe"*: MCCW, 168.

150 *"God forgive us"*: MCCW, 29.

150 *sorcerers and magicians:* Georg Wilhelm Friedrich Hegel, *The Philosophy of History,* trans. J. Sibree (New York: Dover, 1956), 93–96.

150 *"noiseless"*: MCCW, 211.

150 *"ministrations"*: MCCW, 251.

150 *"Egyptian Sphinx"*: MCCW, 464.

150 *"full-blooded"*: MCCW, 213.

150 *"trembled"*: MCCW, 214 (original spelling modernized).

150 *"It has to go"*: MCCW, l.

150 *"there are people"*: Ibid.

150 *"it is Lincoln's"*: Ibid.

150 *"Hell"*: MCCW, 248.

150 *a fool:* Hammond, *Secret and Sacred: The Diaries of James Henry Hammond,* ed. Bleser, 146.

151 *"As Swift"*: MCCW, 274.

151 *"splendid specimen"*: Ibid.

151 *"the Magnificent John"*: Ibid.

151 *"so very agreeable"*: MCCW, 329.

151 *"a bitter"*: MCCW, 274.

151 *"I have always treated him"*: MCCW, 329.

151 *"She has a majestic figure"*: MCCW, 348.

151 *"exceedingly quiet"*: Ibid.

152 *"I wonder"*: MCCW, 408.

152 *"I have fallen"*: MCCW, 284.

152 *"the sweetest"*: MCCW, 348.

152 *"Buck," she said:* MCCW, 430.

152 *In the Summer Garden:* Hodgetts, *The Court of Russia in the Nineteenth Century,* ii, 47–48.

153 *"deviated"*: Ibid., ii, 00.

153 *smile of recognition:* Ibid., ii, 00.

153 *"I am often"*: Mosse, *Alexander II and the Modernization of Russia,* 109–10.

153 *flat and dreary:* Edwards, *The Russians at Home and Abroad: Sketches, Unpolitical and Political, of Russian*

Life Under Alexander II, i, 1; Marquis de Custine, *Empire of the Czar: A Journey Through Eternal Russia* (New York: Doubleday, 1989), 89.

153 *"the Tsar's village"*: Glen Botkin, *The Real Romanovs* (New York: Fleming H. Revell, 1931), 15–18.

153 *"emptied and refilled"*: Ibid., 15.

153 *Six hundred men:* Alexander, *Once a Grand Duke,* 159.

153 *"terrestial paradise"*: Botkin, *The Real Romanovs,* 18.

154 *He was sometimes seen:* Almedingen, *The Emperor Alexander II: A Study,* 137.

154 *dressed entirely in white:* Justin Kaplan, *Mr. Clements and Mark Twain* (New York: Simon & Schuster, 1983), 51.

154 *Mark Twain:* Mark Twain, *The Innocents Abroad* (1869; New York: Library of America, 1984), 309–17.

155 *"Constantine's Eagles"*: Alfred J. Rieber, "Interest-Group Politics in the Era of the Great Reforms," RGR, 64.

155 *payment of a debt:* Mosse, *Alexander II and the Modernization of Russia,* 21.

155 *rejoiced:* Bayard Taylor to Seward, November 28, 1862, in *Life and Letters of Bayard Taylor,* i, 399.

155 *"public"*: Zakharova, "Autocracy and the Reforms of 1861–1871 in Russia: Choosing Paths of Development," RGR, 33.

155 *moved a step closer:* Compare Pipes, *Russia Under the Old Regime,* 295–96; Lincoln, *The Great Reforms: Autocracy, Bureaucracy, and the Politics of Change in Imperial Russia,* xvi; and Zakharova, "Autocracy and the Reforms of 1861–1871 in Russia: Choosing Paths of Development," RGR, 33–34.

155 *thoughtful commands:* Hayek, *The Constitution of Liberty,* 159–61.

155 *"on the threshold"*: Zakharova, "Autocracy and the Reforms of 1861–1871 in Russia: Choosing Paths of Development," RGR, 30.

155 *"is striving"*: Harcave, *Years of the Golden Cockerel,* 172.

155 *"designed to renovate"*: Lincoln, *The Great Reforms,* xvi.

155 *"a body of passive"*: Richard Pipes, "Peter B. Struve: The Sources of His Liberal Nationalism," in *Essays on Russian Liberalism,* ed. Charles E. Timberlake (Columbia, MO: University of Missouri Press, 1972), 68.

155 *"decisive"*: Zakharova, "Autocracy and the Reforms of 1861–1871 in Russia: Choosing Paths of Development," RGR, 31.

156 *Alexander replied:* E. A. Adamov, "Russia and the United States at the Time of the Civil War," JMH, vol. 2, no. 4 (December 1930), 596–07; see also *Life and Letters of Bayard Taylor,* i, 96, 401.

156 *"Russia, alone"*: Albert A. Woldman, *Lincoln and the Russians* (Cleveland: Collier, 1961), 128–29.

156 *to praise the President's:* Ibid., 172.

156 *something was missing:* Rieber, "Alexander II: A Revisionist View," JMH, vol. 43, no. 1 (March 1971), 58.

157 *The Prophet Elijah:* See Turgenev's *Fathers and Children.*

157 *interval of suspense:* EHA, 836.

157 *freshly liberated:* LWEG, ii, 76.

157 *"July 6"*: LWEG, i, 65.

158 *"a certain element"*: Lionel Trilling, *Matthew Arnold* (New York: Harcourt Brace, 1979), 224.

158 *a large book:* Gladstone, *The State in its Relations with the Church,* 2nd ed. (London: John Murray, 1839). See also Macaulay, "Gladstone on Church and State" (April 1839), WLM, vi, 326–80, in which the reviewer demolishes the theory, even as he generously applauds the character and attainments, of the young author.

158 *Disraeli:* LBD, iv, 162–64.

159 *a copy of the* Odyssey: Philip Magnus, *Gladstone: A Biography* (New York: E. P. Dutton, 1954), 136.

159 *"The whole impression"*: LWEG, i, 608.

159 *"Greek-loving Gladstone"*: LWEG, i, 604 (φιλέλλην Γλάδστων).

159 thelesis: LWEG, i, 614 (Θέλησις).

159 *"pilgrimages"*: LBD, iv, 381.

159 *a Roman Triumph:* The Times, Saturday, October 11, 1862, 8.

159 *a banquet:* LWEG, ii, 78.

159 *a toast:* "The Right Hon. W. E. Gladstone, M.P., in Newcastle," *The Times,* Wednesday, October 8, 1862, 7.

14. "Bad Times, Worse Coming"

160 *Yet what had he gotten:* Tolstoy to Countess A. A. Tolstaya, August 7, 1862, TL, 160–63.

160 *personally presented:* The Tsar's aide-de-camp, S. A. Sheremetev, took the letter–Maude, *The Life of Tolstoy: First Fifty Years,* 287; TL, 163 n. 1.

160 *"Have said good-bye":* T, 256.

161 *"I have lived":* Tolstoy to Countess A. A. Tolstaya, September 28, 1862, TL, 169.

161 *"Living two together":* Tolstoy to Countess A. A. Tolstaya, October 8, 1862, TL, 172.

161 *Agatha Mikhailovna:* Kuzminskaya, *Tolstoy As I Knew Him,* 107.

161 *"I can only say":* T, 257.

162 *"My husband":* DST, 5

162 *"It is terrible":* DST, 9.

162 *"He grows colder":* DTW, 85

162 *"something wrong":* DTW, 84.

162 *"If I woke":* DTW, 85 (emphasis in original).

162 *"bad dream":* Tolstoy, *Tolstoy's Diaries,* ed. and trans. R. F. Christian (London: Flamingo, 1994), 150.

162 *"morbid":* T, 252.

162 *"All this commerce":* T, 260.

162 *"The physical side of love":* Ibid.

162 *"When he kisses":* DTW, 83.

162 *the* terem: N. M. Karamzin, *Karamzin's Memoir on Ancient and Modern Russia,* trans. Richard Pipes (Cambridge, MA: Harvard University Press, 1959), 110; Robert K. Massie, *Peter the Great: His Life and World* (New York: Knopf, 1980), 35.

163 *"is so dreadful":* DTW, 82.

163 *"hurts me":* DTW, 83.

163 *"to think that Askinia":* Figes, *Natasha's Dance,* 241.

163 *dreamt:* DTW, 96–97.

164 *"It has come home":* MCCW, 370.

164 *military cloaks:* MCCW, 291–92.

164 *"cold, formal":* MCCW, 418.

164 *"washed away":* MCCW, 412.

164 *"Oh, mother":* MCCW, 406.

164 *"three to one":* MCCW, 360.

164 *"Men":* MCCW, 291.

164 *"I want my wife":* MCCW, 296.

164 *"had to own":* MCCW, 356.

165 *"behavior worthy of the Chivalry":* MCCW, 191.

165 *"And now, Madame":* MCCW, 372.

165 *an invalidism:* MCCW, 422.

165 *dress herself:* MCCW, 382.

165 *"automatic noiseless perfection":* MCCW, 488.

165 *"think for you":* MCCW, 488.

165 *"nervous fainting fits":* MCCW, 286.

165 *"Come, come":* Ibid.

166 *breaks down the moral fiber:* See Mary A. DeCredico, *Mary Boykin Chesnut: A Confederate Woman's Life* (Madison, WI: Madison House, 1996), 72.

166 *"wildly excited nerves":* MCCW, 297.

166 *"D.T.'s opium":* MCCW, 286; see also MCCW, 247.

166 *"they would not":* MCCW, 365–66.

166 *"old man's croak":* MCCW, 377.

166 *"We can't fight":* MCCW, 329.

166 *"Bad times":* MCCW, 377.

167 *"not yet drunk":* "Mr. Gladstone in the North," *The Times,* Thursday, October 9, 1862, 7; LWEG, ii, 79.

167   *it appeared:* Palmerston in fact began to draw back from the idea of intervention after the Union victory at Antietam; but Lincoln did not know this—see McPherson, *Battle Cry of Freedom,* 556.

167   *it was everywhere assumed:* John Bigelow to Seward, in RAL, i, 561; LWEG, i, 79; LBD, iv, 332; Adams, *Great Britain and the American Civil War,* ii, 48.

167   *"Will you pardon me":* ALH, vi, 177.

167   *"The good of the country":* McPherson, *Battle Cry of Freedom,* 569.

167   *"The only safety":* Ibid.

168   *armed train:* Guelzo, *Lincoln's Emancipation Proclamation,* 184.

168   *coal-black horse:* Browne, *The Every-Day Life of Abraham Lincoln,* 524–25.

168   *Drums sounded:* Ibid.

168   *"Come, Hatch":* Ibid., 529–30.

168   *"inherent, and fatal":* Lincoln, "Message to Congress in Special Session," July 4, 1861, SW, 1859–1865, 250. Lincoln here wrestled with a perennial theme in the philosophy of republican government, one that perplexed Polybius, Sallust, Tacitus, and Machiavelli. Are republics doomed to die early and tragic deaths? In establishing the United States, the founders attempted to break the cycle of republican despair, and Lincoln was determined that their experiment should succeed. See Arthur M. Schlesinger, Jr., *The Cycles of American History* (Boston: Houghton Mifflin, 1986), 6–12, 16–20.

168   *"We shall nobly save":* Lincoln, "Annual Message to Congress," December 1, 1862, SW, 1859–1865, 415.

169   *"going out into the dark":* Bismarck to Frau von Bismarck, July 20, 1864, *Gesammelten Werke,* xiv (2), 672.

169   *one bright moment:* "I am now," Lincoln was quoted as saying, "stronger with the Army of the Potomac than McClellan. The supremacy of the civil power has been restored, and the Executive is again master of the situation"—Kelley, *Lincoln and Stanton,* 75.

169   *A sealed envelope:* Sears, *Landscape Turned Red,* 339–40.

Part Two: THE REVOLUTIONS AT THEIR HEIGHT

15. "Whoever Has the Power"

173   *Count Károlyi:* BGE, 65.

174   *by intimate ties:* Gedanken, ii, 63.

174   *"princely solidarity":* Gedanken, i, 339.

174   *"I should like":* Bismarck to Countess von Bismarck, July 28, 1863, *Gesammelten Werke,* xiv (2), 649.

174   *bird-watching:* Gedanken, i, 339.

174   *Wilhelm wanted to go:* Count Charles Frederick Vitzthum von Eckstædt, *Saint Petersburg and London in the Years 1852–1864,* 2 vols. (London: Longmans, Green, 1887), ii, 215; James Wycliffe Headlam, *Bismarck and the Foundation of the German Empire* (New York: G. P. Putnam's Sons, 1899), 194.

174   *"to turn":* Gedanken, i, 340.

174   *"out of Frankfurt":* Gedanken, i, 340.

174   *"As a result":* Bismarck to Countess von Bismarck, August 12, 1863, *Gesammelten Werke,* xiv (2), 650.

174   *prevailed:* Bismarck, *Gedanken,* i, 340.

174   *"Thirty reigning princes":* Ibid.

174   *"worn out," Bismarck said, "by the nervous tension":* Ibid.

174   *tears:* BGE, 75.

174   *smashed a vase:* BMM, 68.

174   *"I went for a walk":* Bismarck to Countess von Bismarck, August 28, 1863, *Gesammelten Werke,* xiv (2), 651.

175   *"I had no heart":* Bismarck to Countess von Bismarck, September 4, 1863, *Gesammelten Werke,* xiv (2), 652.

175 *censorship:* "Foreign Intelligence," *The Times,* Wednesday, November 18, 1863, 6.

175 *He had been intrigued:* Ludwig Bamberger, *Count Bismarck* (Breslau: Günther, 1869), 71; Otto Pflanze, "Bismarck and German Nationalism," AHR, vol. 60, no. 3 (April 1955), 554–55.

175 *"Tory Democracy":* LBD, iv, 551, 553, 559, 564; Carlton J. H. Hayes, "The History of German Socialism Reconsidered," AHR, vol. 23, no. 1 (October 1917), 70; William Harbutt Dawson, *German Socialism and Ferdinand Lasalle* (London: Swan Sonnenschein, 1891), 284; Louis Hartz, *The Liberal Tradition in America: An Interpretation of American Political Thought Since the Revolution* (San Diego, CA: Harcourt Brace, 1983), 178–83. See also Eric Hobsbawm, *The Age of Capital* (New York: Vintage, 1996), 107; Isaiah Berlin, "Benjamin Disraeli, Karl Marx and the Search for Identity," in Berlin, *Against the Current: Essays in the History of Ideas* (Oxford: Clarendon Press, 1989), 267.

175 *Bismarck followed:* Pflanze, "Bismarck and German Nationalism," AHR, vol. 60, no. 3 (April 1955), 555; see also BMS, 178.

175 *"untern Klassen":* Gedanken, i, 290.

175 *educated classes:* Bismarck, *Gedanken,* i, 289; Norman B. Judd to Seward, February 2, 1864, SD NARA M44/ROLL 13.

175 *"In the moment":* Peter Gay, *The Cultivation of Hatred* (New York: W. W. Norton, 1993), 261.

175 *"If a compromise":* BGE, 61.

176 *Ferdinand Lasalle:* Lothar Gall, *Bismarck: The White Revolutionary,* trans. J. A. Underwood, 2 vols. (London: Allen & Unwin, 1986), i, 222; Dawson, *German Socialism and Ferdinand Lasalle,* 167–69; Edmund Wilson, *To the Finland Station: A Study in the Writing and Acting of History* (Garden City, NY: Doubleday Anchor, after 1940), 228–59.

176 *"Give me universal":* BMS, 60.

176 *In that month:* "Foreign Intelligence," *The Times,* Friday, November 20, 1863, 8.

176 *was awakened:* REL, ii, 507.

176 *throat infection:* L, 286.

176 *"Well":* REL, ii, 507.

176 *the Rappahannock in force:* Ibid.

177 *not a question of whether:* James McPherson, *Battle Cry of Freedom: The Civil War Era* (Oxford: Oxford University Press, 2003), 585.

177 *"is the wisest":* McPherson, *Battle Cry of Freedom,* 585–86.

177 *"How":* REL, ii, 520.

177 *"in the air":* REL, ii, 520.

177 *"My troops":* REL, ii, 521.

177 *a "picture":* LO, 241–42.

177 *"Ah, Captain":* REL, ii, 533.

178 *"Let us pass over":* REL, ii, 563.

178 *"Such an executive officer":* REL, ii, 524.

178 *"would be invincible":* L, 306.

178 *Pettigrew's brigade:* L, 321.

178 *experiments in* pleinairisme: Clive Bell, *Landmarks in Nineteenth-Century Painting* (London: Chatto & Windus, 1927), 162.

179 *well formed:* See Edouard Manet, *Le Déjeuner sur l'herbe,* 1863; *Olympia,* 1863 (exhibited 1865).

179 *Goya and Velásquez:* Bell, *Landmarks in Nineteenth-Century Painting,* 166.

179 *the prayer:* Emile Zola, *The Masterpiece,* trans. Katherine Woods (New York: Howell, Soskin, 1946), 147.

179 *"Without any hurry":* Ibid., 147–48.

179 *the nude flourished:* Kenneth Clark, *The Nude: A Study in Ideal Form* (Princeton: Princeton University Press, 1984), 162; Alison Smith, *The Victorian Nude: Sexuality, Morality and Art* (Manchester: Manchester University Press, 1996).

180 *"She is the sort of girl":* Bell, *Landmarks in Nineteenth-Century Painting,* 169.

180 *"pudeur":* Louis-Napoleon's judgment on Manet's painting may be apocryphal. See Alan Krell, "Manet's *Déjeuner sur l'herbe* in the Salon des Refusés: A Re-appraisal," *The Art Bulletin,* vol. 65, no 2 (June 1983), 316.

180 *He purchased:* Ross King, *The Judgment of Paris: The Revolutionary Decade That Gave the World Impressionism* (New York: Walker, 2007), 80.

180 *founded on a contradiction: The Times,* Monday, January 4, 1864, 6; Heinrich von Treitschke, *The Fire-Test of the North German Confederation,* trans. Frederick Arthur Hyndman (London: Longmans, Green, 1870), 21.

180 *a dictator and an emancipator: The Times,* Monday, January 4, 1864, 6.

180 "par la grâce": See, e.g., "Décret Impériale," June 5, 1859, Mac Mahon Dossier, AA, 6yd 57.

181 *a new nation:* The new Italian nation did not, at this time, encompass the city of Rome. In an effort to please his ultramontane Catholic subjects, Louis-Napoleon dispatched French troops to the Eternal City, and by their bayonets was the temporal jurisdiction of the Pope, Pius IX, supported.

181 *1st Division of Infantry: Etat des Services,* May 11, 1872, Bazaine Dossier, AA, 6yd 62.

181 *only his eyes:* The description is based on photographs in the Maréchal Bazaine Dossier in the archives of the French army—AA, 6yd 62.

182 *Hamilton's old counsels:* Edward Mead Earle, "Adam Smith, Alexander Hamilton, Friedrich List: The Economic Foundations of Military Power," in *Makers of Modern Strategy: Military Thought from Machiavelli to Hitler,* ed. Edward Meade Earle (New York: Atheneum, 1967), 135.

182 *"any portion":* President Monroe, "Message to Congress," December 2, 1823, in *The Record of American Diplomacy,* ed. R. J. Bartlett (New York: Knopf, 1956), 182.

182 *John Slidell:* John Slidell, "Memorandum of an Interview with the Emperor at the Tuileries," Thursday, 18th June, 1863, RAL, ii, 12; James Morton Callahan, *Diplomatic History of the Southern Confederacy* (New York: Frederick Ungar, 1964), 184.

182 *Louis-Napoleon:* John Slidell, "Memorandum of an Interview with the Emperor at the Tuileries," Thursday, 18th June, 1863, RAL, ii, 13; Frank Lawrence Owsley, *King Cotton Diplomacy: Foreign Relations of the Confederate States of America,* ed. Harriet Chappel Owsley, 2nd ed. (Chicago: University of Chicago Press, 1959), 446; Beckles Willson, *John Slidell and the Confederates in Paris, 1862–1865* (New York: Minton, Balch, 1932), 175.

182 *"great regret":* John Slidell, "Memorandum of an Interview with the Emperor at the Tuileries," Thursday, 18th June, 1863, RAL, ii, 12.

182 *"a direct proposition":* Ibid., 13; Willson, *John Slidell and the Confederates in Paris, 1862–1865,* 177–78; Burton J. Hendrick, *Statesmen of the Lost Cause: Jefferson Davis and His Cabinet* (New York: Literary Guild, 1939), 319–20; Callahan, *Diplomatic History of the Southern Confederacy,* 185.

182 *"inform Lord Palmerston":* RAL, ii, 31; Owsley, *King Cotton Diplomacy,* 446. It will be seen that Louis-Napoleon, on the advice of his ministers, did not in fact make a "direct proposition" to England for intervention, but rather notified the English Cabinet that "he stood ready at all times to join with England intervention."

182 *elation:* Owsley, *King Cotton Diplomacy,* 451.

16. "This Horrible Massacre of Men"

183 *General Kukel:* MR, 169–70.

183 *"It is a great":* MR, 171.

183 *Kropotkin learned:* MR, 171–72.

183 *"And thus it went":* MR, 213.

184 *cannot be directed autocratically:* Kropotkin's critique of Alexander's revolution anticipated those of Alfred J. Reiber and Richard Wortman, who drew attention to the despotic qualities that undermined the Tsar's liberal reforms—See Alfred J. Rieber, "Alexander II: A Revisionist View," JMH, vol. 43, no. 1 (March 1971), 53–55; Alfred J. Rieber, "Bureaucratic Politics in Imperial Russia," SSH, vol. 2, no. 4 (Summer 1978), 399–413; and Richard Wortman, "Rule by Sentiment: Alexander II's Journeys Through the Russian Empire," AHR, vol. 95, no. 3 (June 1990), 770.

184 *"I soon realized":* MR, 215–16.

184 *"the complex forms":* MR, 216.

184 *who often enslaves them:* Edmund Wilson saw something of this paradox in Karl Marx: "Lucifer was to hover behind Prometheus through the whole of Karl Marx's life: he was the malevolent obverse side of the rebel benefactor of mankind."—Wilson, *To the Finland Station,* 119.

185 *as gloomy:* L, 321.

185 *A spy:* L, 320.

185   *"God grants us":* L, 320.

185   *"push those people":* L, 325.

185   *"Pete" Longstreet's I Corps:* L, 327–30.

185   *the Union itself:* L, 336.

186   *"Up, men":* L, 338.

186   *"General Pickett":* L, 340.

186   *"If I had had":* L, 347.

186   *"Glorious Victory":* SDC, 40.

186   *"I say stop":* Daniel Mark Epstein, *Lincoln and Whitman: Parallel Lives in Civil War Washington* (New York: Ballantine, 2004), 170.

186   *"If there is":* McPherson, *Battle Cry of Freedom,* 574.

186   *took a room:* Whitman to Martha Whitman, January 3, 1863, C, 63.

187   *nursing wounded soldiers:* Epstein, *Lincoln and Whitman,* 131–32; Whitman to Nathaniel Bloom and John F. S. Gray, March 19–20, 1863, C, 82; Whitman to Ralph Waldo Emerson, January 17, 1863, C, 70.

187   *"I am very familiar":* Epstein, *Lincoln and Whitman,* 132.

187   *his "boys":* Whitman to James Redpath, August 6, 1863, C, 122.

187   *"shining beauty":* Epstein, *Lincoln and Whitman,* 135.

187   *"I see the President":* David S. Reynolds, *Walt Whitman's America: A Cultural Biography* (New York: Vintage, 1996), 439.

187   *"a hoosier Michael Angelo":* Whitman to Nathaniel Bloom and John F. S. Gray, March 19–20, 1863, C, 82.

187   *"a pretty big President":* Whitman to Louisa Van Velsor Whitman, October 27, 1863, C, 174.

187   *"Time and again":* Epstein, *Lincoln and Whitman,* 10–11.

187   *"prophetic screams":* LG, 53.

187   *"translucent:* LG, 51.

187   "I speak the password": LG, 50.

188   *"great void":* Matthew Arnold, "Civilisation in the United States," in *The Oxford Authors: Matthew Arnold,* ed. Miriam Allott and Robert H. Super (Oxford: Oxford University Press, 1986), 499.

188   *"no shadow":* Henry James, *Hawthorne,* in James, *Literary Criticism,* ed. Leon Edel (New York: Library of America, 1984), 350.

188   *"formless":* Ralph Waldo Emerson, June 1847, in *Emerson in His Journals,* ed. Joel Porte (Cambridge, MA: Harvard University Press, 1982), 372.

188   *"less brilliant, less glorious":* Alexis de Tocqueville, *Democracy in America,* trans. Harvey C. Mansfield and Delba Winthrop (Chicago: University of Chicago Press, 2000), 9, 459.

188   *it lay in its citizens:* Other nations, Whitman asserted in the preface to *Leaves of Grass,* "indicate themselves in their deputies. . . . but the genius of the United States is not best or most in its executives or legislatures, nor in its ambassadors or authors or colleges or churches or parlors, nor even in its newspapers or inventors . . . but always in its common people"–LG, 5–6.

188   *"Nature's cunningest work":* David S. Reynolds, *Beneath the American Renaissance: The Subversive Imagination in the Age of Emerson and Melville* (Cambridge, MA: Harvard University Press, 1993), 215.

188   *"model artists":* Ibid., 214.

188   *Lady Godiva:* Ibid., 215.

188   "poses plastiques": Ibid., 214.

188   "I hear America": LG, 174.

188   *"unrhymed poetry":* LG, 6.

188   *"essentially the greatest":* LG, 5.

188   *"the broadcloth":* LG, 33.

188   *"hankering, gross":* LG, 45.

17. Dust unto Dust

189   *A coating of snow:* "The Invasion of Schleswig," *The Times,* Saturday, February 6, 1864, 9.

189   *crossed the border:* Norman B. Judd to Seward, February 2, 1864, SD NARA M44/ROLL 13.

189 *Danish dragoons:* A. Gallenga, *The Invasion of Denmark in 1864,* 2 vols. (London: Richard Bentley, 1864), i, 57; "The Invasion of Schleswig," *The Times,* Saturday, February 6, 1864, 9.

189 *The roads were crowded:* "The Invasion of Schleswig," *The Times,* Saturday, February 6, 1864, 9.

189 *bitter cold:* Ibid.; *The Times,* Monday, February 8, 1864; Gallenga, *The Invasion of Denmark in 1864,* i, 56.

189 *to rescue their fellow Germans:* The imperative of liberating German-speaking populations from the dominion of foreign powers and uncongenial governments formed a pretext for conquest of which Berlin was to become fond. Similar claims figured in the justifications offered for the reoccupation of the Rhineland in 1936, the rape of Austria in 1938, the mutilation of Czechoslovakia in the same year, and the invasion of Poland in 1939.

189 *handled roughly:* BGE, 81.

190 *in the hope of retrieving:* John Lothrop Motley to Seward, January 23 1864, SD NARA T157/ROLL 6.

190 *chattered and sang:* "The Invasion of Schleswig," *The Times,* Monday, February 8, 1864.

190 *an ultimatum:* "The Austrian and Prussian Ultimatum," *The Times,* Saturday, February 6, 1864, 9; Adolphus William Ward, *Germany 1815–1890,* 2 vols. (Cambridge: Cambridge University Press, 1917), ii, 147.

190 *The reply:* John Lothrop Motley to Seward, January 23 1864, SD NARA T157/ROLL 6; LLJR, ii, 389.

190 *unity and integrity:* LLJR, ii, 374, 386. Under the terms of the Treaty of 1852, the duchies of Schleswig and Holstein were held to be constituent elements of the Danish Kingdom, and upon the demise of the Danish Crown they were to pass to the Danish heir. At the same time, the "special joint status" of the duchies was to be respected by the Danes.

190 *At Pembroke Lodge: Lady John Russell: A Memoir,* ed. Desmond MacCarthy and Agatha Russell, 2nd ed. (London: Methuen, 1910), 93, 121–22.

190 *Lord Wodehouse:* "The Schleswig-Holstein Question," *The Times,* Thursday, January 7, 1864, 9; LLJR, 386–87; Keith A. P. Sandiford, *Great Britain and the Schleswig-Holstein Question 1848–1864: A Study in Diplomacy, Politics, and Public Opinion* (Toronto: University of Toronto Press, 1975), 78–79.

190 *reduce the size:* Lord Robert Cecil, "The Danish Duchies," in Cecil (afterwards Lord Salisbury), *Essays by the Late Marquess of Salisbury, K.G.* (New York: E. P. Dutton, 1905), 146.

191 *controversial constitution:* John Lothrop Motley to Seward, February 23 1864, SD NARA T157/ROLL 6.

191 *The plea:* Russell, Lord Robert Cecil observed, was in fact urging Denmark "to make everything work pleasantly with Germany"—Lord Robert Cecil, "The Danish Duchies," in Cecil, *Essays by the Late Marquess of Salisbury, K.G.,* 146.

191 *"to swallow the cup":* Ibid., 223, 227.

191 *a diplomatic note:* "Prussia," *The Times,* Saturday, January 9, 1864, 10; BGE, 84.

191 *As he neared:* LHJTVP, ii, 271; LBD, iv, 392.

191 *"I doubt":* Palmerston to Russell, February 13, 1864, LHJTVP, ii, 247–48; LLJR, ii, 390; LBD, iv, 345; see also John Lothrop Motley to Seward, March 7 1864, SD NARA T157/ROLL 6.

191 *Alexander was hostile:* Tsar Alexander's rejection of proposals for concerted European intervention in the American Civil War was an important—arguably the decisive—factor in the decision of Palmerston and Russell not to intervene—Albert A. Woldman, *Lincoln and the Russians* (Cleveland: Collier, 1961), 129. The Tsar's attitude was "an important reason for British refusal [to intervene in the conflict], as, indeed, it was the basis for harmonious decision within the British Cabinet"—Ephraim Douglass Adams, *Great Britain and the American Civil War,* 2 vols. (New York: Russell & Russell, 1925), ii, 43–45, 66; LWEG, ii, 45, 75, 85; LLJR, ii, 350–51.

191 *a cautious man:* The world, Henry Adams observed, thought Palmerston "positive, decided, restless; the record proved him to be cautious, careful, vacillating"—EHA, 870.

191 *"I believe Palmerston":* Victoria to Earl Russell, February 13, 1864, in *The Letters of Queen Victoria, Second Series,* ed. George Earle Buckle, 2 vols. (London: John Murray, 1926), i, 157.

191 *on the march:* Norman B. Judd to Seward, February 27, 1864, SD NARA M44/ROLL 13.

191 *carry the Cabinet:* LBD, iv, 345.

191 *"timidity and weakness":* LLJR, ii, 392.

191 *the Austrian Ambassador:* LHJTVP, ii, 249; Sandiford, *Great Britain and the Schleswig-Holstein Question 1848–1864,* 103.
191 *concluded that England:* "The Schleswig-Holstein Question," *The Times,* Thursday, January 7, 1864, 9.
191 *"England is excessively noisy":* This specimen of the conventional wisdom then prevailing at Berlin and shared by Bismarck was retailed by Norman B. Judd in his letter of February 11, 1865, to Seward, SD NARA M44/ROLL 13.
191 *the English Queen:* LLJR, ii, 392–93; Sandiford, *Great Britain and the Schleswig-Holstein Question 1848–1864,* 87, 93, 100–02, 108–12.
191 *"With regard":* Victoria to Earl Russell, February 13, 1864, in *The Letters of Queen Victoria,* ed. Buckle, i, 153; Earl Granville to General Grey, May 9, 1864, in ibid., i, 183–84.
192 *dusty pavement . . . outstretched limbs:* "The War in Denmark," *The Times,* Monday, May 2, 1864, 11.
192 *Dybböl:* Norman B. Judd to Seward, April 16, 1864, SD NARA M44/ROLL 13.
192 *many a noble house:* "The War in Denmark," *The Times,* Monday, May 2, 1864, 11; Auberon Herbert, *The Danes in Camp: Letters from Sönderborg,* 2nd ed. (London: Saunders, Otley, 1864), 69.
192 *courtesy of the Danes:* "The War in Denmark," *The Times,* Monday, May 2, 1864, 11; Herbert, *The Danes in Camp,* 34–35, 37, 52.
192 *covered with crêpe . . . flaxen hair:* "The War in Denmark," *The Times,* Monday, May 2, 1864, 11.
192 *In that unhappy capital:* See, e.g., MCCW, 330.
192 *"won his three stars":* MCCW, 441.
192 *tall:* Ibid.
193 *"sad Quixote face":* Ibid.
193 *"the hottest of the fight":* Ibid.
193 *"The man was transfigured":* Ibid.
193 *a note of despair:* MCCW, 442.
193 *"Stop!":* Ibid.
193 *"Such rags":* Ibid.
193 *"Not hurt":* Ibid.
194 *"What was that":* MCCW, 443.
194 *"being fallen in":* MCCW, 430.
194 *"Come here":* MCCW, 502.
194 *"to be as happy":* Ibid.
194 *Hood asked Brewster:* MCCW, 509.
194 *"If it amounts to" . . . "light-winged birds":* MCCW, 509–10.
195 *"Our army":* David Herbert Donald, *Lincoln* (New York: Simon & Schuster, 1996), 446.
195 *"I do not":* Lincoln to George C. Meade, July 14, 1863, SW, 1859–1865, 479.
196 *He did not send:* Donald, *Lincoln,* 447.
196 *had done his best:* Lincoln to Oliver O. Howard, July 21, 1863, SW, 1859–1865, 481.
196 *"To avoid":* Lincoln to Henry W. Halleck, September 19, 1863, SW, 1859–1865, 514.
196 *"Lee's army":* Ibid.; Lincoln to Joseph Hooker, June 10, 1863, SW, 1859–1865, 454.
196 *bloody dreams:* Lincoln to Mary Todd Lincoln, June 9, 1863, SW, 1859–1865, 453.
196 *"best of educations":* Donald, *Lincoln,* 428.
196 *in his father's bed:* HLL, 415; Donald, *Lincoln,* 428.
196 *at the age of nine:* Donald, *Lincoln,* 428.
196 *"God bless":* HLL, 2–3.
197 *The President's detractors:* Richard Hofstadter, *The American Political Tradition and the Men Who Made It* (New York: Vintage, 1974), 142–50; Hobsbawm, *The Age of Capital,* 141–42; Thomas J. DiLorenzo, *The Real Lincoln* (New York: Three Rivers Press, 2003).
197 *"on terms":* Lincoln, "Fourth Lincoln-Douglas Debate," Charleston, Illinois, September 18, 1858, SW, 1832–1858, 636.
197 *black equality:* LaWanda Cox, *Lincoln and Black Freedom: A Study in Presidential Leadership* (Columbia, SC: University of South Carolina Press, 1994), 22–24.
197 *"strong measures":* Lincoln to Erastus Corning and others, June 12, 1863, SW, 1859–1865, 460.
197 *"contract so strong":* Lincoln to Erastus Corning and others, June 12, 1863, SW, 1859–1865, 460–61.

197 *a pamphlet: President Lincoln's Views: An Important Letter on the Principles Involved in the Vallandigham Case* (Philadelphia: King & Baird, 1863); *President Lincoln on Vallandigham and "Arbitrary Arrest"* (New York: New-York Tribune, 1863).

197 *more than half a million:* Donald, *Lincoln,* 444.

197 *"name in history":* Lincoln to Michael Hahn, March 13, 1864, SW, 1859–1865, 579.

198 *"How long ago":* Lincoln, "Response to Serenade, Washington, D.C.," July 7, 1863, SW, 1859–1865, 475.

198 *"to the sublimity":* Edmund Wilson, *Patriotic Gore: Studies in the Literature of the American Civil War* (Boston: Northeastern University Press, 1984), 99.

18. Fighters for the Future

199 *Dining in state: Gedanken,* i, 351–52.

199 *Hohenschwangau:* Frances Gerard, *The Romance of Ludwig II of Bavaria* (London: Hutchinson, 1899), xlviii.

199 *"Your Highness":* Ibid., 4.

200 *love of swans:* Henry Channon, *The Ludwigs of Bavaria* (London: Methuen, 1933), 5–8; Gertrude Norman, *A Brief History of Bavaria,* 2nd ed. (Munich: Heinrich Jaffe, 1910), 100.

200 *He could not bear:* Ferdinand Mayr-Ofen [pseudonym of Otto Zarek], *Ludwig II of Bavaria: The Tragedy of an Idealist,* trans. Ella Goodman and Paul Sudley (London: Cobden-Sanderson, 1937), 26; Gerard, *The Romance of Ludwig II of Bavaria,* 19.

200 *threw back his head:* Gerard, *The Romance of Ludwig II of Bavaria,* 38; Channon, *The Ludwigs of Bavaria,* 63. Ludwig seems to have modeled his carriage on that of his hero, Louis XIV, who had, Macaulay says, "a way of holding himself, a way of walking, a way of swelling his chest and rearing his head. . . ."–Thomas Babington Macaulay, "Mirabeau," WLM, v, 627.

200 *Herrenchiemsee:* Eric Pfanner, "Bavaria's Summer Playground," *The New York Times,* Sunday, August 22, 2004, v, 12.

200 *"Find Richard Wagner":* LRW, iii, 216.

200 *ecstasy:* Mayr-Ofen, *Ludwig II of Bavaria,* 29.

200 *Wagner's essay:* Ibid., 30.

200 *He longed:* LRW, iii, 374.

201 *"soulless":* Mayr-Ofen, *Ludwig II of Bavaria,* 32.

201 *"utilitarian man":* Ibid., 33.

201 *"It was this":* Ibid., 31.

201 *When, at last:* LRW, iii, 220.

201 *shed tears:* Mayr-Ofen, *Ludwig II of Bavaria,* 58.

201 *Wagner, bending:* LRW, iii, 222.

201 *beauty of Ludwig:* Channon, *The Ludwigs of Bavaria,* 5–8; Mayr-Ofen, *Ludwig II of Bavaria,* 45; Gerard, *The Romance of Ludwig II of Bavaria,* 23, 37.

201 *"Alas":* Fitzgerald Molloy, *The Romance of Royalty,* 2 vols. (London: Hutchinson, 1904), i, 45.

201 *"Rest assured":* LRW, iii, 222.

201 *"with infatuation":* Mayr-Ofen, *Ludwig II of Bavaria,* 65.

201 *"first beloved":* "He loves me," Wagner said of Ludwig, "with the depth and glow of a first love; he knows and fathoms everything about me, and understands me as my own soul"–Molloy, *The Romance of Royalty,* i, 45. On the πρῶτον φίλον of Plato, see Werner Jaeger, *Paideia: The Ideals of Greek Culture,* trans. Gilbert Highet, 3 vols. (Oxford: Oxford University Press, 1986), ii, 175.

201 *"as to a mistress":* Mayr-Ofen, *Ludwig II of Bavaria,* 66; Molloy, *The Romance of Royalty,* i, 46.

201 *"the moment":* Channon, *The Ludwigs of Bavaria,* 66.

201 *"Shall I":* Mayr-Ofen, *Ludwig II of Bavaria,* 66.

202 *Kissingen:* Guy de Pourtalès, *Louis II de Bavière* (Paris: Gallimard, 1928), 32.

202 *"My solitude":* Molloy, *The Romance of Royalty,* i, 48.

202 *"death-in-love":* LRW, iii, 262.

202 *"I have been":* LRW, iii, 262–63.

202 *velvets, silks:* Molloy, *The Romance of Royalty,* i, 52.

203 *Some anxiety:* "The Nuptials of Miss Kate Chase and Ex-Gov. Sprague," *The New-York Times,* Sunday, November 15, 1863, 8.

203 *He had done as much:* Eric Foner, *Free Soil, Free Labor, Free Men: The Ideology of the Republican Party Before the Civil War* (Oxford: Oxford University Press, 1982), 73–74.

203 *The sound of cheering:* Ishbel Ross, *Proud Kate: Portrait of an Ambitious Woman* (New York: Harpers, 1953), 139.

203 *A crowd:* "The Nuptials of Miss Kate Chase and Ex-Gov. Sprague," *The New-York Times,* Sunday, November 15, 1863, 8.

203 *antipathy:* Peg A. Lamphier, *Kate Chase and William Sprague: Politics and Gender in a Civil War Marriage* (Lincoln, NE: University of Nebraska Press, 2003), 24–25.

203 *a cold:* LO, 90.

203 *"back-stairs influence":* LSWPF, i, 234.

204 *"was left in the hands":* LSWPF, i, 240.

204 *"unity and vigor":* LSWPF, i, 237.

204 *"free and friendly":* LSWPF, i, 243.

204 *other than Seward:* DGW, i, 196.

204 *"he should not have":* LSWPF, i, 244.

204 *The dress:* "The Nuptials of Miss Kate Chase and Ex-Gov. Sprague," *The New-York Times,* Sunday, November 15, 1863, 8; LO, 90; Ross, *Proud Kate,* 142.

204 *"modest and retiring":* "The Nuptials of Miss Kate Chase and Ex-Gov. Sprague," *The New-York Times,* Sunday, November 15, 1863, 8.

204 *social flattery:* Ross, *Proud Kate,* 148.

204 *Her conversation:* Ibid.

204 *Lord Lyons:* Mary Merwin Phelps, *Kate Chase: Dominant Daughter* (New York: Thomas Y. Crowell, 1935), 114.

204 *Each week:* Ross, *Proud Kate,* 125.

204 *The government of Rhode Island:* Sprague was said by some to have bought his offices—See John Niven, *Salmon P. Chase: A Biography* (Oxford: Oxford University Press, 1995), 340; Mary Merwin Phelps, *Kate Chase: Dominant Daughter* (New York: Thomas Y. Crowell, 1935), 126.

205 *Bishop of Rhode Island:* Niven, *Salmon P. Chase: A Biography,* 342.

205 *a drooping aspect:* Ibid., 343.

205 *At fifteen:* Phelps, *Kate Chase,* 125.

205 *"limited":* Ross, *Proud Kate,* 124.

205 *"I have not had":* Niven, *Salmon P. Chase: A Biography,* 341.

205 *As a pledge:* Phelps, *Kate Chase,* 132.

205 *"brandies and whiskies":* Alice Hunt Sokoloff, *Kate Chase for the Defense* (New York: Dodd, Meade, 1971), 87.

205 *"dyspepsia":* Ibid.

205 *"be very cross":* Ibid.

205 *He had receieved:* John G. Nicolay, "Lincoln's Gettysburg Address," in *The Century,* vol. xlvii, no. 4 (February 1894), 597.

206 *"the feelings of the best":* Lincoln, "Address to the Young Men's Lyceum of Springfield, Illinois: The Perpetuation of Our Political Institutions," January 27, 1838, SW, 1832–1858, 32.

206 *To "fortify":* Ibid. (emphasis in original).

206 *Young Italy: The Documentary History of Western Civilization: Metternich's Europe,* ed. Mack Walker (New York: Walker, 1968), 160–69.

206 *Young England:* Robert Blake, *Disraeli* (New York: St. Martin's Press, 1967), 167–89.

206 *"cause be naked":* Lincoln, "Address to the Washington Temperance Society of Springfield, Illinois," February 22, 1842, SW, 1832–1858, 83.

206 *like Bismarck:* Henry A. Kissinger, "The White Revolutionary: Reflections on Bismarck," D, vol. 97, no. 3 (Summer 1968), 890.

206 *read Byron:* HLL, 258, 420.

206 *"hypochondriasm":* HLL, 171; Lincoln to John T. Stuart, January 20, 1841, SW, 1832–1858, 68.

206 *the "divine right":* Benjamin Disraeli, "General Preface to the Collected Edition of His Novels (the Hughenden Edition Preface)," BE, i, xi.

206 *Disraeli:* The romantic qualities of Disraeli's mind and statesmanship are analyzed by Isaiah Berlin in his essay, "Benjamin Disraeli, Karl Marx and the Search for Identity," in Berlin, *Against the Current: Essays in the History of Ideas,* 252–86. Like other romantic nationalists, Disraeli was preoccupied with racial differences. There was, he said, "nothing like Race: it compromises all truths"–Disraeli to Mrs. Brydges Williams, May 14, 1860, LBD, iv, 321. Disraeli sought, through his program of Christian neo-feudal paternalism, to "dish" the Whigs and terminate the "monopoly" of the free-state liberals–LBD, iv, 551–53; Berlin, "Benjamin Disraeli, Karl Marx and the Search for Identity," 267.

206 *Marx:* The romantic character of Marx is analyzed by Edmund Wilson in his essay, "Karl Marx: Prometheus and Lucifer," in Wilson, *To the Finland Station,* 111–19.

207 *Father Jahn:* Hans Kohn, "Father Jahn's Nationalism," RP, vol. 11, no. 4 (October 1949), 419–32; Zoltan Michael Szaz, "The Ideological Precursors of National Socialism," WPQ, vol. 16, no. 4 (December 1963), 924–45.

207 *"deeper and more attractive":* John Henry Newman, *Apologia pro vita sua,* ed. Ian Ker (Harmondsworth, Middlesex: Penguin, 1995), 99.

207 *At noon:* "The National Cemetery Dedication," *The New-York Times,* Thursday, November 29, 1863, 1.

207 *He arrived:* LDD, iii, 221; John G. Nicolay, "Lincoln's Gettysburg Address," in *The Century,* vol. 47, no. 4 (February 1894), 597.

207 *At ten o'clock:* Nicolay, "Lincoln's Gettysburg Address," in *The Century,* vol. 47, no. 4 (February 1894), 602.

207 *After various delays:* Ibid., 602; "The Heroes of July," *The New-York Times,* Friday, November 20, 1863, 1.

207 *skeletons:* Garry Wills, *Lincoln at Gettysburg: The Words That Remade America* (New York: Simon & Schuster, 1992), 33.

207 *military salute:* "The Heroes of July," *The New-York Times,* Friday, November 20, 1863, 1.

207 *uncovered:* Ibid.

207 *some men told:* Ibid.

207 *"dedicatory remarks":* Wills, *Lincoln at Gettysburg,* 35.

207 *"Darling":* Sergei Tolstoy, *Tolstoy Remembered by His Son,* trans. Moura Budberg (New York: Atheneum, 1962), 3.

207 *superstitious regard:* Ibid., 4.

207 *They named:* Ibid.

207 *"free man":* Tolstoy to A. A. Fet, January 23, 1865, TL, 193.

207 *"lucky enough":* Tolstoy to A. A. Fet, January 23, 1865, TL, 193.

208 *"constantly frustrates":* DST, 28.

208 *Lubka:* Aylmer Maude, *The Life of Tolstoy: First Fifty Years* (New York: Dodd, Mead, 1910), 303.

208 *Mashka:* Ibid., 302.

208 *"I am to gratify":* DST, 27 (emphasis in orginal).

208 *"everything collapses":* T, 267.

208 *"I am happy":* T, 269.

208 *"Where is it":* T, 265

208 *"the fatherland":* DST, 24–25.

208 *"I'm not cut out":* DST, 22.

208 *"teacher":* Tolstoy to Countess A. A. Tolstoya, October 1863, TL, 182.

208 *did not know what to teach:* Tolstoy, *A Confession,* trans. Jane Kentish (London: Penguin, 1987), 27.

208 *The belief that:* Tolstoy, *War and Peace,* trans. Rosemary Edmonds (London: Penguin, 1982), 1401.

209 *"I've never felt":* Tolstoy to Countess A. A. Tolstoya, October 1863, TL, 182.

209 *"is not a novel":* Tolstoy to M. N. Katkov, January 3, 1865, TL, 191.

209 *But neither was it:* Tolstoy to Princess L. I. Volkonskaya, May 3, 1865, TL, 194.

209 *"There are marvelous":* Tolstoy to Countess A. A. Tolstaya, January 18–23, 1865, TL, 192.

209 All's Well: Tolstoy to A. A. Fet, May 10–20, 1866, TL, 206.

209 *"Probably":* Tolstoy to A. A. Fet, January 23, 1865, TL, 193.

209 *"I said to myself":* Ibid.

209 *"I am being reborn":* DST, 25.

209 *In the mornings:* Maude, *The Life of Tolstoy: First Fifty Years,* 320.

209 *"a bit of his life":* Ibid., 309.

209 *"aims of art":* Tolstoy to P. D. Boborykin, July–August 1865, TL, 197.

209 *"to make people":* Ibid.

209 *"a matter of complete":* Tolstoy to Countess A. A. Tolstaya, November 14, 1865, TL, 198–99.

209 *"on* The History of 1812": DST. 26.

209 *"He is writing":* T, 272.

209 *"that his mental state":* DST, 26.

209 *"so* clever": DST, 35 (emphasis in orginal).

209 *She relieved him:* Maude, *The Life of Tolstoy: First Fifty Years,* 294.

209 *She cared:* DST, 30.

210 *magnifying glass:* T, 274.

210 *"As I copy":* DST, 42.

210 *"irritable and excited":* Ibid.

210 *"All the parts":* Ibid.

19. That a Nation Might Live

211 "Four score and seven": Lincoln, "Address at Gettysburg, Pennsylvania," November 19, 1863, SW, 1859–1865, 536.

211 *"the last full measure":* Ibid.

212 *he went to bed:* Donald, *Lincoln,* 467.

212 *unsuspecting Danes:* "The War in Denmark," *The Times,* Tuesday, July 5, 1864, 12.

212 *batteries:* Norman B. Judd to Seward, April 20, 1864, SD NARA M44/ROLL 13.

212 *he dispensed with:* Arden Bucholz, *Moltke and the German Wars 1864–1871* (Basingstoke, Hants: Palgrave, 2001), 78–79, 80–81; Walter Goerliz, *History of the German General Staff 1657–1945,* trans. Brian Battershaw (New York: Frederick Praeger, 1956), 83–84; T. N. Dupuy, *A Genius for War: The German Army and General Staff 1807–1945* (Englewood Cliffs, NJ: Prentice-Hall, 1977), 72–73.

212 *retire behind their fortifications:* Norman B. Judd to Seward, February 11, 1864, SD NARA M44/ROLL 13; Herbert, *The Danes in Camp,* 70.

212 *"not crushing":* John Lothrop Motley to Seward, March 7 1864, SD NARA T157/ROLL 6.

212 *Moltke became:* F. E. Whitton, *Moltke* (New York: Henry Holt, 1921), 83; Bucholz, *Moltke and the German Wars 1864–1871,* 97.

212 *The distress:* Herbert, *The Danes in Camp,* 88.

212 *Their capital:* B, 179.

212 *Their military power:* Norman B. Judd to Seward, May 10, 1864, SD NARA M44/ROLL 13.

212 *leveled to the ground:* Ibid.

212 *a pinging sound:* Herbert, *The Danes in Camp,* 190–91.

213 *black coffins:* Ibid., 214.

213 *would fly:* A small portion of northern Schleswig was ceded to Denmark pursuant to the Treaty of Vienna (1864). After the plebiscite of 1920 much of upper Schleswig was returned to Denmark–NCMH, vol. xiv, *Atlas,* ed. H. C. Darby and Harold Fullard (Cambridge: Cambridge University Press, 1970), 143.

213 *"splendid prize":* Lord Robert Cecil, "Foreign Policy," in Cecil, *Essays by the Late Marquess of Salisbury, K.G.,* 220, 229.

213 *"completely master":* Herrmann Kreisman to Seward, August 6, 1864, SD NARA M44/ROLL 13.

213 *Fortune:* Ibid.

213 *Biarritz:* Ibid.

213 *During his sojourn:* John George Louis Hesekiel, *The Life of Bismarck, Private and Political,* trans. Kenneth R. H. Mackenzie (London: James Hogg, 1870), 353.

213 *"We know":* "Foreign Intelligence," *The Times,* Thursday, November 26, 1863, 10.

214 *If they urged:* Ibid.

214 *The budget:* Norman B. Judd to Seward, February 2, 1864, SD NARA M44/ROLL 13.

214 *an emergency supply:* Ibid.

214 *to raise a loan:* Ibid.

214 *less fierce:* Gordon A. Craig, *The Politics of the Prussian Army 1640–1945* (Oxford: Oxford University Press, 1964), 171.

214 *The lawmakers sympathized:* Norman B. Judd to Seward, January 12, 1864, SD NARA M44/ROLL 13.

214 *"bring a relief":* Ibid.

214 *Bismarck, it is true:* Bismarck to Count Bernstorff, February 4, 1864, in "Denmark and Germany," *The Times,* Thursday, February 11, 1864, 9.

214 *"under her zeal":* Norman B. Judd to Seward, February 18, 1864, SD NARA M44/ROLL 13.

214 *"territorial aggrandizement":* Ibid.

214 *"A great many paper missiles":* Lord Robert Cecil, "Foreign Policy," in Cecil, *Essays by the Late Marquess of Salisbury, K.G.,* 223. The dilemma of England was described by Henry Kissinger in *A World Restored:* "An insular power," Kissinger writes, "may fight its wars in the name of the European equilibrium, but it will tend to identify the threats to the equilibrium with threats to its immediate security. Because its policy is defensive and not precautionary, it will make the cause of war depend on an overt act which 'demonstrates' the danger. But the danger to the equilibrium is never demonstrated until it is already overturned, because an aggressor can always justify every step except the crucial last one as the manifestation of limited claims, and exact acquiescence as the price of continued moderation"–*A World Restored: Metternich, Castlereagh and the Problems of Peace 1812–1822* (Boston: Houghton Mifflin, 1973), 163.

214 *"The friendship of England":* Norman B. Judd to Seward, May 28, 1864, SD NARA M44/ROLL 13.

214 *John Bull:* Lord Robert Cecil, "Foreign Policy," in Cecil, *Essays by the Late Marquess of Salisbury, K.G.,* 204–05.

214 *decadent Carthage:* Heinrich von Treitschke, *The Fire-Test of the North German Confederation,* trans. Frederick Arthur Hyndman (London: Longmans, Green, 1870), 27.

215 *"of the most wanton":* Lord Robert Cecil, "Foreign Policy," in Cecil, *Essays by the Late Marquess of Salisbury, K.G.,* 231.

215 *"I wasted several":* B, 173.

215 *a wildness:* "If, by [the] timid language and false love of peace [of the European powers]," Lord Rober Cecil wrote in 1864, "Germany is encouraged to believe that she can set treaties at defiance with impunity, a Continental war will result, in which it is almost impossible that England should not be forced to take a part. . . . In every portion of Europe the combustible materials lie scattered ready for the match. If they are kindled into war, no human power can set bounds to the conflagration, or predict the limits of its rage"–Cecil, "The Danish Duchies," in *Essays by the Late Marquess of Salisbury, K.G.,* 148. The victory over the Danes, the correspondent for *The Times* wrote, was a lesson to all "Bismarcks, present or to come." Could such strongmen add "ever so little and insignificant" a piece of land to the territory governed from Berlin, they would receive "full absolution from a large part of Prussian public opinion." "There is one idea," the correspondent said, "which the true Prussian welcomes more than freedom, progress, or any other watchword of the Liberal Deputies in the Chamber; that idea is the extension of the Prussian state, whether at the expense of Germany or of a neighboring country. . . . We do not pretend to foresee the future, but it requires no great acuteness to discern that a movement has begun in Northern Europe which will lead to changes more important than any since 1815"–*The Times,* May 4, 1864, 10.

215 *"Don't put yourself":* Emile Ollivier, *The Franco-Prussian War and Its Hidden Causes* (Boston: Little, Brown, 1912), 404.

215 *"taste for conquest":* Gedanken, ii, 17–18.

215 *"When I have an enemy":* Gay, *The Cultivation of Hatred,* 254.

215 *"God help":* MCCW, 519.

215 *"like a pall":* MCCW, 501.

215 *"How I wish":* MCCW, 452.

216 *"utterly depressed":* MCCW, 594.

216 *"unbroken wills":* MCCW, 595.

216 *"good child":* MCCW, 601.

216 *"one white man":* McPherson, *Battle Cry of Freedom,* 611.

216 *liquid assets:* Ibid., 437–42.

216 *The Russian navy:* E. A. Adamov, "Russia and the United States at the Time of the Civil War," JMH, vol. 2, no. 4 (December 1930), 586–602; Woldman, *Lincoln and the Russians,* 135–48.

216 *Russia's demonstration of support:* The Tsar, in sending his fleets to the United States, acted out of self-interest as well as principle; in American waters his fleets would be in a stronger position vis-à-vis the British navy than they would be in their home ports. In 1863 the Tsar feared that England and France would intervene in Poland, and that the intervention would lead to war—Adamov, "Russia and the United States at the Time of the Civil War," JMH, vol. 2, no. 4 (December 1930), 602.

216 *"walked with me slowly":* MCCW, 532.

217 *"my sweet Annie":* REL, ii, 421.

217 *Rheumatism:* MCCW, 569.

217 *"Poor lame mother":* MCCW, 450.

217 *"old Revolutionary times":* MCCW, 450.

217 *"the very first man":* MCW, 573.

217 *low bows:* MCCW, 504.

217 *"Poor boy":* MCCW, 586.

217 *tears:* MCCW, 589.

217 *"I would not care":* MCCW, 588 (emphasis in original).

217 *enraged constituents:* MCCW, 568, 578.

217 *He could still:* MCCW, 578.

217 *shrieks:* MCCW, 571.

218 *ominous thudding:* MCCW, 566.

218 *restive:* See, e.g., "Runaways!" *Republican Vindicator,* July 15, 1864.

218 *President Davis's manservant:* MCCW, 535.

218 *"Mary":* MCCW, 564.

218 *"I am to be left":* MCCW, 589.

218 *"This horrid, horrid":* MCCW, 468.

218 *"charged it all":* MCCW, 461.

218 *The proprietor:* MCCW, 462.

218 *"jungle South":* Alfred Kazin, *On Native Grounds: An Interpretation of Modern American Prose Literature* (New York: Reynal & Hitchcock, 1942), 460.

218 *throbbed:* MCCW, 462.

218 *"I knew":* Ibid.

218 *"As she lifted":* Ibid.

218 *without life . . . "in a stony way":* MCCW, 463.

219 *"awful depression":* MCCW, 470.

219 *"sailors who break":* MCCW, 519.

219 *"hospitality":* MCCW, 517.

219 *"Your plan":* MCCW, 514. In fact, James Chesnut continued to protest what he regarded as his wife's social extravagance.

219 *A typical dinner:* MCCW, 515.

219 *Heros von Borcke:* MCCW, 514–15, 529, 548–53, 572, 580–90, 596; Heros von Borcke, *Colonel Heros von Borcke's Journal, 26 April–8 October 1862,* trans. Stuart Wright (Palaemon Press, 1981), 11; Edgar Erskine Hume, "Colonel Heros von Borcke: A Famous Prussian Volunteer in the Confederate States Army," in *Southern Sketches, First Series,* no. 2, ed. J. D. Eggleston (Charlottesville, VA: Historical Publishing, 1935), 23.

219 *"After the battles":* MCCW, 519.

219 *the conversation:* MCCW, 519–20.

220 *"The darling!":* MCCW, 431.

220 *"That is":* MCCW, 555.

220 *Hood:* MCCW, 547.

220 *The "Cause glorifies":* MCCW, 588.

220 *"care for him":* MCCW, 554.

220 *"You foolish child!":* Ibid.

220 *"Why":* MCCW, 555.

20. The Valiant Men

221 *He stood:* T. Harry Williams, *Lincoln and His Generals* (New York: Vintage, 1952), 310; Richard Henry Dana quoted in W. E. Woodward, *Meet General Grant* (New York: Horace Liveright, 1928), 309; Horace Porter, *Campaigning with Grant* (New York: Konecky & Konecky, 2005), 123.

221 *Five days earlier:* PMUSG, 357–58.

221 *"It seems that":* Wilson, *Patriotic Gore,* 138.

221 *barrel of whiskey:* Woodward, *Meet General Grant,* 119.

222 *rode into town:* PMUSG, 106.

222 *old blue army coat:* Woodward, *Meet General Grant,* 123.

222 *"He was actually":* Ibid., 125.

222 *In May 1860:* PMUSG, 106–07.

222 *"I was no":* PMUSG, 118.

222 *"I can't spare":* Williams, *Lincoln and His Generals,* 86.

222 *"The Father":* Lincoln to James C. Conkling, August 16, 1863, SW, 1859–1865, 498.

222 *"Grant":* Williams, *Lincoln and His Generals,* 272.

222 *After dining:* LO, 104.

222 *only once before:* Porter, *Campaigning with Grant,* 19.

222 *"Why, here is":* Ibid.

222 *"quietest little fellow":* Francis F. Browne, *The Every-Day Life of Abraham Lincoln* (New York: N.D. Thompson, 1887), 612.

223 *"nation's appreciation":* PMUSG, 358.

223 *His voice:* John G. Nicolay, *With Lincoln in the White House: Letters, Memoranda, and Other Writings of John G. Nicolay,* ed. Michael Burlingame (Carbondale, IL: Southern Illinois University Press, 2000), 130.

223 *"above all":* PMUSG, 358.

223 *system and discipline:* PMUSG, 364.

223 *auxiliary departments:* Bruce Catton, *Grant Takes Command* (New York: Book-of-the-Month Club, 1994), 138–39.

223 *Grant fixed:* PMUSG, 401.

223 *"makes things git":* Browne, *The Every-Day Life of Abraham Lincoln,* 612 (emphasis in original).

223 *Clausewitz said:* Carl von Clausewitz, *On War,* ed. Anatol Rapoport (London: Penguin, 1982), 150.

224 *headquarters near Meade's:* PMUSG, 359.

224 *coup d'œil:* Clausewitz, *On War,* 141.

224 *The new system:* An elaborate web of telegraph wires made the new system of command possible. In the Army of the United States all the lines converged upon Grant, and they enabled him to advise not only Meade, whenever the two men were separated, but the commanders in the other principal theaters of the war as well. The same principle extended to the commanders to the corps commands. Moltke, in Prussia, refined the technique of attaching to each corps commander a staff officer who could both advise the commander on questions of strategy and maintain communications with the army's principal strategists. Grant adopted a similar technique, though he did not, at first, follow it with inflexible rigor. As a result of his failure to do so, General Burnside, commanding IX Corps during the battle of Spotsylvania Court House, unwittingly surrendered an important advantage he had gained. "I attach no blame to Burnside for this," Grant wrote, "but I do to myself for not having had a staff officer with him to report to me his position"– PMUSG, 409–10, 419.

224 *116,000 Union soldiers:* PMUSG, 452.

224 *continued to hold:* "America," *The Times,* November 18, 1863, 12; PMUSG, 364.

224 *General Sherman:* William T. Sherman, *Memoirs of William T. Sherman,* 2 vols. (New York: D. Appleton, 1875), ii, 31.

224 *"all along the line":* PMUSG, 365–66.

224 *helped . . . to shape:* Donald, *Lincoln,* 498–99.

224 *"Those not skinning":* Williams, *Lincoln and His Generals,* 309; compare PMUSG, 373.

224 *The sun was bright:* Porter, *Campaigning with Grant,* 42.

224 *Battle-stained standards:* Ibid.

224 *sword and a sash:* Ibid., 41.

224 *thread-gloves:* Ibid., 41, 65.

224 *The region:* Ibid., 49.

224 *almost impenetrable:* PMUSG, 392.

225 *Bursting shells:* PMUSG, 407.

225 *chain-smoked cigars:* Porter, *Campaigning with Grant,* 45, 56, 59, 64, 70.

225 *more desperate fighting:* PMUSG, 408.

225 *did not show it:* Porter, *Campaigning with Grant,* 65.

225 *"with almost superhuman":* PMUSG, 96.

225 *"I had known him":* Ibid.

225 *"for an explosion":* Wilson, *Patriotic Gore,* 161.

225 *"determined to butt":* Williams, *Lincoln and His Generals,* 311.

225 *"the grit of a bull-dog":* Donald, *Lincoln,* 501 (emphasis in original).

225 *savage:* Porter, *Campaigning with Grant,* 110.

225 *Muskets crossed:* Ibid., 111.

225 *disappeared:* Ibid., 65.

225 *"purpose to fight":* PMUSG, 419.

226 *"My dear Von":* Heros von Borcke, *Memoirs of the Confederate War for Independence,* 2 vols. (New York: Peter Smith, 1938), ii, 313–14; Hume, "Colonel Heros von Borcke: A Famous Prussian Volunteer in the Confederate States Army," in *Southern Sketches, First Series,* no. 2, 14.

226 *"We must":* L, 410–11.

226 *costly assaults:* PMUSG, 442.

226 *detested the American President:* A. R. Tyrner-Tyrnauer, *Lincoln and the Emperors* (New York: Harcourt, Brace, 1962), xvi, 161.

226 *steadily rejected:* German diplomats naturally made the most of Bismarck's opposition to intervention and prudently overlooked his motives. Bismarck was "true to the Union during the Civil War," Count Bernstorff said, "and averse to any recognition of the independence of the Southern Confederacy, whenever such proposals were put forward from other quarters"—Count Bernstorff, "Abraham Lincoln as the Germans Regarded Him: Address Delivered at Springfield, Illinois, February 12, 1913," NYPL, 18.

226 *"clockwork":* Bismarck to his sister, October 4, 1860, *Gesammelten Werke,* xiv (1), 562.

226 *melancholy of one who:* Bismarck to his wife, July 3, 1851, *Gesammelten Werke,* xiv (1), 230.

227 *"If there is":* Stern, *Gold and Iron,* 89.

227 *"It was borne":* Bismarck to Heinrich von Puttkamer, December 21, 1846, in Gall, *Bismarck,* i, 24.

227 *"As God will":* Headlam, *Bismarck and the Foundation of the German Empire,* 134.

227 *"God's cards":* Gall, *Bismarck,* i, 140.

227 *"see where the Lord":* BMS, 115.

227 *"The will of God":* Lincoln, "Meditation on the Divine Will," ca September 1862, SW, 1859–1865, 359.

228 *"probably it is":* Allen G. Guelzo, *Abraham Lincoln: Redeemer President* (Grand Rapids, MI: William B. Eerdmans, 2003), 463.

228 *kept his theology:* Ibid., 19, 21, 447, 462–63.

228 *"God disposes":* Lincoln, "Address at Sanitary Fair, Baltimore, Maryland," April 18, 1864, SW, 185 -1865, 589.

228 *"plain between":* *Life and Letters of Bayard Taylor,* ed. Marie Hansen-Taylor and Horace E. Scudder, 2 vols. (Boston: Houghton Mifflin, 1885), i, 409.

228 *lecture on Russia:* Ibid., ii, 417.
228 *Lincoln attended:* LDD, iii, 221; Woldman, *Lincoln and the Russians,* 141.
228 *"I think":* Lincoln to Bayard Taylor, December 25, 1863, SW, 1859–1865, 564.
229 *"I should be":* Donald, *Lincoln,* 527.
229 *Miscegenation Proclamation:* McPherson, *Battle Cry of Freedom,* 789.
229 *"seems exceedingly probable":* Lincoln, "Blind Memo," August 23, 1864, SW, 1859–1864, 624.
229 *"some great change":* Donald, *Lincoln,* 527 (emphasis omitted).
229 *The imperial train:* The *Times,* Tuesday, April 25, 1865.
229 *spinal malady:* Cassius Marcellus Clay to Seward, April 24, 1865, SD NARA M35/ROLL 20; MOAR, 152.
229 *word spread:* Cassius Marcellus Clay to Seward, April 24, 1865, SD NARA M35/ROLL 20.
229 *profound depression:* The *Times,* Tuesday, April 25, 1865.
229 *words of courtesy:* Ibid.
229 *frightfully thin:* LGT, 167.
229 *during a foxhunt:* Ibid.
230 *like an old man:* Ibid.

21. Power and Enchantment

231 *Mary Chesnut:* MCCW, 601.
231 *"No room":* MCCW, 604.
231 *"Try something else":* Ibid. (emphasis added).
231 *felt pity:* MCCW, 581.
232 *sobbing bitterly:* MCCW, 610.
232 *came upon Buck:* In the interest of narrative economy I have omitted the interval of time that passed between Mary Chesnut's arrival in Columbia and her coming upon Buck at the head of the stairs.
232 *shone black:* MCCW, 622.
232 *"I have prayed":* Ibid.
232 *ordered the door:* Joshua F. Speed, *Reminiscences of Abraham Lincoln* (Louisville, KY: John P. Morton, 1884), 26.
232 *provoke the President:* Ibid.
232 *"Well, ladies" and the account that follows:* Ibid., 26–28.
233 *tightening around the neck:* "America," *The Times,* Monday, March 13, 1865, 9.
233 *forebodings of defeat:* David Homer Bates, "Lincoln's Forebodings of Defeat at the Polls," *The Century,* vol. 74, no. 4, August 1907), 617–20.
233 *His feet and hands:* HLL, 424.
233 *"tired spot"* LO, 239 n. 55.
234 *"Speed":* Speed, *Reminiscences of Abraham Lincoln,* 28.
234 *Lincoln went early:* "Another Account," *The New-York Times,* Sunday, March 5, 1865, 1.
234 *The wind howled:* SDC, 67.
234 *dark, leaden, soaking:* SDC, 66.
234 *The streets:* "The Inauguration," *The New-York Times,* Sunday, March 5, 1865, 1.
234 *feared mischief:* DGW, ii, 251.
234 *a bodyguard:* William C. Harris, *Lincoln's Last Months* (Cambridge, MA: Belknap Press, 2004), 139.
234 *sharp trot:* SDC, 63.
234 *The lines cut deeper:* SDC, 64.
234 *Rain:* "The Inauguration," *The New-York Times,* Sunday, March 5, 1865, 1; Nicolay, *With Lincoln in the White House,* 175.
234 *Vice President's room:* "The President at Work," *The New-York Times,* Saturday, March 4, 1865, 4; LO, 167.
234 *Thirty-Eighth Congress:* "Adjournment of Congress," *The New-York Times,* Sunday, March 5, 1865, 1.
234 *printed on a half-sheet:* LO, 168.
234 *The newspapermen:* "From Washington," *The New-York Times,* Saturday, March 4, 1865, 1.

234 *Associated Press reported:* "The Inaugural Address," *The New-York Times,* Saturday, March 4, 1865, 4.

234 *Ladies and newspapermen:* "Our Special Account," *The New-York Times,* Monday, March 6, 1865, 1.

234 *"the best of us":* David Herbert Donald, *"We Are Lincoln Men": Abraham Lincoln and His Friends* (New York: Simon & Schuster, 2003), 156, 176.

235 *arm-in-arm:* LO, 166.

235 *consumed too much:* LO, 166; "The Civil War in America," *The Times,* Saturday, March 25, 1865.

235 *"from the ranks":* "Our Special Account," *The New-York Times,* Monday, March 6, 1865, 1.

235 *"There is evidently":* DGW, 252.

235 *A ray of sunshine:* "Our Special Account," *The New-York Times,* Monday, March 6, 1865, 1.

235 *it was determined:* Ibid.

235 *"Don't let Johnson":* Harris, *Lincoln's Last Months,* 139.

235 *A platform:* LO, 167.

235 *"On the occasion":* Lincoln, "Second Inaugural Address," March 4, 1865, SW, 1859–1865, 686 (emphasis in original).

235 *"Probably no other":* Lord Charnwood, *Abraham Lincoln* (New York: Henry Holt, 1928), 439. Mr. Gladstone, who had previously been captivated by the statesmanship of Jefferson Davis, professed to be ravished by the second inaugural address of Lincoln. "I am taken captive," he said, "by so striking an utterance as this." He however qualified his praise, and endeavored to vindicate his judgment, by observing that Lincoln must have grown in office.

236 "With malice": Lincoln, "Second Inaugural Address," March 4, 1865, SW, 1859–1865, 687.

236 *"perhaps more like":* Lord Charnwood, *Abraham Lincoln,* 439.

236 *collapsed:* Donald, *Lincoln,* 568.

236 *Petersburg stench:* CP, 2, 140.

236 *sticky tables:* CP, 2, 7–8.

236 "Oh, my handsome": CP, 143.

236 *The frigate:* This account of the funeral of the Tsarevitch is taken from "The Funeral of the Czarewich," *The Times,* Thursday, June 15, 1865, 6.

237 *"At that time":* Franco Venturi, *Roots of Revolution: A History of the Populist and Socialist Movements in Nineteenth-Century Russia,* trans. Francis Haskell (New York: Knopf, 1960), 348.

237 *"As a rule":* Ibid.

237 *His face was pale:* Ibid., 344.

237 *Dmitri Karakozov:* Ibid.

238 *He had been expelled:* Ibid., 331–32.

238 *"invent some sort":* Ibid., 335.

238 *"abnormality of the social":* CP, 231.

238 *"gave unmistakable evidence":* Richard Pipes, *Russia Under the Old Regime* (Harmondsworth, Middlesex: Penguin, 1979), 297. The radical intelligentsia sought to sabotage Alexander's liberal revolution—See ibid., 296.

238 *"all men will become righteous":* CP, 231.

238 *die before he had accomplished:* Venturi, *Roots of Revolution,* 345.

238 *Monastery of the Trinity:* Ibid.

238 *In March 1866:* Ibid.

22. Muffled Drums

239 *"the other fellow":* LO, 180.

239 *"Thank God":* Browne, *The Every-Day Life of Abraham Lincoln,* 690 (emphasis in original omitted).

239 *the President declined:* Doris Kearns Goodwin, *Team of Rivals: The Political Genius of Abraham Lincoln* (New York: Simon & Schuster, 2005), 715.

239 *"you can't put":* Ibid.

240 *"sold us":* Jay Winik, *April 1865: The Month That Saved America* (New York: HarperCollins Perennial, 2002), 48.

240 *Live torpedoes:* Goodwin, *Team of Rivals,* 718.

240 *The President descended:* Ibid.

240 *When the Marines:* Ibid.; Donald, *Lincoln*, 576.

240 *"I want to see":* Winik, *April 1865*, 119.

240 *A devil was loosed:* Ibid., 108.

240 *whipped by the winds:* Ibid., 109.

240 *A hundred thousand:* Ibid., 110.

240 *"preserve order":* Ibid., 112.

240 *"Glory to God!":* Ibid., 118.

240 *Some of the former slaves:* Donald, *Lincoln*, 576.

240 *"Bless the Lord":* Browne, *The Every-Day Life of Abraham Lincoln*, 691 (original spelling modernized).

241 *"Don't kneel":* Ibid., 691–92.

241 *He entered:* Goodwin, *Team of Rivals*, 719; Winik, *April 1865*, 119.

241 *"This," he said:* Battles and Leaders of the Civil War*, ed. Robert Underwood Johnson and Clarence Clough Buel, 4 vols. (New York: Thomas Yoseloff, 1956), iv, 728.

241 *He spoke softly:* Goodwin, *Team of Rivals*, 719.

241 *"I want no one":* Donald, *Lincoln*, 574.

241 *the Marseillaise:* Goodwin, *Team of Rivals*, 723.

241 *He then requested:* Donald, *Lincoln*, 580.

241 *He took up:* Goodwin, *Team of Rivals*, 723.

241 Macbeth: Michael Knox Beran, "Lincoln, *Macbeth*, and the Moral Imagination," *Humanitas*, vol. 11, no. 2 (1998), 4–21.

241 *his favorite play:* Lincoln to James H. Hackett, August 17, 1863, SW, *1859–1865*, 493.

241 *Lincoln lingered:* Donald, *Lincoln*, 580.

241 *"dark deed":* Goodwin, *Team of Rivals*, 723; Donald, *Lincoln*, 580.

241 *the Weird Sisters:* "Weird" is the old English word for the "principle, power, or agency by which events are predetermined; fate, destiny." In Scotland, "Weirds" were witches or fairies who were supposed to possess the power to foresee and control future events. See *The Oxford English Dictionary*.

242 *tolling of bells:* Epstein, *Lincoln and Whitman: Parallel Lives in Civil War Washington*, 274.

242 *dark, dripping Saturday:* SDC, 306.

242 *lilacs:* SDC, 310.

242 *Their fragrance:* Ibid.

242 *"black, black":* Epstein, *Lincoln and Whitman*, 275.

242 *"noble career":* Gorchakov to Cassius Marcellus Clay, May 16, 1865, SD NARA M35/ROLL 20. The Tsar had not yet returned to Russia from his son's deathbed when he was informed of Lincoln's assassination. After Niks's death, he and the Empress withdrew, for a time, to Darmstadt, the Empress's hometown—"Russia," *The Times*, Saturday, May 13, 1865, 5.

242 *"Tried himself":* Gorchakov to Cassius Marcellus Clay, May 16, 1865, SD NARA M35/ROLL 20.

242 *Mrs. Lincoln:* Cassius Marcellus Clay to Hunter, May 16–18, 1865, SD NARA M35/ROLL 20.

242 *"He was the noblest":* E. M. Almedingen, *The Emperor Alexander II: A Study* (London: Bodley Head, 1962), 205–06.

242 *Now he draped:* Norman B. Judd to Seward, April 27, 1865, SD NARA M44/ROLL 13.

242 *no tears fell:* Ibid.

242 *perfunctory:* Bismarck to Norman B. Judd, April 1865, SD NARA M44/ROLL 13.

242 *Saint Dorothea's:* "Prussia," *The Times*, Saturday, May 6, 1865, 5.

243 *found refuge:* Norman B. Judd to Seward, April 29, 1865, SD NARA M44/ROLL 13.

243 *"the modest greatness":* Remarks of Dr. William Loewe in the Prussian House of Deputies, April 1865, SD NARA M44/ROLL 13.

243 *He asked the Chamber:* Norman B. Judd to Seward, April 29, 1865, SD NARA M44/ROLL 13.

243 *"right and law":* "Address of the Members of the Prussian House of Deputies," April 28, 1865, NARA M44/ROLL 13.

243 *More than two hundred:* Ibid.; "Prussia," *The Times*, Saturday, May 6, 1865, 5.

243 *most eminent members:* Norman B. Judd to Seward, May 2, 1865, SD NARA M44/ROLL 13; compare "Prussia," *The Times*, Saturday, May 6, 1865, 5.

23. Shame

244 *no rain:* "Foreign Intelligence," *The Times,* Wednesday, October 4, 1865, 7.

244 *Asiatic cholera:* "Quarantine at Rome," *The Times,* Saturday, October 7, 1865, 7; "Foreign Intelligence," *The Times,* Thursday, October 12, 1865, 10.

244 *Damascus and Acre:* "Foreign Intelligence," *The Times,* Thursday, October 5, 1865, 10.

244 *Beirut and Jaffa:* Ibid.

244 *Tripoli, Malta, and Gibraltar:* Ibid.; "France," *The Times,* Tuesday, October 3, 1865; "The Cholera in Gibraltar," *The Times,* Tuesday, October 3, 1865, 12.

244 *At Rome:* "Quarantine at Rome," *The Times,* Saturday, October 7, 1865, 7.

244 *startling suddenness:* "Foreign Intelligence," *The Times,* Wednesday, October 4, 1865, 7; "Foreign Intelligence," *The Times,* Wednesday, October 4, 1865, 7; *The Times,* Tuesday, October 3, 1865, 12.

244 Vibrio cholerae: "Vibrio cholerae and Asiatic Cholera," *Todar's Online Textbook of Bacteriology* (Madison, WI: Kenneth Todar University of Wisconsin–Madison Department of Bacteriology, 2005).

244 *Weakened:* "Treatment of Cholera," *The Times,* Friday, October 13, 1865, 12.

244 *had reached Paris:* "Foreign Intelligence," *The Times,* Monday, October 2, 1865, 8; "Foreign Intelligence," *The Times,* Saturday, October 7, 1865, 10.

244 *"Otto's Herculean":* B, 191.

245 *"Black Velvet":* BMS, 43.

245 *mudlarks:* "Foreign Intelligence," *The Times,* Wednesday, October 4, 1865, 7.

245 *The drains:* Ibid.; "Foreign Intelligence," *The Times,* Saturday, October 7, 1865, 10.

245 *drink seltzer water:* "Foreign Intelligence," *The Times,* Wednesday, October 4, 1865, 7.

245 *the Charité:* "Foreign Intelligence," *The Times,* Wednesday, October 11, 1865, 8.

245 *Moulin Rouge:* "Foreign Intelligence," *The Times,* Wednesday, October 4, 1865, 7.

245 *Quai d'Orsay:* Willard Allen Fletcher, *The Mission of Vincent Benedetti to Berlin 1864–1870* (The Hague: Martinus Nijhoff, 1965), 38.

245 *friend of Austria:* Augustus Loftus, *The Diplomatic Reminiscences of Lord Augustus Loftus, P.C., G.C.B., 1862–1879,* 2 vols. (London: Cassell, 1894), i, 42.

245 *"in a very bellicose":* Niall Ferguson, *The House of Rothschild: The World's Banker, 1849–1999* (London: Penguin, 1999), 136.

245 *Biarritz:* "Latest Intelligence," *The Times,* Thursday, October 5, 1865, 12; *Gesammelten Werke,* v, 305–16; Adolphus William Ward, *Germany 1815–1890,* 2 vols. (Cambridge: Cambridge University Press, 1917), ii, 206.

245 *Fearful:* Bismarck to Princess Orlov, October 21, 1865, in Nicholas Orloff, *Bismarck und die Fürstin Orloff* (Munich: Becksche, 1936), 148.

245 *Napoleon III: Gesammelten Werke,* v, 306–11.

245 *The barometer:* "Foreign Intelligence," *The Times,* Tuesday, October 10, 1865, 10.

245 *An autumn storm:* Philip Guedalla, *The Second Empire* (New York: G. P. Putnam's Sons, 1922), 353.

245 *in a poor state:* Adolphus William Ward, *Germany 1815–1890,* ii, 206.

245 *He walked:* Anna L. Bicknell, *Life in the Tuileries Under the Second Empire* (New York: Century, 1895), 200.

245 *His protégé:* Norman B. Judd to Seward, April 16, 1864, SD NARA M44/ROLL 13; John Lothrop Motley to Seward, April 12, 1864, SD NARA T157/ROLL 6.

245 *It was assumed:* John Lothrop Motley to Seward, March 28, 1864, SD NARA T157/ROLL 6.

245 *unpleasant scenes:* Ibid.

246 *quitted the city:* Ibid.

246 *General Frossard:* John Lothrop Motley to Seward, April 5, 1864, SD NARA T157/ROLL 6; John Lothrop Motley to Seward, April 12, 1864, SD NARA T157/ROLL 6; Michele Cunningham, *Mexico and the Foreign Policy of Napoleon III* (New York: Palgrave, 2001), 177.

246 *his right to the throne:* Norman B. Judd to Seward, April 16, 1864, SD NARA M44/ROLL 13.

246 *a trifle fancifully:* Maximilian's claim of descent from Charles V was dubious. See John Lothrop Motley to Seward, April 12, 1864, SD NARA T157/ROLL 6.

246 *Charles V:* Norman B. Judd to Seward, April 16, 1864, SD NARA M44/ROLL 13.

246 *the will of the nation:* Ibid.

246 *twenty-five million francs:* John Lothrop Motley to Seward, March 14, 1864, SD NARA T157/ROLL 6.

246 *liveries:* Ibid.

246 *The prospect brightened:* "Mexicans," Maximilian declared when he assumed the imperial title at Vera Cruz in May 1864, "you have called me among you. Your noble country, by the spontaneous expression of the wishes of the majority, has chosen me to watch over its future destinies. I answer the appeal with joy. . . ."–"Proclamation of Maximilian," Vera Cruz, May 28, 1864, in "The Emperor of Mexico," *The Times,* Wednesday, July 13, 1864, 12.

246 *"You are the white man":* Ibid.

246 *alarmed Americans:* John Lothrop Motley to Seward, March 14, 1864, SD NARA T157/ROLL 6; John Lothrop Motley to Seward, April 12, 1864, SD NARA T157/ROLL 6.

246 *"this continent":* "The Civil War in America," *The Times,* Monday, March 13, 1865, 9.

246 *General Grant had dispatched:* William A. Dunning, *Reconstruction, Political and Economic, 1865–1877* (New York: Harper & Row, 1962), 153.

247 *fruitless tourism:* Cunningham, *Mexico and the Foreign Policy of Napoleon III,* 182.

247 *had recently conferred: Etat des Services,* May 11, 1872, Bazaine Dossier, AA, 6yd 62.

247 *promoted from the ranks:* Bazaine enlisted as a private soldier in March, 1831. Two and a half years later, in November, 1833, Sergeant Major Bazaine, having distinguished himself in the *Légion étrangère,* was raised from the ranks and commissioned a second lieutenant–Ibid.

247 *not exactly known:* BGE, 109; Fletcher, *The Mission of Vincent Benedetti to Berlin 1864–1870,* 39; Chester Clark Wells, *Franz Joseph and Bismarck: The Diplomacy of Austria Before the War of 1866* (New York: Ruseell & Russell, 1968), 302; Ward, *Germany 1815–1890,* ii, 207.

247 *Bismarck was determined:* Bismarck was willing to purchase Austria's interests in the duchies; but Franz Josef was not prepared to sell–See Chester Clark Wells, *Franz Joseph and Bismarck,* 311, and Niall Ferguson, *The House of Rothschild,* 138. The Kaiser similarly refused to sell Venetia to the Italians.

247 *a factitious dispute:* Under the provisional agreement concluded at Gastein in 1865, Prussia was to administer Schleswig and Austria was to govern Holstein. But Prussia "hardly makes a secret," one diplomat observed, "of its intention if possible to annex [both] the Elbe Duchies." Bismarck "means to keep [Schleswig and Holstein] for his sovereign," noted another diplomat, "and in that undertaking he has the support in Prussia of all parties." The object of this policy was not difficult to discern; by humiliating Austria in the matter of the duchies, Bismarck hoped to enable Prussia to make "its long cherished dream of supremacy in Germany a fact"–John Lothrop Motley to Seward, March 20, 1866, SD NARA T157/ROLL 7; John Lothrop Motley to Seward, April 1, 1866, SD NARA T157/ROLL 7; H. Kreisman to Seward, August 6, 1864, SD NARA M44/ROLL 13. See also Loftus, *The Diplomatic Reminiscences of Lord Augustus Loftus, P.C., G.C.B.,* i, 40.

247 *"war to the knife":* Bismarck's phrase–BMS, 81.

247 *sinister bargain:* "Prussia," *The Times,* Saturday, October 14, 1865, 10; *The Times,* Monday, October 16, 1865, 8.

247 *pleased: The Times,* Monday, October 16, 1865, 8.

247 *had extracted:* Shortly after the meeting at Biarritz, Bismarck permitted to appear, in the semi-official *Provinzial Correspondenz,* a statement in which he said that Louis-Napoleon had given him "upon pending questions . . . guarantees for the unaltered continuance of friendly relations between France and Prussia." "It is mainly owing to this fact," the statement continued, "that the question of the Duchies [can] be brought to a solution in conformity with German national and Prussians interests *without European complications.* No doubt exists that the [French] Emperor has resolved to continue the calm, honourable, and *disinterested* policy he has hitherto pursued"– "France and Prussia," *The Times,* Thursday, October 12, 1865, 12 (emphasis added).

247 *Some speculated:* "Prussia," *The Times,* Saturday, October 14, 1865, 10.

247 *kept details of the talks:* Fletcher, *The Mission of Vincent Benedetti to Berlin 1864–1870,* 39.

247 *promise him territorial compensation:* Ibid., 39. A. J. P. Taylor supposes that Bismarck, in exchange for the French pledge of neutrality, promised Louis Napoleon that Prussia would not stand in the way of an attempt by France and Italy to wrest Venetia from the Austrians–BMS, 80–81. See also Ward, *Germany 1815–1890,* ii, 207–08. C. Grant Robertson, by contrast, argued that Bismarck

"accomplished the difficult task of securing Napoleon's benevolent neutrality, without any awkward promissory notes, which could be presented for payment at sight at some future date"—B, 195. Robertson's analysis anticipates that of Henry Kissinger, who argues that Louis-Napoleon left the question of territorial compensation vague because (like many military analysts of the day) "he expected Prussia to lose; his moves were designed more to keep Prussia on its course to war than to bargain for benefits"—Henry A. Kissinger, *Diplomacy* (New York: Simon & Schuster, 1994), 115; see also Alan Palmer, *Twilight of the Habsburgs: The Life and Times of Emperor Francis Joseph* (New York: Grove/Atlantic Monthly, 1995), 143. That Bismarck believed he had secured French neutrality at Biarritz is all but certain, else he would never, in 1866, have denuded Prussia's western frontier of troops in order to fight the Austrians. See, on this point, Loftus, *The Diplomatic Reminiscences of Lord Augustus Loftus, P.C., G.C.B.,* i, 85–86.

247 *Prussia, Louis-Napoleon believed:* Kissinger, "The White Revolutionary: Reflections on Bismarck," D, vol. 97, no. 3 (Summer 1968), 920.

248 *"as calm and smiling":* MCCW, 785.

248 *The town:* MCCW, 789.

248 *Some who had quarreled:* MCCW, 783–85.

248 *a guerrilla campaign:* Winik, *April 1865,* 150.

248 *"General Lee":* MCCW, 788.

248 *"That is a lie":* MCCW, 792.

248 *"I do not":* MCCW, 789.

248 *"Now we belong":* Ibid.

249 *"croaking and dismay":* "The Confederate States," *The Times,* March 7, 1865, 5; compare Herman M. Hattaway, "The Civil War Armies: Creation, Mobilization, and Development," ORTW, 196–97.

249 "Never": MCCW, 779 (emphasis added). The picture of Hood at bay is a composite one; I have compressed into one scene a number of disparate incidents.

249 *black care:* MCCW, 785.

249 *"the torture":* MCCW, 708.

249 *was reviled:* MCCW, 711. "The Civil War in America," *The Times,* Tuesday, March 14, 1865, 5.

249 *"Hood is dead":* MCCW, 698.

249 *"turned as white":* MCCW, 646.

249 *"future in the face":* MCCW, 709.

249 *"She rarely speaks":* MCCW, 792.

250 *so soft:* MCCW, 804.

250 *"beautiful, beautiful":* Ibid.

250 *"fast":* EHA, 904.

250 *"I stood by the fender":* MCCW, 804.

250 *"pretended to be":* Ibid.

250 *If he had been persistent:* Ibid.

250 *"well, I would have":* MCCW, 804–05.

250 *"It was a shame":* MCCW, 804.

250 *In his bedroom-study:* LGT, 128.

250 *After a brisk walk:* LGT, 129.

250 *hollow:* E. A. Brayley Hodgetts, *The Court of Russia in the Nineteenth Century,* 2 vols. (New York: Charles Scribner, 1908), ii, 41.

251 *Her principal consolation:* Some say that the Empress gave way to religious mania after the death of her son. Ibid., ii, 41.

251 *icons:* LGT, 172.

251 *After breakfast:* LGT, 129.

251 *On a spring afternoon:* LGT, 177.

251 *Milord:* Walter G. Moss, *Russia in the Age of Alexander II, Tolstoy and Dostoevsky* (London: Anthem Press, 2002), 90.

251 *sunny:* Ibid.

251 *an overcoat:* "Russia," *The Times,* Monday, April 23, 1866, 10.

251 *The Tsar was in the midst:* Ibid.

24. "Better to Die"

252 *Bismarck opened:* B, 204.

252 *"We have":* Ibid.

252 *railway interests:* Stern, *Gold and Iron,* 80; Craig, *The Politics of the Prussian Army 1640–1945,* 174; Ferguson, *The House of Rothschild,* 130–34.

252 *"a nest":* John Lothrop Motley to Seward, April 17, 1866, SD NARA T157/ROLL 7.

252 *The Viennese:* John Lothrop Motley to Seward, March 20, 1866, SD NARA T157/ROLL 7.

252 *a Prussian descent:* Ibid.; Pflanze, *Bismarck and the Development of Germany,* 294.

252 *less than seven weeks:* Gordon A. Craig, *The Battle of Königgrätz: Prussia's Victory Over Austria, 1866* (Philadelphia: University of Pennsylvania Press, 2003), 7.

253 *"warlike activity":* John Lothrop Motley to Seward, April 1, 1866, SD NARA T157/ROLL 7.

253 *"without any recognizable":* John Lothrop Motley to Seward, April 10, 1866, SD NARA T157/ROLL 7.

253 *Bismarck pretended:* One of the most careful students of the crisis concluded that Bismarck was the aggressor in the war and its conscious instigator—Chester Clark Wells, *Franz Joseph and Bismarck: The Diplomacy of Austria Before the War of 1866,* 476.

253 *partial mobilization:* John Lothrop Motley to Seward, April 17, 1866, SD NARA T157/ROLL 7.

253 *promptly denied:* Ibid.; John Lothrop Motley to Seward, April 1, 1866, SD NARA T157/ROLL 7.

253 *with some warmth:* John Lothrop Motley to Seward, April 17, 1866, SD NARA T157/ROLL 7.

253 *extensive military preparations:* John Lothrop Motley to Seward, April 17, 1866, SD NARA T157/ROLL 7.

253 *"All this":* John Lothrop Motley to Seward, April 17, 1866, SD NARA T157/ROLL 7.

253 *an olive branch:* John Lothrop Motley to Seward, April 18, 1866, SD NARA T157/ROLL 7; John Lothrop Motley to Seward, April 25, 1866, SD NARA T157/ROLL 7.

253 *If, he said:* John Lothrop Motley to Seward, April 25, 1866, SD NARA T157/ROLL 7.

253 *Vienna at once embraced:* John Lothrop Motley to Seward, April 25, 1866, SD NARA T157/ROLL 7.

253 *Italy:* John Lothrop Motley to Seward, May 1, 1866, SD NARA T157/ROLL 7; Palmer, *Twilight of the Habsburgs,* 142.

253 *the Austrians naturally:* John Lothrop Motley to Seward, May 1, 1866, SD NARA T157/ROLL 7; Palmer, *Twilight of the Habsburgs,* 141.

253 *Bismarck took care:* In his eagerness to rally Germany to his cause, Bismarck not only planted articles in newspapers, he also proposed the creation of a Pan-German Parliament, to be elected by universal suffrage.

253 *a German paper:* John Lothrop Motley to Seward, May 1, 1866, SD NARA T157/ROLL 7.

253 *to attack Prussia:* Ibid.; "Austria and Prussia," *The Times,* Wednesday, May 9, 1866, 6.

253 *Ordinary Prussians:* "Prussia," *The Times,* Friday, May 4, 1866, 10.

254 *six army corps:* Joseph A. Wright to Seward, May 9, 1866, SD NARA M44/ROLL 13; "Prussia," *The Times,* Monday, May 7, 1866, 9.

254 *England, France, and Russia:* Joseph A. Wright to Seward, May 16, 1866, SD NARA M44/ROLL 13.

254 *"contented themselves":* John Lothrop Motley to Seward, March 26, 1866, SD NARA T157/ROLL 7.

254 *zenith of its supremacy:* James Truslow Adams, *The British Empire 1784–1939* (New York: Dorset, 1991), 210.

254 *"are much better":* B, 114.

254 *"could not view":* Loftus, *The Diplomatic Reminiscences of Lord Augustus Loftus, P.C., G.C.B.,* i, 99.

254 *"enormous armies":* *The Times,* Wednesday, June 29, 1864, 10.

254 *"in a state":* Ibid.

254 *a volunteer movement:* *The Times,* Monday, April 18, 1864, 9; *The Times,* Monday, April 25, 1864, 8; *The Times,* Saturday, September 30, 1865, 7. See also Anthony Trollope, *Can You Forgive Her?* (1865; London: Penguin, 1986), 76.

255 *Palmerston himself:* Count Charles Frederick Vitzthum von Eckstædt, *Saint Petersburg and London in the Years 1852–1864,* 2 vols. (London: Longmans, Green, 1887), ii, 112.

255 *He had himself:* Elizabeth Gaskell, *The Life of Charlotte Brontë* (1857; London: Penguin, 1985), 78.

255 *"is too weak"*: Palmerston to Russell, September 13, 1865, in Evelyn Ashley, *The Life of Henry John Temple, Viscount Palmerston,* 2 vols. (London: Richard Bentley, 1876), ii, 270.

255 *"faults and recklessness"*: Wells, *Franz Joseph and Bismarck,* 377; Pflanze, *Bismarck and the Development of Germany,* 294.

255 *"The Missus"*: Herbert Maxwell, *The Life and Letters of George William Frederick, Fourth Earl of Clarendon, K.G., G.C.B.,* 2 vols. (London: Edward Arnold, 1913), ii, 310.

255 *"would be an injustice"*: Russell to Clarendon, March 30, 1866, in ibid., ii, 311.

255 *iron cot:* Lieutenant-General Baron von Margutti, *The Emperor Francis Joseph and His Times* (London: Hutchinson, 1921), 45

255 *"I am at"*: Eugen Ketterl, *The Emperor Francis Joseph I: An Intimate Study,* trans. M. Ostheide (Boston: Stratford, 1930), 39.

255 *bath attendant:* Ibid.; Frederic Morton, *A Nervous Splendor: Vienna 1888/1889* (London: Penguin, 1980), 236.

256 *happiest hours:* Henri de Weindel, *Behind the Scenes at the Court of Vienna* (London: John Long, 1914), 95–96.

256 *the Emperor's type:* See Morton, *A Nervous Splendor,* 187.

256 *"How can one"*: Craig, *The Battle of Königrätz,* 5.

256 *One evening:* Joseph A. Wright to Seward, May 9, 1866, SD NARA M44/ROLL 13.

256 *to the police bureau:* Ibid.

257 *pocket knife:* "Prussia," *The Times,* Wednesday, May 9, 1866, 14; Loftus, *The Diplomatic Reminiscences of Lord Augustus Loftus, P.C., G.C.B.,* i, 59–60.

257 *slight contusion:* Joseph A. Wright to Seward, May 9, 1866, SD NARA M44/ROLL 13. Bismarck, forewarned of the possibility of an attempt on his life, had donned a padded undershirt that day, and this may have prevented the bullets from doing him greater injury–Loftus, *The Diplomatic Reminiscences of Lord Augustus Loftus, P.C., G.C.B.,* i, 59.

257 *"I consider"*: Pflanze, *Bismarck and the Development of Germany,* 305.

257 *"Events change"*: Joseph A. Wright to Seward, June 7, 1866, SD NARA M44/ROLL 13.

257 *"Why, after all"*: Loftus, *The Diplomatic Reminiscences of Lord Augustus Loftus, P.C., G.C.B.,* i, 58.

257 *accuse Prussia:* Joseph A. Wright to Seward, June 8, 1866, SD NARA M44/ROLL 13.

257 *they resolved:* BGE, 124–25.

257 *the watchword:* Moritz Busch, *Bismarck: Some Secret Pages from His History,* 2 vols. (New York: Macmillan, 1898), i, 446.

257 *Lord Loftus:* Loftus, *The Diplomatic Reminiscences of Lord Augustus Loftus, P.C., G.C.B.,* i, 60.

257 *"The war"*: Wilhelm J. C. E. Stieber, *The Chancellor's Spy: The Revelations of the Chief of Bismarck's Secret Service,* trans. Jan van Heurck (New York: Grove Press, 1980), 108.

257 *"Who is Europe?"*: Ibid.

257 *"When you start"*: Margutti, *The Emperor Francis Joseph and His Times,* 324.

258 *"The struggle"*: Loftus, *The Diplomatic Reminiscences of Lord Augustus Loftus, P.C., G.C.B.,* i, 60; BGE, 128; Pflanze, *Bismarck and the Development of Germany,* 305.

258 *Army of the Elbe:* John Lothrop Motley to Seward, June 19, 1866, SD NARA T157/ROLL 7.

258 *The Elector himself:* John Lothrop Motley to Seward, July 11, 1866, SD NARA T157/ROLL 7.

258 *George V:* Joseph A. Wright to Seward, June 8, 1866, SD NARA M44/ROLL 13; John Lothrop Motley to Seward, June 19, 1866, SD NARA T157/ROLL 7.

258 *Heros von Borcke:* Hume, "Colonel Heros von Borcke: A Famous Prussian Volunteer in the Confederate States Army," in *Southern Sketches, First Series,* no. 2, 15; Heros von Borcke, *Colonel Heros von Borcke's Journal, 26 April–8 October 1862,* 1–2.

258 *"You must change"*: Hume, "Colonel Heros von Borcke: A Famous Prussian Volunteer in the Confederate States Army," in *Southern Sketches, First Series,* no. 2, 21.

258 *The third element:* Moltke to the Commanders of the First and Second Armies, June 22, 1866, in *Moltke's Correspondence During the Campaign of 1866 Against Austria* (London: His Majesty's Stationery Office, 1915), 47.

258 *Fürstenstein:* Loftus, *The Diplomatic Reminiscences of Lord Augustus Loftus, P.C., G.C.B.,* i, 70.

259 *New Palace:* Lord Ronald Charles Sutherland Leveson Gower, *My Reminiscences,* 2 vols. (London: Kegan Paul, 1883), i, 183–85.

259 *"old hag":* Tyler Whittle, *The Last Kaiser: A Biography of Wilhelm II* (New York: Times Books, 1977), 13, 21.

259 *opposed his war: Gedanken,* ii, 47.

25. The Bloodletting

260 *onlookers groaned:* Moss, *Russia in the Age of Alexander II, Tolstoy and Dostoevsky,* 90.

260 *"Lord, forgive":* Venturi, *Roots of Revolution,* 349.

260 *"bringing out":* MR, 255.

260 *"It was a terrible":* Ibid.

260 *now insane:* Venturi, *Roots of Revolution,* 349.

260 *"on his knees":* Ibid.

261 *a French ideal:* James H. Billington, *The Icon and the Axe: An Interpretive History of Russian Culture* (New York: Vintage, 1970), 234.

261 *Reformers were ousted:* Mosse, *Alexander II and the Modernization of Russia,* 72.

261 *arbitrary arrest:* MR, 252.

261 *counter-surveillance:* Stephen Graham, *Tsar of Freedom: The Life and Reign of Alexander II* (New Haven: Yale University Press, 1935), 207; Edward Crankshaw, *The Shadow of the Winter Palace: Russia's Drift to Revolution, 1825–1917* (New York: Da Capo, 2000), 200.

261 *dancing girls:* MR, 243.

261 *French performers:* LGT, 172.

261 *state budget:* Mosse, *Alexander II and the Modernization of Russia,* 88.

261 *tax farming:* David Christian, "A Neglected Great Reform: The Abolition of Tax Farming in Russia," RGR, 102–14.

262 *closed the Sunday Schools:* Mosse, *Alexander II and the Modernization of Russia,* 110–12.

262 *the nobility of Moscow:* Crankshaw, *The Shadow of the Winter Palace,* 181.

262 *"he had already done":* Venturi, *Roots of Revolution,* 317.

262 *"The right of initiative":* Moss, *Russia in the Age of Alexander II, Tolstoy and Dostoevsky,* 89.

262 *"all-powerful lord":* Larissa Zakharova, "Autocracy and the Reforms of 1861–1871 in Russia: Choosing Paths of Development," trans. Daniel Field, RGR, 35.

262 *fall to pieces:* "And now I suppose you consider that I refuse to give up any of my powers from motives of petty ambition," Alexander told one of those who implored him to grant a constitution. "I give you my imperial word that, this very minute, at this very table, I would sign any constitution you like, if I felt that it would be for the good of Russia. But I know that, were I to do so today, tomorrow Russia would fall to pieces"–Mosse, *Alexander II and the Modernization of Russia,* 112–13; see also Alfred J. Rieber, "Alexander II: A Revisionist View," JMH, vol. 43, no. 1 (March 1971), 43.

262 *He "would fall":* MR, 243.

263 *"Is everything quiet":* Ibid.

263 *crony capitalism:* See Minxin Pei, "The Dark Side of China's Rise," FP (March–April 2006).

263 *"his protectors":* MR, 246.

263 *to enlarge the Empire:* Mosse, *Alexander II and the Modernization of Russia,* 119–33.

263 *of Central Asia:* England watched Alexander's Asiatic policy with unease; the Tsar was coming ever closer to India. The British would soon proclaim Victoria Empress of the subcontinent, in order to show the Tsar that they were quite as serious about their Empire as he was about his.

263 *Legal Tender Act:* McPherson, *Battle Cry of Freedom,* 447.

264 *"skin of ivory":* Maurice Paléologue, *The Tragic Romance of Alexander II of Russia,* trans. Arthur Chambers (London: Hutchinson, 1927), 37.

264 *gazelle:* Ibid., 36.

264 *invited her:* Moss, *Russia in the Age of Alexander II, Tolstoy and Dostoevsky,* 90.

264 *The year before:* Ilsa Barea, *Vienna* (New York: Knopf, 1966), 239.

264 *"Prussia":* Franz Josef, "An Meine Völker," *Wiener Zeitung,* June 17, 1866, 1.

264 *brave corps commander:* John Lothrop Motley to Seward, July 11, 1866, SD NARA T157/ROLL 7.

264 *"I am too little"*: Craig, *The Battle of Königrätz*, 14.

264 *"every tree"*: Joseph Redlich, *Emperor Francis Joseph of Austria* (Hamden, CT: Archon Books, 1965), 323.

264 *"So now"*: Craig, *The Battle of Königrätz*, 14.

265 *"It would"*: Ibid., 79.

265 *"I beg"*: Heinrich Freidjung, *The Struggle for Supremacy in Germany 1859–1866,* trans. A. J. P. Taylor and W. L. McElwee (London: Macmillan, 1935), 228.

265 *Reichenberg (Liberec):* Joseph A. Wright to Seward, July 2, 1866, SD NARA M44/ROLL 13.

265 *was astonished to find:* Gedanken, ii, 32; Craig, *The Battle of Königrätz*, 82.

265 *"Ja"*: Craig, *The Battle of Königrätz*, 82.

265 *"I feel pain"*: Otto Friedrich, *Blood and Iron: From Bismarck to Hitler, the von Moltke Family's Impact on German History* (New York: HarperPerennial, 1996), 102.

265 *He quitted the castle: Gedanken,* ii, 32.

266 *cigars, a French novel:* Bismarck to Countess von Bismarck, July 2, 1866, *Gesammelten Werke,* xiv (2), 716–17.

266 *On the evening of July 2:* Moltke to the Second Army, July 2, 1866, in *Moltke's Correspondence During the Campaign of 1866 Against Austria,* 55.

266 *Moltke . . . was roused:* Loftus, *The Diplomatic Reminiscences of Lord Augustus Loftus, P.C., G.C.B.,* i, 82.

266 *"Gott sei:"* Craig, *The Battle of Königrätz*, 85.

266 *when the cannon began:* Horace Rumbold, *Francis Joseph and His Times* (New York: Appleton, 1909), 281.

266 *At noon:* Moltke to von Wolff, July 4, 1866, in *Moltke's Correspondence During the Campaign of 1866 Against Austria,* 56; John Lothrop Motley to Seward, July 3, 1866, SD NARA T157/ROLL 7.

266 *"Your Majesty"*: Craig, *The Battle of Königrätz*, 111.

266 *"Those are not"*: John George Louis Hesekiel, *The Life of Bismarck, Private and Political,* trans. Kenneth R. H. Mackenzie (London: James Hogg, 1870), 402.

266 *"The campaign"*: Craig, *The Battle of Königrätz*, 122.

267 *Nearly half a million:* Ibid., x–xl.

267 *by storm:* Moltke to von Wolff, July 4, 1866, in *Moltke's Correspondence During the Campaign of 1866 Against Austria,* 56.

267 *Were driven:* Moltke to von Wolff, July 4, 1866, in Ibid.

267 *"Oh, you cowards!"*: Craig, *The Battle of Königrätz*, 133.

267 *in full retreat:* Moltke to von Wolff, July 4, 1866, in *Moltke's Correspondence During the Campaign of 1866 Against Austria,* 56.

267 *"Don't be silly"*: Ward, *Germany 1815–1890,* ii, 287.

267 *A number of his officers:* Ibid.

267 *His troops:* John Lothrop Motley to Seward, July 11, 1866, SD NARA T157/ROLL 7.

267 *"A defeated"*: Craig, *The Battle of Königrätz*, 164.

267 *feverish:* Ward, *Germany 1815–1890,* ii, 288.

268 *"still quivers"*: TE, 101–02.

268 *"the date of doom"*: Ibid.

268 *"It is France"*: B, 206.

268 *peremptory telegram:* Napoleon III to Wilhelm I, July 4, 1866, *Rheinpolitik,* i, 302; *Gedanken,* ii, 33.

268 *council of state:* TE, 104.

268 *Drouyn again:* Ibid.

268 *in French tinged:* Bicknell, *Life in the Tuileries Under the Second Empire,* 25.

268 *Marshal Randon:* TE, 104–05.

268 *The Marquis de La Valette:* TE, 105; Ward, *Germany 1815–1890,* ii, 301.

268 *or so the Empress thought:* TE, 105.

269 *"When the Prussian armies"*: Ibid.

269 *tentatively inclined:* Ward, *Germany 1815–1890,* ii, 300–01.

269 *He ordered a French force:* TE, 106.

269 *reversed his decision:* TE, 107; Ward, *Germany 1815–1890,* ii, 301; Freidjung, *The Struggle for Supremacy in Germany 1859–1866,* 248.

269 *"I am not ready":* BGE, 129; Guedalla, *The Second Empire,* 358.

269 *Footmen:* Margutti, *The Emperor Francis Joseph and His Times,* 173.

269 *halberds:* Ibid., 28.

269 *"No breach":* Ibid., 168; Eugen Ketterl, *The Emperor Francis Joseph I: An Intimate Study,* trans. M. Ostheide (Boston: Stratford, 1930), 47.

269 *"What do you mean":* Margutti, *The Emperor Francis Joseph and His Times,* 38.

269 *"You can take it":* Ibid., 34.

269 *every military review:* Ibid., 41.

269 *"Wekerele":* Ibid., 42.

270 *the neat hand:* Ibid., 49.

270 *regulated:* Ibid., 33.

270 *to inspect the table:* Ketterl, *The Emperor Francis Joseph I,* 45.

270 *looked for his reflection:* Ibid.

270 *disturbing:* Freidjung, *The Struggle for Supremacy in Germany 1859–1866,* 237; compare Rumbold, *Francis Joseph and His Times,* 290.

270 *a telegram from Feldherr:* Freidjung, *The Struggle for Supremacy in Germany 1859–1866,* 237.

270 *dining gardens of the Prater:* Ibid., 252.

270 *The music of Strauss:* Ibid.

270 *"Does not such scum":* Ibid.

270 *terror:* John Lothrop Motley to Seward, July 17, 1866, SD NARA T157/ROLL 7.

270 *"gloom":* John Lothrop Motley to Seward, July 11, 1866, SD NARA T157/ROLL 7; John Lothrop Motley to Seward, July 17, 1866, SD NARA

270 *When the Kaiser drove:* Freidjung, *The Struggle for Supremacy in Germany 1859–1866,* 252.

270 *"Long live":* Ibid.

270 Wiener Abendpost: Ibid., 251.

270 *Zelinka:* Ibid., 258.

271 *"trenches were":* Ibid., 258.

271 *The Prussian Second Army:* Joseph A. Wright to Seward, June 12, 1866, SD NARA M44/ROLL 13.

271 *The railway:* Joseph A. Wright to Seward, June 8, 1866, SD NARA M44/ROLL 13.

271 *First Army:* Joseph A. Wright to Seward, June 12, 1866, SD NARA M44/ROLL 13.

271 *The population:* John Lothrop Motley to Seward, July 24, 1866, SD NARA T157/ROLL 7.

271 *Foreign nationals:* John Lothrop Motley to Seward, July 18, 1866, SD NARA T157/ROLL 7.

271 *Steamships in the Danube:* Freidjung, *The Struggle for Supremacy in Germany 1859–1866,* 258.

271 *gates of the city:* John Lothrop Motley to Seward, July 17, 1866, SD NARA T157/ROLL 7.

271 *the Marchfeld:* John Lothrop Motley to Seward, July 24, 1866, SD NARA T157/ROLL 7.

271 *Pressburg:* Ibid.

271 *"sickening expectation":* John Lothrop Motley to Seward, July 11, 1866, SD NARA T157/ROLL 7.

271 *"It makes me sick":* Bismarck, "Gespräche während der Schlacht von Königgrätz," July 3, 1866, *Gesammelten Werke,* vii, 136.

271 *the telegram:* Ward, *Germany 1815–1890,* ii, 302.

271 *"I will be revenged":* BMS, 85.

272 *The longer the war continued:* Freidjung, *The Struggle for Supremacy in Germany 1859–1866,* 270.

272 *He accepted:* Ward, *Germany 1815–1890,* ii, 305.

272 *"go on to":* Craig, *The Battle of Königgrätz,* 169.

272 *"carried away":* Crankshaw, *Bismarck,* 217

272 *The other powers:* Gedanken, ii, 51; Ward, *Germany 1815–1890,* ii, 312–13.

272 *obstinate:* Gedanken, ii, 45–46.

272 *Bismarck replied:* Gedanken, ii, 46.

272 *The wounding of Austria:* Gedanken, ii, 37, 44.

272 *His nerves:* Gedanken, ii, 43.

272 *relieved of his duties:* Gedanken, ii, 43–44.

272 *join his regiment:* Gedanken, ii, 47.

273 *weeping:* Gedanken, ii, 43.

273 *fall out the window:* Gedanken, ii, 47.

273   *Crown Prince Friedrich:* Ibid. Bismarck's account of his conflict with the King and the generals has been criticized by scholars; but there is reason to believe that, if it is in places open to question, it is in its broad outlines true—See B, 211.

273   *The terms:* John Lothrop Motley to Seward, August 1, 1866, SD NARA T157/ROLL 7.

273   *the greatest part of Schleswig:* (1) A small portion of northern Schleswig was retained by Denmark pursuant to the 1864 Treaty of Vienna. (2) Pursuant to the terms of the 1866 settlement, the inhabitants of upper Schleswig were to vote on the question of union with Prussia or with Denmark. The plebiscite did not take place until 1920—NCMH, xiv, *Atlas,* ed. H. C. Darby and Harold Fullard (Cambridge: Cambridge University Press, 1970), 143.

273   *four million Germans:* Loftus, *The Diplomatic Reminiscences of Lord Augustus Loftus, P.C., G.C.B.,* i, 94.

273   *Frankfurt:* BGE, 134–35.

273   *thirty million florins:* On the amount actually extracted from Frankfurt, see Niall Ferguson, *The House of Rothschild: The World's Banker, 1849–1999,* 152, and Fritz Stern, *Gold and Iron: Bismarck, Bleichröder, and the Building of the German Empire,* 90–91.

273   *"Surely":* Ernest Alfred Vizetelly, *The Court of the Tuileries 1852–1870* (London: Chatto & Windus, 1912), 299.

273   *Prussian superstate:* John Lothrop Motley to Seward, July 17, 1866, SD NARA T157/ROLL 7; John Lothrop Motley to Seward, July 24, 1866, SD NARA T157/ROLL 7; Joseph A. Wright to Seward, July 26, 1866, SD NARA M44/ROLL 13.

273   *salvation of Europe:* Metternich made the prediction to Lord Loftus—Loftus, *The Diplomatic Reminiscences of Lord Augustus Loftus, P.C., G.C.B.,* i, 69.

273   *"Each weakening":* Henry A. Kissinger, *A World Restored: Metternich, Castlereagh and the Problems of Peace 1812–1822,* 59.

273   *"In 1866":* William L. Shirer, *The Rise and Fall of the Third Reich: A History of Nazi Germany* (New York: Simon & Schuster, 1960), 95.

273   *Prussian Germany:* Joseph Roth, "Clemenceau," in Roth, *Report from a Parisian Paradise: Essays from France, 1925–1939,* trans. Michael Hoffmann (New York: W. W. Norton, 2004), 261.

274   *"a matter of detail":* Fletcher, *The Mission of Vincent Benedetti to Berlin 1864–1870,* 99.

274   *But he agreed to ask:* Freidjung, *The Struggle for Supremacy in Germany 1859–1866,* 281.

274   *Count Benedetti:* Fletcher, *The Mission of Vincent Benedetti to Berlin 1864–1870,* 109; Ward, *Germany 1815–1890,* ii, 314; Busch, *Bismarck: Some Secret Pages from His History,* i, 448.

274   *"Louis shall":* B, 208.

274   *But the crafty Junker:* Freidjung, *The Struggle for Supremacy in Germany 1859–1866,* 281–82.

274   *German civil war:* Bismarck was at once the Abraham Lincoln and the Jefferson Davis of the German civil war. Like Lincoln, he sought to unify a nation; like Davis, he sought to withdraw his own region from one federal system (the Austrian-dominated German Confederation) and bring it within the fold of a new one (the North German Confederation, afterwards the German Reich)—Carl N. Degler, "The American Civil War and the German Wars of Unification: The Problem of Comparison," ORTW, 55.

274   *refused to push it:* Bismarck in 1866 attained to Clausewitz's strategic ideal: "A prince or general who knows exactly how to organize his War according to his object and means, who does neither too little nor too much, gives by that the greatest proof of his genius. . . . It is the exact fulfillment of silent suppositions, it is the noiseless harmony of the whole action which we should admire, and which only makes itself known in the total result"—Clausewitz, *On War,* 242.

274   *The purest type:* On the contrast between Bismarck's "practicable aims" and *Caesarenwahnsin,* see G. P. Gooch, "Bismarck's Legacy," FA, XXX (1952), reprinted in *Otto von Bismarck: A Historical Assessment,* ed. Theodore S. Hamerow (Boston: D. C. Heath, 1966), 97.

274   *"hour of fate":* TE, 110.

274   *"seemed so utterly":* TE, 110–11.

275   *"My soul":* TE, 111–12.

275   *Public opinion:* TE, 111; Ward, *Germany 1815–1890,* ii, 315.

275   *"painted Jove":* John Lothrop Motley to Seward, July 17, 1866, SD NARA T157/ROLL 7. Motley's allusion is to Dryden's *Annus Mirabilis.*

275   *"hatched from a cannon ball":* Barbara W. Tuchman, *The Guns of August* (New York: Bonanza, 1982), 7.

275 *national industry:* Mirabeau said: "La guerre est l'industrie nationale de la Prusse."

275 *Richelieu:* Kissinger, *Diplomacy,* 112, 116–17.

275 *"ces maudits":* Treitschke, *The Fire-Test of the North German Confederation,* 21.

275 *"moral shock":* TE, 111.

275 *He could neither walk:* BGE, 129.

275 *At Vichy, he and Drouyn:* Freidjung, *The Struggle for Supremacy in Germany 1859–1866,* 297.

275 *Mainz:* Loftus, *The Diplomatic Reminiscences of Lord Augustus Loftus, P.C., G.C.B.,* i, 96; Ward, *Germany 1815–1890,* ii, 315–16; Freidjung, *The Struggle for Supremacy in Germany 1859–1866,* 295.

275 *Archduchess Charlotte:* Cunningham, *Mexico and the Foreign Policy of Napoleon III,* 189.

275 *Cuirassiers:* Vizetelly, *The Court of the Tuileries 1852–1870,* 332.

275 *belonged to Marie-Antoinette:* Ibid., 330.

275 *withdraw the French expeditionary force:* John Lothrop Motley to Seward, May 15, 1866, SD NARA T157/ROLL 7.

276 *He published:* Headlam, *Bismarck and the Foundation of the German Empire,* 279; Freidjung, *The Struggle for Supremacy in Germany 1859–1866,* 296–97.

276 *Belgium?:* Freidjung, *The Struggle for Supremacy in Germany 1859–1866,* 299–300; Headlam, *Bismarck and the Foundation of the German Empire,* 281–83.

276 *"Bismarck thinks":* Tolstoy to Y. S. Samarin, January 10, 1867, TL, 211.

276 *"the blood-letting" . . . "old jades":* Tolstoy to Y. S. Samarin, January 10, 1867, TL, 211.

277 *2nd Panzer Regiment:* Anthony Beevor, *Stalingrad* (London: Penguin, 1999), 17.

277 *Riding with them:* Hume, "Colonel Heros von Borcke: A Famous Prussian Volunteer in the Confederate States Army," in *Southern Sketches, First Series,* no. 2, 16.

277 *Order of the Red Eagle:* Ibid.

277 *(largely ineffective):* Geoffrey Wawro, *The Franco-Prussian War: The German Conquest of France in 1870–1871* (Cambridge: Cambridge University Press, 2003), 61.

277 *The crowd hailed:* B, 222.

277 *captured guns:* Loftus, *The Diplomatic Reminiscences of Lord Augustus Loftus, P.C., G.C.B.,* i, 109.

277 *"But I have beaten":* Stern, *Gold and Iron,* 94.

277 *indemnify or pardon:* Gedanken, ii, 44, 69–70.

277 *ministerial responsibility:* Craig, *The Politics of the Prussian Army 1640–1945,* xiv; Michael Foot, "The Origins of the Franco-Prussian War and the Remaking of Germany," NCMH, x, 579; Stern, *Gold and Iron,* 93–94.

277 *A relic:* Gedanken, ii, 67–69; Craig, *The Politics of the Prussian Army 1640–1945,* 174–79. Niall Ferguson rightly observes that Bismarck "abandoned his original commitment to William I that he would assert the monarch's unqualified control over the military budget; for, although the military budget of the North German Confederation and later the Reich was never voted on annually, it was still voted on periodically"—Ferguson, *The House of Rothschild,* 150–51. But this was a hollow victory for the free-state liberals, for under the new régime there was neither genuine ministerial responsibility nor effective legislative supervision of the army, which continued to be controlled almost exclusively by the old Prussian military caste. Under the constitution of the Reich, ministers could be dismissed only by the Kaiser, not the legislature; and the lawmakers had no power to initiate legislation. Under Wilhelm II, even the Minister of War was largely a cipher; the army was controlled almost entirely by the sovereign's military cabinet and the General Staff. In the last phases of World War One, the Reich was virtually a military dictatorship under General Ludendorff—Hans Speier, "Ludendorff: The German Concept of Total War," in *Makers of Modern Strategy: Military Thought from Machiavelli to Hitler,* ed. Earle, 308–15.

278 *"sacred right":* Joseph A. Wright to Seward, September 3, 1866, SD NARA M44/ROLL 13.

278 *"right of the German":* Bismarck, "Sitzung der Kommission des Abgeordnetenhauses," August 25, 1866, in *Die gesammelten Werke,* x, 276–77.

278 *zu leben:* Gedanken, ii, 71.

278 *militant:* Bismarck's philosophy of "blood and iron" was influenced by the the romantic theories of Johann Gottfried Herder, Johann Gottlieb Fichte, and Justus Möser. It was at the same time an early version of the idea of *Lebensraum*—living space—which Friedrich Ratzel, Karl Haufshofer, and Adolf Hitler subsequently propounded. In the romantic theory, a nation was not an agglomera-

tion of individuals, of private souls: it was a living organism, an "unanalysable organic whole," one which, if it were to survive, must feed at times upon the flesh of other nations–See Isaiah Berlin, *Against the Current: Essays in the History of Ideas,* 10–13, 342–46; Abram L. Harris, "Sombart and German (National) Socialism," JPE, vol. 50, no. 6 (December 1942), 818–19; Otto Pflanze, "Bismarck and German Nationalism," AHR, vol. 60, no. 3 (April 1955), 560; George Santayana, *Egotism in German Philosophy* (New York: Charles Scribner's Sons, 1916), 68–69.

278   *"a national force":* Jacob Burckhardt, *History of Greek Culture,* trans. Palmer Hilty (New York: Dover, 2002), 161.

278   *restrain the military chiefs:* "It was the fatal weakness of the German Empire," Winston Churchill wrote, "that its military leaders, who knew every detail of their profession and nothing outside it, considered themselves, and became, arbiters of the whole policy of the State. . . . Everything in Germany had been sacrificed to the military view. On every occasion [after the fall of Bismarck] the General Staff had had their way." This "intense and mighty organism" was "at once the strength and ruin of the German Empire," for in Germany "there was no one to stand against the General Staff and to bring their will-power and special point of view into harmony with the general salvation of the State"–Winston S. Churchill, *Thoughts and Adventures* (New York: W. W. Norton, 1991), 104, 108–09. Bismarck failed to create a system which nurtured future leaders, ones capable of carrying on his policy. "It was the great flaw in Bismarck that he did not parallel Moltke's officer-corps by a corresponding race of politicians who would identify themselves in feeling with his State and its new tasks, would constantly take up good men from below, and so provide for the continuance of the Bismarck action-pulse forever"–Oswald Spengler, *The Decline of the West: An Abridged Edition,* ed. Helmut Werner and Arthur Helps, trans. Charles Francis Atkinson (Oxford: Oxford University Press, 1991), 386. Henry Kissinger points out that Bismarck's "very success committed Germany to a permanent tour de force. It created conditions that could be dealt with only by extraordinary leaders. Their emergence in turn was thwarted by the colossus who dominated his country for nearly a generation. Bismarck's tragedy was that he left a heritage of unassimilated greatness. . . . a great man tends to stunt the emeregence of strong personalities"–Kissinger, "The White Revolutionary: Reflections on Bismarck," D, vol. 97, no. 3 (Summer 1968), 890, 921.

278 278   *"Future years":* SDC, 80–81.

278   *"a few stray":* SDC, 81.

278   *"the leading actor":* SDC, 310.

278   *"a Nationality":* SDC, 314

278   *"the peculiar color":* SDC, 69.

279   *"The current portraits":* Ibid.

279   *"Today, alas":* Paléologue, *Roman tragique de l'Empereur Alexandre II,* 30–31.

279   *He went to Putbus:* Gedanken, ii, 76.

279   *"When he sits still":* BGE, 142.

Part Three: FREEDOM AND TERROR

26. Towards the Abyss

283   *burned towns:* MCCW, 796, 800.

283   *"This is Sherman's":* MCCW, 800.

283   *"Nature":* MCCW, 800.

283   *"There was poverty":* MCCW, 805.

283   *in ruins:* MCCW, 802–03.

283   *the old Colonel:* MCCW, 814–15.

283   *They had enough:* MCCW, 805.

283   *Scipio:* MCCW, 815.

284   *"the habit of all":* MCCW, 809.

284   "There remains": William Faulkner, *Light in August,* in Faulkner, *Novels, 1930–1935,* ed. Joseph Blotner and Noel Polk (New York: Library of America, 1985), 442.

284 *"a hundred"*: MCCW, 774.

284 *Rawlins Lowndes:* MCCW, 807.

284 *"perfect wreck"*: MCCW, 818.

284 *"A feeling"*: MCCW, 814.

284 *"are nights"*: MCCW, xli.

284 *to go for a walk:* LGT, 191–92.

285 *"But I don't need"*: LGT, 191.

285 *"dear Angel"*: S. Konovalov, "The Emperor Alexander II and Princess Ekaterina Dolgorukaya (Yurievskaya): Nine Letters," *Oxford Slavonic Papers* (1964), vol. 11, 94ff.

286 *curious faraway look:* Maurice Paléologue, *The Tragic Romance of Alexander II of Russia,* trans. Arthur Chambers (London: Hutchinson, 1927), 62.

286 *"looks into another"*: Robert Blake, *Disraeli* (New York: St. Martin's Press, 1967), 522.

286 *"Why"*: Paléologue, *The Tragic Romance of Alexander II of Russia,* 141.

286 *the Pan-Slavs:* George F. Kennan, *The Decline of Bismarck's European Order: Franco-Russian Relations, 1875–1890* (Princeton: Princeton University Press, 1980), 32–33.

286 *There was a low door:* Paléologue, *The Tragic Romance of Alexander II of Russia,* 41.

286 *In Nicholas's study:* Nicholas I had two studies in Winter Palace, one on the ground floor and one on the third floor. Some scholars believe that the assignations took place in the study on the ground floor–Paléologue, *The Tragic Romance of Alexander II of Russia,* 41; Walter G. Moss, *Russia in the Age of Alexander II, Tolstoy and Dostoevsky* (London: Anthem Press, 2002), 116.

287 *Tsarskoe Selo:* Paléologue, *The Tragic Romance of Alexander II of Russia,* 63.

287 *his alternative world:* Prince Kroptkin spoke of the Tsar's "double life"–MR, 244. The pattern is familiar enough. The tsars were constantly falling into the habit of a double life. Ivan the Terrible, for a time, withdrew from Moscow altogether. He later divided his principality into two parts; in the one, the traditional customs and institutions of Muscovy were preserved, while in the other the Tsar created a private fantasy world. In this secondary domain, Ivan acted upon the "hellish inspiration" that seized him in middle life, and was free to delight in blood and in other forms of perversity. The dreamworld of Catherine the Great, though it was milder in nature, was scarcely less fantastic. The story of the horse was a crude simulacrum of a more complicated drama of escape. The Empress feared to undertake a thorough reformation of her Empire; she relaxed the more odious feature of the patrimonial state without, however, doing away with it altogether, and like other tremulous despots she bought off potential enemies with public treasure, lavishing on the more dangerous grandees large grants of land. These corrupt expedients did not satisfy Catherine's lofty ideals of reason and order, and in an elaborate charade she played the part of Empress-*philosophe,* drafting make-believe laws for a make-believe Russia. The last of the omnipotent tsars, Josef Stalin, retired for long intervals to his roses and mimosas, as well as to his books, as though he were a private scholar who aspired only to cultivate his mind and his gardens in tranquility, and not a cruel tyrant who sent millions to their deaths–See N. M. Karamzin, *Karamzin's Memoir on Ancient and Modern Russia,* trans. Richard Pipes (Cambridge, MA: Harvard University Press, 1959), 112; Richard Pipes, *Russia Under the Old Regime* (Harmondsworth, Middlesex: Penguin, 1979), 119, 174; and Simon Sebag Montefiore, *Stalin: The Court of the Red Tsar* (New York: Knopf, 2004), 65, 74, 93–99, 121, 133–35, 522–23, 542–43, 567–568, 580, 623–24.

287 *"Count Shuvalov is out driving"*: Blake, *Disraeli,* 624.

287 *"Schu"*: Ibid., 647.

287 *"prepared one reactionary"*: MR, 242.

288 *"A couple of bears"*: MR, 243–44.

288 Verwundet: LRW, iv, 190. It is not certain whether Nietzsche heard the musical phrase only, or whether he heard the accompanying words also. The music forms part of the third act of *Siegfried.*

288 *Friedrich Nietzsche:* Nietzsche had met Wagner once before, in Leipzig; it was on that occasion that the composer extended to him an invitation to visit him at Triebschen.

288 *"One thing"*: LRW, iii, 510.

288 *"the other peoples"*: LRW, iv, 39–40.

289 *Bayreuth:* LRW, iv, 262–63.

289   *"Dionysian power"*: Friedrich Nietzsche, *The Gay Science,* trans. Walter Kaufmann (New York: Vintage, 1974), 327–28.

289   "Pater Seraphicus": LRW, iv, 259.

289   *"At that time"*: LRW, iv, 356.

289   *"contest"*: LRW, iv, 192.

289   *"made the Meister"*: Ibid.

289   *"I'd let go"*: Friedrich Nietzsche, *On the Genealogy of Morals and Ecce Homo,* trans. Walter Kaufmann (New York: Vintage, 1989), 247 (emphasis in original).

289   *"secret work"*: Ibid., 254.

289   *"heights"*: Ibid., 263.

289   *reflexive asceticism:* Nietzsche described the asceticism of the philosopher as a form of protective coloration: "for the longest time philosophy would not have been *possible at all* on earth without ascetic wraps and cloaks, without an ascetic self-misunderstanding." The philosopher was forced to disguise himself as an ascetic priest—a type for which Nietzsche had no sympathy. He expressed the hope that the winged creature would eventually escape from its gloomy caterpillar of asceticism, but outwardly at least was true to the ascetic type—Ibid., 115–16 (emphasis in original).

290   *"a philosopher and solitary"*: Friedrich Nietzsche, *The Will to Power,* trans. Walter Kaufmann and R. J. Hollingdale (New York: Vintage, 1968), 3.

290   *the artist knows not:* "This seems to me to be almost the norm among fertile artists—nobody knows a child less well than its parents do—and it is true even in the case, to take a tremendous example, of the whole world of Greek art and poetry: it never 'knew' what it did"—Nietzsche, *The Gay Science,* 327. Nietzsche refined the philosophy of Pindar, who said, "Become what you are." "To become what one is," Nietzsche said, "one must not have the faintest notion *what* one is." Nietzsche, *On the Genealogy of Morals and Ecce Homo,* 254.

27. Unripe Fruit

291   *Count Benedetti:* Count Benedetti, *Ma Mission en Prusse* (Paris: Henri Plon, 1871), 315.

291   *still talked:* "France and Spain," *The Times,* July 8, 1870, 5.

291   *Rarely had the peace of Europe:* E. B. Washburne to Hamilton Fish, July 19, 1870, SD NARA M34/ROLL T-70; Lord Newton, *Lord Lyons: A Record of British Diplomacy,* 2 vols. (London: Edward Arnold, 1913), i, 294.

292   *La Granja:* "News in Brief," *The Times,* Tuesday, July 5, 1870, 12.

292   *Prince Leopold:* "Prince Leopold," *The Times,* Monday, July 11, 1870, 10.

292   *by a remote affinity:* George Bancroft to Hamilton Fish, July 23, 1870, SD NARA M44/ROLL 16.

292   *stout and easygoing:* George Santayana, *Persons and Places: The Background of My Life* (New York: Scribner's, 1944), 77.

292   *Don Juan Prim:* George Bancroft to Hamilton Fish, July 12, 1870, SD NARA M44/ROLL 16.

292   *Portuguese Princess:* "Prince Leopold," *The Times,* Monday, July 11, 1870, 10.

292   *was reluctant:* Leopold initially declined the offer of the Crown—Edward Crankshaw, *Bismarck* (London: Penguin, 1990), 260; see also *Bismarck and the Hohenzollern Candidature for the Spanish Throne,* ed. Georges Bonnin, trans. Isabella A. Massey (London: Chatto & Windus, 1957), 9, and Robert Howard Lord, *The Origins of the War of 1870: New Documents from the German Archives* (New York: Russell & Russell, 1966), 18–19. Prince Leopold's younger brother, Frederick, was also considered for the Spanish throne; but he was averse to the idea.

292   *Bernhardi:* B, 265; *Bismarck and the Hohenzollern Candidature for the Spanish Throne,* 19; Lord, *The Origins of the War of 1870: New Documents from the German Archives,* 17.

292   *"reptile funds"*: B, 260; BGE, 166.

292   *In the last days of June:* BGE, 168.

292   *tepid approval: Bismarck and the Hohenzollern Candidature for the Spanish Throne,* 10.

293   *"Had they"*: EHA, 937.

293   *poison:* Office, Adams said, "was more poisonous than priestcraft or pedgagogy in proportion as it held more power . . . [the] poison was that of the will,—the distortion of sight,—the warping of

mind,–the degradation of tissue,–the coarsening of taste,–the narrowing of sympathy to the emotions of a caged rat"–EHA, 1054.

293 *"I suppose"*: Henry Adams to Henry Cabot Lodge, Nov 15, 1881, in *Henry Adams: Selected Letters,* ed. Ernest Samuels (Cambridge, MA: Belknap Press, 1992), 164–65.

294 *expiatory pilgrimage:* EHA, 740.

294 *"denser, richer"*: Henry James, *Hawthorne,* in James, *Literary Criticism: Essays on Literature, American Writers, English Writers,* ed. Leon Edel and Mark Wilson (New York: Library of America, 1984), 351.

294 *"less a sufferer"*: Alfred Kazin, *On Native Grounds: An Interpretation of Modern American Prose Literature* (New York: Reynal & Hitchcock, 1942), 49.

294 *"speak out plainly"*: Ibid., ix.

294 *"exile"*: Ibid., 5.

295 *"May God"*: Stanford Family Collection, Iris and B. Gerald Cantor Center for Visual Arts, Stanford University.

295 *"there cannot be"*: SDC, 132.

295 *"mechanical consolidation"*: EHA, 1035.

295 *The French Emperor:* Thomas W. Evans, *The Second French Empire,* ed. Edward A. Crane (New York: D. Appleton, 1903), 160.

295 *Three days before:* Baron Mercier de Lostende to Gramont, July 3, 1870, *Origines Diplomatiques,* xxviii, 19; B, 266; Lord, *The Origins of the War of 1870,* 25–26; BMS, 118.

295 *"Le vin"*: Ernest Alfred Vizetelly, *The Court of the Tuileries, 1852–1870* (London: Chatto & Windus, 1922), 394.

296 *Can-Can:* Geoffrey Wawro, *The Franco-Prussian War: The German Conquest of France in 1870–1871* (Cambridge: Cambridge University Press, 2003), 26.

296 *"constitutional minister"*: "France," *The Times,* Tuesday, July 5, 1870, 9; Theodore Zeldin, *Emile Ollivier and the Liberal Empire of Napoleon III* (Oxford: Clarendon Press, 1963), 1.

296 *the state of France:* George Bancroft to Hamilton Fish, July 14, 1870, SD NARA M44/ROLL 16.

296 *look to America:* George Bancroft to Hamilton Fish, July 16, 1870, SD NARA M44/ROLL 16; "The Crops in France," *The Times,* Wednesday, July 6, 1870, 10.

296 *Bazaine had returned:* Etat des Services, May 11, 1872, Bazaine Dossier, AA, 6yd 62.

296 *Ollivier arrived:* Napoleon III to Ollivier, July 5, 1870, *Origines Diplomatiques,* xxviii, 36; "France and Spain," *The Times,* Friday, July 8, 1870, 5.

296 *Ollivier might seem:* The Times, Saturday, July 16, 1870, 8; B, 264.

296 *The pre-eminent figure:* The Times, Saturday, July 16, 1870, 8.

297 *the proposed* entente: James Wycliffe Headlam, *Bismarck and the Foundation of the German Empire* (New York: G. P. Putnam's Sons, 1899), 319. Napoleon III contemplated also an alliance with Italy; but negotiations with the Cabinet of Florence reached an impasse when questions concerning the temporal powers of the Pope and the status of Rome as a fief of the Church were raised. The Italians wished to see Rome the capital of a united Italy; Louis-Napoleon, whose troops upheld the papal jurisdiction with bayonets, was reluctant to take a step which might cost him the support of his Ultramontane subjects–Michael Foot, "The Origins of the Franco-Prussian War and the Remaking of Germany," NCMH, x, 600; Eric Hobsbawm, *The Age of Capital* (New York: Vintage, 1996), 103–04.

297 *"imperil the interests"*: *The Times,* Thursday, July 7, 1870, 9, 12.

297 *"with your support"*: Ibid.; Lord, *The Origins of the War of 1870,* 42.

297 *cheers:* Ollivier to Napoleon III, July 6, 1870, *Origines Diplomatiques,* xxviii, 58–59; *The Times,* Thursday, July 7, 1870, 12; *The Times,* Saturday, July 9, 1870, 12.

297 *casus belli:* It was at this time that Gramont began to inform French diplomats abroad that, if Prussia insisted on the Hohenzollern candidature, *"c'est la guerre"*–Gramont to General Count Fleury, July 6, 1870, *Origines Diplomatiques,* xxviii, 64.

298 *other thoughts:* MR, 236.

298 *"It often happens"*: MR, 237.

298 *A visit to Moscow:* MR, 264–67.

298 *The noble families:* MR, 264.

298   *"the intruders":* Ibid.

299   *"That is the sort":* MR, 25.

299   *"A couple of":* MR, 264.

299   *Yet he did not love:* MR, 250–51.

299   *In the house next door:* MR, 266.

299   "Very grave news from Spain": Gramont to Benedetti, July 3, 1870, *Origines Diplomatiques,* xxviii, 20.

299   *Shortly afterward:* Gramont to Benedetti, July 7, 1870, *Origines Diplomatiques,* xxviii, 86; Benedetti to Gramont, July 8, 1870, *Origines Diplomatiques,* xxviii, 112.

299   *every imaginable argument:* Benedetti to Gramont, July 11, 1870, *Origines Diplomatiques,* xxviii, 218–19.

300   *restoration of his health:* His illness, he said, was of a "bilious character"–Moritz Busch, *Bismarck: Some Secret Pages from His History,* 2 vols. (New York: Macmillan, 1898), i, 25.

300   *recalled him:* George Bancroft to Hamilton Fish, July 12, 1870, SD NARA M44/ROLL 16; "France, Prussia, and Spain," *The Times,* Thursday, July 14, 1870, 5; Le Sourd to Gramont, July 12, 1870, *Origines Diplomatiques,* xxviii, 253.

300   *La Barberina:* Thomas Carlyle, *History of Friedrich II of Prussia, called Frederick the Great,* 10 vols. (London: Chapman & Hall, 1872), v, 258–61, vi, 186, 189; BMS, 112.

300   *"is interested in furnishing":* BMS, 112–13.

300   *"repeatedly pacing":* Busch, *Bismarck: Some Secret Pages from His History,* i, 446.

300   *in his office:* Ibid., i, 21, 448–52.

300   *writing table:* Ibid., i, 450.

301   *studious in fomenting:* Lord, *The Origins of the War of 1870,* 53, 95, 107.

301   *"As a matter of fact":* Busch, *Bismarck: Some Secret Pages from His History,* i, 24–25.

301   *"That the unification":* David Wetzel, *A Duel of Giants: Bismarck, Napoleon III, and the Origins of the Franco-Prussian War* (Madison, WI: University of Wisconsin Press, 2001), 66; Hans Rothfels, "Problems of a Bismarck Biography," RP, vol. 9, no. 3 (July 1947), 374.

301   *"That German unity":* Wetzel, *A Duel of Giants,* 66–67.

301   *"We can set":* Ibid., 67.

28. The Viper Casts Its Skin

302   *"This dispatch":* Thomas W. Evans, *The Second French Empire,* ed. Edward A. Crane (New York: D. Appleton, 1903), 164.

302   *"What has happened":* Wetzel, *A Duel of Giants,* 138.

302   *The withdrawal:* Gramont to Benedetti, July 12, 1870, *Origines Diplomatiques,* xxviii, 255.

303   *"It will not be":* Evans, *The Second French Empire,* 164.

303   *threw down his sword:* Philip Guedalla, *The Second Empire* (New York: G. P. Putnam's, 1922), 409.

303   *The Empress, too:* Ibid. Eugénie believed that war with Prussia was inevitable and could not be avoided–TE, 137.

303   *telegraphed to Gramont:* Napoleon III to Gramont, July 12, 1870, *Origines Diplomatiques,* xxviii, 260–61.

303   *"Never have we been":* Evans, *The Second French Empire,* 168.

303   *He had been left out:* Roger Price, *The French Second Empire: An Anatomy of Political Power* (Cambridge: Cambridge University Press, 2001), 429.

304   *"My children":* Honoré de Balzac, *Eugénie Grandet,* trans. M. A. Crawford (London: Penguin, 1955), 157.

304   *"conscious of being":* Wetzel, *A Duel of Giants* 147.

304   *Bismarck, too:* Fritz Stern, *Gold and Iron: Bismarck, Bleichröder, and the Building of the German Empire* (New York: Vintage, 1979), 130.

304   *"with a threatening":* Sidney Whitman, *Personal Reminiscences of Prince Bismarck* (New York: D. Appleton, 1903), 28.

304   *Queen Augusta's:* Gedanken, ii, 86–87.

304   *"My first thought":* Gedanken, ii, 84–85, 88.

305 *encounter with Benedetti:* Lord, *The Origins of the War of 1870*, 84–85; Hedwig von Olfers Abeken, *Bismarck's Pen: The Life of Heinrich Abeken*, trans. Mrs. C. E. Barrett-Lennard and M. W. Huper (London: George Allen, 1911), 252; "The War," *The Times*, Monday, July 18, 1870, 9.

305 *"might have embroiled":* Lord, *The Origins of the War of 1870*, 86; see also "The War," *The Times*, Monday, July 18, 1870, 9.

305 *Benedetti could not:* Lord, *The Origins of the War of 1870*, 86–87.

305 *"Well, Sire":* Ibid., 87; see also Benedetti, *Ma Mission en Prusse*, 372.

305 *"It seems to me":* Lord, *The Origins of the War of 1870*, 87; Benedetti to Gramont, July 13, 1870, *Origines Diplomatiques*, xxviii, 293–94.

305 *"Be kind enough":* "The War," *The Times*, Monday, July 18, 1870, 9; George Bancroft to Hamilton Fish, July 14, 1870, SD NARA M44/ROLL 16.

306 *The "position":* Whitman, *Personal Reminiscences of Prince Bismarck*, 133.

306 *Was the army ready:* Lord, *The Origins of the War of 1870*, 100.

306 *"The tug":* Lincoln to Lyman Trumbull, December 10, 1860, SW, 1859–1860, 190.

306 *"rather sternly":* Abeken, *Bismarck's Pen*, 255.

306 *more gentle:* George Bancroft to Hamilton Fish, July 19, 1870, SD NARA M44/ROLL 16.

306 *an ongoing negotiation:* Gedanken, ii, 91.

306 *"Ems, 13 July":* "France, Prussia. and Spain," *The Times*, Thursday, July 14, 1870, 5.

306 *"If I not only":* Lord, *The Origins of the War of 1870*, 101. Earlier in the week, *The Times* compared Prince Leopold's candidature to "a red flag waved before the eyes of a bull"—"France," *The Times*, Monday, July 11, 1870, 12.

307 *He got drunk:* Alice Hunt Sokoloff, *Kate Chase for the Defense* (New York: Dodd, Meade, 1971), 115.

307 *"You know":* Ibid., 118.

307 *"happiness of a wife":* Ibid., 138–39.

307 *"acquiesce cheerfully":* Ibid., 156.

307 *"sadly disconnected":* Ibid., 120.

307 *"would feel":* Ibid., 124.

307 *"I would not":* Ibid., 132–33.

308 *"I will* not": Ibid., 120 (emphasis in original).

308 *Mr. Worth:* Ibid., 134.

308 *But her dress was now:* Ibid., 114–15.

308 *"I almost hate":* Ibid., 158–59 (commas added for clarification).

308 *"Jephtha's daughter":* Henry Adams to Charles Milnes Gaskell, March 7, 1870, in *Henry Adams: Selected Letters*, ed. Ernest Samuels (Cambridge, MA: Belknap Press, 1992), 112.

308 *Jephtha:* Judges 11:30–40.

309 *"Public Insult":* Le Soir, July 14, 1870, 1.

309 *arrived at the Tuileries:* "Latest Intelligence," *The Times*, Friday, July 15, 1870, 12.

309 *"slap in the face":* James F. McMillan, *Napoleon III* (London: Longman, 1991), 158–59; Lord Edmond Fitzmaurice, *The Life of Granville George Leveson Gower, Second Earl Granville, K.G.*, 2 vols. (London: Longmans, Green, 1905), ii, 34; "The War," *The Times*, Wednesday, July 20, 1870, 5.

309 *"It is now":* Evans, *The Second French Empire*, 180–81.

309 *red silk:* Vizetelly, *The Court of the Tuileries, 1852–1870*, 130.

309 *influence of drugs:* Wawro, *The Franco-Prussian War*, 26.

310 *"Napoleon has no option":* George Bancroft to Hamilton Fish, July 14, 1870, SD NARA M44/ROLL 16.

310 *"depth of French feeling":* *The Times*, Friday, July 8, 1870, 9. "France," Louis-Napoleon said, "has slipped out of my hand. I cannot rule unless I lead. . . . I have no choice but to advance at the head of public opinion which I can neither stem nor check"—Michael Foot, "The Origins of the Franco-Prussian War and the Remaking of Germany," NCMH, x, 598.

310 *"la Guerre":* "France and Prussia," *The Times*, Saturday, July 16, 1870, 9. According to legend, Eugénie boasted that she had finally got her "little war" (*"ma petite guerre"*); but she herself always denied this, and others have offered evidence that the quotation was fabricated by her enemies. See Thomas W. Evans, *The Second French Empire*, 167; TE, 121–22.

310 *reeking hot:* "The War," *The Times*, Friday, July 22, 1870, 5; "The War," *The Times*, Saturday, July 23 1870, 10.

310 *"After the first battle":* "The War," *The Times,* Friday, July 22, 1870, 5.

310 *Soldiers went about:* "The War," *The Times,* Monday, July 18, 1870, 9.

310 *Marie Sass:* "The War," *The Times,* Saturday, July 23, 1870, 10; Roger Price, *The French Second Empire: An Anatomy of Political Power* (Cambridge: Cambridge University Press, 2001), 438.

310 *Garde Impériale: Etat des Services,* May 11, 1872, Bazaine Dossier, AA, 6yd 62.

310 *Josefa de la Peña:* Bazaine to the Minister of War, July 10, 1865, Bazaine Dossier, AA, 6yd 62.

310 "Nous marchons": Philip Guedalla, *The Two Marshals* (New York: Reynal & Hitchcock, 1943), 136.

29. Dead or Victorious

311 *"rosiest humor":* Abeken, *Bismarck's Pen,* 256.

311 *"incredible napping":* Ibid., 257–58.

311 *slept poorly:* Ibid., 256, 263.

311 *"It is terrible":* "The War," *The Times,* Saturday, July 23, 1870, 10 ; "The War," *The Times,* Thursday, July 21, 1870, 9.

312 *The little Corsican:* Lord, *The Origins of the War of 1870,* 108.

312 *"forty millions":* George Bancroft to Hamilton Fish, July 16, 1870, SD NARA M44/ROLL 16.

312 *in perfect order:* George Bancroft to Hamilton Fish, July 23, 1870, SD NARA M44/ROLL 16.

312 *"was neither confusion":* George Bancroft to Hamilton Fish, August 2, 1870, SD NARA M44/ROLL 16.

312 *more than a million:* George Bancroft to Hamilton Fish, July 23, 1870, SD NARA M44/ROLL 16.

312 *"His mien":* John Van der Kiste, *The Romanovs 1818–1959* (Stroud, Glós: Sutton, 2003), 75.

313 *"an inward":* Blake, *Disraeli,* 683.

313 *"an insolent expression":* Stephen Graham, *Tsar of Freedom: The Life and Reign of Alexander II* (New Haven: Yale University Press, 1935), 208.

313 *A teenaged girl:* MR, 426.

313 *A teenaged boy:* MR, 427.

313 *In the 1870s Tolstoy:* Aylmer Maude, *The Life of Tolstoy: First Fifty Years* (New York: Dodd, Mead, 1910), 386.

313 *There were moments:* MR, 430–31.

313 *"Don't speak":* MR, 430.

313 *drank to excess:* Van der Kiste, *The Romanovs 1818–1959,* 67.

314 *an elevator:* Paléologue, *The Tragic Romance of Alexander II of Russia,* 123.

314 *"a true Russian":* Ibid., 168.

314 *"completely dominated":* Ibid., 79–80.

314 *"I congratulate you":* Ibid., 80; Alfred J. Rieber, "Alexander II: A Revisionist View," JMH, vol. 43, no. 1 (March 1971), 44. Bismarck rightly considered Shuvalov's appointment to the London embassy "a species of honorable exile"—Kennan, *The Decline of Bismarck's European Order: Franco-Russian Relations, 1875–1890,* 70–71.

315 *"big Utopian Babbler":* Robert K. Massie, *Dreadnought: Britain, Germany, and the Coming of the Great War* (New York: Ballantine Books, 1992), 83.

315 *"England, beware":* Whitman, *Personal Reminiscences of Prince Bismarck,* 30.

316 *"World-Historical people":* Hegel, *The Philosophy of History,* trans. J. Sibree (New York: Dover, 1956), 37, 47, 78, 341–42.

316 *"German Spirit":* Ibid., 341.

316 *"that if Germany":* Fitzmaurice, *The Life of Granville George Leveson Gower, Second Earl Granville, K.G.,* ii, 37.

316 *who believed that Germany:* "The universal error of the two generations after the Congress of Vienna was to exaggerate the strength of France among the Great Powers"—A. J. P. Taylor, *The Struggle for Mastery 1848–1918* (Oxford: Oxford University Press, 1971), 17.

316 *found the prediction:* By contrast, Lord Robert Cecil, afterwards Lord Salisbury, perceived the German threat as early as 1862; and he wrote presciently of the German problem in the October 1870 number of the *Quarterly Review*—Andrew Roberts, *Salisbury: Victorian Titan* (London: Weidenfeld & Nicolson, 1999), 121–22. Yet even Salisbury continued to regard France as England's most likely foe.

316 *Belgium:* Lord Newton, *Lord Lyons,* i, 302.

316 *"the outworks":* Thomas Babington Macaulay, *History of England,* WLM, iv, 51–52.

316 *Lord Palmerston put:* Barbara Tuchman, *The Guns of August* (New York: Bonanza, 1982), 18.

316 *slyly released:* "The War," *The Times,* Thursday, July 28, 1870, 5.

316 *photographic copies:* Busch, *Bismarck: Some Secret Pages from His History,* i, 47.

317 *autograph manuscript:* George Bancroft to Hamilton Fish, July 27, 1870, SD NARA M44/ROLL 16.

317 *With the release: The Times,* Monday, July 18, 1870, 8; George Bancroft to Hamilton Fish, July 27, 1870, SD NARA M44/ROLL 16; E. B. Washburne to Hamilton Fish, July 29, 1870, SD NARA M34/ROLL T-70.

317 *Bismarck:* In 1867 Bismarck decided against going to war with France over the question of Luxembourg in part because he feared that Prussia would appear the aggressor, and would draw on itself the antipathy of Europe.

317 *"French Bismarck":* Wawro, *The Franco-Prussian War,* 33.

317 *"the stupidest man":* Alistair Horne, *The Fall of Paris: The Siege and the Commune 1870–1871* (New York: St. Martin's Press, 1966), 36.

317 *"France seeks":* "The War," *The Times,* Monday, July 18, 1870, 12.

317 *The marriage:* Frances Herman Jackson and Mary McNease Kinard, *A Silence After Trumpets: The Story of Sarah Buchanan Preston* (Spartanburg, SC: The Reprint Company, 1998), 205.

317 *"Poor wounded":* MCCW, 813.

318 *Dixie School writers:* C. Vann Woodward, *Origins of the New South 1877–1913* (Baton Rouge: Louisiana State University Press, 1971), 167.

318 *"Everybody knows":* MCCW, 815.

318 *"to protect niggers":* Eric Foner, *Reconstruction: America's Unfinished Revolution, 1863–1877* (New York: Harper & Row, 1988), 276.

319 *Not all the gains:* Ibid., 602–03.

319 *"brief moment":* Ibid., 602.

319 *"They have taken":* MCCW, 829.

319 *"Dem wuz":* Vann Woodward, *Origins of the New South 1877–1913,* 167.

319 *J. P. Morgan's:* Richard Hofstadter, *The Age of Reform, from Bryan to F.D.R.* (New York: Vintage, 1955), 232.

319 *The strike spread:* Foner, *Reconstruction: America's Unfinished Revolution, 1863–1877,* 583.

320 *just sixteen percent:* Eric Hobsbawm, *The Age of Capital* (New York: Vintage, 1996), 138.

320 *"broken down":* EHA, 976.

320 *"was never meant":* EHA, 1063.

320 *Walter Scott:* W. J. Cash, *The Mind of the South* (New York: Vintage, 1991) 65.

321 *Henry Vaughan:* Frank D. Ashburn, *Peabody of Groton: A Portrait* (Cambridge, MA: Riverside Press, 1967), 89.

321 321 *"was ashen":* TE, 141.

321 *His hair:* Vizetelly, *The Court of the Tuileries, 1852–1870,* 133.

321 *"Is it true?"* TE, 141.

321 *resigned fatalism:* TE, 142.

321 *The air was heavy:* Evans, *The Second French Empire,* 190.

321 *"I gave it":* TE, 142.

321 *"I had no doubts":* TE,143.

322 *sadness:* Evans, *The Second French Empire,* 190.

322 *"No, don't expect . . . smoking":* Ibid.

322 *The Prince Imperial:* Vizetelly, *The Court of the Tuileries 1852–1870,* 379.

322 *The Empress:* "The War," *The Times,* Saturday, July 30, 1870, 5.

322 *dead or victorious: The Times,* Thursday, August 11, 1870, 6.

322 *the Cross:* Guedalla, *The Second Empire,* 415.

322 *The whistle blew:* Details concerning the departure of the Emperor can be found in Ernest Alfred Vizetelly, *My Days of Adventure,* available on the Internet; Thomas W. Evans, *The Second French Empire,* 191; and Philip Guedalla, *The Second Empire,* 418.

322 *In the camps:* The morale of the French camps is evoked by Emile Zola in his 1892 novel *La Débâcle.*

323   *Rue Serpenoise:* Ferdinand Foch, *The Memoirs of Marshal Foch,* trans. T. Bentley Mott (Garden City, NY: Doubleday, 1931), xxxiii.

323   *"of a man utterly":* Ibid.

323   *"the old woman":* Wawro, *The Franco-Prussian War,* 136.

323   *no plan of campaign:* Ibid., 66.

323   *The Emperor spoke:* Ibid., 74.

323   *A fortnight after:* Vizetelly, *The Court of the Tuileries 1852–1870,* 397; James F. McMillan, *Napoleon III* (London: Longman, 1991), 161.

324   *blew their brains out:* Wawro, *The Franco-Prussian War,* 85.

30. *"Déchéance! Déchéance!"*

325   *the footmen:* Vizetelly, *The Court of the Tuileries, 1852–1870,* 44.

325   *"I saw":* TE, 180.

325   *The German invasion:* Wawro, *The Franco-Prussian War,* 86–137.

325   *fought back tears:* Guedalla, *The Second Empire,* 417.

325   *"In a flash":* TE, 180.

325   *"When I reached":* TE, 181.

325   *A strange light:* TE, 181–82.

325   *"I felt":* TE, 180.

326   *"The dynasty":* Ibid.

326 326   *Eugénie wore:* Vizetelly, *The Court of the Tuileries, 1852–1870,* 97.

326   *"The sun was":* TE, 12–13.

326   *fascinations of power:* TE, 20.

326   *"Even as a girl":* TE, 61.

326   *"What stirred me":* TE, 62.

326   *"The sky was ablaze":* TE, 16.

327   *"almost virile":* "The War," *The Times,* Wednesday, July 20, 1870, 5.

327   *"used to irritate":* TE, 66.

327   *Emile Ollivier:* TE, 185.

327   *"Madame":* TE, 182.

327   *"Frenchmen!":* "The War," *The Times,* Monday, August 8, 1870, 5.

328   *"visionaries":* MR, 308.

328   *The only credential:* MR, 306.

328   *"a closely united":* Ibid.

328   *"did I meet":* Ibid.

328   *"Gradually":* MR, 302.

328   *"to the people":* MR, 252, 301.

328   *"as doctors":* MR, 302.

328   *"I am taking":* Alexander, Grand Duke of Russia, *Once a Grand Duke* (New York: Cosmopolitan Book Corp.–Farrar & Rinehart, 1932), 47; Joyce Carol Oates, "Tragic Rites in Dostoevsky's *The Possessed,"* GR, vol. 32, no. 3 (Fall 1978), note 8.

329   *"had lilywhite hands":* George F. Kennan, *Russia and the West Under Lenin and Stalin* (Boston: Little, Brown, 1961), 23.

329   *Dumas:* Bismarck developed "a consuming passion for the novels of Dumas"–BMS, 135–36.

329   *Eugène Sue:* The philosophy of Michael Bakunin's *Catechism of a Revolutionist,* Edmund Wilson observed, drew on the inspiration of the virtuous avengers of the oppressed portrayed by Dumas *père,* Schiller, and Eugène Sue. Bakunin managed, Wilson wrote, "to fuse into a single ideal the romantic attitudes of [Sue's] Rodolphe, [Schiller's] Karl Moor, [Dumas's] Monte Cristo and Macaire"–Edmund Wilson, *To the Finland Station: A Study in the Writing and Acting of History* (Garden City, NY: Doubleday, 1940), 276.

329   *Nicholas Chernyshevsky:* MR, 301.

329   *They read the Gospels:* MR, 322.

329   *Marx and Lasalle:* MR, 305.

329 *In a little room:* MR, 274–75.

329 *willing to suffer:* MR, 275, 278, 283–85.

330 *sour:* MR, 276.

330 *undress uniform:* Busch, *Bismarck: Some Secret Pages from His History,* i, 53, 78.

330 *cup of tea:* Except where otherwise noted, the account in this section of Bismarck's experiences while traveling with the army is drawn from Moritz Busch, *Bismarck: Some Secret Pages from His History,* i, 53–78.

331 *"Let me play":* Whitman, *Personal Reminiscences of Prince Bismarck,* 93.

331 *"My temperament":* BMS, 178.

331 *The French weapon:* Wawro, *The Franco-Prussian War,* 52.

331 *"squandering":* Otto Friedrich, *Blood and Iron: From Bismarck to Hitler, the von Moltke Family's Impact on German History* (New York: HarperPerennial, 1996), 169.

331 *new steel guns:* Wawro, *The Franco-Prussian War,* 57–58.

331 *imperturbably calm:* George Bancroft to Hamilton Fish, August 2, 1870, SD NARA M44/ROLL 16.

331 *had not such iron nerves:* Abeken, *Bismarck's Pen,* 349.

332 *"quickens his clearness":* George Bancroft to Hamilton Fish, August 2, 1870, SD NARA M44/ROLL 16.

332 *"love of fighting":* Gedanken, ii, 92.

332 *"dry":* Gedanken, ii, 92.

332 *"Negative Capability":* Keats to George and Thomas Keats, December 21, 1817, in *The Letters of John Keats,* ed. Maurice Buxton Forman (London: Oxford University Press, 1952), p. 71. Fritz Stern drew attention to the applicability of Keats's dictum to Bismarck's character in *Gold and Iron: Bismarck, Bleichröder, and the Building of the German Empire,* 49.

332 *"a very moderate":* Sidney Whitman, *Personal Reminiscences of Prince Bismarck* (New York: D. Appleton, 1903), 85.

332 *deny himself even doubt:* Bismarck would perhaps have liked to have been able to deny himself doubt. "If I had to choose the form in which I would prefer to live again," he once said, "I am not so sure that I should not like to be ant." The ant, he observed, knew only "perfect subordination, discipline, and order"; it did not know doubt—Sidney Whitman, *Personal Reminiscences of Prince Bismarck* (New York: D. Appleton, 1903), 334–35.

332 *the state of feeling:* E. B. Washburne to Hamilton Fish, August 8, 1870, SD NARA M34/ROLL T-70.

332 *had not known such a day:* Ibid.

332 *rain was falling:* Ibid.; "The War," *The Times,* Tuesday, August 9, 1870, 7.

332 *Parisians stood about:* E. B. Washburne to Hamilton Fish, August 8, 1870, SD NARA M34/ROLL T-70.

332 *unfortunate Ollivier:* E. B. Washburne to Hamilton Fish, August 12, 1870, SD NARA M34/ROLL T-70.

332 *read his words:* Ibid.

332 *"The country has been":* Ibid.

332 *fierce gesticulations:* The Times, Tuesday, July 5, 1870, 5.

332 *temper:* "The Spanish Difficulty," *The Times,* Saturday, July 9, 1870, 12; E. B. Washburne to Hamilton Fish, August 12, 1870, SD NARA M34/ROLL T-70.

333 *"Come down":* E. B. Washburne to Hamilton Fish, August 12, 1870, SD NARA M34/ROLL T-70.

333 *The old man pursued:* In this account of Lee's journey to Lexington I adopt the conjectures of Freeman, who having sifted the evidence thought it likely that Lee wore his gray uniform, and that he was refused hospitality on the day he reached the crest of the Blue Ridge—REL, iv, 226–27.

333 *"I consider":* REL, iv, 258.

334 *"We have no":* REL, iv, 278.

334 *"I have":* REL, iv, 296.

334 *"I find it so hard":* REL, iv, 297.

334 *prejudices of his age:* It is no less painful to find Walt Whitman speaking in a similar vein. See David S. Reynolds, *Walt Whitman's America: A Cultural Biography* (New York: Vintage, 1996), 469–74.

335 *"Teach him":* REL, iv, 505.

335 *"Doctor"*: REL, iv, 206.
335 *"We failed"*: REL, iv, 402.
335 *"Misfortune"*: REL, iv, 464.
335 *"to visualize"*: REL, iv, 170–71.
335 *"My interest"*: REL, iv, 345.
335 *The heavy cavalry:* Guedalla, *The Second Empire,* 420.
336 *the Sun King:* Thomas Babington Macaulay, *History of England,* WLM, iii, 572–73.
336 *Marshal Bazaine:* Ordre Général, Armée du Rhin, August 12, 1870, Bazaine Dossier, AA, 6yd 62; Décret Impériale, August 12, 1870, Bazaine Dossier, AA, 6yd 62.
337 *"absolutely stupefying"*: *The Times,* Friday, August 26, 1870, 7.
337 *Châlons:* "Emperor at Châlons," *The Times,* Thursday, August 18, 1870, 7.
337 *insulted his name:* Alistair Horne, *The Fall of Paris: The Siege and the Commune 1870–1871* (New York: St. Martin's Press, 1966), 47.
337 *"I seem to have abdicated"*: Michael Howard, *The Franco-Prussian War: The German Invasion of France, 1870–1871* (London: Routledge, 2001), 185; McMillan, *Napoleon III,* 163.
338 *"never reach"*: Emile Zola, *The Downfall,* trans. W. M. Sloane (New York: P. F. Collier, 1902), 54; see also TE, 190.
338 *Makeup had been:* McMillan, *Napoleon III,* 163.
338 *Once:* TE, 200.
339 *at Metz:* Nietzsche, *On the Genealogy of Morals and Ecce Homo,* 270.
339 *"seemed as if it"*: Walter Kaufmann, *Nietzsche: Philosopher, Psychologist, Antichrist,* 4th ed. (Princeton: Princeton University Press, 1974), 26.
339 *"earth trembled"*: Rüdiger Safranski, *Nietzsche: A Philosophical Biography,* trans. Shelley Frisch (New York: W. W. Norton, 2003), 68.
339 *"sees everywhere"*: "Here," Nietzsche said, "when the danger to [the Greek's] will is greatest, *art* approaches as a saving sorceress, expert at healing"–Friedrich Nietzsche, *The Birth of Tragedy and the Case of Wagner,* trans. Walter Kaufmann (New York: Vintage, 1967), 59–60 (emphasis in original); compare Nietzsche, *On the Genealogy of Morals and Ecce Homo,* 270.
339 *"would never dream"*: Nietzsche, *On the Genealogy of Morals and Ecce Homo,* 270.
339 *nervous breakdown:* Ibid., 222.
339 *He traveled: The Portable Nietzsche,* ed. Walter Kaufmann (Harmondsworth, Middlesex: Penguin, 1983), 104.
340 *"godlike selfhood"*: He "that is richest in the fullness of life," Nietzsche said, is the Dionysian man; he that is weakest is the romantic man–Nietzsche, *The Gay Science,* 328.
340 *"cadaverous perfume"*: Nietzsche, *On the Genealogy of Morals and Ecce Homo,* 270.
340 *did not say yes:* Ibid., 271–73.
340 *dancing naked:* So his peeping landlady in Turin averred. See Lesley Chamberlain, *Nietzsche in Turin* (New York: Picador, 1998), 216; Safranski, *Nietzsche: A Philosophical Biography,* 370.
340 *a new mode of myth:* Compare Nietzsche's assessment of the art of Hugo and Wagner–Nietzsche, *The Will to Power,* 436.
340 *"Zarathustra"*: Nietzsche, *On the Genealogy of Morals and Ecce Homo,* 306.
340 *threw himself:* Kaufmann, *Nietzsche: Philosopher, Psychologist, Antichrist,* 67; Safranski, *Nietzsche: A Philosophical Biography,* 316; Chamberlain, *Nietzsche in Turin,* 208.
340 *"Hit her in the face"*: CP, 53.
340 *"made his way screaming"*: CP, 54.
340 *"He was coming from the pub"*: Maude, *The Life of Tolstoy: The First Fifty Years,* 258–59.
341 *"relentless"*: Nietzsche, *On the Genealogy of Morals and Ecce Homo,* 274–75.
341 *annihilation:* Ibid., 261.
341 *segregation of the sick:* Ibid., 124.
341 *Dionysian dowry:* Ibid., 266.
341 *fraternity boy:* Karl Löwith, *From Hegel to Nietzsche: The Revolution in Nineteenth-Century Thought,* trans. David E. Green (New York: Columbia University Press, 1991), 303.
341 *"repels and disgusts"*: Nietzsche, *The Gay Science,* 161–62.
341 *"horned-beast"*: LRW, iv, 597.

341 *"To think German"*: Nietzsche, *On the Genealogy of Morals and Ecce Homo*, 263.
341 *"I know my fate"*: Nietzsche, *On the Genealogy of Morals and Ecce Homo*, 326.
341 *"The Empress!"*: Vizetelly, *The Court of the Tuileries, 1852–1870*, 44.
341 *her diadem:* Ibid., 398.
341 *and she inquired:* E. B. Washburne to Hamilton Fish, August 11, 1870, SD NARA M34/ROLL T-70.
341 *"Unfortunately"*: Ibid.
341 *Washburne:* PMUSG, 117–21; W. E. Woodward, *Meet General Grant* (New York: Horace Liveright, 1928), 189.
342 *"Yes"*: E. B. Washburne to Hamilton Fish, August 11, 1870, SD NARA M34/ROLL T-70.
342 Cabinet Noir: Vizetelly, *The Court of the Tuileries, 1852–1870*, 147.
342 *took chloral:* Guedalla, *The Second Empire*, 418.
342 *"kept me"*: TE, 193; see also Horne, *The Fall of Paris*, 49.
342 *Chevreau:* TE, 192, 194.
342 *There she learned:* Guedalla, *The Second Empire*, 428.
342 *"No"*: TE, 194–95.
342 *"Why didn't"*: TE, 195.
343 *fell upon her knees:* Ibid.
343 "Déchéance! Déchéance!": Guedalla, *The Second Empire*, 428.
343 "Vive la République!": Vizetelly, *The Court of the Tuileries, 1852–1870*, 406.
343 *"Anything rather"*: Ibid., 405.
343 *extinct:* E. B. Washburne to Hamilton Fish, September 5, 1870, SD NARA M34/ROLL T-70.
343 *proclaimed a Republic:* Ibid.
343 *"Go, go"*: Vizetelly, *The Court of the Tuileries, 1852–1870*, 407.
343 *"Her Majesty"*: Ibid.
344 *A few faithful:* TE, 197.
344 Salon Bleu: Vizetelly, *The Court of the Tuileries, 1852–1870*, 160.
344 *Ominous sounds:* Horne, *The Fall of Paris*, 57.
344 *the Louvre:* Ibid., 58.
344 *hackney cab:* TE, 208.

31. *Vinum Daemonum*

345 *But he could not rid himself:* Unless otherwise indicated, the quotations in this section are taken from Tolstoy's book, *A Confession*, which has been reprinted many times.
346 *"I was literally"*: Aylmer Maude, *The Life of Tolstoy: Later Years* (New York: Dodd, Mead, 1910), 5.
346 *"a kind man"*: Ibid., 66–67.
346 *"steppes of Kansas"*: Maude, *The Life of Tolstoy: First Fifty Years*, 397.
346 *"made me believe"*: Maude, *The Life of Tolstoy: Later Years*, 94.
346 *"The priests"*: Maude, *The Life of Tolstoy: First Fifty Years*, 343.
347 *a heavy burden of debt:* Zakharova, "Autocracy and the Reforms of 1861–1871 in Russia: Choosing Paths of Development," RGR, 31; Boris Mironov, "The Russian Peasant Commune After the Reforms of the 1860s," SR, vol. 44, no. 3 (Autumn 1985), 466.
347 *"more liberal"*: Pipes, *Russia Under the Old Regime*, 167; see also Daniel Field, "The Year of Jubilee," RGR, 52–53.
347 *repressive atmosphere:* MR, 311.
348 *"What then"*: Maude, *The Life of Tolstoy: Later Years*, 238–83.
348 348 *But Tolstoy rejected:* Ibid., 9, 70.
348 *"was a Christ"*: Albert A. Woldman, *Lincoln and the Russians* (Cleveland: Collier, 1961), 251.
348 *"It is absurd"*: Maude, *The Life of Tolstoy: First Fifty Years*, 346.
348 *The sun was setting:* Abeken, *Bismarck's Pen*, 290.
348 *"I am God's"*: Wetzel, *A Duel of Giants*, 15.
349 *not "a clod"*: Wawro, *The Franco-Prussian War*, 253.
349 "exclusive *right*": SS, 194 (emphasis added).

349 *Moltke maintained:* SS, 223.

350 *"cap the volcano":* SS, 227.

350 *"draw the fangs":* SS, 199.

350 *"gets more buzzardlike":* SS, 194.

350 *Confronted with:* B, 274.

350 *"What some day":* SS, 190.

351 *on short rations: The Times,* Monday, August 22, 1870, 6.

351 *no salt:* Wawro, *The Franco-Prussian War,* 241.

351 *Bazaine retired:* Guedalla, *The Two Marshals,* 180. The story of Bazaine's games of billiards is per-haps apocryphal–Ibid., 189–90.

351 *so precarious:* Busch, *Bismarck: Some Secret Pages from His History,* i, 132.

351 *The Chancellor conceived:* TE, 236–39.

352 *"Let us all":* Winston Spencer Churchill, *The Second World War,* 6 vols. (Boston: Houghton Miffllin, 1948–53), iv, 647. Churchill there describes the fall of Admiral Darlan.

352 *At the end of October: État des Services,* May 11, 1872, Bazaine Dossier, AA, 6yd 62; "The Fall of Metz," *The Times,* Saturday, October 29, 1870, 5.

352 *pacing the garden:* Busch, *Bismarck: Some Secret Pages from His History,* i, 172.

352 *"almost certainly":* Stern, *Gold and Iron,* 146.

352 *full and sensual:* Vizetelly, *My Days of Adventure,* available on the Internet; "The New French Gov-ernment," " *The Times,* Tuesday, September 6, 1870, 8.

353 "Mademoiselle, voulez-vous": Wawro, *The Franco-Prussian War,* 286.

353 *"at a draught":* Busch, *Bismarck: Some Secret Pages from His History,* i, 227.

353 *"And their treacherous":* Ibid., i, 167. Otto Friedrich supposes that the words were stimulated "by too much Burgundy"; and Gerhard Ritter notes that Bismarck's most Draconian utterances were often made "over a glass of wine"–Friedrich, *Blood and Iron,* 190; SS, 222. Busch states that the remark in question was made at teatime, but this scarcely proves the sobriety of the speaker. Not wine but brandy–which Bismarck carried with him in a flask–was the most likely culprit, if alco-hol was indeed the inspiration of his words.

353 *"Count Bismarck":* Lord Fitzmaurice, *The Life of Granville George Leveson Gower, Second Earl Granville, K.G.,* ii, 41 (emphasis added).

353 *a deep impression:* Busch, *Bismarck: Some Secret Pages from His History,* i, 167; see also SS, 222.

353 *total war:* Some historians argue that the term "total war" does not apply to the American Civil War. See Mark E. Neely, Jr., "Was the Civil War a Total War?" ORTW, 50–51.

353 *"The proper strategy":* Busch, *Bismarck: Some Secret Pages from His History,* i, 128.

353 *"You know how":* Carl N. Degler, "The American Civil War and the German Wars of Unification: The Problem of Comparison," ORTW, 68–69.

353 *Bismarck had at first:* Busch, *Bismarck: Some Secret Pages from His History,* i, 80.

353 *"The more Frenchmen":* Ibid., i, 167.

354 *prepare public opinion:* Michael Howard, *The Franco–Prussian War: The German Invasion of France, 1870–1871* (London: Routledge, 2001), 353.

354 *"shot and stabbed":* Friedrich, *Blood and Iron,* 190.

354 "femme entretenue": LRW, iv, 272.

354 *"to write to Bismarck":* Ibid.

354 *Richard Hornig:* Desmond Chapman-Huston, *Ludwig II: The Mad King of Bavaria* (New York: Dorset, 1990), 138.

354 *"Sophie got rid of":* Ibid., 137.

355 *"Heaven":* Ferdinand Mayr-Ofen [pseudonym of Otto Zarek], *Ludwig II of Bavaria: The Tragedy of an Idealist,* trans. Ella Goodman and Paul Sudley (London: Cobden-Sanderson, 1937), 172.

355 *"Only spiritual love":* LRW, iii, 244.

355 *"of all mire":* Chapman-Huston, *Ludwig II,* 174.

355 *"by the pure and holy":* Ibid., 179.

355 *"holy and pure":* Ibid., 174.

355 *"Accursed":* LRW, iii, 244.

355 *"On the mountains":* Chapman-Huston, *Ludwig II,* 163.

355 *"Romanticism is disease":* Johann Peter Eckermann, *Gespräche mit Goethe* (Leipzig, 1837), Thursday, April 2, 1829.

355 *He would escape:* LRW, iv, 290.

355 *He would leave:* LRW, iv, 306; Mayr-Ofen, *Ludwig II of Bavaria,* 222.

355 *He once confided:* Ibid.

32. "You Have a New World"

357 *The fifth anniversary:* For the items of news which absorbed the country on the fifth anniversary of Lincoln's death, see *The New-York Times,* Wednesday, April 13, 1870, through Sunday, April 17, 1870.

357 *"notable bad men":* "The Erie Scandal," *The New-York Times,* Saturday, April 16, 1870, 4.

358 *"Whig interpretation":* Herbert Butterfield, *The Whig Interpretation of History* (London: G. Bell, 1959).

358 *morally complicated:* Crankshaw, *Bismarck,* 413–14.

358 *proclamation: Proclamation des nuen deutschen kaiserreiches,* 18 January 1871.

358 *A tremendous* "Hoch": Abeken, *Bismarck's Pen,* 333.

359 *"so cold":* Wawro, *The Franco-Prussian War,* 282.

359 *the most unhappy:* BGE, 182.

359 *territorial title:* Foot, "The Origins of the Franco-Prussian War and the Remaking of Germany," NCMH, x, 601.

359 *refused to shake:* B, 288.

359 *Half a million:* George Bancroft to Hamilton Fish, September 24, 1870, SD NARA M44/ROLL 16.

359 *Favre:* Horne, *The Fall of Paris,* 241.

359 *Bismarck prevailed:* Stig Förster, "The Prussian Triangle of Leadership in the Face of a People's War: A Reassessment of the Conflict Between Bismarck and Moltke, 1870–71," ORTW, 139.

359 *At the behest:* SS, 224.

360 *"I don't like":* Wawro, *The Franco-Prussian War,* 304.

360 *a concession to Moltke:* Förster, "The Prussian Triangle of Leadership in the Face of a People's War," 134.

360 *Shortly after:* E. B. Washburne to Hamilton Fish, March 1, 1871, in Washburne, *Franco-German War and Insurrection of the Commune* (Washington, DC: Government Printing Office, 1878), 148–49.

360 *asked for a light:* Friedrich, *Blood and Iron,* 206.

360 *"the old and cruel":* BGE, 185.

360 *"Professor Gladstone":* G. P. Gooch, "Bismarck's Legacy," *Foreign Affairs,* XXX (1952), reprinted in *Otto von Bismarck: A Historical Assessment,* ed. Theodore S. Hamerow (Boston: D. C. Heath, 1966), 99.

360 *"I have":* Gladstone to Lord Granville, December 10, 1870, in Lord Fitzmaurice, *The Life of Granville George Leveson Gower,* ii, 71.

361 *"represents":* Crankshaw, *Bismarck,* 304.

361 *a book:* The book is dated 1871.

361 *twisting his mouth:* The American painter Jervis McEntee, who encountered Arnold at a party in New York, said that the poet had an "ugly mouth which he twists about in a strange manner"– Jervis McEntee Diaries, March 6, 1884, in The Jervis McEntee Papers, 1850–1905, Archives of American Art, Smithsonian Institution. I am indebted for this reference to Mrs. Sedgwick A. Ward.

361 *There was no poetry:* Lionel Trilling, *Matthew Arnold* (New York: Harcourt, Brace, 1977), 404–05.

361 *"Are there":* Walt Whitman, *Democratic Vistas* (Amsterdam: Fredonia, 2002), 14–15.

362 *Louise Michel:* Horne, *The Fall of Paris,* 270, 298.

362 *Afterwards he was:* Ibid., 271–72.

362 *"No blood":* Ibid., 273.

362 *Georges Clemenceau burst:* Ibid.

362 *A red flag:* E. B. Washburne to Hamilton Fish, March 27, 1871, in Washburne, *Franco-German War and Insurrection of the Commune,* 169.

362 *The greatest terror:* E. B. Washburne to Hamilton Fish, April 6, 1871, in ibid., 178.

362 *A Committee:* Horne, *The Fall of Paris,* 333–35.

362 *hunted down:* E. B. Washburne to Hamilton Fish, April 6, 1871, in Washburne, *Franco-German War and Insurrection of the Commune,* 178.

362 *placards:* E. B. Washburne to Hamilton Fish, April 14, 1871, in ibid., 182.

363 *"Paris":* Horne, *The Fall of Paris,* 388.

363 *Mr. Washburne:* The account of Washburne's visit to Darboy is drawn from E. B. Washburne to Hamilton Fish, April 23, 1871, in Washburne, *Franco-German War and Insurrection of the Commune,* 188, and E. B. Washburne, *Account of the Sufferings and Death of the Most Rev. Darboy, Late Archbishop of Paris* (New York: Catholic Union of New York, 1873).

364 *towards Marshal Bazaine:* Etat des Services, May 11, 1872, Bazaine Dossier, AA, 6yd 62.

364 *Raoul:* David Hume, *The History of England,* 6 vols. (Indianapolis: Liberty Fund, 1983), ii, 226, 244.

364 *"l'affaire Bazaine":* Bazaine Dossier, AA, 6yd 62.

364 *"A mort":* "The Bazaine Trial," *The Times,* Friday, December 12, 1873, 3.

365 *"à mort et à la":* Jugement au nom due people Française . . . Conseil de Guerre Permanent séant à Versailles, December 10, 1873, Bazaine Dossier, AA, 6yd 62; *Etat des Services,* January 30, 1874, Bazaine Dossier, AA, 6yd 62.

365 *Pursuant to the Code:* Bazaine Dossier, AA, 6yd 62.

365 *Borodin:* MR, 328.

365 *sheepskins:* MR, 327.

365 *silk undergarment:* MR, 342.

365 *rye bread:* MR, 325.

365 *His efforts were soon ended:* MR, 330–42.

Epilogue

366 *"What always seemed":* John Russell Young, *Around the World with General Grant,* ed. Michael Fellman (Baltimore: Johns Hopkins University Press, 2002), 157.

367 *The Tsar acquiesced:* Alfred J. Rieber, "Alexander II: A Revisionist View," JMH, vol. 43, no. 1 (March 1971), 57; George F. Kennan, *The Decline of Bismarck's European Order: Franco-Russian Relations, 1875–1890* (Princeton: Princeton University Press, 1980), 32–33, 35.

367 *Russia was dissatisfied:* Kennan, *The Decline of Bismarck's European Order,* 37–38.

367 *steel-plated carriages:* Frederic Hamilton, *The Vanished Pomps of Yesterday* (Garden City, NY: Doubleday, 1934), 163–64.

367 *lined the railway tracks:* Alexander, Grand Duke of Russia, *Once a Grand Duke* (New York: Cosmopolitan Book Corp.–Farrar & Rinehart, 1932), 38.

367 *the nihilists:* Ibid., 57.

367 *"Strange":* W. E. Mosse, *Alexander II and the Modernization of Russia,* rev. ed. (New York: Collier, 1970), 138.

367 *One day:* Maurice Paléologue, *The Tragic Romance of Alexander II of Russia,* trans. Arthur Chambers (London: Hutchinson, 1927), 164–66.

368 *The Tsar insisted:* Alexander, *Once a Grand Duke,* 48, 50.

368 *"His Majesty":* Ibid., 50.

368 *"I am so happy":* Mosse, *Alexander II and the Modernization of Russia,* 145.

368 *"To the Winter Palace":* LGT, 411.

368 *went towards the victims:* Alexander, *Once a Grand Duke,* 60.

368 *"Thank God":* Mosse, *Alexander II and the Modernization of Russia,* 146.

368 *Drops of black blood:* Alexander, *Once a Grand Duke,* 59.

369 *Katya . . . "gave one shriek":* Ibid., 59–60.

369 *a reactionary course:* Larissa Zakharova, "Autocracy and the Reforms of 1861–1871 in Russia: Choosing Paths of Development," trans. Daniel Field, RGR, 37.

369 *As for Katya:* John Van der Kiste, *The Romanovs 1818–1959* (Stroud, Glos: Sutton, 2003), 250–59.

369 *"This buries":* MR, xvi.

370 *"spiritually exalted":* DST, 556.

370 *"he enjoys himself"* Ibid.

370   *"would soon be":* Ibid.

370   *"my dear husband":* DST, 584.

370   *"I thank you":* T, 669.

370   *"What you need":* T, 671.

370   *At Kozelsk:* Ibid.

370   *"The old boy's":* T, 679.

370   *"God":* T, 680.

370   *"What about":* T, 687.

371   *After 1871:* Kennan, *The Decline of Bismarck's European Order,* 97–99; George F. Kennan, *The Fateful Alliance: France, Russia, and the Coming of the First World War* (New York: Pantheon, 1984), xv; Henry A. Kissinger, "The White Revolutionary: Reflections on Bismarck," D, vol. 97, no. 3 (Summer 1968), 920–21.

371   *He foresaw:* SS, 229.

371   *It was a premonition:* SS, 230.

371   *Bismarck preferred:* It is true that Bismarck assumed a bellicose posture towards France during the war scare of 1875; but the Chancellor, Niall Ferguson observes, may "never have intended anything more than to beat the militarist drum for domestic political reasons"–Niall Ferguson, *The House of Rothschild: The World's Banker, 1849–1999* (London: Penguin, 1999), 219. See also Kennan, *The Decline of Bismarck's European Order,* 98.

371   *their entente:* Alexander II may have secretly authorized a limited military collaboration with France in the 1870s. Rumors of such an informal alliance may explain the wariness with which Bismarck regarded the Tsar in the latter part of the decade. Bismarck, with his penchant for blaming intriguing females for his difficulties, alluded darkly to the sinister influence which Katya exercised over the mind of the Tsar–Kennan, *The Decline of Bismarck's European Order,* 42–45, 71. Count Charles Frederick Vitzthum von Eckstædt alluded to an even earlier, more shadowy Franco-Russian *entente* in his *Saint Petersburg and London in the Years 1852–1864,* 2 vols. (London: Longmans, Green, 1887), ii, 134–35.

372   *the Staff came into its own:* Stig Förster, "The Prussian Triangle of Leadership in the Face of a People's War: A Reassessment of the Conflict Between Bismarck and Moltke, 1870–71," ORTW, 117, 139.

372   *authoritarian nationalism and paternalistic socialism:* Abram L. Harris, "Sombart and German (National) Socialism," JPE, vol. 50, no. 6 (December 1942), 805–35; Carlton J. H. Hayes, "The History of German Socialism Reconsidered," AHR, vol. 23, no. 1 (October 1917), 62.

372   *not responsible:* G. P. Gooch, "Bismarck's Legacy," FA, vol. 30 (1952), reprinted in *Otto von Bismarck: A Historical Assessment,* ed. Theodore S. Hamerow (Boston: D. C. Heath, 1966), 98; Geoffrey Barraclough, *The Origins of Modern Germany* (New York: W. W. Norton, 1984), 456; Michael Foot, "The Origins of the Franco-Prussian War and the Remaking of Germany," NCMH, x, 601; Henry A. Kissinger, "The White Revolutionary: Reflections on Bismarck," D, vol. 97, no. 3 (Summer 1968), 922.

372   *"Give the workingman":* Henry W. Littlefield, *History of Europe Since 1815* (New York: Harper & Row, 1963), 99; William Harbutt Dawson, *German Socialism and Ferdinand Lasalle* (London: Swan Sonnenschein, 1891), 167–68; William Harbutt Dawson, *Bismarck and State Socialism: An Exposition of the Social and Economic Legislation of Germany Since 1870* (London: Swan Sonnenschein, 1890).

372   *"subservient":* BMS, 203. Compare F. A. Hayek, *The Constitution of Liberty* (Chicago: University of Chicago Press, 1960), 257–66, 502.

372   *"Whoever has":* BMS, 203.

372   *broke his nation's:* Peter Gay, *The Cultivation of Hatred* (New York: W. W. Norton, 1993), 265.

372   *The leader who is strong enough:* A. J. P. Taylor oddly, though not very convincingly, dissents from this reading of the evidence. "No doubt [Bismarck's constitution]," Taylor wrote, "was a poor thing by the standards of modern democracy in Great Britain or France. . . . Yet, in the last resort, it came to much the same." (BMS, 96). It did? Surely Gordon Craig's analysis is more persuasive: Bismarck and his fellow opponents of constitutional government, Craig wrote, "were able successfully to block the introduction into Germany of what were considered in western countries to be the minimal requirements of representative government, namely the principle of ministerial

responsibility and effective parliamentary control over state administration and policy" (Craig, *The Politics of the Prussian Army 1640–1945,* xiv). Bismarck was reluctant to establish genuine constitutional restraints on power in Germany in part because such restraints would have operated against *him.* It was a wise policy of Solon and Washington to relinquish power after they made their revolutions; Bismarck, like Cromwell and Bonaparte, like Julius Caesar and Augustus Caesar, was a hedonist of power, and he clung to it.

372   *"Had it not been":* David Wetzel, *A Duel of Giants: Bismarck, Napoleon III, and the Origins of the Franco-Prussian War* (Madison, WI: University of Wisconsin Press, 2001), 15–16.

373   *"It must come":* Duff Cooper, *Haig* (Garden City, NY: Doubleday, 1936), 38–39; Hajo Holborn, "Moltke and Schlieffen: The Prussian-German School," in *Makers of Modern Strategy: Military Thought from Machiavelli to Hitler,* ed. Edward Meade Earle (New York: Atheneum, 1967), 198–200.

373   *"Majesty":* Winston S. Churchill, *The World Crisis, 1911–1918* (New York: Free Press, 2005), 168.

374   *"the veneer":* Winston Spencer Churchill, *The Second World War,* 6 vols. (Boston: Houghton Miffllin, 1948–53), i, 58, 60.

374   *Hans von Seeckt:* Ibid., i, 44–47.

374   *Adolf Hitler:* This account of Hitler's relation with the House of Wagner is drawn from Frederic Spotts, *Hitler and the Power of Aesthetics* (Woodstock, NY: Overlook, 2002), 246–62.

375   *"Incredible!":* LRW, iv, 587.

375   *dissolved in tears:* LRW, iv, 544

375   reichsdeutsch: Friedrich Nietzsche, *On the Genealogy of Morals and Ecce Homo,* trans. Walter Kaufmann (New York: Vintage, 1989), 248.

375   *he insisted on calling:* Lesley Chamberlain, *Nietzsche in Turin* (New York: Picador, 1998), 214.

375   *"it became":* EHA, 813.

376   *"brilliant journal":* Edmund Wilson, *Patriotic Gore: Studies in the Literature of the American Civil War* (Boston: Northeastern University Press, 1984), xiii, 279.

377   *did not become a slave empire:* "Since the Civil War," Adolf Hitler said in 1933, "in which the Southern States were conquered against all historical logic and sound sense, the American people have been in a condition of political and popular decay. . . . The beginnings of a great new social order based on the principle of slavery and inequality were destroyed by that war, and with them also the embryo of a future truly great America"–Harry V. Jaffe, *A New Birth of Freedom: Abraham Lincoln and the Coming of the Civil War* (Lanham, MD: Rowman & Littlefield, 2000), 73.

Acknowledgments

I HAVE PARTICULARLY TO THANK Adjutant Gouffin, of the Archives de l'Armée française, in the Château de Vincennes; the librarians of the New York Public Library; the staff of the National Archives and Records Administration; Bruce Nichols and Elizabeth Perrella of Free Press; and Michelle Tessler of Tessler Literary Agency. I am grateful, too, to Michael F. Bishop, who read the manuscript with great care and offered valuable comments, and to Ann Adelman and Edith Lewis for their help in preparing the typescript for the press. My greatest debts are to my wife and to the other members of my family.

Index

About the Author

Michael Knox Beran is the author of a study of Robert Kennedy, *The Last Patrician,* a *New York Times* Notable Book of 1998, and a study of Thomas Jefferson, *Jefferson's Demons,* a selection of the Book-of-the-Month Club and the History Book Club. Born in Dallas, Texas, he was educated at Columbia, Cambridge, and Yale Law School. A lawyer, he lives in New York with his wife and daughters.

2- 19- 08